DATE DUE

DEMCO 38-296

Chancellorsville

Books by Stephen W. Sears

The Century Collection of Civil War Art

Hometown U.S.A.

The Automobile in America

Landscape Turned Red: The Battle of Antietam

George B. McClellan: The Young Napoleon

The Civil War Papers of George B. McClellan:
Selected Correspondence, 1860–1865

To the Gates of Richmond: The Peninsula Campaign

For Country, Cause & Leader:
The Civil War Journal of Charles B. Haydon

Chancellorsville

Chancellorsville

STEPHEN W. SEARS

HOUGHTON MIFFLIN COMPANY

BOSTON   NEW YORK

For information about permission to reproduce selections from this book,
write to Permissions, Houghton Mifflin Company, 215 Park Avenue South,
New York, New York 10003.

For information about this and other Houghton Mifflin trade and reference
books and multimedia products, visit The Bookstore at Houghton Mifflin
on the World Wide Web at http://www.hmco.com/trade/.

Library of Congress Cataloging-in-Publication Data
Sears, Stephen W.
Chancellorsville / Stephen W. Sears.
p.   cm.
Includes bibliographical references and index.
ISBN 0-395-63417-2
1. Chancellorsville (Va.), Battle of, 1863.   I. Title.
E475.35.S43   1996
973.7'33 — dc20   96-31220
CIP

Printed in the United States of America

QUM 10 9 8 7 6 5 4 3 2

For Sally,
once again and always

CONTENTS

MAPS

Maps by George Skoch

INTRODUCTION

CHANCELLORSVILLE holds a unique place on the roll of America's great battles. It was the most complex campaign of the Civil War. It witnessed the most intense and concentrated few hours of fighting of the entire war. It ranks as the most remarkable of Robert E. Lee's victories — and the most disheartening of Union defeats. And for the Southern Confederacy the fate of Stonewall Jackson turned Chancellorsville into the most hollow of victories.

Late April of 1863 saw the Union aggressively on the march in both the western and eastern theaters of war. In the West, U.S. Grant opened his climactic campaign against the Mississippi citadel of Vicksburg. In the East, the start of Joe Hooker's much-heralded campaign against Lee in northern Virginia riveted attention all across the two nations at war. Hooker's campaign plan was inspired — "decidedly the best strategy conceived in any of the campaigns ever set on foot against us," said Confederate soldier and historian Porter Alexander — and his opening maneuvers were brilliantly successful. After the war, when he looked back on his time of command at Chancellorsville, Joe Hooker could only shake his head in disbelief. "I won greater success on many fields in the war," he wrote, "but nowhere did I deserve it half so much. . . ."

General Hooker may be excused that particular conceit. He had prepared the Army of the Potomac well and himself well, and aided by an intelligence coup he put his army in a position to fight the battle exactly as he wanted. Calculated on that basis, he might rightfully have expected victory to follow. When the myths that have long obscured his generalship at Chancellorsville are cleared away, it becomes plain that however much Joe Hooker sinned, on this battlefield he was more sinned against, by inept lieutenants and simple happenstance.

General Lee, on the other hand, snatched victory from impending defeat through the courage of his absolute conviction that the men of his Army of Northern Virginia could not be beaten by any number or combination of Yankee soldiers. He believed these men, and their generals, could do whatever he asked of them, however bold. And bold he was in maneuvering and fighting in the tangled Wilderness around the Chancellorsville crossroads, and at least on this battlefield he was proven right.

Primary sources previously unavailable or unused cast a great deal of new light on this campaign. These sources range from General Hooker's papers to many score letters and diaries of officers and men of both armies. In later years men who fought at Chancellorsville (and historians who listened to them) tended to paint the scene with their own tones. The intent of this narrative history is to restore campaign and battle to its original colors.

Nearly 200,000 men fought here, and nearly one in six was a casualty. When it was over, the Yankees who had crossed the Rappahannock with such high expectations ten days earlier were back north of the river, licking their wounds. General Lee had surely won the battle, a North Carolina soldier observed, but he wondered to what purpose. Here were the two armies back in their old camps on opposite sides of the river, very much as if nothing had happened, and "how much more does it look like peace than before. . . ."

Robert E. Lee was unsatisfied as well. He would bury the dead and reorganize his battered army and set off northward, toward Pennsylvania, to capitalize on what he had won so spectacularly on the great battlefield of Chancellorsville.

Chancellorsville

1

The Revolt of the Generals

T HE TWO GENERALS were ushered into the president's office on
the second floor of the east wing of the White House in midafternoon. It was Tuesday, December 30, 1862, and the purpose of their
interview with Mr. Lincoln was, to say the least, highly irregular. It was
their considered opinion that General Burnside was about to lead the
Army of the Potomac to disaster, and they saw it as their duty to prevent
this from happening.

The two made a decidedly odd pairing. Brigadier General John Newton looked the very picture of a professional soldier. He was forty, tall and
stiffly erect and with a determined look about him. Descended from a
First Family of Virginia, Newton had graduated from West Point second
in class twenty years before, entered the elite Corps of Engineers, and
stayed resolutely at his post when Virginia left the Union in 1861. In the
Army of the Potomac he had compiled a careful combat record, rising to
the command of a division in William F. Smith's Sixth Corps of William
B. Franklin's Left Grand Division. While Newton was not entirely unfa-
miliar with the ways of Washington — his father had been a congressman
from Virginia for twenty-nine years — he would express himself uncomfortable about approaching the president this way. Indeed, when he
came up to the capital that morning from army headquarters on the
Rappahannock, General Newton had not had the least thought of going
anywhere near the White House.

His companion, by contrast, was quite at home in this setting. Brigadier General John Cochrane, commander of a brigade under Newton,
forty-nine years old and entirely lacking in soldierly bearing, was a political operator to his fingertips. Where John Newton was F.F.V., John Cochrane was Mozart Hall politico. He had served two terms as a congressman
from New York City just before the war. A conservative Democrat, he

raised a regiment in 1861 and rode into the army on the coattails of the Republican administration's call for bipartisan support of the war effort. Cochrane soon enough rose from political colonel to political general and proved adept at wire-pulling in Washington. As recently as October he had been sent to the capital by the then commanding general of the Army of the Potomac, George B. McClellan, to lobby for McClellan's reappointment as general-in-chief of the Union armies. In this cause Cochrane enlisted a Cabinet secretary, Salmon P. Chase, and the country's largest newspaper, the *New York Herald,* and spoke directly to Mr. Lincoln on the subject. In the event, his efforts were unavailing, and within a month McClellan was displaced as army commander by Ambrose Burnside. Now, on this December afternoon call at the White House, Cochrane, with Newton in tow, was conspiring to see Burnside displaced as army commander.

Cochrane and Newton had not concocted this intrigue by themselves. They merely represented the latest — and boldest — evidence of a generals' revolt in the Army of the Potomac aimed at Burnside's overthrow. The two ringleaders of the revolt were Cochrane's and Newton's immediate superiors, Major Generals William Franklin and William Smith.

Ten days earlier, on December 20, Franklin and Smith, going without scruple over Burnside's head, had opened a private correspondence with the president on the subject of grand strategy. Disdaining the army's current campaigning on the Rappahannock (General Burnside's approach, said Franklin and Smith, "cannot possibly be successful"), they argued for a return to McClellan's approach to Richmond by way of the Virginia Peninsula — a campaign that had consumed five months that spring and summer and been sharply repulsed by the Confederates. Lincoln had never cared for McClellan's approach, and he told the two dissident generals that he could not see how their proposed return to the Peninsula would overcome what he called "the old difficulty."

In due course General Burnside would turn up the names of seven of his officers conspiring to overthrow him, but in truth just then there were thousands more in the Army of the Potomac who had lost faith in the commanding general. This was an army scarred by repeated failures on the battlefield, yet no previous failure had seemed so senseless and so pointless as Fredericksburg, fought on December 13. Never had the troops fought more gallantly than in their repeated stormings of Marye's Heights behind the town; never was gallantry so obviously and so visibly wasted. On Marye's Heights the Rebel general Longstreet remarked that so long as his ammunition held out and they kept coming, he would kill every Yankee soldier in Burnside's army, and for a time, until darkness intervened, it seemed that he might. Federal casualties were 12,653, greater even than on that terrible day at Antietam Creek in September, and nothing whatever was gained. December 13, 1862, was beyond doubt the worst day in the experience of the Army of the Potomac.

It was General Burnside announcing his intention to resume the campaign that had sent Newton and Cochrane hurrying to Washington. From army headquarters at Falmouth on December 29 came orders for the troops to prepare to march, carrying three days' rations and sixty rounds of ammunition. No details of Burnside's plan were given, but clearly it would mean another crossing of the Rappahannock and another battle at or near Fredericksburg. Later Generals Franklin and Smith would have difficulty recalling the purpose of Newton's and Cochrane's trip to the capital. Franklin testified that he "had no idea . . . the President, or anybody else who had any power" would be visited; Smith said he simply could not remember what his two subordinates had in mind. Yet the fact that with the army under marching orders a general of division and a general of brigade were granted leaves by their superiors to travel to Washington suggests these memory lapses were more convenient than real. The far more credible assumption is that William B. Franklin and William F. Smith knew exactly what their two generals were planning, and in fact had put them up to it.[1]

On reaching the capital that morning of December 30, Cochrane had Newton wait at the Metropolitan Hotel while he hunted up someone of influence to listen to their tale. He went first in search of the head of the Senate's Committee on Military Affairs, Henry Wilson of Massachusetts, and Congressman Moses F. Odell of New York, member of the powerful Joint Committee on the Conduct of the War. But Congress was in recess for the holidays and both men had left town. Nothing daunted, Cochrane determined to take his case directly to the top, to the White House. When he arrived there he encountered an old New York acquaintance, Secretary of State William H. Seward. He told enough of his story to Seward to persuade him to get them in to see the president. While Seward was arranging the appointment, Cochrane hurried back to the Metropolitan to collect the no doubt startled Newton. Now, in midafternoon, the two generals found themselves face to face with their commander-in-chief.

Poor Newton was in a dilemma. As the senior officer he had to take the lead, and what he wanted to say — what he truly believed — was that the Army of the Potomac was demoralized because it had lost all confidence in General Burnside. Should it again suffer defeat on the Rappahannock, which he believed was imminent, it would not be (as he later told the Joint Committee on the Conduct of the War) "a mere defeat, as before, but it would be a destruction." Newton would have been comfortable enough saying this to a civilian, say an influential member of Congress, but "to come square out" to his commander-in-chief was a very different matter. Should he appear to be criticizing his superior with intent to have him relieved (which was just what he and his fellow dissidents devoutly hoped would happen), he could be charged with "manifestly improper" conduct and cashiered. As Newton later confessed, he found himself "in a very delicate position in this conversation." He hemmed and hawed and talked all around the subject and hoped that somehow the president would understand that the army was indeed dispirited and would then investigate matters for himself.

Lincoln saw quickly enough what was really on Newton's mind, and wondered out loud if there might be some intent here "to injure" General Burnside. Quickly, desperately, Newton said that was the furthest thing from his mind. It was his intent only to stress "the condition of the army." At this point Cochrane weighed in to smooth things over. This was not unlike the give-and-take of political negotiation, an art John Cochrane was entirely familiar with, and he soon steered the conversation to the higher plane of selfless duty, with motives of purest patriotism. He confirmed by "personal observation" what General Newton had said of the condition of the army; surely the president could see such testimony as evidence "of patriotism and of my loyalty to the government. . . ." Mr. Lincoln recognized a practiced political hand at work, and no doubt with a sigh "resumed his ordinary manner." By Cochrane's account, the president said he was glad they had visited him, "and that good would come of the interview." With that the two generals took their leave.

From the perspective of those in the army plotting to overthrow General Burnside, something good did indeed emerge from the interview. At 3:30 that afternoon a telegram went out from the War Department to General Burnside on the Rappahannock. "I have good reason for saying you must not make a general movement of the army without letting me know," it read, and it was signed, "A. Lincoln."[2]

* *

AMBROSE EVERETT BURNSIDE was not chosen to replace General McClellan, back in November, because he displayed any obviously striking military talents. Other generals had served in the Army of the Potomac longer than he, and much more capably. His only sustained fighting record with this army, before commanding it, was in the Maryland campaign that September, in which he hardly distinguished himself. Before agreeing to accept the post, on November 7, Burnside had earlier twice rejected Lincoln's efforts to put him in McClellan's place. He told the president he was simply not qualified to lead a great army — certainly not as qualified as his friend General McClellan.

Such frankness was one of the attractions of this appealing man. He not only accepted full responsibility for the Fredericksburg disaster, but sent his statement to the newspapers to ensure its wide circulation. A fellow Potomac army general, Gouverneur K. Warren, rendered a widely accepted verdict on General Burnside: "A good fellow certainly, manly, honest, and comely." In addition to his personable nature, Burnside was without political connections or ambitions — an important considera- tion in this highly politicized army — and was well liked by the men in the ranks. This latter was a most important consideration, for there was real concern in Washington about how the troops would react to the dismissal of their beloved "Little Mac." Ambrose Burnside might not have been the best man for the job of commanding general, but he was surely the safest one in the peculiar circumstances of wrenching General McClellan out of the army he was so much a part of.

Having praise for Burnside the man, Gouverneur Warren went on to take the measure of Burnside the soldier, and found him wanting: "But of only moderate mind and attainments, who has made our cause suffer more in battle than any other Genl. . . ." Observers concluded that Burn- side's humility, which he displayed publicly so often that it was played up by the newspapers, amounted to self-fulfilling prophecy. George Gordon Meade, commanding the Fifth Corps, thought this trait a major factor in Burnside's troubles. "Another drawback," he told Mrs. Meade, "was a very general opinion among officers and men, brought about by his own assertions, that the command was too much for him. This greatly weak- ened his position." Neither Warren nor Meade was part of the cabal formed against Burnside, yet they saw clearly the army commander's wounds, and the sharks circling for the kill.[3]

Burnside was startled by Lincoln's telegraphed order to make no advance without first consulting him. He believed no one outside the high command of the Army of the Potomac knew his plans; the telegram must mean there were military operations elsewhere requiring his coop- eration. He replied that he was rescinding orders already issued, and would come up to Washington the next day to consult. Morning of the last day of the year 1862 found him in the president's office.

Lincoln came directly to the point. Certain general officers of the Army of the Potomac had called on him — he did not reveal their names — to say that the army was moving to the attack, and that the attack "would result in disaster." By Burnside's testimony, he was too surprised at this to remember everything the president told him of the visitors' story, yet he did record one very important element of that story that Newton and Cochrane would neglect to mention in recounting their December 30 call on the president. According to Burnside, the president "said that he had understood that no prominent officer of my command had any faith in my proposed movement." It is highly unlikely that Generals Newton and Cochrane had sufficient contact with every "prominent officer" in the army to risk making such a ringing judgment on their own. But generals of the station of William Franklin and William Smith certainly had those contacts — and would have been glad enough to offer this glittering nugget to their two subordinates before sending them off to Washington on their mission.

Burnside launched into an earnest explanation of his planned movement. In the December 13 battle he had thrown pontoon bridges across the Rappahannock directly in front of Fredericksburg. This time he planned to cross a flanking column a half-dozen miles downstream from the town, and to make a show of crossing above the town as well. All this would be combined with a powerful raiding force of cavalry slicing in behind the Confederates from the west to cut their communications with Richmond. The plan displayed a good deal more imagination than Burnside's earlier head-on lurch across the river, yet the president was uneasy about it. What he had been told of the attitude of Burnside's generals troubled him, and Burnside provided small comfort with the admission that "some of my general officers" did indeed have what he termed "misgivings" about the operation.

Lincoln said he wanted to hear what his advisers, Secretary of War Edwin M. Stanton and General-in-Chief Henry W. Halleck, had to say on the subject. Unveiling his streak of humility, Burnside said that if both his officers and his men lacked confidence in him, he thought he should resign his command. And since he was on the subject, he added that as far as he could tell, there was a definite lack of confidence in the army toward both Secretary Stanton and General Halleck. Taken all together, there was very little in this conversation to give Mr. Lincoln much encouragement about the military picture.[4]

The day's events had generated in General Burnside a rising anger, and that evening, in his room at Willard's Hotel, he composed a forthright letter to the president. What he had said that morning ought to be on the record, he thought. He began by asserting that Secretary of War Stanton "has not the confidence of the country." To which he added, "The same opinion applies with equal force in regard to General Halleck." It was, he observed pointedly, "of the utmost importance" that both secretary of war and general-in-chief possess "the confidence of the people and the army." From that it was but a tiny step to the inference that General Burnside thought both men should resign.

As for himself, Burnside left no doubt about what he thought. Because he was so out of step with his general officers, brought on no doubt by their "lack of confidence in me," it would be in the best interests of the president and the country that he resign. "In this case it is highly necessary that this army should be commanded by some other officer, to whom I will most cheerfully give way."

January 1, 1863, New Year's Day, promised to be a milestone for Abraham Lincoln. The Emancipation Proclamation, with his signature that day, would mark out a new direction for the war and for the country. The signing ceremony was scheduled for noon. First, however, the president had to meet with Burnside, Stanton, and Halleck at the War Department to discuss what was to be done, if anything, with the Army of the Potomac.

This strategy meeting deeply disappointed him. Burnside began by handing his newly written letter of resignation (and comment) to the president, who read it and without a word returned it to him. That was not enough for Burnside. He was Burnside the Honest, believing he owed it to Stanton and Halleck to tell the whole truth of what he had told the president. He announced his opinion that neither they (nor he) had the confidence of the army and of the country. The anti-Burnside cabal would claim that Burnside brazenly told Stanton and Halleck to their faces that they should resign. Halleck blandly denied that any such thing was said in his presence, which was true enough but evasive. No one at this conference was so obtuse as to miss Burnside's unsubtle hint that they as well as he ought to resign.

Lincoln's silence closed debate on the matter of resignations, and then they became sidetracked over the identity of the president's December 30 visitors. The more he reflected on it the angrier Burnside had become at these talebearers who (he thought) had betrayed him, and he wanted them cashiered. Halleck was equally indignant in calling for their dismissal, but the president refused to give up the names.

When he tried to turn the discussion to Burnside's plan of campaign, Lincoln gained no better results. Burnside still wanted to make the movement despite his high command's opposition, and consequently he wanted specific approval and support from Washington. Stanton would not commit himself on such military matters. Halleck spoke only in the most general terms of an advance on the Rappahannock, insisting that it was the responsibility of the general commanding on the scene to plot the time and place and nature of the movement. Soon they were back where they began. "No definite conclusion was come to, during

7

the conference, in reference to the subject of a movement," Burnside testified.[5]

Here was another of those moments that had frustrated President Lincoln so often during the long months of General McClellan's command. Here again, the president could not get an army, or a general, to move or to act or to do anything he wanted. After the meeting he wrote a letter to General Halleck. The general-in-chief, he said, knew what Burnside wanted to do and knew the situation on the Rappahannock. "If in such a difficulty as this you do not help, you fail me precisely in the point for which I sought your assistance." He wanted Halleck to go with Burnside to the army, look over the ground there, confer with the generals, and come back with a definite opinion "that you *do* approve, or that you do *not* approve the plan. Your military skill is useless to me, if you will not do this."

The post of general-in-chief in the American army was not then well defined; whatever definition it had was due to the man who happened to be holding it at the time. McClellan had manned the post during the winter of 1861–62 and did so actively, working closely with his generals in the field to formulate plans and coordinate movements. Henry Halleck played the role differently. He hated the job, for one thing, and remained in it only out of a sense of duty. He saw himself essentially as chief clerk of the army, making sure that things were done in proper form and by the book, that military policies — established by others — were carried out in the most efficient way possible.

In a letter to Burnside a few days later, Halleck nicely stated this attitude. Yes, he wrote, there should be a general advance on the Rappahannock. Yes, he would support such a move. Yes, there were various avenues of approach, all of them with merit. "The character of the movement, however, must depend upon circumstances which may change any day and almost any hour." As he saw it, it was simply not his job to do what the president wanted, to go into the field and pass judgment on specific operations. In his response to the president's letter, he said that if he was required to obey these instructions he wanted to be relieved from the post of general-in-chief. Recognizing that once again he was stymied, Mr. Lincoln wrote across the file copy of his letter to Halleck, "Withdrawn, because considered harsh by Gen. Halleck." The net result of the New Year's Day strategy meeting was the proffered resignations of his two top generals.[6]

* *

WHEN HE returned to his headquarters at Falmouth on the Rappahannock, General Burnside was unable to contain either his anger or his anguish. Rather than taking a stoic, determined stance toward his intractable command, he poured out his troubles without reservation to anyone who would listen. Soon enough the commanders of the three grand divisions — William Franklin, Edwin Sumner, and Joseph Hooker — knew all about his trip to Washington, and so did a half-dozen other general officers. General Meade wrote his wife on January 2 that Burnside even read to him the letter of resignation he had offered the president, not only detailing his own reasons for resigning but hinting that the general-in-chief and the secretary of war ought to resign as well. Whatever Burnside hoped to gain by this spasm of confession, its larger effect was to further weaken his already shaky control over the army's officer corps. "God only knows what is to become of us and what will be done," Meade concluded.

Franklin and his cohort "Baldy" Smith were meanwhile doing their best to drum up support within the officer ranks for changing the line of campaign from the Rappahannock to the Peninsula. General Franklin, Meade wrote, "is very positive in his opinion that we cannot go to Richmond on this line. . . ." With Burnside equally adamant in support of the Rappahannock approach, the Franklin-Smith cabal recognized that its best hope lay in seeing Burnside resign, to be succeeded by the general many in the officer corps believed should never have been relieved — George B. McClellan. Surely a condition of McClellan's return would be the freedom to choose his own line of advance in Virginia. No one could imagine this being anything but a return to the Peninsula.

Gouverneur Warren, in command of a brigade under Meade, was certain that after Fredericksburg there was but one answer to the army's command problem: "We *must* have McClellan back with unlimited and unfettered powers. His name is a tower of strength to everyone here. . . ." General McClellan was then the army's highest ranking general on active duty, although at the moment he was without a command and posted in New York City writing a voluminous report on his fifteen months as head of the Army of the Potomac. McClellan had shaped that army in his own image, convincing those in the ranks to identify personally with him and with his leadership. "I am to watch over you as a parent over his children," he announced to his troops; "and you know that your General loves you from the depths of his heart." Many had taken him to their hearts, and many still felt that way. "He is still admired by the army & spoken of with love & confidence," wrote Colonel William H. Withington of the 17th Michigan ten days after Fredericksburg. "Burnside is liked of course, who could not help liking Burnside but they feel as though McClellan was their man." George W. Lambert of the 14th Indiana was more direct. The slogan "McClellan is the man," he wrote, "is a great deal more unanimous now than it was before this grand failure."[7]

Even stronger and more lasting was McClellan's impact on the Army of the Potomac's officer corps. The officer ranks, from grand division down through corps, division, and brigade, were honeycombed with men who owed their places to General McClellan. They were imbued with his very careful, very cautious, very restrained style of command, a style that set a high premium on obedience to the letter of orders and a low priority on individuality and initiative. The Army of the Potomac was the Union's shield, McClellan had said: it must never under any circumstances be put at serious risk; it must always be preserved to fight another day. If McClellan and his disciples could be said to have a motto, it was "Better safe than sorry."

To be sure, while a majority of these disciples (like General Warren) might long for the day of McClellan's return, they would do their duty (as they conceived it) under General Burnside. The cabal led by Franklin and Baldy Smith set a course to undercut the commanding general, to force him out to clear the way for the return of their favorite. This revolt of the generals might be limited in size, but should it make headway it was unlikely to encounter much opposition from within the officer corps of the army. General Burnside had few diehard supporters.

The contretemps in the high command soon was the talk of Washington. General Samuel Heintzelman, in charge of the capital's defenses, recorded in his diary on January 5 that General Halleck had described for him Burnside's plan to cross the Rappahannock, "when two Generals came to town, saw Mr. Lincoln & he sent orders not to do it." Heintzelman had his own sources of inside information, and added, "I heard since that Genls. Newton & Cochrane who got leave from Gen. Franklin were the officers." He could not understand how "such conduct is tolerated."

On the same date, Sam Ward, a veteran Washington lobbyist, was writing of the latest reports he had picked up from the army — that General Burnside had offered his resignation to the president, and recommended that Stanton and Halleck also resign. Speculating that major change was imminent for the Army of the Potomac, Ward introduced another name into the witches' brew at the high-command level — Major General Joseph Hooker.

"You will recollect that I told you long since of Hooker," Ward reminded his correspondent, "and if possible he would through his unscrupulous action succeed in ousting everyone above him." He named Hooker the new favorite of the Republican radicals, one who "will answer their purposes." Had he seen this last remark, Joe Hooker would have nodded in agreement.

General Hooker wanted just as devoutly as any in the Franklin-Smith cabal to see Burnside overthrown, only with a notably different outcome. He had as little use for McClellan in army command as he had for Burnside, and so he operated independently of the cabal. Joe Hooker had long since come to think of Joe Hooker as the best man to lead the Army of the Potomac. He had expected to be McClellan's successor; indeed, back in November, only by threatening to give Hooker the command had the administration persuaded Burnside to take it. (Ambrose Burnside actively disliked very few people, and Joe Hooker was one of the few.)

After that setback Hooker plotted his campaign more carefully. He made sure the press was aware of the addled state of the high command. Even before Fredericksburg he denounced Burnside's generalship in an interview with Henry Villard of the *New York Tribune*. "His language was so severe and, at the same time, so infused with self-assurance," Villard later wrote, that he was sure the general was trying to use him "for his own glorification and for the detraction of others."

Hooker was shrewd enough to give equal attention to the politics of the case. A lifelong Democrat, even an anti-abolitionist, he now paid homage to radical Republicanism without a backward glance. He cultivated in particular Treasury Secretary Chase and Secretary of War Stanton, whom he took to be the most influential Cabinet members. The Fredericksburg disaster seemed to confirm everything Hooker had been saying. When Congress's Joint Committee on the Conduct of the War investigated the management of that battle, Hooker in his testimony was unsparing of Burnside's shortcomings. For good measure, he also found fault with General Franklin's part in the fighting, thus putting down a potential rival. The radical Republicans who dominated the committee found much to applaud in Hooker's testimony. As Sam Ward observed, promoting Joe Hooker's candidacy for army command suited the committee's purposes very nicely — and suitably braced Hooker's confidence. On January 17 Marsena R. Patrick, the army's provost marshal, recorded in his diary, "Hooker says he can have command of this Army when he will say the word. . . ."[8]

* *

THE FREDERICKSBURG defeat of December 13 had acted like the bursting of a dam, flooding Lincoln with problems that taken together threatened to swamp his presidency. The Army of the Potomac, the

Union's principal army, was fighting under its fourth commander in little more than eighteen months and had suffered its worst defeat yet. The bitter divisions within its high command, brought by fractious generals directly to the White House, spilled over into the newspapers and generated partisan debate. The Joint Committee on the Conduct of the War's investigation of Fredericksburg was also widely reported in the press, further heating the debate. "Many of these attacks," editorialized the *New York Times* on January 13, "are obviously and avowedly made in the interest of the late Commander of the Army of the Potomac; while all of them have . . . the effect of disheartening the loyal North, and giving encouragement to the rebellion."

Reforms were urged on the president. He was advised to set up a high-level Military Council to furnish sound military advice (from such as General McClellan) and thereby spread the responsibility for decision-making. A Republican caucus in Congress sent a delegation to the White House to demand a shakeup and reconstruction of the Cabinet, which might or might not improve the management of the war but beyond any doubt represented a threat to Mr. Lincoln's leadership. The president adroitly maneuvered out of harm's way, yet he knew the threat had only been postponed, not eliminated.[9]

For many in the North Fredericksburg became a vivid symbol of all that was wrong with the way this war was being waged. It was fresh ammunition for those on the home front with antiwar sentiments, and for the newspapers that fanned those sentiments. Colonel Lucius Fairchild of the 2nd Wisconsin wrote his wife on December 30 that after the battle many in the Army of the Potomac "were most heartily tired of the war, & would be willing to accept peace on most any terms. . . . I think the *fight* is out of the men." Colonel Fairchild blamed outside influences for much of this. "A very great deal of the discouragement comes from the North — from Northern papers & from Northern speakers — who to save their own selfish ends would sacrifice all things." Rather than finding encouragement in the newspapers, he wrote, the men read "nothing but howlings against the Administration — against our Generals — detailing all the North *has not* accomplished — instead of what it has. . . ." And he added, "I am sorry to have cause to think all this — but I must believe what I see. . . ."

The Emancipation Proclamation created further problems for the administration. While it strengthened support for the war among antislavery and radical Republican forces across the North — and promised to bring thousands of black soldiers into the ranks to fight for their freedom — at the same time it seriously weakened coalition support for the war among Democrats. Emancipation promised a social revolution that few were ready for; a war for Union was one thing, a war to end slavery seemed something very different.

Strong feelings were expressed on the subject in the Army of the Potomac. New Englander Edwin O. Wentworth saw by the newspapers, he told his wife, "that we hail the nigger proclamation with pleasure, and are *willing* to die, all of us, if thereby the nigger can be freed. This is a d——d lie! The army is enthusiastic to go home." The 75th Ohio's Lieutenant Colonel Robert A. Constable was discharged from the service "for disloyalty" after publicly denouncing the Proclamation. As one of his men explained it, Constable had said he "did not come out to fight to free the damned niggers, so he got a free pass to Ohio. . . . Id hate to be in his situation." A New Jersey soldier wrote home that his regiment used to cheer Mr. Lincoln at reviews, "but if he were to appear today the men would be just as eager to receive him with groans."

Pessimism became the common coin for many at home. According to the New York diarist George Templeton Strong, "The way the Dirt-Eaters and Copperheads and sympathizers and compromisers are coming out on the surface of society . . . shows that the nation is suffering from a most putrescent state of the national blood. . . ." The *Chicago Tribune*'s Joseph Medill believed that "The people are growing exceedingly tired of the war and are becoming very much discouraged." Medill was sure there would be an armistice stopping the fighting during 1863. "Well what then?" he asked. "Why, we have to fight for a *boundary* — that is all now left to us. . . ." Governor Oliver Morton of Illinois was of a like mind. Morton described forces in the states of the Old Northwest that would dictate an armistice and strike a bargain with the Confederacy for a new Union "upon the condition of leaving out the New England states; this they believe the Rebel leaders will accept, and so do I." Such despairing talk as this was fueled by a sobering statistic announced in Congress in mid-January. In the North the cost of the war was now running at $2.5 million a day, "Sundays included," a figure so much beyond the government's income that the deficit was growing $1.9 million every day.[10]

At the center of this galaxy of problems, and linked to all of them, lay the army. Victory on the battlefield contained the promise to change everything, restoring morale in the army and on the home front, making all the sacrifices seem worthwhile. Once the army problem was solved, other problems might suddenly seem smaller. But as 1863 began Union victories remained elusive. At the turn of the year, at Murfreesboro in Tennessee, Federals and Confederates fought to bloody exhaustion, and when it was over so little had changed that neither side had a legitimate claim to victory. To the west, along the Mississippi, Federal operations against the citadel of Vicksburg began badly and future prospects there were clouded in uncertainty. In the eastern theater, unless General Burnside could after all generate some kind of victorious campaign on the Rappahannock, the promise was only stalemate — stalemate following months of costly, empty campaigning.

Mr. Lincoln possessed a clear and stark view of what he called the "awful arithmetic" required of the general who commanded the Army of the Potomac. He observed to his secretary, William Stoddard, that at Fredericksburg the Potomac army had lost 50 percent more men than the enemy army, yet if the two should refight that battle, with the same result, every day "through a week of days," the enemy army would be wiped out and the Potomac army would still be "a mighty host." As Stoddard recorded it, the president said that "No general yet found can face the arithmetic, but the end of the war will be at hand when he shall be discovered." Even at that, however, there was the further question: Would the men in the ranks of the Army of the Potomac face the awful arithmetic?

Generals Newton and Cochrane had painted a picture for the president of these men as demoralized, and hinted at the unthinkable — that in another battle under Burnside they might simply refuse to fight. A great deal of talk like this was running through the army. To be sure, there was never a moment in the life of this army (or of any army) when the men in it did not complain about one thing or another. To complain was a soldier's right, and to claim demoralization sometimes had its uses. Captain Henry Abbott of the 20th Massachusetts recorded with sardonic amusement an incident during the recent Fredericksburg battle. "A runaway soldier," he wrote home, "coming full tilt from the town is stopped by the guard at the bridge. 'For God's sake, don't stop me,' the soldier cries, 'I'm demoralized as hell.'"[11]

Yet it was different now. In the month or two after Fredericksburg evidence that the fighting men of the Army of the Potomac were indeed demoralized was everywhere. One cause of this had been the peculiar visibility of the December battle. The repeated, murderous charges against Marye's Heights occurred in a veritable amphitheater, within sight and hearing of scores of thousands. What happened at the same time offstage, in William Franklin's Left Grand Division, was not so easily seen or known. Burnside had expected Franklin to execute a powerful turning movement against the enemy's flank. Franklin instead displayed all the storied caution of his mentor, General McClellan, and the turning movement dribbled away ineffectually. That left the frontal attacks on Marye's Heights to be seen, and remembered.

Corporal Edward H. Wade of the 14th Connecticut explained it to his homefolks: "The last battle was a wholesale slaughter and they *never* can get the troops into another such a field." Corporal Wade's regiment was part of the Second Corps, and in mid-January when Burnside reviewed that veteran corps he was (as one officer phrased it) "coldly received by the men." Called upon for the usual three cheers for the general commanding — routine during the days of McClellan — the troops' response was stony silence.

There was a second and even stronger reason for the widespread demoralization. The system that bound these individual soldiers collectively into an army had broken down. The most fundamental needs were not being met. The men were fed badly, clothed badly, housed badly, cared for badly. They were not paid on anything remotely resembling a proper schedule. Hubert Dilger, captain of Battery I, 1st Ohio Light Artillery, would in desperation write directly to President Lincoln to complain that his men had not been paid in almost seven months. Nor was this an extreme case; there was not a man in Burnside's army who could say his pay account was up-to-date and current. For soldiers trying to support a family on their army pay, this was a crisis.

In the matter of pay the fault lay with the War Department (and the Treasury) in Washington, but there was much else wrong that was the fault of the high command of the Army of the Potomac. A hospital steward working near the army's main supply base at Aquia Landing on the Potomac almost casually described for his mother "a convalescent camp that is killing the boys off at the rate of 15 or 20 a day." The sick there were living (and dying) on an unvarying diet of hardtack, salt pork, and black coffee. This diet was bad enough for men who were well; for anyone with dysentery or typhoid it could kill. A few miles away, in the Aquia Landing warehouses, were the vegetables and fresh fruit and soft bread and broths and concentrated milk needed to make them well, and all of it out of reach.

Massachusetts's Lieutenant Henry Ropes, writing home on January 5, said he was able to offer a visitor to camp from Boston nothing but bad beef and worse coffee — "Although when he goes to Headquarters he dines on canvasback ducks and champagne." By way of contrast, Lieutenant Ropes continued, "The men suffering a great deal for lack of fresh food and sufficient variety. Diarrhoea and scurvy almost universal." There were indeed hundreds of cases of scurvy, a disease well known to be the result of diet deficiency and well known to be curable, yet men died of scurvy anyway.[12]

In part the problem here was corruption in the commissary department, with thieving quartermasters lining their pockets by the private sale of "extras" from the warehouses. That winter, wrote a bitter regimental historian, many a supply officer enriched himself for life. But as much as anything else, the fault was bureaucratic incompetence and indifference. Mounds of requisition forms and miles of red tape smothered the system, and there seemed to be no one with authority enough and regulations enough — and dedication enough — to unsnarl the tangle. Army hospitals, for example, were miserable places to begin with, badly equipped, unsanitary, even unheated because no one had thought to order proper stoves. Patients in them suffered frostbite that winter. "I do not believe I have ever seen greater misery from sickness than exists now in our Army of the Potomac" was how a War Department medical inspector-general summed it up after a January visit to the Rappahannock front.

In harsh fact, the officer corps of the Army of the Potomac, from General Burnside on down, was failing dismally in that most fundamental duty of an officer — to take care of his men. Too many officers, it was observed, were hardly models of good conduct. Indeed, according to a report to the Senate on January 7, no fewer than 411 commissioned officers of the Potomac army were absent without leave. In the opinion of Captain John T. Boyle of the 96th Pennsylvania, "The men have caught the infection from the officers and seem to have lost much of their fire and energy." Brigadier General Carl Schurz, who led a division made up largely of German troops and who wrote regularly to Mr. Lincoln about the state of affairs in the army, was unsparing on this topic. The worst of it was, he told the president, "the spirit of the men is systematically broken by officers high in command." He saw desertions "increasing at a frightful rate." Take all this together, General Schurz warned, "and you will not be surprised when you see this great army melt away with frightful rapidity."

At the other extreme of rank, Private Robert Goodyear of the 27th Connecticut thought the man in the ranks had reached his breaking point. "The soldier of today has a keen perception . . . ," he wrote. "Abused, humbugged, imposed upon and frequently half-starved and sick, he sees himself made a mere tool for political speculators to operate with. Led on to slaughter and defeat by drunken and incompetent officers, he has become disheartened, discouraged, demoralized."[13]

* *

ABIDING PROOF of the Potomac army's demoralization is in the numbers — the numbers of men deserting from the Rappahannock camps in the weeks after the Battle of Fredericksburg and heading for home. They were deserting at the known risk of severe punishment if caught, up to and including execution by firing squad. They went anyway, and in numbers unprecedented in the army's history.

The Army of the Potomac, to be sure, had always been plagued by the category labeled "absent" on the returns. It was a catchall category, a total of all the men carried on the rolls but not present and accounted for in camp. Some of these men were away from the army legitimately, on furlough or on detached service, such as recruiting duty in their home states. A considerably larger number were the seriously sick and wounded who had been sent north on the sound enough theory that they might recover faster under the care of their homefolks. While these men too were said to be absent by authority, they were out from under direct army control and few of them displayed much eagerness to return to the service. During the Peninsula campaign General McClellan had complained that of the 40,000 listed as absent at least 20,000 were recuperating men "fit for duty" but not back with the army, and that situation had not been resolved in the months since then. The third group in the absent category were the true deserters, the absent without leave, who were not going to return to the army under any circumstances if they could possibly help it.

"I think that if Uncle Sam don't settle this war pretty quick that it will play out for the deserters is a going out by great numbers . . . ," John E. Ryder of the 24th Michigan wrote home on January 4. It seemed that every letter writer in the army had something to say about this suddenly current topic. Sanford N. Truesdell of the 122nd New York, for example, reported that desertions "are of daily occurrence in almost every Regt. in the field, and sometimes in squads of fifteen or twenty at a time, and they are very rarely brought back." One cause of their going, he thought, was disgust with the Emancipation Proclamation. Charles H. Brewster of the 10th Massachusetts observed that in his division there were two courts-martial operating "in full blast" trying nothing but cases of desertion. "They have apprehended from 2 to 300," he wrote, "and I sincerely hope they will shoot about one half of them." Brewster noted that new regiments containing men who had been paid sizable bounties to enlist "are much the worst in this respect." Bounty-men deserters, he thought, fully deserved the death penalty.[14]

Brigadier General Marsena Patrick, Army of the Potomac provost marshal, was driven to distraction by the rush of deserters. What particularly troubled Patrick was the organization of it. Would-be deserters would arrange to have civilian clothes sent to them from home, then slip out of camp after dark, change into their new garb, and head north with little fear of being identified. On any night any unit on picket duty might find dozens of discarded uniforms in the bushes. The more brazen passed themselves off as Confederate deserters, thereby getting a parole and a free ride out of the army. Late in January a cavalry patrol stumbled on and captured no less than 400 deserters near the supply base at Aquia Landing who were building rafts to ferry themselves across the Potomac to safety in Maryland. Confederate sympathizers operated a sort of underground railroad to provide safe houses for deserters on their way north. One such Southerner, caught in the act, was tried by a military court, sentenced to six months' hard labor, and saw his house burned to the ground. Another "undisguised rebel," a Dr. Stewart, supplied slaves' rough work clothes to deserters before sending them across the Potomac into Maryland.

General Patrick was convinced that one of the factors contributing to the army's demoralization, the late pay or little pay, ironically had a direct connection to the desertion rate. Whenever men did finally get paid, Patrick found, it only encouraged them to desert by providing resources for their escape. He recorded in his diary on January 17 a visit from a Third Corps provost marshal who told him, "The Excelsiors are determined to run if they can get a chance, having been paid off today." The Excelsior Brigade — 70th through 74th New York regiments — was one of the better combat outfits in the army. One of the Excelsiors, writing home about this time, insisted "I will never go home on the French leave, but there is a great many leaving in that way." Should more troops be paid off, Patrick predicted "very large desertions & no possibility of staying them."[15]

An order to each regiment and battery to list its absentees and classify them as absent with or without authority produced an unprecedented result. While the overall number of absentees, 85,908, was about the same as the previous November, when Burnside became army commander, the breakdown of the total was very different now. In November the bulk of the men not with the army were the sick and wounded from the severe and continuous fighting of the summer and fall. Now the proportion of sick and wounded had fallen, and the proportion of deserters had risen dramatically. It was found that of the men carried on the rolls of the Army of the Potomac in the field, on the Rappahannock, at the end of January, no fewer than one in ten was a deserter. By report, they "were scattered all over the country," and the rate of desertion had reached 200 a day. The total on January 31 came to 25,363, a veritable corps of deserters. Indeed, this was second only to the Sixth Corps, the largest then with the army.

S. M. Carpenter, a correspondent for the *New York Herald,* wrote his editor from Falmouth that everywhere he looked he found men demoralized and deserting by scores. "Evil days have befallen us, and no one seems at hand to deliver us. God grant that the Army of the Potomac may not continue to degenerate until its power of resuscitation is wholly lost."[16]

* *

THE REVOLT among his generals helped steel Ambrose Burnside to action, regardless of the consequences, if for no other reason than to face them down. The result has come down in the annals of the Army of the Potomac as the Mud March. The episode seemed proof that ill fortune was the lot of this unhappy commanding general. In the judgment of a regimental surgeon, "The Fates have certainly completed his destruction in the Army."

After the president suspended his late December offensive, General Burnside concluded that his plan for crossing the Rappahannock downstream from Fredericksburg was compromised, and determined on another scheme. This time he would cross on the upstream side at Banks's Ford to turn Fredericksburg's defenses from the west, and he would act as quickly as possible. On January 20 he issued an address to the troops. "The commanding general announces to the Army of the Potomac that they are about to meet the enemy once more," it began, and by midday the march upriver was well begun. The way was led by Burnside's two most outspoken detractors, grand-division commanders Franklin and Hooker.

From the moment the march orders were issued Franklin and the Sixth Corps' Baldy Smith opened a litany of complaint. Some of this they registered with Burnside himself, some with anyone who would listen. Colonel Charles S. Wainwright of the artillery visited Franklin's headquarters the day before the movement began and recorded in his diary, "Both his staff and Smith's are talking outrageously, only repeating though, no doubt, the words of their generals. . . . Franklin has talked so much and so loudly to this effect ever since the present move was decided on, that he has completely demoralized his whole command, and so rendered failure doubly sure. . . . Smith and they say Hooker are almost as bad." Even during the march this disaffected talk continued, Wainwright noted. "The whole army seems to know what they have said, and their speeches condemning the move were in the mouths of everyone."[17]

On the evening of the first day's march it began to rain, a full-fledged winter nor'easter, coming down hard and cold and windblown, and it continued for more than forty-eight hours. The ground thawed and flooded and the army became quickly and hopelessly stuck in the mud. The infantry might have made some progress if it had gotten off the roads and into the woods, but the wheeled vehicles — the guns and the wagons and the ambulances and especially the hulking pontoon trains for the bridge crossings — were literally stopped in their tracks.

"At dark we went into park," quartermaster Samuel Partridge reported. "The ground was so soft that the wagons settled to the hub, and the mules over the fetlock." In the pontoon trains teams were doubled, then tripled, with in addition as many as 150 infantry manning ropes, but all to little effect. A newspaperman was reminded of a gang of Lilliputians trying to move "huge-ribbed Gulliver." Infantry were also put to work corduroying the roads. George Nichols of the 32nd Massachusetts thought it an endless task: "Each regiment would march off to some fence and make a grand charge on it and then march off each with a rail on his shoulder. We realized that day at least, that we were in the Army of 'Honest Abe' the rail splitter."

General Alpheus Williams wrote his daughter afterward, "It is solemnly true that we lost mules in the middle of the road, sinking out of sight in the mud-holes. A few bubbles of air, a stirring of the watery mud, indicated the last expiring efforts of many a poor long-ears." Across the river the Confederates watched and jeered and put up signs taunting the mired Yankees. Colonel George H. Sharpe, soon to become the Potomac army's intelligence chief, noted with professional interest that at least one Rebel sign-painter seemed to have full details on the movement. "Burnside and his pontoons stuck in the mud," his sign read. "Move at 1 o'clock, 3 days' rations in haversacks."[18]

At last Burnside recognized the futility of it and ordered the troops back to their camps. The return was as difficult as the advance had been. Straggling was heavy, and an uncounted number of men deserted and were never seen again. Guns and wagons and pontoons by the scores had to be left until the roads dried and they could be moved. Veterans of the Army of the Potomac would look back on the Mud March as the nadir of their military experience. Observers at the time wondered if anything could ever be worse. "Burnside rode along yesterday and was followed by hooting and yells," Lieutenant Henry Ropes wrote on January 23. "The troops are in a dreadful state." General Burnside, Ropes thought, "has brought the Army to the verge of mutiny and the country to the worst case it has ever been in."

Traveling with the army during these adventures was Henry J. Raymond, editor of the *New York Times,* who was appalled by the turmoil in the high command. He learned of the backstairs maneuvering in the officer corps for McClellan's return; of the lack of confidence in Burnside ("because he lacks confidence in himself," one officer said); of Generals Franklin and Smith undercutting their superior at every opportunity. And from the *Times*'s army correspondent William Swinton editor Raymond got an earful of Joe Hooker's broadsides aimed at everyone in sight.

General Hooker, Raymond was told, "has talked very openly about the absurdity of the movement . . . , denounced the commanding general as incompetent, and the President and Government at Washington as imbecile and 'played out.'" Nothing would go right, so Hooker said, "until we had a dictator, and the sooner the better."

Raymond shared these findings with General Burnside, and by the time he was back at his Falmouth headquarters the general was seething. Even before the Mud March, he told Raymond, he had considered relieving Franklin and Smith; only the need to keep the movement on schedule stayed his hand. Now he was free to act, and he determined to crush the revolt of the generals with one blow. General Order No. 8, "By command of Maj. Gen. A. E. Burnside," dated January 23, was an extraordinary document.

Heading Burnside's list of targets was Joe Hooker, whom he ordered dismissed from the service for (among other things) "having been guilty of unjust and unnecessary criticisms of the actions of his superior officers." Also dismissed was Brigadier General William T. H. Brooks, one of Baldy Smith's division commanders, whom Burnside had put in arrest earlier in the month for insubordination.

By this time Burnside had learned the identity of the two talebearers who visited the president on December 30, and Generals John Newton and John Cochrane were also dismissed from the service. William Franklin and Baldy Smith and Colonel J. H. Taylor, of Franklin's staff, being "of no further service to this army," were relieved of their commands and ordered to Washington for reassignment. By now thrashing about in all directions, Burnside relieved two lesser officers, an action he later admitted was done in error.

As soon as the order was drawn up, Burnside showed it to the *Times*'s Raymond and to his medical officer, Dr. William H. Church. While Raymond applauded the document, especially its condemnation of Hooker, he wondered if that general might be tempted to raise the troops of his command in mutiny against his dismissal. Let Hooker try it, Burnside said grimly, and he would "swing *him* before sundown." He was ready to issue General Order No. 8 on the spot until Dr. Church reminded him that such major command changes could not take effect without President Lincoln's approval. Burnside promptly telegraphed the president that he was coming up to Washington with "some very important orders, and I want to see you before issuing them."[19]

* *

NEWSPAPERS REACHING the Union camps on the Rappahannock just at this time carried a front-page story of sobering interest to the dissident generals. Reading between the lines, it was evident that the army administration in Washington and President Lincoln had (so to speak) fired a warning shot across the bows of the officer corps of the Army of the Potomac. The papers announced that on January 21, while the army was wallowing through the Mud March, the president had approved the verdict of a general court-martial sitting in Washington that found Major General Fitz John Porter guilty as charged and cashiering him from the army.

The Porter court-martial had carried with it the odor of notoriety from the moment it convened on December 3, 1862. General Porter was charged with failure to obey lawful orders and with misbehavior before the enemy at the Second Battle of Manassas, fought in late August, during which he commanded the Fifth Corps. The Federals were beaten and Porter was accused of being the primary cause of it. He was also on trial for something more shadowy than that. Fitz John Porter had been George McClellan's virtual alter ego throughout that general's time of command. Consequently, he was whispered to be the virtual personification of McClellanism, the taint now said to be infecting the Army of the Potomac.

As the Porter court-martial progressed, through December and into January, evidence of that taint seemed to grow plainer day by day. There was the report of failings at the Battle of Fredericksburg by McClellan disciple William Franklin; the well-publicized generals' revolt against Burnside; the widespread demoralization within the army; the cries for McClellan's restoration. The nine-member court sitting in judgment of Porter was hardly blind to such signals. The makeup of the court was the work of Secretary of War Stanton and was suspect; Porter complained that he would need "proof strong as holy writ" to win his case. After the judges' verdict but before it was announced, Porter wrote to General McClellan, "the court began to smell your return to power and were influenced by it in their decision." It was a prophetic analysis.

Whatever the merits of the specific charges against General Porter — his cashiering would be reversed, after a rehearing, twenty-three years later — he was silently declared guilty of another military crime. On the day the verdict was announced, the Potomac army's Captain Charles

Russell Lowell recognized the deeper significance of the case. Porter's "frame of mind was un-officer-like and dangerous," Lowell wrote. "This sort of feeling was growing in the army, and the Government and the Country felt that it must be stopped. Porter was made the example." Mr. Lincoln, by approving the Porter verdict, underlined its message: any officer of the Army of the Potomac who dared to direct his loyalty elsewhere than to the general commanding did so at his peril.[20]

On January 23, in Falmouth, Generals Franklin and Smith lunched with the commanding general. Baldy Smith recalled with pleasure the fare being a boned turkey that someone in Rhode Island had sent the general. Burnside seemed "very variable in spirits — at times almost gay and then relapsing into moodiness," and Smith was particularly struck by one remark. "You will presently hear of something that will astonish you all," Burnside promised. He offered the conspirators no further hint of the fate he had planned for them.

The next morning Burnside reached the White House and presented the president with an unhappy choice. He handed him General Order No. 8 and with it his resignation of his major general's commission. He said he did not want to embarrass the president, or to stand in opposition to him, but a choice must be made. The only way he could continue in command of the Army of the Potomac would be without the officers named in the order. The president must either endorse General Order No. 8 or accept his resignation. As he had done at their earlier meeting when Burnside first offered to resign, Lincoln said he would consider the matter and speak with his advisers, and asked Burnside to return the next day.

That Saturday evening President and Mrs. Lincoln held a reception at the White House, which a newspaper reported was "unusually well attended." Among the guests was Henry Raymond, the *New York Times* editor, who buttonholed the president to report on his recent visit to the army. Raymond was at particular pains to relay *Times* correspondent Swinton's conversation with Joe Hooker. He quoted Hooker's unsparing comments on Burnside and on the administration and on Mr. Lincoln himself, as well as his view that what the country needed was a dictator and the sooner the better. The president put his hand on Raymond's shoulder and spoke in his ear, so as not to be overheard: "That is all true — Hooker does talk badly; but the trouble is, he is stronger with the country to-day than any other man."[21]

On Sunday morning, January 25, when the president called Secretary Stanton and General Halleck to his office at 10 o'clock, it was not in fact to seek their advice about the command of the Army of the Potomac. Mr. Lincoln had already decided that question without any need for discussion, as had become his habit when making command changes in this army. At the time, and later, much would be said about who participated in this command decision and what was said and what candidates were put forth, but the truth of the matter is that Mr. Lincoln took the decision himself, without counsel and advice. He simply announced to Stanton and Halleck the choice General Burnside had presented him, and said that he was relieving Burnside and giving the command of the Army of the Potomac to Major General Joseph Hooker.

Burnside was called in and told of the decision. He was not surprised and most probably felt relief; it seemed to him the best solution to what had become an intractable problem. He pledged to the president "that neither he nor General Hooker would be a happier man than I would be if General Hooker could gain a victory. . . ." He was persuaded not to resign his commission but instead to take a thirty-day leave. (In time Burnside would be assigned to the western theater, in command of the Army of the Ohio.)

The generals' revolt could claim success in its primary purpose, the overthrow of Ambrose Burnside. Without its conspiratorial efforts the Army of the Potomac would almost certainly have fought a second battle, at the turn of the year, along the Rappahannock. In that event perhaps General Burnside might have retrieved his reputation and restored spirit to his army. Or, on the contrary, the consequence might have been the destruction of his army, as General Newton predicted. However that may be, the Franklin-Smith cabal was sorely disappointed that for all its efforts it did not end up with the commanding general of its choice.

In due course every member of the cabal would have reason to regret his participation. John Newton would be transferred from the Army of the Potomac to the western theater the next year and would end the war at a backwater posting in the Florida Keys. John Cochrane resigned his commission within the month, citing his health, and returned to the New York political wars. William Franklin was severed from the Army of the Potomac the same day Hooker was appointed to command it. He afterward served in the West with steadily diminishing results and spent most of the last year of the war "awaiting orders." Baldy Smith, too, would be exiled from the Army of the Potomac, and in March saw his major general's commission expire in the Senate. After service in the western theater he returned to the Potomac army, but, like Franklin, he ended the war "awaiting orders." Smith spoke for his fellow conspirators when he wrote, of their efforts that winter, "the results followed me through the war."

Mr. Lincoln, on this twenty-fifth of January 1863, having determined that just then Joe Hooker was stronger with the country than any other of his generals, had to hope that he was the right general to command this shaken army. For all his failings, General McClellan had been right about one thing. The Army of the Potomac was indeed the Union's shield, and right now it desperately needed its demoralization reversed and its confidence restored.[22]

2

General Lee Knows His Business

O N T H E E V E N I N G of January 5, 1863, from the steps of the Confederate White House in Richmond, Jefferson Davis addressed a crowd that had come to welcome his return from a tour of the western theater. The president was in good spirits. Everywhere in the West, he announced, the enemy "have been beaten, and I trust they will be beaten in future." In the East, "our cause has had the brightest sunshine fall upon it. . . . Our glorious Lee, the valued son, emulating the virtues of the heroic Light-Horse Harry, his father, has achieved a victory at Fredericksburg, . . . and driven the enemy back from his last and greatest effort to get 'on to Richmond.'" He remarked, to appreciative laughter from the crowd, that some of the enemy had in fact gotten on to Richmond — "as captives, not as conquerers."

In a more serious vein, Mr. Davis warned his audience that the Confederacy faced a ruthless foe, "the offscourings of the earth. . . . The Northern portion of Virginia has been ruthlessly desolated — the people not only deprived of the means of subsistence, but their household property destroyed, and every indignity which the base imagination of a merciless foe could suggest inflicted, without regard to age, sex or condition. . . ." Yet the South would prevail and must prevail; the fighting was a crucible "in which we are being tested, in order to cement us together. . . . If the war continues, we shall only grow stronger and stronger. . . . With such noble women at home, and such heroic soldiers in the field, we are invincible."

President Davis, of course, had more worries than his rallying-cry speech might suggest, but one worry he did not have just then was Robert E. Lee and the Army of Northern Virginia. Since June of 1862, when General Lee assumed command of that army, and officially settled on its name, this son of Revolutionary War hero Light-Horse Harry Lee had taken the measure of every Union general he faced. In the Seven Days' Battles in June, on the Peninsula, he humbled George McClellan and drove the Army of the Potomac away from the gates of Richmond. Then he turned on the Yankees' newly assembled Army of Virginia and its newly appointed commander, John Pope, and in August at the Second Battle of Manassas broke Pope and sent him flying into the defenses of Washington. Marching into Maryland in September, Lee gained a second victory against McClellan, at Sharpsburg on Antietam Creek, albeit a Pyrrhic victory that forced him to turn back to Virginia with his bloodied army. In December at Fredericksburg against Burnside, the newest Union commander, Lee so positioned the Army of Northern Virginia that it was invincible.

Four campaigns in six months, under General Lee's direction, had cost the Confederacy 50,100 casualties. As Mr. Davis pointed out, however, Lee made a mockery of the Yankees' "on to Richmond" battle cry. He shifted the war from Richmond's doorstep to Washington's, then beyond the Confederacy's frontier into Maryland, and finally back to the disputed ground along the Rappahannock, halfway between the two capitals. Of this record even the hypercritical *Charleston Mercury* had to admit, "General Lee knows his business and that army has yet known no such word as fail." Anything even remotely resembling a generals' revolt in the Army of Northern Virginia was unimaginable.[1]

As 1863 began, fifty-six-year-old Robert E. Lee was at the peak of his powers. He was supremely confident of his army and of himself. Fredericksburg had to rank as a remarkably easy victory. From his vantage point on the heights behind the town, watching the serried ranks of the enemy smash to pieces against his defenses, he had turned to General Longstreet and said, in virtual exultation, "It is well that war is so terrible — we should grow too fond of it!"

Lee's confidence in himself was drawn, understandably enough, from the certain knowledge that he had outgeneraled every opponent in every battle. On the Peninsula, studying McClellan's actions and finding him cautious to a fault, he boldly divided his smaller army in the face of McClellan's larger one and put him to flight with intimidating, aggressive attacks. Of John Pope he was openly contemptuous, calling him a "miscreant." Again he divided his army in the presence of the enemy, maneuvered around and about poor Pope until he had him befuddled, then drove him from the Manassas field. At Sharpsburg Lee fought a battle he did not have to fight because he saw McClellan was once again his opponent. A week before taking his stand at Sharpsburg, he discussed

McClellan with a subordinate. "He is an able general," Lee said, "but a very cautious one." True to form, he outgeneraled cautious McClellan, although it cost him almost a third of his army to prove his superiority.

So costly was Sharpsburg that for the first time since he took command Lee had to surrender the initiative. Now General Burnside would determine the time and place of the next battle. This did not seem to trouble Lee. When he learned of McClellan's dismissal and replacement by Burnside, he remarked (again to Longstreet), "I fear they may continue to make these changes till they find some one whom I don't understand." Burnside's Fredericksburg attack presented Lee with nothing he could not understand, except perhaps why it was ever made.

Having faced down and beaten the likes of George McClellan (twice), John Pope, and Ambrose Burnside, Lee expressed no concern that in Joseph Hooker he would finally meet an equal. It was Lee's habit to read every Northern newspaper he could lay his hands on, thereby gaining a good deal of valuable intelligence; the Northern press had little respect for military secrets. When he found these papers referring to his newest opponent as "Fighting Joe" Hooker, Lee was amused and contemptuous. In his correspondence he spoke derisively of "Mr. F. J. Hooker."

To be sure, self-confidence is an essential ingredient for any general's chances of success — the lack of it severely handicapped General Burnside — yet in this instance Robert E. Lee's self-confidence was edging into overconfidence. When the spring campaign began his overconfidence would expose him to grave danger.[2]

* *

FREDERICKSBURG WAS one of the older towns in the Old Dominion; the first settlers there marked out their places at the head of navigation on the Rappahannock in 1671. In 1860 the census counted just over 5,000 inhabitants. It had its modest historical associations — the home of Mary Washington, mother of the first president, the home of John Paul Jones, the law office of James Monroe, the Rising Sun Tavern where Revolutionary patriots once gathered — and its handsome brick buildings and gracious country seats spoke of its colonial heritage. In this second year of civil war, however, Fredericksburg was a devastated place. When President Davis told his Richmond audience of northern Virginia being "ruthlessly desolated" by the Yankee invaders, Fredericksburg was the prime example of what he meant.

During Burnside's assault in December the Federal guns on the north bank laid a crushing bombardment on Fredericksburg to clear the way for the river crossing. When Federal infantry moved in, it was the signal for Confederate artillery to open on the town. Most of the residents had fled, and damage was confined to property. Yet the ruthless desolation Mr. Davis spoke of was caused not by artillery fire, as bad as that had been, but rather by Burnside's Yankees gone quite out of control. They apparently decided the citizens of Fredericksburg had sown the seeds of war and deserved the whirlwind, and they acted like an army of mercenary soldiery sacking a captured walled town in the Middle Ages.

Men from some of the best regiments in the Potomac army stole what they could and wantonly ruined what they could not carry away. They smashed mirrors and hacked rosewood pianos to pieces with axes and slashed paintings and clothing with bayonets and hurled whole libraries into the muddy streets. "Fredericksburgh given up to pillage . . . ," a New York officer admitted. "The soldiers seemed to delight in destroying everything." Later, after the Confederates had reoccupied the town, Alabamian John Tucker walked the streets and recorded in his diary, "Never looked at so dilapidated a place in my life. Houses burned down & Shot to pieces, furniture destroyed, fences burnt up & general destruction of every species." In their letters home Rebel soldiers took to describing the Yankee army as the Vandal host.

Although Fredericksburg lay within easy range of the Federal guns on Stafford Heights across the river, and Confederate troops were in plain sight on the streets of the town, there was no immediate threat to the citizens after the December battle. Those who had nowhere else to go returned and tried to pick up their lives. Some found their homes uninhabitable, and all found trials of one sort or another. Mayor Montgomery Slaughter could only shake his head at the scene. "There is scarce one thing that makes life pleasant and comfortable that the Vandals have left behind or have not destroyed," he told a Confederate officer. Sympathetic Rebels took up collections for the needy of Fredericksburg. Stonewall Jackson's headquarters staff gave $800, the Washington Artillery of New Orleans $1,391, and A. P. Hill's division contributed more than $10,000.[3]

Taking its rise in the Blue Ridge, the Rappahannock River follows a southeasterly course, with many twists and turns, to a point above Fredericksburg where it turns due east. Shallows here mark the head of navigation on the river. Its chief tributary, the Rapidan, enters from the southwest a dozen miles above the shallows. As it passes Fredericksburg the Rappahannock resumes its southeasterly course, which it follows, with more twists and turns, to Chesapeake Bay, ninety-two miles by river from the town. Yankee gunboats from the Chesapeake only approached to within some twenty miles of Fredericksburg at their peril against Rebel

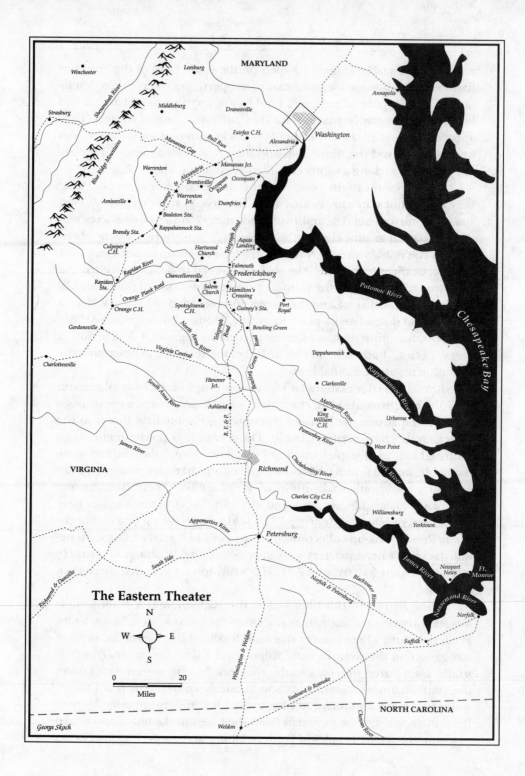

Winchester
Leesburg
MARYLAND
Strasburg
Middleburg
Dranesville
Annapolis
Shenandoah River
Blue Ridge Mountains
Manassas Gap
Bull Run
Fairfax C.H.
Washington
Manassas Jct.
Alexandria
Warrenton
Orange & Alexandria
Brentsville
Occoquan
Amissville
Warrenton Jct.
Occoquan River
Dumfries
Bealeton Sta.
Rappahannock Sta.
Brandy Sta.
Telegraph Road
Aquia Landing
Culpeper C.H.
Hartwood Church
Potomac River
Rapidan River
Falmouth
Chancellorsville
Fredericksburg
Rapidan Sta.
Orange Plank Road
Salem Church
Hamilton's Crossing
Spotsylvania C.H.
Guiney's Sta.
Port Royal
Orange C.H.
North Anna River
Bowling Green
Gordonsville
Virginia Central
Telegraph Road
Bowling Green Road
Tappahannock
Rappahannock River
Charlottesville
Clarksville
Chesapeake Bay
South Anna River
Hanover Jct.
Mattapony River
King William C.H.
Urbanna
James River
Ashland
Pamunkey River
R. F. & P.
West Point
York River
VIRGINIA
Richmond
Chickahominy River
Charles City C.H.
Williamsburg
Appomattox River
Yorktown
Petersburg
Richmond & Danville
South Side
James River
Newport News
Ft. Monroe
Norfolk & Petersburg
Blackwater River
Nansemond River
Norfolk

The Eastern Theater

N
W E
S

0   20
Miles

Wilmington & Weldon
Suffolk
Seaboard & Roanoke
Chowan River
NORTH CAROLINA
George Skoch
Weldon

shore batteries. The Federal navy's main role that winter and spring was guarding the Army of the Potomac's base at Aquia Landing and the supply line that ran north from there by way of the Potomac.

The town of Fredericksburg, stretching for a mile and a quarter along the south bank of the river, was itself quite indefensible, but the high ground behind it was defensible indeed, as the battle in December had demonstrated. An irregular chain of hills forms a broad arc behind Fredericksburg, extending from Banks's Ford on the river three and a half miles above, falling back to 130-foot-high Marye's Heights directly back of the town and a mile from the river, then curving forward in gentle folds toward the river downstream. From there a string of low heights ranging from a quarter to a half mile from the river reaches all the way to Port Royal, eighteen miles downriver. Below Port Royal the Rappahannock broadened into an estuary too wide for practical bridging by an army. This chain of hills, twenty-five miles in length following all its bends and angles, formed General Lee's defensive position.[4]

The two armies settling in facing each other across the Rappahannock supplied themselves over the same railroad, the Richmond, Fredericksburg & Potomac. This line dated back to the 1830s and ran due north from Richmond to Fredericksburg, before the war crossing there on a high trestle bridge. From the river the line angled northeast to Aquia Landing on the Potomac, where river steamers connected it to Washington. Its original total length was seventy-five miles, all of it single track. As the armies swept back and forth across Virginia in 1862, the railroad's Rappahannock bridge was burned, rebuilt, then burned again; now only its stone piers remained. The Yankees had put the section of the line north of the river into running order to supply their army from the Aquia Landing depot.

Lee's supplies came to him in part directly over the fifty-six miles of the line running from Richmond to Hamilton's Crossing, a depot five miles southeast of Fredericksburg. The track from Hamilton's Crossing into the town lay within easy range of the Federal guns across the river and was unusable. Additional supplies from the interior of the state arrived over the Virginia Central, which connected with the Richmond, Fredericksburg & Potomac at Hanover Junction, thirty-three miles south of Hamilton's Crossing.

At the time of Burnside's December offensive, Lee did not order elaborate fortifications thrown up on the heights behind the town, perhaps on the theory that the less obvious the strength of his defenses, the better the chances of luring the Federals into attacking them. In the event, the natural strength of the position, in particular a stone wall fronting a sunken road at the base of Marye's Heights, was enough to stand off repeated frontal assaults. Now, however, Lee reversed himself. He had twenty-five miles of Rappahannock line to defend and certain problems with his army to resolve before he could think of recapturing the initiative. For the time being, his actions would be in reaction to the enemy's. "I have hoped from day to day to have been able to discover what it contemplated, and to be guided in my movements accordingly," he told President Davis on January 13. Meanwhile, he would so strengthen his defenses that the enemy would think twice before attacking him anywhere.

Major Sandie Pendleton of Stonewall Jackson's staff reported a week later that the men were "working as busily as beavers along our front, not in anticipation of the Yankees' crossing the Rappahannock River but lest they may." Fieldworks sprang up on every stretch of high ground between Banks's Ford and Port Royal. At the base of every hill, in imitation of the Marye's Heights position, a trench was dug five feet wide and two and a half feet deep, with the dirt piled up as a parapet in front. On the hilltops redoubts were prepared for artillery. These were in numbers "far exceeding the number of our guns," Pendleton admitted; it was supposed that there would be time enough to call up batteries to any point where the Yankees might cross.

Young Pendleton was a student of the Napoleonic Wars, and this long bristling line of defenses reminded him of what he had read of the famous Lines of Torres Vedras, which the Duke of Wellington built in 1810–11 to frustrate the French invaders of Portugal. Indeed, he believed the Lines of Torres Vedras "could not compare" with the lines General Lee had erected along the Rappahannock. He recalled, too, that it was these defenses of Wellington's that enabled him finally to expel the invaders. In this new war, Sandie Pendleton predicted, the Confederate defenders would "deal death broadcast to the Yankees, should their curiosity tempt them to an investigation." At least one Yankee was convinced. On picket duty one day he called across the river, "You needn't be throwing up dirt there, we don't intend to come that way again!"[5]

The problems General Lee had to resolve that winter were new problems for him, requiring new solutions. The Army of Northern Virginia faced a serious shortage of food for its men and of forage for its animals. To be sure, the Confederate commissary department had never been known for its generous rations, and Colonel Lucius B. Northrop, commissary general and Jeremiah-like prophet of doom, had long been the bane of every general in the field. Now, however, the shortages were immediate, severe, and apparently without end. They strongly affected General Lee's ability to make war.

At the beginning of the year Lee had just over 91,000 men under command who had to be fed, and horses to the number of about one for every four of those men which also had to be fed. The countryside around Fredericksburg was nearly picked clean of food and especially of forage, and so almost everything the army needed was carried over the single-tracked Richmond, Fredericksburg & Potomac Railroad. About half the supplies came from Richmond; the other half were delivered to the R.F. & P. at Hanover Junction by the Virginia Central. While there might be periodic shortages at the source for one kind of army supplies or another, the real problem — and the problem most baffling in its solution — was the delivery system.

Because it lacked adequate sidings on its fifty-six miles of track between Richmond and Hamilton's Crossing, the R.F. & P. could move only a single train at a time, going and returning, over the line. Because its locomotives, rolling stock, and track were in poor condition, that single train was neither a long one nor could it travel at any speed. All this combined to limit the railroad to sending but two trains a day to the army. With the army's animals alone requiring each day 90 tons of hay and 5,000 bushels (107 tons) of corn, there was no possibility that two trains a day could adequately supply both the men and the animals of the Army of Northern Virginia. Nor did the railroad make any special effort to meet the crisis. Instead it was business as usual, the policy of its superintendent, Pennsylvania-born Samuel Ruth, who in these months was giving as little support to the Confederacy as he dared.[6]

An almost worse consequence, at least for a general of Lee's aggressive instincts, was his inability to stockpile a reserve of supplies that would allow him maneuvering room to seize the initiative. Robert E. Lee was unblinkingly realistic about how the South might win its independence. Victory on the battlefield was the surest path to the peace table, he believed, and the best chance to achieve victory was to force the enemy to march to his drum. At Fredericksburg he had had to march to Burnside's drum, but was saved from any embarrassment by the Yankees' disastrous tactics. Whatever Lee's view of Joe Hooker, he had to consider that the next battle might not be so easily won.

In the meantime, he could see no way to prevent Hooker from determining the time and place of that next battle. Lee found this frustrating. Food and forage were dictating to him. "Genl Hooker is obliged to do something," he wrote his daughter on February 6. "I do not know what it will be. He is playing the Chinese game. Trying what frightening will do." Later that month he told his wife, "I do not know what more they will do but am waiting on them. . . . I owe Mr. F. J. Hooker no thanks for keeping me here in this state of expectancy."[7]

If sufficient winter forage could not be gotten to the army's horses, it was decided to take the horses to the forage, or at least closer to the forage supply than they were at present. On Christmas Eve the order went out to all but twelve of the artillery batteries that they must relocate well to the rear of Fredericksburg. Soon new artillery camps were established around Bowling Green and Chilesburg and Hanover Junction, twenty to thirty miles to the south. Here some forage was still to be found in the countryside, and more might be obtained by wagon from Hanover Junction and other depots on the Virginia Central, thereby relieving the overworked Richmond, Fredericksburg & Potomac. Considerably farther to the south, along the Virginia–North Carolina border, 630 replacement artillery horses for the Army of Northern Virginia were wintering where forage was plentiful. When it came time that spring to reunite the army, General Lee had to caution his artillery commander, William N. Pendleton, not to bring up the teams "faster than you can forage them."

The artillerists found that recruiting their animals was no easy task even in the new camps. Deliveries of forage continued erratic, and it was a rare day when the full ration was available. More often it was enough to keep the animals alive but too weak to work. Georgian Frank Coker of the Sumter Artillery wrote home in mid-March that if the Yankees crossed the river and his battalion was called up to Fredericksburg, there would be serious problems. "Our horses are so poor and disabled that not more than half of the batteries can be taken," he thought. "The balance will remain here in camp." Their best hope was that the enemy would delay long enough for the spring grass to supplement the skimpy forage ration.

For the gunners themselves, however, the new camps were a welcome change. Lieutenant Ham Chamberlayne of Crenshaw's Virginia battery admitted that there was a certain monotony about any winter quarters. "But our present camp ground which we will probably occupy for some time to come, at least reminds one less of war and more of Virginia as it was than any I have seen," he wrote his mother. They were welcomed warmly by their Bowling Green neighbors, and "occasionally blessed to the extent of a party where elderly spinsters and very young girls not unmixed with the substantial comforts of chicken salad cold mutton & celery backed by domestic wine & coffee are offered as a fair exchange for our delectable society, our slang, our camp jokes & our never-before-heard-of wishes for peace." Virginia hospitality did much to smooth the rough edges off army life that winter.

For Private Robin Berkeley, going into a new camp near Hanover Junction with the Amherst Artillery was almost like going home. Young Berkeley had enlisted from Hanover County in 1861 and his homeplace was within such easy reach that the first evening after their arrival he and his cousin got passes and were there in time for supper. "Home people were very much surprised to see us," he noted in his diary. For a ten-day period in January he made the summary entry, "We spent this time in camp, going out nearly every night to visit homefolks, friends and neighbors." The young ladies of Hanover County made social lions of the artillerymen, and they returned the welcome by putting on an elaborate dinner party in the officers' mess tent that Berkeley described as "a grand success." General Pendleton, chief of artillery, was one of the guests, "and no one enjoyed the dinner, and the ladies, . . . more than the old General did." For a well-satisfied Private Berkeley, these were months spent "enjoying ourselves in many ways. . . ."[8]

The cavalry, with the largest complement of horses in the army, also had to disperse to obtain its supply of forage. Wade Hampton's brigade was in such poor condition as to horses that it could not even function, and had to be sent well south, below the James River, to recruit. Its recovery was so slow that Hampton would not rejoin the army until the spring campaign was over. A second brigade, under William E. Jones, was posted far to the west, in the Shenandoah Valley. The brigade under W.H.F. "Rooney" Lee, the general's son, found forage in Essex and Middlesex counties, on the Rappahannock far downstream. The brigade of Fitzhugh Lee, the general's nephew, was posted in Culpeper County, well upstream. The vaunted Confederate cavalry was thus reduced to just two brigades actually serving with the army.

When he was not worrying about forage for his animals General Lee had to worry about food for his men. Writing privately to his eldest son, he said that both men and animals "have suffered much from scarcity of food & I fear they are destined to move. I am doubtful whether I shall be able to sustain my position. . . ." To Secretary of War James A. Seddon he was more circumspect: "I am more than unusually anxious about the supplies of the army, as it will be impossible to keep it together without food." During January and February Lee reduced the number of troops he had to feed by almost one quarter. This was dictated more by events in coastal Virginia and North Carolina than by the food shortage; yet the troops remaining at Fredericksburg, on short rations as it was, could be grateful that they did not have to share what they had with three additional divisions.

In December, from their foothold on the North Carolina coast, the Federals had suddenly become aggressive, raiding inland as far as Goldsboro to tear up four miles of track and burn a bridge on the important Wilmington & Weldon Railroad that served Richmond — and Lee's army. Lee sent Robert Ransom's division of North Carolina troops to the rescue. Then, in mid-February, it was reported that a sizable force of Federals had left the Rappahannock and taken ship at Aquia Landing. This force, identified as the Ninth Corps, was tracked to Newport News at the tip of the Virginia Peninsula.

Virginia's southeastern coast, her "deepwater corner," had long been held by the Yankees, causing the Davis government constantly to cast nervous glances over its shoulder. It was well and good that McClellan's 1862 campaign on the Peninsula had been beaten off, but McClellan left behind a solid base — Fort Monroe and Newport News at the tip of the Peninsula, Norfolk and Suffolk just to the south — from which the Yankees might launch another advance on the capital, or perhaps open a new front in North Carolina. Secretary of War Seddon wrote Lee on February 15 that he doubted any full-fledged attack would come from this quarter in the winter season, yet "it is well to be guarded fully and in time." Lee agreed to send additional forces to counter the threat posed by the Ninth Corps.

For this purpose he selected two of the crack divisions in his army, George Pickett's and John Bell Hood's. Pickett and Hood, and Ransom's division as well, were part of the Army of Northern Virginia's First Corps, James Longstreet commanding, and Lee obligingly sent "Old Pete" along to take charge of this new war front. The enemy's intentions were by no means clear, he told Longstreet, "but we should be prepared to concentrate to meet him wherever he should advance in force." In so doing, Lee reduced his rationing needs on the Rappahannock — and his fighting force — by just over 20,000 men.[9]

Late in January the Confederate commissary made official what had been unofficial for some time and cut the troops' ration. The daily issue was now 4 ounces of bacon and 18 ounces of flour, to which was added occasionally (or as one man put it more accurately, "semi-occasionally") an issue of rice, sugar, or molasses. This was one third the standard meat ration. Lee told Secretary Seddon that while he did not believe the men were demoralized by this, "still, I do not think it is enough to continue them in health and vigor, and I fear they will be unable to endure the hardships of the approaching campaign."

"The Yankees say that we have a new gen'l in command of our army & say his name is *General Starvation* & I think for once they are about right," Sergeant W. R. Montgomery of Georgia's Phillips Legion reported. "We generally draw rations for three days at a time & eat them up in two, & do without untill we draw again." Other men did it differently, concluding that the ration made two not very substantial meals per day and testing their ingenuity to scratch out a third. Some were simply philosophical. Private Edgar Allan Jackson of the 1st North Carolina wrote home on March 10, "have just finished my supper, which consisted of bread and water — a very poor supper, but, nevertheless, this is all that we have to eat." Perhaps to reassure his homefolks, he added, "I am in excellent health. . . ."

There were more inventive solutions. Widely favored was a concoction known as "cush." The contents of cush varied, depending on what was available at the moment, but it started with bacon grease and water. Georgian Shepherd Pryor described a typical cush recipe for his wife: "After preaching, I then fixed dinner and ate. What would you think wee had? Il say myself: the bread that was left from breakfast crumbled in a spider, some water & a little grees stewed down was our dinner to day. The name of the dish I think is cush. . . ." Originally cush included pieces of beef, making a sort of hash, but meatless cush was now the rule. Another standby was a dough of flour and water or bacon grease fried until brown, or wrapped around a ramrod and held over the fire. The molasses ration, when there was one, added considerably to the cooking options. Of familiar peacetime pleasures, however, there were few. "I could not get any of the everjoyful to make an eggnog," Georgian Thomas Hightower told his fiancée during the holidays, "neither could I get any eggs."[10]

Yet the Confederate soldier was nothing if not resourceful, and he found novel ways to supplement this meager diet. Captain Pryor was on picket duty with his company one February day when they spotted a family of rabbits in a hillside brier patch. A well-aimed barrage of rocks produced a supper of roasted rabbit. In a similar vein, artilleryman Frank Coker wrote his wife, "The boys have amused themselves for the last two days catching snowbirds, and have taken large numbers of them." About twenty-five of the juncos were considered a mess, he explained. "They call them *Confederate gobblers*. It is all the gobblers the poor fellows get, anyway."

Other hunters were not so successful. Two junior officers in Jubal Early's division borrowed a boat to go duck hunting on the Rappahannock, but the landlubbers lost control of their craft and were blown across the river and into a Yankee prison camp. "This was a caution to all persons disposed to sporting," General Early observed. That spring the run of shad on the Rappahannock was a godsend, and hungry Rebels seined them in by the wagonload. In March, when scurvy appeared in the ranks, General Lee himself ordered out details to gather such antiscorbutics as wild onions, garlic, sassafras buds, and poke sprouts.

For a time men had been able to fend off hunger by "buying little nicknacks," as a Georgian put it; "I now spend my money as fast as I drawd it." It was a time of growing inflation, however, causing a Virginia gunner to complain that it required "two months' pay to buy a quart of onions at the sutler's." In any case, the countryside around the camps was soon enough picked clean of provender, and then nothing was more welcome than a package from home. Soldiers pleaded with their home-folks for anything they could spare, and were rewarded by a flood of boxes containing foodstuffs of every description. Any man leaving camp on army business or furlough always returned laden with edibles to share with his company. Leonidas Torrence of the 23rd North Carolina wrote his brother, who had promised a visit to camp, "If you come bring us a good supply of Cheese Butter and Fruit. Bring some Red Pepper, Whis-key and Soap."

For a time that winter the 3rd Georgia was on even shorter rations than usual, thanks to fellow Georgians from the 18th infantry. The 3rd was posted on the extreme left of the army, twenty miles or more from the railroad. This required the drivers of its commissary wagons to lay over during each supply run, the usual lay-over spot being right next to the encampment of the 18th Georgia. One dark night while the drivers slept their wagons were quietly and completely emptied. The men of the 18th Georgia, Alfred Zachry of the 3rd concluded sourly, "were the most noted and successful *foragers* in Gen. Lee's army. . . ."

Thus by one means or another the Army of Northern Virginia man-aged to stay fed, if far from well fed, and only on a day-to-day basis. In good season the people at home would get in the corn and wheat crops needed by the army, Captain Elias Davis of the 10th Alabama predicted to his wife. "I believe that our cause is just, and believing it to be just, I am confident that God will not allow us to be starved into submission."[11]

* *

LEE'S INFANTRY needed little encouragement, nor did many of them even wait for orders, to go into winter quarters. They burrowed into the ground, added walls of logs and a fireplace, and from a ridgepole draped shelter tents for a roof. Furnishings were equally makeshift. Private Tor-rence explained to his sister that his hut "has a verry nice Brick Chim-ney built with sticks and mud. We have verry nice Mahogony Bedsteads made of Pine poles and a great many other fine articles to tedious to mention." Harrison Griffith of the 14th South Carolina described this domicile as combining "the best qualities of both a cave and a house, . . . and the owner was pretty well secured against the assaults of the winter weather. . . ." Winter's assaults were frequent in the Old Dominion that year. Private William Hill of the 13th Mississippi, the quintessential com-pany clerk, kept a journal in which he carefully detailed daily weather conditions. On fourteen days in the first three months of 1863 Private Hill recorded a significant snowfall.

Boys from the Deep South found the snow a new and exhilarating experience. After the first heavy fall, a foot or so on January 28, they were out rolling in the drifts and pelting everyone in sight with snowballs. Soon the more calculating took charge, and casual snowball fights became snowball battle royals. On January 31, for example, the long roll called William Wofford's Georgia brigade to fall in for duty. Orders were issued to fill haversacks with snowballs and form line of battle, and behind its color guards the brigade marched two miles to the camp of Joseph Kershaw's South Carolina brigade. "We were in line of battle on a hill and Kershaw's formed and come out to fight us," Georgian Jim Mobley wrote his brother. "The field officers was on their horses and when they come against us, they come with a hollar! and, Benjamin, Great God, I never saw snow balls fly so in my life." The order to open fire was given at 100 feet. Charge and countercharge were spirited by the Rebel yell. Combat was hand-to-hand, prisoners were taken. "I tell you it beat anything . . . ," Mobley exclaimed. "There was 4000 men engaged on both sides, and you know it was something!"

In these wintry battles alliances were formed, broken, re-formed. "Louisianians attack us with Snow Balls," Captain John Melhorn of the 10th Virginia noted in his diary on February 24. "We whip them back, & then unite and attack the North Carolinians." A brigade of South Carolinians made a surprise dawn snowball assault that overran a neighboring brigade at breakfast, and to the hungry victors went the welcome spoils. General Lee came out of his headquarters tent to watch the skirmish, and was reportedly struck several times. At least one of these fights turned ugly, with cavalry charging infantry. There were several injuries, men ridden down or unhorsed, and guns were taken up before cooler heads prevailed and a truce declared.

After his first snow battle Private Edgar Allan Jackson wrote home, "I received one ball from some huge double-jointed Irishman on my jaw, which nearly keeled me over; I soon rallied and returned ball for ball." Two months later his homefolks would be notified that Private Jackson had fallen before a Yankee bullet on this same battleground.[12]

"Picket, Picket, Picket. Mud, Mud, Mud. Rain, Rain, Rain." So Captain Melhorn began his diary entry for January 21, nicely summing up the soldier's refrain on the Rappahannock that winter. Jed Hotchkiss, Stonewall Jackson's cartographer, described the daily routine for his wife: "one picket marches out and another marches in, the Yankee campfires send up piles of smoke away off on the Stafford shore, we build our fires, eat our meals, read the papers, talk and work in the most humdrum way imaginable, . . . a dreamy sort of existence, a sort of trance. . . ."

Battalion drills, the time-honored device for keeping soldiers busy, were seldom possible in the snow and mud, which at that time of year seemed to be all that northern Virginia offered. The 5th Louisiana was one regiment excused from drill for want of shoes. Reviews, another institution of camp life, had no better fortune. A. P. Hill's division, 10,000 strong, staged a review in an icy rain that did nothing for anyone's temper or good health. A few days later, on January 10, it was the turn of Fitz Lee's cavalry brigade to be reviewed. Jeb Stuart, the cavalry's commander, planned it as a grand event, with the army's high command and a number of ladies in attendance to watch the cavaliers go through their paces. But it rained throughout, hard and steadily, visibility was limited to 50 yards, and the ladies stayed home. "I have little patience with such vanity," a man on Longstreet's staff wrote, "and I think Fitz Lee and his command agree with me."

Musicales and theatricals were far more welcome diversions. "The McLaws Minstrels," a star turn from Lafayette McLaws's division, played three times a week to standing-room crowds in a makeshift theater in Fredericksburg. The Minstrels, from William Barksdale's Mississippi brigade, charged a modest admission fee that went toward erecting a monument in Jackson, Mississippi's capital, to commemorate General Richard Griffith, the brigade's first commander, killed on the Peninsula. The Mississippi brigade was multi-talented. In addition to the Minstrels, there was the "Barksdale Euterpian and Thespian Club," which took its inspiration from Euterpe, the Greek muse of lyric poetry and music. The Euterpians performed *Cox and Box* and scenes from *Julius Caesar* to appreciative audiences. The club's musical program, rated "very good" by one listener, featured the "Howitzer Glee Club," drawn from the 1st Company, Richmond Howitzers, one of McLaws's divisional batteries.

The single most elaborate theatrical performance that winter was staged by the Washington Artillery of New Orleans. Programs were printed in Richmond, and the beleaguered Richmond, Fredericksburg & Potomac managed to run a special train from the capital for the occasion. Ranking officers and civilian dignitaries filled the front rows. The featured performance was "Po-ca-hon-tas, or, Ye Gentle Savage," a farce that brought down the house "any number of times." The bands of the 12th and 16th Mississippi furnished the music, and the evening concluded on a rousing note with their joint rendition of "The Bonnie Blue Flag."

These Mississippians were an exception to the rule that Confederate bands generally left a good deal to be desired musically. Regimental bands were not a high priority in the Confederate army, where riflemen were always more needed than bandsmen, and many bands were pickup volunteer groups with more enthusiasm than skill. It was freely admitted that when it came to regimental bands, the Yankees had the edge. Consequently, when a Federal band came down to the river one mild afternoon and presented an impromptu concert, Rebel soldiers crowded along the south bank to listen. The Yankees ran through their repertoire of Northern tunes and patriotic airs, including "Yankee Doodle." Then a Johnny Reb called across, "Now give us some of ours!" The band obliged, swinging into "Maryland! My Maryland!," "The Bonnie Blue Flag," and of course "Dixie." The concert closed with a sentimental favorite of both armies, "Home, Sweet Home." It was a moment the men on both sides of the river never forgot.[13]

For much of its course between the two armies the Rappahannock was less than 150 yards wide, said to be "easy hollering distance," and the opposing pickets wasted little time declaring an unofficial truce. It would remain in force, unviolated, for four and a half months. Inevitably a good deal of banter was exchanged. Not long after the Fredericksburg battle a Federal called across to the pickets of the 37th North Carolina to ask if there was "a sorry corporal" over there they would be willing to trade for General Burnside. If not, he said, would they accept the general in an even swap for a broken-down horse? Following the Mud March the Rebel pickets were quick to ask the sodden men of the Sixth Corps, "When are you coming over again?" and "Have you got your mules out of the mud?" There were frequent good-natured comparisons of rations and the discomforts of picket duty and the merits of their respective officers.

It was not long before the pickets were trading more than talk. Sergeant Edmund S. Stephens of the 9th Louisiana explained the new trade to his parents: "We taken boxes and other such articles as would answer, fixed sails to them and send them across to the Yankees and exchange Tobacco & cigars for coffee & tea. . . ." Newspapers were another popular medium of exchange. One lucky Federal encountered a Rebel so desperate for coffee that he would trade whiskey for it. More typical was the transaction recorded by a Pennsylvania soldier on January 6: two pounds of Union coffee for ten of Confederate tobacco. Officers tried to break up this nautical commerce but without notable success; supply and demand was at work here in a classical way. The best time to catch officers unaware, the men found, was at first light, and in those dim hours the cross-river trade flourished.

Sergeant Stephens went on to describe the adventures of a man in his company, Ezra Denson, who was not satisfied with this arm's-length trade. He found a piece of flotsam and paddled across to the north bank to do his trading in person. Denson reported that the Pennsylvanians he encountered "were very kind, social and invited him back." On the subject of the war, however, he found them "disgusted, discouraged & dissatisfied, could not digest old Lincoln's action calling for Negro Troops." It was mutually agreed that the two armies should meet halfway "and shake hands and never fire another gun."[14]

Like the Federals across the river, the Confederates found winter quarters to be a breeding ground for disease. The limited rations led inevitably to scurvy. Clerk William Hill recorded a dangerous outbreak of scarlet fever — eighty-six cases — in his Mississippi brigade, and a scourge of pneumonia as well. He counted six men dead of pneumonia in a ten-day period. The most feared scourge that winter, however, was smallpox. Quarantine was established with the first confirmed cases and the disease was contained, but not without cost. The February medical report for Jackson's Second Corps listed almost a hundred cases of smallpox, of which thirty-one died. "This disease has been very fatal," a hospital steward wrote. The sick list was considerably lengthened by the harsh weather in these months, and only when spring came and the army went on campaign would there be a measurable improvement in its health.

For a thousand or so men of the Army of Northern Virginia, one event of winter quarters that year was remembered above all others — they went home on furlough. To stimulate morale it was decreed on January 5 that a limited number of furloughs would be granted, "preference to be given to those who first enlisted and who have the most urgent business," as clerk Hill recorded it. This produced a blizzard of applications and promised a decision-making nightmare and was soon abandoned, replaced by a furlough system of two men per company or battery, drawn by lot. Length of stay was tied to distance traveled. Private Robert A. Moore of the 17th Mississippi, for example, drew a furlough by lot in March. Nineteen days at home in Holly Springs required of him twenty-seven days of travel. "Left home, relatives & friends this morning & know not when I shall meet them again," he wrote in his diary on April 16. Private Moore did not in fact meet them again; he would be killed that fall in the fighting at Chickamauga.[15]

That winter, too, the Army of Northern Virginia got religion. What came to be called the "great revival" swept through the Rappahannock camps. "We are having a glorious time about now . . . ," a man in Stonewall Jackson's command wrote his family. "Gen. Jackson (God Bless him) has given us the privilege to be exempt from Morning's Drill in order that we may attend preaching. . . . We all sit around on the ground and listen to the sweet sound of the Gospel." (Jackson vigorously supported the revival. His only "apprehension of his country's cause," according to his chaplain, was the sin that infected the army and the people; "If he commanded a *converted army,* he would feel confident.")

Clerk Hill kept a careful record of the revival's progress in his Mississippi brigade. The chaplains "have got up a very interesting revival," he wrote on February 19; "from 40 to 50 soldiers are at the mourners bench every night." Each week right up to the start of the spring campaign, he made note, "The revival still continues." Sunday, March 15, particularly caught his attention: "The Baptists immersed 21 soldiers this morning, the Methodists immersed 9 and sprinkled 30, the Presbyterians sprinkled 7."

The great revival displayed little of the perfervid emotionalism that had marked revivals in rural America in the years before the war. The hard and bloody battles of 1862 had made these men veterans and tempered them spiritually. They listened attentively to the preaching, and "to the sweet sound of the Gospel," and the believers then made profession, or reaffirmation, of their faith. Sometimes this was done with no more ceremony than a handshake with the preacher. It was a common thought in this army that God had blessed them with victories since General Lee took command, and the great revival was their way of expressing their thanks.[16]

"You have heard various rumors about the suffering of the men in the army," Colonel Frank M. Parker of the 30th North Carolina wrote his wife. "I tell you I never saw men looking better; they all look hard, and fit enough for good work." He admitted rations were "rather scarce," but thought they got along on them. But he added, "I am sorry to say that we have a good many deserters from the army, several from my own Regt."

The demoralization that caused men to desert from Burnside's army in great numbers was seldom a factor in cases of desertion from Lee's army. That winter the Army of Northern Virginia was not a legion of pessimists. These troops could boast of their heritage of victories. They had no reason to feel any lack of confidence in their generals. To be sure, there were some who deserted because of the short rations — three Rebel deserters who swam the Rappahannock, a Pennsylvania cavalryman reported, "give a woeful tale of destitution of their army" — yet they were comparatively few in number. By far the largest share of the deserters from the Rebel army were conscripts.

General Lee left no doubt of the link between conscription and desertion in a letter he wrote to Secretary of War Seddon on February 11. During the month of January, Lee reported, the army had lost 1,878 men by death, discharge, and (the most of them) by desertion. Only 708 entered the army that month, and Lee listed them as 421 newly enrolled conscripts — and 287 conscripts who had deserted, been caught, and returned to the army. "I beg you to use every means in your power to fill up our ranks," he urged Seddon. For his own part, Lee took the blunt action of ordering armed details from each brigade to go back to their places of enlistment and ferret out deserters and return them to the ranks. In spite of his best efforts, the army's March 31 return listed 5,953 men "absent without leave."[17]

The conscripts, most of them, were men who had stayed at home during the rush of volunteers to the colors in 1861. The Conscription Act of April 1862 had now brought them into the army, and a certain element, from motives sincere or selfish, was deserting at the first opportunity. On March 21, for example, Lieutenant Edmund Patterson of the 9th Alabama discovered that a conscript in his company had deserted during the night from his picket post. He found the man's tracks in the snow leading down to the bank of the Rappahannock. This Private Green had only just joined the company, and Patterson wondered if perhaps he had been opposed to the war on principle. In that case, Patterson wrote, "I can't blame him much . . . if conscripted, I don't know but that I would do as he did, leave between two days without telling anybody goodbye." If it were otherwise, however, he had no sympathy: "Goodby Green, I wish you no bad luck. But I would rather be lying out there in the old field wrapped in my blanket filling a soldier's grave, than to be in your condition."

General Dorsey Pender complained that conscripts in his North Carolina brigade were deserting in droves, and that back home the deserters were being welcomed and offered safe haven. Richard M. Pearson, chief justice of the state's supreme court, had declared the state powerless to enforce conscription or arrest deserters, and reluctant warriors among North Carolina's conscripts had concluded that if they could reach home they might sit out the war with impunity. "Letters are received by the men, urging them to leave; that they will not be troubled when they get home," Pender reported. ". . . Our regiments will waste away more rapidly than they ever have by battle."

In his determination to stanch the drain on his army caused by desertion, General Lee took extreme measures. At sundown on January 11, for example, two men of the 16th Virginia were executed by firing squad for desertion. On February 28 Bartlett Malone of the 6th North Carolina entered in his diary, "And Mr. Portland Baley of Company D 6th Regiment N.C. Troops was shot to death to day at 2 oclock with musketry." On March 16 Malone reported, "And Mr. Stons of Co. F 57 N.C. Regiment was shot to death to day with musketry." On March 21 four men of the 5th North Carolina were publicly flogged for desertion, and two of them died.

These events were carefully staged to inspire second thoughts in anyone who might be contemplating desertion. Usually the entire brigade of the condemned man was drawn up on three sides of a square to witness the execution. Spencer G. Welch, surgeon of the 13th South Carolina, narrated such a scene for his wife: "A man was shot near our regiment last Sunday for desertion. It was a very solemn scene. The condemned man was seated on his coffin with his hands tied across his breast. A file of twelve soldiers was brought up to within six feet of him, and at the command a volley was fired right into his breast. He was hit by but one ball, because eleven of the guns were loaded with powder only. This was done so that no man can be certain that he killed him. . . . These severe punishments seem necessary to preserve discipline."

On February 20, writing to his wife, General Frank Paxton, commander of the famous Stonewall Brigade, confessed that he was depressed by a recent verdict of court-martial. "Four of my brigade have been sentenced to be shot — three for desertion and one for cowardice," he told her. ". . . Such spectacles witnessed in the quiet of the camp are more shocking than the scenes of carnage upon the battle-field. I am sick of such horrors." In this instance justice would be tempered by mercy, sparing General Paxton this particular horror. On the day set for the executions, Jefferson Davis pardoned the condemned men.[18]

*   *

IF ROBERT E. LEE was at the peak of his powers as 1863 began, Stonewall Jackson was at the peak of his fame. Readers of Southern newspapers had grown accustomed to seeing Jackson referred to as the "hero of the war." He had been front-page news almost from the beginning. His nickname, which seemed to fit him perfectly, stemmed from his role in the first battle at Manassas in 1861 and spread through the newspapers and made him instantly identifiable. Instead of Thomas J. he was "Stonewall" to everyone across the Confederacy — everyone except his men, who called him "Old Jack." His fame redoubled after his bold campaign in the Shenandoah Valley in 1862. It was the first good news for the South after months of bad news. The *Richmond Whig* knew no bounds in telling how Jackson's handful of citizen-soldiers marched 500 miles, fought a dozen battles, "defeated four Generals — routed four armies — captured millions of dollars worth of stores &c. . . ." Southerners like the Charleston diarist Mary Chesnut marveled: "Stonewall is a regular brick! going all the time — winning his way wherever he goes."

Correspondent Peter Alexander, writing in the *Southern Literary Messenger* for January 1863, explained to his readers that on the battlefield the seemingly ordinary Jackson came alive: "becomes a hero . . . full of fire and energy, quick as lightning and terrible as the thunderbolt. . . . He is the idol of the people, and is the object of greater enthusiasm than any other military chieftain of our day." Jackson's well-known and fervid piety also struck a chord with Southerners. Newspaperman George Bagby called him "a Presbyterian who carries the doctrine of predestination to the borders of positive fatalism — the very man to storm the infernal regions in case of necessity." Now, with Longstreet on detached duty in southeastern Virginia, Jackson had no rival as Lee's chief lieutenant.[19]

In addition to his stature as Confederate hero, it was customary to compare the grim and dour warrior Jackson with Oliver Cromwell, the Lord Protector. Thus his staff was surprised and delighted when the general accepted winter quarters of a decidedly un-Cromwellian nature. His Second Corps held the right of the army's lines as far as Port Royal, and Jackson took for his headquarters an estate called Moss Neck, overlooking the Rappahannock eleven miles below Fredericksburg. The English-style manor house was one of the handsomest in the district. Its owner, Richard Corbin, a most modest aristocrat, wore his uniform of private in the 9th Virginia cavalry in welcoming Jackson to Moss Neck. The estate's office, a building separate from the main house, served Jackson as both quarters and military office. It contained a country gentleman's library and the walls were decorated with hunting trophies and numerous sporting and racing prints. In this unlikely setting Old Jack carried on army business with no more notice than if he were in his usual spare field tent.

Particularly uncharacteristic was Jackson playing host at Christmas dinner at Moss Neck. Lieutenant James Power Smith of his staff was in charge of the arrangements, and the fare he collected, contributed by the general's admirers, added up to what Smith unabashedly called "a famous dinner." There were no fewer than three turkeys, a ham, a bucket of oysters, pickles and biscuits, cake, even wine. General Lee headed the guest list, which included artilleryman William Pendleton, cavalryman Jeb Stuart, Majors Charles Venable, Charles Marshall, and Walter Taylor of Lee's staff, Majors Heros Von Borcke, John Esten Cooke, and John Pelham of Stuart's command, Jackson staff members, and a number of others. Service was provided by the staff mess boy in white apron. General Lee was amused by the unwonted display, and chided Jackson that all this was just playing soldier; to see how soldiers really lived they must visit him in his field-tent headquarters. The irrepressible Stuart, the only fellow officer who ever dared make sport of Jackson, pointed with mock horror at the aproned waiter and at the wine on the general's table, and insisted that the rooster imprinted on the cake of butter, a gift from a neighboring estate, must be Old Jack's coat of arms. On this day at least the Cromwell of the Confederacy unbent.

Distinguished foreign visitors arrived at Moss Neck to study the general and learn his views, for Jackson was greatly admired abroad. Francis Lawley, correspondent for the *Times* of London, and Frank Vizetelly, artist for the *Illustrated London News,* represented the English press. The Marquis of Hartington and Colonel Charles Joseph Leslie, chairman of the military committee of the House of Commons, had connections with the Palmerston government. Colonel Leslie apparently had better success than most in getting comment from the reticent Jackson, for after a week's stay in camp he said he regarded Stonewall Jackson as the best-informed military man he had met in America.[20]

*   *

FOR SOUTHERN newspaper readers the one truly fabulous figure in Confederate gray was beyond doubt Major General James Ewell Brown Stuart. Jeb Stuart, who turned thirty that winter, had won renown for his cavalry corps and for himself with one dashing exploit after another. On the Peninsula he led a cavalry detachment on a 100-mile expedition entirely around McClellan's army, and a newspaper asked if the history of warfare had ever seen "so daring a deed." In the Second Manassas campaign he had raided behind Federal lines, capturing, among other things, General Pope's headquarters baggage. Less than a month after the battle at Sharpsburg he struck into Pennsylvania in again making a complete circuit of McClellan's Army of the Potomac. These feats made Stuart famous, and he relished the fame, but behind all the trappings was a superb combat leader and an exceptional collector of military intelligence. Jeb Stuart was as well one of the rare Confederate generals who could work with Stonewall Jackson without striking sparks.

It was primarily for intelligence-gathering that Lee was now using Stuart's cavalry. The Federals' main supply route ran from Washington down the Potomac to Aquia Landing, then by rail to Falmouth, but they also moved supplies south to Falmouth over the Telegraph Road that paralleled the Potomac. That winter Stuart made the Telegraph Road a frequent target. He did so to disrupt the enemy's communications, to gather intelligence, to give his men exercise and experience — and to make off with military riches. Less than a week after the Fredericksburg battle, for example, he sent Wade Hampton behind the Federal lines on a raid that netted 150 prisoners and 20 wagonloads of booty.[21]

At the turn of the year Stuart personally led the kind of raid that burnished his fame. Setting out on December 26, swinging well upstream to cross the Rappahannock at Kelly's Ford, he turned back eastward to strike the Telegraph Road at Dumfries, twenty miles to the rear of Falmouth. He had with him 1,800 troopers and four guns. For the troopers easily the most satisfying result of the Dumfries raid was the capture of nine sutler's wagons filled with a luxury of food and drink. (A few days later Yankee pickets on the Rappahannock would make anxious inquiries across the river "relative to their sutlers captured by Gen. Stuart.") Balked by a strong force of infantry at Dumfries, Stuart made what was now almost a patented move. Rather than withdrawing as he had come, he sent off in an unexpected direction — due north.

Near the village of Occoquan Stuart's column met and routed a force of Pennsylvania cavalry and overran the Yankees' camp, collecting more spoils of war and burning what they could not take with them. They pressed on to Burke's Station on the Orange & Alexandria Railroad, just fifteen miles from Washington. Capturing the station's telegraph office intact, Stuart put his own operator on the line to eavesdrop on Federal efforts to track him. When he had heard all he needed, he addressed a telegram to the chief quartermaster in Washington, Montgomery Meigs, complaining about the quality of the mules he was capturing; they could hardly pull the wagonloads of booty. He signed his name in proper military form.

Against a floundering pursuit Stuart made a leisurely withdrawal, riding well west and south, recrossing the Rappahannock a dozen miles above Kelly's Ford where he had started. He was back in Fredericksburg on New Year's Day. With him were 200 prisoners, 200 horses, 100 arms, 20 wagons filled with plunder. One of his troopers described it as the "longest, most dangerous and most brilliant Expedition that the Cavalry has yet given to an admiring public." The Richmond press was indeed admiring, especially of Stuart's jaunty telegram to Washington. Federal general Alpheus Williams, leading infantry in pursuit of Stuart, had a different view of the episode. "Thus we let a few thousand cavalry ride through our lines while our cavalry is cut up into small parties of fifty or a hundred scouring around the country to little or no purpose," he observed. ". . . Everybody much disgusted at the result. . . ."[22]

When in February General Lee learned from his scouts and spies that the Federal Ninth Corps had embarked from Aquia Landing for southeastern Virginia, he wondered if perhaps it signaled the movement of a large part or even all of Hooker's army. In common with the dissident Union generals, Confederate rumor frequently had the Army of the Potomac returning to the Peninsula. There was the strong possibility, Lee wrote President Davis on February 18, "that the Federal army under General Hooker is abandoning its present position between the Rappahannock and the Potomac. The greater portion which has so far left has descended the Potomac." Even as he ordered Hood's and Pickett's divisions southward to meet the threat, he continued efforts to find out what remained in front of him across the Rappahannock.

While Lee's spies had been able to track Union shipping movements easily enough, they were less forthcoming about troop strengths. He finally had to resort to direct action. The cavalry must probe the Federal lines north of the river to find out what lay behind them. The assignment went to the general's nephew, Fitz Lee. On February 24 cavalryman Lee, with elements of the 1st, 2nd, and 3rd Virginia cavalries, some 400 men in all, crossed the Rappahannock upstream at Kelly's Ford and the next day took up their march eastward along the Warrenton Post Road. This time there would be no evading the enemy forces. Lee made straight for their lines with the deliberate purpose of finding out their strength.

Initially all the advantage lay with Lee, for he knew where he was going and the Federals did not. Their cavalry pickets, having to cover the flank and rear of the army, were spread thin. In the vicinity of Hartwood Church the Rebel troopers charged through the Yankees' outer picket line, through the reserve pickets, and up against infantry lines within five miles of Falmouth. They inflicted 36 casualties against a loss of 14, and took 150 prisoners.

Having discovered that solid masses of infantry remained around Falmouth, Fitz Lee withdrew and recrossed the river comfortably ahead of his pursuers. His findings persuaded General Lee to revise his estimate of the situation. He was satisfied, he told Secretary of War Seddon, that the Ninth Corps might operate in the Peninsula area "while General Hooker pursues this route. The army in front of us at present is certainly very large." There was another lesson from the Hartwood Church skirmish. Hooker had tightened his army's security. "Its approaches are so closely guarded that it is difficult to penetrate its lines," Lee noted. Spies had not been able to find out what he needed to know, forcing him to call on his cavalry. To be sure, Fitz Lee succeeded well enough, yet there was the possibility that next time the Yankees might do better at concealing what they were up to.[23]

* *

WHILE GENERAL LEE confronted nothing like the command upheaval marking the Army of the Potomac in these weeks, he did have a good deal of revising and sorting out to do among his general officers. With Longstreet and his staff and three of his divisions absent, Lee himself took direct command of the two First Corps divisions, Lafayette McLaws's and Richard H. Anderson's, still remaining with the army. Each of these divisions required a new general of brigade. Thomas Cobb, killed at Fredericksburg, was replaced by William Wofford, a veteran of hard fighting at Sharpsburg. Carnot Posey, another Sharpsburg veteran, took over the brigade of the transferred W. S. Featherston.

Officer casualties had cut a swath through Jackson's Second Corps. To replace Maxcy Gregg, killed at Fredericksburg at the head of his South Carolina brigade, Lee promoted one of Gregg's regimental commanders, Samuel McGowan. Five other generals, wounded in various 1862 battles, were not yet sufficiently recovered to resume command. Dick Ewell, who lost a leg in the Second Manassas campaign, was still healing and Jubal Early continued as head of his division. Isaac Trimble, wounded at Second Manassas, was promoted to the command of Jackson's old division, but Trimble would be unable to return in time to lead it in the spring campaign; it went instead to Raleigh Colston.

Another of Jackson's divisional commands, that of D. H. Hill, became vacant when Hill was transferred to his native North Carolina. The recuperating Edward "Allegheny" Johnson, wounded in the Valley campaign, was assigned Hill's division, but like Trimble, Johnson did not recover in time. His division would be led into action that spring by the hard-fighting Robert Rodes. Charles Field, wounded at Second Manassas, was replaced in brigade command by Virginian Harry Heth. The brigade of Alexander Lawton, who had been wounded at Sharpsburg, went to Georgian John B. Gordon. Finally, promotions had created two further brigade vacancies. Robert F. Hoke took over Trimble's North Carolina brigade, and William "Extra Billy" Smith led Jubal Early's Virginia brigade. (In civilian life Smith had often collected extra post office payments for his mail-coach business; thus he was "Extra Billy.")

Of these ten generals — three of division, seven of brigade — it appeared that all of them had sufficient experience to be likely to meet their command responsibilities, with the possible exception of Raleigh Colston, heading Jackson's old division. On the Peninsula Colston had seen only limited action, and no action since. He had served with Jackson on the faculty of the Virginia Military Institute before the war, however, which was enough to gain him Old Jack's recommendation.

Another V.M.I. man that Jackson favored now became the subject of considerable embarrassment to him. John R. Jones, leading a Second Corps brigade, was accused of cowardice during the Fredericksburg fight, where he was said to have hidden behind a tree. It was recalled that at the very outset of the Sharpsburg battle Jones had left the field after supposedly being stunned by an artillery burst overhead. The officer who made the Fredericksburg case refused either to prefer charges or to retract them, and much to Jackson's irritation there the matter rested.

When the spring campaign opened, General Jones was still with his brigade.[24]

With three of his divisional commands already in the process of change, Stonewall Jackson, to the annoyance of General Lee, resumed an ugly feud with his fourth general of division, A. P. Hill. Their feud had flared into the open in the Maryland campaign of the previous September, when the march discipline that Hill applied to his division did not suit Jackson. This Jackson stated in no uncertain terms, and high-tempered Powell Hill did not suffer the rebuke gladly. Charges were filed, and Hill demanded to be heard in military court. The episode was blown out of all proportion from the beginning, and now it had become a matter of amour-propre, and neither man would back away from what promised to be a serious collision.

Lee's legendary tact was stretched to the breaking point trying to mediate this tangle, which just grew more tangled. Hill would say only that he was doing everything possible "to guard myself against any new eruption from this slumbering volcano." Jackson stiffly announced to Lee, "I respectfully request that Genl. Hill be relieved from duty in my Corps." Lee finally resorted to silence; he would do nothing in the case in the hope that eventually, somehow, the issue might wither away. When in due course the spring campaign began, Jackson and A. P. Hill were as much at loggerheads as ever, but they still held their respective commands. Lee had at least achieved that much.[25]

For all his problems finding food for his men and forage for his animals and keeping conscripts in the ranks and coping with eccentric subordinates that winter, General Lee did achieve one major gain painlessly. He successfully reorganized his artillery. While the artillery arm of the Army of Northern Virginia had never lacked for bold individual exploits, overall its record in the 1862 campaigns was checkered. The essential difficulty was organizational. In the crisis of battle the guns were not always where they were most needed, or not in sufficient numbers, or not on hand at the right moment.

The most notorious instance of this failing was Malvern Hill on July 1, during the Seven Days' Battles, when the Federal guns slaughtered Lee's attacking infantry while no fewer than thirty-five Rebel batteries stood idle at the rear, lacking orders. Under their original organization, the army's batteries were assigned individually to brigades and, later, additionally to divisions, and were controlled by the individual brigade and division commanders. Broader needs in battle were supposed to be met from an artillery reserve, but the reserve was held at the rear of the army and lacked effective field control; in the heat of action its batteries could seldom be gotten to the proper place in strength and in good time. After Malvern Hill a reform was begun by grouping batteries into battalions, but this was done unevenly and there was still little tactical independence of command. Although there were outstanding examples of Confederate gunnery at Second Manassas and at Sharpsburg and most recently at Fredericksburg, these had largely been in defensive roles, where flexibility was not the most pressing need. For General Lee, who was always offensive-minded, the system needed further refinement.

The chief of artillery, William Pendleton, enlisting the aid of his "most judicious artillery officers," Porter Alexander of the First Corps and Stapleton Crutchfield of the Second, submitted a reorganization plan to Lee on February 11. There were to be four regular artillery battalions, most containing four batteries, assigned to each of the corps. In addition, each corps was to have a reserve of two battalions. Two more battalions would serve as a general army reserve under Pendleton.

While each of the eight regular battalions reported to a divisional commander, each was also subject to overriding orders from Lee or from the corps commanders for larger tactical roles — the roles also intended for the corps reserve battalions and the general army reserve battalions. The plan called for additional officers and for promotions at the battalion level, promising further tactical flexibility. The primary gain of the new system was to give more tactical control to the artillerists themselves; this, Pendleton pointed out, ought to correct the current "insufficient scope for field officers of artillery." In short, control of the guns in battle was shifting to the men most expert in how to exercise it.

In addition to these tactical improvements, General Lee was intent on improving the quality of his ordnance. As he observed dryly to Secretary Seddon, a contest between a Confederate 6-pounder smoothbore and a Yankee 12-pounder Napoleon "is very unequal, and, in addition, is discouraging to our artillerists." Before long most of the 6-pounders were on their way to the Tredegar Iron Works in Richmond to be recast as hard-hitting Napoleons. While not every 6-pounder in the army would be thus transformed, enough of them were that nearly every battery commander could face the spring campaign with the confidence that he would not be outgunned at every turn. It remained to be seen, however, whether their demands for better-quality ammunition would be met as well.[26]

To pass the time during his slow recuperation from the leg wound suffered at Second Manassas, General Isaac Trimble composed plans for crossing the Rappahannock and seizing the Yankees' supply base at Aquia Landing and then marching on Washington, and sent them to General Lee. In his response Lee confessed that he had been thinking along the same lines himself. "I know the pleasure experienced in shaping campaigns, battles, according to our wishes . . . ," he told Trimble on March 8. "The idea of securing the provisions, wagons, guns of the enemy, is truly tempting, and the desire has haunted me since December." Yet to attempt a crossing in the Fredericksburg area against the massed Federal batteries would be to risk unacceptable casualties. He could envision an upstream turning movement, he said, although "the distance from there to Aquia is great."

But such offensive planning was for the future. For the present he was hamstrung by provisions, forage, transportation. The Army of Northern Virginia simply lacked the freedom to move as he wanted. Sadly, bitterly, Robert E. Lee had to admit that attempting any offensive at present would be "unpropitious, in my judgment. . . . I cannot jeopardize this army."

Another of Lee's generals, Georgian Lafayette McLaws, thought the scene along the Rappahannock was decidedly curious. He had just come from an inspection tour in Fredericksburg, he told his wife, "and I found the command there all in good spirits, the men playing ball, the band playing, some fishing, and all so unconcerned about the enemy as if there was no war, no enemy within a thousand miles. . . ." Yet all the time the enemy was in plain sight, "visible on the other side, parading and drilling and moving about in large masses." It was a strange sort of war, McLaws concluded, and apparently the unwarlike scene would continue until the Yankees decided to make the first move.[27]

3

Joe Hooker Takes Command

MAJOR GENERAL Joseph Hooker's reputation preceded him, and to the general's misfortune his reputation was suspect. Whenever Joe Hooker's name was mentioned, tongues wagged and heads were shaken. Certainly some of this was deserved — as Mr. Lincoln said, Hooker did talk badly — but more of it was exaggerated, and all the gossip obscured the fact that General Hooker understood a good deal more about commanding the Army of the Potomac than any general who had held that post before him.

The talk about Hooker had begun during his West Point days, when he offset an excellent academic record with numerous demerits for misconduct; even then Joe Hooker was likely to speak first and regret it later. The demerits dropped him to a ranking of twenty-ninth (of fifty) in the class of 1837. During the Mexican War Hooker gained an exceptionally wide range of experience, serving as chief of staff for five different generals. None was a professional soldier, and all depended on Major Hooker to manage their commands. "When you see occasion for issuing an order, give it without reference to me," one of them told Hooker. "You understand these matters." In addition, Hooker led their troops into battle often enough to win three brevets for gallantry. He ended the Mexican War a brevet lieutenant colonel with an invaluable fund of experience in both managing forces in the field and leading men in combat.

In what was to become a typical pattern, Hooker squandered these credits by opening his mouth, testifying for one of the political generals in a bitter dispute at war's end with the commanding general, Winfield Scott. Scott was not one to forgive or forget. However, it was in California in the 1850s that Hooker's reputation became a staple of gossip. Both during his army service there and after he resigned his commission in

1853 it was said he gambled and drank and otherwise took up dissolute ways. The old army was a tightly knit petty aristocracy where officers were expected to hew to strict social conformity and display the proper gentlemanly virtues, and by this standard rough-edged Joe Hooker was less than proper. What was worse, he was a bachelor in an era when marriage was sanctified and middle-aged bachelorhood was regarded as suspect on the face of it.

The reputation that preceded Hooker from California was summed up by General McClellan in his recollections, in which he described Hooker's moral character as "of the worst; . . . his course in California had been such as to forfeit the respect of his comrades — that he was then a common drunkard & gambler." That Joe Hooker enjoyed a game of cards played for money was true enough, but that was neither unique in the army nor evidence of an all-consuming interest. To term him a common drunkard was as untrue as it was damaging.

The allegation that Joe Hooker drank to excess was the hardiest of any charge against him, and John Hay, President Lincoln's secretary, thought he knew why. In his diary Hay recorded dining with General Hooker in Washington in the fall of 1863. Hooker drank very little, "not more than the rest who were all abstemious," Hay noted, "yet what little he drank made his cheek hot and red & his eye brighter. I can easily see how the stories of his drunkenness have grown, if so little affects him as I have seen." During Hooker's wartime service there would be credible investigators who disproved the drunkenness charges, yet appearances continued to deceive.[1]

The other burden from California days that Hooker carried into the Civil War was a long-standing dispute with Henry W. Halleck. As General Halleck explained it, Hooker was hostile to him even yet because "I know some things about his character and conduct in California. . . ." Hooker's explanation was different and more concrete. By his account, while in army service in California Halleck joined a law firm specializing in land claims, and Hooker called him out in no uncertain terms for "schemes of avarice and plunder" regarding the landholdings of acquaintances of Hooker's. "Indeed I indulged in still harsher language which seems never to have been forgotten," he added. (Joe Hooker was never chary with his language.) However all that may be, the gulf between the two men was so wide that when Hooker was given command of the Army of the Potomac, he stipulated that he would have no dealings with the general-in-chief. He would deal only with President Lincoln. As to General Halleck, Hooker told the president, neither the Army of the Potomac nor its new commander "expected justice at his hands."[2]

When forty-six-year-old ex–Lieutenant Colonel Hooker reached Washington from California two months after Fort Sumter and sent his credentials and several glowing testimonials to the White House, he was optimistic about his prospects for a place in the Union army. Lincoln sent the papers on to the army and asked if General-in-Chief Scott "would like Col. Hooker to have a command." The general-in-chief would not; he had not forgotten Hooker standing against him in Mexico. Thus the army went to war without Joe Hooker, but he refused to let that erode his self-confidence. Soon afterward he was presented to Mr. Lincoln. "I was at Bull Run the other day, Mr. President," he said without preamble, "and it is no vanity in me to say that I am a damned sight better general than any you had on that field." The president's response is not on record, but on August 3, 1861, the Senate confirmed Joseph Hooker's nomination as brigadier general.

During the sixteen months that followed, Hooker advanced from command of a brigade to a division, a corps, then a grand division. In that time no general officer in the Potomac army saw more combat. On the Peninsula he fought at Williamsburg and Seven Pines; and in the Seven Days at Oak Grove and Glendale. His division was in the thick of the battle at Second Manassas, where John Pope termed him "gallant and chivalric." In Maryland Hooker led the First Corps at Turner's Gap and at Antietam, where his gallantry was conspicuous and he was wounded. He commanded the Center Grand Division under Burnside, and at Fredericksburg took part in the storming of Marye's Heights.

Along the way the newspapers began to call him "Fighting Joe." This came about by accident — a typesetter mistook the lead-in on a piece of reporter's copy, "Fighting — Joe Hooker," and reset it as a heading — but it was perfectly appropriate. He was truly a fighting general, and everyone acknowledged it. With Fighting Joe in command his men had no illusions about what to expect. "We are to have hard marching and hard fighting for when Old Jo fights he will win a splendid victory or suffer a terrible defeat," Captain Henry F. Young of the 7th Wisconsin assured his wife.

Hooker disliked the nickname Fighting Joe, and asked the press not to use it. In an interview after taking command of the army he complained that the public might think "that I am a hot headed, furious young fellow, accustomed to making furious and needless dashes at the enemy." His reasoning suggests more than simply the nickname's affront to his dignity. Clearly General Hooker was giving careful thought to the way battles in this war had been conducted, to those repeated "needless dashes at the enemy."

In every battle where he was engaged he had either led a frontal attack as ordered or defended against a frontal attack by the enemy. At Williamsburg on the Peninsula, for example, his division lost 1,575 men in consequence of a futile, unsupported frontal attack. At Second Manassas, after protesting Pope's orders, he led a frontal assault and termed it "a useless slaughter." At Antietam his First Corps lost a third of its men in a head-on slugging match with Stonewall Jackson. At Fredericksburg he told Burnside, in a manner "ungentlemanly and impatient," that the Marye's Heights assault was senseless. Sent in anyway, he fought until "I had lost as many men as my orders required me to lose," then suspended the assault. Now the general commanding, he could reshape the army's battle tactics. Fighting Joe Hooker was determined to find a better way to direct an offensive against the Army of Northern Virginia.[3]

On January 26, 1863, one day after appointing Hooker to Burnside's place, President Lincoln composed a masterly and remarkably candid letter to his new army commander. Unlike his counterpart Jefferson Davis, who seldom had to concern himself with the management of his principal army, Mr. Lincoln seemed never to be free of concern about the Army of the Potomac. Several times previously he had composed similarly thoughtful letters to General McClellan, pressing that cautious captain to act on his opportunities. He failed with McClellan, and dismissed him. Now he had a general who by all accounts was as different from McClellan as night from day. Joe Hooker appeared to be rash instead of cautious. He talked too much and too indiscreetly. On his climb to the high command he had acted less than honorably toward his fellow generals, or so it seemed. A congressional friend who discussed the matter with Lincoln that day recorded in his diary, "the President did not know what better to do than to appoint Hooker. . . ."

The president in his letter went directly to the point: "I think it best for you to know that there are some things in regard to which, I am not quite satisfied with you," he wrote. "I believe you to be a brave and skilful soldier, which, of course, I like. I also believe you do not mix politics with your profession, in which you are right. You have confidence in yourself, which is a valuable, if not an indispensable quality. You are ambitious, which, within reasonable bounds, does good rather than harm." However, during General Burnside's time of command, he went on, "you have taken counsel of your ambition, and thwarted him as much as you could, in which you did a great wrong to the country. . . ."

Recalling what *New York Times* editor Henry Raymond had told him two days previous, Mr. Lincoln spoke further to Hooker's habit of indiscretion. "I have heard, in such way as to believe it, of your recently saying that both the Army and the Government needed a Dictator. Of course it was not *for* this, but in spite of it, that I have given you the command.

Only those generals who gain successes, can set up dictators. What I now ask of you is military success, and I will risk the dictatorship."

While pledging him the administration's support, the president had a warning for his general: "the spirit which you have aided to infuse into the Army, of criticising their Commander, and withholding confidence from him will now turn upon you. I shall assist you as far as I can, to put it down. Neither you, nor Napoleon, if he were alive again, could get any good out of an army, while such a spirit prevails in it."

"And now, beware of rashness. Beware of rashness, but with energy, and sleepless vigilance, go forward, and give us victories."[4]

* *

ON JANUARY 26, a Monday, while President Lincoln in Washington was writing his letter to General Hooker, in Falmouth the Army of the Potomac was once again going through the ritual of changing commanding generals. At an early hour Burnside called Hooker to headquarters and officially turned over the command. Both men issued general orders, Burnside's last, Hooker's first. Burnside thanked the troops for their courage, patience, and endurance, and urged them to give "to the brave and skillful general who has so long been identified with your organization" their full support and cooperation "and you will deserve success." Hooker reminded the army that he had shared both its glories and its reverses, and said the enemy was its inferior in every respect; "let us never hesitate to give him battle wherever we can find him." He closed by conveying to the late commander "the most cordial good wishes for his future."

Afterward Burnside called in certain of his generals for a personal farewell. There were champagne toasts, in which he hinted at his resentment at the way the command change had been engineered. Provost Marshal Patrick noted in his diary that night, "I thought proper to reply, and prevented any thing unpleasant from taking place. . . ." By noon Ambrose Burnside was gone from the army he had commanded for just over two and a half months.[5]

Newspaperman Noah Brooks, recalling a visit to the Potomac army's winter camp, described General Hooker as "by all odds, the handsomest soldier I ever laid my eyes upon . . . : tall, shapely, well dressed, though not natty in appearance; his fair red and white complexion glowing with health, his bright blue eyes sparkling with intelligence and animation, and his auburn hair tossed back upon his well-shaped head. . . . He was a gay cavalier, alert and confident, overflowing with animal spirits, and as cheery as a boy." Joe Hooker had long been waiting for this moment, and he took to army command as if he were born to it.

Among the men in the ranks, the immediate response to the announcement of the change in command was relief that there was a change. "We was very glad to hear that Burnside had been relieved as he was played out and the boys had no confidence in him at all . . . ," Horace Emerson of the 2nd Wisconsin wrote home on January 31. Among the rank and file Hooker was better known than any other general in the army. Most of them welcomed his appointment. Even McClellan loyalists admitted that, after their hero, he was the best choice. Sergeant David Leigh, a New York artilleryman, expected Hooker would be "very busy getting everything in order. He is just the man to do it too, he wont stand for no nonsense from any body." Captain William Folwell of the engineers wrote home on February 3, "I think the Army will receive Gen. Hooker with confidence. Burnside ruined his own cause by excessive modesty. I think Hooker not likely to commit such an error." John E. Ryder of the 24th Michigan was another admirer of the general's confident attitude. By report, Hooker said "he was afraid the rebs would run before he got a chance to fight them, but I think that if that is Gen. Hooker's worst failing it isn't very bad."

The Yankee soldiers had a favorite ditty, "Marching Along," that contained the lines

> *For McClellan's our leader, he is gallant and strong.*
> *For God and our Country, we are marching along.*

Soon they were singing

> *For Joe Hooker's our leader, he takes his whiskey strong.*
> *For God and our Country, we are marching along.*[6]

Officers of elevated social background seemed most disturbed by the implications of Joe Hooker's raffish reputation. Captain Henry Livermore Abbott, of the Boston Abbotts, for example, wrote his father on January 27, "Hooker is nothing more than a smart, driving, plucky Yankee, inordinately vain & I imagine from the way he has converted himself to the Administration, entirely unscrupulous." Lieutenant Henry Ropes, another Bostonian, termed Hooker "a doubtful Chief. . . . I have little confidence in his honesty of purpose and fear he may risk all to gain a great name." Charles Francis Adams, Jr., 1st Massachusetts cavalry, grandson and great-grandson of presidents, wrote of his new army commander while looking down his nose: "a man who has not the confidence of the army and who in private character is well known to be — I need not say what."

Officers who had fought alongside Hooker in the field viewed him with more balance. Blunt-spoken John Gibbon of the Second Corps admired Hooker for his gallant bearing and coolness under fire and for his approachable manner, although he had no doubt that Hooker had gained his post by intrigue. George G. Meade, as fair-minded as any general in the Army of the Potomac, regarded Hooker more favorably than did most of the old regulars. "I believe Hooker is a good soldier," he told his wife; "the danger he runs is of subjecting himself to bad influences. . . ." Whatever the general's habits in former times, Meade said, "since I have been associated with him in the army I can bear testimony of the utter falsehood of the charge of drunkenness." Artillerist Charles Wainwright had no doubts about Hooker as a fighter, but thought him untested as a tactician. "I am asked on all sides here if he drinks," Wainwright confided to his diary. ". . . I never saw him when I thought him the worse for liquor. Indeed, I should say that his failing was more in the way of women than whiskey."

Colonel Wainwright's observation about Joe Hooker's bachelor habits was already common enough among the gossips in Washington, where the long-standing term for a prostitute and the general's name were linked with a wink and a smirk. During the war years a section of Washington's Second Ward filled with brothels was known as Hooker's Division. Yet another element of Joe Hooker's reputation had preceded him.[7]

The public and the press viewed the command change with the same mixed response as the army. No one doubted that Hooker could, and would, fight. But was he of sufficient character to command a great army? "Injudicious Hooker!" wrote the New York diarist George Templeton Strong. "Perhaps he is the fated knight that is to break the spell under which that army has lain enchanted so long. If he fail, a heavy penalty awaits him. . . ." Elizabeth Blair Lee, of the politically powerful Blair clan in Washington, regretted the appointment: "still it may do — for he has the gift of appreciating clever men & maybe to use them — if so he will get along & well — but I think he lacks every thing but courage. . . ." The *New York Times* recorded the reaction in the army, and expressed what was the most typically held view of Fighting Joe Hooker: "Every one, however, feels that the new General will do one of two things, and that right speedily — destroy the rebel army, or his own."[8]

On January 27, the day after taking command, General Hooker was in Washington meeting with his superiors. Major decisions were promptly taken; clearly indecision was not going to characterize Joe Hooker's administration. Up to this time, command of the Army of the Potomac had always included overall responsibility for defending Washington.

The moment he heard of Hooker's appointment, however, Sam Heintzelman, in immediate charge at Washington, went to General Halleck and protested. He pointed out that for much of 1862 Hooker had served in his Third Corps; Hooker's "whole reputation was gained under my command," Heintzelman said, and so it would not do now for him to be under Hooker's command. Heintzelman urged that Washington be made a military department separate from the Army of the Potomac.

In fact this suited Joe Hooker's ideas very nicely, and he welcomed the change. The defense of Washington had always been considered a millstone around the neck of the Potomac army commander, and Hooker was just as glad to be rid of it. It was going to require all his time and effort, he testified, just "to place the Army of the Potomac in proper condition for field service before the coming of spring." By this one stroke Hooker's command was reduced by 62,000 men.[9]

They next addressed command problems. Two of Hooker's fellow grand-division chiefs were already disposed of on Burnside's recommendation. William B. Franklin was relieved by the same order that appointed Hooker, as was Edwin Sumner. Old Sumner, tired and burned out, disgusted with all the "croaking" in the high command, welcomed his relief. The immediate problem was the Ninth Corps, which had been associated with Burnside since its formation and was likely to remain so. It seemed best for the morale of all concerned to remove his old command from the Potomac army, and the Ninth Corps was ordered to the Peninsula. (It was this movement, with its mundane rationale, that caused the Confederates to counter the move with Longstreet and half his army corps.) Hooker seized on the transfer to rid himself of another of the late conspirators. He regarded Baldy Smith as the "evil genius" of the generals' revolt, and expecting no loyalty from that quarter, he sent Smith away in temporary command of the departing Ninth Corps.

Hooker also met privately with the president and promised that despite "apprehensions" about the state of the army he would enter into his duties cheerfully. His sole condition was that the president stand between him and the general-in-chief. Apparently Lincoln raised no objection to this, for Henry Halleck remarked that henceforth Hooker "ignored me entirely." And when he returned to Falmouth and his new command, General Hooker carried with him Mr. Lincoln's letter of advice and reproof.[10]

Presently, sorting out the army paperwork left by his predecessor, Hooker came on a copy of General Order No. 8 of January 23, carelessly left behind by Burnside's adjutant. The discovery that Burnside had tried to have him cashiered put Hooker in a rage. Provost Marshal Patrick recorded him swearing, "Burnside shall eat it, or he will have his ears, as soon as the war is over. . . ." So as to make Burnside "more conspicuous than he had ever been before," Hooker leaked a copy of General Order No. 8 to the *New York Herald,* which published it some weeks later. (When Mr. Lincoln wondered how it had gotten into the newspaper, an unrepentant Hooker told him. "I considered it a great wrong to its author in withholding it from the public," he said.)

Hooker's response to the president's letter was colored by this discovery of Burnside's order. A few days after Lincoln handed him the letter, Hooker recalled, "I informed him personally of the great value I placed upon the letter notwithstanding his erroneous views of myself, and that sometime I intended to have it framed and posted in some conspicuous place for the benefit of those who might come after me." The president's erroneous views, Hooker was sure, were the result of "cowardly calumnies" spread by General Burnside in his final act before leaving the command. If Hooker remembered speaking of dictatorships to *New York Times* reporter Swinton, he made no mention of it, then or later. He explained away any talk of a dictator as "ridiculous," and thought that on reflection Lincoln probably agreed. Had he not already demonstrated the rein he kept on his ambition by giving up command of the Washington garrison, thereby reducing the size of his army by at least one quarter?

Whether Joe Hooker would take heed of the president's cautions remained to be seen, but in any event there is no reason to doubt his claim that Lincoln's letter "filled me with satisfaction." He would preserve it with care, and ensure its eventual publication.[11]

* *

IF GENERAL HOOKER in his labors thought he could not count on the cooperation of General-in-Chief Halleck, he offset that lack by cultivating Secretary of War Edwin M. Stanton. Not many generals got along with the abrasive, abusive Stanton, but Hooker addressed him as an equal and confided in him, and usually was able to muster his support. In one instance, however, he was unable to budge Stanton. On January 26, as one of his first acts, Hooker telegraphed the War Department, "It will be a great happiness to me to have Brig. Gen. Stone ordered to report as chief of staff."

Joe Hooker displayed considerable courage in asking for Charles Stone, for in 1862 that general had been imprisoned on Stanton's order for more than six months for alleged disloyalty. The charge was trumped up and wholly false, and Stone had finally been released, but Stanton's suspicions were not allayed. He refused the request, and Hooker had to give up his effort to rehabilitate poor Stone.

Hooker's second choice for chief of staff was in some ways as unconventional as his asking for Stone. He appointed Major General Daniel Butterfield to head his staff. Butterfield had not attended West Point nor had he made the army his career. By training and experience he was a business executive, having run the eastern division of the American Express Company, of which his father, the noted express company pioneer John Butterfield, was part owner. To be sure, military management was one of Dan Butterfield's interests. He had long been active in militia affairs in New York, and early 1863 would see the publication of his manual *Camp & Outpost Duty for Infantry*. In 1862 he had devised a special bugle call for directing his brigade in battle, and then turned a disused cavalry call into "Taps," the Army of the Potomac's haunting lights-out call. He was also not without influence in Washington's higher circles of power.

On the Peninsula and afterward Butterfield had displayed considerable bravery under fire, belying his diminutive appearance. And like Joe Hooker, he was a convivial sort and a bachelor, and Hooker found him good company. Finally, Dan Butterfield was available. After he commanded the Fifth Corps under Hooker's direction at Fredericksburg, Burnside had displaced Butterfield with the more senior George Meade. From the beginning, Butterfield's appointment as chief of staff drew the scorn of many of the army's old guard. Nevertheless, it was a clear signal of Hooker's intentions. As he saw it, his most immediate task was to rejuvenate the Army of the Potomac, to shake it up and reorganize it and raise its morale, and in Dan Butterfield he had a skilled administrator to help him with the task.[12]

At the time of Hooker's accession the Army of the Potomac was organized into four grand divisions, of two army corps each. The upheaval of Burnside's departure threw this organization into disarray. Hooker's advance to commanding general left one grand-division post vacant, and the relief of Franklin and Sumner created two more vacancies. Only Franz Sigel's Grand Reserve Division (Eleventh and Twelfth corps) was untouched. Filling these vacancies would require considerable shuffling all down the chain of command, and Hooker promptly resolved the matter by abolishing the grand divisions, declaring them unwieldy, "impeding rather than facilitating" army business. Certainly of equal weight was his awareness that experienced general officers were in short supply, at least in the lower reaches of the high command. This was already problem enough as it was.

From March 1862, when the Potomac army embarked on its first major campaign, on the Peninsula, to January 1863 and Hooker's taking command, the turnover of brigade commanders — due to battle losses, transfers, resignations, and other causes — numbered fifty. In addition, twenty-five generals in higher postings — division and corps — were gone from the army. In part this was a weeding-out process highly beneficial to the army, but it also meant that numerous officers would be facing up to new responsibilities in new postings.

When Joe Hooker led the Army of the Potomac on campaign that spring, he would have under him in the infantry four new corps commanders, four new division commanders, and nineteen new brigade commanders. Of these nineteen brigades, thirteen were led by colonels, too new to the post to have even the proper brigadier's rank. Just six of the nineteen were professional soldiers. Indeed, in the Army of the Potomac as a whole, less than one third of the brigade commanders were professionals.[13]

General Sigel was most unhappy with the abolition of the grand divisions, for it left him merely in command of his old corps, the Eleventh. Sigel had fled the German States in the aborted revolution of 1848 and become a leading figure in the large German community in St. Louis, where in 1861 he staunchly supported the Union cause. The Army of the Potomac, especially the Eleventh Corps, contained a good many first- and second-generation German soldiers, and Franz Sigel was their hero. "I fights mit Sigel," they proudly boasted. Their hero, however, was now more senior than any major general in the Potomac army (including Hooker), and he felt entitled at least to its largest corps, and the Eleventh Corps was far from that. "The reduction of my command . . . ," he announced, "makes it exceedingly unpleasant and dispiriting for me to remain longer in my present command. . . ." When Mr. Lincoln observed that he had given General Sigel the best command that he could "and desires him to do the best he can with it," Sigel left in high dudgeon.

Had Hooker been sympathetic to the "I fights mit Sigel" sentiment in the Eleventh Corps, he would have advanced the senior divisional commander, Carl Schurz, to Sigel's place. Schurz, another 'Forty-eighter, was as well known to the German community as Sigel, and he had served in the corps since its formation, and the men would certainly not have hesitated to change their boast to "I fights mit Schurz." But Hooker had little use for Schurz's generalship — "I would consider the services of an entire corps as entirely lost to this army were it to fall into the hands of Maj. Gen. Schurz," he told Secretary Stanton in his usual outspoken manner — and in any event he needed to use the Eleventh Corps to resolve another thorny seniority problem.

When he promoted Daniel Sickles to head the Third Corps, Hooker stepped on the toes of Oliver Otis Howard, a divisional commander in the Second Corps. Howard hastened to inform Hooker that his commission as major general predated Sickles's and that therefore he should have at least an equivalent command. Hooker took the point, and to keep the Eleventh Corps out of Carl Schurz's hands he gave it to Howard. The men of the Eleventh Corps, "the only compact representation of the 90 or 100,000 Germans who have entered the Army," Schurz complained to President Lincoln, had expected they "would remain in the hands of one of their own. . . . They look at me as their natural head and representative."

In his new post, Otis Howard later admitted, "I was not at first getting the earnest and loyal support of the entire command." Nor was he the sort to turn the situation around by the force of his personality. Howard was a West Pointer and courageous enough — he had lost his right arm leading his brigade at Seven Pines on the Peninsula — but he was not strong-willed and forceful in command. Howard's passion was religious orthodoxy. "I think he is the most earnest and devoted Christian I ever saw," a man in the Second Corps wrote of Howard; he reported the general was forever distributing religious tracts and Bible verses among his troops. The man found this refreshing in an all-too-often godless army, but among the Germans of the Eleventh Corps, many of whom were freethinkers, the activities of "Old Prayer Book" were not so welcome. All in all, it was an unpromising appointment on Hooker's part. The Eleventh Corps would go on campaign under a general it neither liked nor trusted, and Howard was marching quite out of step with his command.[14]

Hooker's appointment of Dan Sickles to head the Third Corps caused much shaking of heads among the army's old guard. Sickles was a political general, a former Democratic congressman and veteran of New York City's political wars who recruited and then led the celebrated Excelsior Brigade. Sickles made up for his lack of military training by acting on the battlefield with reckless courage, and was much admired for it by his men. Hooker felt he had witnessed enough of Sickles in action to warrant the promotion.

The advance of a political general to corps command was disturbing enough to the old guard without the additional fact that Dan Sickles was, in a word, notorious. In 1859, in broad daylight a block from the White House in Washington, Sickles had shot down and killed his wife's lover. Worse, the lover was Philip Barton Key, son of the author of "The Star-Spangled Banner." Sickles's trial was the most sensational of its day. After lurid testimony he was acquitted by reason of temporary insanity, a pioneering defense that one of his attorneys, Edwin M. Stanton, helped construct. Sickles then proceeded to compound his notoriety by taking Mrs. Sickles back to his bed and board. There were those in the officer corps who shuddered at the prospect of Joe Hooker, Dan Butterfield, and Dan Sickles at the same headquarters.

The other decisions Hooker took regarding the army's high command were not the sort to stir controversy. John F. Reynolds, wholly capable and widely admired, remained as head of the First Corps. John C. Robinson, a veteran brigade commander, advanced to a division under Reynolds, as did James S. Wadsworth, a political general of the Republican persuasion who had been military governor in Washington; this would be Wadsworth's first combat command. Reynolds's third division was under the veteran Abner Doubleday. Two regimental commanders were moved up to fill brigade vacancies in the First Corps.

The Second Corps under Darius N. Couch was the best-officered corps in the Potomac army. Couch was the most senior of the corps commanders. His generals of division were Winfield Scott Hancock, John Gibbon, and William H. French; only two vacancies at the brigade level needed to be filled. By contrast, the Third Corps saw seven of its thirteen command posts changed under Hooker. In addition to Dan Sickles himself, one of the Third Corps divisions went to another political general, Hiram G. Berry of Maine. Like Sickles, however, Berry had learned his trade by fighting, starting as colonel of the 4th Maine, and Hooker was satisfied to promote him to head the division he himself had once led. David B. Birney and Amiel W. Whipple (the only West Pointer in the group) led the other two Third Corps divisions. Five new brigade commanders were promoted from within the corps.

The Fifth Corps, once Fitz John Porter's, was now George G. Meade's, and no one questioned Meade's ability to command an army corps. Charles Griffin, Andrew A. Humphreys, and George Sykes were Meade's generals of division. Sykes, who commanded the Potomac army's entire complement of regulars, had three brigade commanders to break in.

The Sixth Corps also had a new commanding general, replacing Baldy Smith — John Sedgwick, probably as much admired in the ranks as Hooker himself; "Uncle John" Sedgwick was known to take care of his men. Three West Point veterans headed the divisions in the Sixth Corps: Albion P. Howe and two of the generals so displeasing to Burnside, John Newton and William T. H. Brooks. Five of the nine Sixth Corps brigades would be led in the coming campaign by men new to their jobs.

Despite the appointment of New England Yankee Howard to lead the Eleventh Corps, the corps as a whole retained a decidedly German flavor, with such names in command as Von Gilsa, Von Steinwehr, Buschbeck, Schurz, and Schimmelfennig. Schurz, Von Steinwehr, and Charles Devens, who was new, commanded its divisions, and there was one new brigade commander. Henry W. Slocum's Twelfth Corps, with only two divisions, required but one change, at brigade. Slocum's divisions were headed by Alpheus S. Williams and John W. Geary.[15]

In the same order abolishing the grand divisions, General Hooker pressed a sweeping reorganization on his cavalry arm. For the first time, Federal cavalry would be unified in a single corps under a single command. In this the Yankees were some fifteen months behind the Rebels, who had unified their cavalry force as early as October 1861. From that time forward, Jeb Stuart's troopers had literally ridden rings around the Yankees, but apparently it did not occur to anyone before Joe Hooker that the first step in challenging Stuart on anything like equal terms was at least to match him organizationally. Under McClellan, Pope, and Burnside, the cavalry was scattered throughout the army, to be employed by the various generals of division and corps. With Hooker's order Federal cavalrymen spoke of being emancipated, of being given new life.

George Stoneman, formerly head of the Third Corps, was put in command of the new cavalry corps. Under Stoneman were three divisions, of two brigades each, headed by Alfred Pleasonton, William W. Averell, and David McM. Gregg. These six brigades contained twenty-one regiments of volunteer cavalry. John Buford led a reserve brigade of five regiments of regulars. Henceforth the seven infantry corps would each be limited to no more than one squadron (two companies) of cavalry for use as orderlies and messengers; in practice one corps lacked even that complement of troopers.

Hooker's reform was merely the first step toward gaining equality with the Confederate cavalry, but it was an essential first step. It also suggested that Hooker might be planning some singular role for his newly unified cavalry. However that might be, it remained to be seen whether the newly liberated Federal captains of cavalry could actually match their Southern counterparts in action.

One year earlier, when the Army of the Potomac campaigned on the Peninsula, none of these eight corps commanders — seven infantry and one cavalry — headed a corps. Only two (Couch and Sedgwick) led divisions then; the other six led brigades. Only Couch and Reynolds had exercised the responsibilities of corps command in battle, and only in a single battle, Fredericksburg. And of course the general commanding was leading an army for the first time.[16]

Oddly enough, having initiated the unification of his cavalry, General

Hooker took exactly the opposite course with his artillery. The Federals' artillery was considerably superior to the Rebels' in every materiel aspect, but it had not kept up with the Rebels in tactical deployment. In the 1862 battles both armies had seen occasions when not enough guns were in the right place in time because of a lack of unified, flexible artillery command. The Confederates moved first to repair this lack, and that winter Lee's artillery-battalion reorganization continued the reform. The response of McClellan and Burnside had been to increase the tactical authority of Henry J. Hunt, the Army of the Potomac's wholly capable chief of artillery. Now, to Hunt's surprise and dismay, Hooker stripped him of this authority.

When General Hunt proposed to further expand the grouping and tactical control of the army's batteries during battle — according to Hooker, Hunt "was very anxious to have a Corps made of it, and himself placed in command" — Hooker insisted that the local commanders should control the guns. In his days commanding a brigade and then a division, he recalled, "I found that my men had learned to regard their batteries with a feeling of devotion, which I considered contributed greatly to our success. . . ." This close accord between infantry division and its assigned batteries would be lost, Hooker thought, if the batteries were regrouped and fought under the direction of an outsider — even if the outsider was the chief of artillery and his purpose was to be able to respond to some larger issue in the fighting.

Henry Hunt was a McClellan disciple and strong-willed and outspoken, and he seems to have argued the matter hotly with the new commanding general. "He showed so much ill feeling," Hooker later wrote, "that I was unwilling to place my artillery in his charge." Hunt was ordered to restrict himself to administrative duties only; in battle he was expected to "be about" but to direct batteries only for a specific purpose and on Hooker's specific authority. It was a case of two strong personalities in conflict, to the almost certain weakening of the army's artillery arm.[17]

One further Hooker appointment, buried obscurely in a routine listing of headquarters staff, was as important as any he made during his reorganizing efforts. It noted that Colonel G. H. Sharpe, 120th New York infantry, was to be deputy provost marshal. George H. Sharpe's posting was a good deal more lofty than that, for he was in fact Joe Hooker's chief of intelligence, charged with establishing what came to be known as the Potomac army's Bureau of Military Information. While Dan Butterfield's later assertion that when Hooker took command "we were almost as ignorant of the enemy in our immediate front as if they had been in

China" was a considerable exaggeration, it did at least suggest the size of Sharpe's task — to develop virtually from scratch a coherent, reliable intelligence-gathering operation.

General McClellan had been first to utilize intelligence-gathering, as organized by the Chicago private detective Allan Pinkerton. Pinkerton's group, however, simply collected raw intelligence, which it passed on to the commanding general in bulky reports with no effort at evaluation. Furthermore, the methods Pinkerton used to estimate the size of Lee's army were faulty on every count, resulting in wildly inflated numbers. Yet even this inflation failed to keep pace with McClellan's own inflation of the enemy numbers. Inept as he was, Pinkerton was hardly responsible for the "phantom army" that General McClellan faced at every turn.

When McClellan was dismissed in November 1862 Pinkerton departed as well, claiming that he was the general's private employee. Only one of Pinkerton's men, John Babcock, stayed on during Burnside's tenure, but Babcock was unusually capable and would prove invaluable in Sharpe's new bureau. Except for Babcock, the Bureau of Military Information was an entirely new organization, with no ties to the discreditable intelligence record of the past.

The decision to put Sharpe at the head of the B.M.I. was Dan Butterfield's, or at least Butterfield took credit for it. Sharpe had raised the 120th New York and was serving as its colonel, but he was not the typical regimental colonel. At thirty-five he was older than many of his rank, and with a law degree from Yale, better educated than most. Before the war he had a thriving law practice in upstate New York, where he probably was acquainted with Butterfield and perhaps with Provost Marshal Patrick as well, under whom the B.M.I. would be organized. Just ten days after Hooker took command, Patrick received from the general a directive to "organize and perfect a system for collecting information as speedily as possible. . . ." On February 10 Patrick recorded in his diary an interview with Sharpe regarding the "secret service department." "He appears well," he wrote of lawyer Sharpe, "& I think he would be a pleasant man to be associated with. . . ." The next day Sharpe was the new deputy provost marshal.

Beyond the usual sources of information about the enemy gathered by interrogating prisoners, deserters, contrabands, and refugees from the "other side," Sharpe's bureau would for the first time coordinate intelligence from a variety of other sources, including infantry and cavalry reconnaissance, signal stations, and the aerial balloon corps. Most important and most novel, Sharpe set about recruiting scouts from the army and spies from among the local population to infiltrate Lee's army and report directly on its position and strength. Finally, all this intelligence from all sources would be in ordered and evaluated form. For the first time in its history, the Army of the Potomac had promise of a true picture of the Rebel army it was going to fight.[18]

* *

JOE HOOKER'S attack on the desertion problem was immediate and vigorous. He recognized that unless the disaffected were blocked from leaving, and a start made at returning those already gone, he would have little chance of checking the demoralization among the rank and file. On January 30 every regiment and battery was directed to list its absentees by name, and to specify which ones were absent without leave and to furnish a physical description of each. These findings were to be at headquarters no later than February 7. The War Department put local authorities in the North to the task of rounding up deserters, offering a cash bounty for captures. All express company packages were routed to the provost marshal's office for inspection, to cut off the supply of civilian clothes going to would-be deserters from their homefolks. The navy increased its patrols on the Potomac so as to close off that escape route to Maryland. Security was stepped up on all roads leading into Washington.

First priority meanwhile went to securing the Rappahannock camps. Hooker made his intentions clear in a stern order to Provost Marshal Patrick on January 28: "The practice of permitting any person to move about through the lines of the Army, without scrutiny and examination, must be stopped." Picket lines were strengthened and drawn more tightly around the army, allowing no one to head north from the encampments without ironclad authority. It was announced that anyone not responding to a sentry's summons would be shot without further challenge.

All this was the stick in Hooker's carrot-and-stick effort, and it was effective. In just the first week of his regime, even before many of the measures could take effect, 467 deserters were brought back into the army. As early as February 6, twelve days after he took command, Hooker was saying that "desertions from this army are now at an end, or nearly so. . . ." By that barometer of army opinion, soldiers' letters and diaries, this was not an idle boast. By mid-February most writers in the ranks had fallen silent on the subject of desertion.

As the carrot in the process, President Lincoln issued on March 10 a proclamation granting amnesty to any Yankee soldier absent without leave if he returned by April 1. There would be no penalty beyond loss of pay. At Hooker's suggestion, as a matter of fairness the amnesty was extended to deserters already in custody or awaiting sentence. The American consul-general in Montreal was confident that amnesty would have a good effect on what he described as the "many hundreds" of deserters who had fled to Canada. By March 31 the return of the Army of the Potomac listed just 1,941 men as absent without leave. In January deserters had made up 30 percent of the absentees; now they were less than 4 percent.[19]

At the same time, Washington took a new and radical step toward filling the ranks. Congress passed and on March 3 President Lincoln signed the Enrollment Act, making all eligible men in the North between ages twenty and forty-five liable for military service. In thus embracing conscription the North was a year behind the South, and months would pass before the first draft call, but now a policy was set and a start made.

The response to the Enrollment Act in the Army of the Potomac was derisive satisfaction. "We were all glad when we heard of the passage of the Conscript Law and only hope they will enforce it," Ed Weller of the 107th New York told his father. "Let a lot of those home guards, as we call them, come down here and go through what we have and they will not croak quite so much about the Army and why it does not do more." John Ryder of the 24th Michigan wrote his mother that by report some at home had said they would die before they would serve; "I guess Uncle Sam can fetch them and if they wish they can die here. . . ." Even if it produced no immediate reinforcements, the Enrollment Act at least seemed to promise that in the future the burden of saving the Union would be shared more equally.[20]

General Hooker meanwhile had offered a carrot of his own in the form of an enlightened furlough policy. In the same directive requiring lists of the absentees, he laid out his new furlough plan — two men per hundred (which in practice worked out for convenience to two per company), drawn by lot, each pair to return before the next pair could leave, but only commencing after the regiment or battery had passed a rigorous inspection. Leaves would be for ten days to the mid-Atlantic states, fifteen days to Maine, New Hampshire, and Vermont, and to Ohio and the states to the west.

"I think the granting of furloughs has done much good to this army," Lieutenant Chester Leach of the 2nd Vermont wrote his wife. It cut down on desertions, he thought, "& it also has a tendency to make the men try & do well, for they know that if they dont their chance for a furlough is slim." Because of the furloughs "I think this army would be worth more in the field today. . . ." Hooker reported that President Lincoln was dubious about the plan, predicting that too many of the furloughed men would never come back. Hooker pleaded for a three-week trial, and was prideful when it proved successful.

Of course nothing in an army ever works faultlessly, as a bitter Sanford Truesdell of the 122nd New York discovered. Furloughs for his company were suspended when it was found that the man in line ahead of Truesdell "had skedaddled to Canada." He calculated that it would now be "until the end of 'Three years, or the close of the war'" before he got home.[21]

Dan Butterfield could take credit for another lift in the army's morale, although that was not the original intent of his innovation. On the Peninsula the previous summer General Phil Kearny, as hard a fighter as any in the Potomac army, had devised a diamond-shaped patch of red flannel for the men of his division to wear, to distinguish his own troops from those of other generals and to better control straggling. Kearny's men soon found it safer to stay in the ranks than to face their general's wrath. Phil Kearny was dead now, killed in the Second Manassas campaign, but the men of his old division still pridefully wore the Kearny patch in his memory. Like the Germans of the Eleventh Corps who boasted "I fights mit Sigel," the men of Kearny's division — led now by David Birney — regarded the red diamond as a badge of honor.

Butterfield went to Hooker with the idea of giving each of the seven corps in the Army of the Potomac its own distinctive badge. The men would affix the badge to their caps, and it would also be painted on the corps wagons, ambulances, and artillery vehicles. Like Kearny, Butterfield's primary goal was better battlefield control, an idea Joe Hooker enthusiastically supported. Hooker remembered likening every march of McClellan's army to a defeat, from all the straggling: "When you enquired of the men the corps to which they belonged, they would tell you any one but the true one." Whatever the intent, the real gain of the corps badges was unit pride — in Dan Butterfield's words, "aiding in the 'esprit de corps' and elevation of the morale and discipline of the army. . . ."

For the badge of the First Corps Butterfield selected a disc. For the Second Corps it was a trefoil, for its resemblance to the shamrock beloved by the many Irishmen in the corps. Kearny's old division was in the Third Corps, and so a diamond became the Third's badge. Butterfield had once passed out medals in the shape of Maltese crosses to his militia regiment, now in the Fifth Corps, and he made a Maltese cross the badge of that corps. The badge of the Sixth Corps was a Greek cross, that of the Eleventh a crescent, that of the Twelfth a star. As a further identification, in each corps the badge in the First Division was red, the Second Division white, and the Third Division blue. While the badges were being made up and issued, Hooker let it be known that each regimental flag might be inscribed with the names of all the battles the regiment had fought in. For Fighting Joe Hooker, soldier's pride had meaning and purpose.[22]

To repair the many things that had gone wrong with the running of this army, General Hooker gave sharp spurs to his inspector-generals. He increased their numbers and their authority, and before long every regiment and every battery in the army was subject to a thorough going-over by a tough-minded inspector. Those that failed lost their furlough privileges, for both men and officers, and had to pass a re-inspection to get them back. It was announced that additional furloughs would be awarded those outfits that passed their initial inspections.

It seemed that no one in the Army of the Potomac could escape Joe Hooker's inspector-generals, or in fact the sharp eye of the general himself. The concept was simple enough — as General Alpheus Williams put it, "Everybody must be active, each one above inspecting to see that those below are doing their duty" — but it was effective only when the general commanding and his staff and his inspectors pressed the matter. By pressing they cleaned up the hospitals and the campsites and improved camp sanitation. Paydays were re-established and new clothing issued. The corrupt were rooted out of the commissary department. Boards of inspection searched out and dismissed incompetent officers.

No single act of Hooker's boosted morale more quickly than the announcement, on February 7, that soft bread would henceforth be issued to the troops four times a week. Fresh potatoes or onions were to be issued twice a week, and desiccated vegetables once a week. Any commissary officer failing to meet these standards had to furnish written proof that his depot lacked the necessary stocks; any depot lacking stocks was advised that it had better have an explanation. Brigade bakeries were established, and any company lacking a company cook was ordered to get one. Joe Hooker announced, "My men shall be fed before I am fed, and before any of my officers are fed," and clearly he meant it. "Gen. Hooker seems to be gaining the confidence of the army completely," Captain William Folwell of the 50th New York engineers wrote home on February 18. "His 'soft bread' order reaches us in a tender spot. . . ."[23]

Stocking the depot warehouses proved to be no problem. In striking contrast to the situation south of the Rappahannock, food, forage, munitions, and stores of every sort poured into the Army of the Potomac that winter in a growing flood. To supply his army General Hooker could call on Herman Haupt and Daniel C. McCallum, two of the best railroad men in the country, North or South. It is no surprise that for General Lee the thought of seizing the Yankees' supply riches was "truly tempting."

Haupt and McCallum devised an ingenious and strikingly efficient supply system for Hooker's army on the Rappahannock. Trains of freight cars loaded with army stores arriving over the Baltimore & Ohio at

Washington were routed to Alexandria, the head of deep-water naviga-tion on the Potomac. There the loaded cars were run onto special tracked railroad "floats" and towed the sixty miles down the Potomac to Aquia Landing. At Aquia, on newly built wharfs and a new spur track, the cars were rolled off the barges onto the rails of the northern section of the Richmond, Fredericksburg & Potomac to complete the journey to Falmouth. From Washington to Falmouth by rail and water took just twelve hours, and just one unloading. On average, 140 cars with a total capacity of 800 tons were unloaded at Falmouth every day. Provisions, forage, and transportation were the worst of General Lee's problems that winter; they were the least of General Hooker's.[24]

No previous commander of the Army of the Potomac was ever as security-conscious as Joe Hooker. Amidst his barrage of changes and reforms and reorganizations he set about securing his army against what he saw as the irresponsibilities of the Northern press. If he had his way, he told Secretary Stanton, he would "choke the newspapers." Their cor-respondents, he later assured a military historian, "were the authors of more mischief in an Army than I can represent to you." His first step was to halt the trading of newspapers during flag-of-truce meetings with the enemy. Northern editors, in Hooker's view, were far more indiscreet than their Southern counterparts, and General Lee was gaining a great deal more in these exchanges than he was.

Hooker's next move was to fire a warning shot at the members of the press covering the army. He was infuriated to read, in the *New York Herald* for March 14, of "unmistakable preparations now being made for a speedy movement of the army," which "no one in the army doubts will come at the earliest possible moment." The *Herald*'s Potomac army cor-respondent was Edwin F. Denyse, and on Hooker's order he was arrested. That Denyse's story was totally wrong was irrelevant; the next time, Hooker said, he might get it right. Denyse was tried by a military commis-sion in the provost marshal's office and sentenced to six months' hard labor. Having made his point about military secrets in no uncertain terms, Hooker commuted Denyse's sentence to permanent banishment from the army.

Joe Hooker could not single-handedly bring full responsibility to the Northern press, but at least he made a start. His most innovative move, coming just as the army started on its spring campaign, was to require correspondents to include their names with any stories that saw print. Failure to do so, by the reporter or his editor, would see him banished and his paper banned from sale in the army. At the time the anonymity of correspondents was standard newspaper practice. Now, thanks to Joe Hooker, bylines would become standard practice. Being publicly responsible for what they wrote, Hooker said, had to be the better way. Follow the rules, he told the reporters, sign your stories, and they would be free "to abuse or criticise me to their hearts' content."[25]

*   *

THE YANKEE soldiers went to ground in winter quarters as quickly as did the Rebels. With the same materials to work with, the quarters looked much the same on both sides of the river — typically a hole in the ground with log walls, roofed over with shelter tents. A shelter tent alone would never get a man through the winter, Sergeant Matthew Marvin of the 1st Minnesota explained. "So we all put in our best lick to build something better that is a house about 12 ft long 6 wide & 4 high shingled with 6 tents & a fire place in the side." As an Ohio man put it, this structure served as sitting room, bed chamber, dining room, parlor, and kitchen, "without the trouble of walking up and down stairs." The art was in the fireplace-building, to provide heat without smoking out the inhabitants. A squad of the 24th Michigan solved the problem by stealing a parlor stove from a nearby "secesh" house, which kept them both warm and well fed. In his diary Nathaniel Parmeter of the 29th Ohio casually observed that his fireplace boasted a chimney made of bricks pulled from a local courthouse, "the second one built in the U.S."

Some were moved by a craving for quarters with architectural distinction. Samuel Fiske of the 14th Connecticut described the scene for readers of the *Springfield Republican* under the heading "Studies in Architecture": "My own building is a severe classic, without ornament, rather low and heavy, inclined to the Doric, or perhaps even to the Egyptian order. . . . Some model after a heathen temple, some after a Yankee woodshed, some after an Indian wigwam, and some after a woodchuck's hole."

Any hardships found in these varied quarters were not shared by the army's officers. Their spacious wall tents, heated by stoves, were neatly laid out fronting on company streets, along with the necessary cook and mess tents. Colonel Wainwright, the First Corps' chief of artillery, reported that his tent was floored with cedar boughs and "a good piece of Brussels carpet," and his mess presided over "by a French cook." All was snug and comfortable; "I know of no tent anywhere that looks so nice and inviting."

Whatever the level of comfort, it was achieved at the expense of the Virginia countryside. With each passing week the landscape grew more barren. A diarist in the 93rd New York, Lieutenant Robert S. Robertson, pictured the scene: "It looks hard to see this section, so beautifully covered with woods & groves when we came here, now a wilderness of stumps, and intersected by corduroy & mud roads. . . . The fences and landmarks are completely destroyed, and the forests are cut away for the camp fires." By his estimate, by the end of March thirty square miles of timber, on both sides of the river, had been cut away by the two armies. "Such is war — even without fighting!"[26]

Once the troops were sheltered, their thoughts naturally enough turned to food. Men in Union blue, unlike those in Confederate butter-nut across the Rappahannock, had few worries about actual shortages in their rations, but before Hooker's reforms they were growing heartily sick of them, or at least of hardtack. Legends would gather around hardtack — about its tensile strength, its nutritional value, its date of manufacture. Hardtack was flour-and-water biscuit or pilot bread, baked into a hard cracker, some three inches square and half an inch thick. There were numerous recipes for making it allegedly palatable. The 2nd Wisconsin's Horace Emerson had a brother serving in one of the western armies, to whom he offered advice on "a dish we are very fond of in this Army. Here it is. Soak your hard tack in water, and fry them in pork fat untill brown. We call the thing a *Son of a Bitch*." Fried or baked hardtack concoctions had other names as well: "skillygalee," "lobscouse," "dunder-funk," "dung-slide." Hooker's edict on issuing soft bread was welcomed in many regiments with cheers.

Yankee soldiers had filled the mails with pleas to their homefolks to send them food to supplement the tiresome diet of salt pork, hardtack, and coffee. Corporal Edward H. Wade of the 14th Connecticut made up a typical want-list for his sister: "I wish among other things you would send me a few links of unfried sausages, a mince pie, a little tin box of butter, a loaf of rye bread, and some kind of cake — any kind you may happen to have on hand. Put in a little cheese, and a little tea." He added, with a touch of desperation, "If you think of *anything* that you think I would like, why just put it in." Private Edwin O. Wentworth of the 37th Massachusetts thanked his wife for the box of good things she had sent, and suggested that the next time she include some whiskey "to keep off the chills . . . it is impossible to get any here." He thought his captain would probably wink at the transaction; "still, if you send me any, you had better enclose it in a loaf of bread. . . ."

Hooker's regulation that all express packages were to be inspected by the provost marshal's office put a crimp in whiskey smuggling, but there were other ways for a resourceful soldier to get a drink. Samuel S. Par-tridge, quartermaster of the 13th New York, explained one way in a letter to his brother: "Preserved fruits are not contraband. Brandy Peaches are preserved fruit. . . . Sutler swears to his manifest of Brandy Peaches — Inspector sees the Brandy Peaches. Brandy Peaches sell at $3 or $4 per bottle. The purchaser pours the syrup in cups, adds a little water and finds he has a good Brandy cocktail." The last step, Partridge noted, was to throw away the peaches and the bottle.

Lieutenant Henry Ropes of the 20th Massachusetts, who earlier dismissed General Hooker as "a doubtful Chief" lacking in honesty of purpose, now had to admit that he misjudged him. "Hooker is doing a great deal to improve the Army," he wrote his father on March 14. ". . . Provisions are plenty and stores of all kinds are brought up and everything is done to make the troops more comfortable." Lieutenant John V. Hadley of the 7th Indiana agreed, although he was suspicious of the motive behind the changes. "Our situation is now good," he wrote home. "Our culinary condition has been much improved. Soft bread, Potatoes, onions, Molasses, beans, beef, and butter are among the things we now eat. Like a herd of poor oxen they are fattening us for the slaughter. We eat and sleep and wait patiently for the time. . . ."[27]

Waiting and dull routine bred boredom. Private Henry Howell of the 124th New York reported his duty was guarding brigade headquarters. "It takes twelve men and a corporal up there to take care of a few trees and salute the officers as they pass," he wrote; "these are all the orders we have, but it is military I suppose." General Hooker was well aware that a soldier with time on his hands was a soldier with time to think about his troubles, and he instituted a rigorous schedule of drills and exercises and instructions, weather permitting.

"We are reviewed and inspected one day and inspected and reviewed the next, and so it goes all the while," wrote a Massachusetts soldier. ". . . We can hear nothing but drum, drum, drum from sunrise till dark." Chester Leach of the 2nd Vermont described the routine for his wife. He listed company skirmish drills in the morning and battalion or brigade drills in the afternoon. "Today we had a Division review in the forenoon & a Battalion drill in the afternoon, & this evening we have had a recitation of Tactics, which I suppose will be in order for the times to come." The drilling and the instructing also profited the many line officers taking up new posts. The 1st Minnesota, for example, was now under its lieutenant colonel, and at first things did not go smoothly. "The Lt. Col. commanding," wrote Sergeant Marvin after battalion drill on February 16, "made three or four boches & once got us tangled up so that we had to make ½ doz. nonmilitary movements to get us untangled. . . . We drilled miserable. . . ."[28]

* *

UNDER JOE HOOKER'S exuberant prodding, spirits began to rise in the Rappahannock camps. With the general's blessing a number of officers sent for their wives and children to join them in their quarters, lightening everyone's mood. "Once in a while we hear the baby cry and the rattle of ladies' tongues remind us of home," wrote a sergeant in the 32nd Massachusetts. On March 12 the Third Corps celebrated a wedding, Captain Daniel Hart of the 7th New Jersey taking as his bride Miss Ellen Lammond of Phillipsburg, New Jersey. General Hooker headed the guest list, which included most of the Third's ranking officers. Dan Sickles hosted the reception at corps headquarters, and there was dancing and celebration and even a fireworks display.[29]

The major event of the Potomac army's social season, however, was planned for March 17, St. Patrick's Day, as commemorated by Brigadier General Thomas Francis Meagher's Irish Brigade. An arbor of evergreen boughs decorated brigade headquarters, before which were tables piled high with cakes and an enormous wooden tub, painted green, filled with a near-lethal punch containing eight baskets of champagne, ten gallons of rum, and twenty-two gallons of Irish whiskey. To start the festivities, each man in the brigade received March 17th's standard issue: two gills of whiskey.

The Irishmen turned no one away from their celebration, which was attended by the army's ranking officers and their guests, and no one went home hungry or sober. There were foot races, sack races, mule races, boxing matches, and a greased pole with $50 and a fifteen-day pass atop it. (The winner filled his pockets with sand to supply the necessary traction.) A one-mile steeplechase course was laid out on the parade ground, with fences and water-filled ditches, and the racing was wild and violent. By the time the races were over one man and two horses were dead and there were more than a few broken bones. Toward afternoon Private Charles Goddard observed that all the officers were getting progressively drunker, and all of them were mounted, "and it was not safe for a private who had to take it on foot or not at all, so I took my leave. . . ." All in all, St. Patrick's Day 1863 was a day few in the Army of the Potomac — and certainly no one in the Irish Brigade — would forget.

General David Birney, commanding First Division, Third Corps, determined not to fall behind the Irish Brigade in merrymaking. In the words of one of his colonels, Regis de Trobriand, "He gave, in his turn, a fête, which made an epoch in the remembrances of the division." Birney's fête was held on March 27, and was similar to St. Patrick's Day in its entertainments, although not quite so awash in liquor. There was a variety of foot races for the men, and horse racing for the officers. A pontoon train served as a grandstand, and the spectators — 15,000 by one count — were headed by General Hooker and staff and guests.

"How they managed to scare up such a number of females I cannot imagine," Colonel Wainwright observed. Prominent among them was the lovely Princess Salm-Salm, the former "Miss Leclerq," circus rider and actress, who by Wainwright's account was attractive enough "to stand very well in the eyes of General Joe." Prince Felix Salm-Salm, formerly of the Prussian cavalry, commanded the 8th New York. Unfortunately, the prince was one of several riders thrown during the steeplechasing, and broke his arm. In spite of this, General Birney's fête was considered a success, and a rather more orderly success than what had been staged by the Irish Brigade. "The affair went off exceedingly well for this country," Colonel Wainwright thought, "where we are not much accustomed to these sports. . . ."[30]

Among Yankee soldiers something out of the ordinary, something special, was referred to as a "Big Thing." For example, H. N. Hunt, writing to his wife, described the case of two corporals in the 27th Connecticut who were sharing quarters at Falmouth that winter when one of them fell sick and on examination was discovered to be a woman. "She was a private when she enlisted but promoted to corporal," Hunt noted. ". . . The boys say that the 2nd corporal was a 9 months man and the 1st no man at all. . . . Big Thing in the Army." In a similar case, tentmates in the Sixth Corps were discovered to be a man and wife after she contracted typhoid and confessed to the surgeon. She had maintained the disguise for two years, and been promoted from the ranks for "marked bravery" at Antietam.

Nor were these cases the least of the phenomenon. Quartermaster Partridge recorded that in the 118th Pennsylvania "Corporal Blank" reported sick one evening and was sent to the hospital tent for examination, "said examination causing a great commotion among the doctors and hospital attendants. . . . In the course of the night Corporal Blank gave birth to a fine boy — a genuine child of the Regiment."

On record are no less than three other such events in the Army of the Potomac that winter and spring. "A very singular circumstance has given rise to considerable talk in the 107 Pa. Regt.," Lieutenant Colonel Elijah Cavins confided to his wife on January 19. A corporal recently promoted to sergeant for gallantry at Fredericksburg had given birth, and Colonel Cavins asked, "What use have we for women, if soldiers in the army can give birth to children?" Thereafter babies were born to a corporal in a New Jersey regiment in the First Corps and to a corporal in a Massachusetts regiment in the Sixth Corps. Private Solomon Newton reported of the Sixth Corps baby that the new mother was said to be the wife of the regimental orderly, "but I dont believe it. . . . She must have seen some hard times and heard some awful talk, for there was only one knew she was a woman. . . ."[31]

How these women had disguised their presence for so long — indeed how four of them had also managed to conceal their pregnancies — no doubt furnished the troops with many an evening's campfire gossip. For more active amusement, like the Confederates across the river they engaged in snowball battles, although for the Yankees snow was hardly the novelty it was for those from the Deep South. With the coming of warmer weather the sport of choice was baseball.

Gershom Mott's brigade in Joe Hooker's old division staged a sort of brigade series. First, nine officers of the 5th New Jersey challenged a nine from the rest of the brigade, but "got left." The next day it was the turn of the 2nd New York to carry out the challenge; the New Yorkers "got left also." A man in the Sixth Corps reported that Brigadier General Joseph Bartlett "frequently plays ball with the boys and is said to be a good player." The records do not show that Major General Abner Doubleday of the First Corps fielded an outstanding nine, however.[32]

As the men began to feel better about themselves and their army, some of them set out to infuse their new spirit into the people back home. The peace party in the North — the Copperheads, commonly compared by the troops to the poisonous vipers that struck without warning — found no support in the Army of the Potomac. In the opinion of Pennsylvanian James Miller, they had "done more to dishearten the army and prolong the war than ten times their number could have done if they had been in the rebel army."

General Solomon Meredith of the Iron Brigade — five western regiments from Indiana, Michigan, and Wisconsin, as good a brigade of fighting men as any in the army — delivered a rousing speech on the subject at dress parade on March 26, and "the ground shook." Then, wrote George Fairfield of the 6th Wisconsin, "we adopted a preamble and resolutions denouncing the copperheads." He added, "No opportunity given for negative. . . ." Resolutions from like-minded regiments and brigades appeared in hometown newspapers all across the North. As a man in the 33rd New York explained to his family, the goal should be "to set some of these copperhead *Cowards & Traitors* to thinking & shame them into the Union ranks. . . ."[33]

* *

"I DO not think it possible that such a change could have taken place for the better as has been effected in the short space of two months," the 2nd New Jersey's Sergeant Edmund English wrote. "From a dissatisfied and almost mutinous mob, we have become a good and well-disciplined army second to none." Sergeant English's view was echoed up and down the chain of command. The Second Corps' General Darius Couch stated forthrightly that the commanding general, "by adopting vigorous measures stopped the almost wholesale desertions, and infused new life and discipline in the Army." Captain Henry Abbott of the 20th Massachusetts, so disapproving of Hooker at his appointment in January, looked at the general's policy on furloughs and admitted, "I must give Hooker the credit of saying that this step is the very best for the army that could be taken. . . ."

Captain Folwell of the engineers admired the discipline Hooker instilled: "We feel the reins tightening up every day more and more." According to Sergeant Charles Ward of the 32nd Massachusetts, "We are ready for a fight & the men never have been so well & looking so fleshy & in so good spirits as now. . . . We hope Joe will do something with us this time." The *New York Times* summed up by saying that the Army of the Potomac "is about as much Hookerized as it was at one time McClellanized."[34]

Virtually everyone agreed — and virtually everyone was surprised — that in only two months Joe Hooker had engineered a miraculous recovery. Fighting Joe, of raffish reputation and headstrong impulses, had proved himself to be an efficient administrator, an innovative reformer, a practiced military executive. As the *Times* suggested, comparisons to the McClellan era were inevitable, especially to that general's infusions of spirit to the Army of the Potomac after the debacles at Manassas in July 1861 and again in August 1862.

The comparisons were more apparent than real, however. After First Manassas McClellan inherited not an army but a collection of raw regiments waiting and wanting to become an army. The men were more confused and untrained than demoralized, and in eight months McClellan administered the training. And at Second Manassas the men of the Potomac army felt they were not defeated and demoralized so much as they were outgeneraled. What they desperately wanted was a new general; once they were given "Little Mac" they were ready to fight again.

At no other point in the war was the Army of the Potomac so dangerously low in spirit and morale as in the winter of 1862–63. Not only had the men lost all confidence in their commanding general, they had no confidence that the high command even knew what it was doing. All the essential ties that bound the army together were unraveling. Each two or three days the equivalent of a regiment deserted and went home; every day the rate of desertion reached a new high. When General Schurz warned Mr. Lincoln that he must not be surprised "when you see this great army melt away with frightful rapidity," he was recording a literal truth.

The first essential for recovery had been simply a change of command, giving the men at least the promise of something better. Unlike

Burnside, Hooker expressed no doubts of himself or of his ability to command a great army, and his confidence was infectious. Most important, he grasped at once that nothing he did in command was more important than getting the machinery of the army operating as it was supposed to. He demonstrated to even the men in the rear ranks that he cared about their well-being. Joe Hooker understood that a soldier's pride was a vital asset, and when he boasted publicly that he was leading "the finest army on the planet," he was addressing that pride.

In a letter home on March 25, the 7th Maine's Lieutenant Colonel Selden Connor cast a thoughtful veteran's eye on the rejuvenated army around him. General Hooker, he wrote, was daily gaining strength and popularity with the rank and file. "The army never was in better shape than now; I think it lacks the *enthusiasm* that pervaded it when we commenced the Peninsular Campaign, but it has a cool, dogged determination which perhaps is better." Then he added a thought that was on many minds just then regarding Fighting Joe Hooker: "We hope and expect that he will not be found wanting when the day of trial comes."[35]

4

The Highest Expectations

W HEN CONFEDERATE cavalryman Fitzhugh Lee made his raid on
the Army of the Potomac near Hartwood Church in the last week
of February, one of the Federal cavalry divisions sent in futile pursuit was
commanded by William W. Averell. Fitz Lee and William Averell, cadets
together at West Point in the mid-1850s and close friends, had gone their
separate ways in 1861 to become opposing brigadiers of cavalry. Now, as
Lee slipped his pursuers and went back across the Rappahannock, he left
a note to be delivered to his old friend. "I wish you would put up your
sword, leave my state, and go home," it read. ". . . If you won't go home,
return my visit, and bring me a sack of coffee."

Neither Averell nor Joe Hooker was amused. Hooker was blunt with
his cavalry generals. "You have got to stop these disgraceful cavalry 'surprises,'" he told them. "I'll have no more of them. I give you full power
over your officers, to arrest, cashier, shoot — whatever you will — only
you must stop these 'surprises.'" Should they fail to, he warned, "I will
relieve the whole of you and take command of the cavalry myself!"
Averell, being the particular offended party, said he wanted to accept Fitz
Lee's challenge and go straight for the Rebel cavalry across the river.
That suited Hooker's purposes very nicely. It ought to put a halt to
enemy raiding and so keep his own movements secure, and it would be a
good test for the newly reorganized cavalry arm. Soon enough General
Averell had his orders — cross the Rappahannock and "attack and rout
or destroy" Fitzhugh Lee's cavalry brigade.

William Woods Averell was thirty years old and had seen more cavalry
fighting, against hostile Indians, when serving in the Mounted Rifles in
the late 1850s than thus far in this civil war. That was typical of cavalrymen in the Army of the Potomac. And those who did fight were regularly
trounced by Jeb Stuart's troopers. Looking back on the first two years of

the war, a veteran Federal cavalryman remarked that in those days there seemed only three choices when engaged with the enemy — "surrender, die, or run." Hooker was determined to change all that, and Averell was willing enough to try. He told his troopers to sharpen their sabers and be ready to use them. The question was how well he could carry off this newfound aggressiveness.

The Federals' new intelligence bureau, headed by Colonel George Sharpe, made Averell's task easier by exactly locating Fitz Lee's cavalry brigade for him. Interrogation of prisoners and a report from a resident spy of Sharpe's who lived right in the middle of the Rebel army south of the Rappahannock placed Lee's brigade at Culpeper Court House, fifteen miles by road southwest of the crossing at Kelly's Ford. Lee had crossed the Rappahannock upriver at Kelly's to make his February raid on the Yankee camps. Now Averell would cross there and throw down the gauntlet to his old friend who had become his nemesis.

For this duty Averell had the two brigades of his cavalry division, led by Colonels Alfred Duffié and John B. McIntosh, consisting of three Pennsylvania regiments and one each from Massachusetts, Rhode Island, New York, and Ohio. From the cavalry reserve came two regiments of regulars, 1st and 5th United States, under Captain Marcus A. Reno. For artillery support there was the 6th New York Independent battery, six 3-inch Ordnance rifles, under Lieutenant George Browne. The nine regiments of horse and the battery totaled 3,100 men.

Colonel Sharpe's Bureau of Military Information gave Fitz Lee "near 3,000" horsemen, although reports placed from 250 to 1,000 of them around Brentsville, some distance north of the Rappahannock. This worried Averell, and he detached 900 men to guard his flank and rear. By this excess of caution he reduced his numbers facing the far greater threat in his front by nearly a third. By late evening on March 16 General Averell's forces were assembled at Morrisville, a half-dozen miles short of Kelly's Ford. He set March 17 as the day of battle. While the rest of the Army of the Potomac celebrated St. Patrick's Day, the cavalry would attempt to "rout or destroy" Fitz Lee's marauding brigade.[1]

Fitzhugh Lee, the twenty-seven-year-old nephew of the commanding general, had a full measure of the cavalry-fighting experience that Averell lacked. He had played a part in all of Jeb Stuart's exploits and possessed Stuart's full confidence. By happenstance Stuart would witness this day's fight, but he left its management entirely to Lee. That a fight was imminent Lee had little doubt. Headquarters reported the Yankee cavalry leaving its camps on March 16, and scouts reported its arrival at Morrisville. The Yankees' objective, however, was not yet clear. From Morrisville they might attempt to cross at Kelly's Ford, or cross farther upstream at Rappahannock Bridge on the Orange & Alexandria Railroad, or they might continue westward toward the Shenandoah Valley. Lee reinforced his picket post at Kelly's Ford with forty sharpshooters, positioned reinforcements for the picket post at Rappahannock Bridge if need be, and waited at Culpeper Court House for the Yankees to reveal their hand.

Under cover of darkness Averell sent a 100-man party ahead to Kelly's Ford, intending that at first light on the seventeenth it take the Rebel pickets there by surprise and storm the crossing. He made an odd selection of picked men for this important task. A few were regulars from the 5th U.S., but most were from the 4th New York cavalry — Dickel's Mounted Rifles, a German unit of undistinguished record. During Fitz Lee's Hartwood Church raid in February, for example, "with the greatest alacrity, they broke by individuals to run to the rear," as a regimental historian phrased it. Perhaps Averell thought this disgrace would inspire Dickel's Mounted Rifles to thirst for revenge, but if so he was disappointed. When the main body reached Kelly's Ford at daylight, it found the Mounted Rifles dismounted and sheltering in a sunken road near the ford, exchanging a desultory fire with the Rebels on the opposite bank.

The means to blast his way across Kelly's Ford was at hand in Lieutenant Browne's battery of Ordnance rifles, but General Averell feared the noise of the guns would alert Fitz Lee's main body. A party sent downstream to outflank the defenders soon returned, balked by the high water and swift current. Averell concluded his only choice was to force a passage under fire right at the ford. On both banks the Confederates had cut down trees to form woody entanglements called abatis. At the picket post, in rifle pits and in a dry millrace along the south bank, the primary defenders were eighty-five troopers under Captain W. A. Moss, 4th Virginia cavalry. Moss's little force was well sheltered and firing across a river only 100 yards wide, and it was formidable beyond its numbers.

Twice Averell's intrepid chief of staff, Major Samuel E. Chamberlain, led the 4th New York troopers of the advance party in charges into the river, and twice they broke and scrambled back under the enemy's fire. Chamberlain's horse was three times wounded and he himself was shot in the face. Undaunted, he next collected a party of 1st Rhode Island troopers for a third charge, but with no better result. Chamberlain's horse was hit again, this time mortally, and he was knocked out of the saddle with a bullet through his cheek into his neck. He was dragged out of the water and onto the bank. There, bloodied but not the least bowed, in a fury, he emptied his pistol at the Rhode Islanders fleeing past him.

In the meantime axmen had hacked apart the abatis to widen the approach to the ford, the covering fire was redoubled, and the Rhode

Islanders were rallied for another charge. Major Chamberlain's place at their head was taken by Lieutenant Simeon A. Brown. Of eighteen men in Brown's lead party only he and three others made it across the river, but that was enough. The defenders fled the rifle pits and millrace at their approach, and Lieutenant Brown waved his saber and shouted reinforcements across, and soon enough Kelly's Ford was secured. Captain Moss's Virginians ran back to their horses to escape, but twenty-five of them were not quick enough and were captured. Only at 7:30 A.M. did Fitz Lee at Culpeper learn the enemy was at Kelly's Ford, and had won the crossing there. He put his troopers on the ford road at a rapid trot.[2]

It took some time for General Averell to get his entire command and his battery across the ford and reorganized and the ground reconnoitered. Only at midmorning was he ready to advance to his chosen field of battle, open ground a mile's march beyond Kelly's Ford. Subtracting the guarding force left north of the Rappahannock, and the loss of men and horses in the fight at the crossing, he had some 2,050 men under command. Averell chose the defensive deliberately. He expected that Fitz Lee, with a detachment of his own north of the river, would accept the challenge with a roughly equal force — and that he would attack. It was noon when the Confederate advance guard was sighted, coming up behind a high stone fence in the farm field of C. T. Wheatley.

General Averell was right about Fitz Lee's aggressiveness but wrong about his numbers. The lack of forage had seriously weakened Lee's cavalry brigade, and by Lee's account, in addition to various detachments, he had been forced to detail "a large part of the command to go to their homes for fresh horses. . . ." Counting his picket force at Kelly's Ford and a battery of horse artillery, Lee began March 17 with barely 1,000 men. He advanced from Culpeper with barely 800 troopers. With him in expectation of battle were Jeb Stuart, who happened to be nearby on a court-martial case, and a second fabled figure of the Confederacy, Major John Pelham, known throughout the South as "the gallant Pelham."

Major Pelham was twenty-four, from Alabama, the head of Stuart's battalion of horse artillery. He had resigned from West Point's class of 1861 to join the Confederacy, and in more than sixty engagements, beginning with First Manassas, had given new meaning to the mobile use of field artillery. It was Robert E. Lee himself, in his report on Fredericksburg, who applied the adjective "gallant." Youthful, handsome, dashing, Pelham was the very stuff of heroes, and it was perfectly in character that while on a visit to a young lady in the neighborhood he would hear of the impending cavalry fight and hurry to the scene. Although without official duties on this battlefield, both he and Stuart would manage to get into the fight.

The stone fence in Mr. Wheatley's field looked to Averell like a good anchor for his defensive line, and he had two regiments — the 4th Pennsylvania and the now notorious 4th New York — dismount to seize it. The troopers were uncomfortable in their infantrymen's role and (as Averell put it) "did not come up to the mark at first," but with the general and his staff prodding them toward the enemy fire, and with another detachment outflanking the position, the Rebel advance guard was soon driven off and the Yankees took over the stone fence. Seeing this as he came up with his main body of cavalry — 1st, 2nd, 3rd, 4th, and 5th Virginia — Fitz Lee turned to Stuart and asked, "Hadn't we better take the bulge on them at once?" Stuart agreed, and Lee gave the order to charge to the 3rd Virginia's Colonel Thomas H. Owen.

Colonel Owen preceded his charge with a squadron of sharpshooters advancing as skirmishers to beat down the enemy fire. They found themselves badly outgunned, however, and began to falter under the combined fire of Yankee cavalry carbines and Lieutenant Browne's 3-inch rifles. At that Jeb Stuart dashed forward, waving his plumed hat and yelling, "Confound it, men, come back! Don't leave me alone here." The sharpshooters held their ground then, and the 3rd Virginia began its charge.

The Virginians came slanting fast across the field in a column four riders abreast. The Federals behind the stone fence made poor targets, and the fence had no openings and was too high to jump, and the troopers turned their horses to the left and galloped along the fence seeking a gap, whooping and firing their pistols and taking losses in return. Reaching the Wheatley homestead, the 3rd was joined by the 5th Virginia, and the two regiments at last found a gateway in the fence there and rushed forward to try and turn the Federal position.

Now Major Pelham was at the gateway too, with no reason for being there but the excitement of the chase, standing in his stirrups and holding his saber high and shouting the men forward. Then a shell from one of Lieutenant Browne's guns burst overhead and Pelham was on the ground, apparently unmarked but insensible. He was carried from the field and a surgeon found he had been struck in the back of the head by a shell fragment. He did not regain consciousness, and presently he died. "Our loss is irreparable," Jeb Stuart would mourn. In due course the gallant Pelham would lie in state in the Capitol in Richmond, and then he was returned to Alabama by slow train as the South mourned.[3]

Pelham's fall came at the peak of the Virginians' charge. The right of the Federal line, where the assault was now focused, was defended by the

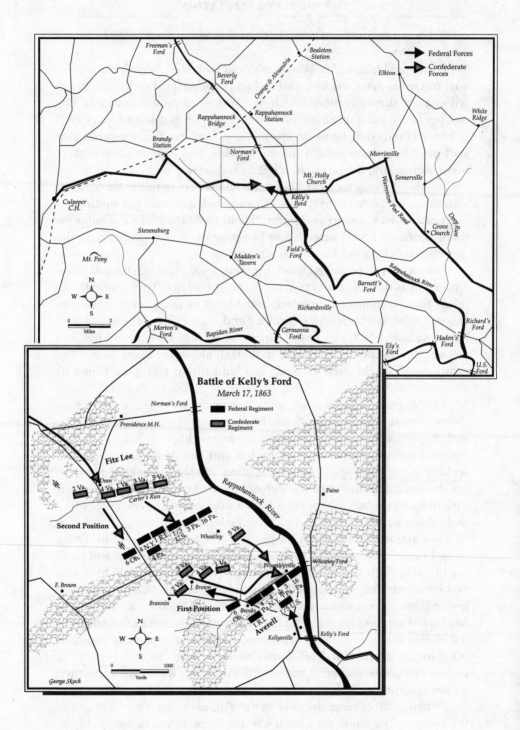

Federal Forces
Confederate Forces

Freeman's Ford
Bealeton Station
Elkton
Beverly Ford
Orange & Alexandria
White Ridge
Rappahannock Bridge
Rappahannock Station
Brandy Station
Norman's Ford
Morrisville
Somerville
Culpeper C.H.
Mt. Holly Church
Kelly's Ford
Warrenton Post Road
Grove Church
Deep Run
Stevensburg
Madden's Tavern
Field's Ford
Rappahannock River
Mt. Pony
Barnett's Ford
N
W   E
S
Richardsville
Richard's Ford
0   2
Miles
Morton's Ford
Rapidan River
Germanna Ford
Haden's Ford
Ely's Ford
U.S. Ford

Battle of Kelly's Ford
March 17, 1863

Federal Regiment
Confederate Regiment

Norman's Ford
Providence M.H.
Fitz Lee
Dean
2 Va.   4 Va.   3 Va.   5 Va.
Carter's Run
Rappahannock River
Paine
Second Position
4 N.Y. 1 R.I. 1/5 U.S. 3 Pa. 16 Pa.
5 Va.
6 Oh.   4 Pa.
Wheatley
3 Va.   4 Va.   1 Va.
Wheatleyville
Wheatley Ford
F. Brown
2 Va.   J. Brown
4 Pa. 3 Pa.
1 R.I. 4 N.Y. 1 Pa.
Brannin
First Position
6 Oh. Brooks
1 R.I.
1/5 U.S.
Averell
Kellysville
Kelly's Ford
N
W   E
S
0   1000
Yards
George Skoch

16th Pennsylvania, fighting dismounted in and around the Wheatley house and outbuildings. These Pennsylvanians, like the defenders behind the stone fence, demonstrated that a trooper firing his carbine coolly from good cover was easily a match for a mounted cavalryman, even a charging one. Colonel Owen's attack was checked and then turned back, and the survivors drifted back across the field in disorder. The 3rd Virginia would lose 44 men this day (and 51 horses), more than a quarter of its strength, mostly in this charge. The 5th Virginia, less heavily engaged, lost 11 men and 29 horses.

Manning the other end of the Federal line, Colonel Alfred Napoleon Alexander Duffié, late of the 4th Chasseurs d'Afrique, in command of Averell's First Brigade, decided this was the moment for a charge of his own. Duffié, a St. Cyr graduate and a veteran of years of cavalry service abroad, had resigned from the French army in 1861 to offer his services in this new war. He was a cavalry traditionalist, expert with the saber, and now he led the 1st Rhode Island, 6th Ohio, and elements of the 4th Pennsylvania and 5th U.S. out into the field in a deliberate challenge. Facing Duffié was the balance of Fitz Lee's brigade, the 1st, 2nd, and 4th Virginia.

The unexpected audacity of Duffié's challenge seemed to take the Confederates by surprise, and with his wider line threatening to overlap their narrower one, they could only maneuver and parry and fall back. A sharp counterattack did succeed in capturing eighteen of the Rhode Islanders, but still Fitz Lee had to recall his command back through a strip of woods and into the next field for another stand.

To General Averell, Colonel Duffié's impetuousness in ordering his charge outweighed its favorable result, and he sent strict orders that any officer assigned a position was not to leave it without an explicit order from him or a staff man acting for him. The Federal cavalry reforms, it seemed, did not include independence of mind. Two further developments served to feed General Averell's caution. Prisoners reported Jeb Stuart was on the field, causing Averell to assume Confederate reinforcements were not far behind. As if in confirmation, a locomotive whistle sounded from the Orange & Alexandria a few miles away; surely it signaled the reinforcements' arrival. That was what Fitz Lee wanted Averell to think when he ordered the engineer to run his locomotive back and forth with much whistling. It was a Confederate ruse already grown old in this war, but it found a willing believer in William Averell.

The two lines of horsemen paused 600 yards apart, and Fitz Lee again ordered a charge. Averell remained on the defensive, holding his troopers to their places. Firing from the back of a stationary horse promised considerably more accuracy than from the back of a galloping one, and the casualties soon reflected that fact. Lee's troopers also took losses when they rushed within canister range of Lieutenant Browne's guns. The charge collapsed in swirling confusion and loss. Captain Reno's U.S. regulars, in ideal position on the flank for a countercharge but hamstrung by Averell's order, watched in frustration as the Rebels fell back out of range half a mile. Lee's horse artillery was up now, and it dueled with the Federal battery while Lee desperately sorted out his forces for what was beginning to look like a last stand.

Just then the Battle of Kelly's Ford was William Averell's for the taking. Except for Duffié's unauthorized charge, he had steadfastly remained on the defensive. Now a hell-for-leather charge by his entire command had every chance to "rout or destroy" Fitz Lee's whole cavalry brigade, as ordered. It was 5:30 P.M. and Averell had to make a decision, and it was his imaginings — and the Rebel cavalry's fearsome reputation — that decided him. He had his bugler sound recall and broke off the action and turned back to Kelly's Ford and crossed over to the north bank.

A Federal surgeon remained behind with two men too badly wounded to move, and Averell gave him a sack of coffee and a note for delivery to Fitz Lee. "Dear Fitz," it read, "Here's your coffee. Here's your visit. How do you like it? . . ."[4]

His riposte no doubt gave great satisfaction to General Averell, but his excessive caution left it a battle without an outcome. As Joe Hooker put it, "He was sent to perform a certain duty, and failed to accomplish it from imaginary apprehensions." Kelly's Ford was the first true cavalry-versus-cavalry battle of the war for the Army of the Potomac — "a brilliant and splendid fight," one man called it — and for a moment it had given promise of a startling victory.

Averell lost 6 men killed, 50 wounded, and 22 missing, for a total of 78. Fitz Lee's aggressiveness cost him considerably more: 11 killed, 88 wounded, 34 missing, 133 in all. Stuart and Lee in their reports boasted of pushing the invaders back across the Rappahannock. Perhaps, however, they admitted privately to second thoughts about these Yankee troopers, who before the recall order clearly had the best of the fighting. Certainly that raised morale among the long-suffering Federals, although they expressed puzzlement at their general for breaking off just when they were on the verge of seizing the victory they all hungered for.

Whatever claims each side made for Kelly's Ford, there was an unspoken outcome of the day's fighting there. To Confederate eyes, the Federal cavalry was now an active force, one to be reckoned with in the future. The sight of Yankee troopers massed at Kelly's Ford, or anywhere else on the flanks of the armies, would no longer be thought unusual;

their objective, whatever it might be the next time, would have to be taken seriously. That new awareness was to be a major factor in the campaign to come.[5]

* *

THE NORTHERN press was highly complimentary of General Averell's fight at Kelly's Ford. The Rebels, said the *New York Tribune,* "express astonishment at the splendid fighting of our cavalry. . . . The effect of the fight upon the tone of our entire army has been admirable." According to the *Herald,* "The cavalry are in good spirits over their affair. . . ." Averell's newspaper victory came as a welcome counter to the press criticism leveled at the cavalry only a few days earlier. On March 16 the *New York Times,* for example, had fulminated against what it termed "another of those utterly disgraceful incidents with which this war has abounded. . . ." This latest disgrace was summed up by a Vermont soldier in a letter home: "It seems the rebels have got a new trade, that is stealing Brigadier Generals. I think they done it up first rate."

The stolen brigadier was Edwin H. Stoughton, snatched from his bed in the early morning hours of March 9 by John Singleton Mosby and his Partisan Rangers, and it cruelly embarrassed the cavalry supposed to be guarding General Stoughton. On that dark and rainy night, Mosby and twenty-nine Rangers slipped through the cordon of cavalry patrols and picket lines and took over General Stoughton's posting at Fairfax Court House, just fifteen miles from the White House. Mosby's real target was Colonel Percy Wyndham, the local cavalry commander who after repeatedly failing to catch Mosby had termed him a common horse thief. Colonel Wyndham, to his good fortune, was in Washington that night.

Mosby settled instead for Brigadier General Stoughton, commander of that sector of Washington's outer defenses. When he came to write his memoirs a half century later, Mosby would say that he awakened the sleeping Stoughton with a slap on the backside. However that may be, being captured in his own bed was humiliating enough for the general. Compounding the insult, Mosby's little party of irregulars also made off with 2 captains, 30 privates, and 58 of the best horses in the Union stables, all without a shot being fired. When he heard of it Mr. Lincoln was sardonic. "I can make a much better Brigadier in five minutes," the president said, "but the horses cost a hundred and twenty-five dollars apiece."[6]

"Mosby has covered himself with honors" was Robert E. Lee's response to the affair. With winter turning to spring and bringing the promise of campaigning weather, General Lee was growing increasingly impatient at his inability to control or direct events. He recognized

Mosby's Partisan Rangers as one means to at least distract the Federals, but just then distraction seemed to be the limit of his ambitions. General Hooker, he told Mrs. Lee, "is reported to be all ready & only waiting upon the weather. I wish I could say the same for ourselves. We are scattered, without forage & provisions, & could not remain long together if united for want of food."

Lee at first had read the advance of Averell's Yankee cavalry across Kelly's Ford on March 17 as the opening of Hooker's spring offensive. That evening, before getting any reports of the engagement or of Averell's withdrawal, he telegraphed James Longstreet at Petersburg to return his two First Corps divisions, under Hood and Pickett, to the Rappahannock. As Lee reckoned it, he would need every man he could find to contend with the Army of the Potomac. The next day, however, after receiving Jeb Stuart's overheated version of events at Kelly's Ford ("Enemy is retiring. He is badly hurt. We are after him. His dead men and horses strew the roads."), Lee countermanded the order and told Hood and Pickett they were not needed after all.

The response to his first telegram to Longstreet had been prompt. In less than twenty-four hours Hood's division moved north through Richmond to Ashland on the railroad forty-five miles from Fredericksburg. This exercise (as it proved to be) seemed to instill in General Lee a confidence in the speed with which he might reunite his army in an emergency — and perhaps an overconfidence in how much advance notice he would have of the Federals' movements. Next time, too, he would wait to be certain the alarm was real before acting.[7]

Lee and Longstreet were carrying on an almost daily correspondence in these weeks about how best to employ the divisions detached from the Army of Northern Virginia. The first of the First Corps divisions sent south, Robert Ransom's in January, had since been parceled out for the defense of Charleston and to guard the North Carolina coast. Although he considered Ransom's two brigades as only on loan from his army, Lee accepted it as a long-term loan and did not count them in any immediate plans for contending with Hooker on the Rappahannock.

Hood's division and Pickett's, however, were a different matter. So was the role of Longstreet. Old Pete was Lee's deeply trusted lieutenant, a key player in every contest Lee had fought, and the two divisions contained thousands of the best fighting men in the army. It was unimaginable that General Lee would accept battle — if he had any choice in the matter — without them, and without Longstreet.

Joe Hooker had recently, and gladly, relinquished the responsibility of guarding Washington with the Army of the Potomac, but Robert E. Lee remained liable for the defense of *his* capital, and indeed all of North

Carolina as well. Lee's responsibilities also extended to the Shenandoah Valley and to the area to the west that the federal government, at least, had declared to be the Unionist state of West Virginia. It was to guard Richmond that Longstreet was sent south with Hood's and Pickett's divisions in February, when the Federal Ninth Corps was detected shifting from the Rappahannock to the Virginia Peninsula. Then, soon after the Kelly's Ford fight, Ninth Corps troops were seen by spies to embark at Newport News, at the tip of the Peninsula. Confederate authorities deduced they were setting out for an operation somewhere along the North Carolina coast, and were alarmed.

But on March 30 Lee wrote to Longstreet, in exasperation, "I fear that the enemy, by a systematic propagation of falsehood, has been able to deceive us, and that the report of troops from Newport News going to North Carolina was purposely spread to conceal their movement west." That was indeed the case. Two of the three Ninth Corps divisions had sailed north to Baltimore, where they entrained for Kentucky. So the employment of Longstreet's two detached divisions once again became a subject for debate.[8]

The strategic situation confronting General Lee had by now grown infernally complicated. Everywhere he looked the Confederacy appeared to be outmanned. In middle Tennessee William Rosecrans's Federal army occupied a highly threatening position at Murfreesboro. In Mississippi U. S. Grant's army and the Federal navy together posed a grave threat to Vicksburg. On the Rappahannock Hooker's Army of the Potomac, certainly a great deal larger than Lee's army even when it was united, continued to mystify, successfully concealing its intended path to Richmond, or even if Richmond was its target. In southeastern Virginia the Yankees at Fort Monroe and Norfolk and Suffolk remained a threat, perhaps to Petersburg, perhaps to the important North Carolina railroads. Federal arms menaced Charleston, cradle of the Confederacy.

Richmond hoped that General Lee might have answers, might know how to relieve the pressures from these various directions. And finally there was the certain knowledge gnawing at Lee that his men were getting nowhere enough to eat, and that only he was capable of finding the solution to that particular problem.

In the midst of these times demanding decisive actions, Lee fell seriously ill. As early as March 6 he had written to Mrs. Lee that he was "in indifferent health . . . & feel almost worn out, so that I fear that I may be unable in the approaching campaign to go through the work before me." A few days later he complained that "Old age & sorrow is wearing me away, & constant anxiety & labour, day & night, leaves me but little repose." After two weeks or so his symptoms worsened to "a heavy cold," then "a violent cold." At the insistence of his medical director, he moved from his field-tent headquarters into the nearby country house of William Yerby. Only on April 5 could Lee write his wife that he believed he was finally on the mend, but only after episodes of severe pain in his chest, back, and arms that "came on in paroxysms." His doctors, he said, "have been tapping me all over like an old steam boiler before condemning it."

From the general's description of his symptoms, he likely suffered from pericarditis, an inflammation of the membranous sac around the heart. It is also likely that angina pectoris was present, the disease of the heart that seven years later would cause his death. This episode, at the end of March 1863, was the first sign of the affliction. As late as April 12 he was writing, "I hope in a few days I shall be as well as ever. . . ."[9]

Perhaps because he was distracted by his illness and by all the competing demands being made on him — or perhaps simply because he was reluctant that spring to commit himself to a single defensive course of action — Robert E. Lee let Longstreet's two divisions slip away from his control. This became true gradually, and literally. At the time of Averell's incursion at Kelly's Ford on March 17, Hood's division was standing on alert to return to the Rappahannock, and might have reached there in thirty-six hours. Pickett's division would not have been far behind. Six weeks later, however, Hood and Pickett were 130 miles distant from Lee's army and would need a full week or more to reach it in an emergency. It was General Lee's gravest miscalculation in nearly a year of army command.

Oddly enough, the southeastern Virginia–eastern North Carolina war front was the scene of as much bemusement and indecision by one side as by the other. The Federals' outposts in coastal Virginia, at Fort Monroe and Newport News on the Peninsula and at Norfolk and Suffolk to the south, could serve them well as jumping-off points for advances on Richmond or the railroad center of Petersburg. In addition, their troops at Suffolk and at outposts on the North Carolina coast — Edenton, Plymouth, Washington, New Bern — were constant threats to the vital Confederate seaboard railroads. It was from New Bern that Yankee raiders had damaged the Wilmington & Weldon the previous December, causing great alarm in Richmond.

That, however, was the extent of Yankee aggressiveness. In the bitter wake of McClellan's failed Peninsula campaign, Washington had steadily lost interest in this theater of war. Except for the naval blockade, the Federals' only focus on the Atlantic seaboard was Charleston. At Charleston, in truth, prospects were strategically barren: the port was already securely blockaded, and capturing the city would have only the symbolic value of reclaiming the spot where war began.

Washington's strategic myopia was not readily apparent in Richmond. President Davis, Secretary of War Seddon, and General Lee responded quickly to any provocation in this theater, such as the movement of the Ninth Corps to the Peninsula. Indeed, the general in command on the scene, James Longstreet, argued for a campaign there in preference to, or at least in advance of, one on the Rappahannock. Losing Petersburg or the seaboard railroads, he insisted, "would cut off most of the supplies that we depend upon for our sustenance."

Pointing to Hooker's "grand army" and then to the Yankee detachments along the coast, Longstreet called for a Confederate strategy that would concentrate against "his detachments and then make a grand concentration on the grand army." Old Pete went so far as to urge Lee to pull back from his position on the Rappahannock if it became necessary to fend off Hooker until southeastern Virginia and eastern North Carolina were made secure.[10]

Ever present in Lee's calculations in these days was the skimpy ration for his men. He reminded Secretary Seddon that 4 ounces of bacon "of indifference quality" and a pint of flour a day were simply not enough for a soldier to fight on. It "will certainly cause them to break down when called upon for exertion." Finding that complaining to the commissary in Richmond produced excuses instead of rations, General Lee took more direct action. He told Longstreet to obtain "all the supplies possible of forage and subsistence . . . and turn all the energies of your department in that direction." With the capital apparently now free of danger of attack by the Ninth Corps, and with Hooker's army apparently again quiet, Longstreet's primary assignment would be to act as the Army of Northern Virginia's new commissary at the source — the fields and smokehouses of the farmers and planters of North Carolina and Virginia.

Under Lee's direction Longstreet held command of the Department of Virginia and North Carolina. Under him in North Carolina was D. H. Hill who, to keep the Federals at bay while he collected the abundant supplies of the region, invested their garrisons at New Bern and Washington. Harvey Hill's sieges would fail to capture any Yankees, but they did secure great quantities of bacon and corn for the army.

Longstreet meanwhile focused his foraging efforts on the rich agricultural district around the Blackwater River in southside Virginia, south of the James and west of Suffolk. His challenger there was the commander of the Suffolk garrison, Major General John J. Peck. General

Peck was the most capable Union officer in this theater of war, and by aggressive patrolling he held sway over everything east of the Blackwater. To obtain any supplies there Longstreet would have to be equally aggressive, and for that task he wanted Hood's and Pickett's men.

The situation now began to drift out of hand and into the grip of a relentless but contradictory logic all its own. As it became clear that Richmond was not in danger after all, General Lee came to regard Hood's and Pickett's troops as a sort of self-rationing mobile reserve. From their postings around Richmond they might come to him on the Rappahannock, or they might go to Longstreet's support, as the situation dictated.

Yet at the same time, Lee found he must greatly increase the rationing of his army if he was to do battle with the enemy that spring. Only Longstreet could obtain those rations — and only if he had Hood and Pickett to drive the Yankees away from the rich stocks of bacon and corn on the Blackwater. Rather than being poised for a quick return to the Rappahannock should Hooker suddenly advance, these two crack divisions — and their commander — would be locked in a confrontation with General Peck's Yankees at Suffolk. Longstreet put the dilemma clearly in a dispatch to Lee on March 19. He could only collect the necessary supplies, he said, "If I can use my forces; but if the two divisions are to be held in readiness to join you, or even one of them, I can do nothing."[11]

While Lee did not entirely surrender his better judgment to all of Longstreet's ideas — he refused to consider giving up the Rappahannock position as Old Pete suggested, and refused his request for reinforcements, and turned away a proposal to send Longstreet's men to reinforce the Tennessee line — he did display an incautious acceptance of much of his lieutenant's thinking. Lee felt, for example, that the divisions of Hood and Pickett ought to act solely as guards while others gathered, but still he allowed them to become fully involved at Suffolk when Longstreet said it was the only way. Longstreet at first spoke of rapidly seizing Suffolk in a coup de main, but in the event he settled for besieging the place. Lee acquiesced.

On April 4 Longstreet was telling Lee, "I hope to be able to finish with the operations in this section in time to join you. . . ." A week later he was laying siege to Suffolk. It was the peculiar logic of the moment that persuaded him. He could hardly post his men unprotected in front of the enemy's fortifications, and so ordered them to dig in. He showed no desire to spend lives to press the matter to a conclusion, and Lee agreed that the prize would not be worth the cost. After all, Longstreet explained to Secretary Seddon, "The principal object of the expedition was to draw out supplies for our army." Certainly in that respect, and by that logic, Longstreet's Suffolk operation could not be faulted. In due course he estimated it would be late May before all the acquired supplies could be hauled away.[12]

* *

BEFORE THE RAILROAD came to Fredericksburg twenty-five years before the war, the focus of the town was its network of roads that dated from colonial and early national times. The Rappahannock might link Fredericksburg to the coast and the outside world, but it was the local highways and byways that travelers and planters and small farmers depended upon. Now, in 1863, the two armies supplied themselves from the railroad, but they too were dependent on the road network if they were to maneuver to advantage.

The Telegraph Road came down from the north, from Alexandria, and passed through Fredericksburg en route to Richmond. It was dirt and unimproved, bridging the larger streams and fording the lesser ones, and travel on it was hard going in rainy seasons. The Bowling Green Road was considered better for wagon travel between Fredericksburg and Richmond; running well to the east of the Telegraph Road much of the way to the capital, it was also known as the Old Stage Road. To maintain his fortified positions along the Rappahannock east of Fredericksburg, General Lee depended on the River Road and its extension, the Port Royal Road.

Of the road network to the west of Fredericksburg, the chief highway used by the Federals north of the Rappahannock was the Warrenton Post Road. It ran from Falmouth, a mile and a half upstream from Fredericksburg, through Morrisville and Bealton Station to Warrenton at the foot of the Bull Run Mountains. South of the river, a group of investors back at the time of the War of 1812 had financed construction of the Orange Turnpike, connecting Fredericksburg with Orange Court House thirty-six miles to the west. They improved their turnpike with gravel so it would be passable in all seasons and charged a toll for its use.

In 1816, to cater to traffic on the newly built Orange Turnpike, George Chancellor opened a tavern ten miles from Fredericksburg where the Ely's Ford Road intersected the Turnpike. It was a substantial building of brick, two and a half stories high, with accommodations for travelers. Mr. Chancellor ambitiously named his tavern and its outbuildings Chancellorsville. While his settlement never grew into its name, it was at least one of the more prominent landmarks in Spotsylvania County. George Chancellor died in 1836 and over the years Chancellorsville slipped into a genteel decline. The tavern room closed with the

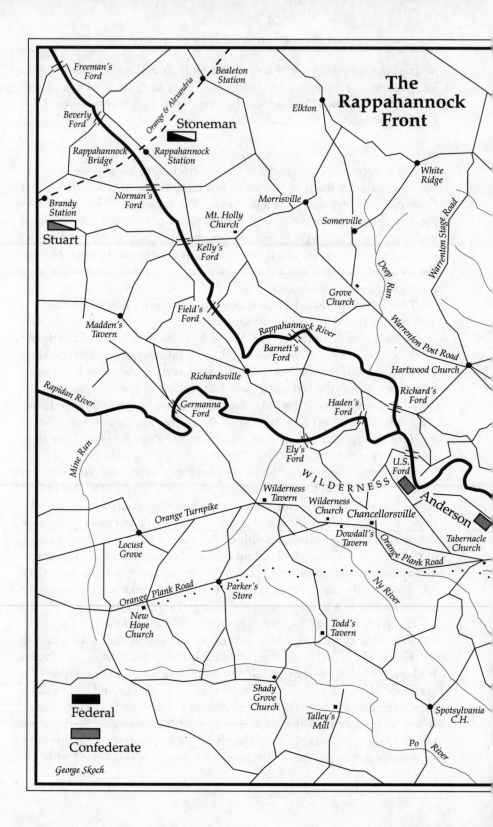

The Rappahannock Front

Freeman's Ford
Bealeton Station
Elkton
Beverly Ford
Orange & Alexandria
Stoneman
White Ridge
Rappahannock Bridge
Rappahannock Station
Brandy Station
Norman's Ford
Morrisville
Somerville
Warrenton Stage Road
Stuart
Mt. Holly Church
Kelly's Ford
Grove Church
Deep Run
Field's Ford
Madden's Tavern
Rappahannock River
Barnett's Ford
Warrenton Post Road
Richardsville
Hartwood Church
Rapidan River
Germanna Ford
Haden's Ford
Richard's Ford
Mine Run
Ely's Ford
U.S. Ford
WILDERNESS
Anderson
Wilderness Tavern
Wilderness Church
Chancellorsville
Orange Turnpike
Dowdall's Tavern
Tabernacle Church
Locust Grove
Orange Plank Road
Ny River
Orange Plank Road
Parker's Store
New Hope Church
Todd's Tavern
Federal
Shady Grove Church
Confederate
Talley's Mill
Spotsylvania C.H.
Po River

George Skoch

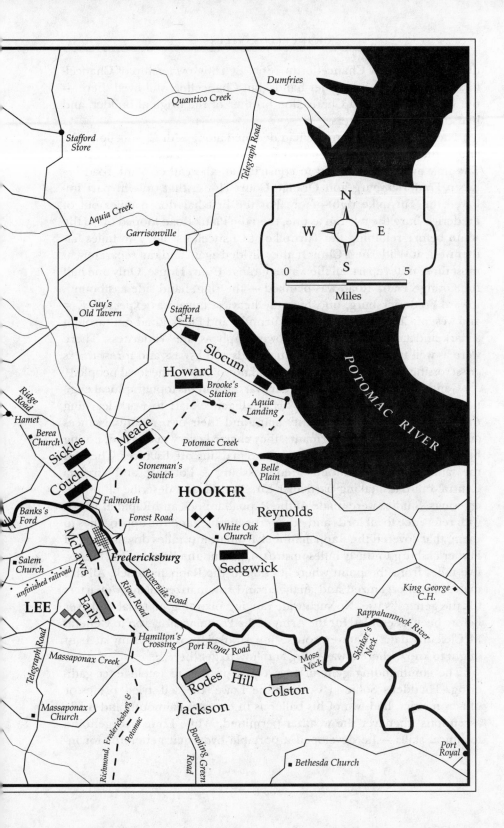

Dumfries

Quantico Creek

Stafford
Store

Aquia Creek

Garrisonville

N
W   E
S

0   5
Miles

POTOMAC RIVER

Guy's
Old Tavern

Stafford
C.H.

Slocum

Howard

Brooke's
Station

Aquia
Landing

Ridge
Road

Hamet

Berea
Church

Sickles

Meade

Potomac Creek

Belle
Plain

Couch

Stoneman's
Switch

HOOKER

Banks's
Ford

Falmouth

Forest Road

White Oak
Church

Reynolds

McLaws

Salem
Church

Fredericksburg

Sedgwick

King George
C.H.

unfinished railroad

LEE

Early

River Road

Riverside Road

Rappahannock River

Skinker's
Neck

Telegraph Road

Telegraph Road

Hamilton's
Crossing

Port Royal Road

Moss
Neck

Massaponax Creek

Richmond, Fredericksburg & Potomac

Rodes

Hill

Colston

Massaponax
Church

Jackson

Bowling
Green
Road

Port
Royal

Bethesda Church

death of the widow Chancellor in 1860. By 1863 ownership of Chancellorsville had fallen into other hands, but Chancellors still lived there — the widow of Stanford Chancellor, brother of the original builder, and her son and six daughters.

The old Orange Turnpike had declined along with Chancellorsville, and in the 1850s it was taken over by the Orange Plank Road Company. The new owners proceeded to construct an all-weather plank road between Fredericksburg and Orange Court House that only in part followed the Turnpike right-of-way. For the first half-dozen miles out of Fredericksburg the two ran as one, then the Plank Road looped off to the south before rejoining the Turnpike at Chancellorsville. Two miles farther west, at Wilderness Church, they divided again and ran separately, at most three miles apart, all the way to Orange Court House. Only one half the Orange Plank Road was planked — the right-hand side eastbound, toward Fredericksburg, on which the heaviest travel was expected. East and west of Chancellorsville both Turnpike and Plank Road ran through a dark and tangled woodland known simply as the Wilderness. There were as well numerous little country roads and byways and forest tracks crisscrossing the region, many of them known only to the local people.[13]

General Hooker put Gouverneur Warren and his topographical engineers and George Sharpe and his intelligence staff to work learning this road network. Using county maps and their own reconnaissances and information from informants, they charted every main road, noting bridges and fords and other features and marking off distances. They did the same for the Richmond, Fredericksburg & Potomac and Virginia Central railroads, taking particular care to note and describe all bridge crossings. Studies were made of the Rappahannock and Rapidan rivers, with reference to all fords and other crossing sites and the approaches to them, that covered the Rappahannock from twenty miles downstream of Fredericksburg to thirty miles upstream, and up the Rapidan for twenty-five miles from the point where it entered the Rappahannock. All this material was organized and analyzed and summarized at headquarters for the general's use. No such wide-ranging planning material had ever before been assembled for the Army of the Potomac, not even in General McClellan's day. Whatever course Joe Hooker took, his army at least ought to know where it was going and how to get there.[14]

The commanding general gave equal priority to intelligence-gathering. Thaddeus Sobieski Constantine Lowe, the self-styled professor of aeronautics, had two of his balloons in camp at Falmouth and made ascensions whenever the weather permitted. While Lowe had genuine technical skills — he developed a portable hydrogen generator for inflating his balloons that gave the aerial corps considerable mobility — he was at heart more carnival promoter than skilled military observer. "From an ascension made at 5 oclock P.M. I found the enemy in large force South & S.E. from the city . . ." was typical of his observation reports. General Hooker wrote across this one in exasperation, "What does the Professor call a large force?"

By contrast, when the army's chief engineer Cyrus Comstock began making ascensions in Lowe's balloon, he might report, as he did on February 27, "The enemies camp back of Fredericksburg, which I thought on the 24th not larger than a brigade, may contain two or three brigades. . . ." Professor Lowe continued his haphazard ways, and before the spring campaign opened Captain Comstock took over management of the balloon corps. Thaddeus Lowe became, in effect, aeronaut without portfolio.[15]

In the meantime, Colonel Sharpe's Bureau of Military Information was setting up an espionage network to spy on General Lee's army as it had never been spied on before. The results were extraordinary. Late in February, for example, Milton Cline, a sergeant recruited from the 3rd Indiana cavalry, managed to tour the Rebel encampments along the Rappahannock from one end to the other, most likely taking the guise of a Mosby irregular. He identified and located nearly all of Lee's major units.

A second important find of Sharpe's was a civilian named Isaac Silver, best described as a resident spy. The Northern-born Silver lived on the Orange Plank Road just three miles east of Chancellorsville, and knew his way around all the Confederate camps. His first report, in mid-March, located and identified units down to brigade level, gave details of fortifications and artillery postings, and estimated strengths. Silver's report reached Sharpe through another local Union man, Ebenezer McGee, who apparently had a secret route for crossing the Rappahannock. Isaac Silver gave promise of further information: "I cannot say but little more at present try to let your messenger come onst more if possible before the battle," he wrote. "I will try to be better posted about the rebble armey."

On March 15 Sharpe and his assistant, John Babcock, submitted the B.M.I.'s first report on the Army of Northern Virginia. Under the new system it incorporated information from all sources: from spies and scouts, from the balloon corps, from interrogations of prisoners and deserters and refugees and contrabands. The report identified all of Lee's divisions and counted all but three of his brigades. It noted Longstreet's departure and correctly named his First Corps divisions sent south. D. H. Hill was correctly reported to be commanding in North Carolina, but without taking any of his troops with him. The artillery was located in its winter quarters in the vicinity of Hanover Junction.

Most noteworthy, when compared to the McClellan-Pinkerton era, the B.M.I. objectively and realistically attempted to estimate Confederate numbers. This first such effort was in fact something of a conservative underestimate, but that was a refreshing change from the hugely inflated numbers of the past. As more information reached him — the B.M.I. was hardly a month old — Sharpe predicted further reliability in his counts, and he was as good as his word. By the time the spring campaign opened, Joe Hooker would know almost as much about Robert E. Lee's army as Lee himself knew. On April 22 a visitor to headquarters could write with confidence that the commanding general knew "all that it is necessary to know in regard to the enemy, every regiment and brigade, division, etc., all their latest arrivals and departures, etc., all collated, compared from many sources, and fully confirmed. The secret service of Gen. Hooker is far superior to anything that has ever been here before."

Colonel Sharpe's report offered one further revelation: the Potomac army's chief signal officer "is in possession of the full code of signals used by the enemy's Signal Corps. . . ." At the time both armies were using signal flags for their daily message traffic, and since the flag stations had to be at high points for visibility, each side could easily watch the other's signaling from across the river. Both used comparatively simple alphabetic codes rather than true encipherment, and with enough patient effort the Yankee signalmen had figured out the code the Rebels were using.

But there was even more to it than that. Not long afterward, it was learned from a captured Confederate signal officer that Lee's signalmen had broken the Yankees' code and could read *their* flag messages. Chief of Staff Daniel Butterfield filed away that intriguing bit of information for future use.[16]

* *

"GENL HOOKER seems to have postponed his movements till the next fair day," General Lee wrote his wife on March 21. That was true enough in principle, except that General Hooker never planned to move before the first of April. In sending Averell's troopers across the river on March 17, he had contemplated nothing more than a fight between cavalries. Hooker knew as well as Lee that in that season in the Old Dominion even the best-prepared and best-equipped army was hostage to the weather. One hard rain turned Virginia roads to bottomless mud and made rivers like the Rappahannock and Rapidan run too deep and fast for even cavalry to ford safely. By April there was hope that showers might replace storms, and that the warm temperatures might dry the roads rapidly.

As he made ready for the spring campaign, Joe Hooker was facing a potentially disruptive manpower problem, one that threatened the revival he had so skillfully directed. His March 31 return credited the Army of the Potomac with 133,627 men equipped and present for duty. Included in that total were 114,442 infantrymen, and General Hooker's problem was that 37,200 of them — very nearly a third — were scheduled to leave the army during the next three months.

Back when the war was young, two Northern states, New York and Maine, had enlisted a number of regiments slated for the Army of the Potomac for two years rather than the more common three-year term. Thus in the spring and early summer of 1863 thirty-three New York and two Maine regiments, all told close to 20,500 men, were due to be discharged. To be sure, not all these men were expected to be lost to the army permanently. It was thought that many would re-enlist — but only after getting out and going home and collecting the sizable bounties being offered to anyone agreeing to join up in this third year of civil war. But once home they would certainly be lost to this spring campaign at the least. "The large bounties," Hooker explained to the army's adjutant general, ". . . seem to be uppermost in their minds, and they will be likely to hold back for their recurrence. At all events, they are unwilling to re-enlist now."

Much would depend on how soon Hooker could launch his campaign. Only five of the two-year regiments were due out in April, but there would be thirteen out in May and seventeen in June. Some number of these were sure to be lost to the army. As for the others, Hooker and his generals had to ask themselves how hard such troops would fight if they were thrown into battle knowing that in a matter of days or a week or two they would be free of the army and back home in the embrace of their families. The Sixth Corps' General John Sedgwick, for one, had no doubts on the matter. "No troops with but a few days to leave," he wrote home, "are going to risk much in a fight." Furthermore, since by law mustering-out had to take place where each regiment enlisted, they might have to be started home as much as a week before their time was up.

As if the subject were not already complicated enough, heated disputes soon roiled many of these regiments over exactly when their enlistments were up. The men took the date to be two years from when they had signed their enlistment papers in their home states. The War Department, to the contrary, insisted that enlistment only began on the date the regiment was accepted into Federal service. Since in many instances it had taken no little time to fill up the ranks, the two dates might be weeks apart. As a consequence, as spring wore on the Army of the Potomac would find itself facing actual mutiny over this issue.

The matter, and the confusion, was not limited to the two-year regiments. There were twenty-five other regiments — sixteen from Pennsylvania and nine from New Jersey — that had signed up for nine months' service during the crisis in the Union's fortunes the previous summer and fall, when Lee won at Second Manassas and marched into Maryland. The time of these 16,700 nine-months' men was also up in April, May, and June. Here again, much depended on when Hooker could take the offensive. With a total of sixty infantry regiments thus in limbo, Joe Hooker would have to keep one eye on the weather and the other on the calendar as he planned his campaign.[17]

The fresh thinking applied by Hooker and his staff in these weeks included a hard look at the army's logistics. Joe Hooker's acquired distaste for frontal attacks like Fredericksburg was leading him to consider a campaign primarily of maneuver, which in turn was leading him to see how better to supply a mobile army in the field.

The first key link in the Potomac army's logistical chain was its main supply base at Aquia Landing, on the Potomac. Provost Marshal Patrick was responsible for guarding Aquia, and he complained in his diary that there was "nothing to prevent them from making a dash upon our Depot & destroying it before we can get any thing up there to defend it." Indeed, General Lee was already casting covetous looks at Aquia's supply riches. Presently Aquia Landing was well fortified and guarded by a pair of batteries and one of the navy's gunboats and a detachment of infantry. For this seemingly safe duty, General Patrick had a goodly share of the soon-to-be-discharged two-year regiments, thus solving two problems with one assignment.[18]

Within a week of taking command of the army, Hooker had begun experimenting with making it more mobile. On February 3 a so-called Light Division (more properly, a light brigade) was formed and detailed for special service with the Sixth Corps. In time enlarged to five regiments and an attached battery, the Light Division was designed to travel light and fast so as to respond rapidly in an emergency. With the encouragement of Dan Butterfield, who had long been interested in the matter of "marching and feeding a large army beyond a given distance from its base of supplies," the effort was made to extend these lessons of mobility to the full army. Barely a month after the Light Division was organized, a board made up of its commander and four of his regimental officers was given the task of finding some "means of carrying an increased amount of rations by the troops over the three days' usually carried."

The American military of the time was quick to adopt anything French, from Captain Claude Minié's bullet designed for a rifled musket to the gaudy uniforms of the Zouaves and the handy 12-pounder Napoleon fieldpiece, and so the French idea of a "flying column" was an appealing one. The army's chief quartermaster in Washington, Montgomery Meigs, saw to it that a paper on the flying column by one Alexis Godillot, described as "an extensive manufacturer of clothing and equipments for the French army," was translated and distributed to the Potomac army's high command. In M. Godillot's scheme, the troops would carry with them eight days' rations and "thus do away with all wagons." Pack animals would carry necessary additional equipment. The fast-moving column would "march forward, overthrow the enemy, take his works, . . . break up his camps, and keep always advancing. These are the tactics which the French army employs with success."[19]

The challenge here was transposing the idea of the flying column from its French setting — M. Godillot's model column contained but 2,500 men — to an American army corps which in General Hooker's army averaged nearly 16,000 men. The Light Division's board of officers experimented with packing the infantryman's knapsack and haversack in various ways, tested them on practice marches, and concluded that Yankee soldiers could indeed carry eight days' rations in place of the standard three days' — and would be less fatigued in the bargain.

What was required was strict discipline in what the men were allowed to take with them on the march. They had to leave all personal items behind, and all clothing but a single change of shirt, drawers, and socks. They could take one half of a two-man shelter tent and a blanket, but no overcoat. In the knapsack was to be five days' worth of hardtack, coffee, sugar, and salt, plus the change of clothing. A lighter load — three days' cooked rations of bacon or pork, plus hardtack, coffee, and sugar — was designated for the haversack. Line officers' rations and gear would be carried by their servants. Two mules per regiment would pack cooking gear and beans, rice, and desiccated vegetables. Beef on the hoof for five days would accompany the column, to be butchered as required.

With knapsack and haversack properly packed, with rifle, cartridge box, and sixty rounds of ammunition, a man in a flying column was expected to set off on campaign with a 45-pound load. In theory this was a pound or so less than the old way, but there were men who had their doubts about that. "We were even advised," George Fairfield of the 6th Wisconsin noted in his diary, "to throw away our testaments as we should have to carry 8 days rations." Trains of pack mules would carry the infantry's small-arms ammunition.

By cutting down the infantry's wagon trains to ambulances and wagons carrying reserve supplies, it was thought the flying column would be more self-contained and less road-bound than before; if called upon, it might march cross-lots or through woodlands with ease. Certainly the duration of any operation could be greatly increased, allowing General Hooker far more flexibility in his planning. The wheeled artillery and its ammunition trains would remain largely road-bound, and if January's Mud March had any lesson, it was that pontoon trains for river crossings needed reasonably dry roads if they were to move at all. But the infantry ought to be freer-moving than ever before.

Orders putting the flying-column plan into effect went out to all commands, along with the new requirements for eight-day rationing. The most troublesome change appeared to be increasing mule trains at the expense of wagon trains. Captain Daniel D. Jones, a First Corps quartermaster, was a conservative who did not think much of the new arrangement. "It strikes me," he wrote, "more like a whim started by Hooker based upon old California notions than a really practical idea." The First Corps' chief of artillery, Colonel Charles Wainwright, was more tolerant of the idea, but raised a practical question about it. Neither the mules nor the muleteers had any experience in packing loads like this. Wainwright watched a demonstration on how to pack a half-dozen mules with three boxes of ammunition each. "Now there is great amusement in the trains, trying to get the mules accustomed to their new burdens, and the men used to their animals. . . ." Time and patience might bring both parties around, but he wondered if there would be enough of either.[20]

During all this time, Joe Hooker did not slacken efforts to instill soldier's pride in his men. Like General McClellan, he appeared before the troops at every opportunity, and like McClellan, he cut a superbly martial figure on horseback. Hooker had a different approach at reviews, however. After a review of the First Corps early in March, Lieutenant Samuel C. Hodgman wrote home, "Hooker did one thing that McClellan could not have done & that was to pass through & among all the troops without a single cheer being given him — not that he is disliked but the boys dont like to cheer him until he has done something." Hooker must have felt the same way, for he had told his generals to stop the practice, begun in McClellan's time, of ordering the men to cheer on cue each time the commanding general appeared.

Yet Hooker was generous and open-handed with his praise. At a review on April 2, for example, he singled out the colonel of the 13th Massachusetts and said to him, "Give them my compliments. They are the best looking regiment I have seen." That got back to the men of the 13th in no time at all. A week later Hooker gave the men of the 16th Michigan "the praise of having the nicest and cleanest kept ground of any Regt. in the Army of the Potomac," as a man in the 16th proudly recorded it. Not long afterward it was the 24th Michigan's turn. "Colonel Morrow, you have a fine regiment, a fine regiment, fine as silk," said the general. John Ryder of the regiment wrote that "the Col. felt so well over it he let us lie still for 2 days, having nothing but dress parade."

At least so far as the men of his army were concerned, Fighting Joe Hooker's stock was rising fast. And by Joe Hooker's account, by early April the Army of the Potomac "was in condition to inspire the highest expectations."[21]

5

My Plans Are Perfect

P RIVATE HALL TUTWILER was posted at the War Department in Richmond, and on April 3, 1863, he wrote excitedly to his sister, "We had a dreadful riot here on yesterday, & they are keeping it up today, but they are not near as bad today. . . ." He went on to explain that the day before he had gone out into Cary Street where "a large number of women had broken into two or three large grocery establishments, & were helping themselves to hams, middlings, butter, and in fact every thing eatable they could find." Many of the rioters, he reported, were armed with pistols, Bowie knives, hatchets, or hammers. "As fast as they got what they wanted they walked off with it. . . . It was the most horrible sight I ever saw. . . ."

The scene Private Tutwiler watched had begun peaceably enough on the morning of April 2 as a demonstration in Capitol Square by a large group of women and boys. Their message was simple. "We want bread!" they called out to Virginia's governor, John Letcher, when he spoke calmingly to them from the steps of the governor's mansion on the square.

It was, in truth, a riot waiting to happen. Food prices had escalated wildly, with the grocery bill for a typical Richmond family in early 1863 running at least ten times what it had been two years earlier. There was ruinous competition between the army and the citizenry for available supplies, with the government's price for the food it impressed much less than the market price. President Davis had declared March 27 a day of fasting throughout the Confederacy, causing government clerk J. B. Jones to remark in his diary, "Fasting in the midst of famine!" Hungry Richmonders read in their newspapers of a recent bread riot in Salisbury, North Carolina, where a group of women, most of them soldiers' wives, had cowed shopkeepers into providing food at the below-market government price. Governor Letcher's platitudes fell on deaf ears. The choice, a demonstrator warned, was "bread or blood!"

The crowd spilled out of Capitol Square and into Cary Street and Main Street, growing in size and temper until it became an unreasoning mob. Foodstuffs were its first target. Grocery store and bakery windows were smashed and shelves emptied. The City Hospital yielded 310 pounds of beef to the rioters. After food stocks were carried away, the more lawless pillaged shoe stores and clothing stores and jewelry stores. On Main Street the rioters were confronted by a detachment of the city guard and tried to barricade the street with a heavy dray cart.

Now Jefferson Davis appeared on the scene. He climbed onto the dray and managed to quiet the throng. However just they thought their cause, he said, this was riot and plunder and must be ended. "You say you are hungry and have no money," Mr. Davis cried. "Here is all I have," and he threw them a handful of coins. Then he took out his watch and glanced meaningfully at the militiamen behind him. "We do not desire to injure anyone, but this lawlessness must stop." They had five minutes to disperse, he told them; otherwise they would be fired upon. For a time the mob was silent and unmoving. Then the captain of the guard called out the drill, beginning with "Load!" That was enough, and slowly the crowd broke up and drifted away.

The next day there were scattered demonstrations, but more troops were at hand and authority was restored without further trouble. The Richmond Bread Riot was over, with several of the ringleaders in arrest. The incident greatly alarmed the authorities, however, and the City Council made significant improvements in its welfare programs for the poor. Pleas were made to the press to limit reporting of the affair. Secretary of War Seddon ordered that "nothing relative to the unfortunate disturbance . . . be sent over the telegraph lines in any direction for any purpose."[1]

On April 10, just over a week after the Richmond Bread Riot, President Davis issued a proclamation to his fellow Southerners. In seconding the resolution of the Confederate Congress, he urged the people to forgo their old cash crops of cotton and tobacco in favor of a more patriotically motivated agriculture. The army and its animals — and the people of the cities — needed above all foodstuffs and livestock and forage. "Let your fields be devoted exclusively to the production of corn, oats, beans, peas, and other food for man and beast," Mr. Davis urged; "let corn be sown broadcast for fodder. . . ."

Yet however much this new spirit might increase supplies of these essentials, it would not really touch the root of the problem, the reason General Lee's men on the Rappahannock were on less than half-rations and being victualed only on a day-to-day basis, and at that were always hungry. As the foraging efforts of Longstreet's and D. H. Hill's men in southside Virginia and eastern North Carolina were demonstrating (between them in a matter of weeks they would collect 1.3 million pounds of bacon), there were not then any real shortages at the source. The problem was transportation.

For Lee's army in particular, the problem was the utter inadequacy of its single-track railroad supply line. Through that spring the Richmond, Fredericksburg & Potomac continued limping along on its two-trains-a-day schedule, without the hope of anything better. Superintendent Samuel Ruth's heart might not be in the Confederate cause, yet even an R.F. & P. superintendent of impeccable loyalty could not have turned the situation around any time soon. There was simply not enough trackage or depot facilities or locomotives or rolling stock to give the Army of Northern Virginia all the food and forage it required — and to give General Lee the logistical freedom of action he so urgently wanted.[2]

Robert E. Lee was tempting fate in these April weeks. Longstreet with a quarter of the army was 130 miles distant, becoming ever more entangled in a siege that Lee surely realized could not be broken off as quickly as need be should he have to reunite the army. Yet he made hardly any effort to hurry his lieutenant, rarely even communicating with him once Suffolk was under siege. Only on April 27 would he inquire politely, "Can you give me any idea when your operations will be completed and whether any of the troops you have in North Carolina can be spared from there?" General Lee seemed serenely confident and otherwise preoccupied, especially with recapturing the initiative. For six months and more he had had to follow the Yankees' lead, and now he was restive in the role.

In the long view of events, Lee believed, the South was nearing a moment of great opportunity. He reflected on the matter in a letter to his wife. "I do not think our enemies are so confident of success as they used to be," he told her. "If we can baffle them in their various designs this year & our people are true to our cause . . . I think our success will be certain." He hoped soon to establish the army's supplies "on a firm basis. On every other point we are strong." Confederate success on the battlefield would bring in the fall "a great change in public opinion at the North. The Republicans will be destroyed & I think the friends of peace will become so strong as that the next administration will go in on that basis." To General Lee the proper course was clear: "We have only therefore to resist manfully." That he was willing and indeed anxious to do.

Already he had put the army on notice to send off surplus baggage and to reduce transport needs "to the lowest limit," and to expect no more leaves, in anticipation of "a resumption of active operations by the 1st of April." On April 2 he sent President Davis a situation report, outlining Longstreet's movements and speculating on Hooker's. He had been unable to crack the Federals' tightened security on the Rappahannock, he told Mr. Davis, but he supposed "their object is to deceive us, and that they may, while intending to act on the defensive, have re-enforced other points for offensive operations." He would not be able to confirm this suspicion, however, "until we are able to make some aggressive movements."[3]

His first thought for an aggressive movement was in the Shenandoah Valley, "which I think will draw General Hooker out. . . ." However that might be, the Federal general in the lower Valley, Robert Milroy, had threatened draconian measures against the inhabitants there, and General Lee was eager to suppress Milroy just as he had suppressed John Pope the summer before for the same sort of transgressions. A week later he wrote Secretary Seddon with another and even more aggressive proposal. Should Hooker's army remain on the defensive, as he was predicting, the best way to relieve Federal pressures in other war theaters — he mentioned in particular the Vicksburg area and Charleston — "would be for this army to cross into Maryland." He admitted this was not possible at the moment, for want of sufficient transportation and a reserve of supplies. "But this is what I would recommend, if practicable."

Preliminary to any march northward, and to discomfit the notorious General Milroy, Lee and his lieutenants in the Shenandoah Valley and in the mountain country to the west planned a dashing raid aimed at the Union's vital Baltimore & Ohio Railroad. The Valley commander, leading a detached brigade of Stuart's cavalry corps, was William E. Jones, universally known as "Grumble" Jones for his feuding, cantankerous nature. Lee's lieutenant in western Virginia was John D. Imboden. At the same time, Fitzhugh Lee's cavalry brigade would distract General Milroy with a raid of its own into the Valley. Mosby's partisans, too, would harass the Yankees.

"I think these operations will draw Milroy from Winchester and the Valley to the northeast," Lee explained, "open that country, for a time, at least, to us; enable us to drive out horses, cattle, &c., and afford an opportunity to our citizens . . . now suffering under oppression and robbery." The seized supplies would help victual the army when it advanced into Maryland. To prepare the way for this invasion, Lee brought up a pontoon train and ordered a bridge to be built at Germanna Ford on the Rapidan. The Jones-Imboden raid was planned for mid-April, when the high waters should recede and the roads should dry.[4]

If the opposing army continued to lie quiet and concealed on the north bank of the Rappahannock, Lee told Mr. Davis, it was "all-important that we should assume the aggressive by the 1st of May. . . ." At the very least, he said, "the Valley could be swept of Milroy, and the army opposite me be thrown north of the Potomac." Having swept Milroy away, he would then continue north through Maryland, just as he had done the previous September. Supplies for such an advance would come from Longstreet and from the planned raid into northwestern Virginia. If there was to be a showdown battle, something always in General Lee's thoughts, let it be on Northern soil.

Lee had only recently learned, from Northern sources, of the infamous Lost Order — his marching orders for the previous fall's Maryland campaign, lost by mischance and found by McClellan — that had caused him to accept battle at Sharpsburg before he was ready. The Lost Order explained a great deal: apparently it was only chance that had frustrated his plans on that bloody field that bloody September. Perhaps next time — perhaps this time — Dame Fortune would smile on the South.[5]

Remarkably, while talking of assuming "the aggressive," General Lee had at his elbow the latest return for his army. Dated March 31, it showed just over 61,500 men of all arms "present for duty." This was the main army, on the Rappahannock and in its artillery camps to the south, and did not include Longstreet's detached First Corps divisions. Except for a continuing influx of conscripts, Lee could expect no reinforcements from elsewhere. By the end of April his total force would barely exceed 65,000.

At the time, Lee had no settled opinion of Hooker's numbers across the river, although he suspected that Washington was requiring his opponent to give up troops to other war theaters. Later in April, when his secret service reported the strength of the Army of the Potomac to be from 150,000 to 160,000, he would mark that down as "very much exaggerated." He had at hand, he said, another report giving Hooker 90,000 rank-and-file infantry. By whatever belief and by whatever measure, however, Lee had to assume that the army he confronted had something approaching double his own numbers.[6]

To be sure, this was hardly new in General Lee's experience. Only at the start of the Seven Days' Battles the previous June, outnumbered 105,900 to 94,400, had he been anywhere close to achieving parity with the enemy. He fought at Second Manassas in the shadow of becoming hugely outnumbered, and at Sharpsburg with but one man for every two of McClellan's. Although outnumbered again at Fredericksburg, that battle had been instructive: fighting defensively, he beat off the more numerous enemy with comparative ease. Since Lee was giving so little priority to hurrying Longstreet back to the Rappahannock to be ready to receive Hooker's attack, he apparently assumed that when and if that attack came he would again receive it behind fortifications. In that event, being outnumbered two to one would be no great disadvantage.

This suggested a second assumption on Lee's part: that Fighting Joe Hooker — Mr. F. J. Hooker — was no more of a general to worry about than his predecessors. Lee had respected George McClellan as an officer and a gentleman, but took cruel advantage of what he recognized as McClellan's timidity. He had only contempt for John Pope and suppressed him contemptuously. Lee expressed no recorded opinion of Ambrose Burnside, perhaps because his tenure was so brief, but Burnside's direction of the Fredericksburg assaults did nothing to earn him anyone's respect. Evidently General Lee expected no surprises from Hooker either, even if that general might command an army twice the size of his own.

From his reading of Northern newspapers Lee had gleaned the interesting fact that his opponents — or at least General McClellan — greatly and consistently overestimated the size of the Confederate army. This was indeed one of McClellan's delusions, and it was he who had given it out to the press. McClellan's subsequent excessive caution in battle reflected this belief, and knowing of the delusion had given Lee one more edge on the battlefield. So far as he knew, the Federals were still inflating the size of the Army of Northern Virginia. He could not know that since the arrival of Colonel Sharpe and his Bureau of Military Information this was one battlefield advantage he would no longer enjoy.

One final assumption of Lee's also stemmed from his reading of Northern newspapers. The press had made no secret of the imminent discharge of the two-year and the nine-month regiments from the Army of the Potomac, or of the passage of the conscription bill. By April it was a common opinion in the Confederate officer corps that Fighting Joe Hooker would not fight until these short-term men were discharged and his ranks refilled by drafted men. Now this became General Lee's opinion as well. On April 16 he wrote President Davis that he might in good season take the offensive on the assumption that Hooker's army would "be weakened by the expiration of the term of service of many of his regiments, and before new recruits can be received." It would therefore be safe to leave Longstreet to his foraging for some time yet.

From the sum of these various assumptions about his opponent — all of them mistaken — Robert E. Lee took reinforcement for his confidence — indeed his overconfidence — in himself and in his army and in his ability to control events. In consequence, he would be far from prepared to meet his opponent when the campaign opened, and so would face a danger graver than any he had faced before.[7]

* *

THERE WAS no lack of self-confidence across the river, where Joe Hooker set about planning his campaign. At the end of March he went up to Washington and in his conversations at the White House invited the president to visit Falmouth and review the army and discuss what was to be done with it. On April 3 Mr. Lincoln telegraphed his acceptance, saying he would arrive by steamer at Aquia Landing on Sunday, the fifth. "Our party will probably not exceed six persons of all sorts." Hooker replied that evening, "I am rejoiced to learn that you have appointed a time to visit this Army and only regret that your party is not as large as our hospitality."

The president seldom left wartime Washington except to visit his army, and the visits always rejuvenated him. Midway through his stay at Falmouth he would admit as much to newspaperman Noah Brooks. "It is a great relief to get away from Washington and the politicians," he said, and then added, "But nothing touches the tired spot."

Lincoln and Mary Lincoln and their son Tad, who turned ten the day the trip began, and their guests spent the first night on the Potomac aboard the little steamer *Carrie Martin* and arrived at Aquia Landing on Sunday morning, April 5. Hooker had a special train waiting at the wharf, its presidential boxcar draped in flags and gay bunting. Dan Butterfield established the party in three large hospital tents at Falmouth headquarters. There had been a freak spring snowstorm and the ground was too wet for a review that day. It was announced that instead the cavalry corps would be reviewed on Monday.

Monday's review of Stoneman's corps was described by Attorney General Edward Bates of the president's party as simply "the grandest sight I ever saw." Excited comparisons were made with the storied French legions of Marshal Murat. The 10,000 horsemen, "stretched out right and left as far as the eye could carry," as one officer put it, made an impressive sight indeed, one never before seen in America. First Mr. Lincoln and General Hooker and staff reviewed the ranked cavalrymen as they posed at rest. Then it was the turn of the troopers to wheel smartly in their thousands past the reviewing party, guidons snapping and bands playing. Newspaperman Brooks thought the vast, seemingly endless column winding over the hills along the Rappahannock and away out of sight looked "like a huge serpent." Rebel soldiers crowded the heights opposite to see what they could of the panoply. That made Provost Marshal

Patrick very nervous. He complained in his diary that Confederate gunners "have had us in plain sight all day, & if they had desired, could have dropped a shell amongst us."[8]

Over the next days it was the infantry's turn for review. The review on April 8 was especially spectacular, with no less than 75,000 men in four army corps — Couch's Second, Sickles's Third, Meade's Fifth, and Sedgwick's Sixth — striding for hours on end past the presidential party. The soldier's pride Joe Hooker had worked so hard to instill was plain to see. Still, it was a wearying experience for those in the rear ranks. "We had our knapsacks on six hours in the middle of the day," Private Henry Howell wrote in his journal afterward. ". . . It was a big thing but we do not want to see many more such days." The men thought Mr. Lincoln looked tired and careworn, but he was attentive to the marchers and seemed to enjoy himself. "I dont know whether he took off his hat to me or not," a veteran in the Fifth Corps remarked, "but he took it off."

The president did in fact enjoy himself hugely that week. He admired the musical flourishes of the Eleventh Corps' expert German drum and bugle corps, and the precision marching of Duryée's Zouaves, although he did wonder if their crimson pantaloons might make them conspicuous targets on the battlefield. General Hooker pointed out the five western regiments of the Iron Brigade as they strode past, and the westerner president nodded. The Iron Brigade's Solomon Meredith, Lincoln observed, is "the only Quaker General I have in the army."

On the way to one of these reviews in an army ambulance, Mr. Lincoln listened with growing amusement to the driver trying to manage his fractious mules. Finally he leaned forward and tapped the driver on the shoulder and inquired if the man was an Episcopalian. The puzzled driver said no, he was a Methodist. "Well," Lincoln said, "I thought you must be an Episcopalian, because you swear just like Governor Seward, who is a churchwarden."

It is not recorded if the president noticed how the army received his escort for the occasion, a detachment of Rush's Lancers. These bandbox cavalrymen affected bright red streamers on the tips of their lances, which looked to irreverent infantrymen like nothing so much as turkey wattles. "Whenever they passed the infantry every one began to gobble," an engineer officer reported. "It was extremely annoying to them, particularly as they were a fine regiment, under perfect discipline, and always performed most effective service."[9]

It was said, General Meade wrote his wife on April 9, that the president "has been brought here for relaxation and amusement. . . ." That was true enough, but there were as well serious discussions between president and commanding general about the coming campaign. Its importance was intensified by news of a Federal repulse at Charleston. Lincoln ordered his thoughts in a memorandum.

In the present circumstances, he wrote, "there is *no* eligible route for us into Richmond." Argument over the Rappahannock route or the James River route "is a contest about nothing. Hence our prime object is the enemies' army in front of us. . . ." In pointed contrast to what General Lee was then saying, Mr. Lincoln had no thought that "by raids towards Washington he can derange the Army of the Potomac at all," nor could he by other, more distant operations. The Federals, on the other hand, "have such operations which may call him away, at least in part." Lincoln was opposed to assaulting Lee in his Fredericksburg entrenchments, as Burnside had done, "but we should continually harass and menace him, so that he shall have no leisure, nor safety in sending away detachments. If he weakens himself, then pitch into him."

Dr. Anson Henry, an old friend of Lincoln's, listened to these discussions and noticed that General Hooker demonstrated respect for the president's "sound judgment & practical sense, and will act in accordance with his suggestions in good faith for the reason that they meet with his own views in the main." Dr. Henry recognized how different Hooker's attitude was in this regard from General McClellan's, who always "seemed to try to go counter in every particular to the President's suggestions." Clearly Mr. Lincoln had determined to take a firmer stand with this general than he had with his predecessors. For his part, Joe Hooker seemed perfectly willing to take the commander-in-chief into his confidence. Certainly nothing dampened his brash assurance of ultimate success. Lincoln was heard to say to him, "If you get to Richmond, General . . . ," at which point Hooker interrupted, "Excuse me, Mr. President, but there is no 'if' in the case. I am going straight to Richmond if I live."

Darius Couch of the Second Corps was the most senior of Hooker's generals, recognized as his unofficial second-in-command. On April 10, the day he was to return to Washington, the president sent for Couch to come to Falmouth headquarters. He found Lincoln and Hooker alone in the general's tent, deep in conversation. After they discussed the strategic situation for a time, the president prepared to depart. He paused and then spoke with marked emphasis, giving Couch the impression he had been called in especially to hear this. "I want to impress upon you two gentlemen," Lincoln said, "in your next fight put in all of your men."

"The only cheering thing I have seen this half year," Attorney General Bates wrote a friend upon returning from Falmouth, "is Hooker's army. He has renewed it, in courage, strength, spirit, confidence. He told me with emphasis that he had as many men as he wanted, & as good men."

He had learned how unwise it was to praise generals in advance, Bates went on. "But seeing what Hooker has done in the rehabilitation of that army, I do not doubt that he will use it as effectively as he has reformed & inspired it."[10]

* *

THE PROBLEM facing Joe Hooker was as simple as it was daunting. The two armies were in plain sight of each other, separated by a major river, and he had to find a way to transport his army across that river and then find there a promising battlefield. The terrain at and downstream from Fredericksburg was favorable for laying pontoon bridges, when supported by the formidable Federal artillery, but the attackers would then face the defensible high ground back from the river. Burnside's fate in December was a grim object lesson. Upstream from Fredericksburg the high ground diminished, but the terrain there favored opposing any crossing attempt right at the water's edge. Hooker began to ponder the problem even as he worked to revive and restore his army.

During his early weeks of command his first thought, in planning for an offensive, was to turn Lee's right, downstream from Fredericksburg. By that route he thought he might outflank the Rebel defenders and strike for their railroad supply line. He had his engineers study the idea of towing floating bridge sections up the Rappahannock to such sites as Skinker's Neck or the Seddon house, respectively sixteen and seven miles by river below the town. They also examined a variation on this theme, one contingent to cross far downstream at Port Royal and a second near where Burnside had crossed in December, so as to strike simultaneously at the enemy's flank and front.

Arguing against this downstream approach was the extensive line of fortifications that Lee soon threw up on the hills behind the river all the way to Port Royal. With careful planning and under covering fire from the Union heavy artillery, gaining a lodgment along the wide plain on the south bank was certainly feasible. But any attempt to break through these imposing defenses anywhere between Banks's Ford and Port Royal might well result in a second Fredericksburg. There was the risk too that shifting the line of advance well to the east would uncover Washington for a Confederate counterstroke from the west.

Still, the downstream approach survived searching discussion during the president's Falmouth visit. No doubt Mr. Lincoln believed it was worth close examination, for back in November he had proposed a version of it to Ambrose Burnside. That general had rejected it, but Joe Hooker was more respectful of his commander-in-chief's ideas. Because the protection of Washington was always uppermost in Lincoln's mind, a considerable force from General Heintzelman's garrison there — the better part of eight brigades of infantry and eleven batteries of artillery — was readied to march toward Warrenton to block the western approach to the capital. Upon the president's return Heintzelman issued orders for the march.[11]

After pondering the matter further, however, Hooker came around to the belief that no Rappahannock crossing would ever succeed "except by stratagem." In consequence, he drew up a second plan very different from the first. It took its direction from fresh intelligence about the enemy.

Colonel Sharpe and his Bureau of Military Information continued to refine the count of the numbers in Lee's army, and equally important, to analyze that army's condition. From testimony solid enough to "authorize the judge to rule," said lawyer Sharpe, it was certain that the Rebel soldier's ration was "1 pint flour & ¼ lb bacon or pork per diem." In addition to this "tea cup of flour and patch of bacon," Sharpe noted, there were reports of an issue of a little sugar or rice "about once in three weeks." It was further reported that supplies at Fredericksburg were so low that rations were drawn on a virtual day-to-day basis. "The subsistence of the Southern Army," Sharpe concluded, ". . . seems to be nearing the point of total failure."

Sharpe's analysis suggested that at least for the time being General Lee would have to remain on the defensive because of supply problems. The spy Isaac Silver provided confirmation. Silver's report, smuggled across the river on April 1 from his place in the midst of the Rebel camps, mentioned Lee's order sending off excess baggage and urging the army into fighting trim, but said he had heard nothing of any actual plans for a movement. "They are making no preparations to move eneyware that I can learn," he wrote. ". . . I do not think they intend to move away soon."

Wholly dedicated as he was to avoiding frontal assaults and "needless dashes at the enemy," Joe Hooker gave the highest priority to finding some way to flush Lee out of his Fredericksburg fortifications. The slaughter of the December battle there still haunted him. "They could destroy men faster than I could throw them on their works," he testified of that experience, and vowed never to repeat it. At Second Manassas he had led a division in a frontal attack, then repeated the experience at Antietam with a corps, then repeated it yet again at Fredericksburg with a grand division. He was sure there had to be a better way to fight and win on the battlefields of this war than with head-on assaults. Of all Joe Hooker's new ideas about army command, this thought was as innovative as any of them.

The Confederates' supply crisis seemed to offer the answer to his

needs. Without a stockpile of supplies, Hooker reasoned, Lee would be forced to react immediately to any cut in his railroad lifeline between Fredericksburg and Richmond. He would have to either move out to restore it quickly or retreat to a new source of supply. The one thing he could not do was stay where he was, behind his fortifications.

Retreat would mean falling back due south along the Richmond, Fredericksburg & Potomac toward Richmond, or else in a southwesterly direction, toward Culpeper Court House and Gordonsville and a new rail supply line, the Orange & Alexandria. To sever the Confederates' lifeline General Hooker had at hand what amounted to a secret weapon, so far as the Army of the Potomac was concerned — General Stoneman's newly organized cavalry corps.[12]

On April 12, a Sunday, Dan Butterfield arrived at the White House to present Hooker's new plan. Hooker was so conscious of security that he ordered his chief of staff to show it to no one but the president. That left Secretary of War Stanton looking "black as a thundercloud," Butterfield recalled: "anger and displeasure and disappointment were plainly expressed as if by words. . . ." Only when they were alone did Mr. Lincoln study Hooker's handiwork. "After giving the subject my best reflection," it began, "I have concluded that I will have more chance of inflicting a serious blow upon the Enemy by turning his position on my right. . . ."

The key to Joe Hooker's new plan was severing Lee's communications with Richmond with his "Dragoon force," as he called Stoneman's cavalry corps. The idea was not unlike Burnside's aborted effort at the turn of the year. Stoneman was to cross the Rappahannock far upstream, in the vicinity of Rappahannock Bridge on the Orange & Alexandria, swing south through Culpeper Court House and Orange Court House and Gordonsville, brushing aside the slight opposition expected there, then turn back south by east to strike the Richmond, Fredericksburg & Potomac at Hanover Junction.

It was his expectation, Hooker said, that when Lee learned his lifeline was cut he would give up his Fredericksburg lines and retreat. From his position astride the railroad Stoneman would "hold him and check his retreat until I can fall on his rear — or if not that, I will compel him to fall back by the way of Culpeper and Gordonsville over a longer line than my own with his supplies cut off." In that event, Richmond would be open to the Federals.

After the cavalry had marched, Hooker's infantry would threaten crossings at several points to unsettle the enemy. Hooker did not specify his actual intended crossing point once the enemy fell back, and might not yet have decided on one; events would dictate his choice. In any case, this shift to the right, westward, obviated the need for Heintzelman's movement with the Washington garrison. Hooker set the opening of the operation for the next day, April 13. "I hope, Mr. President, that this plan will receive your approval." The president telegraphed that the plan was received "and will be conformed to."[13]

Fighting Joe Hooker brimmed with confidence in these days. On one of his Washington visits he told a congressional supporter, the abolitionist senator Charles Sumner, that he "did not mean to drive the enemy, but to bag him." To a visitor at headquarters he reinforced the point: he intended "to destroy Lee's army or his own within a week." In expectation of ultimately driving into Richmond, he arranged for the navy to transport a million and a half rations up the Pamunkey River to supply the troops on their final approach to the Confederate capital. He called on the railroad man Herman Haupt to be prepared to rebuild the rail bridge across the Rappahannock at Fredericksburg and to keep the R.F. & P. in operation behind the army as it drove southward. He told him, Haupt recalled, "that when he did move he expected to advance very rapidly. . . ."

General Hooker's confidence — his overconfidence — was in truth more solidly grounded than General Lee's. In just two and a half months he had restored his army's faith in itself and in its commander. He had obtained, for the first time in two years of war, a clear and unblinking portrait of the opposing army. He had baffled his opponent as to his own plans. And those plans were far more intelligently drawn and far more innovative than anything that had gone before. Joe Hooker might be forgiven, then, for assuring a group of his officers, "My plans are perfect, and when I start to carry them out, may God have mercy on General Lee, for I will have none."[14]

* *

THE SAME day that Dan Butterfield delivered the new plan of campaign to the White House, George Stoneman received his marching orders from the commanding general. Hooker's instructions were detailed and explicit, leaving General Stoneman no room for any misunderstanding of the cavalry's role — or how important it was to the plan as a whole. Later Hooker was typically outspoken on the subject. "I had worded my instructions so strongly," he wrote, "I thought that they would wake up a dead man to his true condition."

Stoneman was told what route to take and told just what to do when he reached the Virginia Central and then followed it to the Richmond, Fredericksburg & Potomac at Hanover Junction, thirty-five miles behind Lee's lines — "destroying along your whole route the railroad bridges, trains, cars, depots of provisions, lines of telegraphic communication,

&c." He was told to take all necessary tools and equipment of destruction. He was fully instructed how to harass and delay Confederate forces whenever and wherever they were encountered. "Moments of delay will be hours and days to the army in pursuit." Finally, he was told, "Let your watchword be fight, and let all your orders be fight, fight, fight. . . ." Stoneman was reminded that his cavalry corps was "the initiative in the forward movement of this grand army"; upon him "must depend on a great measure the extent and brilliancy of our success. Bear in mind that celerity, audacity, and resolution are everything in war. . . ."

Leaving but one brigade of cavalry with the main army, Stoneman would have the rest of his corps with him on the expedition — 9,895 troopers in all, plus four batteries of horse artillery. Fitz Lee's Confederate brigade, placed at Culpeper and counted as 2,000 strong by Colonel Sharpe, was not expected to be any problem for a force of this size. Indeed, Stoneman should comfortably outnumber the "5,000 sabers, and those badly mounted," said to be the total for the Confederate army. He was to take rations and forage for eight days, and was instructed to communicate with headquarters "as often as necessary and practicable." Stressing the point, Hooker told Stoneman that meant at least a daily report. The main army, he promised, would make connection with the cavalry before its supplies were exhausted.

Beyond that no timetable was specified. Presumably Hooker would advance with the infantry in pursuit as soon as Lee reacted to the discovery that his supply line was cut. There was no certainty about how much delay Stoneman's troopers could inflict on the retreating enemy, but however that might be, there was every chance that at the least the movement would draw Lee out from behind his fortifications. And that would give Joe Hooker his chance. Stoneman issued orders for the march upriver to commence at daylight the next day, Monday, April 13.[15]

To mislead about his real objective, Stoneman had been told to drop word that the cavalry was bound for the Shenandoah Valley to pursue Grumble Jones's Confederate force there. Now Dan Butterfield had an inspiration. He remembered Colonel Sharpe's report that Yankee signalmen had broken the Rebels' signal-flag code — and that the Rebels had returned the compliment — and he concocted a ruse.

On the afternoon of April 13 Butterfield wrote out a message for signal officer Samuel Cushing to send by flag from his station directly across the river from Fredericksburg. "Our cavalry is going to give Jones & guerillas in the Shenandoah a smash," it read. "They may give Fitz Lee a brush for cover. Keep watch of any movement of infantry that way that might cut them off & post Capt. C."

By couching his ruse in casual signalman-to-signalman talk, Butterfield hoped to allay the suspicions of enemy interceptors, and his hope was rewarded. The next day a Federal signal station intercepted (and decoded) a Confederate flag message that began, "Dispatch received from Yankee signal flag," followed by Butterfield's ruse message in full. From that Butterfield could feel confident that his planted signal would reach Confederate headquarters.

What he could not know was how readily Robert E. Lee would take the bait, and act on it. "I learn enemy's cavalry are moving against you in Shenandoah Valley; will attack Fitz. Lee in passing," Lee telegraphed Grumble Jones on April 14. ". . . General Stuart, with two brigades, will attend them. Collect your forces and be on your guard." And in due course, Dan Butterfield's bit of deception would produce additional results beyond anything he had imagined for it.[16]

Meanwhile, on April 13, the largest cavalry force the war had yet seen was on the move, opening Joe Hooker's spring campaign. From their camps at Falmouth and from as far away as Aquia Landing column after column of horsemen filled the roads leading upriver. The weather that Monday was clear and pleasant and the roads were dry, and there was no undue delay. By nightfall the columns were converging on Morrisville, on the Warrenton Post Road nineteen miles northwest of Falmouth. A force of infantry — Adolphus Buschbeck's brigade from the Eleventh Corps and the 91st Pennsylvania from the Fifth Corps — was sent along to secure the upstream fords as they were reached.

At the same time, back at Hooker's headquarters, a circular went out to the seven infantry corps. By Tuesday evening, it ordered, knapsacks must be packed with five days' rations and haversacks with three. Sixty rounds of ammunition would be issued per man, and an additional eighty rounds per man carried by pack mule. Preparations must be complete by Wednesday morning, April 15. "Corps Commanders will require every servicable man to march with the column," James Miller of the 111th Pennsylvania wrote home, "so you see that all we lack of being pack mules is a little in the length of ears." Henry Young of the 7th Wisconsin told his wife, "There is all kind of rumours in camp about our destination but the fact is if Old Jo knows himself he also knows how to keep the secret. . . ."

To preserve the secret, Hooker had the Washington postmaster hold up all mail from the Rappahannock for twenty-four hours "for very urgent reasons." The Potomac Flotilla was asked to send two gunboats up the Rappahannock to Port Royal to engage the Confederate batteries there as a diversion. General Heintzelman's Washington command took over patrolling the Telegraph Road north of Falmouth that had been the duty of Stoneman's cavalry. Hooker sent a copy of Stoneman's orders to the president, with a note. "I send you this in order that you may know what I am about. I have no time to write at length. J. H."

"We move very shortly, are nearly ready and our hopes are strong," Alexander S. Webb, a staff officer with the Fifth Corps, wrote his wife on April 14. ". . . We must we shall whip this time and mark my words, 'Things look more like outwitting the Rebels than I ever saw them.' We will either go up the spout or we will whip them terribly. No half way."[17]

The good weather held on April 14, but General Stoneman spent the daylight hours cautiously orchestrating an elaborate scheme for crossing the Rappahannock at four widely separated fords, none of them defended by more than a small Rebel picket post. Hooker's pointed reminder to Stoneman that "celerity, audacity, and resolution are everything in war" apparently had gone unnoticed.

At Kelly's Ford and Rappahannock Bridge, Stoneman stage-managed noisy day-long demonstrations while at two fords far upstream Benjamin F. "Grimes" Davis crossed his brigade and began to work his way down the south bank. But the day was gone before Davis could uncover the crossings for the rest of the cavalry. That evening Pennsylvania cavalryman Samuel Cormany noted worriedly in his diary, "Looks like rain. . . ."

At 2:00 A.M. on April 15 the rain came, and for twenty-four hours it poured down in torrents. "It is, in truth & reality, a terrible rain," General Patrick recorded in his diary. To make matters worse, the storm came out of the Blue Ridge to the west, where it had already put the headwaters of the Rappahannock in flood. By day's end the river at Rappahannock Bridge had risen seven feet. Stoneman hastily recalled Grimes Davis from the south bank, and Davis only narrowly escaped having his command cut off by the Rebels. As it was, he saw twenty-five of his men captured and several others drowned trying to swim their horses back across the swollen river. "I was wet to the hide," trooper Cormany wrote disgustedly. Cavalry general John Buford reported that at midnight on April 15, "The country at that hour was like a sea."[18]

Before he had word of Stoneman's pullback to the north bank of the river, General Hooker was optimistic that his plan of campaign was well begun. If Stoneman had succeeded in getting all his cavalry across the Rappahannock, he assured President Lincoln, "the storm and mud will not damage our prospects." In another forty-eight hours they should be astride the railroad in Lee's rear. He would demonstrate with the infantry on the present line, and "if they should fall back, shall pursue with all the vigor practicable." By evening on April 15, however, Hooker had later word from Stoneman, and he passed on the discouraging news to Washington.

Mr. Lincoln's reply was tinged with the weary acceptance that nothing had changed after all. He had heard all this so often before from his generals. "General S. is not moving rapidly enough to make the expedition come to anything," he observed. "He has now been out three days, two of which were unusually fair weather, and all three without hinderance from the enemy, and yet he is not 25 miles from where he started." Stoneman had sixty miles to go, and another river, the Rapidan, to cross, "and will be hindered by the enemy. By arithmetic, how many days will it take to do it? I do not know that any better can be done, but I greatly fear it is another failure already."

Two days later, when all the facts were in, Hooker wrote the president that as much as he regretted what had happened, he could find nothing in Stoneman's conduct "requiring my animadversion or censure. We cannot control the elements." He had ordered Stoneman to remain where he was, he said, "holding himself in readiness to march as soon after the roads and rivers will permit. . . . I still hope to turn his movement to some good account." Then he added, in what was surely the most significant outcome of the operation, "We have no reason to suppose that the enemy have any knowledge of the design of General Stoneman's movement."[19]

* *

IN THAT surmise Joe Hooker was quite right. The Federals' move had been reported to General Lee on the evening of April 13, and early on the fourteenth Jeb Stuart warned headquarters that Yankee cavalry was once again menacing Kelly's Ford. Lee responded more circumspectly than he had the month before when the enemy first appeared at Kelly's. He alerted General Pendleton to ready his reserve artillery for possible action, but this time he issued no call to Longstreet in southside Virginia to return his divisions. Indeed, he waited three days to inform Longstreet of the development, and then it was without comment. "The enemy's cavalry are again on our left," he told Old Pete on April 17. ". . . Nothing, however, has been ascertained." He was taking the intercepted Yankee flag message — Dan Butterfield's ruse — as the most likely explanation for the reappearance of Federal cavalry along the upper Rappahannock.

Lee's most immediate concern was for Grumble Jones in the Shenandoah Valley, and whether this enemy movement might unhinge the plans for the Jones-Imboden raid against the Baltimore & Ohio. He telegraphed Jones that his earlier warning, based on the intercepted dispatch, was now confirmed. The Yankees had appeared just as the dispatch promised: "main body of enemy's cavalry is moving via Liberty toward Warrenton, with the intention to march into Shenandoah Valley against you. . . . Be prepared."

He shifted his own cavalry to meet the threat. Fitzhugh Lee's brigade, which had moved up to the Blue Ridge ready to cross into the Valley to support Jones and Imboden, was called back to a blocking position on the upper Rappahannock at Amissville. To replace Fitz Lee on the army's left, the brigade of his cousin, Rooney Lee, had already been brought over from the far right to Culpeper Court House. These two brigades of cavalry, General Lee decided, would suffice to "attend" the Yankees. The Jones-Imboden raid would go ahead as planned, although now without Fitz Lee's diversionary strike against the Vandal general Milroy. After these actions General Lee rested, and waited and watched.[20]

The attraction of Dan Butterfield's ruse was simply that it seemed to disclose something definite — and something apparently confirmed — about the Yankees' intentions. So effective were Hooker's security measures that Lee was reduced to guessing what his opponent might do. Jeb Stuart moved cavalry headquarters to Culpeper to confront Stoneman, and gave it as his opinion that the enemy's move up the Rappahannock was a diversion. Stoneman's cavalry, said Stuart, was diverting attention away from Hooker's plan to shift his army to the Peninsula and repeat McClellan's campaign of 1862.

Lee doubted this. He did not believe Hooker would dare leave Washington uncovered, or that Washington would permit him to, with a Confederate army as close as the Rappahannock. But if this was not in fact a move to the Shenandoah, he told Stuart, perhaps it was designed "to draw us out from our present position, either to disclose our force, or enable them to seize upon Fredericksburg, rebuild the bridges across the river, &c." Mr. F. J. Hooker might be attempting nothing more than a variation on Burnside's attack the previous December.

Days passed and there was no further movement by the Federals, and General Lee could find out nothing from his scouts. "I have been able as yet to learn nothing which goes to show the real intention of the enemy," he complained to Stuart on April 19. Now he began to think it was a move to the Valley after all — but one that had been frustrated. "It appears to me that he is rather fearful of an attack from us than preparing to attack," he observed. Stoneman was not crossing the Blue Ridge as planned because of "the apprehension that you will plunge into the rear of their army and cut up their line of communications." He wanted Stuart to remain alert and endeavor "to ascertain what his movement means." For that purpose Stuart shifted Mosby's partisans well to the north and west, to keep watch on Stoneman's force and raid it at any opportunity.

So it happened that in this state of continued indecision, the Army of Northern Virginia's entire cavalry force remained far to the west of the main army. The gap on the left between Lee's infantry and his cavalry was some·twenty miles wide — a gap largely empty of Confederate troops of any sort. Furthermore, Mosby's Rangers, Lee's primary scouting force north of the Rappahannock, had been pulled well away from their usual haunts close by the Yankee camps. Dan Butterfield's planted message was paying unexpected dividends.[21]

Amateur strategists were as baffled as General Lee. "The enemy appear very restless," Captain William Calder of the 2nd North Carolina wrote home on April 20; "they withdraw their pickets and then post them again, keep trains constantly running back and forth, and send up a balloon two or three times a day. I reckon they are trying to fool somebody. . . ."

To be sure, inquisitive Confederate pickets had found out quickly enough from gullible Yankees about the order for marching rations. "It is really strange how the rebs get notice of our intended movements," a Michigan soldier observed. Just one day after the order to pack knapsacks and haversacks, he went on, Rebel pickets were calling across to ask where they were going with their eight days' rations. "Guess they will make your shoulders ache before you march a great ways with them," they sympathized. But since the Yankee soldiers had no idea what direction they might be ordered to take, this information had limited usefulness. In fact, when days passed and no march was made, it had the effect of one more diversion.

This spilling of information by the riverside picket lines attracted the attention of Provost Marshal Patrick, and before long, on the Federal side at least, there was a change. Officers were ordered to stand watch with their men on picket duty and shut off the cross-river talk the moment it began. Within a week after Stoneman's cavalry marched upriver, General Lee was complaining that Yankee officers were walking the picket lines "to prevent any communication with our men."[22]

Meanwhile, the Northern press had again sent Joe Hooker's temper past the boiling point. He read in the *Philadelphia Inquirer* a tale of cloak-and-dagger doings on the Rappahannock. An underwater telegraph cable, so the paper claimed, had been discovered running from a house on the Falmouth waterfront to the south bank, no doubt delivering all the army's secrets to the enemy. Hooker demanded that Washington track down the source of the story — which was in fact nothing more than fevered imagination on the *Inquirer*'s part — so that the culprit might be banished from the army's camps.

General Hooker's temper was just then already at a boil over another newspaper story, this one in the *Washington Chronicle*, that revealed to the world — and thus to the enemy — the exact size of his army. It seemed

that an incautious army surgeon in Washington had showed a correspondent a report on the health of the Army of the Potomac, a report the
surgeon later sheepishly admitted contained numbers "susceptible of
further calculation." What the report showed was the number of sick and
the "ratio of sickness per 1,000" for each of the army's major commands
— which it conveniently listed — based on the latest return. "Already all
the arithmeticians in the army have figured up the strength . . . belonging to this army," Hooker raged to Secretary Stanton. "The chief of my
secret service department would have willingly paid $1,000 for such
information in regard to the enemy. . . ."

The figure the arithmeticians quickly produced was 159,329, the
"aggregate present" in the Potomac army. To Hooker's good fortune,
however, this most serious of security leaks was mishandled by the Confederates. The story appeared in the *Chronicle* on April 17, but more than
a week would pass before a report of it reached Richmond, and then in
nonspecific, summary form. General Lee learned only on April 26 that
Hooker's strength was stated "to be from 150,000 to 160,000." That, he
decided, was "very much exaggerated." It was only on May 10, two eventful weeks later, that he discovered the leak had been entirely credible. As
for Joe Hooker, this leak and the tall tale of the submarine telegraph
cable led him to issue his edict, dated April 30, that henceforth all
newspaper stories from the Army of the Potomac must carry the reporter's byline. It would prove to be a small but important step toward a
responsible press.[23]

The grass was greening in the camps south of the Rappahannock and
the weather was milding, and Rebel officers and enlisted men grew full of
speculation. On April 12 General Lafayette McLaws wrote his wife, "It is
the general belief that we will move before very long but in what direction is not known." Two weeks brought him a fresh rumor: "A considerable number of persons are of the opinion that the enemy are leaving the
other side of the river." James T. McElvany of the 35th Georgia was
convinced there would be no further fighting on this line. "I don't think
the yankees will cross. Surely they have better sense. . . ." Lieutenant
Ham Chamberlayne of Crenshaw's battery thought the news good and
the time ripe. "The European loan, & the news from Charleston &
Vicksburg has made us all hilarious and we are anxiously expecting Lee's
order for us to move," he wrote home on April 16; "then the machine
goes to work which never failed yet and we look forward to Maryland, my
Maryland."

From their letters, men in the rear ranks had a rather less exalted
view of matters than Lieutenant Chamberlayne. Private J. J. Wilson of the
16th Mississippi, Carnot Posey's brigade, headed an April letter home

"Camp Starvation" and thankfully reported all quiet on the Rappahannock. He felt that if the Yankees did try to cross, "Gen. Lee is wide awake and will not let them get off as well as they did before." But even another repulse at Fredericksburg would not put an end to it. "I am getting very tired of this war but I have lost all hopes of it stoping any time shortly." Private Wilson, however, did not want his people to think he had lost his resolve. "I am used to hardship," he insisted. "I can do with eating once a day now just as well as I used to with eating three meals. . . ."[24]

Colonel Alfred Scales, commanding the 13th North Carolina in A. P. Hill's Light Division, believed he had the best possible line on Confederate intentions. On April 19 he wrote his wife, "Gen. Jackson has sent for his wife & that looks as if we might stay here at least a week or two."

The next day Anna Jackson arrived at Guiney's Station on the morning train, bringing with her five-month-old Julia, the daughter the general had never seen. Jackson was at the station to greet them. Mrs. Jackson treasured her husband's first glimpse of his daughter. "Catching his eager look of supreme interest in her," she wrote, "she beamed her brightest and sweetest smiles upon him in return. . . ." Jackson installed them at William Yerby's, where General Lee had recently recuperated, and spent each dusk to dawn with them. On April 23 the Reverend Beverly Tucker Lacy baptized the child, and Jed Hotchkiss of the staff heard Old Jack say it was "very fine, very fine."[25]

* *

ON APRIL 15, as the Army of the Potomac's infantry stood poised to march, an engineer on the headquarters staff, Washington A. Roebling, wrote his father, "Although the chances are that the move will take place tomorrow or next day, everybody is still in utter ignorance as to the direction of our march; that fact alone speaks volumes in favor of Hooker's management and discretion, and is without parallel in the previous history of the war." Hooker maintained the secrecy, saying nothing even to his generals. He continued the alert from day to day, hoping Stoneman's cavalry would go on as planned, urging him to cross the river "at the earliest practicable moment." He appreciated the general's impatience, Stoneman replied, and was just as impatient himself to advance, but by all reports "the river is swimming still." There was no way he could cross his artillery and pack trains.

Fortune seemed to be frowning on them, Captain William L. Candler of Hooker's staff wrote on April 24. After several drying days it had started to rain again. "It seems as though it were never to stop raining; the longer it rains the harder it seems to come down." Candler found the mood at headquarters grim: "every one is moving around in an aimless, nervous way, looking at the clouds and then at the ground, and in knots trying to convince themselves that it is going to clear off and they will be able to move day after to-morrow."[26]

There was the same anxiety in Washington, and on April 19 President Lincoln had made a flying visit to Aquia Landing to discuss the case with General Hooker in person. He brought with him his chief military adviser, Henry Halleck, but because Halleck and Hooker were not on speaking terms the president brought Secretary of War Stanton along as well, with whom Hooker was on the best of terms. Hooker had abruptly changed his campaign plan since their last meeting, at Falmouth, and apparently Mr. Lincoln was at Aquia to find out what he could expect from his general.

One subject for discussion was the Federal force in southeastern Virginia, at Suffolk and at Fort Monroe on the Peninsula. Secretary Stanton offered Hooker "general control" of these troops so they might act in perfect concert with the Army of the Potomac. Hooker declined to command at such a distance, but he did secure agreement that General Peck and his superior, General John A. Dix, would move aggressively against Longstreet's Confederate divisions in southside Virginia. It was essential that they pin Longstreet down, Hooker said, not allow him to break off and come to Lee's aid when the army advanced from the Rappahannock. Henry W. Bellows, head of the U.S. Sanitary Commission, was with Hooker the day of the president's visit and found the general straining at the bit. "He is determined *to smash the enemy or be smashed*," Bellows told a friend afterward. "There is fire in his eye!"[27]

Stymied by the weather, Hooker decided once more to recast his campaign plan. Still committed to stratagem, he now turned his attention to the upstream Rappahannock crossings. Between Fredericksburg and the point where the Rapidan empties into the Rappahannock there were two practical crossing points. The first of these, half a dozen miles upriver by road, was Banks's Ford, the objective in Burnside's Mud March in January. Seven miles' march above Banks's was U.S. Ford. In company with his engineers, General Hooker personally inspected both crossings. It was immediately apparent that laying a pontoon bridge at either site, against determined enemy fire, would be a formidable task. It was also apparent that General Lee was going to contest any such crossing attempts.

At Banks's Ford, wrote Captain William Folwell of the engineers, "It will be *impossible* to construct the bridge under the fire which will be from 3000 yards of rifle pits and a four-gun battery at short range." The scene at U.S. Ford (which took its name from the nearby abandoned United States Gold Mine) was much the same — extensive Rebel rifle pits on the south bank, backed by redoubts for artillery. "Possibly they may have been contrived on the scarecrow principle . . . ," Captain Folwell observed, "but they look ugly." When the inspection tour was finished engineer Stephen Weld noted in his diary, "I do not think that General Hooker liked either place as a crossing for the army."

Lieutenant Weld was quite right in thinking Hooker had no enthusiasm for forcing a crossing at either Banks's Ford or U.S. Ford. Either would be a perfect example of one of those needless dashes at the enemy he had determined to avoid as army commander. Both these fords, however, were important to the new plan of campaign — his third plan — taking shape in his mind. Rather than trying to smash his way across, he would make use of them by a stratagem.[28]

Once again, General Hooker's newest plan of campaign was shaped by the newest intelligence from across the river. The picture of Lee's army painted by the Bureau of Military Information was sharpening and taking on additional detail. An April report by the B.M.I.'s John Babcock carefully charted what had been learned of the makeup and strength of the Rebel forces.

Babcock correctly identified Lee's six divisions and 26 of his 28 infantry brigades. He listed 116 regiments of infantry, of an actual total of 130. Of Lee's 56,200 infantrymen marked present for duty that April, Babcock's count of their numbers reached 49,800; only the two unlocated brigades, from Longstreet's peripatetic First Corps, escaped his notice. Most remarkably, in Babcock's system of calculation the Confederate infantry regiments averaged 429 men; their actual average was 432. And by the time the campaign opened, the B.M.I. would identify both missing brigades.[29]

For Hooker it was as important to know the whereabouts of Lee's forces as their strength, and the B.M.I. furnished him that information as well. Here the spy Isaac Silver proved invaluable. Silver's farm, on the Orange Plank Road just east of Chancellorsville, was squarely at the center of the area of Confederate occupation most difficult for the Federals to observe. Stonewall Jackson's positions, from Fredericksburg eastward, were many of them in open areas easily seen from Yankee observation stations and from Professor Lowe's balloons. It was the two divisions of Longstreet's First Corps, Richard Anderson's and Lafayette McLaws's, posted west and south of Fredericksburg in heavy woods, that were the hardest for Colonel Sharpe's B.M.I. to penetrate. And with this latest shift in plans, it was the location of Anderson's and McLaws's men that most interested General Hooker. Isaac Silver's report, carried to headquarters on April 15 by Ebenezer McGee, was a gold mine of information.

Within supporting distance of the pickets at Banks's Ford, according to Silver, was the Rebel brigade of Cadmus Wilcox. To the west, at U.S. Ford, was Carnot Posey's brigade, with two batteries. "They are very much scattered," he wrote, from U.S. Ford on the Rappahannock to Ely's Ford on the Rapidan. These were Posey's men and, he thought, William Mahone's. He counted 2,500 troops close by each ford, with another 1,000 to 1,200 camped around the Grady house, less than three miles south of U.S. Ford. All these troops were from Anderson's division. Silver added, "there is no other standing troops" from Grady's eastward as far as the road to Spotsylvania Court House — almost five miles. He reported the next concentration of troops to be along the Telegraph Road, due south of Fredericksburg. Without exception, he added, their battery horses "is in low order," and there were "no stores of enny amount" at Hamilton's Crossing on the railroad; "In fact it appears their eating is near run out. . . ."

In March Sharpe's soldier-spy Milton Cline had reported "a considerabell force" at the Chancellorsville crossroads; since then, by this new account, it had moved out, leaving Chancellorsville unguarded. By Isaac Silver's observation, then, Lee's farthest defenses upriver from Fredericksburg were shallow rather than in-depth, and they were focused only on the crossings at Banks's Ford and U.S. Ford. The flank and rear of the Army of Northern Virginia were wide open.[30]

Although he liked to speak confidently of "bagging" the opposing army and showing no mercy in a showdown struggle, Fighting Joe Hooker had all along privately assumed the battle would be one of pursuit. In nautical terms, it would be a stern chase. By cutting Lee's communications he would force him out of his Fredericksburg defenses and into retreat, then cross the Rappahannock and pursue and (he hoped) catch Lee in the open and fight him.

Now, with this new intelligence in hand, he decided on a very different course. Stoneman's cavalry mission would go on as planned, but it would be the main army that would slash in behind the enemy's lines with quickness and maneuver. Infantry rather than cavalry would immediately threaten Lee's lifeline, forcing him into battle directly rather than by the tactic of pursuit — and forcing him into battle on Hooker's terms rather than Lee's. This was the most radical of General Hooker's three plans of campaign, and the boldest and most daring. None of Hooker's predecessors had thought of anything so innovative.

At the heart of Hooker's new scheme was a grand turning movement. He would march secretly upriver along the north bank with three army corps — perhaps 40,000 men — storm the Rebel picket post at Kelly's Ford and lay a pontoon bridge, cross the Rappahannock, repeat the process at the Rapidan crossings, and march back downriver to Chancellorsville and the flank and rear of Lee's army. To fix Lee's attention meanwhile, he would post two corps to cross the river just below Fredericksburg. The remaining two corps would act as a mobile reserve to reinforce success wherever it developed. The flanking march back down the south bank of the Rappahannock from Kelly's Ford would uncover U.S. Ford and Banks's Ford for crossing reinforcements and to shorten his own communications.

By marching with eight days' rations in the flying-column pattern, Hooker would have his flanking column at Chancellorsville in four days, leaving it four days to operate independently and to fight the decisive battle. In any event, seizing U.S. Ford and Banks's Ford would allow the column to be resupplied in good season.

For Joe Hooker, the beauty of his new plan was its promise of stealing a long march on Robert E. Lee. Butterfield's signal ruse had drawn the Rebel cavalry far to the west, opening a twenty-mile gap and leaving a good crossing site, Kelly's Ford, guarded by only a picket post. The spy Isaac Silver had shown the road to Lee's rear was clear of any opposition. Stoneman's raiders were to carry out their original orders as soon as might be, to further divert attention from the turning movement and to ensure destruction of the enemy's supply line. Now as then, this was essential. In meeting Hooker's thrust, Lee would have to act in the knowledge that his communications with Richmond were cut.

To be sure, sending Stoneman on his raid left but a single brigade of cavalry to operate with the infantry of the flanking column, but this did not unduly worry Hooker. He did not believe cavalry could perform effectively in the thickly wooded Wilderness south of the river. "The only element which gives me apprehension with regard to the success of the plan is the weather," he told Mr. Lincoln. "Now much will depend on it."[31]

*   *

IN WORKING out this final plan, Hooker had under command 134,800 fighting men of all arms. This was not, as he well knew, as impressive a total as it seemed. The two-year and the nine-month regiments were causing headaches. Already five of the April 1861 regiments were on their way home or about to leave. The 7th New York, the most celebrated of the prewar militia units that had joined up right after Fort Sumter, set off for Manhattan and mustering-out on April 26. "I hear their hurrahing before I come off picket," a diarist in a neighboring regiment wrote. Other short-term regiments, however, saw their celebrations end abruptly. "The 130th Penn. lay close to us, and they are in our

Brigade," Corporal Edward Wade of the 14th Connecticut wrote home on April 25. "Their time is out on Wednesday next and if they dont feel happy, then I dont know what it is to be happy." But these happy Pennsylvanians, nine-months' men, ran up against an unyielding War Department, which announced that by its calculations they still had another month to serve.

In similar circumstances the 1st New York determined to stand up for its rights. The 1st was a veteran outfit of good reputation, serving in Phil Kearny's old division and at Glendale on the Peninsula suffering more casualties than any other Yankee regiment in that fierce battle. The New Yorkers said they had signed their papers for two years on April 22, 1861, and now their time was up. The army said their service began when they took up a posting in Federal service at Fort Monroe on May 25; they would only be mustered out on May 25, 1863. "The First N.Y. Volunteers stacked their arms and declared their term of enlistment had expired," a diarist in their brigade reported. "The 17th Maine Vols. are guarding the First N.Y. Vols. who are all under arrest." The matter would end peacefully and the men of the 1st New York would serve out their time — or their extra time — but not before their wartime casualty roll saw eighty names added to it.

Throughout the army, generals shifted short-term men to behind-the-lines postings — provost marshal units, guards for depots and communications, headquarters assignments, labor battalions, ambulance details — or simply left them in camp. Most two-year regiments contained some number of three-year men as well (men who were now truly embittered at their lot), and in their skeleton units they were shifted to the rear.

General Andrew A. Humphreys, commanding a division in the Fifth Corps, had to wonder how his men would stand up in a fight when six of the eight regiments were nine-months' men, all of them due out in May. Brigadier Gabriel R. Paul of the First Corps had a similar concern: all five of his regiments had signed up for nine months, and four of the five would be facing battle for the first time. Nearly half of William H. French's Second Corps division was made up of short-termers or new regiments. Nearly half of Carl Schurz's Eleventh Corps division would be seeing battle for the first time. The most unusual case was that of the 20th Maine, which reported eighty-four cases of smallpox and would spend the next weeks in camp in quarantine. General Hooker would later say that he began his campaign with 40,000 troops he considered of doubtful or at least uncertain quality. That gave him one more reason to try and fight his battle with his men behind defenses.[32]

Yankee deceptions continued. "I must play with these devils before I can spring," Hooker explained to General Peck. On April 22 two brigades from Abner Doubleday's First Corps division marched downriver to a point opposite Port Royal. They carried pontoon boats with them, making no effort at concealment. Doubleday intended to cross and raid into Port Royal, but his infantrymen were baffled trying to assemble the canvas pontoons and he gave up the effort. Before retiring, the Federals produced much threatening activity. The next day a second detachment did cross over to Port Royal on a brief raid, capturing a dozen prisoners, seven horses, eight mules, and the mail of the Confederate Second Corps. Upriver, Colonel Buschbeck's Eleventh Corps infantry remained highly visible opposite Kelly's Ford, and General Stoneman's cavalry was seen farther upriver around the Orange & Alexandria Railroad crossing. At Falmouth Professor Lowe's two balloons, *Eagle* and *Washington,* made ascensions whenever the weather permitted, so that the Confederates would attach no particular significance to seeing them aloft.

In the military terminology of the day, such feints and deceptions were designed to "amuse" the enemy while concealing serious movements. In this instance, General Lee was genuinely amused. "The enemy is making various demonstrations either to amuse themselves or deceive us, but so far they have done us little harm," he wrote his wife on April 24. After great flurries of activity at the Rappahannock's upper crossings, he told her, they then appeared downriver. "Formed in line of battle, threw out skirmishers, advanced their artillery, brought up their wagons, built up large fires, & after dark commenced chopping, cutting, & sawing as if working for life. . . . Their expeditions will serve for texts to the writers for the Herald, Tribune & Times for brilliant accounts of grand Union victories. . . ."

While he had no doubt all this downriver activity was merely a deception and that if "a real attempt is made to cross the river it will be above Fredericksburg" (as he told Stonewall Jackson), Lee did nothing more than alert his guarding forces at Banks's Ford and U.S. Ford. Hooker, he concluded, would probably attempt nothing more bold than what Burnside had attempted in his Mud March in January.[33]

"We have a clear, bright, breezy day," Captain Folwell wrote home on April 25. "The ground and the roads are drying off wonderfully fast." The Rappahannock continued to run high, but in General Hooker's new scheme of things that was less important than the troops being able to travel the roads without hindrance. Forty-eight hours of dry weather ought to be sufficient, he thought, and privately he set the start of operations for April 27. "Hooker seems very confident of success, but lets no one into his secrets," General Meade, commander of the Fifth Corps, wrote his wife on the twenty-sixth. "I heard him say that not a human being knew his plans either in the army or in Washington."

As long as no one on his side of the river knew anything of his plans, Hooker reasoned, no one on the other side could know either. That was vital. It was equally vital that operations begin now, before very many more of the short-term troops departed. He sensed too that a campaign that sprawled all across the landscape, as his did, would challenge him and his generals as they had never been challenged before. It was a challenge Fighting Joe Hooker relished. Years later, looking back on the moment, he remembered, "I felt at the beginning of the campaign that I had eighty chances in one hundred of being successful. . . ."[34]

6

Army on the March

I T WAS THE LAST Sunday in April, the twenty-sixth, and morning services at Stonewall Jackson's headquarters were well attended and especially notable. Jackson and Anna Jackson and the staff were joined for the occasion by General Lee and other officers of rank, including even Jubal Early, not usually known for his piety. Some 2,000 rank and file attended as well, and heard the Reverend Lacy, whom Jackson had appointed "chaplain general" to the Second Corps, preach the parable of Lazarus and the rich man. Mrs. Jackson found the sermon "earnest and edifying." Diarist Jed Hotchkiss recorded the day "pleasant, with a fresh breeze." The war seemed far away. That afternoon the staff of Alfred Iverson's North Carolina brigade made plans to celebrate "King of May Day" the following Friday with speeches and ceremonies. Fishermen in butternut crowded the riverbank to take their Sunday suppers from the spring run of Rappahannock shad.[1]

At Army of the Potomac headquarters on the other side of the river there was too much to do to take time for Sunday services. The army had marching orders for the next day, April 27. The headquarters tents were pitched in a pleasant grove on high ground along the Forest Road east of Falmouth, opposite Fredericksburg but out of range of the Rebel batteries there. On Saturday the commanders of the Fifth, Eleventh, and Twelfth corps had been alerted for Monday's movement. Now, in the tent of the army's adjutant general, Seth Williams, the actual orders of march were prepared under General Hooker's direction and marked "strictly confidential." Before now there had been no hint of his plans from security-conscious Joe Hooker. Even today corps commanders Meade, Howard, and Slocum learned nothing of the general's intentions beyond the fact that they were to have their commands at Kelly's Ford by 4 o'clock Tuesday afternoon, without revealing themselves to the enemy.

They, and indeed most all the Potomac army's generals, might have echoed Gouverneur Warren, Hooker's chief engineer, when he later testified, "I did not know any of his plans until I saw them being carried into operation."[2]

If Joe Hooker was preoccupied with secrecy, it was with good reason. He knew that his long flanking march would be risky in the extreme. It had "no reasonable chance of succeeding . . . ," he later insisted, "unless conducted with secrecy and despatch." There could be great danger should the Confederates learn of the march in time to put up a strong fight at either or both the Rappahannock and Rapidan river crossings and seize the initiative against his divided army.

Wherever he looked Hooker saw threats. The press could not be trusted to respect military secrets, as it had recently demonstrated with the story in the *Washington Chronicle* revealing the numbers in the Army of the Potomac. Hooker did not even trust the security of the telegraph lines. He told General Peck at Suffolk that he dared not telegraph him details of his plan because the wires "are so often tapped." Washington, he was sure, was overrun by Rebel agents. He liked to tell the story that no sooner had the War Department decided to evacuate McClellan's army from the Peninsula the previous August than it was announced "through posters on the walls of Richmond." There were many in the capital, Hooker warned Mr. Lincoln, whose fidelity could not be trusted. "It almost makes me tremble," he told the president in describing his plan of campaign, "to disclose a thing concerning it to anyone except yourself."

In truth he was greatly overestimating General Lee's secret service, which in these months was far less effective than Hooker's own Bureau of Military Information. Yet at the same time he was not underestimating the need to secure his turning movement from prying eyes. Hooker planned every aspect of the march with security in mind, and in the event, his efforts were astonishingly effective.[3]

The very composition of the flanking column was dictated by security considerations. All the units that had been camped closest to the Rappahannock since December — and which had manned the picket lines along the riverbank in those months — were kept in place. Any gaps in the picket lines were certain to be noticed by the Confederates the moment they appeared. During the opening of the campaign, therefore, John Reynolds's First Corps, holding the extreme left of the army's line downstream from Falmouth, was to make no move. The same was true of the next corps in line, John Sedgwick's Sixth. In and around Falmouth, Darius Couch's Second Corps and Dan Sickles's Third were also initially to remain in their camps. The march upriver of Stoneman's cavalry corps, begun on April 13, had long since been noted by the enemy, and Jeb Stuart had the Yankee troopers on the upper Rappahannock under observation. They too would remain in place for the time being.

The forces making up the flanking column were those whose winter encampments were most distant from the Rebels. The two divisions of Henry Slocum's Twelfth Corps were at Aquia Landing on the Potomac and at Stafford Court House, six miles to the west. The camps of Otis Howard's Eleventh Corps were between Stafford Court House and Brooke's Station on the railroad. George Meade's Fifth Corps was along the railroad between Brooke's Station and Falmouth. Simply because of their postings, then, these three corps would make up the column that was to march far upriver to Kelly's Ford, cross the Rappahannock and then the Rapidan, then pass around the flank and rear of the Confederate army. Their march, depending on the route, would range from forty to fifty-five miles.

Had he had more choice in the matter, or had he shaped his final plan earlier and thus bought time for a quiet shifting of forces, General Hooker would have assembled this flanking column differently. The Fifth was a veteran corps, having served in the Army of the Potomac from the Peninsula onward and with a proven leader in George Meade, and was certainly up to the challenge of the flank march. Howard's Eleventh Corps and Slocum's Twelfth, however, were the stepchildren of the Army of the Potomac. Formed in the murky confusion of warfare in the Shenandoah Valley and far western Virginia, they came to the Potomac army from John Pope's much-maligned Army of Virginia in the reorganization following Pope's defeat at Second Manassas. Although that was seven and a half months ago, neither corps felt a sense of belonging.

Slocum's Twelfth was the second-smallest corps in the army, with just 13,450 men counted in its two divisions on the April 30 return. Slocum and his generals of division, Alpheus Williams and John Geary, were competent enough, but their troops had faced the roughest kind of fighting against Stonewall Jackson in the Valley, at Cedar Mountain in the Second Manassas campaign, and at Antietam. During the army's winter crisis the Twelfth Corps had the highest percentage of deserters of any corps. Had he been able to, Hooker would likely have found a less demanding role for the Twelfth.

He would without a doubt have assigned a different role to the Eleventh Corps. It was the smallest in the army, its three divisions averaging barely 4,300 men. These men had suffered under a most mediocre succession of generals since their enlistment in 1861, and they had fought with a singular lack of success in the Valley and at Second Manassas. The Eleventh had yet to fight a battle under the banners of the Army of the Potomac, and its assignment there had not been welcomed. Its numerous German regiments were regarded with distrust and suspicion, and many in the army (and in their own corps) referred to them by the slurring term "Dutchmen." General Howard was an unknown quantity both to his men and to the commanding general. Still, the need for security was paramount, and the Eleventh Corps was slated to march with the Fifth and the Twelfth. As the campaign developed, Hooker posted the Eleventh as far as possible from probable scenes of fighting.[4]

As Hooker viewed it, "despatch" was every bit as important as secrecy to the success of his plan. Kelly's Ford was a twenty-three-mile march from Falmouth, and from the camps of the Eleventh and Twelfth corps, north and east of Falmouth, the march would stretch to as much as thirty-six miles. Hooker's schedule allotted just thirty-six hours for the flanking column to reach Kelly's. His goal, he said, "was to mobilize my column as much as practicable." The French flying-column scheme the high command had been developing for some weeks would be tested to its limits.

To speed the march the artillery was cut back, the three corps taking only nine of their assigned twenty batteries. Ambulances were limited to two per division. The reserve of small-arms ammunition would be packed by mule. There would be beef on the hoof for five days. There would be wagons only to carry forage for the animals. Because the Eleventh and Twelfth corps would march on separate roads the first day, they would bring their reserve trains with them as far as the turnoff for Banks's Ford, in position to resupply once the flanking column opened that crossing on its march back downriver. So as not to clutter the march routes, the Fifth Corps left its reserve trains near its Falmouth camps. The regulation that the men carry eight days' rations in knapsacks and haversacks was to be strictly enforced. Also to keep the march route clear, and to further promote secrecy, the pontoon-bridge train needed for the Kelly's Ford crossing would be brought roundabout from Washington over the Orange & Alexandria to Bealeton Station, north of Kelly's. Dan Butterfield and the headquarters staff were doing their best to cover every contingency.

The corps commanders were told they could leave their short-term men on duty in the rear. In the Fifth Corps one two-year regiment was already gone and a second was soon to go, but the half-dozen nine-month regiments due out in the latter half of May were expected by stern General Meade to stay the course. Howard's Eleventh Corps had lost only one two-year regiment, but in the days to come eleven of the remaining twenty-seven regiments would be going into battle for the first time. The Twelfth Corps was short one two-year regiment and had three nine-month regiments scheduled for muster-out within two weeks; five other regiments were facing their first battle. Subtracting the mustered-out regiments and the artillerymen left behind, the flanking column — the optimistically named flying column — totaled 39,795 fighting men.

There was serious concern, however, about the numerous new troops and nine-months' men — more than a quarter of the total — in the flying column. Captain John D. Wilkins, commanding a regiment of regulars in the Fifth Corps, expressed this concern in an April 27 letter to his wife. "I cant say that I am at all sanguine at going into a fight with these *nine month* men," he told her. "I only wish that I could have a little more confidence. . . ." Joe Hooker was equally concerned.[5]

Under the best of circumstances, Hooker had decided, those thirty-six hours — from Monday dawn to Tuesday evening, April 28 — were about as long as he could expect his turning movement to remain a secret. He hardly hoped to steal a longer march on Robert E. Lee. Although his intelligence service confirmed that Dan Butterfield's ruse had created a twenty-mile gap on the Confederate left, from U.S. Ford to the Orange & Alexandria Railroad, the Rebel pickets at Kelly's Ford would surely report the Yankee crossing there if they could not stop it.

The issue would then be clear — how swiftly the flanking column could march back downriver toward Chancellorsville, matched against how swiftly General Lee could reinforce his left to meet it. At risk was a battle for the Rapidan crossings. To raise the odds in his favor, Hooker would simultaneously launch a powerful threat against the Confederates' right in their works at Fredericksburg. His goal, he told the president, was "keeping them in their places, and if they should detach heavy forces to attack the troops coming down the river, to storm and carry those works and take possession of the enemy's short line of retreat."

Once again it was the position of the army's winter camps — camps established in Burnside's regime — that dictated the movements of the other Federal wing. In making up his striking forces for the campaign, Hooker wrote later (with considerable bitterness), "it was necessary to conform to the condition of my encampment, irrespective of the qualities of soldiership of the officers in command." The main weight of the left wing — the Fredericksburg half of the operation — would be borne by John Sedgwick's Sixth Corps and John Reynolds's First, whose postings formed the Federal lines downriver from Falmouth.

With four divisions and more than 23,600 men, the Sixth Corps was by far the largest in the army; it was almost twice the size of the smallest, Howard's Eleventh. Sedgwick was to lay pontoon bridges and force a passage of the river two miles below Fredericksburg at Franklin's Crossing, where William B. Franklin's Left Grand Division had crossed during the December battle. At the same time, Reynolds would force a second passage, at Fitzhugh's Crossing, not quite two miles farther downstream. Hooker timed these two crossings for the small hours of Wednesday morning, April 29 — just about when he supposed General Lee would have the news that the Federals were crossing the Rappahannock far upstream at Kelly's Ford.

Initially Dan Sickles's Third Corps would be positioned to support Sedgwick and Reynolds. Darius Couch's Second Corps would meanwhile quietly and secretly shift two of its divisions upriver to the centermost of the crossing sites, Banks's Ford and U.S. Ford. Couch's third division, under John Gibbon, encamped directly opposite Fredericksburg in plain sight of the enemy, was not to stir. In due course Sickles's Third and Couch's Second corps would act as a general reserve, to be thrown into action as the situation dictated. Joe Hooker wanted to operate by the old military maxim, reinforce success. (In a typical bit of army perversity, the Light Division, specially formed that winter to demonstrate the theory of the mobile, fast-moving flying column, was retained in the Sixth Corps rather than being put at the head of the upriver flanking column.)[6]

*　*

"MONDAY MORNING was bright and pleasant though rather too cool for comfort, the boys appeared in good spirits and ready for the march." So wrote Private Justus Silliman of the 17th Connecticut, Eleventh Corps, of the first day — the first day at last — of Joe Hooker's spring campaign. April 27 did indeed prove to be a fine spring day, the third such in a row. Like many another Yankee soldier that morning, Captain Charles Bowers of the 32nd Massachusetts wrote a hurried letter to his wife. "I may be too sanguine, I know I have been again and again disappointed, but I certainly never felt so confident of success as I do now," he told her. ". . . I have seen defeats enough, I want to witness one good substantial victory."

Otis Howard's Eleventh Corps was scheduled to lead the flanking column, and it was shortly after sunrise when the first of his three divisions strode out on the road westward from Brooke's Station at 5:30 A.M. By six the other two divisions were also on the road. The troops had stripped the tent roofs from their log huts to shelter themselves on campaign, giving the abandoned camps the look of miniature ancient ruins. For security reasons there was none of the trash burning that usually marked the breaking up of camp. Nor was there any music or any march calls. Sergeant John Cate of Adolph Von Steinwehr's division wrote his wife, "Not a drum was beat or a bugle blast was heard, and the men were not allowed to holler or cheer." Before long the word went through the ranks that this time they were out to fool Johnny Reb.

The plan for the first day's march had the Eleventh Corps picking up the Telegraph Road north of Falmouth, then turning from that into the Warrenton Post Road and following it to Hartwood Church, a crossroads country church eight miles west of Falmouth. The Twelfth Corps faced the longest march on April 27, especially its Second Division that had wintered near Aquia Landing on the Potomac. The Second Division was commanded by John W. Geary, who at six feet six inches was the tallest general in the Army of the Potomac. Setting off at daylight, Geary fell in behind Alpheus Williams's Twelfth Corps division at Stafford Court House. They too followed the Telegraph Road for a time, then turned right into the Ridge Road that intersected the Warrenton Post Road at Hartwood Church. The Fifth Corps, from its winter quarters closest to Falmouth, had the day's shortest march to Hartwood Church and did not start until late morning.[7]

The landscape desolated by the wintering army was softened by the greening grass and the emerging wildflowers and the blossoming peach and cherry trees of April, but hour by hour the marching grew wearying. The country east of Falmouth was rough and broken, and in low places there were still sloughs from the recent rains. In a letter home General Williams of the Twelfth Corps described the roads as "terrible . . . my pioneer corps was busily at work cutting new roads all through the pines. . . ." For the marchers, however, the greatest burden that day was the burden they carried — their knapsacks and haversacks laden with eight days' rations.

In the winter's flying-column experiments in packing for eight days, the high command had concluded that only the strictest discipline would limit the infantryman's load — rifle, sixty cartridges, rations, clothing, shelter — to 45 pounds, matching the former march standard for carrying only three days' rations. Room for the additional rations was found by eliminating the overcoat, carrying only one half a shelter tent, limiting clothing to one shirt, one pair of drawers, and one pair of socks, and no personal gear at all.

There may have been a Yankee soldier here and there who adhered strictly to this spartan regimen, but on the evidence of the first day's march they were rare indeed. Veterans hardened by experience believed anything left in camp would be stolen before their return, and left nothing behind. Rookies in their innocence considered it their duty to pack everything they had ever been issued. It was not uncommon that day for men to start out carrying 60-pound loads.

These resolutions lasted only as long as it took to reach the first rest halt. Then there was a general overhauling of loads, further refined at each subsequent halt. "Overcoats blankets and tents which had been thrown away by those in advance lined the road and covered the ground at their halting places," reported the 17th Connecticut's Private Silliman. "I do not think a hundred thousand dollars would more than have covered the loss. . . ." The track of the Army of the Potomac to Kelly's Ford could have been traced by the trail of overcoats alone. "The Negros & poor white people followed behind & picked up what they wanted," the Fifth Corps' James Houghton noted in his journal. Every Virginian in Stafford County, white and black, might have had a U.S. Army blanket or overcoat if so inclined.

That evening around Hartwood Church only small cooking fires were permitted. Footsore stragglers came in until well after dark. Most men were too tired to bother pitching their shelter tents, and those who still had blankets immediately rolled up in them and went to sleep. Before he slept a Fifth Corps surgeon climbed a small rise and was struck by the sight of an army at rest: "The many fires came up like the lights of a city and then in the fog and smoke the fires looked singular, fading away in the near distance."[8]

This march of nearly 40,000 troops and nine batteries of artillery and assorted trains over some forty miles of roadways east, north, and west of Falmouth could hardly be concealed from patriotic Virginians living in the area. Joe Hooker's solution to that was to post house guards at every point where agents or scouts or anyone else loyal to General Lee might signal across the river that the Federal army was on the move. Pickets had standing orders to watch for nighttime signal lights and such things as suspicious daytime patterns in the setting of window blinds in houses overlooking the river. Those caught signaling, or suspected of signaling, were put in arrest by provost marshals.

The widespread house-guarding extended along the route of the flanking column as it moved on upriver, largely by troops of Darius Couch's Second Corps. Captain Thomas Livermore's company of the 5th New Hampshire was posted at a cluster of houses by an old mill with instructions "to keep the inhabitants from leaving the vicinity." With Yankee ingenuity the New Englanders soon had the mill operating and took their fee in the form of freshly ground cornmeal for hoecakes, a welcome change from hardtack. These New Hampshiremen and Pennsylvanians from the 81st regiment guarded no fewer than forty-one houses and picketed every road in the vicinity of U.S. Ford. The renowned Irish Brigade, also from the Second Corps, performed similar duty near Banks's Ford. The cavalry confined "a large number of citizens" in a country church until the army had passed. "We found the people very generally full of smothered rebellion, but quite civil," wrote Colonel Edward Cross of the 5th New Hampshire.

These security measures were so tight and so effective that General Lee had not a hint of the march upriver of the three Yankee army corps. Here Dan Butterfield's planted message paid its final dividend. When his ruse drew Mosby's force of Partisan Rangers to the north and west to watch Stoneman's cavalry corps, it left the country north of the Rappahannock between Stafford Court House and Kelly's Ford — the country through which the flanking column was marching — entirely empty of partisan scouting parties.[9]

In the camps around Falmouth that Monday everything was staged to look like army business as usual. In early morning Professor Lowe's balloon *Washington* rose majestically from Stafford Heights a mile back of the river. With an enormous portrait of the first president on one side and the name in ornate red, white, and blue lettering on the other, it looked more like a carnival attraction than a machine of war. At 10 o'clock on the parade ground behind the town Dan Sickles's Third Corps staged a review for a party of distinguished visitors from Washington that included Secretary of State Seward, Governors Abner Coburn of Maine, Joel Parker of New Jersey, and Horatio Seymour of New York, and a number of foreign diplomats. General Hooker and staff joined them, and afterward the party was served luncheon at army headquarters.

That afternoon Hooker took time to compose a lengthy letter to Mr. Lincoln marked "confidential." "The following is what I have done and what I propose to do," he wrote, and went on to spell out his plan for the grand turning movement. "I write in great haste as I leave for Kelly's Ford tomorrow morning and am busy in making the necessary preparations."

As he wrote, a telegram arrived from Washington with the quiet query the president had so often addressed to previous battlefields — "How does it look now?" "I am not sufficiently advanced to give an opinion," Hooker telegraphed. "We are busy. Will tell you all as soon as I can, and have it satisfactory."

In the evening Hooker called in General Couch, by seniority his second-in-command, and explained the plan of campaign in detail, "in view," as Couch put it, "of an accident befalling him." He would also meet personally with Henry Slocum, who in his absence was to command on the right. There is no record, however, of his undertaking a similar face-to-face sharing of confidences with John Sedgwick, who by seniority would be responsible for the Fredericksburg half of the operation. This was surprising, for as Hooker certainly knew, this was to be General Sedgwick's first taste of the responsibilities of independent command.[10]

Across the river in the Confederate camps Monday's routine also went on undisturbed. There were the usual drills, and at General William Barksdale's headquarters close by Fredericksburg there was a ceremony at noontime. Barksdale's Mississippi brigade held a reception for two home-state representatives to the Confederate Congress, Senator A. G. Brown and Representative Ethelbert Barksdale, the general's brother. There was a serenade by the band of the 13th Mississippi, and speeches were made and toasts drunk. "Everything was exceedingly quiet on our side," a Georgian in Jubal Early's division remembered. "No orders to be ready to march, no rations to be cooked, no camp rumors disturbed the repose of the season."

At his headquarters on the Mine Road south of Fredericksburg General Lee (like General Hooker) wrote a long letter to his president that Monday. He told Mr. Davis of his continued concern about supplies for the army, which left him "unable even to act on the defensive as vigorously as circumstances may require." He reported the enemy's cavalry still camped on the upper Rappahannock, its intentions unclear, and that he had learned of reinforcements for General Hooker. That, he supposed, "would indicate a forward movement of the Federal Army." He hoped the president could soon arrange matters so as to free Longstreet from operations in southside Virginia, "as I may be obliged to call him back at any moment." That evening Lee remarked to one of Stonewall Jackson's staff that Hooker intended to advance, and would have done so the previous Friday but for the rain. Despite this he issued no preemptive call for Longstreet's return.[11]

* *

By TUESDAY, April 28, it was evident to everyone throughout the Army of the Potomac that the long-awaited campaign was under way at last. Men who had not written their last letters the day before hastened to do so now. "We are advancing upon the enemy," the 6th Wisconsin's Lieutenant Colonel Rufus R. Dawes wrote home. "I doubt not that we must have a bloody, desperate battle. I leave this where I have perfect confidence it will be sent to you in case I am killed, and only in that event. I loved you dearly, sincerely. . . . I dont believe you will ever think lightly of the love of a man, who if he had few other merits, gave his life freely for his country and the *right*."

In their bivouacs around Hartwood Church the men of the flanking column were roused well before dawn by their officers without resort to reveille. At 4:00 A.M. the Eleventh Corps, again designated to lead, took up its march. "There was no singing or shouting allowed in the ranks," wrote Private Silliman, "and everything was conducted quietly." By sunrise the road was open for Alpheus Williams and John Geary to follow with their Twelfth Corps divisions. Finally came George Meade's Fifth Corps. The day began mild but cloudy, with the threat of rain.

One of General Meade's regiments, the 5th New York, Duryée's Zouaves, was badly divided over the matter of its impending discharge. About half the men had signed up for two years and were due to be shipped home in a few days. The rest were three-year men who were understandably bitter at their comrades' good fortune while they faced another year's service attached to a regiment of strangers. Stragglers had been plentiful on the previous day's march, and most never turned up at Hartwood Church and were marked down as deserters. This morning, when Duryée's Zouaves set out again, they were short twenty more three-year men who had deserted during the night.

The march from Hartwood Church to Kelly's Ford was fourteen miles, and unlike the day before the entire flanking column was crowded onto a single road. For nearly half the distance its track was westward along the Warrenton Post Road. Turning from that into a country road past Crittenden's Mill, the column was scheduled to reach Mt. Holly Church, a mile and a half from Kelly's Ford and hidden from the enemy, by late afternoon. Joe Hooker, who came up with the marchers at midday, was soon swearing and "full of dire anger" over their pace.[12]

Because at this point the flanking column was a good five miles from the nearest Rebel picket post on the river, there was no objection when the troops spontaneously raised a cheer for the commanding general when he appeared. Fighting Joe Hooker, wrote Private William Aughinbaugh of the 5th Ohio in his journal, "is a red smooth-faced person, and reminded me of descriptions I have read of old English squires, although he is not so portly as I imagine one of those to be." Hooker acknowledged the tribute cheerfully enough, but no doubt his red-faced choler was due to his seeing the clotted condition of the flanking column as he passed up its length. When he reached its head he had sulfurous words for General Howard.

The Eleventh Corps had been put on lead because it was the smallest in the army and thus supposedly the swiftest. It had been made even smaller by the dispatch on April 13 of Adolphus Buschbeck's brigade to stand watch at Kelly's Ford, leaving barely 11,000 men in its ranks. Because of General Howard's laxness, however, the Eleventh Corps was hobbled by its trains, especially a lumbering mile-long string of wagons far in excess of the number authorized for the march. The Eleventh's 125 wagons were five times the number with the following Twelfth Corps. To be sure, a few of these were delivering the eight days' rations to Buschbeck's brigade, but most had been slipped in by quartermasters to carry extra rations and baggage supposed to have been left behind. General Williams, whose division was marching immediately behind, complained of repeatedly running up against Howard's trains. That

Tuesday Williams's men spent an hour standing and waiting for every two hours they marched. In late morning it began to rain, not hard enough to turn the road to mud but steadily enough to soak every man's load and make it that much heavier. By nightfall, wrote Private Aughinbaugh, they were "a sore, worn-out body of men," who thought they had marched at least five miles too far that day for the loads they had to carry.

In the end, Otis Howard's inattention to his orders created more of a nuisance than a problem on April 28. By 4:30 that afternoon, only half an hour after Hooker's deadline, the Eleventh Corps was bivouacking at Mt. Holly Church. The Twelfth and Fifth corps also camped there or along the road from Crittenden's Mill. General Howard remembered the episode as "my first mortification of this campaign." Events would show that it did not cause him to change his ways, however. And events would give the men of the Eleventh Corps cause to regret their oversized supply train.[13]

During the afternoon Joe Hooker issued orders for a time from Morrisville, four miles north of his flanking column at Mt. Holly Church and seven from his cavalry at Bealeton Station on the Orange & Alexandria. From Bealeton he might communicate with Dan Butterfield back at army headquarters by telegraph via Warrenton Junction and Washington. For an offensive plan as complicated as this one, rapid sure communications were vital. As the army advanced, communications links were extended to keep pace with every movement in every direction.

During the winter the Signal Corps had established a network of signal-flag stations along the north bank of the Rappahannock paralleling the Confederate fortifications on the south bank. The central station — Station F — was at the Phillips house on Stafford Heights, midway between Falmouth and Potomac-army headquarters. When the campaign opened, the chief signal officer, Captain Samuel T. Cushing, was ordered to supplement the flag system at Station F by extending a telegraph wire downstream to Franklin's Crossing, the proposed site of the Sixth Corps' bridges. Upstream a wire was to go first to Banks's Ford and then be extended to U.S. Ford, keeping pace with the troops; in due course, from one or both of those upstream crossings, communications would link up with the right wing at Chancellorsville. By Day Two these telegraph links were in place except for the one to U.S. Ford, which went into operation on the evening of April 29.

By traveling with the flanking column on April 28, General Hooker assured himself there would be no command slip-ups in the right wing at least as far as Kelly's Ford. On the twenty-ninth he would return to headquarters for the crossings of the left wing. As soon as the flanking column reached Chancellorsville he planned to join it, leaving Chief of

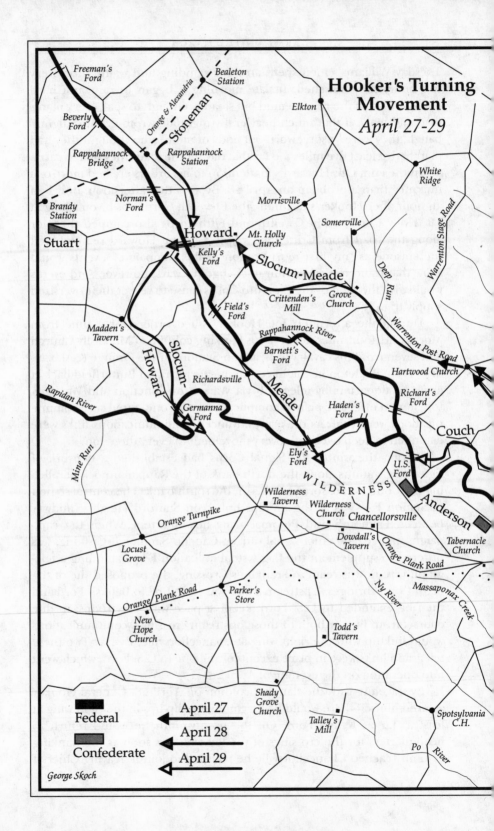

Hooker's Turning Movement
April 27-29

Freeman's Ford
Bealeton Station
Elkton
Beverly Ford
Orange & Alexandria
Stoneman
White Ridge
Rappahannock Bridge
Rappahannock Station
Morrisville
Somerville
Brandy Station
Norman's Ford
Howard
Mt. Holly Church
Stuart
Kelly's Ford
Slocum-Meade
Deep Run
Warrenton Stage Road
Field's Ford
Crittenden's Mill
Grove Church
Madden's Tavern
Howard
Slocum-
Rappahannock River
Warrenton Post Road
Barnett's Ford
Hartwood Church
Richardsville
Meade
Richard's Ford
Rapidan River
Germanna Ford
Haden's Ford
Couch
Mine Run
Ely's Ford
WILDERNESS
U.S. Ford
Anderson
Wilderness Tavern
Wilderness Church
Chancellorsville
Orange Turnpike
Dowdall's Tavern
Tabernacle Church
Locust Grove
Orange Plank Road
Orange Plank Road
Parker's Store
Ny River
Massaponax Creek
New Hope Church
Todd's Tavern
Shady Grove Church
Spotsylvania C.H.
Talley's Mill
Po River

Federal — April 27
Confederate — April 28
April 29

George Skoch

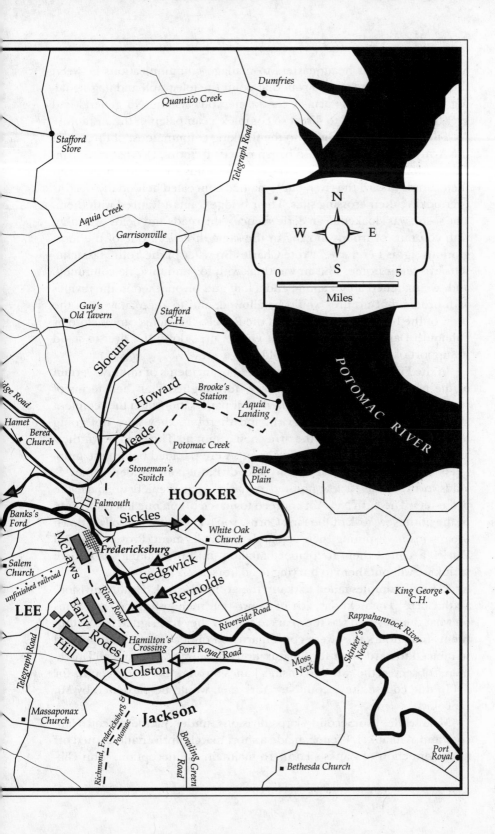

Dumfries

Quantico Creek

Stafford
Store

Aquia Creek

Garrisonville

Telegraph Road

Guy's
Old Tavern

Stafford
C.H.

Slocum

Howard

Brooke's
Station

Aquia
Landing

POTOMAC RIVER

N
W   E
S

0   5

Miles

Ridge Road

Hamet

Berea
Church

Meade

Potomac Creek

Stoneman's
Switch

Belle
Plain

HOOKER

Falmouth

Banks's
Ford

Sickles

White Oak
Church

McLaws

Fredericksburg

Sedgwick

Salem
Church

unfinished railroad

LEE

Early

River Road

Reynolds

King George
C.H.

Rappahannock River

Rodes

Hamilton's
Crossing

Riverside Road

Hill

Colston

Port Royal Road

Moss
Neck

Skinker's Neck

Telegraph Road

Massaponax
Church

Jackson

Richmond, Fredericksburg & Potomac

Bowling Green Road

Bethesda Church

Port
Royal

Staff Butterfield at headquarters to manage communications between the two wings of the army. From that point the telegraph and flag signaling would serve as the army's central nervous system. No general had ever before attempted to direct so complex a campaign in this fashion.[14]

That Tuesday, in addition to the flanking column, most of the rest of the Army of the Potomac also began quietly to move. Downstream from Falmouth Sedgwick's Sixth Corps and Reynolds's First advanced from their camps toward the river, but remained concealed behind the heights overlooking their crossing sites. Their bridge trains advanced with them. The scene was cloaked in an eerie silence, "the roads and fields swarming with columns of troops moving in the same direction, one of the most glorious sights I ever saw," wrote Charles Brewster of the 10th Massachusetts in a letter home. The air was thick with fog and mist, he continued, and "we marched about a mile and a half and bivouacked in the ravines with orders that no fires would be allowed, and to keep away from the brow of the hill, and out of sight of the Rebels." From his camps close by Falmouth Dan Sickles brought the Third Corps down the river to stand in support of Sedgwick and Reynolds.

In the First Corps the day was marred by incidents of mutiny. Certain of the two-year men of the 24th New York argued that their terms of service had begun when they signed their papers, not when the regiment was accepted into Federal service, and therefore they were not going to spend these last days in the army being shot at. They laid down their arms. Promptly two Wisconsin regiments were paraded before the mutineers with loaded muskets, and the division commander, James S. Wadsworth, made "a few pointed remarks" that seemed to shake the protesters. The 24th New York agreed to march off on one last campaign. In the 26th New York of the First Corps, 100 two-year men also laid down their arms in disputing their actual date of enlistment. Provost Marshal Patrick assigned them to a labor battalion until the matter was settled: "think we will put them to burying dead horses. . . ."

(These examples failed to daunt the 20th New York, Howe's division, Sixth Corps. The next day, 201 of its two-year men grounded their arms on what they insisted was two years to the day they had signed up. Within twenty-four hours they were court-martialed on a charge of mutiny and sentenced to hard labor for the duration of the war. "They are all Dutchmen," observed the 5th Wisconsin's James Strong. "So that accounts for it." In due course these 20th New York men would be pardoned by Mr. Lincoln.)[15]

Meanwhile, two Second Corps divisions, under Winfield Scott Hancock and William H. French, made a short march upriver and turned off in the direction of Banks's Ford. To maintain the deception, John Gibbon kept the corps' third division in its camps, and on its picket lines, opposite Fredericksburg. On the approaches to Banks's Ford engineers labored in concealment to repair the roads. "We had men sawing off stumps with hand saws in order not to alarm the Rebel pickets who were lounging around their fires across the Rappahannock a few hundred yards off," William Folwell of the 50th New York engineers noted in his diary.

During the day the signal officers at Station F reported Confederate infantry drilling "as usually seen from this station. Animals are grazing on the plains opposite. See nothing as yet unusual." In a message smuggled across the river the spy Isaac Silver reported, "Wee have not herd your drums nor no movement at all." It was the opinion in the Rebel army, Silver added, that the Federals would shift their operations to some other line. "I think your time is good. . . ." The B.M.I.'s Colonel Sharpe, questioning the latest deserters from the other side, confirmed that the three divisions of Stonewall Jackson's corps posted downstream from Fredericksburg — A. P. Hill's, Robert Rodes's, and Raleigh Colston's — were still in their places and had no orders to move. That night Provost Marshal Patrick recorded in his diary, with considerable satisfaction, "So far, I think the rebels have not the slightest idea what we are about today. Even the pickets know nothing about it."[16]

By this Tuesday, too, Colonel Sharpe put the finishing touches on his detailed order of battle for the Army of Northern Virginia. He located and counted its strength brigade by brigade. Joe Hooker accepted the figures as "reliable information," and assured one of his generals, without qualification, "We know the strength of the enemy in front. . . ." Hooker's confidence in his intelligence service was not misplaced. The B.M.I.'s latest count of Lee's infantry came to 54,600, just 1,600 short of its actual numbers. In estimating Lee's artillery at 243 guns, the B.M.I. overcounted by just 23.[17]

* *

TWO WEEKS EARLIER, Colonel Adolphus Buschbeck's Eleventh Corps brigade — 27th and 73rd Pennsylvania, 29th and 154th New York — had taken position opposite Kelly's Ford in support of Stoneman's cavalry raiders. When Stoneman remained along the upper Rappahannock to wait for the flooded river to subside, Buschbeck's infantrymen remained too. In common with the pickets downriver, they promptly arranged an unofficial truce with the Confederate picket post on the south bank. These Virginia cavalrymen from Rooney Lee's brigade were happy enough to honor the truce, for they were heavily outnumbered by the 2,000-man Yankee brigade. As the days passed and the Federals set up their camps and made no threatening moves, the Rebel observers began to regard them with growing indifference.

Throughout the afternoon of April 28 Buschbeck's men kept up the deception, giving no hint of the arrival of the flanking column a mile and a half in their rear. Thus at 6:00 P.M. the Confederate pickets were caught totally by surprise when out of Marsh Run, 500 yards below the ford, came a flotilla of canvas pontoon boats, each manned by fourteen paddlers from the 154th New York. Without pause they splashed straight across the river. At the same time, the north bank blazed with covering fire laid down by sharpshooters from the 73rd Pennsylvania. These New Yorkers in the boats had never been under fire before, but they bent to their paddles and reached the far shore unharmed. The Rebel troopers managed one wild volley and stood their ground only "until the first boats reached the shore, when they suddenly took to their horses and fled," as Major Charles Howard, the general's brother, described it.

The pontoon-bridge train had arrived that morning from Washington over the Orange & Alexandria exactly on schedule, and teamsters hauled it from Bealeton Station to Mt. Holly Church to coincide with the arrival of the flanking column. With the bridgehead secured and with General Howard detailing a thousand men to help with the labor, Captain Cyrus Comstock and the 15th New York engineers soon had the pontoons positioned and fixed in the river and began lashing down the planking. By 10:30 that night the bridge was completed and the 17th Pennsylvania cavalry clattered across to picket the far shore. General Hooker was on hand to observe. With Carl Schurz's division leading the way, through the night by the light of torches the Eleventh Corps tramped across the Rappahannock into what until then had been Confederate ground.[18]

It was a very dark night and the large meadow on the Kelly homestead beyond the ford was blanketed in fog and mist, and before long General Schurz suspected that his guide was as lost as he was. The suspicion was confirmed when Schurz heard a familiar voice in the fog, that of the colonel of the 82nd Illinois who he knew was leading the rear guard. The entire division, 4,000 men, had been marching in a circle. "We struck matches, examined our compasses, and then easily found our way . . . ," Schurz wrote.

It was soon reported to him, however, that one of his staff sent to find a way across the dark meadow had been seized by prowling Rebel cavalry. The captive was Captain Jules Schenofsky, a Belgian, one of the numerous refugees from Europe's armies who had found a place in the Army of the Potomac. Captain Schenofsky, it seemed, had a cavalier attitude about being a prisoner in this war. He volunteered to his captors that the entire Eleventh Corps was across the river, and gave its numbers as 14,000 men and six batteries of artillery. "He seemed frank and honest, as well as communicative," Jeb Stuart remarked. Fortunately, thanks to Hooker's rigid security measures, Captain Schenofsky did not know as much as he might have, such as where the flanking column was headed, but he knew enough.

The Confederate pickets who earlier managed to escape from Kelly's Ford were cut off from any chance to warn the picket posts farther downstream. Instead they headed westward to Rooney Lee's cavalry headquarters at Brandy Station, on the Orange & Alexandria. From there Lee dispatched the 13th Virginia cavalry to the scene to find out what the Yankees were up to. It was these troopers who picked up the voluble Captain Schenofsky. Jeb Stuart, at his headquarters at Culpeper Court House a half-dozen miles down the line from Brandy Station, had word of the Kelly's Ford crossing by 9:00 P.M. on April 28.

That intelligence, and whatever else Stuart learned that night, would be slow reaching General Lee in Fredericksburg. From Culpeper Stuart communicated with Lee over roundabout telegraph links via Gordonsville and Richmond, and at least one of the stations in this network closed down at night. For want of a nighttime telegraph operator, General Lee remained in the dark about the Federals' turning movement for twelve hours after it was discovered.

The first thirty-six hours of his campaign, from Falmouth to Kelly's Ford, had gone precisely as General Hooker planned it. Except for John Gibbon's division at Falmouth, a portion of the artillery, and the reserve trains and the cavalry, the entire Army of the Potomac, more than 100,000 strong, had marched as ordered over these two days without revealing itself to the enemy. Joe Hooker felt confident that he had stolen a long march on Robert E. Lee. In a new set of orders to the generals in the flanking column he now revealed the second phase of the campaign, to begin the next day. Their final target, he told them, was Chancellorsville. "The general desires that not a moment be lost until our troops are established at or near Chancellorsville. From that moment all will be ours."[19]

* *

SHORTLY AFTER daybreak on Day Three, Wednesday, April 29, Lieutenant James Power Smith of Stonewall Jackson's staff entered Lee's tent at army headquarters to wake the general. Jackson had sent him to report, Lieutenant Smith said. The enemy was advancing, crossing the Rappahannock below Fredericksburg in force under cover of fog on the river. "Well, I thought I heard firing, and was beginning to think it was time some of you young fellows were coming to tell me what it was all about," Lee said cheerfully. "Tell your good general that I am sure he knows what to do. I will meet him at the front very soon." Within moments the rest of Lee's army was awakened as well when the bell in the tower of the Episcopal church in Fredericksburg began tolling urgently.[20]

Joe Hooker's plan for his left wing on April 29 called for seizing bridgeheads at Franklin's Crossing and Fitzhugh's Crossing, below Fredericksburg, under cover of darkness in the small hours of the morning. As soon as infantry crossing in pontoon boats secured a hold on the far shore, engineers would lay the bridges — three at Franklin's Crossing for the Sixth Corps, two at Fitzhugh's for the First Corps. They were to be completed by 3:30 A.M., half an hour or so before first light. The darkness ought to shield the attackers from any interference by the enemy, or so Hooker assumed. In the event, the cover of darkness only added to the hopeless tangle the operation had become before it even started.

At Franklin's Crossing William T. H. Brooks's division of the Sixth Corps was selected to lead the assault. "Bully" Brooks was blunt and temperamental to such a degree that amiable Ambrose Burnside had relieved him for insubordination after Fredericksburg. Thus to begin with, General Brooks was not the sort to take kindly to being ordered about by the equally temperamental Henry W. Benham, head of the army's Engineer Brigade and in overall command of the bridging operation. To make matters worse, just as the various boat parties and assault parties and support parties were trying to find their way to their starting places in the inky darkness, Brooks discovered that Benham was drunk — literally falling-down drunk.

Lieutenant Stephen M. Weld of Benham's staff was appalled. "I found General B. drunk as could be, with a bloody cut over his left eye, and the blood all over that side of his face and forming a disgusting sight altogether," Weld wrote in a letter home that day. "He had fallen down and cut his face. Soon after he reeled in his saddle, and in trying to shake hands with General Pratt, he fell right off his horse on to the ground." Benham's jumbled orders added to the chaos, and he soon got into a shouting match with Brooks and with Brooks's brigade commander David Russell, whom he tried to put in arrest. Lieutenant Weld saw him in another dispute with one of Sedgwick's staff, "yelling out in a loud tone of voice and Goddamning him. This, too, right on the bank of the river and when he had been cautioning every one to keep quiet."[21]

Eventually, at first light, the officers on the scene ignored Benham and took matters in hand themselves. Boat parties moved the pontoons to the water's edge, carrying them supported on long poles. Troops in General Russell's brigade from the 49th, 95th, and 119th Pennsylvania formed assault parties of forty-five men to a boat, with four men of the Engineer Brigade to row. It was becoming light now, but to the good fortune of the attackers a thick blanket of fog on the river formed a perfect shield for the assault. The first wave of twenty-three boats pushed off and immediately disappeared in the fog. Their progress could be traced by the splashing of oars, the sound of the boats grounding on the gravelly shore, then flashes of dim red in the fog and a rattle of musketry. Then came the echoing sounds of cheering.

Beyond the water's edge on the Confederate shore was a steep bluff, and beyond that an open plain — the fields of the Bernard homestead, Mansfield, stretching half a mile to the main Rebel line on high ground. The plain lay within easy range of the Union artillery on the north shore and was occupied only by pickets of the 54th North Carolina, posted in rifle pits atop the bluff. The fog made it impossible for them to mount any kind of defense against the landing, and after a volley or two the North Carolinians ran for their lives as the Pennsylvania boys charged up the bluff toward them. "The secesh wir scamping across the fields at a tearing pace," a Federal wrote. ". . . It was the greatest fun we have ever had, but at first it was considered the most desperate thing we had ever undertaken." Soon the boats were back to ferry across the rest of Russell's brigade. The 54th North Carolina escaped with the loss of only two men captured. The engineers immediately set to work laying their bridges, and by 9:45 A.M. all three were down.

Despite General Benham's antics — and thanks to the providential fog — the Sixth Corps had its bridgehead at the cost of just one man killed and ten wounded. These eleven Pennsylvanians would be counted as the first casualties of the Battle of Chancellorsville.[22]

Downstream at Fitzhugh's Crossing, Benham's plan for Reynolds's First Corps to cross before first light had also fallen apart before it started. Benham himself did not appear there until close to 9 o'clock, long after the plan had gone awry, and in his absence apparently no one understood what needed to be done. When he finally did reach the crossing site, Benham was not a figure to inspire confidence. Rushing up to John Reynolds, his old Mexican War comrade-in-arms, he exclaimed, "Hurrah, Josh! Hurrah for here and Buena Vista!" The generals on the scene, like those at Franklin's Crossing, had already resolved to act on their own.

James S. Wadsworth's division had been chosen to make the crossing, and Wadsworth picked the Iron Brigade of westerners — 2nd, 6th, and 7th Wisconsin, 19th Indiana, 24th Michigan — to be his spearhead. Wadsworth was a political general, a wealthy New York landowner and early convert to Republicanism who the previous fall had run for governor (and lost) in New York State. He had served as military governor of Washington but this was his first field command, and he was eager to do the right thing by his men.

It was the engineers' plan to move the pontoon boats silently by hand down to the shore soon after midnight. Seventy-two men were detailed to carry each boat. General Wadsworth watched this operation for a time, saw his men struggling and slipping on the muddy road, and decided that it was too much of a load for soldiers to bear. He ordered the boats brought back and reloaded on their bridge-train wagons. There were forty of these hulking wooden pontoons to manhandle, and all the train's mule teams had to be harnessed and the teamsters collected, and by the time the first twenty of the pontoons were finally hauled down to the river it was full daylight. Everything was anxiety and suspense, reported James Latta of the Iron Brigade: "the whole affair appeared to be badly managed & every one anticipated a signal failure."

The fog was lifting now, and on the far shore pickets of the 13th Georgia opened fire the moment this tempting target was revealed. The Rappahannock here was only 150 yards wide, and the effect of their fire was immediate. "Crack, smash, whiz, ping, came the musketry . . . ," wrote Lieutenant Colonel Rufus Dawes of the 6th Wisconsin. "*Such* a skedaddling of negroes, horses, extra duty men of the pontoons never before was seen. Our generals looked blank." The Iron Brigade, standing by to make the crossing, was ordered down to the shoreline to return the fire. But the Rebels were sheltered in their rifle pits on the bluff and overlooked the Yankees on the shore, and it was obvious that musketry alone would not beat down their fire.[23]

The First Corps' artillery chief, Colonel Charles Wainwright, already had his guns deployed to cover the crossing, and as soon as it was clear enough to see Reynolds ordered him to open fire on the far shore. On high ground to the rear Wainwright had posted seven batteries of 3-inch rifles, thirty-four guns in all, and for closer work he put two batteries of smoothbore Napoleons on a low rise near the shoreline. The Federals' combined infantry and artillery barrage was overwhelming. "Soon one man jumped out and ran," Lieutenant Weld wrote, "then another, and soon all along the line men could be seen running from houses, ditches and rifle-pits. Then our artillery would open and make the rascals scatter. I saw one round shot knock a rebel head over heels."

These Confederates, dug in on the Pratt family's property called Smithfield, were from Jubal Early's division, and they were badly outgunned. Most of Lee's artillery was still in winter quarters to the south, and Early had but two batteries, with six rifled pieces between them, to meet Wainwright's challenge. In the rifle pits on the bluff the 13th

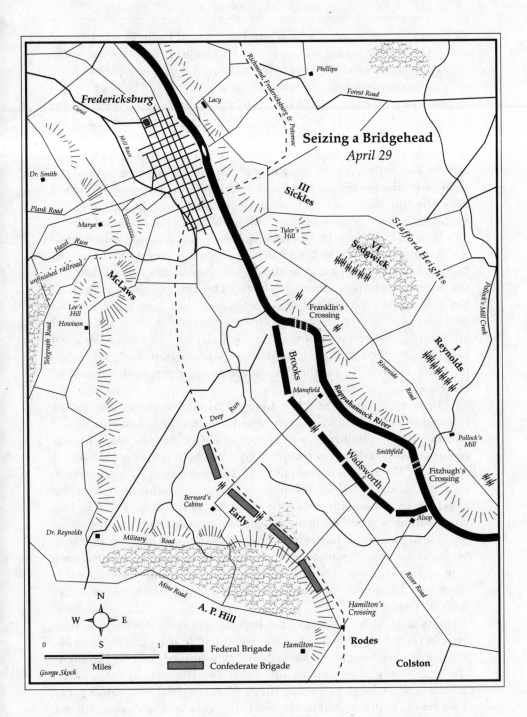

Seizing a Bridgehead
April 29

Fredericksburg

Phillips

Lacy

Richmond, Fredericksburg & Potomac

Forest Road

Canal

Mill Race

Dr. Smith

III
Sickles

Plank Road

Marye

Tyler's Hill

VI
Sedgwick

Stafford Heights

Hazel Run

unfinished railroad

McLaws

Lee's Hill

Howison

Franklin's Crossing

I
Reynolds

Riverside Road

Pollock's Mill Creek

Brooks

Mansfield

Rappahannock River

Telegraph Road

Deep Run

Wadsworth

Smithfield

Pollock's Mill

Fitzhugh's Crossing

Bernard's Cabins

Early

Alsop

Dr. Reynolds

Military   Road

Mine Road

River Road

A. P. Hill

Hamilton's Crossing

N
W   E
S

Rodes

0   1

Hamilton

Colston

Miles

█ Federal Brigade

▬ Confederate Brigade

George Skoch

Georgia ran low on ammunition and was relieved by the 6th Louisiana, and started for the rear. "We never lost but one man while we was in the rifle fight," claimed Georgian Henry Walker. "But when we went to base, they swept our boys down like they was chaff."[24]

John Reynolds was a hard fighter and an impatient one, and he was not happy with what he was seeing. The general, wrote Colonel Wainwright of the events of the day, "has sworn pretty hard when things did not go to suit him. . . ." Reynolds decided that direct action was needed, and he sent orders for the Iron Brigade to force a crossing in the pontoon boats abandoned at the water's edge when the Rebels first opened fire. The 6th Wisconsin and the 24th Michigan got the call. "Such a feeling of horror as came over us," admitted Lieutenant Colonel Dawes. "To be shot like sheep in a huddle & drown in the Rappahannock was the certain fate of *all* if we failed, or *many* if we succeeded." Shucking off knapsacks and haversacks, the two regiments double-quicked down to the water and tumbled into the boats. The rest of the Iron Brigade and Colonel Wainwright's gunners redoubled their covering fire as the oarsmen sent the craft into the river with furious strokes. General Wadsworth, apparently contrite over the delay he had caused, spurred his horse into the water and leaped into one of the lead boats, swimming his horse behind. "It was the fiercest regatta ever run in this country," Dawes said.

The worst of their casualties were taken getting under way. Dawes counted fifteen of the Wisconsin men hit in the first moments of the crossing. Captain William Speed of the 24th Michigan saw two of his sergeants and a private in his company go down before they even reached the boats. "The balls flew about like hail," he remembered. But soon they were across and splashing ashore and charging up the bluff, and the Rebels there threw down their rifles in surrender or ran for the rear. The Wisconsin men and the Michigan men would argue for years over who was first to plant their flag on this enemy ground, but however that may be, the victory was complete. At the sight of their waving banners a roar went up from the north bank. "And then such cheering & shouting you never heard," the 6th Wisconsin's Colonel Edward Bragg told his wife. "Everybody was crazy."[25]

In its fight on both banks of the Rappahannock on April 29 the Iron Brigade recorded 57 men killed and wounded. In the Confederate rifle pits the 6th Louisiana had 7 killed and 12 wounded, and 78 captured. The 13th Georgia gave up an additional 28 prisoners. By their sturdy resistance at Fitzhugh's Crossing they had delayed the First Corps some three hours, but by noontime the two bridges there were completed and reinforcements streamed across. Soon enough Reynolds's men and

Sedgwick's from above linked up, extending the Federal bridgehead two and three-quarter miles along the south bank. By stealth and then by firepower, Joe Hooker had gained a solid foothold against Lee's center.[26]

* *

STONEWALL JACKSON had spent the night with his wife and child at William Yerby's, where at an early hour Jubal Early's aide found him and reported the Federals' crossing. Jackson was soon on the scene, a Georgian in Early's division wrote, "galloping round with his glass viewing the enemy's position and numbers from every available direction. When Jackson would pass, we had to get up on the embankment with swords drawn to keep the men from cheering. We did not want the enemy to know our position."

The Yankee gunners had the range now, and shells were bursting close enough to raise concern for the general's safety. He ignored the fire and calmly continued his reconnaissance. To the astonishment of his men, Old Jack had this morning exchanged his old and faded and rather seedy uniform for a brand-new one, and "his unusually spruce appearance excited much attention and remark. . . ." When he finished the inspection, Jackson sent a note to his wife to prepare to leave immediately for home and safety. The Reverend Lacy saw Mrs. Jackson and the baby off on the morning train for Richmond. At the same time, for the second time in five months, Fredericksburg's citizens fled from the threat of Federal guns.

Jubal Early had already ordered his four brigades forward to a defensive line along the R.F. & P. tracks, which at this point ran parallel to the river and about a mile from it. Early set a line of pickets a half mile in advance along the River Road, overlooking the enemy's bridgehead. After conferring with General Lee, Jackson brought up Robert Rodes's division on Early's right at Hamilton's Crossing. Later A. P. Hill's division came up to a position behind Early, and Raleigh Colston marched up from his posting downriver at Moss Neck to form behind Rodes. Whatever the Federals' intentions here, they would face Jackson's entire Second Corps, some 38,000 strong in infantry. The day was cloudy and warming, with the threat of rain, very much like the day before.[27]

It was never General Lee's intention (nor had it been in December) to seriously oppose a Rappahannock crossing at the water's edge. The powerful Federal artillery on Stafford Heights would make a defense there too costly. He was satisfied to meet the attackers behind his fortifications on the high ground, with all the advantages of position. As to this crossing, Lee's first impression was that it was just what he had predicted two weeks before — the distraction by the Yankee cavalry on the upper Rappahannock so their infantry might "seize upon Fredericks-burg" by throwing bridges across there. If that was indeed the case, it was a scheme only marginally more imaginative than Burnside's in December. Lee telegraphed Richmond early that morning that "taken with the reports received from our left it looks like a general advance," although he could not yet be sure this was the main effort. "Troops not wanted south of James River had better be moved in this direction. . . ."

Whether or not this was the Federals' main effort, artillerist Porter Alexander had no doubts that it was serious. "It was clear that the building of this bridge meant business," he wrote later of his first thoughts that morning, "& that we were about to try the fortunes of another great battle." That would certainly be Stonewall Jackson's choice. A rumor was making the rounds, chaplain Lacy told him, that they would have to fall back in the face of this enemy offensive. "Who said that?" Jackson demanded. "No sir, we have not a thought of retreat. We will attack them!"

While considerable numbers of Federals were clearly visible along the north bank of the river, the actual buildup on the Confederate shore was hidden from view by the bluff there. Lee approved the massing of Jackson's corps in front of the two crossings, called up his artillery battalions from their winter camps, and pressed Richmond for Longstreet's return, although he surely recognized that his failure to obtain any advance warning of the Yankees' move meant there was little chance Longstreet's two divisions could reach him in time to make a difference. It looked as if he would have to play his hand with the cards he had dealt himself. Now he had to wait for Mr. F. J. Hooker to reveal the rest of his hand.[28]

One of Hooker's cards was turned up at midmorning when Jeb Stuart's dispatch at last reached Fredericksburg over the Confederate telegraph network. Stuart told Lee what he had found out the previous evening at Kelly's Ford. Thanks to the talkative Captain Schenofsky, the Yankee force at Kelly's was identified as General Howard's "division," 14,000 strong and with six batteries, "making toward Gordonsville." Lee passed this on to Richmond, along with his surmise that Stoneman's cavalry would probably cross farther up the Rappahannock and make Gordonsville and the Orange & Alexandria and Virginia Central railroads its targets.

Although now, on Day Three, Hooker's turning movement had been discovered and finally reported to Lee, the secret of its target — Lee's army rather than Lee's communications — was still a secret. Lee warned the War Department, "I have nothing to oppose to all that force up there except the two brigades of cavalry under Genl Stuart." He asked that all available troops in Richmond be sent forward "as rapidly as possible by rail and otherwise." They should be directed, he said, to Gordonsville.

From Early's position General Lee rode upriver to Lafayette McLaws's section of the line guarding Fredericksburg. In December Burnside had crossed his heaviest force here, marching through the town to assault Marye's Heights. This time there was no sign of an attempt to cross opposite the town. At McLaws's headquarters at about noon Lee had a long conversation with this Georgian who commanded one of the two divisions of Longstreet's still with the main army; the second was Richard Anderson's. In Longstreet's absence McLaws and Anderson reported directly to Lee and his headquarters staff.

General Lee, McLaws wrote his wife that night, "was very confident of his ability to beat back the enemy should our troops behave as well as they have usually done." The enemy was reported to have "crossed above us & below us," the commanding general explained. "Who is to blame is useless to inquire now. . . ." Lafayette McLaws was known more for dependability than for boldness in battle, and apparently Lee thought it necessary to brace and inspire him and his men to the task ahead. "General McLaws," he said, "let them know that it is a stern necessity now, it must be Victory or Death, for defeat would be ruinous."[29]

* *

IT WAS DAWN that Wednesday morning when Joe Hooker's flanking column took up its march from Kelly's Ford. Hooker himself turned back to army headquarters, assigning Henry Slocum to command the right wing in his absence. Alpheus Williams moved up to take Slocum's place at the head of the Twelfth Corps. The plan today was for the flanking column to divide, Meade's Fifth Corps taking a left turning just beyond Kelly's on a road that paralleled the Rappahannock and ran southeasterly to cross the Rapidan at Ely's Ford. The Twelfth Corps, followed by Howard's Eleventh, would continue straight on southward from Kelly's toward Culpeper Court House for four miles before also turning off southeasterly to strike the Rapidan farther upstream at Germanna Ford. Alfred Pleasonton's cavalry brigade would escort the march. Once across the Rapidan, the three corps were to reunite at Chancellorsville on Day Four. General Slocum's marching orders for April 29 called for both columns to seize their Rapidan crossings before nightfall.

Rising ground south of Kelly's Ford formed a kind of amphitheater, and as brigade after brigade came down to the bridge and crossed over and then formed up for the day's march, General Williams found "the picture was indeed exciting." Long winding lines of infantry converged on the crossing, while on the south bank "brigades were breaking masses and filing up the hills. Batteries of artillery and heavy columns of cavalry were forming large solid squares, which, seen from the elevations in advance, looked like great black blocks on the green surface, massed by some unseen power." All this to the accompaniment of a crackle of small-arms fire as the Yankee cavalry pickets pushed aside the thin screen of Rebel troopers keeping watch on the scene.[30]

Day Three would also see George Stoneman's cavalry corps finally set off on its much-delayed raid behind Confederate lines. Stoneman was directed to have his troopers across the river before 8:00 A.M. so they might get out ahead of the infantry column and screen its movements and gain a good start on their mission. By his reports, Stoneman had been primed for the move for more than a week, waiting only for the waters to recede; in fact only when the order came on April 28 did he start preparing. Stoneman was all night collecting his forces and his trains and issuing rations, and 8 o'clock came and went before the first Yankee trooper arrived at Kelly's Ford. Now infantry had priority on the pontoon bridge. Only when it was across and on its way did the cavalry take to the bridge or splash across the nearby ford. When all were across the engineers had orders to take up the bridge and carry it along for further use by the Fifth Corps. By day's end the Kelly's Ford crossing, which had accommodated more than 47,000 fighting men during the previous twenty-four hours, was entirely empty of Yankees and their works.[31]

Hooker expected that if his turning movement encountered opposition on the Rapidan it would be strongest at Germanna Ford. The B.M.I. reported the Confederates were building a bridge there. Hooker told Slocum to lead with his best troops. With the Twelfth Corps replacing the Eleventh in the van, Slocum named the veteran brigade of Thomas H. Ruger — 3rd Wisconsin, 27th Indiana, 2nd Massachusetts, 13th New Jersey, 107th New York — as his spearhead. Screening and scouting out front was the 6th New York cavalry.

South of the Rappahannock was pretty country, thought the Eleventh Corps' Justus Silliman. The road was good, and there were numerous well-stocked, well-fenced farmsteads with fields planted in grain. From their "thriving appearance" it was obvious that armies had not been through here before. At one farm gate smiling slaves offered buckets of cold water to the marchers. At another, "quite a collection of very substantial looking females" gawked at this seemingly endless column of Yankee soldiers. "What a great gob of men," one of them exclaimed. "This little affair kept up our spirits for a time," Private Silliman remarked. By now, in their diaries and letters home, the men had stopped complaining about the loads they were carrying. They had already stripped their packs down to size, and today they would consume the third of their eight days' rations, and somehow the whole business seemed more manageable than it had on Monday.

During the morning the 13th Virginia cavalry continued shadowing and sparring with the Yankee column marching southward from Kelly's Ford. To Jeb Stuart at his Culpeper Court House headquarters, it still seemed most likely this Yankee infantry — Howard's "division," he thought — was bound for Gordonsville by way of Culpeper. Probably it would cooperate with Stoneman's cavalry corps advancing down the railroad from its posting around Rappahannock Bridge.

To meet this substantial threat to Confederate communications Stuart continued holding his two cavalry brigades to the west, on the railroad between Culpeper and Brandy Station. It was not until 1:00 P.M. that Stuart learned the enemy's infantry was not advancing beyond Madden's Tavern, where the road to Germanna Ford branched off. He set out at once with Fitz Lee's troopers to investigate this new development. In the meantime, George Meade's Fifth Corps had made its turning toward Ely's Ford undetected. Halfway through Day Three, the essential secret of Joe Hooker's turning movement was still intact.[32]

A week or so earlier the Confederates had dispatched a party of pioneers, with a guarding force of infantry and cavalry, to Germanna Ford to build a bridge that General Lee wanted for his proposed march north into Maryland. Before the war a trestle bridge had crossed the Rapidan here, but during 1862's maneuverings it was burned, leaving only the tall stone piers in the streambed. The pioneers set up a sawmill and fashioned stringers to rest atop the piers and had cut planking and were preparing to start their bridge-building in these last days of April.

About 11:00 A.M. on this April 29 an old man who lived near the Rappahannock hurried up to the bridge site to say that Yankees were across at Kelly's Ford and marching this way in force. The bridge-builders insisted this could not be so; the cavalry pickets on the river would surely have sent them warning. The old man was equally insistent, saying he "knew a Yank when he saw one." Cavalryman Frank Robertson was sent up the road toward Madden's Tavern to investigate. He had gone perhaps a mile and was about to dismiss the old man's story when suddenly around a curve ahead came a squadron of Yankee cavalry. Lieutenant Robertson spun about and put spurs to his horse, pursued by cries of "Come here, Johnny!" and "Stop, you damned Reb!" and a fusillade of carbine fire.

Reaching Germanna Ford at a gallop, Robertson shouted a warning to his men and (as he put it) "crossed the river in plunges." The small party of pioneers and guards on the north bank took up their rifles and managed to drive off the pursuing troopers. At the sound of the firing General Ruger brought his brigade up fast and deployed for battle. He sent his two lead regiments into skirmish formation at the double-quick, the 3rd Wisconsin to the left of the road and the 2nd Massachusetts to the right. Pushing through scrub-oak thickets to the bluffs overlooking the river, they swept up the thirty Rebels trapped on the north bank without firing a shot.

On the south bank, however, the Confederates took cover in a road cut and made a fight of it. There was a bend in the river here and they were on the inside of the bend, and the Yankees simply extended their skirmish line around the outside of the bend until they had an enfilading fire of the defenders. "A few attempted to escape by running up the road, but our riflemen brought them down every time, and in a few minutes they hung out a white cloth . . . ," General Williams wrote. "We counted 125 prisoners." These were Mississippians from Carnot Posey's brigade and Virginians from William Mahone's. Barely a handful of the bridge-building party escaped. The Federal loss was one man killed and four wounded.[33]

The Rapidan was running high and very fast, and the main channel along the southern bank was a good four feet deep. Men likened it to a millrace. On Slocum's order Williams sent his lead division wading across. The water came up to the men's armpits and they held their rifles high, cartridge boxes slung on fixed bayonets, and plunged yelling through the icy torrent. "Never mind your pocketbooks, boys, but keep your powder dry," General Slocum called out. Two men were swept away and drowned. It was a spirited scene, Williams recalled, and Arthur Lumley, special artist for the *New York Illustrated News,* "made a pretty sketch of it." (Unfortunately, he added, Lumley would lose his entire portfolio of sketches during the ensuing fighting.) At 3:30 Slocum reported the seizure of Germanna Ford to Hooker and estimated that the rest of his column would be across the river by nightfall.

Crossing at the ford this way was both slow and dangerous, and there were the pack trains to consider, and the Twelfth Corps' engineers hit on the idea of finishing the job the Confederate bridge-builders had begun. All the stringers and the planking were conveniently at hand, and all the necessary tools. When they floated the first stringer out from the south bank, preparatory to hoisting it to the top of the first pier, it became so tightly wedged against the base of the pier by the rush of water that the idea of a footbridge began to look like the better solution.

A second, parallel stringer was lodged against a boulder eight feet upstream from the pier and held there firmly by the current. Planking was spiked down, and then the process was repeated alongside the next pier. Once the main channel with its racing current was spanned, it was simple enough to assemble new piers for the footbridge from the rocks in the shallows along the north bank. In less than two hours they were done, and the rest of the Twelfth Corps and all the Eleventh and all the pack trains crossed. Bonfires lighted the way. "This bridge built in this way, on the water," a proud engineer remembered, "was solid enough to support, dry shod, all the troops and the ammunition mules and horses."

"The rain began to fall before night," wrote General Williams, "but as we were all pretty wet and my boots full of water, it mattered little and the men were as cheerful as in gayest sunshine." In fact the last troops in the Yankee column were not across Germanna Ford even by midnight and perhaps not all were in a cheerful mood by then, but at least their boots were not full of water. From their bivouacs on the south bank Chancellorsville was less than ten miles away.[34]

*   *

IT WAS late morning, after Slocum's two corps had started off, before George Meade's Fifth Corps took up its march from Kelly's. Being last in line, it was unobserved by Stuart's cavalry scouts as it turned off on the road to Ely's Ford. Charles Griffin's division had the lead, followed by George Sykes's regulars. From Kelly's Ford to Ely's Ford was just over ten miles. The 8th Pennsylvania cavalry scouted the route ahead.

Meade's third division, under Andrew Humphreys, remained behind at Kelly's to help the engineers take up the pontoon bridge there and to act as a general rear guard. It was originally intended that the bridge would be reused at the Ely's Ford crossing, but there were so many delays at Kelly's during the day, especially the crossing by Stoneman's lumbering cavalry corps, that the bridge train was not ready to march until 11:30 that night. If the Fifth Corps was going to be across the Rapidan by nightfall as ordered, it would have to wade.

It was late afternoon when General Meade rode up to join his advance guard inspecting the scene at Ely's Ford. Except for a dozen mounted Rebel pickets watching them from the far shore, the place was deserted. Meade quickly sent his Pennsylvania troopers splashing across the river, and the pickets turned and trotted off down the road toward Chancellorsville. Ely's Ford fell into Federal hands bloodlessly.

At 5:00 P.M. Meade reported the crossing to Hooker. "The ford is deep and I fear impracticable for infantry," he added. "I shall try it and by means of rafts try to set my men over." However, when he learned that Slocum was already across at Germanna Ford, Meade realized that he had no time to build rafts and could not wait for his pontoon train, and he ordered the troops to cross at the ford the best way they could.

"The water was about three feet deep or a little more," Sergeant Charles Ward of Griffin's division explained in a letter home, "and we took off our pants, slung clothes & ammunition on our shoulders &c and after getting over, we went to the top of a hill . . . and pitched a tent & built good fires." James Houghton of the same division described "all the yelping and yelling mingled in with some horid oathes; any one would think that the devels school was out for noon." Ely's was a rough and rocky ford and the current was swift, and men were tumbled off their feet, only to fetch up against a lifeguard line of cavalrymen stationed across the river downstream. The young drummer boy of the 146th New York, Jimmie Shaw, lost his grip on the man carrying him across and sailed off downriver clinging to his drum right past the cavalry lifeguards. He was finally rescued when his colonel, Kenner Gerrard, rode into the river and scooped him up.

This being largely unspoiled country, the men found plenty of fence rails to stoke their bonfires. Captain Jonathan Hager of the regulars thought it a strange and eerie scene. It was dark now, and on the far shore the bonfires cast great leaping shadows. "The men in their drawers," he wrote, "looked more like ghosts than hearty solid warriors." When it began to rain few cared about the added discomfort. "The men dried their clothes, boiled their coffee, laughed over the incidents of the day, and at 10 o'clock the camp was silent in sleep. . . ."[35]

"By dint of great exertion" — but in fact with exaggerated deliberation — General Stoneman had finally gotten his cavalrymen, now 7,400 strong, across Kelly's Ford by 5 o'clock that afternoon. There he called a halt to confer with his officers so as to gain what he described in his report as "a thorough understanding of what we were to do and where we were each to go."

The day before, at Morrisville, Hooker had handed Stoneman a new set of instructions that modified his original April 12 instructions for the raid. Their basic thrust was unchanged — Stoneman was to disrupt and destroy Lee's railroad lifelines, both the Richmond, Fredericksburg & Potomac and the Virginia Central, and block his retreat. The difference now was that he would divide his force into two columns. Stoneman's assertion that he thoroughly understood his new orders, and that he shared his grasp of them with his officers, would prove to be a considerable overstatement.

Stoneman and his advance got no farther that evening than Madden's Tavern on the Culpeper Road, four miles beyond Kelly's. Some of his men paused on the way to plunder the home of the Kelly who gave his name to Kelly's Ford. "He is said to be a rank rebel, who fired on our men as they were crossing," a Pennsylvania cavalryman said in justification.

Except for a brief brush with the 13th Virginia that was keeping watch on the Yankee advance, Stoneman made no contact with the enemy on April 29. Had he reached Madden's Tavern a few hours earlier he might have performed a real service that day by driving off Jeb Stuart's command that was probing for information there.

It was midafternoon when Stuart reached Madden's from Culpeper. Sighting the column of Yankee infantry marching easterly, toward Germanna Ford, he lashed out to break into the column and take prisoners for identification. For this purpose he was fortunate to hit the seam where the Eleventh Corps followed along on the tail of the Twelfth. Stuart's men came back with prisoners from both corps, and for good measure some from Meade's Fifth Corps. Apparently Meade had sent a party cross-country to make contact with Slocum. Stuart hurried back to Culpeper with this important intelligence, but arrived too late to telegraph it to General Lee; once again, a section of his roundabout telegraph link with Fredericksburg had shut down for the night.[36]

Between 5 and 6 o'clock that afternoon the survivors of the bridge-building detail at Germanna Ford, and the cavalry picket at Ely's, reached the camps of Richard Anderson's division to report Yankees on the Rapidan. Couriers quickly carried the news to General Lee at headquarters. By 6:30 Lee was pondering its meaning.

While it added substantially to Stuart's morning report of Federal infantry across the Rappahannock at Kelly's Ford, this was still very incomplete intelligence. It spoke only of Federal cavalry seen at the two Rapidan fords, and of some infantry at Germanna. None was identified. "Their intention, I presume, is to turn our left, and probably to get into our rear," Lee telegraphed Jefferson Davis. What was not yet clear was whether this was a direct threat to his army or only reinforced cavalry intent on raiding in the rear areas. Was this Stoneman and Howard? Was Gordonsville still a Yankee target? Jeb Stuart's report, which would have ended the uncertainty, was lying unsent in a telegraph office waiting for daylight on April 30.

Lee sent dispatches that evening to Generals McLaws and Anderson, holding the center and left of his lines. McLaws was to shift to the position back of Fredericksburg, where the Federals had been repulsed in December, and also to prepare to change position the next day "to strengthen our left." Anderson, whose brigades under Carnot Posey and William Mahone were posted the farthest west, toward the Rapidan, was ordered to take "the strongest line you can" in the vicinity of Chancellorsville to meet any advance by the enemy from the Rapidan crossings. Like McLaws, Anderson was to be ready to change position "in consequence of the enemy having come in between us and General Stuart." Before he actually committed any additional troops to the left, however, Lee would have to await fuller information in the morning. Thus General Hooker would begin Day Four with the initiative still firmly in his grip.

When he told Mr. Davis that evening, almost ruefully, "Our scattered condition favors their operations," Robert E. Lee came as close as he ever came to acknowledging that he had miscalculated enemy intentions that spring of 1863. By allowing Longstreet to besiege Suffolk he virtually precluded one quarter of his army from engaging in the fighting on the Rappahannock. In his overconfidence he underestimated his opponent, failing to anticipate either Hooker's movements or their direction. In falling for a ruse he left his army poorly positioned to meet the attack when it came. His earlier warning to General McLaws of the "stern necessity" of the moment might have been a warning to himself as well.[37]

* *

BY NOON on April 29 Joe Hooker was back at his Falmouth headquarters from Kelly's Ford. He had to be delighted with his campaign so far. His particular concern, the weather, had so far caused him no concern. By day's end every formation in the Army of the Potomac would be exactly where he had planned it to be. The flying-column experiment seemed successful. The turning movement had exceeded even his most optimistic expectations. Dan Butterfield's hoax message had opened the way: not only had the column crossed the Rappahannock on schedule and without opposition, it had then seized both crossings of the Rapidan with trifling loss — and again exactly on schedule. Hooker could not know it, but his flanking column had been on the march for no less than sixty hours before General Lee issued his first order in regard to it.

"They have been taken napping, undoubtedly . . . ," General Patrick remarked in his diary after talking to Hooker. "Unless they are a great deal stronger than I think they are, they *must* be driven if Hooker gets across & in their rear, by their left flank — & I think he will." Or as Dan Butterfield put it with nice brevity in a message to John Sedgwick that afternoon, "Everything goes beautifully above."

A headquarters link with the flanking column was secured when General Meade's cavalry made a side excursion to Richard's Ford on the Rappahannock, a mile above where the Rapidan enters, and captured the unsuspecting 35-man Confederate picket post there. The link would be strengthened and shortened the next day by way of U.S. Ford. But even now Hooker had notice of the successes of Slocum and Meade.

Darius Couch's two Second Corps divisions — Hancock's and French's — had moved up to Banks's Ford in secrecy the day before. Now, on April 29, they continued on upstream to U.S. Ford, repairing the road as they went for a pontoon train to follow. On Hooker's instructions, today Couch's men marched and worked with no effort at concealment. With both right and left wings of his army safely across the river, Hooker was happy enough to give General Lee another crossing (or another diversion) to worry about. By Hooker's schedule, Dan Sickles's Third Corps would follow Couch's track on April 30. Together Couch's and Sickles's five divisions would add up to a 30,400-man reinforcement slated for the turning movement.

Sergeant Franklin Marcha, 122nd Pennsylvania, Third Corps, was confident that their turn had finally come. "We expect to meet the enemy tomorrow," he confided to his diary that night, "when the ball will be opened & the union army will *show* old Jeff Davis that the last Fredericksburg battle did not in the least discourage the troops."[38]

While the First and Sixth corps crossings below Fredericksburg had certainly not gone as planned that early morning, in the end their lodgment was made perfectly secure. By nightfall all of Wadsworth's division and all of Brooks's were across the river — 16,800 fighting men, along with Battery D, 2nd U.S. Artillery. In support on the northern shore stood an enormous array of artillery, ninety-six pieces in all, and the other five divisions — 23,800 men — of the two corps. There seemed no danger that the lodgment could be driven into the Rappahannock.

A gunner in one of the supporting batteries marveled at the spectacle. Through the afternoon masses of men funneled down to the bridges to cross in dense columns. Right and left stretched guns in battery. Two balloons floated high overhead, and signalmen cast their urgent flag messages. "And then in addition to this," the gunner wrote, "when I mention the singing of birds, the leafing of trees, and the mildness of the day, you can imagine what a magnificent sight there is presented for the admiration and enjoyment of us soldiers."

By report from his pickets across the river, Sedgwick told Hooker that evening, the enemy was massing primarily against Bully Brooks's division on the right of the bridgehead. General Wadsworth on the left at Smithfield was feeling aggressive. "I think we should make a bold dash south westerly at daylight," Wadsworth urged, and John Reynolds endorsed the idea. This, however, was contrary to Joe Hooker's battle plan.

Dan Butterfield, speaking for the general, explained to Sedgwick that if the enemy was indeed massing forces in front of Brooks that was all to the good. The maneuvers of the flanking column "now in progress the general hopes will compel the enemy to fight him on his own ground" — ground, that is, of Hooker's choosing. "He has no desire to make the general engagement where you are, in front of Brooks or Wadsworth." That, to General Hooker, would only be the senseless December battle all over again. What was instead truly important was "whether or not the enemy are being held in your front."[39]

Intelligence-gathering efforts intensified now that battle lines were drawn. Hooker's complex plan depended for success on knowing Lee's response to each Federal move — where and when he shifted his forces, in what strength and in what place. Every move Hooker had made in these first three days was made according to a carefully worked-out schedule. In the days to come, however, events would increasingly be shaped by circumstances. The more he could learn of the Confederates' movements, the more he could shape those circumstances to his liking. What he wanted, more than anything else (as he told Sedgwick), was to fight by choice and on ground of his own choosing.

Hooker regarded it as vital to know, for example, the whereabouts every minute of Longstreet's two divisions. He telegraphed General Peck at Suffolk to say he had commenced his operations, which might result in Longstreet's divisions being recalled by Lee. That, he told Peck, would "afford you an opportunity to push or hold them." Peck replied that he thought he could hold Longstreet for some time, "which will favor your operations very materially."

Throughout the day Yankee signal stations downstream from Falmouth reported scores of sightings of Confederate troop movements as Jackson assembled his corps to confront the invaders in their bridgehead. At 4:30 P.M. signalman Peter A. Taylor at Station F reported "Twelve Regts. Infantry and sixty wagons & ambulances moving up toward Hamilton's Crossing from below." Professor Lowe in balloon *Washington* hovered over Franklin's Crossing to describe Rebel positions across the river. Aeronaut E. S. Allen in balloon *Eagle* opposite Fredericksburg reported on enemy defenses there. Colonel Sharpe of the B.M.I. interrogated the prisoners taken by Brooks's and Wadsworth's troops. "The present attack was not suspected up to the moment of the completion of the pontoon bridges by officers or men," Sharpe reported. Up until daylight that morning, he added, there had been "no movement" in Jackson's three divisions posted downriver from Fredericksburg.

On Hooker's order aeronauts Lowe and Allen made ascensions after dark to locate Confederate positions by their campfires. Balloon *Eagle* was to be towed by wagon and team the next morning to Banks's Ford to observe the enemy there. What most interested Hooker now was how Lee would react to the flanking column bound for Chancellorsville. How much of Jackson's command could Sedgwick's left wing hold at Fredericksburg? He ordered the most careful watch kept on the roads west of Fredericksburg that led toward Chancellorsville. On Day Four, for the first time in the campaign, he would be making decisions based on the shifting circumstances of the case.[40]

Two years later, testifying on his wartime service before the Joint Committee on the Conduct of the War, Joe Hooker spoke pridefully of this operation carried out with "so much secrecy and despatch that the head of the columns had reached the crossings of the Rapidan before the enemy was apprised of their approach." And, he went on, "soldiers and citizens who give the subject their attention will appreciate the sublimity of their exertions."

Indeed, a British soldier-historian of the day, a Colonel MacDougal, went so far as to compare Hooker's crossing of the Rappahannock and Rapidan with such historic feats as Hannibal's passage of the Rhone, Alexander's of the Hydaspes, Wellington's of the Adour, and Napoleon's of the Po and the Danube. Perhaps more meaningful was the observation on the subject by the thoughtful and perceptive chronicler of Lee's army, artillerist Porter Alexander. In his *Personal Recollections* of the war Alexander wrote, "On the whole I think this plan was decidedly the best strategy conceived in any of the campaigns ever set on foot against us."[41]

7

Day of Decisions

MAJOR GENERAL Richard Heron Anderson of South Carolina was forty-one years old and was in his twenty-first year of army service. A West Point classmate of fellow First Corps generals Longstreet and McLaws, Dick Anderson had fought in Mexico and on the frontier in the old 2nd Dragoons, and had already taken two wounds for the Confederacy in this war. All his service in the Army of Northern Virginia had been under Longstreet, who rated him courageous enough certainly but sometimes indolent about his duties. Now Anderson was facing the greatest challenge of his military life. His division guarded the army's left flank and rear, and by report a Federal force of unknown but he suspected substantial strength was bearing down on him.

Three of Anderson's five brigades formed the extreme left of Lee's Rappahannock River line. Farthest upstream, at U.S. Ford, were William Mahone's Virginians and Carnot Posey's Mississippians. The Alabama brigade of Cadmus Wilcox was at Banks's Ford. E. A. Perry's Florida brigade was on the Orange Plank Road five miles west of Fredericksburg, and Ambrose Ransom Wright's Georgians were on the Telegraph Road eight miles to the south. Whatever direction the Yankee flanking column might take, the first Rebels it would encounter would likely be Dick Anderson and his men.

When he learned in the early evening of April 29 that Federal cavalry, and a sighting of infantry, were as close on his left as the Rapidan crossings, General Lee had been quick to alert Anderson. He told him to fall back from his exposed position at U.S. Ford and take the strongest line he could "so as to cover the road leading from Chancellorsville down the river." To rivet Anderson's attention Lee added pointedly, "I wish you to go forward yourself and attend this matter." By 9 o'clock Anderson had his orders and was acting on them. By midnight he was at Chancellorsville himself and meeting with Mahone and Posey. Leaving a small force to deny the Yankees the U.S. Ford crossing for as long as possible, they had the rest of their men posted across the roads leading to Germanna and Ely's fords. To add weight to his defense, Anderson called up a third brigade, "Rans" Wright's Georgians. "You can imagine how I spent the night, expecting the enemy to come upon us at every moment," one of Mahone's Virginians wrote home. "There was not much sleep for us, I can assure you. . . ."[1]

Nor was there much sleep for Jeb Stuart and his troopers. At some point on April 29 when his telegraphic link with Fredericksburg was working, Stuart had received a directive from Lee. It was necessarily a very general directive, for Lee then knew only that Yankee infantry to the number of 14,000, with six batteries, had crossed the Rappahannock at Kelly's Ford. He charged Stuart with protecting "public property" on the railroad in the direction of Gordonsville — and also with rejoining the main army. However concerned he might be about his communications, General Lee was determined not to have to fight a battle blind, without the eyes of his cavalry.

He left it to Stuart just how to meet these two objectives, and Stuart made an important decision. At Madden's Tavern that afternoon he had gained a good look at the size of the Federal column, and tracked its path toward the Rapidan, and concluded that it was a major threat, or at least an immediate threat, to the main army. Stoneman, with his lethargic movements that day, was yet to reveal his hand. Stuart therefore assigned Rooney Lee the task of shadowing and harassing Stoneman and his raiders, but with only a minimal force — the 9th and 13th Virginia cavalries and six guns of the horse artillery, perhaps a thousand men in all. With the balance of his two brigades Stuart would join Lee at Fredericksburg. Like the good soldier he was, he instinctively elected to march toward the sound of the guns.

With Yankees on the most direct road eastward, Stuart in setting out from Brandy Station and Culpeper had to swing around to the south and cross the Rapidan farther upstream. And if he was not to be cut off he must not delay a moment. With Fitz Lee's brigade and that part of Rooney Lee's not assigned to watch Stoneman, he set off on a night march. It was dark and rainy with a chill wind "as we rode on into the night," recorded Captain Justus Scheibert, the Prussian military observer who had attached himself to Stuart's headquarters. By midnight on April 29 the cavalry column was at Raccoon Ford on the Rapidan, some ten miles above Germanna Ford. "The high, rocky bank could be seen rising majestically as a dark background beyond the river," Scheibert wrote, "while we could scarcely see the leading horseman . . . in the darkness and dead silence. Fortunately, he knew the ford and led us safely to the opposite side." It had been a long day and men and horses were exhausted, and Stuart made a cheerless bivouac in the dripping woods for a few hours' sleep. At first light on April 30 — Day Four — they took up their march again.[2]

In these early morning hours Dick Anderson too made an important decision. Lee's orders of the previous evening had charged him with taking the strongest line he could guarding the way eastward from Chancellorsville — that is, the Orange Plank Road and the Orange Turnpike. Pulling back Mahone's men and Posey's on the U.S. Ford Road during the night, Anderson collected them where it intersected the Plank Road, at Chancellorsville. At daylight Rans Wright's brigade joined them there.

In the cold light of day, however, General Anderson had second thoughts about the place. While he could take blocking positions there across the Germanna and Ely's Ford roads well enough, visibility was poor in this aptly named Wilderness. His flanks might be turned without warning. There was little room for artillery to deploy except right at the crossroads. All in all it looked like a bad place to make a stand, especially as he expected he would be outnumbered. At 6:00 A.M. he started Posey and Wright back along the Plank Road, and Mahone along the Turnpike, to take up a better position in the open three and a half miles to the east, near Tabernacle and Zoan churches. Acting on the discretion in Lee's orders, Dick Anderson determined on his own that there would be no battle for the Chancellorsville crossroads on April 30.[3]

General Lee awakened with a trace of the chest pains that had troubled him earlier in the month, and for a time that morning conducted army business while resting in his headquarters tent. Stonewall Jackson reported to him there to discuss their course. By now Lee had Stuart's delayed dispatch of the day before reporting the strength of the Federals on the Rapidan as three army corps. It gave him, at last, a glimpse of his opponent's intentions. He telegraphed President Davis in Richmond, "Meade, Slocum, and Howard commanded corps. Object evidently to turn our left. If I had Longstreet's division, would feel safe."

Apparently the communications link between Richmond and Longstreet in southside Virginia was no better than between Lee and Jeb Stuart, and it would not be until late this Thursday, thirty-six hours after Lee called for him, that Longstreet learned he was wanted on the Rappahannock. He replied that he must retrieve his trains from their foraging expeditions and disengage his troops from their siege lines at Suffolk, and all that would take time. It would not be until nightfall on May 3 that Longstreet started north with Hood and Pickett.

With Stuart's dispatch in hand, Lee's first concern on April 30 was for

Dick Anderson's division on the Chancellorsville front. He sent Anderson the army's chief engineer, Lieutenant Colonel William P. Smith, along with Captain Samuel R. Johnston of the engineer corps, to help him lay out his defensive line. To brace that line he hurried along Porter Alexander's artillery battalion from its winter quarters. Then Lee rode with Jackson to the Rappahannock to observe the Yankees' bridgehead there. It was now clear that Hooker had divided his army, and that probably the smaller part of it held the lodgment below Fredericksburg. Old Jack proposed that they attack it. Surely, he said, his Second Corps on the scene was larger than whatever force the enemy had managed to get across the river since yesterday.

This same issue had come up following Burnside's repulse back in December, when Jackson proposed a counterattack to drive the beaten Federals into the river. Lee's response now was the same as it had been in December. Any assault launched across the open plain toward the river would face the all-powerful Federal artillery on Stafford Heights. "It will be hard to get at the enemy," Lee observed, "and harder still to get away if we succeed in driving them to the river." Then he added, in deference to his trusted lieutenant, "But, General, if you think you can effect anything I will give orders for the attack." Jackson thought a moment and then asked for time to make a careful reconnaissance of the enemy's position. Lee agreed, and rode back to army headquarters on the Mine Road to wait while Old Jack studied the matter.[4]

* *

IT WAS just after 4:00 A.M., first light, when General Meade put his advance guard, the 8th Pennsylvania cavalry, on the road to Chancellorsville. The morning was foggy and gray with a light rain, described as "cold and disagreeable" by one of Meade's men. From the Rapidan to Chancellorsville by the Ely's Ford Road was five miles. At the four-mile mark, where a byway to U.S. Ford branched off to the north, the Pennsylvania cavalrymen surprised a company of the 12th Virginia of Mahone's brigade on picket duty. Most of the pickets, including their three company officers, had taken shelter from the weather in a country schoolhouse, and they paid for their carelessness. Caught unaware inside their shelter, they were ordered to throw out their guns and surrender. The twenty-five Virginians were mortified to discover they had been taken captive by eight grinning Yankee troopers.

Not everyone on picket duty that morning was so easy a mark. Further on there was a sharp fight at a rough breastworks that only ended with a charge by a full squadron of the troopers. One defender was shot through the head and killed, and Sergeant John Sale and five of his fellows ran off into the woods, where they dodged bullets and tried to find their way to safety. "I thought I was gone," Sergeant Sale admitted, ". . . so we took all our letters and tore them up and made away with our guns and accoutrements so they would not benefit the enemy and started again." Yankee shouts echoed all around them in the dark woods. Finally they found a pathway and a direction and caught up with their regiment just as it was withdrawing from Chancellorsville.

The 12th Virginia soon gained at least a measure of revenge. It was serving as rear guard for Mahone's column on its march along the Turnpike when the 8th Pennsylvania came up again and attempted another charge. Smartly deploying in a double skirmish line across the road, the Virginians sent the troopers scattering, wounding three. They were repulsed, reported General Mahone, "so effectually as to leave us free from any further annoyance. . . ." Colonel Thomas Devin of the cavalry was content to send back to General Meade that he had secured Chancellorsville.[5]

At Ely's Ford Meade had roused his Fifth Corps infantry at 4:00 A.M. but allowed them two and a half hours before the day's march began. Captain Charles Bowers of the 32nd Massachusetts had a resourceful company cook who used the respite profitably. Having expropriated "a good fat hen" along the road the day before, he made what Captain Bowers described as "a nice stew of it. This afforded us a splendid breakfast." Captain Jonathan Hager of the regulars was not so fortunate. His breakfast was "two or three mouthfuls of a compound of fat pork & hard bread fried together." It was welcome enough, he added, "but was terribly insufficient. . . ." However they fared, the men of George Sykes's and Charles Griffin's divisions were on the road by 6:30. Andrew Humphreys's division, so long delayed at Kelly's Ford, was still a day's march behind.

The morning's bag of prisoners had been collected by the cavalry in a little clearing by the side of the road, and when the first of Meade's infantry came up they stopped to gawk at them. It was not often they had a chance to see their foes close up. These Virginians were uniformed well enough, Captain Bowers thought, and contrary to rumor they showed no signs of starvation. He reported that one of them spoke up and asked his captors if they thought General Lee could take Washington. "We told him *no*. Neither can you take Richmond said he, and there is no use your trying."

Hooker required his flanking column to uncover and secure the vital link with the north bank at U.S. Ford, and Meade sent a squadron of his Pennsylvania cavalrymen to scout the road there. The report came back — somewhat garbled, as it proved — that Rebels to the strength of a brigade blocked the way. Meade ordered Sykes's division to clear the road. This proved to be only a long detour, wrote one of Sykes's disgusted men. "We found the rebels had flown." At midmorning they reached U.S. Ford and called across to the Second Corps troops there. Captain William Folwell of the engineers, struggling to haul his bridge train to the crossing site, looked across the fog-bound river and was pleased to recognize "our own men . . . on the *rebel shore*." Having secured the crossing, Sykes turned back to join Griffin at Chancellorsville.

The good news was sent to Hooker: the ford was secured and "General Slocum is moving cautiously but steadily down the plank road toward Chancellorsville. . . . General Meade's Corps is about a mile from Chancellorsville and our cavalry are in advance. They show a small force. . . ." A confident Joe Hooker telegraphed the railroad man Herman Haupt in Washington that he should be prepared to start rebuilding the railroad bridge across the Rappahannock at Fredericksburg two days hence.[6]

Off to the south Henry Slocum's troops were toiling along the Germanna Plank Road toward Chancellorsville. It was toilsome indeed, for this was (as General Williams described it) "an old, worn-out plank road, full of holes and gullies and very slippery from the rain," and much of what planking remained was deeply overlaid with mud. Yet however tiring the marching might be, Williams noticed that there was no straggling. Everyone realized that out there somewhere was Rebel cavalry, and any laggards were likely to end up in Richmond's infamous Belle Isle prison camp.

As he was passing on his way to join Lee, Jeb Stuart attempted to delay Slocum's column, but he had only limited success. Cavalry was seldom very effective fighting alert and well-led marching infantry — infantry riflemen were an overmatch against mounted troopers — and so it was this day. Stuart had sent the 3rd Virginia cavalry under Colonel Thomas H. Owen on ahead during the night to track the Yankees and to try and block their way. This was the same Colonel Owen who had led the initial dashing charge in the big cavalry fight at Kelly's Ford back on March 17. They engaged near the Wilderness Tavern, where the Germanna Plank Road intersected the Orange Turnpike. Owen's troopers first sparred with Duncan McVicar's 6th New York cavalry, with charge and countercharge and men unhorsed on both sides. There was "a spirited fight" for possession of the bridge across Wilderness Run, where McVicar lost one man killed and four wounded, but then the infantry came up and Owen had to give way.

Stuart himself was on the scene now and he opened on the Yankee column with dismounted sharpshooters and a section of horse artillery. General Williams's Twelfth Corps had the advance, and he detached the

28th Pennsylvania in skirmish formation to drive off this annoyance. The affair was over soon enough. They "got up a very brisk engagement, in which we lost a few men and the Rebels more," Williams wrote. "A second regiment succeeded in brushing away both skirmishers and artillery and we were not further molested during the day." Stuart continued on his way, and the Federals plodded on toward Chancellorsville.[7]

Many of the citizens living in the path of the invaders had fled, and whatever they left behind was used up or plundered by the marchers almost as a matter of routine. "We were all surprised at the great quantities of grain that had been sown and was now up and growing finely," Private Silliman wrote. "It made excellent pasture for our horses at every halting place." Artillerist Darwin Cody remarked on the number of abandoned farms they encountered, and added, "Our boys soon rob the hen roosts and bee hives." Troops of the advance broke into Simms's store near the Wilderness Tavern, "extracting every thing valuable therefrom, not even sparing the poor mans account books and due bills which were scattered many miles along the road." Apparently the proprietor of the Wilderness Tavern had more forewarning, for no Yankee reported finding anything in that establishment to slake his thirst.[8]

It was noon when the van of Meade's corps reached Chancellorsville. Slocum's column — Twelfth Corps, followed by the Eleventh — arrived in midafternoon. Chancellorsville, explained General Williams, was "simply a Virginia 'ville' of one large brick house on the northwest corner of cross roads, built by one Chancellor." The Chancellor currently in residence was Fannie Pound Chancellor, widow of the brother of the original builder of the place, George Chancellor. Seven of the widow Chancellor's nine children were with her there — one young son and six unmarried daughters, all of them attractive.

That winter the Chancellor girls had been the apples of every Confederate eye. In the big house they entertained the likes of Dick Anderson and "Little Billy" Mahone and the dashing Mississippian Carnot Posey. Jeb Stuart was a visitor too, and all the girls fell in love with Jeb Stuart. The youngest, fourteen-year-old Sue Chancellor, found him "so nice and always a pleasant word for everyone . . . always so charming. . . ."

All that had come to an end early that morning when the Confederates bid their hasty farewells and marched away, and it was a final end. "Presently, the Yankees began to come, and they said that Chancellorsville was to be General Hooker's headquarters. . . ." Various neighbors fleeing the enemy had sought shelter at Chancellorsville, and there were sixteen people in the house when the Yankees came. Their greeting was cold, one of the Federals reported: "They were not at all abashed or intimidated, scolded audibly and reviled bitterly." Soon they were all

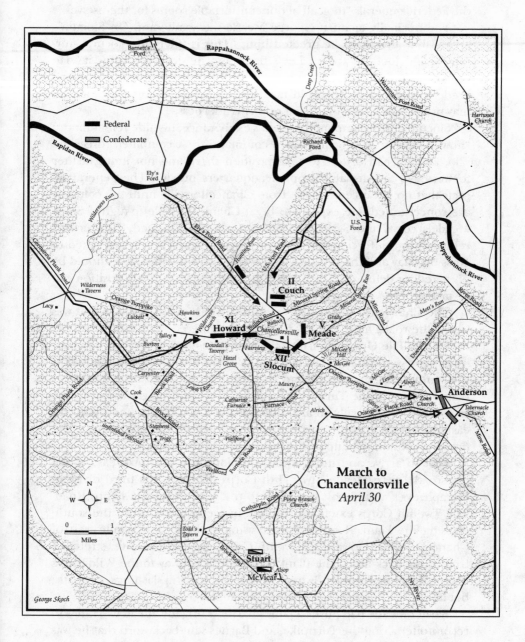

Federal
Confederate

Rappahannock River

Barnett's Ford

Deep Creek

Warrenton Post Road

Richard's Ford

Hartwood Church

Rapidan River

Ely's Ford

U.S. Ford

Wilderness Run

Ely's Ford Road

Hunting Run

U.S. Ford Road

Rappahannock River

River Road

Germanna Plank Road

Wilderness Tavern

Orange Turnpike

Lacy

Luckett

Hawkins

Wilderness Church

Bullock Road

II
Couch

Mineral Spring Road

Mineral Spring Run

Mine Road

Mott's Run

Tulley

Burton

XI
Howard

Bullock

Chancellorsville

Dowdall's Tavern

Fairview

Hazel Grove

V
Meade

Grady

McGee's Hill

Duerson's Mill Road

Carpenter

Brock Road

Lewis's Run

XII
Slocum

Maury

McGee

McGee

Orange Turnpike

Lewis

Alsop

Anderson

Cook

Catharine Furnace

Fumace Road

Silver

Alrich

Zoan Church

Tabernacle Church

Stephens

unfinished railroad

Trigg

Wellford

Orange

Plank Road

Mine Road

Wellford

Furnace Road

Piney Branch Church

March to
Chancellorsville
April 30

N
W   E
S

0   1

Miles

Catharpin Road

Todd's Tavern

Brock Road

Stuart

Alsop

McVicar

Ny River

George Skoch

crowded into one wing of the house, Sue Chancellor remembered, and the Federal generals "took all of our comfortable rooms for themselves."[9]

The normally taciturn George Meade was exuberant. On Slocum's arrival that afternoon he greeted him, "This is splendid, Slocum; hurrah for old Joe! We are on Lee's flank and he does not know it." He urged Slocum to continue his march along the Plank Road toward Fredericksburg, and he would take the Turnpike, "or *vice versa*, as you may prefer," and "we will get out of this Wilderness."·

Slocum curtly dampened Meade's exuberance; his aide remembered "how his face fell." Slocum was to command their combined forces, he said, and he had orders to take position there and not move farther forward. As the dispatch from headquarters put it, "The general directs that no advance be made from Chancellorsville until the columns are concentrated. He expects to be at Chancellorsville to-night." Since Meade's corps and Slocum's were already concentrated, Hooker was referring to reinforcements from the Second and Third corps slated to cross that day and the next at U.S. Ford. Meanwhile the place should be prepared for defense: "The maps indicate that a formidable position can be taken there."

The Chancellor house had been built where it was because that was where the roads met. The Ely's Ford Road entered the crossroads from the north. The Orange Turnpike formed the eastern arm of the crossroads. The western arm was the Orange Plank Road, which looped off to the south at the crossroads and then ran east for five and a half miles before rejoining the Turnpike. Entering two hundred yards east of the crossroads and virtually an arm of it was the River Road, running northeasterly toward the Rappahannock and on into Fredericksburg. The flanking column took up postings covering all these roads.

First to arrive and most advanced, along the Turnpike east of the crossroads, were Meade's two Fifth Corps divisions. His third division, Humphreys's, would halt two miles to the rear on the Ely's Ford Road. The Twelfth Corps extended the line in a curve around to the south, crossing the Plank Road and then swinging back to it a mile west of Chancellorsville. Howard's Eleventh Corps, the last to arrive, stretched from there back along the Plank Road about halfway to the Wilderness Tavern. In some commands trees were felled to form slashings, or abatis, but no serious defenses were begun that night.

Earlier Meade had pushed James Barnes's brigade ahead two miles to reconnoiter along the Turnpike, and Barnes sent back word that he was facing a Rebel line of battle on some high ground back of a little stream called Mott's Run. They looked as if they wanted to make a fight of it, Barnes said (this was Little Billy Mahone's rear guard, in no mood to be further harassed by Yankees that day), and he wanted support. Meade told him to break off and return: the orders were not to bring on a battle. That night he summed up his feelings on the matter in a letter to Mrs. Meade. "We are across the river and have out-manoeuvered the enemy," he told her, "but are not yet out of the woods."[10]

*   *

JOE HOOKER'S decision would draw other critics besides General Meade — especially latter-day critics — yet it was a decision very much in line with his plan of battle. The conditions he wanted for battle were not yet right. He wanted, first, to force Lee out of his fortifications by cutting or threatening to cut his communications, and by report that had not yet happened. When the battle did come he wanted it to be by his choice and at a time and place of his choosing — and, if at all possible, he wanted to fight it defensively. No more reckless frontal attacks; make General Lee do the attacking for once. Hooker wanted to be on the scene himself to command, to study the ground and to make the decisions and to lead by example as he had done on other battlefields. Later, referring to that day, he spoke of "my limited knowledge of the country." Finally, uneasy about the makeup of his flanking column, he wanted it braced by the veteran fighters in Couch's and Sickles's corps.

In any event, Hooker calculated time to be in his favor. His campaign was in its fourth day, and his flying column across the river was self-sufficient for four more days, and U.S. Ford was now in hand as a route for resupply. He expected at any time to hear that Stoneman's raiders had severed the Confederates' railroad lifeline, which ought to put intense pressure on Lee to act. Tomorrow would be soon enough to initiate a further advance. That was his timetable.

Perhaps had Hooker remained with the flanking column instead of returning to Falmouth to oversee Sedgwick's river crossing, he might have cast his eye on the scene at Chancellorsville and decided to abandon his timetable and push ahead that afternoon. Being there, perhaps he would have reacted with an enthusiasm akin to Meade's. But he was not there, and it is not surprising that distant as he was he saw things differently. Thus far his timetable had worked to perfection and he saw no reason to change it. Fighting Joe Hooker's decision to hold his flanking column at Chancellorsville on the afternoon of April 30 was not a decision he had any trouble making.

He was impatient for results from Stoneman, however. That afternoon John Reynolds, whose headquarters on the Federal left had a view of Hamilton's Crossing across the river, reported on Rebel railroad activity. Two trains were seen to come up from the south, and that evening he

181

added, "The railroad seems to be busy to-day." In passing on these messages to Hooker, Dan Butterfield observed, "These dispatches seem to indicate no disturbance to the RR yet."[11]

George Stoneman, when he finally set out on his raid, would consistently move in mysterious ways. He divided his force into halves, giving William Averell 3,400 men with which to disperse the Rebel cavalry said to be off to the west, along the Orange & Alexandria Railroad. (These were the 1,000 troopers Jeb Stuart had left with Rooney Lee.) That done, Averell was to rejoin Stoneman. Meanwhile, with the 3,500 men in the commands of David Gregg and John Buford, Stoneman would open the assault on Lee's communications.

According to Stoneman's official report, he set off from Madden's Tavern at 4:00 A.M. on April 30. The problem of crossing a river on horseback seemed to baffle General Stoneman all that month of April, and when he went into bivouac at 10:00 P.M. after crossing the Rapidan at Raccoon Ford, he had marched all of ten miles. "Our crossing was a grand sight," one of his troopers wrote proudly.

Averell's column moved at a smarter pace that day and got as far as Rapidan Station, where the Orange & Alexandria crossed the Rapidan farther upstream. "Found the opposite side occupied by the enemy in rifle pits with artillery from which they opened fire on our approach," wrote Captain John Tidball of Averell's horse artillery. "Withdrew out of shelling range and encamped in a black jack swamp."

General Averell, cautious by nature, would now be made even more cautious by the discovery of a letter in a captured Confederate mail that put Stonewall Jackson and 25,000 men lying in wait for the Yankees at Gordonsville, just fifteen miles ahead. A prisoner was happy to confirm the tale. The gullible Averell, accepting this as "reliable and important," sent it to headquarters by courier. It was the first piece of intelligence received from the cavalry column. General Hooker's reaction to it is not on record.[12]

Hard-working Yankee engineers were meanwhile turning U.S. Ford into a usable Rappahannock crossing for the army. The hardest and most time-consuming part of the operation proved to be just getting the bridge trains to the crossing site. On April 28 the 50th New York engineers had secretly hauled the two bridge trains from winter quarters to within half a mile of Banks's Ford. The next evening it was decided at headquarters to shift the trains seven miles farther upstream, to U.S. Ford, and General Couch's Second Corps was scheduled to cross there on the thirtieth to join the flanking column. Those seven miles became a nightmare experience for the engineers.

The road was little more than a track through the woods, narrow and twisting, and pioneers had to clear trees so the cumbersome pontoon wagons could negotiate the sharpest turns. During the night, wrote engineer Folwell, "the rain fell rapidly and the road became slippery." The mule teams were doubled to drag the heavy wagons through the deepening mud. One slough was so deep that it had to be bridged before they could advance. At 8:00 A.M. on April 30 they finally reached U.S. Ford, after fifteen hours of grueling labor. Then new approaches down to the riverbank had to be cleared, and General Couch detailed 500 infantrymen to help. It was 1 o'clock that afternoon when the engineers started laying the first bridge, and they completed it in two hours. The band of the 14th Indiana led the way across. "We played Hail Columbia while crossing," bandsman George Lambert noted in his diary, "and the bridge wavered so that we could hardly stand. . . ." Once across they swung into "Dixie." Then Second Corps infantry followed in steady procession. As they marched past the empty rifle pits and gun emplacements on the south bank the men cheered.

Captain Folwell had charge of the second bridge. It was the invention of a man named Waterman, and Mr. Waterman himself was on hand to help with its first test under campaign conditions. The Waterman bridge train was comparatively mobile, for its pontoons were transported disassembled, but the bridge-laying was slower and more complicated than with standard components. Each of the Waterman pontoons had to be assembled out of forty pieces, and then linked together with long iron rods. Finally the balks, or stringers, and the planking were bolted down. "It might have been a good construction for a bridge to lie for a long time in one place," Captain Folwell decided. "It was utterly unfit for the field." The Waterman bridge was too short for the crossing place and had to be pieced out with conventional pontoons, and it was after 8 o'clock that night "when our abutments were staked down on the other shore." Folwell had his reward, however — the "magnificent sight" of an endless column of fighting men "streaming across the flat to the bridge and so on into Dixie."[13]

These troops were the Second Corps divisions of William French and Winfield Scott Hancock — John Gibbon's division was still held at Falmouth — and they bivouacked for the night at the Bullock house, three fifths of a mile from Chancellorsville. While all this was going on, Dan Sickles's Third Corps was on the march to the U.S. Ford crossing "by the shortest road, concealed from view of the enemy." That afternoon Sickles set off from Franklin's Crossing, below Falmouth, in three columns that (as one of his men wrote) "meandered through valleys and over the slopes of rising ground; and no men were allowed to stand or walk upon the crest. . . ." By night they were at the Hamet house on the Warrenton

Post Road, where the road to U.S. Ford branched off. Sickles was under orders to be at the bridges by 7:00 A.M. the next day, May 1. He and Couch together would bring five additional divisions to the concentration of forces at Chancellorsville.[14]

*   *

BACK AT army headquarters near Falmouth, General Hooker spent much of April 30 trying to detect Confederate responses to his offensive. His observation posts were busy but had little new to report. Stonewall Jackson's divisions that were camped downriver from Fredericksburg seemed to have completed their assembly in front of the Federal bridgehead. All the defenses that had repulsed Burnside back in December appeared to be fully manned. After midday visibility improved enough for reports to come in from the balloons, but they detected nothing especially threatening. Professor Lowe, passing on sightings sent him from balloon *Eagle* at Banks's Ford, found no change in the enemy west of the town: "It is hard to estimate their forces, for they are partially concealed in the pine woods, but they are certainly not near as strong as below Fredericksburg." He estimated that "full three-fourths of the enemy's force is immediately back and below Fredericksburg."

Hooker's first thought had been that a demonstration might produce useful intelligence. He sent orders to Sedgwick to make a probing advance toward the railroad at Hamilton's Crossing at 1:00 P.M. The orders were hedged about with cautions, however. He simply wanted to learn if "the enemy continues to hug his defenses in full force. . . ." They were not to assault him in his defenses; if Sedgwick and his generals were certain those defenses were indeed fully manned, that would satisfy the commanding general and no demonstration would be required.

Sedgwick was quick to throw cold water on the scheme. He would of course make the demonstration if ordered, but he said he was already satisfied the enemy was in front of him in full strength. "Genl Reynolds has just informed me that the enemy has shown more force this morning than was employed in December last." If that was not enough, Brooks too reported "a strong force in his front." Sedgwick's dispatch reached headquarters at close to noon, and by now the aerial observers had detected no Rebel movements either above or below Fredericksburg. Jackson's entire corps must be right there — by the B.M.I.'s estimate it contained 33,500 infantry — and Sedgwick had better leave well enough alone. After all, he had but two divisions across the river. "Let the demonstration be suspended till further notice," Hooker wrote across the dispatch.[15]

"I rather think that our demonstration here is merely a feint," Lieutenant Charles Brewster of the Sixth Corps wrote home that day, "but the beauty of the whole thing is that no one knows what is up and if the Greybacks are equally ignorant it is all I ask." Considering the fact that the Yankees in their lodgment on the south bank and the Rebels in their fortifications were but a rifle shot apart, April 30 was a comparatively peaceful day on the Rappahannock. It was so peaceful in fact that Captain Andrew J. Russell, the army's official photographer, crossed the river on a Sixth Corps bridge and set up his camera for a unique set of pictures of the Army of the Potomac during battle. *Harper's Weekly* artist Alfred Waud was there as well, busily sketching the scene at Franklin's and Fitzhugh's crossings.

Some of the two-year men in New York regiments on picket duty made an effort — a self-serving effort — to revive the informal picket-line truce that had been in effect before the campaign. Dorsey Pender, commanding a North Carolina brigade in A. P. Hill's division, wrote his wife that they called across the lines and "asked us not to fire, that they did not want to hurt us and that as they had only three days to serve, they did not want to be hurt." That, he thought, ought to make it all the easier to whip the Yankees.

Not every Confederate shared General Pender's confidence. Sergeant Marion Fitzpatrick of the 45th Georgia, posted in reserve behind Early's division, considered these quiet hours as the quiet before the storm. He was drawn to visit the place where he had been wounded in the December battle against Burnside. "I went a few hundred yds beyond the Rail R. in the old field," he wrote his wife that night. "The field is literally covered with graves now. I saw the arm of a dead Yankee sticking out of a grave that had not decayed." Like many Federal letter writers a few days before, Sergeant Fitzpatrick wanted his wife to have perhaps his last thoughts. "I had hoped for peace but there seems to be no peace for us soon. Do not grieve for me, even if I should fall, but remember me as one dieing to save his country."[16]

In the afternoon Major Thomas Hyde of General Sedgwick's staff made an ascension with Professor Lowe and described the scene as "exceedingly magnificent." Spread out below him was a panorama — "the beautiful green valley of the winding Rappahannock, dotted with country seats and alive with troops; the pontoon bridges; ten-thousand men holding with watchful care the opposite bank; the city off to the right; the batteries of both sides roaring and flashing at each other. . . ."

The late afternoon artillery exchange Major Hyde saw from on high took a toll on the ground. John Reynolds would report First Corps casualties that day of five dead and sixteen wounded, all by artillery. In one instance a shell from a Confederate Parrott rifle struck in the midst of the 13th Massachusetts camped on the north bank and killed a lieutenant, mortally wounded a captain, and took off the right arm and leg of a sergeant. At that General Reynolds turned to his artillery chief, Charles Wainwright, and asked, "Colonel, can you reach those fellows?" Wainwright obliged with a sharp barrage. "Johnnies got the worst of it," an observer decided.

Other such encounters were not as deadly. Washington had declared April 30 National Fast Day, and here and there in the camps an audience was rounded up for its observance. In Colonel Adrian Root's First Corps brigade the men were formed in a hollow square to be addressed by the regimental chaplains. "They were eloquent in their appeals to patriotism," remembered the 16th Maine's Abner Small. ". . . They besought us all to stand firm, to be brave; God being our shield, we had nothing to fear." Just then came several enemy shells from across the river and a general scattering. The chaplains were the first to flee, and the swiftest, their coattails streaming in the wind, "followed by gleefully shouted counsel: 'Stand firm; put your trust in the Lord!'"[17]

At headquarters Dan Butterfield had orders from Hooker to maintain the secrecy of the movement, and not even the president was told of the successful crossings. The press was blacked out too, although imperfectly. Correspondents had arranged by means of codes of innocuous phrases to tip off their editors in New York, in confidence, that the long-awaited campaign was under way. Editors leaked the news to favored political friends, in confidence, who circulated it further, also in confidence. That night General Heintzelman, the shrewd commander of Washington's defenses who always seemed to hear things first, recorded in his diary that he had it from the wife of New York senator Ira Harris that the Army of the Potomac was across the Rappahannock and there was fighting. "Nothing official," he added smugly.

"The army of General Hooker is in motion and has been for several days past," the *New York Herald* editorialized on April 30. ". . . He must win or his fall will be, like that of Lucifer, never to rise again." The *Herald* went on to note that in his testimony before the Committee on the Conduct of the War the general had set himself up as the superior of McClellan and Burnside, and now he has "no alternative before him but victory or death — death in the field or death to his reputation as a military leader."[18]

Headquarters was issuing a flurry of orders. Additional batteries were dispatched across the river to the bridgehead, and earthworks and rifle pits constructed there. The engineers were told to take up one of the three bridges at Franklin's Crossing and one of the two at Fitzhugh's Crossing after dark and transport them upriver to Banks's Ford, to be at hand when that crossing was uncovered by the flanking column's next advance. General Gibbon at Falmouth was alerted to be ready to join the rest of his corps across the river. The telegraph line was ordered extended to First Corps headquarters on the left and across the Rappahannock at U.S. Ford on the right to speed communications. Then, late in the afternoon, Joe Hooker set out with his field staff for the U.S. Ford bridges and the road to Chancellorsville.

His last dispatch of the day from headquarters went to Sedgwick and spelled out his intentions for May 1 — Day Five. Field headquarters would be at Chancellorsville, Sedgwick was told. "It is proposed that the army now at that point will assume the initiative to-morrow morning. . . ." From Chancellorsville the advance would be along the Orange Turnpike and Orange Plank Road to uncover Banks's Ford, thus shortening communications between the two wings of the army. Should the Rebels respond to this by showing "any symptoms of falling back" in front of him, Sedgwick was to drive straight ahead with his entire force, advancing along the Bowling Green and Telegraph roads leading south from Fredericksburg, sweeping the country clear of the enemy between the two highways and the railroad. Hooker wanted John Sedgwick to be aggressive. "Be observant of your opportunities, and when you strike let it be done to destroy."[19]

* *

LIKE HIS opposite number, General Lee spent much of the day on April 30 trying to discern the enemy's intentions. His immediate concern continued to be Dick Anderson's division. "I hope you have been able to select a good line and fortify it strongly," he wrote Anderson in midafternoon. ". . . Set all your spades to work as vigorously as possible." This was a new departure for Robert E. Lee. In eleven months in command of the Army of Northern Virginia he had never before ordered his men on campaign to erect field fortifications.

To be sure, the army had fought purely defensively at Fredericksburg in December, and had fought battles in which defense had a major role, as at Second Manassas and Sharpsburg. And certainly, out of self-preservation, his men had sometimes sheltered behind natural features or hastily thrown-up breastworks. But this was different because it was official: sending engineers Smith and Johnston to help Anderson lay out his fieldworks made it official. Lee was acknowledging that with the weaponry of this war — rifled muskets and rifled cannon — defense could dominate a battlefield.

It reflected too his awareness of the dramatic disparity in numbers in the two armies. Even when Anderson's division was united it contained barely 9,100 men. Equally significant were Lee's instructions to Anderson to cook two days' rations and to collect his baggage and equipage and his trains and send them to the rear. If the situation worsened, General Lee was prepared to give up the Rappahannock position and fall back to some new line.

The position Anderson had selected was a ridgeline three and a half miles east of Chancellorsville along which the Mine Road, running southeast from U.S. Ford to Hamilton's Crossing on the railroad, slanted across both the Turnpike and the Plank Road. It was the highest ground in the area. The brigade of Little Billy Mahone was posted to block the Turnpike at the Baptists' small wooden Zoan Church. The line was extended southeasterly half a mile to the Plank Road by Carnot Posey's brigade. From there it turned south past Tabernacle Church to the raised grade of an unfinished railroad, manned by Rans Wright's Georgians. At first the only guns were the four of Captain Charles Grandy's Norfolk Blues battery. By afternoon, however, Porter Alexander's battalion from the First Corps reserve was at hand with eighteen guns after a hard march from winter quarters. As soon as the engineers had laid out the line the infantry was put to work with shovels and axes. "We were digging and fortifying all night," one of Mahone's men complained.[20]

After writing his dispatch to Anderson, Lee rode again to the Rappahannock front to study the situation there. From the eminence called Lee's Hill, where he had directed the battle against Burnside in December, he examined the Federals across the river for some minutes. Then he abruptly closed his glass and turned to Charles Marshall of his staff and said with assurance, "The main attack will come from above."

Back at headquarters on the Mine Road, he summoned Jackson to hear his report. Jackson said he had studied the enemy lodgment from every angle and had come to agree with the commanding general: "It would be inexpedient to attack there." (Lieutenant Randolph Barton, on the staff of the Stonewall Brigade, always liked to think he played a part in Jackson's decision. That morning he was near the general, who was standing with arms folded, staring fixedly at the Yankee lines, when a shell burst nearby. It startled Barton's horse, which "as luck would have it backed immediately upon General Jackson, who nimbly stepped aside out of the way, saying nothing but giving me a glance as he did so." It was about then, Barton later learned, that Jackson abandoned his plan to attack there. "How much my hammer-headed horse contributed to this conclusion, I do not know, but I am satisfied that the great soldier was at that moment pondering the subject. . . .")

Lee was ready with a new plan. "Move then at dawn to-morrow up to Anderson," he told Jackson. He elaborated in a dispatch to Richmond: "I determined to hold our lines in rear of Fredericksburg with part of the force and endeavor with the rest to drive the enemy back to the Rapidan." Robert E. Lee recognized that in due course he might have to give up the Rappahannock line in the face of this threatening enemy host, but characteristically he was not going to do so without a fight. It was exactly the decision Joe Hooker anticipated he would make.

Lee made his shift to the left a powerful one. The troops closest to Dick Anderson, the division of Lafayette McLaws at the center of the line, were to march that night. McLaws was told to leave one of his four brigades for the defense of the town of Fredericksburg; William Barksdale's Mississippians were selected. Jackson's orders were to leave one division in the lines facing the Federal lodgment — he chose Jubal Early's — and with the rest of the Second Corps — the divisions of A. P. Hill, Robert Rodes, and Raleigh Colston — march west at daylight on May 1. The men would cook two days' rations, and all trains not necessary for combat would be sent to the rear should a withdrawal become necessary. By this division of force General Lee would be massing better than four fifths of his army against Hooker's flanking column at Chancellorsville.[21]

Early that evening Jackson gathered his staff at Second Corps headquarters near Hamilton's Crossing. The prospect of fighting always energized Stonewall Jackson. After one of Hooker's earlier feints he had been heard to mutter, "I wish they would come!" But Colonel William Allan, his chief of ordnance, had never seen the general so animated as he was that evening. "I well remember the elation of Jackson," he wrote afterward. "He seemed full of life & joy. His whole demeanor was cheerful & lively compared with his usual quiet manner." The staff caught the mood. Youthful Keith Boswell and Sandie Pendleton were "full of spirits"; even the usually dour artillerist Stapleton Crutchfield "appeared gleeful." Clearly Old Jack and his lieutenants were primed for battle.

Jackson had already primed himself for this particular assignment. Earlier in the day, when he began to share Lee's doubts about assaulting the Federal bridgehead below Fredericksburg, he had called on his cartographer Jed Hotchkiss for a map of the region to the west bounded by the Rappahannock and Rapidan rivers and extending to the Orange & Alexandria Railroad. No doubt Jackson remembered the previous August when they had nearly trapped John Pope's Yankee army in this triangle between the rivers, and he recognized its strategic possibilities.

After a brief shower in midafternoon the sky cleared and the evening turned pleasant. That night the moon, two nights short of full, shone brightly on columns of silently marching men moving westward from Fredericksburg. The first of Lafayette McLaws's brigades reached Dick Anderson by nightfall, and the other two brigades were on the march by 1:00 A.M. As was customary, Stonewall Jackson ordered his troops to be on the road at first light on May 1, Robert Rodes's division leading. After issuing his marching orders Jackson retired early.

This was Colonel Allan's first campaign as corps ordnance officer, and shortly before midnight he received a summons to report to the general's quarters. He found the headquarters camp quiet and dark at that hour, with only a single sentry on duty and the only light a candle in Jackson's tent. Allan's entrance awakened the general, who politely bid him to take a seat and asked him several questions about where the various ammunition trains were directed to be the next day. "He evidently wished to assure himself that his new Ord. Officer had every thing in proper trim," Allan wrote. "I bade him good night, mounted my horse & slowly rode away from the quiet camp."[22]

* *

THAT THURSDAY afternoon, when he reached Chancellorsville, General Slocum ordered his cavalry escort to scout for the enemy off to the south. Lieutenant Colonel McVicar, commanding the 6th New York cavalry, was told to march toward Spotsylvania Court House until he met resistance, then report back. McVicar, a red-haired, rough-hewn Scotsman, had been scrapping painfully with Rebel cavalry for two days, and he did not welcome the assignment. It looked to him like a "dusty job with results uncertain and perilous." It proved to be all of that.

By nightfall McVicar had made his way to the Brock Road and was less than three miles from Spotsylvania — and unknowingly on a collision course with Jeb Stuart. After his brush with Slocum's infantry earlier in the day, Stuart had turned southward and gone into bivouac near Todd's Tavern, on the Brock Road some two miles behind McVicar's party. The moon had risen now, and Stuart set out with his staff to ride on ahead and report to General Lee for orders. The road ran through dark forest and was deeply shadowed. Suddenly Stuart sensed something. "Things are not quite right up front," he said, and sent an aide forward. The aide came back pursued by Yankee troopers. Stuart's party retreated hastily toward Todd's Tavern and called up Fitz Lee's brigade.

Colonel McVicar saw this narrow road amidst dense woods as no place for a cavalry fight, and led his men into a roadside field on the farm of Hugh Alsop. Mr. Alsop's field was fenced, and the Yankee troopers trained their carbines on the gate through which they had entered. The 5th Virginia was the first to try them there, and was roughly handled. "Our horsemen," the Prussian Scheibert reported, "came roaring back pell-mell in the woods." The 3rd Virginia was next to take up the charge, but cramped by the narrow gateway it too was repulsed.

Measuring the odds, Colonel McVicar concluded it would be only a matter of time before he was trapped in the field and overcome by numbers. Standing in his stirrups, saber held high, he shouted, "Sixth New York, follow me! *Charge!*" They rushed for the gate, the colonel in the lead, and he was within seventy feet of it when he was shot dead off his horse with a bullet through his heart. His column broke through to the road and became tangled in a wild melee with yet another Rebel regiment, the 2nd Virginia. There were losses and prisoners on both sides; the 2nd Virginia's bugler captured his Yankee counterpart. "The old 2nd gave the biggest Rebel yell that night I think I ever heard," Sergeant C. E. Adams remembered. Another man thought "The silent and desolate spot, the moonlight glancing from the sabres, the excitement of the struggle . . . recalled some scene of knightly glory."[23]

Somehow in all this charge and countercharge the way was cleared for both contestants. The New Yorkers gratefully made their way back to Chancellorsville. For Stuart and his command the road was open to Spotsylvania Court House and Lee's army. Federal losses that night came to fifty-one, with thirty-six of them prisoners. There was no official count of Confederate losses, but a man in the 3rd Virginia thought they were "ten or fifteen men." The 5th Virginia lost a number captured in its charge, but in the confusion they were able to escape. The next morning pickets of the 2nd Virginia found the body of Colonel McVicar and buried him on the Alsop farm, marking the grave with a neatly lettered headboard.

There was a lesson for the Yankees in this midnight scrap at Alsop's. It was a vivid demonstration that in the days to come all the roads in the Wilderness beyond the immediate reach of the army were likely to be dominated by Jeb Stuart's cavalry — and that Alfred Pleasonton's troopers were too few in number to challenge that dominance.[24]

Joe Hooker and staff rode up to the Chancellor house at about 6 o'clock that evening, and Hooker assumed field command of his army, or that large portion of it gathered immediately around him. "It was a pleasant, moonlight night," Alpheus Williams wrote. "Chancellorsville house became the center for hundreds of officers (generals and staff). It was a gay and cheerful scene. We had successfully accomplished what we all supposed would be the great work of the campaign. Everybody prophesied a great success, an overwhelming victory. Everybody was full of enthusiastic congratulations."

General Williams wrote this to his family some days after the event, with more than a trace of irony in his tone, yet there was essential truth in his picture of the mood at Chancellorsville crossroads that April 30 evening. "God Almighty could not prevent me from winning a victory tomorrow," Hooker was heard to say, and if that struck the more devout among his listeners as sacrilegious it did at least reflect confidence rather than hope. Except for the newcomers from the Second Corps, the troops there had all been four days on the march against Robert E. Lee and here they were squarely on Lee's flank and rear with scarcely a shot yet fired. Even the hardiest veterans among them had never witnessed such a thing. Surgeon Bacon of Sykes's division recognized the sense of accomplishment. "Thus far the movement is really pretty. We have surprized the enemy and are concentrated in their country . . . ," he wrote in his diary that night. "The men . . . have done all this hard marching without complaint, for they have great faith in General Hooker."[25]

It was this soldier's pride — the soldier's pride he had been carefully nurturing ever since he took command of the army in January — that Joe Hooker was addressing in the general order he issued that evening. "It is with heartfelt satisfaction the commanding general announces to the army that the operations of the last three days have determined that our enemy must either ingloriously fly, or come out from behind his defenses and give us battle on our own ground, where certain destruction awaits him. The operations of the Fifth, Eleventh, and Twelfth Corps have been a succession of splendid achievements."

Later men would look back on this address of Hooker's and shake their heads at his temerity and call him vainglorious and full of bombast — General Williams termed it "a flaming order" — but at the time it was issued it was greeted with enthusiasm. "I heard great cheering in camp . . . ," wrote Private Silliman. "Old Joes complements put us in high spirits & the bands played like all possessed. . . ." Captain Bowers woke up his Massachusetts company to read them the address. "It would have done you good to hear the cheers that went up for fighting Jo. Hooker," he wrote his wife. "They were loud, hearty, sincere."

Even the most cynical veterans seemed willing to give the general the benefit of the doubt. "There is some bumpkin there of course but the main features I think are true," wrote a man in the 14th Indiana. Charles Eoger of the 15th Massachusetts told his wife, "It sounds well & reads well & if that is the case, all right, but they have been 'bagged' so many times & always escape through some hole, I want to see it accomplished to be a firm believer."

In actual fact, Hooker's appraisal — the enemy must ingloriously fly or else come out from behind his fortifications to give battle "on our own ground" — was a precisely accurate statement of the case. Whether certain destruction would be the enemy's fate remained to be seen, of course, but Joe Hooker was not the first general in this war, nor the last, to predict victory.[26]

8

To Repulse the Enemy

I T WAS CALLED the Wilderness of Spotsylvania, or simply the Wilderness, a distinctive tract of Virginia woodland of some seventy square miles. North to south it ran from the Rappahannock and Rapidan rivers to three or four miles south of Chancellorsville. East to west it extended from about Tabernacle Church to beyond Wilderness Tavern. Since colonial times the Wilderness had been the site of a nascent iron industry, but all that remained of it now was Catharine Furnace, a mile and a half southwest of Chancellorsville. Abandoned in the 1840s, the furnace had recently been reactivated to produce iron for the Confederate war machine. It was this iron industry that gave the Wilderness its distinctive character. Most of the first-growth timber had been cut to make charcoal to feed the furnaces and foundries, to be replaced by a second-growth tangle of dwarf pine and cedar and hickory and a scrub oak known locally as blackjack. Undergrowth in this warped and pinched forest grew dense and brambly. Men who fought in the Wilderness would remember it with fear and hatred — a dark, eerie, impenetrable maze.

For the most part it was uneven ground. A series of boggy watercourses cut ravines across it to empty into the Rapidan and Rappahannock or the Ny River to the south — Wilderness Run, Hunting Run, Mineral Spring Run, Mott's Run, Lewis's Run. The low ridgelines between them ran generally north and south, and there were scattered sloughs and marshes, one of them extensive enough to be called Big Meadow Swamp. What cleared ground there was in the Wilderness was mostly along the Turnpike and the Plank Road. The largest clearing, some seventy acres, was at Chancellorsville. There were clearings to the west along the Plank Road at Fairview and Dowdall's Tavern and Wilderness Church. East of Chancellorsville there were more frequent farms along the Turnpike and the Plank Road, including those of the spy Isaac Silver and his courier, Ebenezer McGee.[1]

Military communications, except verbal or by courier, promised to be a particular problem in this Wilderness. In the vicinity of Fredericksburg, on both sides of the river, there was sufficient high, open ground for flag signaling, but in this woodland, ground that was both open and high was a rarity. The Signal Corps would be put to the test to maintain communications between the two wings of the Potomac army.

In all the detailed, careful planning for the spring campaign, Joe Hooker and Dan Butterfield had given no special attention to the Signal Corps branch of their army. They seem to have taken it for granted that the signal units would advance as the army advanced, and without notice perform their progressively more vital role in the wide-ranging battle plan. As it happened, betting on the Signal Corps of the Army of the Potomac was betting on considerably less than a sure thing.

It had been clear enough, back in 1861, that the electric telegraph was going to revolutionize military communications in this war. Harnessing that revolution proved to be another matter. The War Department took control of the North's commercial telegraph network and formed from it the U.S. Military Telegraph, which despite its name was essentially a civilian organization. Initially, the U.S.M.T.'s primary task was handling strategic communications — between army commands and Washington, for example. It used tried and tested Morse-code sending and receiving instruments, powered by heavy lead-acid batteries. For tactical communications — battlefield and intra-army communications — the U.S. Army's Signal Corps had its own tried and tested signal-flag system. But to hold on to its traditional tactical role (and to fend off the rival U.S.M.T.), the Signal Corps needed to develop a field telegraph system of its own.

The Morse system was reliable, certainly, but its cumbersome batteries limited mobility, and its operators had to be skilled and highly trained. The Signal Corps required mobility, and lacked trained operators. For telegraphic operations in the field it thought it had the answer in the Beardslee Patent Magneto-Electric Field Telegraph Machine. The Beardslee machine, invented by George W. Beardslee, was handy and compact, powered by a hand-cranked magneto. Instead of the Morse's sending and receiving keys it had lettered dials with synchronized pointers. Each letter indicated by the pointer on the sender's dial was repeated on the receiver's dial. Operators needed only be literate.

In trials the Beardslee proved handy enough, but its power was limited, and reliability beyond about five miles' distance, even using wire in perfect condition, was questionable. Too, the machines required the most delicate adjustment to remain in proper synchronization. The

Beardslee's only battlefield experience, at Fredericksburg in December, produced mixed results. But the Signal Corps was committed to it, and argued its merits against rival U.S.M.T. operators over the winter.

Hooker's chief signal officer, Captain Samuel T. Cushing, said later that he would have faced the Chancellorsville campaign with more confidence if only he had had advance notice of what was expected of him and his equipment, and could have been better prepared. But with his concern for secrecy General Hooker said nothing more of his plans to Captain Cushing than to the rest of his officers. Cushing received his first orders on April 27, Day One.[2]

The telegraph line he was ordered to install downstream, to Franklin's Crossing, was in operation on Day One and continued to work successfully. The line ordered for upstream reached Banks's Ford the next day, but the Signal Corps' troubles began when Butterfield wanted it extended from there to U.S. Ford, to secure communication with the flanking column when it reached Chancellorsville. Captain Cushing did not have sufficient wire at hand for this extension, and had to take it from a line running from headquarters to Belle Plain on the Potomac, an outpost of the army's supply base. The Belle Plain wire had been in use for four months, Cushing pointed out, and he wanted time to inspect and repair it before sending it into the battlefield. Butterfield refused to allow any delay. In his report, Cushing would complain of orders issued "by one who was unaccustomed to the special details of the service. . . ."

On April 29, the day the flanking column reached the Rapidan, a Signal Corps party strung the Belle Plain wire (wire, said Cushing, "in which I had but little confidence") the seven miles from the Banks's Ford station to U.S. Ford. At first the new link could not be made to work. Captain Frederick E. Beardslee — son of the Magneto-Electric Machine's inventor — was sent to U.S. Ford to make repairs. One problem, young Beardslee reported, was due to an act of God. In an evening thunderstorm the station was hit by lightning, discharging the magnetic field that worked the pointer. He managed to recharge the machine, and by late evening had it operating. But it operated erratically, and only by a patchwork system was headquarters notified that Slocum and Meade had successfully crossed the Rapidan that day.

A telegram that reached headquarters from U.S. Ford at 10:30 that night was marked as originating at 5:30. Butterfield assured Cushing that he was not going to wake the commanding general for any telegram that was five hours arriving; his repose was "worth more than the commissions of a dozen signal officers," he snapped. In fact the offending telegram had arrived promptly enough once the Beardslee machine was finally working, but the operator failed to mark on it the actual sending time.

Butterfield understood nothing of this, however, and angrily ordered U.S.M.T. operators, with more reliable Morse equipment, to relay messages from the Banks's Ford intermediate station.[3]

When General Hooker advanced his headquarters into the field at Chancellorsville on April 30, the pressure on the Signal Corps intensified. Hooker demanded the latest intelligence on enemy movements at Fredericksburg. He wanted his orders to Chief of Staff Butterfield at army headquarters to be executed just as promptly. The Beardslee telegraph did not begin to meet these new demands on it.

For one thing, the distance from Banks's to U.S. Ford was a strain on the Beardslee's range, and breaks in the wire's insulation caused "leaks" that further weakened the signal. The wire had been strung on lances — sharpened poles notched at the top to carry the wire — and all too often carelessly driven artillery batteries or supply wagons knocked the wire down along the forest road. When the harassed Signal Corps lieutenant in charge of the U.S. Ford station, A. B. Jerome, was ordered to run a wire across one of the pontoon bridges at the ford to carry it toward Chancellorsville, the problems multiplied. While Captain Cushing would blame everything on the leaking and sometimes broken wire, Lieutenant Jerome was more candid. The Beardslee machines, he said, frequently became "disarranged" — slipping out of synchronization and producing garbled messages — and were difficult to readjust. There were failings, too, due to "the incapacity of some of my operators." A U.S.M.T. Morse operator at the Banks's Ford station reported, "We handed the Signal folks as much every five minutes as they could transmit in an hour. We were obliged to send most of the messages to Hooker by orderlies. . . ."

For some eighteen hours — from General Hooker's arrival at Chancellorsville on the evening of April 30 until after midday on May 1 — the right wing of the army suffered from a communications blackout, sometimes partial, sometimes total. Some telegrams were hours reaching their destination — as much as five hours or more. Others were garbled by the malfunctioning Beardslee machines. Captain Cushing ordered fifteen miles of new wire from Washington, and on May 1 U.S. Military Telegraph operators with Morse equipment were ordered to replace the Beardslee operators at the U.S. Ford station. By then, however, the damage had been done. For much of Friday, May 1, so far as communications were concerned, Joe Hooker was all but struck blind in the Wilderness.[4]

*   *

PORTER ALEXANDER, commanding one of the First Corps' reserve artillery battalions, had by chance been in Fredericksburg on April 29 when the Federals launched their surprise crossing of the Rappahannock there. His battalion was telegraphed for in its winter quarters near Hanover Junction, and while he waited for it to arrive Alexander applied his engineering skills to helping Dick Anderson fortify his line on the Chancellorsville front. By the next day, twenty-four hours after they were summoned, five batteries of Alexander's were on hand. The horses were jaded, but they somehow managed the haul. Alexander expected they would soon be fighting a defensive battle at this place, and so he carefully "studied out all the secrets of the ground. . . ."

But on May 1 "in a moment all was changed," Colonel Alexander remembered. "Up the road from Fredericksburg comes marching a dense & swarming column of our shabby gray ranks, and at the head of them rode both General Lee & Stonewall Jackson. Immediately we knew that all our care & preparation at that point was work thrown away. We were not going to wait for the enemy to come & attack us in those lines, we were going out on the warpath after them." Porter Alexander wrote those words years later, with the benefit of hindsight knowledge, yet there is no reason to doubt the accuracy of his recollection of the moment. Up to then he had fought in every battle, on every field, with Robert E. Lee, and he knew his man.

Observers like Alexander sensed the high drama in the scene as the Army of Northern Virginia marched off to battle. Lafayette McLaws's division moved first. From its position at Fredericksburg Paul Semmes's brigade had reached Dick Anderson's line the evening before, and by 1:00 A.M. on May 1 the brigades of William Wofford and Joseph Kershaw were on the move. A nearly full moon lighted their path. They marched in their thousands in shadowed silence, without music and without calls. By daylight they too were in position in Anderson's line.

Meanwhile, at first light, three divisions of Jackson's Second Corps were setting out westward. As the light rose so did a white blanket of morning ground fog, giving an eerie dimension to the drama. On the Plank Road a battery of the Richmond Howitzers was halted by the roadside to let A. P. Hill's Light Division pass. Lieutenant Robert Stiles watched the infantrymen loom up suddenly in the swirling mist, striding along silently in their endless column. The only sound as they passed, Stiles remembered, was "the low clatter or jingle of accoutrements." Later on came a small party of mounted officers — General Lee on his way to meet Jackson at the head of the advance. "As he would pass each brigade they would raise a terrible cheer," wrote Private William Dame of the Howitzers. "The old Gen. pulled off his hat & such tremendous cheers as the Rebels gave!"[5]

Lee's decision to give battle on the Chancellorsville front on May 1 rather than on the Rappahannock front — his decision to give battle at all — was calculated at least in part on the nature of the two potential battlefields. Lee the experienced engineer displayed his confidence in the defensive strength of his Rappahannock line by leaving what was not much more than a skeleton force to man it. To defend the six miles of fortifications running from behind Fredericksburg downriver to Hamilton's Crossing, Jubal Early had 11,100 infantry from his own division and from Barksdale's brigade of McLaws's division. To brace this line Lee left 65 guns, nearly a third of the army's artillery. Altogether, counting both infantrymen and gun crews, Early had 12,400 men to hold off the Yankees at Fredericksburg.

Lee ordered the rest of his command there — some 36,300 infantry, with thirty-three batteries — to march west to confront the Yankee turning movement. In the actual advance on May 1 the bulk of the Second Corps, plus a good part of the artillery, would act as a reserve. Dick Anderson's division and Lafayette McLaws's, from Longstreet's First Corps, formed the spearheads. For the day's operation Lee put them under Stonewall Jackson's command.

Jackson reached Anderson's line at Tabernacle Church at 8:30 that morning, well in advance of his troops. Lee's orders to him had not been specific — he was simply to "make arrangements to repulse the enemy" — but in their discussions the previous day Lee had certainly revealed his larger goal (as he told Richmond) of "driving the enemy back to the Rapidan." Jackson, always offensive-minded, determined to repulse the enemy by driving them. So far as Dick Anderson could say, his brush yesterday had been just with Hooker's cavalry, but Lee would have shared with Jackson the contents of Jeb Stuart's telegram identifying three infantry corps in the flanking column. Little Billy Mahone had engaged them only on the Turnpike and it was not known where else Yankee forces might be, but since the Turnpike and the Plank Road intersected at Chancellorsville, Jackson decided to advance in strength along both roadways. That way he was certain to find an enemy to fight.

Old Jack, once again resplendent in his bright new uniform, wasted no time making his wishes known. He told Anderson and McLaws to have the men put away their picks and shovels and take up their arms and fall in without delay for an advance. Nor would he delay long enough for all of his three divisions to arrive, but instead march as soon as possible with the men at hand. His cartographer Jed Hotchkiss arrived and handed out newly made maps to the senior commanders. Jackson himself was not familiar with the ground, but he used those who were to lead the way. Little Billy Mahone and Carnot Posey had spent the winter with their brigades on this ground — both had been regular visitors to the hospitality of Chancellorsville — and only the day before they had marched back from there over the Turnpike and the Plank Road. Now, on May 1, they would lead the march on the way back.

Mahone's brigade would be in the van on the Turnpike, followed by McLaws's three brigades under Wofford, Semmes, and Kershaw. They would be reinforced by the brigades of Cadmus Wilcox and E. A. Perry, of Anderson's division, called in from their postings near Banks's Ford. Artillery support would be provided by six batteries, 24 guns. Two squadrons of Thomas Owen's 3rd Virginia cavalry would cover the northern flank, picketing especially the Mine Road that slanted in from the northwest. This Turnpike column, under Lafayette McLaws's immediate command, totaled just under 13,000 infantry, artillery, and cavalry.

For the column on the Plank Road to the south, Carnot Posey's Mississippians, followed by Rans Wright's Georgians, both from Anderson's division, would lead. Their close support was 14 guns from Porter Alexander's battalion. Their reinforcement was to be Stephen Ramseur's brigade, from Robert Rodes's Second Corps division. Rodes's other four brigades, and A. P. Hill's six, along with eight batteries, were in immediate reserve, with Raleigh Colston's division a more distant reserve. The 4th Virginia cavalry picketed the southern flank. All told, counting the immediate reserves, there were some 27,000 men in the Plank Road column. Jackson commanded it personally.

At 10:30 A.M., with most of his Second Corps troops still several miles distant, Old Jack gave the order to advance. Looking back at the moment, Porter Alexander thought that just then Stonewall Jackson was at the peak of his powers. On that first day of May 1863, he wrote, "as a fighter and a leader he was all that it can ever be given to a man to be."[6]

* *

JOE HOOKER was up early on May 1, "devoting a few hours," he said later, "to gaining information on the country I was in, and its roads. . . ." Like General Lee that morning, he was greeted warmly by his men. It was 7:00 A.M., noted Captain Samuel Fiske of the 14th Connecticut, and "Gen. Hooker is riding along the lines, and the men are cheering him madly." Other bursts of cheering echoed through the Wilderness when at morning roll call there were readings of Hooker's optimistic general order of the evening before. A rumor crackled through the ranks that the cavalry had cut the Rebels' railroad lifeline to Richmond. "Our army is in grand spirits," Captain Fiske thought. Spirits were raised higher in many regiments when, on this first day of May, they were mustered for pay.[7]

General Hooker's plan for Day Five was simple enough — to seize the open heights south of the Rappahannock behind Banks's Ford, outflanking and driving off the Confederate defenders there. Throwing pontoon bridges across at Banks's would reduce the gap between the two wings of the army to half a dozen miles. Gaining the crossing at Banks's was only the secondary purpose of the operation, however. The bridges already in place at U.S. Ford were perfectly adequate for reinforcing and resupplying the army. The primary purpose of the Day Five advance was its promise of outflanking Lee's forces west of Fredericksburg.

Banks's Ford was at the bottom of the most southerly loop of the Rappahannock upstream from Fredericksburg. It was Hooker's thought to approach the ford itself by way of the River Road, while advancing columns simultaneously along both the Turnpike and the Plank Road at least as far as their junction near Tabernacle Church. Any defenders met there would be threatened in front and outflanked from the direction of Banks's Ford. Once again maneuver ought to carry the day. At that point General Hooker's turning movement would be clear of the Wilderness and squarely in the rear of Fredericksburg. It was the final step he had plotted in his advance planning for the campaign.

Hooker had planned for that final step the day before, when still at army headquarters near Falmouth. He arranged for two of the bridges on Sedgwick's front to be taken up after dark for transport to Banks's Ford. John Gibbon's Second Corps division at Falmouth — the only unit in the army that had not yet moved — was alerted to march to Banks's, to cross there when it was seized. Dan Sickles's Third Corps was ordered to U.S. Ford, to cross on May 1 as reinforcement for the Chancellorsville front. John Sedgwick was given directions for a major demonstration below Fredericksburg, also on May 1. When that evening Hooker moved to Chancellorsville to take field command, he turned to the telegraph to coordinate the movements of all these elements. That was when his troubles began.

On the evening of April 30, for example, he issued an order from Chancellorsville for General Gibbon to be at Banks's Ford for a crossing there "tomorrow at 9:00 A.M." It went to the U.S. Ford telegraph station, where a breakdown of the Beardslee machine prevented its being sent until sometime after midnight. When the operator finally sent the order he dated it May 1. When Chief of Staff Butterfield received it, about 8:00 A.M., he could not tell whether Gibbon was supposed to march that morning or the next. He could not get confirmation from Hooker because the telegraph had stopped working again. Knowing none of this, Hooker continued issuing his telegraphic orders. One of the most important, on May 1, was his direction to Sedgwick "to threaten an attack in full force" simultaneously with the advance from Chancellorsville.[8]

The field of operations, Joe Hooker would say in justifying his actions that day, "was in what is called the *Wilderness,* of which I had no adequate conception. . . . I was not prepared to find it an almost impenetrable thicket. It was impossible to maneuver. . . ." Nor, as it turned out, had he an adequate conception of where he would find the enemy or in what force.

Apparently the only fresh intelligence Hooker received about the enemy on his front before starting his advance was a 5:30 A.M. dispatch from Butterfield reporting that according to a deserter who had entered Sedgwick's lines, "Jackson's whole corps is opposite Franklin's Crossing." That meant that only Anderson's division, and perhaps McLaws's, were facing him — that according to the Bureau of Military Information, and thus far the B.M.I.'s analysis had been without flaw. For something more concrete, however, Hooker delayed the advance long enough for his chief topographical officer, Gouverneur Warren, to go out ahead on the Turnpike to reconnoiter.

He delayed, too, in the hope of hearing of any last-minute enemy movements from the Signal Corps observers and from Professor Lowe's balloons. He was disappointed. Nothing could be seen of the Rebels until 9 o'clock because of the morning ground fog, and then when they did sight the movements of Jackson's divisions the failed telegraph prevented their warnings from reaching the commanding general in good season.

Warren returned at 10 o'clock to report that he had been able to go out some three miles, from which point he sighted Rebel breastworks across the Turnpike. When Hooker ordered the march, that from Warren was the sum total of what he knew about where he might find the foe. Since Stonewall Jackson was no better informed about the Federals on May 1, the two contestants would be groping blindly toward each other.

George Meade led the northernmost column, on the River Road, containing two of his Fifth Corps divisions, under Charles Griffin and Andrew Humphreys, and one battery. Meade's infantry strength was 10,850. His other Fifth Corps division, George Sykes's regulars, 4,950 strong, was sent out on the Turnpike supported by two batteries. The divisions of Alpheus Williams and John Geary in Henry Slocum's Twelfth Corps (Slocum had returned to his corps command when Hooker took the field) made up the southernmost column, on the Plank Road. It had 13,450 men and 12 guns. To guard the army's flank and rear, a division and a battery of the Second Corps were to march west and then south toward Todd's Tavern. The three columns of the advance were supposed to link up at their objectives, forming a solid front, and be mutually supporting. The timetable called for "the heights of Fredericksburg to be carried at 2 P.M."

In view of the numbers he commanded at Chancellorsville that May 1 — by day's end, more than 72,000 infantry and thirty-one batteries — General Hooker was committing rather less than an overwhelming force, 29,250 infantry and 26 guns, to his advance. Other units were assigned to follow these spearheads, but none in immediate close support. Originally Humphreys was told to march with Sykes on the Turnpike, but at the last minute he was ordered to go instead with Griffin on the River Road. That left Sykes's center column, at 4,950 men, much the smallest of the three.

Hooker took the slim diet of intelligence received about the enemy on his front that morning to mean that nothing had changed, that Lee was still holding his heaviest forces under Jackson at Fredericksburg. In that event the enemy in front of him should react defensively; he need not fear coming under attack himself. Dan Butterfield soon enough had much better information on Jackson's whereabouts, but the failed communications meant it would be some time reaching the commanding general. On May 1 Fighting Joe Hooker did not expect — and was ill-prepared — to have to risk a serious battle to gain the position he wanted.[9]

* *

AT 10:30 that Friday morning, just as Stonewall Jackson at Tabernacle Church was giving the signal to advance, four miles away at the Chancellor house Joe Hooker gave a like signal. The ground fog had burned off and the day was warming until it was described by many as a perfect May Day. The mood at Chancellorsville was cheerful. General Couch, commanding the Second Corps, wagered a box of cigars with cavalryman Pleasonton that they would be squarely in the rear of Fredericksburg by nightfall. General Williams of the Twelfth Corps said he had never seen his men in better condition, "never more anxious to meet the enemy. . . . Such, I believe, was the condition of almost every corps in the army. Surely we had promise of success."[10]

In George Meade's column on the River Road to the north the 32nd Massachusetts had the lead, and Captain Charles Bowers remarked in a letter to his wife that back home a road like that would be considered "utterly impassable." They struggled along for what he thought was about three miles when the order came to halt and cap muskets and send skirmishers out ahead. Then the march resumed.

Although the River Road when it reached the vicinity of Banks's Ford was only a mile and a quarter from the Turnpike, for much of the way it looped in a broad arc farther to the north, so that from the start Meade's column was diverging sharply away from the center column on the Turnpike. The Wilderness pressed in closely, with only scattered clearings and farms. At one point they passed a newly abandoned Rebel encampment, and Captain Bowers was surprised to see that it looked just like one of their own. "In every respect it was as good a camp as any we have had. . . ." (Rummaging through this campsite, men of the 2nd Maine came upon a packet of photographs of Federal soldiers. Someone recognized a name on one of them as a man in their brigade, and before long Sergeant Walter Carter, 22nd Massachusetts, was handed the pictures he had lost on the Fredericksburg battlefield five months earlier. And scavengers in the 83rd Pennsylvania recovered some of the fancy French knapsacks they had lost at Gaines's Mill the previous June.)

After a time they began to hear the muffled rattle of musketry and the hard boom of artillery through the dense forest off to the right, but what it might mean was a mystery. "We are of course in utter ignorance of the plan," Bowers told his wife, "and many things that appear inexplicable while passing are explained in time."

By midafternoon Meade's column was in sight of the Rappahannock and only a mile or two short of Banks's Ford. "We had reached a point exactly opposite the place we left on Monday," Captain Bowers noticed. "Our balloon was up looking as natural as ever and we could see our old encampments." Just then a staff officer came pelting up through the column to its head, and after a "sudden halt" they were about-faced and countermarched without explanation. Bowers's regiment was part of a command turned off onto a woods road leading southward, and the sounds of the unseen battle grew louder. "The cheers of the combatants as one or the other gained a point were distinctly heard," Bowers wrote. "The musketry at times was fearfully rapid, and it became most exciting to us."

Then again without explanation they returned to the River Road and turned back toward where they had started that morning. By day's end Meade's two divisions were back close to Chancellorsville, without having fired a shot and none the wiser for the day's events. Perhaps the movement "will be made plain by and by," Bowers concluded, "but for the present 'I can't see it.'"[11]

The fighting that Captain Bowers heard had begun mildly enough in late morning on the Turnpike barely a half mile from the Confederates' starting point at Zoan Church. The opening shots were delivered by Lieutenant Colonel Everard Feild's 12th Virginia, renewing its squabble with the 8th Pennsylvania cavalry.

Following their running fight the day before, the Pennsylvania troopers had set up an advanced picket post on the Turnpike three miles beyond Chancellorsville at the homestead of Joseph Alsop. When General Mahone ordered him forward, Feild deployed a substantial skirmish line and chased the Yankee pickets at Alsop's back toward their reserve, bivouacked on a hill half a mile to the rear at the house of an elderly woman named Ann Lewis. Much excited, Mrs. Lewis called out to Captain Charles Wickersham of the cavalry that was camped in her dooryard to come and see the Rebels. Wickersham ran up the stairs and from Mrs. Lewis's window sighted a line of skirmishers in butternut walking deliberately toward him in line across the Turnpike, "followed by three solid lines of infantry."

Mrs. Lewis took shelter in her cellar, and Captain Wickersham went back for help and turned to doing what he could to delay the Rebel advance. He put most of his troopers to fighting dismounted, taking cover first behind a brush fence on the Lewis homestead. As soon as the enemy came within "easy carbine range" they opened fire and the enemy replied, "and a lively skirmish was soon in progress." In the Confederate line an officer was heard to call out, "Hurry up, boys, and get a shot at the Yankee cavalry!" Private Westwood Todd of the 12th Virginia was happy enough for the chance. In infantryman Todd's opinion, "If there is any poetry in fighting it is Infantry fighting Cavalry."

The troopers gave up ground grudgingly, falling back from one ridgeline to the next as their flanks were threatened. "I must say they were stubborn fellows to deal with," one of the Virginians admitted. But cavalry could do nothing more than delay. By about noon, after an hour or more of skirmishing, they had been forced back more than a mile. As the pursuing Rebels emerged from a wood into a large open field, they saw the cavalrymen disappear behind a wide line of blue. The U.S. regulars had arrived.[12]

At cavalryman Wickersham's warning General Sykes had ordered his lead brigade of regulars ahead at the double-quick. Colonel Sidney Burbank had six regiments in his command, but all were woefully understrength and totaled only some 1,500 men. Approaching Mott's Run, where Mahone's Virginia brigade had taken a stand the day before and which it was about to reach again, Burbank briskly deployed three of his regiments to the left of the Turnpike and two to the right. The 17th U.S. was put out in advance as skirmishers. The Federals were on a downslope here and much exposed to the enemy fire. "The shells come thick as they whiz near," wrote a Fifth Corps surgeon. "The impulse is irresistible to duck, and the whole line bows very frequently. I confess I make frequent bows to the rebels." Burbank drove his brigade forward beyond Mott's Run toward the crest of the next ridge. Lieutenant Malbone Watson's Battery I, 5th United States, came pounding up the Turnpike and unlimbered to support the advance.

The regiments on the right had to fight their way through thick woods bordering the road and were hard-pressed to keep pace. They fought blindly, seldom able to see who was firing at them. "After the first fire delivered by the enemy," wrote a man in the 2nd U.S., "we commenced to peg away at the rebels in the timber."

The left of the road by contrast was largely cleared land on the homestead of Reuben McGee, and the Federals found easier going. (The McGee family had been divided by the war. One of Reuben McGee's sons was in the Confederate army, and two others were strongly Unionist, Ebenezer so much so that he served as courier for the spy Isaac Silver.) The well-drilled regulars marched across the McGee property aligned on their colors as if they were on a parade ground. "We advanced up a hill & into a belt of woods," wrote Private George Merryweather of the 11th U.S., "& here the hot work began. . . ." They swept up twenty-seven men of the 12th Virginia who had taken cover behind the McGee house. "We cast our eyes the other way, to the left, and found . . . a solid column on our left and rear," one of Feild's men remembered. "Of course we gave up. . . ."

The shallow valley of Mott's Run was about a mile wide, and the momentum of the regulars' attack pushed the 12th Virginia ahead of them to the crest of the next ridge, putting the fighting back at Mrs. Lewis's. The rest of Mahone's brigade came up to stiffen the Virginians' line. On the Federal side, Sykes advanced Romeyn Ayres's brigade of regulars to brace Burbank's position on the left, north of the Turnpike. From Patrick O'Rorke's trailing brigade, New York volunteer regiments, the 5th New York went to the left and the 146th New York into the woods to help on the right. On the relatively narrow battlefield Lieutenant Watson's 3-inch rifles had to fire over the heads of their own infantry to reach the enemy. Two Confederate guns furnishing front-line support were doing the same.[13]

Virginian Westwood Todd, admiring the "beautiful line" of the Yankee regulars, was struck by a special quality about this battlefield. It was different from the nasty one-sided fighting he had experienced on the Peninsula: "Now we had a fair, square stand-up, open field fight." He would remember it as the "most satisfactory fighting in which I had any share during the war." His company took position behind a rail fence and poured a hot fire into the enemy. One particular Federal captain caught Private Todd's attention by the way he courageously stood his ground and rallied his men and kept them from running. Todd fired at him several times and missed, and an officer borrowed his rifle to take a shot at the captain and he too missed. It seemed that sometimes the brave led charmed lives. In the shifting fortunes of the day Todd's company was marched forward and back until all were exhausted. Then reinforcements arrived and they decided they had done their part that day; "we concluded we would rest on our laurels."

On the Federal side one of the reinforcing regiments was the 14th U.S., and for Captain Jonathan Hager this was the first time he had commanded in battle. When he deployed his men they were in the open and close to Watson's battery and squarely in the line of fire of the Rebel battery. One shell struck amidst the 14th's color guard, wounding five of its nine men. A second hit within ten feet of Captain Hager, showering him with dirt. A third exploded directly under a battery caisson, Hager wrote, "& I thought my time had come." But miraculously the caisson did not explode, and he decided that a "kind Providence protected me." After that he felt no fear. Whatever the day's outcome, he was satisfied (like Private Todd) that he had done his part.[14]

Lafayette McLaws, commanding the Confederate advance on the Turnpike, now pushed his own brigades into the fight to support Mahone. William Wofford's brigade came up on the Lewis farm north of the Turnpike. Paul Semmes's Georgians joined the confused fighting south of the road, where the drifting battle smoke was making it harder than ever to see anything in the dense woods.

Here the 51st Georgia caught the heaviest of the Federals' fire. John Wood of the 53rd Georgia reported the Yankees firing too high to do much harm to his regiment, but "the left of our brigade suffered a sight, especially the 51st. . . ." He estimated it lost at least 100 men — more than all the rest of Semmes's brigade that day. The 51st's colonel, William Slaughter, was mortally wounded, and then his second-in-command, Lieutenant Colonel Edward Ball, was wounded. At about the same time the commander of the Federal regiment opposing them, Captain Salem S. Marsh, 2nd United States, was shot dead with a bullet through his forehead.

McLaws sent an aide to Jackson to say that the Federals were in force in front of him, but that he thought they could be turned from the south by a movement of the column on the Plank Road. Jackson replied that he was bringing forward his artillery for such a movement, and that McLaws was to hold his present position. McLaws established a wide, solid front facing the Federals, outreaching them north and south, and sent formations of skirmishers probing beyond both their flanks.

A dispatch from Jeb Stuart also reached Jackson, saying he had the cavalry positioned south of Chancellorsville to watch the enemy. "I will close in on the flank and help all I can when the ball opens. . . . May God grant us victory." Ever ready to acknowledge such a sentiment, Jackson replied, "I trust God will grant us a great victory. Keep closed on Chancellorsville."

George Sykes, for his part, was feeling considerably less than confident about his situation. It was 1 o'clock now and the battle was two hours old, and he had heard nothing at all from Meade on his left or from Slocum on his right. He could clearly see that he was heavily outnumbered and about to have both flanks turned. He sent Gouverneur Warren, who had come along with the center column as an observer, back to Hooker to explain his predicament. As Sykes put it in his report, the situation was critical. "I was completely isolated from the rest of the army."[15]

* *

THERE WAS nothing in this war more persistently troublesome to field commanders than coordinating the movements of columns of troops on a battlefield that were out of sight of one another. Joe Hooker not only had three such columns under his command that day, but each of his lieutenants heading them — Meade, Sykes, and Slocum — had different ideas on how best to carry out their operations. Then, too, there was the element of surprise. Hooker had anticipated any enemy met on May 1 to be defensive, not aggressive and attacking. Stonewall Jackson, by pressing his advance as he did, totally deprived the Federals of the avenues by which one column was to have communicated and linked up with another. General Sykes was quite right to consider himself completely isolated.

Only two roads, for example, ran between the River Road (and Meade's column) and the Turnpike where Sykes was advancing. The two, the Mine Road and the Duerson's Mill Road, both reached the Turnpike at about Zoan Church, and Sykes was three quarters of a mile short of that point when McLaws's advance blocked his path. (A turnoff from the Mine Road did enter the Turnpike farther west, but Sykes was brought to a halt just short of that, too.) General Meade dutifully sent advance parties down both the Mine and Duerson's Mill roads to meet Sykes halfway, but found no one. An attempt by 8th Pennsylvania troopers and by one of Sykes's staff to reach Meade by going cross-lots ran up against a screen of McLaws's flankers.

Ironically, had he known of Sykes's plight, Meade was ideally positioned, and certainly strong enough, to strike the Rebels squarely in the flank by way of these roads. In that event, two Confederate brigades would have confronted two Federal divisions. Or Meade might simply have marched to the sound of the guns, yet there was nothing in his orders to encourage such independent action. Indeed, there was nothing at all about initiating battle in Hooker's orders. George Meade's expedition on the River Road that day was an exercise in futility.

On the Plank Road to the south Henry Slocum and the Twelfth Corps were experiencing the same futility. Slocum had gotten started at 11 o'clock that morning and about a mile out encountered a Rebel picket post. Rather than brushing it aside and continuing at a marching pace along the highway, Slocum in an excess of caution halted to deploy his two divisions in line of battle, one on each side of the road. This took no little time. Then his 13,450 men tried to advance in some kind of order at some kind of pace through the dense woods bordering the Plank Road.

Rice Bull of the 123rd New York described their adventures in the Wilderness. There was a scrub-pine thicket whose branches were so interlocked that "we could not advance in company front. It was even difficult for a single man to move ahead in the thicket. We broke into columns marching by fours; even then we could not keep that formation. Then we went on as best we could in single file, breaking our way through the pine branches. . . ." A scattering of enemy fire caused little harm but shot and shell "made a terrifying noise as they tore through the tops of the trees."

It was no better for Private William Aughinbaugh of the 5th Ohio. "Our brigade was taken through swamps, woods and brush thickets almost impossible for human beings to get through," he complained. They marched "to and fro for a few hours, always in the worst places, . . . having one man of our regiment wounded by a piece of shell. . . ."

Meanwhile Sykes's center column had marched steadily ahead on the Turnpike until it encountered serious opposition; indeed its last rush was at the double-quick. At the time Sykes and McLaws reached their standoff on the Lewis farm, Slocum on the Plank Road was just emerging into a large clearing on the John Alrich farmstead. There he met the head of Jackson's infantry column, which (like Sykes's column) had been proceeding steadily along the road in marching order. Jackson and Sykes had marched right past each other in opposite directions on the parallel roads. As a result, Slocum on the Plank Road was nearly two miles to the rear of Sykes on the Turnpike. All their efforts to communicate with each other failed.[16]

Hooker had sent out Colonel Joseph Dickinson of his headquarters staff to track Slocum's progress. Dickinson found him on the Alrich farm, just a mile and a half from Chancellorsville, surveyed the scene, and sent back to report that the Twelfth Corps was far short of its objective and already engaging the enemy. At about the same time, 1:30 P.M., General Warren reached Hooker's headquarters to report Sykes's perilous position on the Turnpike.

It had always been Joe Hooker's habit to put himself right at the scene of any fighting, but today, as army commander, he felt obliged to

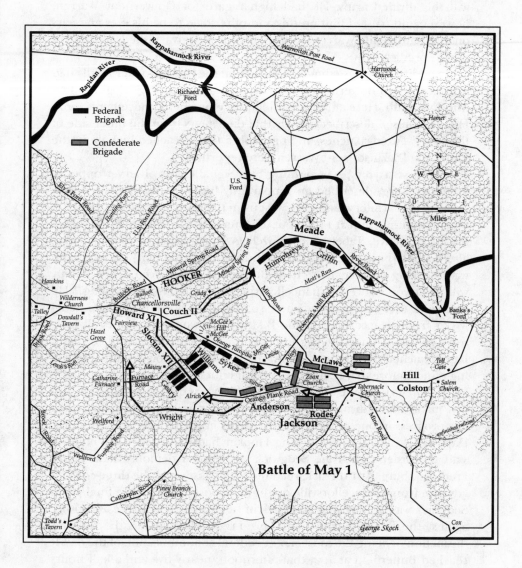

Battle of May 1

Federal Brigade

Confederate Brigade

Rappahannock River

Rapidan River

Warrenton Post Road

Richard's Ford

Hartwood Church

Hamet

Ely's Ford Road

Hunting Run

U.S. Ford Road

U.S. Ford

Rappahannock River

Mineral Spring Road

Mineral Spring Run

V Meade

Humphreys

Griffin

River Road

Banks's Ford

Hawkins

Wilderness Church

Bullock Road

Bullock

HOOKER

Grady

Mott's Run

Mine Road

Talley

Dowdall's Tavern

Chancellorsville

Fairview

Couch II

McGee's Hill

McGee

Orange Turnpike

McGee

Lewis

Dierson's Mill Road

Howard XI

Hazel Grove

Lewis's Run

Slocum XII

Williams

Sykes

Alger

Silber

McLaws

Toll Gate

Hill

Catharine Furnace

Maury

Furnace Road

Geary

Zoan Church

Tabernacle Church

Colston

Salem Church

Brock Road

Alrich

Silber

Orange Plank Road

Anderson

Rodes

Mine Road

unfinished railroad

Wellford

Jackson

Wright

Furnace Road

Wellford

Catharpin Road

Piney Branch Church

Todd's Tavern

George Skoch

Cox

N W E S

0 1
Miles

remain in the rear at headquarters and close to communications links with his divided army. He had high regard for Gouverneur Warren, however, and trusted him on this and other days to be his eyes and ears on the battlefield. Warren furnished him an unvarnished account of Sykes's predicament.

In addition to these timely reports from the front, Hooker finally had word from Dan Butterfield by way of the malfunctioning telegraph link with Falmouth. Here at last was intelligence on enemy movements, or as Hooker himself described it later that day, "news from the other side of the river." Two dispatches, and probably a third, reached him about the same time Dickinson and Warren were reporting.

The first, a 10:25 A.M. sighting by a Signal Corps observer opposite Fredericksburg, described an "apparently heavy" force of Confederate infantry and artillery marching west from the town "toward our right." A second sighting, sent at 11:32, put the enemy column making straight for Sykes's objective, Tabernacle Church. A third dispatch, sent at 12:30, also ought to have reached Hooker if (as Butterfield put it) the telegraph was "working correct now." In it Butterfield announced, "The enemy will meet you between Chancellorsville and Hamilton's Crossing." He estimated that Lee had detached 10,000 to 15,000 troops from Sedgwick's front — according to the B.M.I. these would be Stonewall Jackson's troops — since the fog lifted at 9 o'clock. How many Lee might have detached during the moonlit night and in the fog-shrouded morning hours before that Dan Butterfield did not hazard to guess.

This news from the other side of the river was disturbing enough, and was made more disturbing by Butterfield's puzzling failure to report any progress in one of the key movements in Joe Hooker's program for Day Five. At 11:30 that morning Hooker had telegraphed his chief of staff the order to activate Sedgwick's scheduled demonstration below Fredericksburg. At 1 o'clock, read the order, just when the three-column advance from Chancellorsville ought to be positioned for the final push, Sedgwick was "to threaten an attack in full force . . . as severe as can be" against the Rebels facing him. This 11:30 telegram has the dubious distinction of being the most errant Federal communication of the day. It reached Butterfield at 4:55 that afternoon, nearly five and a half hours after it was sent.[17]

Fighting Joe Hooker, whom Mr. Lincoln had cautioned "beware of rashness," now made a most prudent decision. "I soon discovered," he would later say, "that I was hazarding too much to continue the movement." His center column, by far the weakest of the three, was approaching a crisis. Heavily outnumbered, both flanks being turned, Sykes was at risk of being crushed before Meade or Slocum could support him — if indeed they ever could support him. Sykes's scheduled reinforcement, Hancock's division of the Second Corps, had not yet marched.

Their opponent this day had to be Stonewall Jackson, of fearsome reputation, and if Jackson was in such strength against Sykes as reported, it was likely Slocum and perhaps Meade would be at risk as well. Sykes was short of his day's objective; Slocum was nowhere near his. Whatever Sedgwick had done by way of a demonstration — if he had done anything at all — it had clearly failed to deter General Lee.

Finally, should he go ahead and try to make a fight of it on this ground, Hooker feared that his narrow, road-bound columns could not deploy into line of battle swiftly enough against the enemy's battle lines. If they were outnumbered (as in fact they were), this could be a fatal maneuver. He was, he said, "apprehensive of being whipped in detail."

"From character of information have suspended attack," Hooker telegraphed Butterfield at 2 o'clock. "The enemy may attack me — I will try it. . . ." Warren was sent back out the Turnpike with the decision — "General Sykes will retire to his position of last night. . . ." Other aides hurried to Slocum and Meade with verbal orders to withdraw their columns at the same time.

Colonel Dickinson, invoking his authority as headquarters staff, assured the bristling Slocum that the order to return to Chancellorsville was official, and peremptory. Slocum obeyed grudgingly, saying he had hardly yet begun to fight. Meade turned his column back more in puzzlement than anger. It was clear to him at least that something had gone very wrong with the plan.

Darius Couch of the Second Corps had ridden out to Sykes's battle line on the Turnpike in advance of Hancock's division, and when he learned there of Hooker's order to withdraw he sent one of his staff back to Chancellorsville to try and stay the order. "In no event should we give up our ground," Couch remembered saying.

Such boldness was uncharacteristic of Darius Couch, normally the soul of McClellan-like caution. It no doubt stemmed from his knowing nothing of the facts of the situation. He had only just come on the field and knew nothing of the ground or of the larger questions confronting Hooker that afternoon. The staff man returned with a confirming order for Sykes to pull back without delay, his withdrawal to be covered by Hancock. "We sorrowfully sent in our men," Couch recalled.[18]

"This movement has since been severely criticised by persons fancying that they were judges," Joe Hooker wrote later in his own defense, "apparently having been misled by misapprehensions of the relative forces. . . ." Such criticisms, he went on, "appear trifling to me, as their authors have never seen the ground and know nothing of my surroundings. . . . If situated in like manner again, I do not hesitate to declare, as my conviction, I should repeat the order."

Hooker's judges, blessed with wisdom after the fact, did indeed condemn his May 1 decision. He should never have given up the opportunity to get his army out of the Wilderness and onto the high, open ground south of Banks's Ford, they said. He should have gone resolutely to battle right where he was that afternoon. Their arguments were taken up by latter-day observers. "The advance was stopped," a former staff man declared loftily thirty-five years later. "The battle of Chancellorsville was lost right there." Twenty-five years later General Couch recalled Hooker telling him that day, "It is all right, Couch, I have got Lee just where I want him; he must fight me on my own ground." Couch added, with the prescience of recollection, "I retired from his presence with the belief that my commanding general was a whipped man."

In fact it was the intelligence concerning the enemy that as much as anything else decided Hooker on his course. It was General Hooker, not his critics on that or any other day, who had the clearest picture of what he faced that afternoon.

The heavy columns of Rebel troops seen marching against him had to be from Jackson's corps, which Colonel Sharpe's Bureau of Military Information reported could be as many as 33,500 infantry. The B.M.I. counted Anderson's and McLaws's divisions probably already on the field as 14,700. Thus Hooker could be facing more than 48,000 of the enemy. (Their actual count was 48,300.) He sent out that morning in his three columns fewer than 30,000 men. Their only scheduled reinforcements were Hancock's division (5,800) for Sykes and Howard's Eleventh Corps (13,000) for Slocum. Once on the scene these ought to make for an even match against their opponents — but they would be some time reaching the scene.

Moreover, since Meade had not reported any enemy force in front of him, the Confederates must be concentrated on the Turnpike and the Plank Road; both Sykes and Slocum were therefore likely to be outnumbered even after their reinforcements reached them. Neither was within supporting distance of the other. Nor was it likely that the rest of the Second Corps, and the Third Corps, could come up before the fighting was over. As the first Army of the Potomac commander to have full and accurate intelligence about the Army of Northern Virginia, Joe Hooker was not going to enter a battle by choice as the underdog.[19]

In any event, the ground where Sykes and Slocum were then engaged was hardly worth fighting for. They were contending for nothing more than clearings in the Wilderness, clearings reached over narrow roads through the forest from which reinforcements (as Hooker predicted)

General Burnside's aborted offensive at Fredericksburg in January 1863, called the Mud March, plunged morale in the Army of the Potomac to a new low. Newspaper artist Alfred Waud sketched the bedraggled marchers above. A. J. Russell photographed the rejuvenated Federals below three months later. This is the 110th Pennsylvania at Falmouth on April 24.

Photographer Russell turned his camera on the Falmouth encampment of the 110th Pennsylvania regiment, whose rotund chaplain stands at right. Log huts like these, roofed with shelter tents, housed Yankees and Rebels on both sides of the Rappahannock during that winter.

President Lincoln visited the Army of the Potomac on the eve of the spring campaign. *Leslie's Illustrated Newspaper* artist Edwin Forbes made the sketch above of Lincoln's train cross- ing the military span over Potomac Creek near Falmouth. Below, Forbes drew the president riding alongside General Hooker as the two reviewed the army's cavalry corps on April 6.

Artist Waud did the drawing above, a view from Falmouth on the north bank of the Rappahannock toward Fredericksburg, during the quiet weeks before the campaign. Below, Timothy O'Sullivan photographed Fredericksburg at about the same time. At center are the piers of the demolished Richmond, Fredericksburg & Potomac railroad bridge.

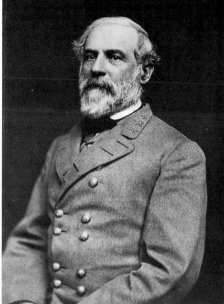

Robert E. Lee

Joseph Hooker

This "sketch from life" of Stonewall Jackson is the work of Confederate cavalryman Robert A. Caskie and dates from 1862.

Forbes's drawing above shows the Falmouth camp of Union aeronaut Thaddeus Lowe. In the foreground is Lowe's apparatus for generating hydrogen to inflate his balloons, and at rear the burned-out ruin of the Phillips house. Below is Waud's view of a New Jersey battery posted to guard the Banks's Ford crossing of the Rappahannock upstream from Falmouth.

Daniel Butterfield

George Stoneman

Stoneman's Yankee cavalry at Kelly's Ford on the upper Rappahannock, drawn by artist Forbes on April 21. A rainstorm rendered this cavalry movement a false start. The Stoneman raiders would not begin their strike behind enemy lines until Day Three of the campaign.

The Chancellorsville campaign opened on April 27 as the Federals marched upriver secretly to cross the Rappahannock at Kelly's Ford. Above, Forbes sketched the troops leaving their winter camps; they have stripped the huts of their shelter-tent roofs. Below is Waud's drawing of the 8th Pennsylvania cavalry securing the Rapidan crossing at Ely's Ford on April 29.

Henry W. Slocum

George G. Meade

In Hooker's intricate plan, Dan Sickles's Third Corps marched upriver on April 30 toward the U.S. Ford crossing to reinforce the main flanking force. Edwin Forbes made this sketch of a double column of Sickles's troops moving along the north bank of the Rappahannock.

Union engineers laid two pontoon bridges across the Rappahannock at U.S. Ford on April 30, and that evening elements of Couch's Second Corps and Sickles's Third crossed and marched toward the Chancellorsville crossroads. Forbes made the sketch above from the Confederate shore. Below is Forbes's view of the Chancellor house, looking northwest. The troops marching at left are on the Orange Plank Road, guarded by the entrenched battery in the foreground.

Hooker ordered in reinforcements to brace his position at Chancellorsville. Above is a Forbes drawing of a column of Couch's Second Corps men on a night march from the U.S. Ford crossing, their path lit by a flaming tree. Forbes also drew the scene below, of Hooker's congratulatory address of April 30 being read to the troops. "Our enemy must either ingloriously fly," Hooker announced, "or come out from behind his defenses and give us battle on our own ground."

A major deception in Hooker's plan was forcing a crossing downstream from Fredericksburg. On the foggy morning of April 29, as sketched above by Alfred Waud, Pennsylvanians of David Russell's Sixth Corps brigade in pontoon boats stormed ashore to seize a bridgehead.

Harry Fenn's pen-and-ink drawing above, after a Timothy O'Sullivan photograph, shows two of the pontoon bridges laid at Franklin's Crossing, the site gained by Russell's troops.

Downstream from Franklin's Crossing, at Fitzhugh's Crossing, John Reynolds's First Corps won a second bridgehead on April 29, sketched below by Waud from the Confederate rifle pits.

The scene at the Chancellorsville crossroads during the battle on May 1 was sketched above by Waud for *Harper's Weekly*. The view is southwest, with the Chancellor house at the right. The troops, from Slocum's Twelfth Corps, pre- pare to march to the scene of the fighting to the east. That fighting, also sketched by Waud, is pictured below. Sykes's Fifth Corps regulars advance to battle along the Orange Turnpike, supported by a gun of the 5th U.S. Artillery.

Richard H. Anderson

Lafayette McLaws

Stonewall Jackson's last portrait, made
some two weeks before Chancellorsville.

Below, seated on Yankee hardtack boxes,
Lee and Jackson plan Jackson's flank march
in the early morning hours of May 2.
Drawing by William Sheppard.

Battles and Leaders of the Civil War

would have great difficulty deploying under fire. The Lewis and Alrich farmsteads had nothing in particular to recommend them as new Federal positions. Already at Mrs. Lewis's Sykes was being outflanked both left and right. At Alrich's Slocum had his right flank threatened by Rans Wright's Georgians starting along the cleared right-of-way of the unfinished railroad to the south. Unless he and Sykes could drive the enemy back two miles or more — something very seldom done in that war against Stonewall Jackson — so as to put the Wilderness behind them, there was little profit in continuing the battle where it was being fought.

Sykes pulled back his regulars with some promptness. They were girding themselves to charge a Rebel battery, said Private Merryweather, "when Gen. Sykes came up & stopped us." As the army fell back, a Fifth Corps field hospital in a toll-keeper's house alongside the Turnpike came under fire. "When the men began to bring their wounded fellow soldiers in they would not stop where I was," surgeon John Shaw Billings wrote. "Shells fell on all sides, one passing through the house, and in five minutes I was the only person left about the place." The wounded were soon evacuated to the Chancellor house.

As any soldier would, Slocum objected to having to break off the contest and withdraw under fire, always a difficult maneuver. "The men went back disappointed, not without grumbling," General Williams wrote, "and it really required some policy to satisfy them that there was not mismanagement somewhere." The orders for the Eleventh Corps to reinforce were canceled just as it started forward.

In the midst of the withdrawal Hooker now sent orders to Couch and Slocum to "hold on to your position till 5 P.M." His intent was not clear — at least not to Couch and Slocum — but apparently by including a deadline he simply wanted to stabilize the relative positions of the two columns before their final pullback. Or possibly he gave thought to holding a line atop the last ridge of high ground in front of Chancellorsville, a little over a mile east of the crossroads. Holding that ridge would deny the Confederates a good artillery position. Be that as it may, General Couch took it as a change of mind. Tell General Hooker, he said "with warmth unbecoming in a subordinate," that it was too late. The enemy was upon him flank and rear, and he was in full retreat.[20]

* *

AT DAYBREAK on May 1 Battery L, 1st New York Light Artillery, went over the Fitzhugh's Crossing pontoon bridge to take position in John Reynolds's First Corps sector below Fredericksburg. At noon Lieutenant George Breck seated himself behind the battery's earthen embrasure to write one of his regular letters to his hometown paper in upstate New

York. "The day is warm and beautiful — a real summer day," he began. "Fleecy clouds are floating in the air, the birds are caroling their sweetest notes, and, as I write, 12 o'clock, everything is very quiet. With the exception of a few musket or rifle shots, there has been no firing to-day." He went on to speculate that hard fighting was surely ahead, but right now on General Sedgwick's front that seemed to be the farthest thought from anyone's mind. As he closed his letter he added a postscript: "P.M. — For the last hour there has been heavy cannonading on the right. All quiet in our front."

This third day in the Yankee bridgehead was the most unwarlike day yet. In their rifle pits and behind their entrenchments the men ate their rations and slept and played cards and smoked their pipes and traded rumors. "All kinds of yarns are afloat at such times as these but I dont believe scarcely any of them," New Yorker Cyrus Stone assured his parents. Most of the rumors and speculations that afternoon centered on the heavy rumble of artillery fire off to the west, and it was generally agreed that Fighting Joe must be after the Rebs today. In a letter to his father, Lieutenant Colonel Selden Connor of the 7th Maine explained, "Hooker is playing a deep game on them this time, and notwithstanding our former ill-success we are hopeful now of the best results."[21]

The Confederates beyond the lines also welcomed the unexpected quiet of the day. When A. P. Hill's Light Division was ordered to march out at first light, one of its quartermasters had to leave behind two wagonloads of fish just seined from the Rappahannock. The marchers were told to take all they wanted for later cooking, but in the end Jubal Early's men inherited a substantial supply of fresh fish. Private Samuel Eaton of Hoke's brigade, Early's division, began his diary entry that day with a culinary note: "Friday 1st of May we had a fine time frying and eating herine. I dried & fryed for a good many. . . ."

Before he left for the other front that morning, General Lee had instructed Early to do his best to conceal the thinness of his forces. If he could not hold the position against an attack he must retreat southward along the railroad to protect the army's communications. If the enemy withdrew any troops on his front, he should strike a balance there and come west with the rest of his men.

Thus not many in Jubal Early's command had time for a fish fry that day. He kept his infantry busy throwing up entrenchments, using whatever implements came to hand, including bayonets and tin plates. To defend Hamilton's Crossing on the railroad he had a fortification constructed of rails and ties taken up from the unused section of the line that lay within range of the Yankee guns across the river. The artillerymen were especially busy, and by night there were 49 guns dug in on the high ground, with another 10 in reserve. One battery was sent downriver to fend off two Yankee gunboats threatening Port Royal. On the right beyond Hamilton's Crossing, where he ran out of infantry, Early posted an English-made Whitworth rifle, a breechloader of exceptional range, to threaten the flank of any Federal advance.

Still, General Early had more ground to cover than men for the task, and he opened his bag of tricks. Details were sent out to build campfires in the rear areas where Jackson's divisions had their fires the night before. Bivouacs of empty tents went up on ground where they could be seen from across the river. Guns were run out in plain sight on every height. "Details were made to build fires along our lines and hollar and hoop and by this means we kept them off . . . ," boasted Georgia private Urbanus Dart. "The boys did not know what to think of the officers when they were told they were on a hollaring detail but appeared to be quite fond of it."

In another of Early's ploys, two well-coached Louisianians from Harry Hays's brigade deserted to the Yankees with a tale to tell. They said that three divisions — Early's, Rodes's, and Colston's — were on Sedgwick's front that day and, more alarming to their interrogators, they told of the arrival of Hood's division, just up from the south.

At dusk the band of the New Jersey brigade in Bully Brooks's division assembled behind the entrenchments on the right and put on a concert of martial music. Before long the Yankee bandsmen were startled to hear a Confederate band across the lines strike up a cheerful rendition of "Yankee Doodle." The Jerseymen responded with "Dixie." "Both armies cheered," wrote Edmund Halsey of the 15th New Jersey. "It was a strange sight and the sun going down at the moment made a deep impression on every one."[22]

At General Sedgwick's headquarters on the north bank of the river the day passed in suspended animation. Observation posts dutifully reported their sightings. Sedgwick telegraphed Butterfield, for example, "Gen. Brooks reports large column of infantry with ambulances & baggage train moving to our right." It was John Reynolds who originated the warning that Hooker would encounter an enemy column advancing west of Fredericksburg. The Sixth Corps' Light Division was sent across the river to strengthen the bridgehead, and troops there were held under arms for the planned demonstration. There was considerable puzzlement when the sound of battle was heard from upriver in the afternoon. How could they act intelligently on their front, Reynolds asked Sedgwick, without knowing "something of what has transpired on the right?"

It was 4:00 P.M. when word finally arrived from General Hooker, and it only caused more puzzlement at Sedgwick's headquarters. Marked 2 o'clock, the dispatch announced that Hooker was suspending his advance and that Sedgwick should "keep a sharp lookout, and attack if can succeed." Hooker assumed Sedgwick had already begun his demonstration as ordered, and it might now be profitably converted into an attack against a weakened enemy front. Sedgwick, for his part, had no idea what he was supposed to do. He replied that he and Reynolds were in agreement that it would be unwise for them to attack now before General Hooker "accomplished some success." They believed the enemy was too strong on their front to dislodge, and they would wreck their commands trying.

The only reply to that, almost an hour later, was the delivery of Hooker's much-delayed 11:30 A.M. telegram ordering the demonstration to open at 1 o'clock. Sedgwick dragged his feet in complying, hoping for some light to be shed on the tangle. At 9:30 that night the fitfully operating telegraph brought him Hooker's order to cancel the demonstration. He had long since told his troops to stand down. From the first, John Sedgwick had never had a very clear picture of what was expected of him in this campaign, and the events of May 1 did nothing to enlighten him.[23]

There was the same sense of a false start in Falmouth. John Gibbon's division there had been roused at 4:00 A.M. and told to pack up for the march upriver, but in all the confusion caused by the telegraph failure General Gibbon spent the day awaiting orders that never came.

His was not a day without event, however. It was reported to him that six companies of the 34th New York in his division had stacked arms and were refusing to serve any longer. Here was another instance of two-year enlistees disagreeing with the War Department on when their two years were up. John Gibbon was old army and a hard man — the Iron Brigade earned its name under his command — and he had no patience or sympathy with such protests. He told the 34th's brigade commander, Alfred Sully, to deal with the case, but Sully replied that he was unable to enforce discipline on the mutineers.

At that Gibbon went to the 34th's camp and confronted the protesters with the 15th Massachusetts, rifles in hand, a regiment Gibbon considered one of the best in the army. He addressed the New Yorkers, telling them that whatever their grievances this was mutiny, and they were no better than "the rebels on the other side of the river." Unless they promptly returned to duty, he said he would order the 15th Massachusetts to open fire "and kill every man it could. . . ." Then he called on every man now ready to do his duty to step forward.

"Gen. Gibbon makes a speech to the 34th N.Y. & they return to their 'allegiance'" was how a diarist phrased it. By ones and twos at first the protesters stepped forward, then more followed, and finally every man stood on the new line. They even started a cheer, but stern Gibbon silenced them. Only when they had taken up their arms and equipment again would their cheers be welcome. That ended the mutiny of the 34th New York. It would serve faithfully in the days to come, and be mustered out the next month.

John Gibbon remembered that he rode away from the scene "trembling at the thought of what might have happened. . . ." Still, he thought the action he had taken should have been taken earlier by Brigadier Sully, and he relieved him on the spot. A court of inquiry would find Gibbon's action unjustified, but Alfred Sully never again served with the Army of the Potomac.[24]

*　*

WHEN HE tried to put the best face on the events of the day, Joe Hooker would tell his chief of staff that he judged all the Rebel cavalry to be "in my immediate presence, which I trust will enable Stoneman to do a land-office business in the interior." In fact his cavalry commander did hardly any business at all on May 1. When it came to General Stoneman obeying his instructions for the raid on the enemy's communications, Hooker would later say, "It is fair to conclude, that he never read them over after they passed into his hands, but carried on the war after his own fashion."

When he decided back in February to make his cavalry an independent corps, Hooker had not looked far for its commander. George Stoneman had been his classmate at West Point and they had served together in California, where Hooker "formed a favorable idea of his promise." During 1862 Stoneman served McClellan as chief of cavalry, a purely administrative post but a logical steppingstone to command the cavalry corps under Hooker. Of that appointment Hooker would say ruefully, "You cannot know men for War until you have had an opportunity to try them."

His directive for Stoneman's raid had certainly been explicit enough about its objective. The commanding general, it read, "considers the primary object of your movement the cutting of the enemy's communications with Richmond by the Fredericksburg route" — the Richmond, Fredericksburg & Potomac Railroad — "and he wishes to make everything subservient to that object." Stoneman was told specifically to cut the line in the vicinity of Hanover Junction. In the supplementary directive given him on April 28, the R.F. & P. remained his primary target, with the additional proviso that he reach it by a more direct route and proceed by forced marches.

It may be supposed that when Hooker handed this April 28 directive to Stoneman at Morrisville, he discussed the raid generally with him, stressing its objectives. This (it may be further supposed) ought to have awakened in Stoneman a sense of enterprise — the enterprise to seize the moment and hurry a picked force 75 miles ahead from Kelly's Ford by forced marches to reach Hanover Junction, where the R.F. & P. intersected the Virginia Central. Tough John Buford and his four regiments of veteran regulars would have been an ideal choice for such a mission.

Within a few miles above Hanover Junction were three good-sized wooden R.F. & P. bridges (as charted by Hooker's intelligence staff), over the North Anna River, Reedy Swamp, and Pole Cat Creek. Burning any one of them would shut down the railroad instantly and for a substantial period. Thus the primary object of the raid would be achieved at the very least by Day Five of the campaign; even as Hooker was observing what a land-office business Stoneman must be doing, one or more of these bridges ought to have been in flames.[25]

His cavalry commander, however, entirely lacked such enterprise. By evening of Day Five his vanguard was only approaching Louisa Court House, on the Virginia Central 34 miles west of Hanover Junction. Moreover, the march he planned for the next day would take him south, not east toward the Junction. General Stoneman was indeed carrying on the war after his own fashion.

May 1 did see him pick up his laggard pace somewhat, as his lead division under David Gregg covered 25 miles to reach Louisa Court House. Even so, Gregg's troopers found time enough for foraging. During the afternoon, Nathan Webb of the 1st Maine recorded in his journal, "we had foraged pretty extensively and every man had his 'extras' in the shape of butter, eggs, milk, dried peaches &c. One man had a two gallon jar of raspberry jam." One brigade was detoured for hours in fruitless pursuit of a Confederate wagon train that reportedly had crossed its path. The net gain for the day was the capture of a twelve-man picket post at Orange Springs.

General Averell, to whom Stoneman had assigned half the raiding force to dispose of the Rebel cavalry in the area, spent the day cautiously sparring with the foe at Rapidan Station on the Orange & Alexandria. The railroad crossed the Rapidan here, and Rooney Lee had posted the 9th and 13th Virginia, with one gun, to guard the place, and from dawn to dusk Averell worried the problem of getting through or around Lee's troopers. By evening Lee had orders to shift his attention to Stoneman's force, and before he withdrew he fired the railroad bridge. John Tidball, in command of a battery of Federal horse artillery, observed in his journal that this "rendered it unnecessary for us to do anything more for its destruction. We however remained in position until dark when we withdrew to our former camp in the swamp."

Averell (unlike Stoneman) at least made an effort to report to General Hooker on the state of affairs with the cavalry. For his trouble he received a sharply worded dispatch from Hooker's headquarters. The commanding general, he was told, "does not understand what you are doing at Rapidan Station." Here was the campaign in its fifth day and it appeared that General Averell with half the cavalry had so far managed to cover just 28 miles on its mission to destroy Lee's communications. Averell was ordered to return with his force without delay to U.S. Ford, and to report to headquarters in person.[26]

* *

THE MOMENT he learned that Hooker's columns were starting to withdraw along the Turnpike and the Plank Road that afternoon, Stonewall Jackson was on them. The lieutenant general commanding "is pressing on up the Plank Road," a dispatch to McLaws announced; ". . . you will press on up the turnpike toward Chancellorsville, as the enemy is falling back. Keep your skirmishers and flanking parties well out, to guard against ambuscade." He pushed Stephen D. Ramseur's brigade from Rodes's division to the front on the Plank Road. Riding ahead to the point of the advance, Bryan Grimes's 4th North Carolina, Jackson intoned over and over, "Press them, Colonel."

Countermarching a large force in contact with the enemy — especially when the enemy is under a Stonewall Jackson — was never an easy maneuver. General John Geary of the Twelfth Corps was moved by the experience to call it "a movement always requiring great tact and delicacy united with firmness of will and purpose." However that may be, Geary and Alpheus Williams were able to extract their divisions on the Plank Road without great difficulty. Their loss on the return to Chancellorsville was only ten killed and wounded. They were fortunate not to have been more closely engaged when Hooker's order reached them. That gave them enough of a head start to evade most of Jackson's pursuit. He encountered "some of the worst swamps and thickets I ever saw," wrote Lieutenant Thomas Hightower of the 21st Georgia. "We pitched around there all day and never saw the first wild Yankee. We saw some who had been killed and a few prisoners."

During the march along the Plank Road artillerist Porter Alexander had boldly pushed Pichegru Woolfolk's Virginia battery right up with the skirmishers in the advance. When Slocum's corps emerged from the forest onto the Alrich farm, Alexander quickly deployed the rest of his guns for battle. "But they soon began to disappear in the woods," he wrote, "& we recognized that they were being withdrawn."

Then with a single gun of Woolfolk's and a squad of infantry skirmishers at his side, Alexander moved cautiously ahead through the enclosing woods until they reached the last bend in the road. Ahead 300 yards was a barricade and a Federal battery. In the far distance, down the straight stretch of road, Alexander could see the Chancellor house "& the black masses of troops about it. . . ." After a brief exchange of shelling he withdrew. It appeared that the whole Yankee army was in front of them.[27]

At the same time on the Turnpike to the north, Sykes's regulars were having to make a fighting withdrawal. They had a considerably longer distance to cover than Slocum's men, and they were more closely pursued. Artillery was right up on the firing line on both sides and suffered accordingly.

A gun crew of the Norfolk Blues, attached to Anderson's division, had one man killed and six wounded, and for a time only three were left to work the gun. The Bedford Light Artillery was also hit hard by the Yankee fire and had a caisson destroyed. "We were pretty badly cut up," Captain Tyler Jordan remembered, "and that night ordered back to refit. . . ." The First Richmond Howitzers went forward in support, wrote Private William Dame, and "every few yards we would meet wounded men coming to the rear and as we advanced farther on we passed men killed in the fight." The Howitzers took position "right by 3 dead Yankees."

For most of the day here the gun duel on the Federal side was carried on by Lieutenant Watson's Battery I, 5th U.S., which suffered two men and five horses hit and a caisson blown up. At Hooker's order to withdraw, General Couch pushed two Second Corps batteries out on the Turnpike along with Winfield Scott Hancock's infantry division. Captain William Arnold's Battery A, 1st Rhode Island, and a two-gun section of Lieutenant Alonzo Cushing's Battery A, 4th U.S., unlimbered in a clearing by the road to help repel McLaws's pursuit. The regulars passed safely through Hancock's line to the rear, and then Hancock and the gun line pulled back in practiced sequence. During this final stage of the countermarch it was primarily Hancock's skirmishers who were engaged. Theirs was nasty woodland sniping in which the 61st New York's Colonel Nelson A. Miles, a future general-in-chief of the U.S. Army, won mention in dispatches.

Thomas Dardin, 16th Virginia, was one of those close on the Yankees' heels, and he was surprised, as they neared Chancellorsville, to see his foes halt abruptly and turn and form a defensive line. "The Yanks gave loud and rapid cheers as they thought they had such a good position. . . ." Dardin and his fellows soon learned the cheering was not an idle boast. According to a Pennsylvanian in Hancock's division, "The rebs came over on the double-quick holloring like savages but we had 3 lines up ther which stoped them very quick." A regular in one of Sykes's brigades added with satisfaction, "The rest of us fired a few volleys which sent our opponents to the right-about. While this was going on I heard a chaplain shouting out behind us: 'Give 'em Hell, boys; give 'em Hell, and the Lord have mercy on their souls.'"[28]

Stonewall Jackson still had one card left to play this Friday. Characteristically it was a move by the flank. He had sent Rans Wright's Georgia brigade swinging off to the left to follow the railroad right-of-way to see what might be done about turning the Federals' southern flank. It was close to 6 o'clock when Wright reached Catharine Furnace, a mile and a half to the south and rear of Chancellorsville. There he encountered Jeb Stuart with the 1st Virginia cavalry and a detachment of horse artillery. A mile or so to the north across Lewis's Run, Stuart said, there were Yankees on the high, open ground of the Hazel Grove farmstead. He thought they might be there in some force, but visibility in this woodland was poor. Wright prepared to give battle, sending forward the 22nd and 48th Georgia behind a screen of skirmishers "through the almost impenetrable forest."

After its recall in midafternoon Alpheus Williams's Twelfth Corps division had marched back past Chancellorsville to take up its old position west of the crossroads. (Private Joseph Akerman made note in his diary that he had seen General Hooker watching from the verandah of the Chancellor house when they marched out that morning, and now he saw him there again as they marched back.) Williams had his men digging in along the northern edge of Hazel Grove. For outpost duty he sent the 123rd New York and the 3rd Wisconsin across the open ground to the south to establish the division's picket line in the shallow valley of Lewis's Run. In this marshy wooded ground they ran suddenly into Rans Wright's advancing skirmishers. "We had some severe conflicts," Williams noted dryly.

The 123rd New York had enlisted the previous September and had done mostly occupation duty in the campaigns since then, and today was its first battle. Earlier, in the woods along the Plank Road, they had encountered a good deal of noise and battle smoke, and shell fragments and minié balls sang through the trees overhead, but as Rice Bull put it, "as the enemy was some distance away our fears were not greatly excited." Now, standing in line of battle in the open at Hazel Grove, without warning a volley was fired at them from the woods ahead "and bullets began to whistle and sing." The man standing next to Private Bull, Jerry Finch, dropped his gun and staggered and went down. "I stooped down and turned him over as he had fallen on his face; when I spoke he gave no answer. He had been instantly killed."

They could not return fire until their skirmishers were out of the way, and for a time they had to endure the continued musketry and then artillery shells began to fall around them. Colonel Archibald McDougall jumped onto a log and waved his sword and shouted, "For God sake, boys, stand your ground! Don't let it be said the boys of Washington County ran!" Finally they were ordered back to the defenses along the northern edge of the Hazel Grove clearing.

Four men of the 123rd were dead and seven wounded. The rest wondered if they had actually hit any among the unseen enemy. Private Bull discovered that a bullet had struck the stock of his rifle and another had gone through the tin coffee pail hanging from his haversack. That night, he wrote, "we felt that we had our baptism of blood and commenced to realize the gravity of our position."[29]

After Porter Alexander's reconnaissance established that the Federals were posted in strength in front of Chancellorsville, Stonewall Jackson had galloped to the left to find out for himself the results of Rans Wright's movement. At Catharine Furnace he met Stuart, and the two generals and their staffs rode forward to a wooded knoll to observe the progress of Wright's attack.

Wright had no guns with his column, and had requested artillery support from Stuart to help dislodge the Federals. Stuart sent him four guns from Major Robert F. Beckham's horse artillery. With much labor Beckham's gunners dragged their pieces up the narrow forest track to the knoll where Stuart and Jackson were watching the fighting. They opened fire and soon enough pushed the Yankee infantry back across Hazel Grove, but in turn they drew a hail of counterbattery fire.

General Williams had his divisional artillery posted at Hazel Grove and at Fairview on his left rear, and it took up Beckham's challenge. The six Parrott rifles of Battery M, 1st New York Light, and four Napoleons from Battery F, 4th U.S., pounded the knoll with a converging fire. "I do not think that men have been often under a hotter fire than that to which we were here exposed," Major Beckham admitted. Watching Yankees saw one of the Rebel caissons explode, throwing a gunner high in the air. One gun was disabled with a shattered axle; men and horses went down. Beckham's sixteen casualties included almost half his gunners. The New York battery would expend 100 rounds in forty-five minutes of steady firing.

"Quite a number of our men were killed & wounded by this unexpected fire," one of Stuart's staff wrote, and it seemed to him that an immediate retreat was in order. Jeb Stuart was in full agreement. "General Jackson," he said, "we must move from here." It was thought miraculous that neither general was hit before they evacuated the knoll. (Earlier that afternoon a Federal barrage in front of Chancellorsville had rained down shell fragments all around General Lee. A shaken witness, Thomas Dardin, wrote, "I think our Generals expose themselves too much.") Even as the party was hurriedly moving off, a piece of shell struck Stuart's adjutant, Major Channing Price, in the leg. Young Price, one of the most promising officers in the cavalry, shrugged it off, insisting that nothing was broken. But an artery had been severed, and in a matter of hours he was dead from loss of blood.[30]

General Williams had a story of his own about war's odd chances. He had taken a log house at Fairview as his headquarters, and it was targeted by Beckham's gunners. One shell (Williams later discovered) struck the chimney's flue and fell down unexploded into the ashes of the fireplace. The next morning, purely by chance, the headquarters cooks decided to prepare breakfast outside. "If the cooks had, as they had done the morning before, used the fireplace for cooking, we should have had an explosion which would probably have spoiled our breakfast and lessened the number of headquarters cooks materially," Williams wrote his family. "Such are the slight accidents that make or mar small as well as great matters."

It was sundown now, and as Wright pulled back his Georgians and Major Beckham withdrew what remained of his battery from the knoll, Friday's fighting was finally over. Joe Hooker's army was back where it had been at the beginning of the day, holding the Chancellorsville crossroads and its communications with U.S. Ford. Robert E. Lee bivouacked his army just to the east, extending from the Mine Road on the north across the Turnpike to the Plank Road.

On the Federal side George Sykes's division had done nearly all the fighting, on the Turnpike, and suffered 261 dead, wounded, and missing. Over half this total was in Colonel Burbank's brigade of regulars who first made contact with McLaws's advance. The Confederates did not record their losses separately for this day, but since the fighting on the Turnpike was generally even before the Federal pullback, McLaws's losses were surely about the same as Sykes's. Between them on May 1 the two sides lost perhaps 600 men.[31]

The day certainly had been a check for General Hooker, and he recognized that. Yet he was neither disheartened nor had he lost confidence in himself or in his plan. Indeed, he had now achieved his two primary aims — to get his army in good position south of the Rappahannock, and to draw General Lee out from behind his Fredericksburg fortifications.

It also appeared to Hooker on this evening of May 1 that he would be fighting the impending battle defensively. When he assured General Couch, "I have got Lee just where I want him; he must fight me on my own ground," it was not the empty posturing Couch later declared it to be. At the end of Day Five of his campaign Joe Hooker's dream was still intact.

At dusk, near the intersection of the Plank Road and the Catharine Furnace Road a mile and a quarter east of Chancellorsville, Robert E. Lee and Stonewall Jackson sat themselves on a fallen log in a little clearing in the woods and began to plan what to do with the initiative Joe Hooker had surrendered to them.[32]

9

My Troops Will Move at Once

G ENERAL ALPHEUS WILLIAMS was a man with varied interests
and an inquiring mind. Before the war he had studied at Yale and
practiced law and run a newspaper and traveled widely, and he had
picked up his military education on his own from service in Mexico and
in the state militia organization in Michigan. He had seen hard service
in the unhappy campaigning of the Twelfth Corps, and made it a habit
to record his experiences in long and richly descriptive letters to his
family. In the late hours of May 1, sitting outside his headquarters in the
Fairview clearing, he reflected on the happenings of the day.

"I sat quite late enjoying the brilliant moonlight," he wrote. In front
of him was a long line of guns, black and menacing, still in battery from
the earlier action. Beyond the gun line, in the sharp shadows on the brow
of the ground overlooking the wooded ravine of Lewis's Run, lay two of
his brigades on guard. Whippoorwills, "thicker here than katydids up
north," whistled their melancholy calls "as if there was nothing but peace
on earth, and save the occasional crack of the rifle away off on the left
there was a solemn stillness which was almost oppressive." General Williams visualized the two great hostile armies lying "within almost the
sound of one's voice, and now and then away off in front I could fancy
the sound of wheels and the tramp of men."[1]

In the Chancellor house a half mile to the east lights burned late.
Now that the battle was finally joined, General Hooker needed to know
what to expect the next day. During the afternoon and evening he had
been seriously distracted by the vagaries in his telegraphic link with
Falmouth. Not only had dispatches been delayed for hours, but when
they did arrive they were frequently and seriously garbled by the malfunctioning Beardslee machines. Dan Butterfield assigned darker motives to these mechanical failings. He suspected his dispatches to the

225

general "have either been mutilated or tampered with," and he had the telegraph lines patrolled. "Put to death instantly any person found injuring them or tampering with them at all," he ordered.

Apparently it was from one of these garbled messages that Hooker got the idea Lee was massing troops to force a crossing of his own at Banks's Ford. Artillery chief Henry Hunt was told to rush batteries from the reserve at Falmouth to cover the ford, and a brigade of infantry was detached from John Gibbon to defend against any crossing attempt. Passing on these orders, Butterfield tried to explain to Hooker that he knew of nothing to support the "supposition of an attack on Banks' Ford." After he put 26 guns in battery there Hunt said, "I think there is no great danger."[2]

The Yankee troops were hard at work with ax and shovel. In a circular to his corps commanders, Hooker called on them to put the lines assigned the previous day "in condition of defense without a moment's delay." The general commanding "trusts that a suspension in the attack to-day will embolden the enemy to attack him." Indeed, that was Joe Hooker's devout wish, as he made clear to a gathering of his generals at the Chancellor house that evening.

Gouverneur Warren, among others, took the occasion to argue for a renewal of the offensive the next day. Warren would, in effect, repeat the maneuvers of that morning, only this time using the northernmost column, on the River Road, to turn the enemy's flank. Hooker rejected the idea; "his original determination to await attack," as Warren put it, was unshaken.

Hooker was concerned, however, about the army's right, or western, flank. He thought it should be contracted and a portion swung back to a more secure position facing west. General Howard, who would be most affected by this, persuaded him to leave the line unchanged out of consideration for the sensibilities of the Eleventh Corps. His men, he said, would be demoralized by any further seeming pullback. Instead, the position of the Eleventh Corps, spread out at some length along the Plank Road, would be strengthened "with breastwork and abatis." As evidence of his confidence, Howard sent back the proffered reinforcement of a brigade and a battery from the newly arrived Third Corps. He wanted it understood that he "needed no assistance." He assured the general (as did Slocum and Couch) that he could hold right where he was.[3]

Another of Hooker's concerns was the whereabouts of James Longstreet's two divisions. He had to assume that Longstreet would be recalled from Suffolk as soon as the Yankees' intentions on the Rappahannock were clear. The question then would be how long it would take Longstreet to reach Lee and by what route he would come.

If Stoneman's cavalry cut the Richmond, Fredericksburg & Potomac and then the Virginia Central as ordered, to come by rail Longstreet's forces could approach only by way of Gordonsville after a most round-about journey. In that event the battle on the Rappahannock would be settled one way or the other before Longstreet could intervene. The campaign was five days old, however, and Confederate trains were still seen arriving at Hamilton's Crossing. What news there was from the cavalry did not inspire confidence. And now came reports by deserters and prisoners that at least Hood's, and perhaps Pickett's division too, had already arrived.

Butterfield was quick to test this supposition with General Peck at Suffolk. In this instance the telegraph worked faultlessly, and in two and a half hours the answer came back that if any of Longstreet's men were in front of Hooker they were only "first installments." As recently as the day before, Peck said, deserters and contrabands had come into his lines from both Hood's and Pickett's divisions. He would confirm and update that intelligence the next morning. Colonel Sharpe of the B.M.I. con-cluded that the deserters who had carried the tale were planted, and he made no change in his order of battle for Lee's army. Nevertheless, General Hooker would continue to look over his shoulder for Longstreet in the days to come.[4]

George Sharpe and John Babcock of the Bureau of Military Infor-mation spent the night patiently interrogating deserters and prisoners from the day's fighting, and in the process produced a striking piece of military intelligence work. Battlefield interrogation was nothing new, certainly — it had been common enough during detective Pinkerton's days with General McClellan — yet Sharpe and Babcock seem to have brought unusual skills to the task. When they finished their night's work — Sharpe was with Hooker at Chancellorsville, Babcock with Sedgwick on the Fredericksburg front — they had a remarkably clear picture of the enemy facing them.

"We have evidence," Sharpe announced, "that Anderson, McLaws, Rhodes & Trimble are in front of us" — that is, in front of Hooker at Chancellorsville. "I think only Early & A. P. Hill are left down there" — that is, facing Sedgwick at Fredericksburg. He did not spell out how he had reached that conclusion, but since Trimble's division (commanded in this battle by Raleigh Colston) did not engage the Yankees on May 1, Sharpe must have found a knowledgeable prisoner, perhaps a staff offi-cer, who knew something of the day's battle plan. Nor did Sharpe explain how he had wormed such information out of the man. In any event, by the next morning he had further refined this intelligence so as to put A. P. Hill on the Chancellorsville front along with Anderson, McLaws, Rodes, and Colston. Except for the one brigade of McLaws's that was with Early at Fredericksburg, this was an exact picture of the Army of Northern Virginia on May 2. In the battle to come, thanks to the B.M.I., Joe Hooker would know whom he was facing (although not necessarily where they were) at all times.

He would also have a good idea of how many altogether he was facing. Colonel Sharpe's strength estimate for the Army of Northern Virginia was now confirmed by a spy, one Joseph H. Maddox, that the B.M.I. had managed to slip into Richmond. Maddox learned, apparently from a commissary source in the Confederate capital, that during the last week in April the daily ration issue to Lee's infantry and artillery was 59,000. (He was unable to learn the issue to the cavalry.) This number nicely mirrored Sharpe's figure, and at headquarters was a welcome certification of the B.M.I.'s work.[5]

Oddly enough, General Hooker's mental picture of the Rebel army was clearer than his picture of his own army. His clouded knowledge, not surprisingly, involved the army's left wing, specifically John Sedgwick's Sixth Corps.

At some point during the communications chaos on May 1, Hooker got it into his head that Sedgwick had withdrawn all the Sixth Corps troops from the bridgehead below Fredericksburg. Since there was nothing to that effect in any dispatch recorded as sent to the commanding general that day, the only explanation for the confusion seems to be yet another malfunction of the Beardslee telegraph machines. For example, the notice that Hiram Burnham's Light Division was crossing to the south bank to reinforce Bully Brooks might have been garbled in sending (as other messages were garbled) so as to make it appear that both had instead crossed to the north bank.

However it happened, it helped push General Hooker to a new tactical decision. It was evident from the day's events that Lee was no longer being fixed in place at Fredericksburg by any threat of Sedgwick's. The deception was over; the battle would now be on the Chancellorsville front. Hooker decided to keep the Sixth Corps on the north bank opposite Fredericksburg (where he then supposed it to be) as a guard for headquarters and the army's supplies — and its supply line — and to bring John Reynolds's First Corps upriver to Chancellorsville.

When he arrived, Reynolds would form on the right rear of Howard's Eleventh Corps, extending the line back to the Rapidan. Thus both flanks would be anchored securely, the left at U.S. Ford on the Rappahannock, the right at Ely's Ford on the Rapidan, and Joe Hooker's mind would be eased.

He moved quickly to implement this tactic. The bridgehead was to be evacuated before daylight, and by midafternoon on May 2 Reynolds ought to be in his new place in the Chancellorsville lines. At 1:55 A.M. Hooker telegraphed Dan Butterfield, "Direct all of the bridges to be taken up at Franklin's crossing and below before daylight, and for Reynolds' corps to march at once, with pack train, to report to headquarters."

As Hooker reckoned it, there ought to be enough time before daylight for Wadsworth's First Corps division (the only troops he believed were still on the south bank) to recross in safety and for the engineers to take up the three bridges — the one at Fitzhugh's Crossing Wadsworth would use, and the two Sixth Corps bridges at Franklin's Crossing. Hooker's reckoning was accurate enough, but for the fact that the Signal Corps' comedy of errors had not yet run its course.

In this instance, with U.S. Military Telegraph operators and their Morse instruments newly in place at U.S. Ford and the station at Banks's Ford, the telegraph itself worked well enough. But somehow, in some way, on this bright moonlit night the courier carrying the dispatch from Chancellorsville the five miles to the U.S. Ford station lost his way. Not until 4:55 A.M. on May 2, three hours after it was written and fifteen minutes before sunrise, did Hooker's orders reach Falmouth. In explaining matters to General Reynolds, Dan Butterfield called this latest communications lapse "one of the most unfortunate that has occurred. . . ."

Since Hooker's order for Reynolds's First Corps was definite and without qualification, it would have to be carried out in daylight regardless of the risk. John Sedgwick, however, was in a quandary regarding the Sixth Corps. The order mentioned taking up the two Sixth Corps bridges at Franklin's Crossing, but nothing about removing any troops there. Sedgwick could not see the logic in leaving Brooks's division in its lines in the bridgehead (now supported by Burnham's Light Division), completely isolated on the enemy's side of the river. Indeed, like so many of General Hooker's orders to him over the last twenty-four hours, it seemed both illogical and dangerous. "I dare not take up the upper bridges as it would relieve the enemy at once, leaving him free to move against Gen. Brooks," he replied brusquely. He noted later, "To this dispatch I received no reply."

The dispatch did go to Hooker at the Chancellor house, but perhaps he only glanced at it, for he missed the reference to Brooks's division. Throughout the course of events on May 2 General Hooker would continue to think that Sedgwick's entire corps was on the north bank of the Rappahannock. But the far more significant consequence of this latest communications fiasco was that the 16,900 men of John Reynolds's First Corps would spend the afternoon hours of May 2 still on the march upriver rather than digging in on the army's right flank at Chancellorsville.[6]

*   *

WHEN HE first came up with Stonewall Jackson during the fighting on May 1, General Lee had listened as Jackson reported on the progress of the advance but offered no suggestions. Clearly he decided his lieutenant had matters well in hand. Lee then reconnoitered off to the right, northward toward the river, riding out some way along the Mine Road with the cavalry pickets. One obvious tactic would be to turn Hooker's left to cut him off from his base across the river. But the enclosing Wilderness argued against it. Just to reach the enemy and deploy over the few narrow roads would be a severe problem. Lee stated it simply — he found "no place fit for attack. . . ."

When he returned from his reconnoiter he sent to Jeb Stuart to find out just who it was they were fighting. Lee explained that the prisoners taken so far were all from Meade's corps (these were Sykes's regulars who were doing most of the Potomac army's fighting that day), and they said that Howard's corps had crossed the Rapidan ahead of them and taken some other road. The day before Stuart had identified three Federal corps as crossing the Rappahannock. "What has become of the other two?" Lee asked. He had still to consider the possibility that this movement was a cover for a Federal column advancing on Gordonsville. He told Rooney Lee to hamper any move in that direction by having his cavalry burn the Orange & Alexandria's bridge across the Rapidan.

As the sun went down and the firing on Rans Wright's front sputtered out, Stonewall Jackson made his way back to the rest of his command. He crossed the Plank Road and went on to the Turnpike, where Captain Alexander Haskell, a staff officer in A. P. Hill's division, guided him to some open high ground from where the Yankee lines were visible. "Ride up here, General, and you will see it all," Haskell told him. With his glasses Old Jack studied the scene for some minutes. "The shells were bursting around us," Captain Haskell observed. In view were three blue lines of battle, solidly entrenched. Their flags could be seen by dozens. As Porter Alexander had witnessed from the Plank Road, it was obvious that the enemy was massing at Chancellorsville in very heavy force.

Jackson returned to the intersection of the Plank Road and the Catharine Furnace Road, a site that by its central location came to serve as the high command's headquarters in the field. Before long General

Lee joined him. A Yankee sharpshooter in a tall pine was harassing a nearby battery, and the two generals moved off to a more sheltered spot in a clearing just to the south and east of the crossroads. Seating themselves on a log there they discussed the day's events and tomorrow's plans. Watching from a distance, an awestruck artillery private remembered how "General Jackson made some gestures with his hands, as he pointed in various directions."[7]

Afterward, when the full significance of this conference in the Wilderness had become apparent, men would scour their recollections for the exact words Generals Lee and Jackson spoke in those evening hours. They were together until after nightfall, and staff men and general officers came and went, and in later years it was hard to remember just who said what or when they said it. Yet there can be no mistaking the general outline of the conversation. Someone would remember Lee asking Jackson, "How can we get at these people?" but the question was rhetorical. He had already decided that.

The afternoon before, Lee made what was for him the fundamental decision of the campaign — he would give battle rather than give up the Rappahannock line — and ordered Jackson to march west to accept Hooker's challenge on the Chancellorsville front. From the way the Yankees had pulled back at almost the first contact — they did not make a sustained fight of it anywhere that day — and the way they had by report strongly entrenched themselves around Chancellorsville, it was obvious that Hooker wanted to fight defensively. He was inviting attack; he was daring Lee to attack. But in so doing he had to give up the initiative, and on the battlefields of this war the initiative was something that had always served Robert E. Lee very well.

Attack he would; Lee hesitated not a moment in making that decision. If he met a check, his line of retreat by way of the Richmond, Fredericksburg & Potomac was still open. Or he might fall back southwesterly by way of Gordonsville. The Federal cavalry was not so far reported on his lines of communication. In truth, Lee's choices were limited: to fight or (as Joe Hooker had already put it) to ingloriously fly.

Too, Robert E. Lee might have had a particular reason for deciding to fight this battle with especial boldness. It was apparent, from the stark choices facing him, that he had underestimated Mr. F. J. Hooker. His opponent's surprise maneuvers had put him in a critical position — and with one quarter of his army absent by his own miscalculation. (Lee would tell Jefferson Davis on May 2 that he had no expectation of Longstreet joining him in time for this confrontation.) Lee was being tested by Fighting Joe Hooker as he had never been tested before, not by McClellan or by Pope or by Burnside, and he had need to rise to the challenge.

Several years later, when an account by a Stonewall Jackson disciple giving Jackson the dominant role at Chancellorsville was shown him, General Lee made a point of setting the record straight. "I am misrepresented at the battle of Chancellorsville in proposing an attack in front, the first evening of our arrival," he wrote in reference to the events of May 1. "On the contrary, I decided against it, and stated to Gen. Jackson, we must attack on our left as soon as practicable. . . ." Thus this discussion in the clearing in the Wilderness on the evening of May 1 was not about what to do, but only about how to do it.[8]

Staff officers were sent to the right toward the river to reconnoiter, so as to confirm Lee's first impression that there was no opening there to exploit. Dick Anderson and Little Billy Mahone, who had spent the winter with their commands encamped in the area, were queried about the terrain the Federals occupied. Lee's decision to "attack on our left" required two vital pieces of intelligence: the location of Hooker's right flank, and a hidden way to reach that flank.

Jeb Stuart now joined the conference, and was sent back to Catharine Furnace to find out what the cavalry had discovered about the enemy positions south and west of Chancellorsville. Stuart, and Jackson too, could testify that the Yankees were at Hazel Grove in force. Fitz Lee and his troopers had been scouting all day farther to the west, and they reported no interference from Yankee cavalry. All the roads, it seemed, belonged to the Confederates.

Indeed, Yankee cavalry was hardly to be seen on May 1. The only troopers who were in action were the 8th Pennsylvania pickets who had tangled that morning with Mahone's advancing column on the Turnpike. Colonel McVicar's unhappy nighttime clash with the Rebels near Todd's Tavern had apparently discouraged Pleasonton from any further reconnaissance efforts. When he probed for the Federal positions Fitz Lee encountered nothing but infantry pickets.

In late afternoon he had skirmished with a regiment from Alexander Schimmelfennig's Eleventh Corps brigade on the Carpenter homestead. Carpenter's was a mile or so south of Wilderness Church where the Orange Turnpike and the Orange Plank Road divided and a full two miles west of Chancellorsville. Somewhere in that area, Fitz Lee reported, was the Federals' right flank.

In his search for information, Stuart remembered that Beverly Tucker Lacy, Jackson's "chaplain general," knew the Wilderness well. The Reverend Lacy had once served a church there, and the Lacy family owned property in the area. He was called for and General Lee queried him on the roads south and west of Chancellorsville (Jackson had by this time retired for the night). Lacy explained that marching by way of

Catharine Furnace it was possible for a column to swing around south by west by north in an arc to reach the Orange Turnpike at Wilderness Tavern, some five miles west of Chancellorsville. If Fitz Lee was right about the location of the Federals' line, that would not only turn Hooker's flank but reach his rear. Furthermore, with Stuart's cavalry in firm control of the roads, the march could be made secretly.

By now Stuart, and Jackson himself, would have confirmed by personal observation that more than just Meade's corps was in front of them. It must be that all three of the corps Stuart had identified the day before — Meade's, Howard's, and Slocum's — were at Chancellorsville. It is unlikely, however, that General Lee was aware that Sickles's Third Corps and two divisions of Couch's Second had also joined Hooker. They had been at pains to conceal their marches, and of their troops only Hancock's were engaged on May 1, with no loss of prisoners.

Even had he known of them, it is unlikely that it would have altered Lee's determination to fight here. He stated the case clearly to Mr. Davis: "It is plain that if the enemy is too strong for me here, I shall have to fall back, and Fredericksburg must be abandoned. If successful here, Fredericksburg will be saved and our communications retained." To test if they were too strong, he would fight. Win or lose, he would go on as planned.

The Reverend Lacy's report seems to have been taken as confirmation of what the cavalry had already sketched out to the two generals. According to Major T.M.R. Talcott of Lee's staff, the flanking movement, at least in its general terms, had by then already been decided upon. Lee had outlined it for Jackson, giving him Stuart's cavalry to shield the march. Specific details on the route would have to wait for daylight. As Talcott remembered it, Old Jack listened attentively "and his face lighted up with a smile while General Lee was speaking. Then rising and touching his cap, he said, 'My troops will move at four o'clock.'"[9]

That night the two generals and their staffs made a simple bivouac in a nearby clearing in a pine thicket. Jed Hotchkiss, Jackson's mapmaker, offered the general his saddle blanket for a bed and they covered themselves with their overcoats, with their saddles for pillows.

Lieutenant James Power Smith, sent earlier to Anderson and McLaws for information on the enemy on their front, returned to the headquarters encampment about 10 o'clock. There was not even a campfire burning. In the moonlight he was directed to General Lee, lying under a pine tree, covered by his military cape. Told that the general had been asking for him, he waked him to give his report. He would remember Lee as completely at ease, even light-hearted on this night before battle. He teased young Smith about the staff's failure to locate a Yankee battery that had annoyed them during the afternoon's fighting. Only then did he let the lieutenant go off to make a rude bed of his own in the silent bivouac.

The chill of the spring morning would awaken Lieutenant Smith before first light, and looking around the bivouac he saw that everyone was asleep except Generals Lee and Jackson. They were warming themselves over a small fire, deep in conversation. When he fell back asleep they were still talking.

Jackson had risen that Saturday morning even before Lee to set the plan in motion. He called first for the Reverend Lacy, who repeated what he had told Lee the night before. Jackson had him mark the roads mentioned on a map, and Lacy obliged him — south by west on the Catharine Furnace Road, west from the Furnace on what he called a "blind road" across to the Brock Road, then north on that to the Orange Turnpike.

When laid down on a map, however, the route appeared to Jackson to pass too close to the enemy's pickets as seen by Fitz Lee's cavalry the day before. Was there not some other route between that one and the long circuit by way of Todd's Tavern? Lacy could not say for sure, but he knew someone who could — Charles C. Wellford, the proprietor of Catharine Furnace. Jackson seized on that. He roused Jed Hotchkiss and sent him with Chaplain Lacy to seek out Wellford. Find out what roads they could use, he told them, and if they were practicable for artillery, and try to procure a local man for a guide.

Hotchkiss and Lacy rode with all speed the two miles to Wellford's house beyond the Furnace. They roused him from his bed and explained what they wanted, and by the light of a candle in his parlor he marked on Hotchkiss's map exactly what they needed. From the Furnace, Wellford explained, he had recently opened a road through the forest southwesterly to the Brock Road in order to haul cordwood and ore for his ironmaking operations. He knew also of a byway that would avoid the enemy's pickets. This would make a shorter route than going around by way of Todd's Tavern, and at the same time shield them from the Yankees' view. Wellford's son could act as a guide. Exclaiming their thanks, Hotchkiss and Lacy raced back to camp.

They found the two generals together and Hotchkiss offered his report. Lee and Jackson were seated at their fire on empty hardtack boxes discarded by the Yankees the day before, and Hotchkiss set out another hardtack box as a table and spread his map and pointed to the route Mr. Wellford had outlined. They had a few questions, but their agreement was obvious: here was the hidden route to the enemy's rear.

The exchange that followed, Jed Hotchkiss wrote, impressed itself "on my mind very forcibly." As he recalled it, "Gen. Lee began by saying, 'Well, General Jackson, what do you propose to do?' Gen. Jackson, moving his finger over the route indicated on the map, said, 'I propose to go right around there.' Gen. L. replied, 'What do you propose to do it with?' Gen. J. said, 'With my whole command.' Gen. Lee then said, 'What will you leave me here to hold the Federal army with?' Gen. J. replied, 'The two divisions that you have here.' After a pause Gen. Lee said, 'Well, go ahead.'"

With no more drama than that in this dawning hour of May 2 the matter was settled. General Lee took paper and pencil and began making notes for the necessary orders. When he was done Stonewall Jackson rose and saluted and said, "My troops will move at once, sir."[10]

*   *

CAPTAIN WILLIAM CANDLER of Hooker's staff was on duty that night at headquarters in the Chancellor house, and in the small hours of the morning he found time to write a letter home. They had been attacked yesterday by Johnny Reb, he began. "Fell back at first to draw him on, then took a position and gave him 'fits'." Candler expected the battle to resume as soon as it was light. ". . . They must come out of their works and attack us in our own position. To-day will tell a big tale. God grant we may be successful. Staff and general all sound as yet."

During these hours there was no pause in preparations to meet the expected attack. The pioneers were ordered to work through the night, felling trees for abatis and clearing fields of fire for the guns. Troops and batteries were shifted to better defensive positions. By daylight or a little after that Saturday nearly every unit was in the position it would occupy for the day. The line, roughly convex in shape, was just over six miles long, guarded by thirty-one batteries and manned by nearly two thirds of the infantry of the Army of the Potomac.[11]

The left was anchored solidly on the Rappahannock at Scott's Dam, just over a mile downstream from U.S. Ford, and shielded the army's communications. The infantry here was Humphreys's division of the Fifth Corps, and there were 28 pieces of artillery by the river or within supporting distance. The rest of Meade's Fifth Corps — Griffin's division and then Sykes's — extended the line for two miles along the Mineral Spring Road to its intersection with the Ely's Ford Road. Meade posted his men in two strongly fortified lines carved out of the forest. In front the ground fell off to the valley of Mineral Spring Run, beyond which was Meade's picket line.

At the intersection of the Mineral Spring and Ely's Ford roads was the farm of Oscar Bullock, the only sizable cleared area in the Wilderness north of Chancellorsville. Because the Wilderness had so few open sites for artillery, Mr. Bullock's farm had become an enormous park for batteries in reserve.

The Bullock house marked the northern edge of a shallow salient that enclosed the Chancellorsville crossroads. Here the line was thickly manned by the two Second Corps divisions of Hancock and French — Gibbon's Second Corps division was still at Falmouth — which extended the salient across both the Turnpike and the Plank Road. In front of the Chancellor house and commanding these key roads was an artillery array of 14 guns. The other half of the salient, facing south and curling back to the Plank Road a mile west of the Chancellor house, was held by Slocum's Twelfth Corps divisions under Geary and Williams. Their line encompassed the strong artillery position at Fairview.

From the Rappahannock to Chancellorsville the line ran south by west. From there it turned west to parallel, then to follow directly, the Orange Plank Road by which Slocum's and Howard's corps had arrived at Chancellorsville two days before. At daybreak on May 2 Birney's division of Sickles's Third Corps filed into the line west of Slocum at Hazel Grove. The other two Third Corps divisions, under Berry and Whipple, served as a general reserve. A line of pickets was set out some 500 yards in front of the salient.

Howard's Eleventh Corps — Von Steinwehr's division, then the divisions of Schurz and Devens — extended the line a mile and a half farther west along the Plank Road from Dowdall's Tavern, past Wilderness Church and the point where the Orange Turnpike branched off, to the farmstead of James Talley. Throughout its length this line was on dominating high ground and faced to the south. Some 500 yards beyond Talley's on the Turnpike it simply ended, where Howard ran out of men. There was no natural feature here on which to anchor a defense, nor any formidable force with which to make a defense, only two regiments and two guns pointing to the west down the narrow road through the dark, silent forest. Fighting Joe Hooker's right flank, in the phrase of the military textbooks, was "in the air."

In these five army corps on the Chancellorsville line there were thirteen divisions, thirty-six brigades — all told, 72,300 troops and 184 pieces of artillery. The strength of this force was multiplied by field fortifications. The Wilderness at least furnished a limitless supply of logs for breastworks and trees to be felled for abatis and obstructions. On this Day Six of the campaign the army still carried three days' rations and had as well a secure route for resupply. Joe Hooker had prayed for the chance to fight his battle defensively, and at every hand was evidence that his prayer was about to be answered.

To be sure, there were causes for concern. Fighting defensively in the Wilderness would not be as easy as Lee's defensive December fight on the open hills behind Fredericksburg. In the minds of the artillerists there was concern that artillery chief Henry Hunt was not on hand to administer sure, centralized control over the guns. Too, there was unease at having to fight blind. The Todd's Tavern cavalry fight had persuaded Hooker, and Alfred Pleasonton, that Stuart's entire cavalry corps was at hand. Pleasonton husbanded his single cavalry brigade in the rear, not daring to reconnoiter. Hooker had tried to correct this lack by ordering in Averell's cavalry brigades from Rapidan Station, but Averell only received the order at 6:30 that morning and would be all day reaching Chancellorsville.

By far the weakest link in Hooker's defensive chain — as Hooker well knew — was Howard's Eleventh Corps. It was not only the smallest in the army but also thought to be the poorest in quality, and Hooker had his doubts about its commander. He posted Howard on the far right to keep him out of the most likely line of fire. Hooker had acted as promptly as he could to bring Reynolds's First Corps to secure this "in the air" flank. Now, by mischance and a bumbling courier, it was unlikely that Reynolds could reach the scene before nightfall. By day's end, however, that flank ought to be secure. By day's end, too, there ought to be cavalry to add to that security.[12]

General Hooker again rose early to ride the lines. His first priority was his first concern, the right. With Dan Sickles of the Third Corps and Cyrus Comstock of the engineers and various staff officers he led a cavalcade of inspection. Hooker rode his favorite horse, a milk-white charger named Colonel, and (as Private Silliman put it) "he made a fine appearance." At every position he was cheered to the echo. Sickles remarked on the "irrepressible enthusiasm of the troops."

It is said that this morning, May 2, 1863, was the last time the Army of the Potomac would ever raise a spontaneous battlefield cheer for its commanding general.

When the party reached the Eleventh Corps lines General Howard joined it and pointed out his dispositions. Because of what Howard described as "much extension" of his line, there were gaps noticeable in the divisions of Carl Schurz and Charles Devens posted farthest to the west. Engineer Comstock took Howard aside and cautioned him, "General, do close in those spaces!" Howard pointed out that everywhere the forest was "thick and tangled; will anybody come through there?" Comstock was quick with his answer: "Oh, they may!"

Otis Howard would later remember that conversation ruefully. Joe Hooker would remember pointing out the weaknesses and how they should be remedied. At the time, however — it was about 8:00 A.M. — he did not repeat his thought of the night before about "refusing" the flank, pivoting it back to make it stronger against a threat from the rear.

Some fortifying had been done on Howard's line, but it was not extensive; each commander seems to have followed his own ideas about military engineering. Clearly General Howard and his lieutenants were relying on the Wilderness as their first line of defense. Where the line ended there was the two-gun section of Captain Julius Dieckmann's 13th New York Independent battery and the two infantry regiments, 54th New York and 153rd Pennsylvania, some 700 men, posted behind a flimsy barricade of saplings and brush. They faced west, and a mile or so farther back, where the corps reserve artillery was posted, there were shallow rifle pits dug at right angles to the Turnpike. Everything else on the line of the Eleventh Corps faced south.[13]

On the left, in the immediate presence of the Rebel army, the fortifying was taken a good deal more seriously. Rifle pits were dug and stout breastworks of logs were put up and packed with dirt. Out front, where the ground fell off, the pioneers felled trees for abatis, their branches forming dense entanglements facing the enemy. Veteran commanders like Meade and Sykes and Couch and Hancock made sure this work was done and done right. Men who had fought on the Peninsula the year before made sage comparisons of the line in front of Chancellorsville with Malvern Hill, where the Yankee guns had inflicted a memorable defeat on Lee's charging infantry. A staff man in the Fifth Corps took note, that Saturday morning, that "Meade says we will not be attacked."[14]

*　*

WHEN CALLED out at first light, the men in Jackson's corps would remember how chilly the dawn was on May 2, and how they shivered and their teeth chattered. Hot coffee and the sun warmed them soon enough, and the day would turn out to be even more pleasant than the day before. As the 1st South Carolina was forming up, General Jackson rode past to the front. "We rose, on the point, I felt, of breaking into the old cheer," remembered J.F.J. Caldwell, "but reading battle in his haste and stern look, we contented ourselves with gazing at him and giving expression to our foolish speculations." When in due course Jackson's corps took up its line of march, "breaking off square to the left," veterans began to speculate with more confidence. "I knew old Jack was going to the rear of old Joe," John Brooks of the 20th North Carolina would insist.

The day's fighting began with a brief but violent artillery exchange in front of Chancellorsville. Ten guns from Willie Pegram's battalion, attached to A. P. Hill's division, opened on two Federal batteries soon after sunrise. The Federal gunners — Pennsylvanians under Captain Joseph M. Knap, firing 10-pounder Parrott rifles — had the best of the duel. "We replied and blew up 2 caissons silencing their battery," gunner James Heazlitt wrote proudly in his diary. If there was any question about the Yankees' position, and about their willingness to fight, it was answered.[15]

Jackson's powerful flanking column included the infantry of three divisions (Rodes, Colston, and A. P. Hill) — fifteen brigades, 29,400 men in all. The artillery complement was twenty-seven batteries, with 108 guns. Three and a half regiments of Stuart's cavalry served as escorts and guards. With artillerymen and cavalrymen, the total in the column came to 33,000.

General Lee would be left with seven brigades in the divisions of McLaws and Anderson — 13,915 infantrymen. Adding the one and a half regiments of cavalry and the gun crews of six batteries (24 guns) gave him a total of 14,900 men of all arms to hold the lines in front of Chancellorsville.

Having ignored the military textbooks and divided his army in the presence of a superior foe in every previous campaign he had fought (except Fredericksburg in December), such a move as this was not unprecedented for Robert E. Lee. But having now divided his army and then divided it again within twenty-four hours, literally under the guns of an army twice the size of his own, *was* unprecedented. Yet as Lee appraised the situation and measured his opponent, the risk became acceptable.

The smallest of the three segments of the army — Jubal Early's 12,400 at Fredericksburg — held a strong position and at the same time was free to maneuver. If pressed too strongly he might fall back down the railroad. If Lee was pressed too strongly at Chancellorsville, Early might come promptly to his support. Furthermore, the tactical situation at Fredericksburg had now reversed itself. At first the Federal crossing there was enough of a threat to pin down the greater part of the Confederate army. That deception now over, it was Early who was pinning down at least some portion of the Union army. And the more Yankees who were seen to leave Early's front (the march of the First Corps upriver that day would be seen and reported), the greater would be Early's freedom to maneuver.

The major risk of the operation was of course to that segment of the army, barely larger than Early's, commanded by Lee himself. He was at the very center of things, knowing he confronted at least three army corps. He willed himself to take that risk because of his confident reading of his opponent's mind.

The suspiciously easy victory of the day before, the reports of the enemy fortifying so strenuously, made it apparent that Fighting Joe Hooker was eager to do his fighting defensively. Instead of making the next move with his dominant force, he was waiting for Lee to move. Consequently, so long as Jackson did not tip his hand too soon that day, that ought to give Lee's little force security from attack. By seizing the initiative — by realizing the initiative was his for the taking — General Lee went a long way toward lowering the odds against him.

The other factor in lowering the odds was Stonewall Jackson. Lee had perfect confidence in his lieutenant. He knew him to be a master of concealment and a genius at exploiting surprise. That had always been his credo. Early in the war one of Jackson's lieutenants remembered him saying, "Always mystify, mislead, and surprise the enemy. . . ." With three divisions at his command, Jackson was certain to overwhelm initially whatever part of Hooker's army he struck, whether its flank or its rear. After that, in the fluid heat of battle in the entangling Wilderness, there was no telling what results might follow. Thus far in the campaign it was Joe Hooker who had put Robert E. Lee to the test. This flanking movement, whatever its outcome, would put Joseph Hooker to the test.[16]

* *

IT WAS a Stonewall Jackson tradition for his "foot cavalry" to set out on a march at first light, but on this day, May 2, 1863, his greatest march, there was delay. Too much to do had been left for morning. Then the artillery duel sent men scrambling for cover. Jackson's corps had started from Fredericksburg the morning before with two days' rations, so there was no delay for that, but still officers wanted their men to get down a good breakfast before they marched. (By habit a good many finished off whatever rations they had before going off to battle, trusting to Providence for replenishment; by evening many would be hungry.) Robert Rodes's division was to head the column, and when Alfred Colquitt's Georgians stepped off in the lead it was close to 7 o'clock, well after sunrise.

Not long afterward, at the point where the Catharine Furnace Road turned off southward from the Plank Road and not far from the night's headquarters bivouac, General Lee stood quietly by the roadside watching Rodes's men march past and turn down the Furnace Road. Jackson rode up, mounted on his rawboned warhorse Little Sorrel. He paused for a brief conversation with the commanding general. Their words — their last words — went unrecorded. Jackson's forage cap was pulled low over his eyes and his expression was intense. He gestured, pointing toward the enemy. Lee nodded, and then Jackson rode on.[17]

The order of march had Rodes's division leading, followed by Raleigh Colston's and then A. P. Hill's. The column carried only its fighting trains — ammunition wagons and ambulances — marching along with the artillery behind their assigned divisions. Colonel Allan's corps ordnance train brought up the rear. There was no baggage or commissary wagons; the men would carry what they ate. Thomas Munford's 2nd Virginia cavalry led the column. Jeb Stuart and Fitz Lee with the rest of the cavalry — 1st and 5th Virginia, half the 3rd Virginia — would advance on the right to secure all roads and byways in the direction of the enemy. Regimental commanders marched at the rear of their units to discourage straggling. The march regimen was standard: one mile in 25 minutes, 10 minutes' rest each hour, a rate of 2 miles per hour. There would be only a 15-minute midday meal break instead of the usual hour, however. Old Jack was balancing his need for speed with his need to have troops fresh enough for an attack when they reached their target.

As it happened, Jackson set out on his celebrated flank march that morning with an imperfect idea of exactly where the enemy's flank was located. His last intelligence put it at about the Carpenter farm, where Fitz Lee's cavalry had skirmished with Yankee infantry the previous afternoon. Carpenter's was on a byway called the Brook Road that ran south from Wilderness Church to the Brock Road. The first half of the march would go by way of the Catharine Furnace Road and Wellford's new extension of it to its intersection with the Brock Road. Turning right (north) on the Brock Road, however, would soon bring the column within a thousand yards of Carpenter's and reveal it to any Yankees who might be there.

It was here that Mr. Wellford had made his second contribution. A turn left on the Brock Road instead of right would in a short distance bring the marchers to the start of a byway that ran west of and parallel to the Brock Road. Anyone following this byway northward would be quite out of sight of the Carpenter homestead. Once past that point, the column could return to the Brock Road and follow it to its crossing of the Orange Plank Road. By turning back eastward on the Plank Road it was just over two miles to Wilderness Church — and, by all accounts, the rear of Hooker's army. As Jed Hotchkiss plotted it for the generals, it ought to be a march of between ten and eleven miles. To maintain secrecy there was no provision for any advance scouting. If the Federals were not where the plan put them, the plan would have to be changed on the fly.[18]

Jackson stayed back for a time to prod the marchers along. "Press forward, press forward," Hunter McGuire, his medical director, remembered him saying to the passing ranks. "See that the column is kept closed and that there is no straggling," he told the officers repeatedly. "Press on, press on. . . ."

There was to be no music and no calls, nor any cheering. A North Carolina soldier recalled Jackson riding past his regiment "at a long gallop," his cap held aloft, and the men, all mute, raising their caps in a return salute. Jackson pushed on to the head of the long column, riding with Robert Rodes and his staff just behind the troopers of the advance. By direction, the staff stopped by Wellford's and brought along Charles B. Wellford, son of Catharine Furnace's proprietor, to act as their guide. Wellford, who early in the war had served in the Confederate artillery, rode with the cavalry at the head of the column.

Porter Alexander, leading his artillery battalion from Longstreet's corps, was also invited to ride with the headquarters party, and he remembered Jackson being "grave & silent, & there was not very much conversation in the party." Then someone remarked on how well represented the Virginia Military Institute was on this march. Jackson himself had taught there, and so had two of his present divisional commanders, Rodes and Colston. Stapleton Crutchfield, Jackson's chief of artillery, was a V.M.I. graduate, as was Thomas Munford of the lead cavalry regiment. Indeed, when they were counted up, the number of brigadiers and colonels of line and staff in the column who were V.M.I. graduates came to more than twenty. At that Jackson turned to Munford and said, "Colonel, the Institute will be heard from today."

The talk of V.M.I. seemed to put Jackson in a reflective mood. He told Munford that he had heard it said (no doubt in a Northern newspaper) that General Hooker had more men than he could handle. He would like to have that problem, he said. Give him half again as many men as he had that day, "and I would hurl him in the river!" The Confederate army's trouble was that it never had the reserves to exploit its successes, Munford remembered him observing. "We have always had to put in all our troops, and *never* had enough at the *time* most needed."

Veterans among the foot cavalry would rank this Chancellorsville flank march considerably less demanding than some of their marches under Old Jack in the Shenandoah the spring before, or during the Second Manassas campaign the previous summer. This May day was breezy and pleasant, and it was not too hot. The roads were soft and damp from the rains, and there was no choking dust. (This was a double blessing: the enemy would not be able to track the movement by the dust they raised.) There were few wells or creeks along the route, however, and the improvident who had not filled their canteens suffered from thirst. "For hours our silent columns swept along the roads at the quick step, now turning to the right, and now to the left . . . ," Captain Harrison Griffith of the 14th South Carolina recalled. "We lost the points of the compass and became about as much bewildered in regard to courses or directions, as we already were in regard to the object of the expedition."

Fifteen brigades of infantry and twenty-seven batteries, with even minimal trains, required a great deal of marching space, and it was only after 11:00 A.M. that the last of A. P. Hill's men set out. Even with the best march discipline — and every man that day knew Old Jack's ideas on march discipline — the narrow roads through the dense forest meant frequent bottlenecks. Four men abreast was the maximum. Any obstruction, any mudhole, any delay of any sort caused the column "to string out & lose distance," as Porter Alexander put it. He spelled it out: "So that, though the head may advance steadily, the rear has to alternately halt & start, & halt & start, in the most heartbreaking way, wearing out the men & consuming precious daylight. . . ." That was the issue — daylight. The hours slipped by, and the flank march became more and more a race against the clock.[19]

* *

WHEN JOE HOOKER returned from the morning inspection tour of his lines, he found several telegrams from Chief of Staff Butterfield. One reported that the movement of Reynolds's First Corps, taking place now in daylight due to the wayward courier, had caught the attention of Rebel gunners. Their shelling was heavy, but he thought Reynolds would be "little delayed in consequence." In a telegram from Suffolk General Peck repeated the intelligence that as of that morning "no brigades have gone from Longstreet's command." That put Dan Butterfield in a good mood, and he wanted the general to share it. "Enemy's pickets," he reported, "called out to ours this A.M., 'You damned Yanks, reckon you've got us this time.'"

Butterfield's optimism about Reynolds's march was premature. The two First Corps divisions on the north bank were ready to start upriver as soon as might be, but Wadsworth's division in the bridgehead was another matter. A good deal of marching and countermarching was undertaken by way of concealment. Just then, noted Charles Wainwright, Reynolds's chief of artillery, "they opened a heavy fire on our bridges, and a very accurate one, too. . . ."

The fire came from half a dozen of Early's rifled guns, and it splintered the planking and wrecked one of the pontoons at Fitzhugh's. Crossing at the moment was the 137th Pennsylvania, an untested nine-month regiment, and to a man they turned and scampered back to the south bank. General Reynolds dryly described the incident as "causing them to take the double-quick." Soon enough the engineers had a new pontoon in place and the planking patched, and the nervous Pennsylvanians led the rest of Wadsworth's division across safely. But it was only at 11:00 A.M. that Wadsworth set out for Chancellorsville behind the rest of the corps.[20]

The Federal aeronautical corps was also having its troubles on Day Six. Professor Lowe had been ordered into the air at sunrise, but at the altitude he favored there were stiff winds that hampered observation. Not only did the wind drive the *Washington* downward against its tether, but caused it to revolve so rapidly that Lowe could not focus his glass. The *Eagle* had been towed upstream to Banks's Ford, four miles from where Jackson began his flank march, but once there aeronaut E. S. Allen complained that "the wind at present is too strong for me to get up." When he finally did get aloft, Allen had the same difficulty focusing his glass as did Lowe. Furthermore, the unmilitary Allen (unlike Lowe) confessed unease at his amateur status. It would be well, he thought, "to send an officer here to make an ascension as they could judge better of the movements than myself."

Confederates in Jackson's column reported seeing a Yankee balloon — it was the *Eagle* — and assumed that if they could see it, it could see them. Yet such were conditions aloft that not a single report reached General Hooker that day from the aeronautical corps that an enemy column was marching to the south and west of Chancellorsville.[21]

For a little more than a mile after it left the Orange Plank Road, the Furnace Road ran westerly through dense, concealing forest. Nearing Catharine Furnace, the road crossed a stretch of high, open ground, then dropped down to cross Lewis's Run. At the Furnace Mr. Wellford's newly opened section turned due south, following the valley of Lewis's Run for three quarters of a mile past the Wellford homestead before turning west again into the concealing forest.

That first opening, near the Furnace, was three quarters of a mile from the Hazel Grove clearing to the north, and visible to any Yankee observers posted there. Beginning at 8 o'clock that morning those observers, perched in tall trees, began reporting to General David B. Birney, whose Third Corps division occupied Hazel Grove, that a steady procession of Rebel troops, with artillery and trains, was crossing that open space from the east "toward the right." Birney passed the reports up the chain of command.

For about an hour and a half (time enough for Jackson's troops to cover three miles) there was no response to these reports. They went through Dan Sickles's Third Corps headquarters and on to the Chancellor house, and both Sickles and Hooker were absent on their inspection tour. On his return Sickles went forward to observe from Hazel Grove and then got Hooker's approval to bring up a section of rifled guns to shell the enemy column.

At 10 o'clock Lieutenant Robert Sims's Battery B, New Jersey Light, opened with two 10-pounder Parrotts. Over the next hour the other four guns of Sims's battery joined him. The Rebels were seen to double-quick across the opening under the shellfire. Dan Sickles, never shy in reporting results, claimed the enemy's trains and artillery "hurried past in great confusion, vainly endeavoring to escape our well-directed and destructive fire."

Earlier Jackson had taken the precaution of having Rodes detach a regiment from his lead brigade to stay behind and secure this exposed area. The 23rd Georgia was detailed. The shelling caused no casualties among the Georgians, nor among the marchers, although it was a considerable annoyance. Orders went back to the heavy corps trains at the rear to take a more roundabout route to avoid this danger. The corps ordnance and ambulance trains obediently turned into the Catharpin Road that ran well to the east of the Furnace Road and intersected the Brock Road well to the south at Todd's Tavern. The rest of the column continued to hurry past the Furnace with all due speed.[22]

Back at the Chancellor house Joe Hooker began dictating dispatches. The first, to General Howard, was intended as a follow-up to his inspection of the Eleventh Corps. He began by noting that "the disposition you have made of your Corps has been with a view to a *front* attack by the enemy. If he should throw himself upon your flank," Howard was cautioned, ". . . examine the ground and determine upon the position you will take in that event, in order that you may be prepared for him in whatever direction he advances." Howard should also have heavy reserves "well in hand to meet this contingency." Then, after examining Birney's sighting reports, Hooker added a postscript: "We have good reason to suppose that the enemy is moving to our right. Please advance your pickets for purposes of observation as far as may be safe in order to obtain timely information of their approach."

Brigadier General James Van Alen of the staff signed the dispatch and marked it 9:30 A.M. and sent it to Howard by courier. Hooker then determined to issue a circular to the same purpose for both Slocum and Howard, apparently to strengthen his message. To the point about preparing for a flank attack and positioning heavy reserves to meet one, he added this straightforward appraisal: "The right of your line does not appear to be strong enough. No artificial defences worth naming have been thrown up, and there appears to be a scarcity of troops at that point, and not, in the general's opinion, as favorably posted as might be." The

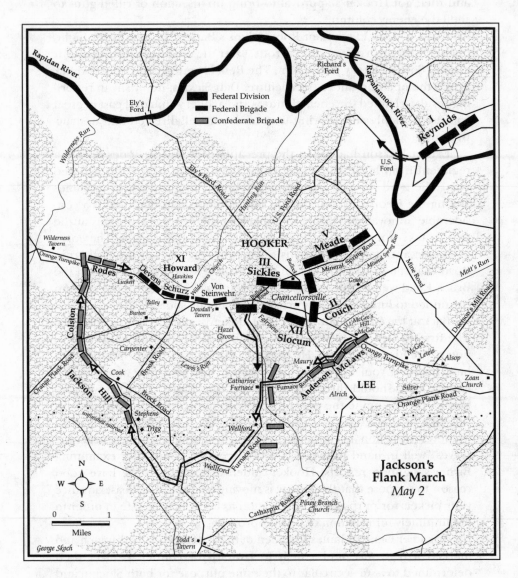

Rapidan River

Rappahannock River

Richard's Ford

Ely's Ford

U.S. Ford

I
Reynolds

Federal Division
Federal Brigade
Confederate Brigade

Wilderness Run

Ely's Ford Road

Hunting Run

U.S. Ford Road

Mineral Spring Run

Mine Road

Mott's Run

Wilderness Tavern

Orange Turnpike

Rodes

Luckett

XI
Howard

Hawkins

Devens

Schurz

Wilderness Church

Von Steinwehr

HOOKER

Bullock Road

V
Meade

Mineral Spring Road

III
Sickles

Bullock Road

Chancellorsville

II
Couch

Gravly

McGee's Hill
McGee

McGee

Dickerson's Mill Road

Colston

Talley

Burton

Carpenter

Cook

Dowdall's Tavern

Hazel Grove

Lewis's Run

Fairview

Catharine Furnace

Furnace Road

XII
Slocum

Anderson

Maury

McLaws

Orange Turnpike

Alrich

LEE

Silver

Lewis

Alsop

Zoan Church

Jackson

Hill

Brook Road

Stephens

unfinished railroad

Trigg

Wellford

Wellford Furnace Road

Piney Branch Church

Catharpin Road

Todd's Tavern

Jackson's
Flank March
May 2

N
W   E
S

0   1
Miles

Orange Plank Road

Orange Plank Road

George Skoch

postscript sent to Howard about the enemy seen "moving to our right" was then incorporated as the closing paragraph of the circular. It too was marked 9:30 and sent off. No doubt Joe Hooker believed this was warning enough (as he said of his earlier orders to Stoneman) to "wake up a dead man to his true condition."[23]

It was less than two miles from the Chancellor house to Howard's headquarters at Dowdall's Tavern, and the courier delivered Hooker's dispatch by 10 o'clock or a little after. Howard had been up late the night before, and after the early morning inspection he tried to catch up on his sleep. He told Carl Schurz, one of his generals of division, to receive dispatches and to wake him with anything important. Schurz quickly grasped the importance of Hooker's warning, awakened Howard, and they had an animated conversation about it on the front porch of the tavern. As they talked, a second courier arrived from headquarters with the circular "of virtually the same purport," as Schurz phrased it.

General Schurz would claim that he argued "most earnestly" with Howard that they should respond to the warning by facing substantial forces west and strengthening their reserves. When just then it was reported to them that from the high ground around the Talley house a column of unidentified infantry could be seen some two miles away, moving westward (this was Jackson passing the opening at Catharine Furnace), Schurz said it flashed through his mind that they were opposed in this campaign by Stonewall Jackson, "the great flanker." However much hindsight influenced that particular recollection, it is clear enough that here was one general in the Eleventh Corps who suspected they might be in danger.

Howard did not. His recollection of the day grew so clouded that twenty-five years later, in an article on the battle, he insisted he never saw any warning dispatch from Hooker. That in fact he did see it is certain (in addition to Schurz's testimony, the dispatch itself, receipted for, was preserved in the Eleventh Corps files), but it is equally certain that it made virtually no impression on him.

Within an hour, at 10:50, he replied to Hooker. He reported the sighting from the Talley house, and added, "I am taking measures to resist an attack from the west." That was reassuring to General Hooker no doubt, but the sum total of Howard's measures was posting Signal Corps captain Davis E. Castle on the Turnpike a mile west of Dowdall's Tavern. Castle was told to communicate with Howard's headquarters by flag, reporting "all movements of the enemy as I could see them. . . ." No troops and no guns were repositioned. Otis Howard continued to trust to the densely tangled Wilderness to protect his position.[24]

The Confederates' movement seen off to the south led Hooker to ask where they had come from. He ordered a reconnaissance to the east, where the enemy had halted after the previous day's fighting. Dan Sickles's Third Corps, the army's reserve, was called on for (as Sickles grandly put it) "two reliable regiments, led by circumspect and intrepid commanders."

Berry's division — Joe Hooker's old division — furnished the 11th Massachusetts and the 26th Pennsylvania. The Pennsylvanians went out the Plank Road a short way, pushed aside a Rebel picket line, and encountered two lines of battle supported by artillery. They fell back with the loss of two dead and four wounded. The 11th Massachusetts ran into a similarly solid defense on the Turnpike. The 11th's lieutenant colonel, Porter D. Tripp, complained that the sharpshooters detailed to him "shamefully ran away from the enemy's fire," requiring him to substitute skirmishers armed with old smoothbore muskets. With that handicap they sparred with the opposing pickets for some hours.

Thus it was reported to General Hooker that the enemy to the east was showing no lack of resolve. The Rebel postings here were a mile or so from Chancellorsville on a ridgeline east of Mott's Run known locally as McGee's Hill. They were actively entrenching and also seemed to be actively threatening. Guns in battery between the Turnpike and the Plank Road would abruptly open on the Federal lines with a barrage of shells. Skirmishers probed forward as if looking for a weak spot, and commands for assembly could be plainly heard. Captain Bowers, in Meade's line to the left, wrote his wife, "Three times to-day we have been in line expecting the enemy was approaching. But as yet it is quiet here," and he added, "any force attempting to pass would be terribly cut to pieces."[25]

Having secured his right flank, as he thought, Hooker turned to his left wing. The morning shelling of Sedgwick's position had been reported by Butterfield. With Colonel Sharpe's latest intelligence in hand, Hooker telegraphed, "Sedgwick is all right. He has but Ewell's division in his front; the balance is here." (Sharpe had told him Jubal Early now led Dick Ewell's division, but Hooker called it Ewell's by habit.) He then dictated the day's instructions for relay to Sedgwick. Butterfield was to tell him "if an opportunity presents itself with a reasonable expectation of success, to attack the enemy in front." Sedgwick was assured that "reliable information" put only Early's division at Fredericksburg. "It is impossible for the general to determine here whether it is expedient for him to attack or not. It must be left to his discretion."

This was the sort of discretionary order Hooker might have safely given to a John Reynolds or a George Meade — it was exactly the sort of discretionary order Lee customarily gave Stonewall Jackson — but it was not an order welcomed by John Sedgwick. A West Point classmate of Hooker's (and of Jubal Early), Sedgwick was a bachelor who had made the army his life, and his family. He was "Uncle John" to his men, perhaps the best-liked and most widely respected general officer in the Army of the Potomac. But constitutionally Sedgwick was a McClellan disciple, careful and cautious and conservative, greatly solicitous of his men, entirely competent but happiest carrying out direct orders.

He had been wounded at Glendale on the Peninsula and wounded three times at Antietam. It was at Antietam that something had gone out of John Sedgwick. His division there was led into an ambush by bumbling old Edwin Sumner and wrecked by Stonewall Jackson's flank attack. In less than fifteen terrible minutes 2,200 of Sedgwick's men had been shot down. He was not at all responsible for this debacle, but it scarred him and left him more careful and cautious than ever. Later Joe Hooker would say regretfully that Sedgwick simply lacked confidence in his own soldiership. Whatever the case and whatever the cause, he was not temperamentally suited to the independent command he was now being asked to exercise over the Federal left wing.

In any event, from the start General Sedgwick had never been clear about the left wing's role in this campaign, and certainly Hooker's recent very confusing orders, delivered over the erratic telegraph link, had only added to his bewilderment. The Confederate defenses on his front looked strong, and he was not sure that just one division manned them.

Nevertheless, if the commanding general ordered him directly that day to attack the enemy, he would obey promptly. Instead he was told to make the judgment for himself, to decide whether an attack was "expedient," whether there was a "reasonable expectation of success." He did not like to have to decide these things, and so on May 2 he took no action at all in response to his discretionary orders. He thereby missed a glittering opportunity to change the course of the campaign.[26]

* *

BY A CURIOUS coincidence, at almost the same moment Hooker sent Sedgwick the order to attack Early at his discretion, Lee decided to send Early an order for action at *his* discretion. Lee wanted Early to judge for himself if the enemy was weakening his forces on the Fredericksburg front. If so, he was to leave a small holding force there and join Lee before Chancellorsville with the rest of his command. He added a suggestion for handling the reserve artillery in the event Early thought a movement the wisest course. This was essentially the same discretionary order

Lee gave Early the day before, except on that occasion he had explained it to him personally. Today, fully occupied with events in front of Chancellorsville, he sent his chief of staff, Colonel Robert Chilton, to deliver the order to Early verbally.

The ideal chief of staff reads his chief's mind and mirrors his words, but this was one aspect of the job that Robert Chilton had never mastered. Twice during the Seven Days' Battles on the Peninsula Chilton had misinterpreted orders dictated by Lee, hampering Confederate offensives. During the Maryland campaign the previous fall, the Lost Order was lost on Chilton's watch, and due to his laxness the loss was not discovered. Now, in the midst of the Chancellorsville crisis, Chilton twisted Lee's discretionary order to Early into a peremptory order. He told Jubal Early to leave a single brigade at Fredericksburg, send the greater part of the reserve artillery to the rear, and march with the rest of his command to join General Lee, and to do so immediately.

Jubal Early was cantankerous and irreverent and famously profane — General Lee called him "my bad old man" — and when he wrote later of this order being "very astounding" to him he was surely putting a polite gloss on his reaction at the time. He and William Pendleton, chief of the artillery reserve, sharply questioned Chilton. Did not General Lee understand that if they pulled out the bulk of their men and guns the enemy would be on their heels and seize the entire Fredericksburg line? The Yankees had given up only part of their bridgehead that morning, and masses of their troops remained on both sides of the river. Chilton insisted the order was peremptory. "The Colonel said he assumed General Lee understood all this . . . ," Early wrote. With that "Old Jube" could argue no further. He and Pendleton prepared to withdraw their forces.

Early realized that he would have to shorten the line the Confederates were defending at Fredericksburg. He left in place the 21st Mississippi of Barksdale's brigade, McLaws's division, already picketing the town's waterfront, and detailed Harry Hays's Louisiana brigade of his own division to hold the rest of the abbreviated position. With his remaining three brigades and the rest of Barksdale's brigade he began to pull out. Pendleton left fifteen of his guns in the strongest of the artillery emplacements and started the rest down the Telegraph Road to the rear. When the movement was completed it would leave fewer than 3,000 men to defend Fredericksburg.[27]

Although both Early and Pendleton did their best to disguise the withdrawal, Federal observers quickly picked it up. In daylight and with clear weather there was not enough concealment to fool the Signal Corps telescopes. (Professor Lowe would manage to get aloft in the

Washington after midday, but the few observations he made simply confirmed what ground observers had already reported. Lowe complained of wind "so flawy" that it blew him nearly to earth from a thousand feet.)

As early as 10:45 A.M. an observer opposite the bridgehead was reporting movements of the Rebel infantry. Butterfield wrote on the dispatch, "Report this to Genl. Sedgwick & ask if it is likely a move to reinforce their troops at Chancellorsville." Soon sightings were flowing in steadily, and were sent directly to Sedgwick. By 2:30 that afternoon, for example, signalman James Hall at Station F at the Phillips house was being specific in his reporting: "Sixteen pieces of artillery seen moving on the Ridge road . . . and in the direction of Chancellorsville. Five wagons accompanying the batteries. Four regiments of infantry seen retiring from Sedgwick's front."

By that time John Sedgwick had every good reason, under his discretionary orders, to be pushing Bully Brooks's division forward against Early's lines along the River Road below Fredericksburg. Burnham's Light Division was at hand for immediate support. He had sufficient artillery to open the way, and there were the divisions of Albion Howe and John Newton to bring across the river to exploit Brooks's gains. But Sedgwick did nothing more than question Butterfield about his report of the Rebels' strength in Fredericksburg. "What information have you on that subject?" he asked. He appeared to be paralyzed without the stimulus of a direct order. When Butterfield telegraphed Hooker the obvious (obvious to everyone but John Sedgwick) — "I think the enemy are evacuating Sedgwick's front" — it bore with it Butterfield's virtual shrug of resignation.[28]

Unaware that his chief of staff had created potential disaster in the army's rear at Fredericksburg, General Lee spent the slow-paced Saturday hours waiting with his usual apparent calm. On his immediate front he issued orders directly to McLaws and Anderson, as he had since Longstreet was sent south. He quickly shifted brigades to fill gaps left by Jackson's departure.

The position, following the ridgeline of McGee's Hill, extended northward on the right as far as the Mine Road. Slanting from there south by west and paralleling the enemy's position, it crossed the Turnpike and traced the Catharine Furnace Road to its intersection with the Plank Road, and then beyond for some distance as a guard for the Furnace Road. Field fortifications were thrown up for a little over a mile of this three-mile distance to cover the Turnpike, the Plank Road, and the ground between. The artillery was concentrated to cover the two key highways.

Lee instructed his officers to be aggressive on their picket lines but not to draw the enemy into battle; the last thing he wanted that day was an attack on this isolated segment of the army. McLaws and Anderson were told to hold where they were while Jackson "would operate to the left and rear." Cadmus Wilcox at Banks's Ford was told to thin out his brigade there as much as possible so as to be ready to reinforce the Chancellorsville front. He could not tell what Wilcox faced, Lee said, "but at this distance it does not appear to me that your whole force is necessary to guard that front." It also looked to him as if the Federals reported marching upriver on the north bank — this was Reynolds's First Corps — were headed toward U.S. Ford and were not any immediate threat to Wilcox.

Lee had issued his orders and there was nothing to do now but wait. He took advantage of the lull to write a long dispatch to President Davis. He explained the position of the two armies. The enemy, he said, "seems to have concentrated his strength for this effort." General Hooker's army at Chancellorsville was "in a position remarkably favorable for him. We were unable last evening to dislodge him. I am now swinging around to my left to come up in his rear."

If the outcome here was not successful, he told the president, he might have to fall back along the Orange & Alexandria or the Virginia Central, but in any event "I will be in position to contest the enemy's advance upon Richmond." He expressed neither optimism nor pessimism about the forthcoming battle, but he did observe that if only he had all his command with him, and was well supplied with provisions and forage, "I should feel easy. . . ." Lacking these advantages, however, led him to admit that "the advantage of numbers and position is greatly in favor of the enemy." All in all, it was not the sort of dispatch to make Mr. Davis feel easy.[29]

* *

IN CONTRAST to General Lee, security-conscious General Hooker said nothing at all to his president on May 2. He ordered Butterfield to telegraph nothing to the War Department. Nevertheless, Washington was awash in rumors of fighting on the Rappahannock that had reached the capital through unofficial channels. Secretary Stanton chided Hooker by telegraph for a letter making the rounds in Washington written by General Van Alen that fully described the Federals' position at Chancellorsville. "Can't you give his sword something to do, so that he will have less time for the pen?" Stanton asked. Hooker's brash address to his army had also made its way to Washington. In his diary

General Heintzelman noted reports that the army was across the Rappahannock "& the 'Tribune N.Y.' has a full account mentioning every corps & where it is." He added, "I would try that correspondent." But for Washington's citizenry the most telling signs were the scores of army ambulances waiting at the Potomac wharves, a certain indication of a battle to the south.

At the Chancellor house Joe Hooker was waiting on events with an air of confidence. Provost Marshal Patrick listened to him discuss his plans, and entered in his diary his belief that "the game was all in our hands." The commanding general, Colonel Robert McAllister wrote his wife that morning, "is in fine spirits and says our success is assured."

Surgeons had taken over several first-floor rooms in the Chancellor house to treat the wounded, which included two Confederates with leg wounds requiring amputation. The Chancellor women in the house volunteered to nurse them and their offer was accepted. At noon the headquarters staff took a luncheon of bread and tea. Among the party was a General Fogliardi, an observer from the Swiss army, who bustled about displaying great interest in the progress of the battle. He toasted the staff with a sociable glass of brandy. General Hooker, as had become his habit, abstained.

Out on the battle lines the scene was equally calm. In the clearings behind their entrenchments men speculated on the spatters of rifle fire or the occasional boom of cannon heard beyond the dense woods. After he inspected the Twelfth Corps front, General Williams stopped by the headquarters of one of his brigadiers, Joseph Knipe, on the Plank Road. "As no orders came," Williams wrote, "I took a long nap. I found Gen. Slocum there with his staff, and what with his and mine and Knipe's we formed a large group of officers and orderlies, all of us pretty much engaged in sleeping."[30]

All that was lacking to make Joe Hooker's day complete was word that Stoneman's cavalry had broken Lee's communications. Then the game would truly be in his hands. In that event, whether Lee gave battle that day or not, he would certainly have to retreat without delay to restore his supply line. If by inviting attack Hooker was giving up the initiative, Stoneman's success would surely regain it for him.

That word eluded Hooker once again. Today marked the fourth day of Stoneman's foray, and he had yet to send back a report of any sort. In desperation Butterfield telegraphed the Federal garrison at Yorktown on the Peninsula to learn if any news of the cavalry had reached there. That day or the day before, Butterfield explained, Stoneman ought to have reached and destroyed the Richmond, Fredericksburg & Potomac. "Use every possible means to get any information," he pleaded. Late in the day he had his answer, but from a closer source. Sedgwick's pickets traded for that morning's Richmond papers, clear proof that at least the morning train had reached Hamilton's Crossing without difficulty. After hours of unavailing effort, Butterfield admitted defeat: "Tell Gen. Hooker that we have heard nothing of the operations of our cavalry."

George Stoneman would end the day nearly as far from Hanover Junction and the R.F. & P. as he began it. He spent some time planning the capture of Louisa Court House against virtually no opposition. There he tore up five miles of track of the Virginia Central, a task of only secondary importance in his orders. He sent two companies of the 1st Maine cavalry toward Gordonsville, where Rooney Lee's troopers pounced on this inadequate force and captured two thirds of it. By day's end Stoneman had collected his forces farther south yet, at the hamlet of Thompson's Cross Roads on the South Anna River. They had dropped on this countryside like a shell, he told his lieutenants, and next day he intended "to burst it in every direction. . . ."[31]

Following his 9:30 warning to Howard that there was reason to think "the enemy is moving to our right," Joe Hooker displayed a curious indifference to the matter. He seemed willing to let Lee play out his hand without disturbance. Dan Sickles, aggressively chafing for action, was not content with simply shelling the enemy sighted near Catharine Furnace. He kept petitioning Hooker to let him attack. Hooker finally agreed, but only at noon and only with careful hedging. Sickles was "to advance cautiously" in order to "harass the movement."

Sickles called for David Birney's division, which from its position at Hazel Grove was closest to the enemy at the Furnace. For a spearhead Sickles gave him Berdan's Sharpshooters. Hiram Berdan's two-regiment brigade was the Potomac army's crack unit, specially recruited from across the North and specially outfitted in plumed hats and uniforms of dark green. Every man was rated a marksman with the Sharps breechloader. To act as lead skirmishers in an operation of this sort, against an enemy outpost in difficult country, was exactly what the unit had been created for. Backed by Birney's lead brigade, Berdan's men crossed Lewis's Run and pushed southward in the creek valley toward Catharine Furnace where the enemy had last been seen.

It was approaching 1 o'clock by now and Jackson's column had been passing this point for some five hours. So belated was the Federals' reaction that their target was moving swiftly out of reach. Already all of Rodes's, Colston's, and A. P. Hill's infantry had crossed the Furnace clearing, and all that remained was a part of one of the Second Corps reserve artillery battalions and its train. Indeed, upon the Yankees' approach, the tail of this train not yet at the Furnace was turned off on a rough track to the east that bypassed the clearing entirely and rejoined the Furnace Road below the Wellford house. Jackson's ordnance train under Colonel Allan and the corps ambulance train had earlier taken a wider detour by way of the Catharpin Road to Todd's Tavern. Dan Sickles was due for a disappointment. The prey had flown; the chance had been missed.[32]

Colonel Emory F. Best's 23rd Georgia had been left at the Furnace to discourage any advance by the Yankees toward the exposed flanking column there. Best had advanced his regiment some 300 yards north of the Furnace clearing, where it waited without event until midday. Then Berdan's Sharpshooters approached in skirmish formation, supported by what looked to Colonel Best like a full brigade of infantry.

A Pennsylvanian in one of the supporting regiments watched the sharpshooters operate. They crept through the high swamp grass bordering Lewis's Run and tried to make the Rebels in the woods ahead show themselves. One of Berdan's men raised his cap on a ramrod to draw fire. "He then gave a leap and fell on the grass as if dead. This caused several Rebs to look out from their hiding places. . . ." However effective this tactic might be it was slow work, and the Georgians held their ground long enough for the last of the trains to turn off southward at the Furnace clearing toward Wellford's. Then they fell back to the Furnace, taking a stand in one of the foundry buildings.

Here Best's men got some much-needed support from Captain James Brooke's Virginia battery, pulled out of the last artillery battalion in Jackson's column. One of Brooke's gun crews checked the Yankee advance with three quick rounds of canister and then pulled back to Wellford's with the rest of the battery to engage the Federal guns supporting the assault. With his flanks threatened Colonel Best had to pull back as well, leaving a company as a rear guard at the foundry building to hold off the pursuit as long as possible.

"Whenever they showed a head they got a crack shot," wrote Lieutenant George Marden of the sharpshooters. Chaplain Lorenzo Barber, armed with a Sharps, came up with the advance. "The sight of a *butternut* looking through a barn window at four hundred yards was too much for him," Marden wrote; ". . . he blazed away and the rebs dropped out of sight like so many prairie dogs. . . . In a few moments the rebs showed a white rag and came in; 56 of them including the Maj. & Chaplain."

At 1:30 Sickles reported his progress to headquarters. Only as they approached the Furnace could the Federals finally see that the Rebel column, instead of moving westward, was in fact turning southward. That discovery offered a whole new perspective on events. "The enemy column is still moving south," Sickles explained. "For the past five or ten minutes only their wagon train is in sight." He told of his skirmishers advancing and of one of his batteries breaking the column "several times." Then Dan Sickles leaped to a conclusion. "I think it is a retreat. Sometimes a regiment then a few wagons — then troops then wagons. . . ."[33]

This fighting around Catharine Furnace became a magnet, attracting fresh troops from both sides. Lee told Dick Anderson to extend his line south and west in support, and Anderson sent forward Carnot Posey's Mississippians and Rans Wright's Georgians. Four companies of Tennesseans from A. P. Hill's division who had been on picket duty and were trying to catch up with their brigade took a hand in the action. The trailing brigades in Hill's division, under James Archer and E. L. Thomas, turned back to lend their support if needed. On the Federal side Sickles ordered in the rest of Birney's division and readied Amiel Whipple's to support it. Then he called on his neighboring corps, the Eleventh and Twelfth, for assistance. With his quarry gone, Sickles seemed to be fighting just for the sake of fighting.

Somehow the reinforcements were little help to the 23rd Georgia, which was being relentlessly pursued by Berdan's Sharpshooters. The line of the unfinished railroad ran through the Wellford property, and Colonel Best had his men take cover in a shallow cut the railroad builders had left. One of them related their fate with brevity: "We held them back in front, but our line was too short."

While one contingent of sharpshooters pinned down the Georgians with their accurate fire, the rest swung around to the right and outflanked them. Best shouted to his men to get out if they could, and he and some others managed to escape, but most would not dare the fire and surrendered. Lieutenant Marden asked the prisoners "why they did not run away as I thought they might have done so. They replied that the balls came too close whenever they showed themselves." Marden added, "It was a most splendid affair and the praise of the Sharpshooters was in everybody's mouth."

The 23rd Georgia suffered only three wounded on May 2, but had 296 captured. Colonel Best was later court-martialed (unfairly it would seem) and dismissed from the service. In the best tradition of a forlorn hope, his regiment had successfully held the Yankees away from Jackson's trains. Except for one caisson that broke down, every gun and every vehicle in the column escaped.

The prisoners were herded to the rear. "The boys chaffed them a good deal, giving them the laugh for getting caught," a man in the Twelfth Corps wrote. The Georgians retorted with warnings for anyone who cared to listen. "You may think you have done a big thing just now," one of them said, "but wait till Jackson gets round on your right." Another was considerably more direct: "You'll catch hell before night."[34]

* *

WHILE THE TAIL of Jackson's flanking column was fighting off its tormentors, the head was moving forward swiftly and silently and secretly. At 1:30 that afternoon, about the time Dan Sickles signaled Hooker that the Rebel army was in retreat, Stonewall Jackson was searching out the right flank of Hooker's army.

After it reached the Brock Road beyond Wellford's, Jackson's column had been guided by young Wellford along the back roads that took it out of sight of the Carpenter farm. Each byway that came in from the right, toward the Federals, was sealed off by Jeb Stuart's cavalry. The column re-entered the Brock Road at the house of a free black named Cook, and after just over a mile it reached the crossing of the Orange Plank Road. As the plan was formulated early that morning, an advance eastward on the Plank Road for some two miles ought to turn the enemy's right.

Dutifully the advance party of Tom Munford's 2nd Virginia cavalry, leading the column, turned into the Plank Road to reconnoiter. Before long the troopers encountered a small Yankee cavalry picket, which turned and hurried off. One of the Virginians remembered his captain passing the word "that Jackson was in the rear which caused every man to do his duty." They opened fire and pursued at a gallop, but they were under orders to observe rather than fight, and about a mile and a half down the highway they halted and set out a picket of their own. On their left was a high, open knoll, and the captain climbed it for an observation. What he saw sent him pelting back toward the Brock Road and Fitzhugh Lee. Lee hurried forward for a look. He would never forget the moment: "What a sight presented itself before me!" Back he went at a gallop for General Jackson.

Finding Jackson at the head of Rodes's infantry, Fitz Lee said to him, "General, if you will ride with me, halting your column here, out of sight, I will show you the enemy's right." Accompanied only by a courier, Jackson followed the cavalryman. They turned up the track to the knoll, in a clearing on the farm of a man named Burton, and there spread out before them, not 700 yards distant, was the Yankee army.

From the knoll at Burton's Jackson could see straight along the

Orange Plank Road three quarters of a mile to where it was joined by the Orange Turnpike at Wilderness Church. The two roads met at an angle of about 35 degrees, and from the intersection it was possible to see half a mile east and about the same distance west along the Turnpike before the Wilderness closed in and cut off the view. "There were the lines of defence, with abatis in front, and long lines of stacked arms in rear," Fitz Lee remembered. "Two cannon were visible in the part of the line seen. The soldiers were in groups in the rear, laughing, chatting, smoking, probably engaged, here and there, in games of cards, and other amusements. . . . In rear of them were other parties driving up and butchering beeves."

At the extreme left of this vista was the Talley homestead, and at the extreme right Dowdall's Tavern, residence of Melzi Chancellor, a son of the founder of Chancellorsville. What Jackson was seeing, although he could not know it, was the better part of Otis Howard's Eleventh Corps. Jackson had to assume that since yesterday, when Fitz Lee reported the enemy's flank to be at Carpenter's a mile or so due south of the troops he was now observing, they had withdrawn to this new line along the Turnpike and the Plank Road. In that event, this must indeed be Hooker's right flank, although how far west beyond Talley's it might extend he could only guess.

It was also clear that any assault by way of the Plank Road against this position would be little better than a frontal assault, albeit at an oblique angle. To carry out the plan Jackson would have to alter it so as to strike from beyond the flank. However far beyond Talley's the line ran, on a narrow road through the forest it could not be too formidable in any case.

Unnoticed by the Yankees, Old Jack studied the scene through his binoculars for perhaps five minutes, responding to Lee's remarks with complete silence. Finally he turned to his courier and said tersely, "Tell General Rodes to move across the old Plank Road, halt when he gets to the old Turnpike, and I will join him there." The courier turned his horse and was gone, and then still without a word to Fitz Lee Jackson followed him.[35]

Jackson was soon back with the column passing up the Brock Road. "When he came back from the view," wrote Porter Alexander, "there was a perceptible increase of eagerness in his air. . . ." Robert Rodes already had the troops up and marching northward toward the Orange Turnpike. It was a mile and a half to the Turnpike, and then Rodes swung east for half a mile to the farm of John Luckett and halted. No Federals blocked his way or were in his sight. They had marched just under twelve miles.

Stonewall Jackson paused to scribble a brief dispatch for General Lee. Marking it "Near 3 P.M." he wrote, "The enemy has made a stand at Chancellor's which is about 2 miles from Chancellorsville. I hope as soon as practicable to attack. I trust that an ever kind Providence will bless us with great success." In a postscript he added, "The leading division is up & the next two appear to be well closed."[36]

10

They Were Flying in Great Disorder

I N T H E 14th South Carolina in A. P. Hill's division, far back in the flanking column, there was little notion of what they were doing that May 2 or where they were going. It was late afternoon and they were toiling along the Brock Road when a cavalryman came tearing down the road toward them on some urgent errand. Infantry never missed an opportunity to gibe cavalry. "We're going to have a fight, boys, for the cavalry's going to the rear!" was the call. The trooper grinned and called back as he passed, "You're right this time. Our men are advancing on them now!"

In his 3 o'clock dispatch to General Lee, Jackson had noted that his two trailing divisions were well closed up. While this was true enough, the column was so slender and so long and so road-bound that deploying it from marching formation to fighting formation was exasperatingly slow. To make matters worse, the clearing at Luckett's was hardly 400 yards wide north to south, which meant that most of the deploying had to be done in deep woods. It also had to be done in complete silence — no calls, no shouted commands, everything directed with care by gesturing staff officers. As soon as they were placed the men sank down gratefully. Captain W. H. May of the 3rd Alabama remembered the chief occupation as sleeping. Others chewed on their cornbread or whatever rations they had and speculated and waited, with the certainty of Old Jack's veterans, for the fight to start.

The first line as deployed over the next hours was entirely Robert Rodes's troops — from left to right the brigades of Alfred Iverson, Edward O'Neal, George Doles, and Alfred Colquitt. Straddling the Orange Turnpike and at right angles to it, Rodes's line of battle extended some three quarters of a mile to each side and contained some 7,800 men in a double rank. A skirmish line of sharpshooters was pushed out ahead 400 yards, concealed in the dense woods.

Two hundred yards to the rear was a second line — Dodson Ramseur's brigade from Rodes's division on the right, then two brigades from Raleigh Colston's division under Edward Warren and John R. Jones. A third line, north of the Turnpike, contained the brigades of Francis Nicholls, of Colston's division, and Harry Heth, of A. P. Hill's division; another of Hill's brigades, James Lane's, was deployed in column on the Turnpike.

About a third of Jackson's force was not in this attack formation. Frank Paxton's Stonewall Brigade, Colston's division, had been detached to secure the Orange Plank Road to the south. A. P. Hill's remaining three brigades were too far to the rear to bring up in time, as was the mass of the artillery. Indeed, the only place to use artillery in this woodland seemed to be the road itself. Four sections of Stuart's horse artillery lined up on the Turnpike, ready to advance with the troops. The 2nd Virginia cavalry was posted to guard the far flanks. In immediate reserve in the center on the Luckett homestead was Thomas Carter's artillery battalion.

This force with which Stonewall Jackson intended to make his attack consisted of some 21,500 infantry and 8 guns, and it took half the afternoon to arrange everything to Jackson's satisfaction. He was determined to attack on the broadest possible front, taking the maximum advantage of his numbers against what was sure to be a very narrow-front enemy defense.

Jackson's instructions for the assault were based on his earlier reconnaissance of the enemy lines visible from the Burton farm. The ground at Talley's farm on the Turnpike was seen to be the highest in the area, commanding everything to the east at least as far as Dowdall's Tavern, the farthest point he had been able to see. Thus the position at Talley's, as Rodes put it in his report, "was to be carried at all hazards. . . ." His entire line, Rodes was told, must "push ahead from the beginning," taking the Turnpike as guide. The artillery would keep pace to beat down any strongpoints. There must be no pause under any circumstances. The lead brigades were authorized to call directly on the trailing brigades for support as needed.

In no previous battle had Stonewall Jackson ever had the time and opportunity to plan an assault with such care. A half mile ahead beyond the forest lay the foe, all unsuspecting. It was like some long-ago tactical lesson learned in a classroom at West Point, now miraculously made real, on a real battlefield.[1]

What was not known, as the deployment continued, was the what and where of the enemy's extreme right flank, west of Talley's. To remedy that, Jeb Stuart sent two of his young lieutenants, Frank Robertson and Walter Hullihen, "to see what was in the road in front."

Once beyond their own skirmishers the two rode cautiously through the brush alongside the Turnpike for some 200 yards, Robertson wrote, "when we concluded to go to the edge of the road & see what we could see. Hullihen was climbing a sapling & I was standing up on my saddle, both looking down the road where we saw two guns, with gun crews at their posts." Glancing across the road, they were startled to see, not 50 yards away, three Yankees, "guns in hand, staring stupidly at us." Not wasting a moment, they slipped into their saddles and turned back to report their sightings. "Why those 3 Yanks neither challenged nor shot, is one of the mysteries yet to be solved," Robertson concluded. "May have been foreigners — certainly damned fools." However that may be, the reconnaissance precisely located both the Yankees' flank and their picket line.

Captain Marcellus Moorman, in command of one of the horse batteries on the Turnpike, sought out Jackson — his onetime V.M.I. instructor — to clarify his orders. "Yes, Captain," he was assured, "I will give you the honor of going in with my troops." As they talked they could hear artillery rumbling off to the east. Jackson asked the artillerist how distant it was. Moorman said he thought five or six miles. "I suppose it is General Lee," Jackson said, and added matter-of-factly, "Time we were moving."[2]

* *

DAN SICKLES'S report that the Rebels were in retreat reached the Chancellor house about 2 o'clock or so. Quickly it made the rounds of the high command. Darius Couch would recall Hooker telling him "between 2 and 3 P.M." that Lee was retreating "in the direction of Gordonsville." Lieutenant Colonel Alexander Webb, of Meade's staff, wrote his wife that afternoon, "the enemy has started his trains to the rear & is we believe in retreat." Most importantly, if that conclusion reached as far as Fifth Corps headquarters on the left, it surely also reached the Eleventh Corps on the right. General Howard would later explain to a friend, "I was deceived at the time of Jackson's attack, and did believe, with all the other officers, that he was making for Orange Court House." The messenger who brought him those tidings was Captain Alexander Moore, of Joe Hooker's staff.

At about 3 o'clock Captain Moore presented himself at Howard's headquarters at Dowdall's Tavern with a request from Sickles for support. Presumably Moore told Howard of Sickles's effort to pursue the enemy's trains. But Howard, remembering Hooker's 9:30 order to keep a strong reserve at hand, replied that he had no troops he could spare.

Moore was back an hour later with an order from the commanding general to send support to Sickles. Certainly then, if he had not before, Moore described the Rebels' retreat southward. Howard complied by sending off the only brigade he had in reserve, Francis Barlow's. Then, for good measure, he decided to lead Barlow to the scene himself. Considering the unsettling reports then flooding into the Eleventh Corps, Howard's decision to leave his headquarters ranks as one of the more obtuse decisions taken that day.

Unimaginative, unenterprising, uninspiring, a stiflingly Christian soldier, Otis Howard was the wrong general in the wrong place with the wrong troops that day. In the face of uncertainty — and May 2 was a day of many uncertainties — his way was to close his mind to everything but judgments and orders from his superior.

During the month since he had replaced the beloved Franz Sigel in command of the Eleventh Corps, the spirit inherent in their "I fights mit Sigel" war cry had gone out of the men, and Howard lacked the resources to restore it. Perhaps his decision that afternoon to lead Barlow's brigade into a potential fight was his way of demonstrating leadership by personal example. To be sure, the men of the Eleventh Corps had entered on this campaign willingly enough, as a way of proving their mettle and earning their place in the Army of the Potomac, but what they needed was the best sort of leadership that army had to offer. They got instead the poorest sort.

Unfortunately for them, too, the general commanding under Howard on the army's far right flank, Charles Devens, was another of the poorest sort. Devens, out of the Harvard Law School and the Massachusetts militia establishment, had taken over the division just a week before the campaign began, displacing the popular Nathaniel McLean and reducing McLean to command of a brigade. Devens was a harsh disciplinarian with a lofty Bostonian's view of non–New Englanders, an attitude that particularly did not sit well with the five of his nine regiments that were German or part German. (Nor did it sit well with the numerous Ohioans in his command. Presumably only his 17th Connecticut met the test for General Devens.)

Devens shared with Howard the belief that information of military importance flowed only down the chain of command, not up it. In any case, May 2 was not a good day for General Devens to begin with. The day before his horse had carried him into a tree, badly bruising his leg, and he was resting off his feet in his headquarters at the Talley house. On the testimony of several of his officers, he was easing the pain that day with brandy, which improved neither his temperament nor his judgment.[3]

There was other evidence that the Confederates were retreating than just Dan Sickles's observations. Although he had no word yet regarding Stoneman, there was every reason for Hooker to think the cavalry had by now carried out its orders to destroy Lee's railroad lifeline. Certainly there had been time enough. In that event, with the R.F. & P. wrecked, Lee's course would have to be toward Orange Court House and Gordonsville and the Orange & Alexandria if he hoped to restore his supply line. Sedgwick's threat to the R.F. & P. would also steer Lee toward the west. It was logical that Lee would start his trains and his reserve artillery first (just as Sickles was reporting), then disengage his infantry, probably under the cover of night, and follow with it tomorrow.

Finally, Colonel Chilton, Lee's chief of staff, had unwittingly furnished some of the most convincing evidence of all that a retreat was under way. Chilton's misinterpreted order from Lee that started Early's infantry and Pendleton's guns out of Fredericksburg produced a flood of sightings by Yankee observers on the ground and in the air. Butterfield passed these on to Hooker one after another, until he could say with confidence, at 4:45 P.M., that the enemy was evacuating Sedgwick's front. There is no small irony in the fact that this botched order of Lee's contributed substantially to the success of Stonewall Jackson's flanking operation.

Even before all this evidence of retreat was in his hands, Hooker took an important step to act on it. At 2:30 a circular went out from headquarters to all corps commanders. "The Major General commanding," it read, "desires that you replenish your supplies of forage, provisions and ammunition to be ready to start at an early hour tomorrow." The moment Lee's main army set off on its retreat, Joe Hooker would be after it.[4]

*　*

AFTERWARD, in the months and years to come, a number of soldiers from the Eleventh Corps would come forward to insist they had detected Stonewall Jackson's flanking column on Day Six in plenty of time to meet and halt it. But when they reported these sightings to their generals they were ignored or laughed at or called coward. They described the sightings in books and articles and interviews, and declared themselves prophets without honor; history would be different, and men would be alive today, if only they had been listened to.

It is quite true that the secret of Jackson's flanking column was not perfectly kept — with 33,000 men and 108 guns, could not be perfectly kept — and it is quite true that warnings that should have been heeded were shamefully ignored. Yet it is also true that among these witnesses were those who larded their testimony with what they learned and understood only after the fact. What was actually seen of Jackson's forces by the Federals on May 2 was a good deal less, and a good deal more ambiguous, than hindsight claimed.

It is the fact of the matter that between the time Jackson's column set out until it began to deploy in midafternoon on the Orange Turnpike half a mile from Howard's right, the only time and the only place it could have been seen by anyone in the Eleventh Corps was when it crossed the clearing at Catharine Furnace. The column was indeed sighted at the Furnace from Devens's headquarters at the Talley house more than two miles away — and at that distance no one (as Devens noted) could even tell which army it belonged to.

In their march between the Furnace clearing and the Turnpike, Jackson's men were concealed every step of the way by at least a mile and a half of the Wilderness — and for good measure tightly screened by Stuart's cavalry — from any observers in Howard's command. As Major Norvell Cobb, 44th Virginia, expressed it at the time, "The country being wooded & thick, and his troops masked by a cavalry force which skirmished with the enemy, all got by, undetected."

Yet Colonel John C. Lee of the 55th Ohio (for example) would claim in later years that as early as midday on May 2 his pickets south of Talley's spotted the passing column of Confederates. Three times Lee took his story to General Devens, and three times it was rejected. "You are frightened, sir!" Devens finally exclaimed in exasperation, adding the insult that western colonels seemed to be more scared than most. Lieutenant Colonel Charles W. Friend, 75th Ohio, said he went to both Devens and corps headquarters with a similar story and was laughed at and warned not to bring on a panic. From the same perspective (looking south from the center of Devens's line) Colonels William P. Richardson, 25th Ohio, and William H. Noble, 17th Connecticut, would retail similar stories and similar responses.

At the time, before hindsight and the humiliation of their wrenching experiences later that day warped their view, what these various officers actually reported was less alarming. It was what their pickets had been reporting to them ever since they took up this line two days earlier — repeated sightings of parties of Rebels, pickets and scouts, mostly Stuart's men, sealing the byways and probing the Federals' positions. A threatening enemy was indeed being seen out there in the deep woods and on the narrow tracks, but at that time and place what was seen did not include any marching infantry and artillery.

Had Hooker retained more cavalry with the army — or had Alfred Pleasonton acted aggressively with the cavalry he had — Stuart's troopers would have had a more trying time on May 2 and Jackson's column would likely have been spotted at an early hour. What cavalry there was on the Federal flank was hopelessly outclassed.

Howard had been assigned two small cavalry squadrons of the 17th Pennsylvania and a contingent of the 1st Indiana, and they could do nothing in this situation. Their picket on the Orange Plank Road that was chased early in the afternoon by Tom Munford's Virginia troopers, for example, never came close to sighting Jackson's column. When General Devens complained, "I wish I could get someone who could make a reconnaissance for me," his cavalryman said with candor, "General, I can go further, but I can't promise to return."[5]

Beginning at 3 o'clock or so there was a series of actual sightings of Jackson's forces that by any measure ought to have jolted Devens and Howard — and Hooker — into action. Alpheus Williams of the Twelfth Corps was (as he put it) "a disbeliever in the retreat." On his own account he sent several experienced scouts from his command all the way across to the army's right to see what they could find. By the simple expedient of climbing the tallest tree in the area they sighted Rebel troops massing beyond Howard's line. Williams passed on their report to his corps commander, Henry Slocum, "who, I believe, reported the facts to Gen. Hooker." Williams heard nothing further of the matter.

At the farthest extreme of the Eleventh Corps was the brigade of Leopold Von Gilsa, and two of Von Gilsa's officers, looking to the west, raised the alarm. Lieutenant A. B. Searles, on picket duty, described the "queer jumble of sounds" he could hear in the forest in front of him, and sent back a warning. His courier came back with a caution from General Howard that Lieutenant Searles "must not be scared of a few bushwhackers. . . ." Major Owen Rice, in command of Von Gilsa's picket line and therefore, it would seem, someone worth listening to, sent back a warning that was blunt and unqualified: "A large body of the enemy is massing in my front. For God's sake make dispositions to receive him." By Von Gilsa's account, when he took this dispatch to Howard's headquarters he was received with taunts.

Sometime later there was an actual collision between the picket lines of Von Gilsa and Rodes, with shots exchanged and Captain Dieckmann's section of 3-inch rifles, marking the end of Howard's line, firing two rounds apiece. Signalman Castle flagged this to Howard's headquarters at 4:30. According to Castle, the report was "not credited" and no attention was paid to it.

Like Alpheus Williams, Carl Schurz, holding the center of Howard's line, was a disbeliever in the retreat theory. He told his battery commander, Captain Hubert Dilger, to scout out a place to post his guns to meet a possible attack from the rear. Dilger, a veteran of the German wars in the Baden Mounted Artillery, was known as "Leatherbreeches" for the fancy doeskin pants he favored, and he believed in personal reconnaissance. He rode off well to the north and west to see what the ground was like.

It was early enough that Jackson's deployment was just beginning, and Dilger penetrated as far as a view of the Luckett clearing, which just then was a solid mass of Rebel troops. Spotted by Munford's cavalry, he galloped off madly to the north and east along obscure forest tracks and made good his escape. At last he found a track that led him to the Chancellor house. As a mere captain of artillery he was not permitted to see the general commanding, and a contemptuous major of cavalry on duty there told him to take his story back to the Eleventh Corps. When finally he reached Dowdall's Tavern he found General Howard absent on his errand with Barlow's brigade, and no one on the staff would give his story a hearing. Leatherbreeches rode back to his battery weary and dejected, and cautioned his gun crews not to take the horses to water but to keep them close at hand.[6]

These messengers, reporting sightings seemingly firm enough to raise an alarm at every headquarters in the chain of command, had the misfortune to arrive in the midst of or after the welter of vague picket-line sightings so annoying to Howard and Devens. The generals interpreted these new sightings as just more of the same; like Aesop's fable, the cry of "Wolf!" was being heard at every hand.

One warning in particular, Major Rice's dispatch about the enemy massed in his front, earned an extra discount for coming from an untested nine-month regiment, the 153rd Pennsylvania. Furthermore, after Howard went off with Barlow's brigade at 4 o'clock, there was no one in charge at the Eleventh Corps to investigate such matters. (Howard, in any case, had investigated none of them before he left.) Charles Devens, increasingly fortified with brandy, simply threw up his hands at the continued interruptions.

But more than anything else, all these sightings, whether vague or specific, could now be explained by the belief in an enemy in retreat. The maps showed the Orange Plank Road and the Orange Turnpike, never more than three miles apart, running straight to Orange Court House and the road to Gordonsville. Lee in retreat must be detouring to the south and west around the Federal army to reach these roads; any Rebels seen to the west of Howard must be merely a rear guard posted by the army Fighting Joe Hooker had predicted would ingloriously fly. Devens caught this attitude perfectly when he told the alarmed Colonel Lee that since he had received no warnings from corps or army headquarters, there was nothing alarming about these various sightings. Headquarters, to generals like Devens and Howard, was the font of all knowledge.

Although both generals claimed they passed on the sighting reports to the Chancellor house, there is no record of which and how many were received. Certainly none are known to have been credited by the general commanding. Hooker would say that interrogation of prisoners from the 23rd Georgia taken at the Furnace produced the identification of Jackson's column, but this came too late to do any good. After the morning warnings, there is no record of any further warnings sent from headquarters to the Eleventh Corps. Hooker seemed satisfied that his 9:30 messages to Howard, and Howard's response, had secured the army's right flank.[7]

Joe Hooker had been heavily engaged in every battle the Army of the Potomac had fought against Robert E. Lee and Stonewall Jackson, and it is surprising that he was not more alert that day for one of their unconventional battlefield moves. But the reports of Lee's retiring from the Rappahannock line — and they seemed to be reports with substance — overtook the caution he had felt in the morning. The Army of Northern Virginia retreating would write a climax to what thus far had been a brilliantly successful campaign, and in his confidence Hooker accepted that as his due.

He became preoccupied with pressing support for Dan Sickles's fight at the Furnace. Soon two of Sickles's three divisions were involved. Barlow's brigade from the Eleventh Corps went in as support on the right. The divisions of Williams and Geary of the Twelfth Corps were sent in to attempt to turn Lee's line where it guarded the Furnace Road. Pleasonton's cavalry brigade was advanced to pursue should there be a breakthrough. The force grew until it included some 25,000 men, and for a time, late in the afternoon, there was some sharp fighting between the Twelfth Corps and the brigades of Rans Wright and Carnot Posey.

In his preoccupation with Sickles's operation, Hooker forgot — or ignored — the fact that his movement of troops to the south vacated more than a mile of the Chancellorsville line. The Eleventh Corps was now quite alone on the right flank.

Hooker went on to issue new orders to Sedgwick and the left wing, and to prepare the army to pursue the retreating foe. With Sickles's reports in hand, he telegraphed Sedgwick to seize Fredericksburg "with everything in it, and vigorously pursue the enemy. We know that the enemy is fleeing, trying to save his trains. Two of Sickles' divisions are among them." That moment — it was 4:10 P.M., Saturday, May 2, 1863 — may be taken as Fighting Joe Hooker's supreme moment of the Chancellorsville campaign.[8]

*   *

GENERAL DEVENS'S unconcern about the Eleventh Corps, and about his division in it, was not at all shared by his lieutenants. They were in a dilemma. They could not change the alignment of their troops without orders, and they feared demoralizing or panicking the men with dire predictions. The best they could do was to keep everyone alert.

Colonel Robert Reily of the 75th Ohio, for example, called his regiment together and announced that a great battle was in the offing. "Some of us will not see another sunrise," he said. "If there is a man in the ranks who is not ready to die for his country, let him come to me, and I will give him a pass to go to the rear, for I want no half-hearted, unwilling soldiers or cowards in the ranks to-night." It was said that no member of the regiment present that day would easily forget Colonel Reily's remarks. The colonel was one of those who would not see another sunrise.

Carl Schurz, a general of division with independence of mind enough to act on his own, quietly realigned three of his regiments to face west, covering a woods road leading northwest to Ely's Ford on the Rapidan. A few trees were felled to further block the road. It was at least a gesture toward guarding the corps' rear. Also there was a line of shallow rifle pits near Dowdall's Tavern that might be manned against an assault from the west. Basically, however, the Eleventh Corps remained strung out for a mile and a half facing south. To raise morale, General Schurz had his musicians — the German regimental bands were the best in the army — play patriotic and martial music during the afternoon.

Among those whose duty it was to guard this line there was a decided lack of aggressiveness. The Wilderness itself seemed to intimidate. The picket line that faced west, for example, which Howard would afterward insist was posted "from a half to three quarters of a mile beyond my front," was in fact sighted by the Confederate scouts hardly 200 yards beyond its own line. And a cavalry patrol sent out on the Ely's Ford woods road where the 26th Wisconsin was posted came back in only ten minutes to assure the Wisconsin men "that it was all right" and then trotted off to the rear to rest.[9]

The order for Barlow's brigade to support Sickles's movement left the Eleventh Corps manning its lines with fewer than 11,000 men. About two thirds of these were German or of recent German descent — to the rest of the army, "Dutchmen" who spoke comical English if they spoke English at all and who had never shared in this army's trials. The army's attitude ranged from one man's irritation that the Germans "were allowed their lager beer & ale when no other part of the army could get any," through intolerance for the numerous abolitionists and free-thinkers in their ranks, up to unthinking outright contempt for anyone foreign, an outgrowth of the anti-immigrant Know-Nothing politics of the 1850s.

To be sure, the Potomac army had peculiar notions of "foreignness" — Meagher's Irish Brigade was no less foreign than Von Gilsa's German Brigade, but no comparable stigma attached to the Irish — and there was no accounting for it. The best solution to all this, for the Dutchmen, would be a strong showing in this their first battle with the Army of the Potomac.

Even under better circumstances, the odds in favor of such a showing were not very good. Of the Eleventh's twenty-three regiments on the line just then, eight of them — nearly a third — had never been in battle before. And the remaining fifteen could hardly boast of sterling records. Not one of them had been on the winning side in any battle since their enlistments. It was the simple fact that nothing really good had ever happened to this corps.

Its fighting men, already crowded in their lines by the confining Wilderness, found the crowding made all the worse by the 125-wagon supply train that (contrary to orders) General Howard had permitted his quartermasters to bring along. The teamsters added to the swarm of noncombatants filling every open space close behind the lines. Amidst this was the corps' herd of beef cattle, with today chosen for the issue of fresh meat. In their diaries and letters a good many men would remem-ber the calm of that Saturday afternoon, with arms stacked and bands playing and the "sweet and tantalizing scent of the boiling meat" in every encampment. In midafternoon, wrote Thomas Evans of the 25th Ohio, Devens's division, "there was a feint made on our right after which the band played us a national air. Thus, as we supposed, we were secure from danger, such was the near-sightedness of our commander."[10]

Myopic indeed describes Charles Devens and Otis Howard in com-mand that day. Neither personally investigated any of the reports of Rebel activity on their front, and Howard compounded his negligence by leaving his command for two critical hours. Neither sent anyone from their staffs to investigate the reports. Devens, either through drink or intolerance of his lieutenants, failed in that most fundamental duty to protect his men from danger. Howard, having promised his superior that morning to take measures "to resist an attack from the west," took not one meaningful measure. A bitter Joe Hooker would charge that "my instructions were utterly and criminally disregarded."

The general belief at the Chancellor house that Lee was retreating, and Hooker's order to Howard to give up his reserve brigade for the pursuit, in no way repealed the 9:30 warning or Howard's duty to act on it. That 9:30 warning to Howard was in force for a full five hours before word reached Howard that the enemy might be retreating, and he did nothing in all that time. Had he taken the action his reply gave Hooker every right to assume he had taken — refusing Devens's division so as to face west with better than a third of the corps — this tale of retreat would have been rendered relatively harmless. Jackson's attack might still have been a surprise, but it would surely have been blunted to some degree.

Hooker's failing that day was not having enough cavalry with the army to guard it against surprise. He would defend his dispositions by saying that in the constricting Wilderness cavalry had no scope to operate, which was true enough but revealed a fundamental misunderstanding on his part. For all the drama of mounted men charging and countercharging, the paramount role for cavalry in this war (the role Jeb Stuart understood instinctively) was intelligence-gathering. Hooker's plan to raid Lee's communications was a sound enough tactic, certainly; his failing was not balancing Stoneman's needs with his own.

Lee and Jackson discovered Hooker's weakness in cavalry and made it a key element in the flanking plan. Thus Jackson's march security, except for the unavoidable sighting at Catharine Furnace, was faultless. And beyond a doubt Dame Fortune was smiling on the South this day.

For the Federals it was pure mischance that John Reynolds's First Corps was not dug in on the army's right flank. Then the Federals misinterpreted the sighting at the Furnace. Even Colonel Chilton misinterpreting Lee's order proved to be a blessing in disguise. But most of all, it was surely good fortune for the Confederacy that when Stonewall Jackson finally signaled the charge, he was aiming squarely at the ineptly led Eleventh Corps of the Army of the Potomac. And, in the final irony, it was because Joe Hooker had recognized that ineptitude that the Eleventh Corps was posted where it was.

It was about 5:45 and the sun was low in the west and many of the Yankees were cooking supper when Von Gilsa's regiments on the far west of the line heard a bewildering commotion in the woods in front of them. They could hear what sounded like bugles but the rest was just growing but unidentifiable noise. Suddenly quail in numbers came beating through the treetops, and then there was a rush of frantic deer and rabbits straight toward them out of the woods; one man claimed he saw a bear among the fleeing game.

The men whooped and pointed at the sight, and then they heard the crackle of gunfire and the blood-curdling banshee screech of the Rebel yell coming from in front and from left and right to the limits of their hearing. Then they knew. Years afterward, thinking back on it, Thomas Evans wrote, ". . . Jackson was on us and fear was on us."[11]

* *

AT 5:30 that afternoon, on the Orange Turnpike, Stonewall Jackson sat his horse alongside Robert Rodes and Major Eugene Blackford of the skirmishers. Jackson turned and asked, "Are you ready, General Rodes?" Rodes's "Yes, sir!" was prompt. Without pose or gesture Jackson said quietly, "You can go forward then."[12]

At a nod from Rodes, Major Blackman had his bugler sound the call and it was taken up urgently up and down the line. The men went forward quickly, shouldering their way through the matted vines and briers and tangled underbrush, through the Wilderness General Howard thought impenetrable by an army. There was half a mile of this to reach the Yankee line. It was hard going, but no one straggled. "The command was given forward march, guide right," wrote North Carolinian John Brooks of Iverson's brigade in the front line. "In less than ten minutes our pickets commenced firing on the enemy and five minutes more our line of Battle gave them a volley that will last them until peace is made."

George Doles's Georgia brigade, straddling the Turnpike, smashed head-on against the outlying Yankee defenses. Two of Von Gilsa's German regiments, 41st and 45th New York, posted along the Turnpike aligned to face south, were surprised and turned so quickly that they ran without firing a shot. The section of Captain Dieckmann's guns pointing west down the road touched off their loaded rounds and managed to fire a second round, but then the charging Georgians were on them and shot down the battery horses and the gunners left their pieces and ran.

In the woods north of the road Von Gilsa's only regiments facing west, 54th New York and 153rd Pennsylvania, managed to stand a few minutes longer. "I fired into the thicket, others did likewise, reloaded and fired again," Pennsylvanian Francis Stofflet wrote in his diary. Doles rapidly shifted the 21st Georgia to turn this flank. "We were ordered forward and the boys all gave a few keen yells and said they intended to have some Yankee crackers before they slept that night," Lieutenant Thomas Hightower of the 21st Georgia told his fiancée.

With that the New Yorkers on the threatened flank broke and went to the rear. The 153rd Pennsylvania was a nine-month regiment that had

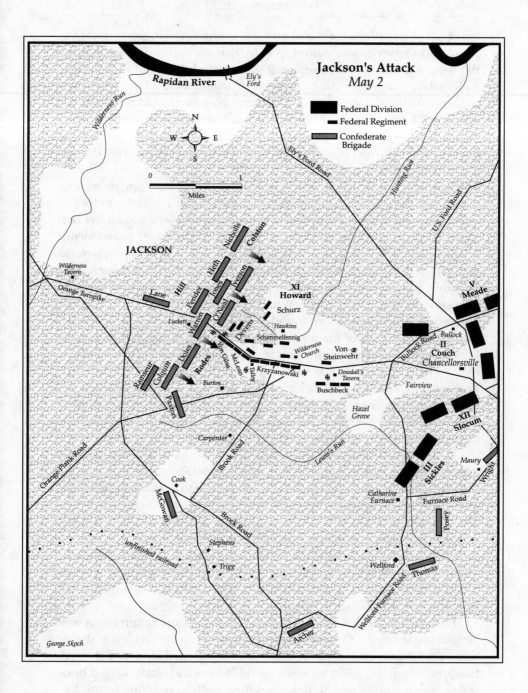

Jackson's Attack
May 2

Rapidan River

Wilderness Run

Ely's Ford

Ely's Ford Road

Hunting Run

U.S. Ford Road

Federal Division

Federal Regiment

Confederate Brigade

N
W — E
S

0   1
Miles

Wilderness Tavern

JACKSON

Orange Turnpike

Lane

Hill

Pender

Heth

Nicholls

Colston

Jones

O'Neal

Iverson

Luckett

Warren

Doles

Van Gilsa

McLean

Talley

Devens

Hawkins

Schimmelfennig

Wilderness Church

XI
Howard

Schurz

Von
Steinwehr

Ramseur

Colquitt

Rodes

Burton

Krzyzanowski

Dowdall's Tavern

Buschbeck

V
Meade

Bullock Road

Bullock
II
Couch
Chancellorsville

Fairview

Paxton

Carpenter

Brook Road

Hazel
Grove

Lewis's Run

XII
Slocum

Cook

McGowan

Brock Road

Catharine
Furnace

III
Sickles

Maury

Furnace Road

Wright

Posey

unfinished railroad

Stephens

Trigg

Wellford

Wellford Furnace Road

Thomas

Archer

Orange Plank Road

George Skoch

never been in battle before, and now the troops on both sides of it were gone, and the order was passed to save themselves. For Private Stofflet the issue was clear: "Well, the rebels surrounded us and our entire brigade was in danger of being captured or annihilated." They were pursued by a hail of fire from behind and from both flanks and there was no stopping. "It was futile now," he wrote, "and my only anxiety was how to escape capture and where to find my company and regiment." In just ten minutes Von Gilsa had lost 264 men, half of whom were captured, including two of his four regimental commanders.[13]

Colonel John C. Lee of the 55th Ohio, the next regiment in line after Von Gilsa's brigade, galloped back to the Talley house for help. He found General Devens sitting his horse in front of his headquarters but stubbornly unwilling to act without instructions from higher authority; Howard was absent, and no word reached him from corps headquarters. Lee pleaded for permission to change front to meet the attack. His brigade commander, Nathaniel McLean, looked inquiringly at Devens, who said nothing. Finally McLean told Lee, "Not yet."

Back at his regiment, Lee found a full-blown crisis. The Rebel battle line had crashed out of the forest into the Talley clearing and McLean's Ohio brigade — three regiments along the Turnpike facing south, two in reserve behind them — was hopelessly out of position. Again Colonel Lee spurred back to the Talley house, and again Devens was silent. McLean resignedly waved Lee back to his command. Afterward Lee and a fellow colonel, William P. Richardson of the 25th Ohio, insisted that General Devens was too befuddled by drink to know what he was doing.

The 75th Ohio was posted to the rear of the main line, acting as a general reserve for Devens's division, and Colonel Reily changed front to the west without waiting for orders. He even tried to advance to meet the attack, but his ranks were repeatedly broken by fugitives from the front. Some men from Von Gilsa's shattered brigade stopped and joined Reily in his stand; most hurried on toward the rear. Dole's Georgians and on their left Edward O'Neal's Alabamians came on at the double-quick, greatly overlapping the ragged line of Ohioans. The leading section of Stuart's horse artillery added canister to the storm of fire and Colonel Reily was killed and his line collapsed.

The remains of the Ohio brigade (when the 17th Connecticut was assigned to them the Ohioans had shrugged and gone on calling themselves the Ohio brigade) fell back 500 yards and rallied around divisional headquarters at the Talley house. General Devens had finally stirred himself to action and he and McLean and their staffs were trying frantically to stem the tide. Devens was soon wounded in the foot and helped from the field, and the line was outflanked on the left and then it broke apart.

The crews of the four remaining guns of Captain Dieckmann's battery made no effort to wheel their pieces around but instead limbered up and fled without firing a shot. Four of McLean's five colonels were dead, wounded, or captured, and 688 of his men. "In 15 minutes we were all cut to pieces," Thomas Evans remembered. "There was no place left us but to flee for our lives which we did with a right good grace." Luther Mesnard of the 55th Ohio could hardly believe what he was seeing. "To the right or left or in front as far as I could see, everything was fleeing in panic," he wrote. "It seemed to me that the whole army had gone to pieces. . . ."

The 17th Connecticut's Major Allen Brady, according to Private Silliman, "was some excited, said he did not know what to do as he had no orders." This was the 17th's first battle, and the major's command was supposed to be supporting Dieckmann's battery, but that was gone now and everyone was facing in the wrong direction to meet the swarming Rebels. "They had nearly reached the house when he ordered us to make for the woods," Private Silliman wrote. "His order was promptly obeyd though I believe there were but few who started before the order was given. Many of us stuck to the major however as he made about as good time as any of us through the woods." Eventually the scattered fragments of the regiment washed up far to the rear at the Chancellor house. When there was time for a count it was found that the colonel was wounded, the lieutenant colonel was dead, and all told the regiment had lost one in five of those who began the day.[14]

* *

LIKE RUSHING waters from a burst dam, Jackson's massive assault came boiling out of the woods into the next open ground to the east along the Turnpike. This was the large, irregularly shaped clearing surrounding Wilderness Church and the intersection of the Plank Road and the Turnpike. The Baptist chapel, a modest white-painted frame building, was set back 150 yards from the road in a little grove. Beyond it, a quarter mile farther to the north, was the Hawkins farmstead. To the east, close by the Plank Road, was Dowdall's Tavern, headquarters of the Eleventh Corps. Carl Schurz's division held this ground, supported on the east by the last of the corps' units then in line, Adolphus Buschbeck's brigade of Adolph Von Steinwehr's division. Beyond Buschbeck there were no Federal troops anywhere in sight for more than a mile.

General Howard, just returning to his headquarters after leading Barlow's brigade to join Sickles at the Furnace, would remember this moment in the metaphor of a great storm: "It was a terrible gale! The rush, the rattle, the quick lightning from a hundred points at once; the roar, redoubled by echoes through the forest. . . ." Fugitives from Devens's division rushed headlong past and through Schurz's men, spreading panic like a contagion. The sight stunned Howard. Devens's men, he told his wife, "immediately gave way, broke up & ran upon the other troops with such momentum that they gave way too. Such a mass of fugitives I hav'nt seen since the first battle of Bull Run." (Otis Howard, who had commanded a brigade in that battle, recognized a rout when he saw one.)

Schurz's division was called the most foreign in the Potomac army, eight of its ten regiments being German. The brigade commanders were Alexander Schimmelfennig and Wladimir Krzyzanowski, and there were colonels named Mahler and Hecker and Braun and Peissner and Van Hartung. (The Pole Krzyzanowski's appointment as brigadier general was not confirmed by the Senate, it was said, because no one in that body could pronounce his name.) Four of the regiments had never been in combat before, and for the most part morale was fragile. "I fights mit Sigel" had been this division's particular watchword, and resentment ran high against his successor as corps commander.

Although Schurz had earlier shown foresight in facing three of his regiments to the west on the Hawkins farm, it proved only enough to delay Jackson's juggernaut for a matter of minutes. At Hawkins's the 82nd Ohio, 58th New York, and the 26th Wisconsin, one of the new regiments, traded volley for volley with the enemy until they were outflanked and had to fall back. They did so, at least, in good order. The 26th Wisconsin's Adam Muenzenberger wrote his wife of his first-battle ordeal and concluded, "The fault of it is this: Sigel isn't with us any more, and the others are merely humbug generals." Over 40 percent in his regiment were casualties.

To the south, between Wilderness Church and the Plank Road, the scene was utter chaos. Officers trying to pivot their regiments to meet the assault had neither time nor space to do so. Masses of men and pack mules and horses and wagons from Howard's inflated trains bowled over what formations there were and broke them up. In its desperate flight Dieckmann's battery of four guns took to the fields to escape and became tangled in a wattle fence and was captured intact by the jubilant Rebels.

Along the Plank Road the Germans of the 119th New York, in their first battle, saw nine of the twelve men in the color guard shot down. Their colonel was Elias Peissner, who General Schurz contended was the natural son of the celebrated and eccentric king of Bavaria, Ludwig I, but an estimable soldier for all that. Peissner was hit by two bullets and killed and the regimental line collapsed and went to the rear. "The rest run like deer, saying they wanted Gen. Sigel and no other," a man in the 119th complained.[15]

The strongest Federal showing on this Wilderness Church line was made by Leatherbreeches Dilger and his Battery I, 1st Ohio Light Artillery. Dilger placed his six Napoleons on a little rise near the Plank Road and opened an effective fire on Jackson's legions as they broke into the clearing. One of his gunners, Private Darwin Cody, described the scene for his parents. "Our supports was all germans," Cody wrote. "They run without firing a gun. Such yelling I never heard before as the Rebs made. Our Battery was soon left alone." Ahead was a solid line of menacing infantry, stretching beyond sight left and right. Dilger held them there, firing until the enemy was within a hundred yards, then fell back and unlimbered again. "We gave them double canister which soon checked them in the center. . . . Then the Rebels soon commenced to charge on our Battery . . . to get one of the guns. They shot the wheel horses, then we was done. We done all we could to save it. . . . I say dam the DUTCH."

For a time the corps reserve batteries opened as well, firing over the heads of their own infantry. Then they were masked by the fugitives rushing in front of the guns and finally they went to the rear. The battery of Captain Michael Wiedrich lost two of its pieces when it did not pull back fast enough. Leatherbreeches Dilger sent his remaining Napoleons to the rear except for one piece that he kept back to try and hold the Plank Road. Meanwhile, around Dowdall's Tavern, the Eleventh Corps was making its last stand.

General Howard and his officers had rushed into the stream of fugitives trying (as he put it) "to arrest the tide." Howard took up an abandoned stand of the national colors, gripping the staff with the stump of his right arm, and rode with it recklessly toward the fight, hoping by example to inspire a rally. His horse, he told his wife, became panicked by the firing "and stood so straight on his hind legs, that I had to come down — but I was soon up again." One of his staff was killed at his side. "I presume I have never been more exposed then in the last battle, but a kind Providence has succored me," he would write. However derelict in his command duties, Otis Howard lacked nothing in personal courage.

Correspondent Thomas Cook of the *New York Herald* was watching. "On the one hand," Cook wrote, "was a solid column of infantry retreating at double quick from the face of the enemy; on the other was a dense mass of beings who had lost their reasoning faculties, and were flying from a thousand fancied dangers . . . ; battery wagons, ambulances, horses, men, cannon, caissons, all jumbled and tumbled together in an apparently inextricable mass, and that murderous fire still pouring in upon them."[16]

* *

STONEWALL JACKSON'S men were exultant. They had seen their enemies retreat before, but never was it like this. "You never saw such a grand sight in your life," Robert Garnett of the 21st Virginia exclaimed in a letter to his brother. "We came up in rear of the yankees late on Saturday evening. You never saw such a charge as we made upon them, we soon got them routed and then it was a perfect foot race. . . ." They tried to stand behind some rifle pits, a Louisianian wrote, "but they were soon routed from them and we pressed on driving them from three successive lines. They were flying in great disorder. . . ." The historian of the 1st North Carolina remarked how "the thick woods through which we were passing was like a strainer, letting the lean and lesser Dutchmen escape, while we secured the fat ones."

Robert Rodes made a striking figure leading this triumphant rush. With his sweeping mustaches and martial bearing he had the look of a Viking warrior of another century. Rodes's bold dash on every battlefield had brought him quickly up through the ranks from company captain of the Alabama Warrior Guards to brigadier general in command of D. H. Hill's old division. His record this day marked him for further promotion. Rodes's battle cry, delivered in a clarion voice heard over the din, was exactly in character: "Forward, men, over friend or foe!"

Driving forward, Rodes's division soon became disordered by the stretches of woodland in its path and by the spurts of resistance it met, and by the sweet taste of victory. Porter Alexander watched "men singly & in groups, firing, stopping to load, & then pressing forward again." Colonels and captains took over direction of the assault when it outdistanced higher commands. Colston's second line closed up on Rodes and in many places the two lines became intermixed, causing greater disorder. A. P. Hill's third line in the rear seldom found targets.

On the left, northern, flank, Iverson's North Carolina brigade repeatedly turned the outmanned Federal positions, so that B. B. Carr of the 20th North Carolina termed it simply "a running fight." From the woods, he wrote, "we emerged charging with a yell over their cooking detail routing their rear line which retreated with firing only a few shots at us, a great many of them not taking their guns which were stacked. . . . The attacking forces by time night came on was a disorganized rabble, every one his own commander doing as pleased him but going forward all the time." A Federal officer down with a wound had a similar impression. The Rebels, Hartwell Osborn wrote, rushed past him "with very little attention to line formation and clad in as motley an array of uniforms as could be imagined; but they were all disciplined and eager to go on. . . ."[17]

Afterward, in the shock of defeat, soldiers in the Eleventh Corps would try to burnish their corps' honor with accounts of how regiments had stood and fought until overwhelmed by superior numbers, then retreated in orderly fashion. This was certainly true enough, yet there were at least as many regiments that were so surprised they fell prey to unreasoning panic, even leaving their rifles behind. Numerous Confederate accounts speak of finding these stacked arms, and General Harry Heth, of A. P. Hill's division, was even specific about it. When his brigade reached the Wilderness Church clearing, he recalled, "not a Federal soldier was to be seen. I passed over a line of muskets stacked; this line of muskets was, I think, 200 yards in length."

General Heth also took account of the campfires and the simmering camp kettles he saw. "We had no time to plunder," Oliver Hamilton of the 38th North Carolina wrote, "and picked up but little more than some fresh cooked beef which they had left sitting in the boilers . . . and of which we were greatly in need." Most Confederate accounts of the attack speak of this welcome Yankee beef ("We *of course* would appropriate a portion of it," one man explained), and the officers seem not to have objected. As General Iverson put it in his report, "Hungry men seized provisions as they passed the camps of the enemy, and rushed forward, eating, shouting, and firing." Nor was beef the only plunder. A wounded, bloodied Rebel encountered by the advancing 14th South Carolina called out, "Oh boys, they are running! They are running! They've got the shoes, too, and I got a pair!" As he held up his prize for all to see he was cheered for it.[18]

The fleeing Yankees might not have recognized it, but Jackson's assault was overbalanced on the left. All the outflanking was being done by Iverson's and O'Neal's brigades to the north. This was due to the sudden caution of Alfred Colquitt on the right. By Rodes's account, Colquitt had been carefully instructed not to be concerned about his right flank. South of him, on the Orange Plank Road, was the Stonewall Brigade and Stuart's cavalry, placed there specifically to guard the southern flank — Colquitt's flank — from any interference by the enemy.

Yet the battle had hardly opened when Colquitt halted his brigade and faced to the south, announcing that his advance had sighted Yankee cavalry and infantry on his flank. Dodson Ramseur, whose brigade had been crowded out of the front line for lack of space and was behind Colquitt, impatiently scouted ahead half a mile and reported "not a solitary Yankee was to be seen." He urged Colquitt to follow instructions and push on; let him rely on Ramseur and the force on the Plank Road as his guard. Colquitt reflected on this and at length resumed his advance.

What he (or his skirmishers) had actually seen remains a mystery. No Federal cavalry was anywhere in the area, and the only foot soldiers might have been pickets from Schurz's division, scarcely a threat to a brigade of infantry. Colquitt's timidity did not weaken the sledgehammer effect of Jackson's blow, but had he advanced in concert with the rest of Rodes's line, turning this other Federal flank, no doubt a considerably larger portion of the Eleventh Corps would have been taken. At least there was one Yankee that day who thought so. "A yankey Colonel that we took prisoner," wrote James Coghill of the 23rd North Carolina, "said that if we had to have kept on we would have captured the whole army. . . ."

Howard attempted his last stand with the last of his force, the brigade of Adolphus Buschbeck. Four days earlier the 154th New York under Buschbeck had paddled alone across the Rappahannock under fire to seize Kelly's Ford, but that experience paled in comparison with this one. The New Yorkers took position with the rest of the brigade in some shallow rifle pits near Dowdall's Tavern that had been dug earlier and faced west. Some stalwarts from Devens's and Schurz's divisions joined the fight here to bring the total in Buschbeck's line to perhaps 4,000.

Their position covered a thousand yards from end to end, but soon enough Rodes easily outflanked them on the north. In twenty minutes Howard's last line was turned like all the others. The 154th New York's James Emmons wrote that their volleys "would mow a road through them every time but they would close up with a yell . . . they drove us at last we run you better believe." Forty percent of Emmons's comrades were killed, wounded, or missing. The 495 casualties in Buschbeck's brigade included three of the four regimental commanders down with wounds.[19]

As he rode close behind his swiftly advancing forces, Stonewall Jackson would call to every officer he encountered, "Press forward! Press forward!" By the account of Captain Robert E. Wilbourn, the general's signal officer, "All the orders I heard him give were simply a repetition of this order." When he came up with Major Robert Beckham, whose horse battery was blazing away with canister right up alongside the infantry, Jackson leaned down to shake the hand of the startled Beckham and tell him, "Young man, I congratulate you!" To Rodes too he offered congratulations for gallantly conducting the drive. "I had never seen Gen. Jackson so well pleased with his success as that evening," Wilbourn wrote. "He was in unusually fine spirits and every time he heard the cheering of ourselves which was the signal of victory he raised his right hand a few seconds as if in acknowledgment of the blessing and to return thanks to God for the victory."

Old Jack might well give thanks. In just an hour and a half his surprise attack had flanked and overwhelmed the Eleventh Corps and driven it a mile and a quarter and routed it from its last feasible defensive position. From Dowdall's Tavern it was less than two miles to the Chancellor house, and there was no knowing if the Confederate drive could be stopped short even of that point. The sun was down now, however, with perhaps forty minutes of evening twilight remaining. Just then (as Porter Alexander put it) daylight was worth a million dollars a minute to the fortunes of the Confederacy.[20]

11

The Fate of Stonewall Jackson

A S HE WAS preparing his assault on the Eleventh Corps, Stonewall Jackson received a dispatch by courier from General Lee. Lee assured his lieutenant that at the first sign of "any engagement which may take place in rear of Chancellorsville," he would vigorously demonstrate on his front with infantry and artillery so as to keep Hooker from pulling any troops from there to oppose Jackson. When finally the thunder of Jackson's attack was heard across the four miles or so separating the two segments of the army, there was considerable relief on McGee's Hill. "Thank God! There are Jackson's guns," exclaimed Little Billy Mahone. Lafayette McLaws rode his lines calling out, "Yell, men! Yell! Jackson is in their rear, make them think we are very strong here." As Corporal Lewis Warren of the 10th Georgia recalled it, "We yelled, we were glad to know that Jackson was at his old tricks again. . . ." To his commanders Lee passed the word: "Press them heavily everywhere."

With Wright's and Posey's brigades already fully engaged near Catharine Furnace, Lee's order was taken up most vigorously by Mahone on the Plank Road and by William Wofford on the Turnpike. McLaws told his skirmishers to engage and threaten, "but not attack seriously." Wofford's Georgians had their blood up, however, and had to be restrained. They withdrew, McLaws reported, "in good spirits, after driving the enemy to their entrenchments."

Mahone's brigade was equally aggressive. The skirmishers of his 6th Virginia not only "felt the enemy warmly" but came back with the regimental flag of the 107th Ohio. If Mahone can be taken at his word, that makes this one of the more remarkable stories of the day. The 107th Ohio, from McLean's Ohio brigade, had fled from Jackson on the army's extreme right all the way across to the army's extreme left, where it promptly lost its flag to troops under Lee. May 2 was the Ohioans' first battle, and one they would not soon forget.[1]

At some point during the afternoon Lee learned (no doubt to his dismay) that his discretionary order to Early in Fredericksburg, through some "misapprehension" on the part of Chief of Staff Chilton, had become an order for Early "to move unconditionally." How Lee learned this is not on record. Very likely it was by dispatch from a worried Jubal Early, making a point of acknowledging the commanding general's peremptory order to withdraw his division from the town.

Lee hastened to send a corrective order. This too is not on record, but Early showed it to artillerist Pendleton, who noted (perhaps diplomatically) that it expressed "apprehension that his wishes had been misunderstood." However that may be, Early was leading his division onto the Plank Road west of Fredericksburg "a little before dark" when Lee's dispatch reached him. Any withdrawal was again left to his discretion. Soon enough a report came from the brigade still in Fredericksburg that decided him. The Yankees were driving in force from their bridgehead toward the River Road below the town. The army's reserve artillery was at risk. "I determined to return at once to my former position," Early wrote.

Throughout the afternoon and early evening of Day Six, General John Sedgwick sat at his headquarters on Tyler's Hill on the north bank of the Rappahannock in a seeming state of bemusement as one Confederate unit after another was seen to leave their lines on the south bank. Even Dan Butterfield telling him "enemy evacuating your front" failed to prompt Sedgwick to move. What finally stirred him was Hooker's order — his peremptory order — to "capture Fredericksburg with everything in it, and vigorously pursue the enemy."

Hooker sent this at 4:10 P.M., but the Signal Corps had only marginally improved its service that day and the dispatch was some two hours reaching Sedgwick. Also true to form, it contained an ambiguity: General Sedgwick was to "cross the river as soon as indications will permit" to attack as directed. Since the commanding general obviously did not understand the position of the Sixth Corps, Sedgwick called for his horse and rode to army headquarters near Falmouth to discuss the matter with Chief of Staff Butterfield.

They seem to have agreed that whatever Hooker meant by this, his basic intent was clear. The Sixth Corps should cross its two remaining divisions, break through the weakened enemy lines, capture Fredericksburg, and pursue the enemy wherever he might fly. At 7 o'clock, just as Stonewall Jackson was tearing through the Eleventh Corps, Butterfield telegraphed the Chancellor house that Sedgwick was advancing as ordered.

At the same time, from Fredericksburg, a courier came pelting after Jubal Early with the plea for help. Early turned his division back promptly enough, but he had to hope that Harry Hays's Louisiana brigade could hold out until he reached his old lines. He had to hope, too, that even then they would be strong enough to hold off this new Yankee offensive.[2]

* *

JUST TO the east of Dowdall's Tavern the Wilderness closed in, leaving the Orange Plank Road as the primary corridor of escape for Howard's wrecked corps. A woods road slanted off southeasterly to the Hazel Grove clearing, but the Plank Road, running straight east toward Chancellorsville, was the route of choice for the fugitives that evening. This narrow corridor ran for half a mile before the forest gradually gave back to form ever-larger clearings, first at an old schoolhouse, then at Fairview, finally at the Chancellor house. When Colonel Buschbeck's line collapsed, the stream of fugitives here became a torrent.

By some fluke of acoustics the roar of Jackson's assault did not immediately reach Federal headquarters at the Chancellor house. Or perhaps the banging of Lee's guns and those at Catharine Furnace drowned out the firing to the west. In any event, General Hooker was sitting on the Chancellors' front porch with Captains Harry Russell and William Candler of his staff when at about 6:30 a commotion down the Plank Road attracted Captain Russell's attention. He stepped out into the road and focused his glass, and after a moment he shouted, "My God, here they come!"

General and staff quickly mounted and rode fast toward the right to identify this rush of men and vehicles. To their astonishment it proved to be the outriders of Devens's routed division. Amidst the clamor and babble of explanations could be heard repeated cries of "*Alles ist verloren!*" Hooker and the staff and the headquarters cavalry detail tried to halt the flight but without the slightest success.

A man in the 94th New York who came upon the scene a few minutes later tried to catalog it: "Men on foot on horseback on mules & in teams were rushing & piling back for dear life telling all kinds of yarns & we began to think that there was another Bull Run. . . . Some had no caps some not coats all going for dear life, teams & droves of cattle all rushing back to the rear. After a while we found out that the 11th Corps composed of *Dutchmen*, the Blenkerites & Sigelites, had stampeded shamefully. . . ."[3]

The commanding general — he was Fighting Joe Hooker now — realized that whatever enemy had set off this panic was sure to be not far behind, and that these fugitives gave no promise of stopping any time soon. He needed artillery, and he called on Captain Clermont Best, the artillery chief of the Twelfth Corps who had guns at Fairview, to wheel them into battery facing west. For infantry he turned to the only troops left in reserve near the Chancellor house, Hiram Berry's division of the Third Corps. This was Hooker's old division, and unabashedly he rallied its troops for old times' sake. "It was there that 'Old Joe' galloped up and called for us his *old division*. Up we went to the front the boys cheering and swearing," William Wiley remembered. "Throw your men into the breach!" Hooker shouted to General Berry. "Receive the enemy on your bayonets! — don't fire a shot! — they can't see you!"

Colonel Robert McAllister, commanding the 11th New Jersey in Berry's division, wrote his wife of "the gallant Hooker. . . . The order came down the line: 'Double quick!' Three times three cheers resounded in the air. The boys were ready and willing for the fight. . . ." As they dashed past Hooker sitting his big white warhorse, he would call out, "Receive 'em on your bayonets, boys! Receive 'em on your bayonets!" This was the Fighting Joe of a half-dozen battlefields. Later another man saw him at one of Best's batteries, "working like an enlisted man at the guns." If personal inspiration could save the day, Joe Hooker was the man of the hour.[4]

The crushing of the Eleventh Corps did not entirely become the skedaddle the newspapers would report. On the Plank Road Leatherbreeches Dilger was turning the infantry tactic of "fire and fall back" into an artillery tactic, firing a round or two of canister, dragging his single gun back 50 or 100 yards and firing again, measurably slowing the pursuit. A hundred or so infantrymen of the 61st Ohio, Schimmelfennig's brigade, stayed alongside Dilger in support. There were regiments and parts of regiments that went back in decent enough order, fully armed, under officers' control, then took up defensive positions in the rear as ordered. Yet for each of these stories there was another story — or two or three stories — of utter demoralization and uncontrollable panic. It seemed that every failing and every injustice piled on this corps for the past two years now broke it into pieces.

Rushing into the Chancellorsville clearing, panicked men surged northward over every byway, crying out for directions to the bridges and safety across the river. Many had thrown away their rifles and torn off their corps badges to become anonymous. Old-timers seeing this flight who had served on the frontier were reminded of cattle and buffalo stampedes. To others it seemed the blind flight of sheep. One desperate German approached General Hancock and asked the way to the pontoon bridges. The reply of Win Hancock, a master of profane invective, was not thought seemly enough for his biographer to record. It is recorded that other fugitives kept running right through the Second Corps lines and into the Confederate lines beyond. Amidst this din and confusion the band of the 14th Connecticut blared out "Yankee Doodle" and "The Red, White, and Blue" and "The Star-Spangled Banner" over and over.[5]

The high command's greatest concern was that the Eleventh Corps' contagion would infect other units, and encounters became episodes of danger and even death. William Aughinbaugh of the 5th Ohio, Slocum's corps, was in line trying to arrest the flight "and had succeeded in stopping several hundred, when a large party came up and fired into us and rushed through us, . . . scattering the men in every direction." According to Private Cody of Dilger's battery, "Gen. Hooker soon ordered the 12th corps to kill every man that run in the 11th. I saw a number of officers and privates shot trying to break through the guard. It served them right. . . ." General Williams saw Joe Dickinson of Hooker's staff "riding fiercely about, pistol in hand, and occasionally discharging it at some flying Dutchman." Sergeant Lucius Swift of the 28th New York recorded that on orders "four or five were shot down. Colonel Cook was a dead shot and I saw him shoot one with a navy revolver at twenty rods; the man fell on his face. When they saw that we were in earnest, they stopped. . . ."[6]

Later, when a final count of the Dutchmen could be made, it was found that of the nearly 11,000 in line when Jackson struck, just over 2,400 were casualties — just under 22 percent. The assault was so sudden, and so enveloping, that nearly a thousand of these were prisoners. Nine guns were lost.

Otis Howard was described by one of his lieutenants as "full of mortification & disgust." Howard himself would admit, "I wanted to die. . . . That night I did all in my power to remedy the mistake, and I sought death everywhere I could find an excuse to go on the field." The loss in Jackson's attacking force on May 2 was only some 800. Most discouraging for those of Howard's men with a sense of corps pride, there was no chance for redemption. For the rest of the campaign the Eleventh Corps would be posted far from harm's way.[7]

Staff couriers at the Chancellor house raced off through the gathering dusk with their urgent messages. The high open ground immediately to the right, at Fairview and beyond at Hazel Grove, was now at risk, and the troops who had been responsible for holding it were with Dan Sickles around Catharine Furnace. Witnessing the outriders of defeat from the right, Slocum had Williams's Twelfth Corps division recalled to reoccupy its position guarding Fairview. Sickles was ordered to return to Hazel Grove with his two Third Corps divisions from the Furnace. Barlow's brigade of Howard's corps had gone the farthest, and was the last to return.

In the other direction, Reynolds's First Corps from downriver was told to come forward as soon as it could cross at U.S. Ford. General Meade, on his own initiative, shifted his Fifth Corps forces to secure the army's communications with the river. The task facing them all, in Hooker's words, was "to seize, and hold, at all hazards" the high ground from which the Rebels might threaten the army's center.

By now the Confederates were almost as disorganized by victory as the Federals by defeat. Colston's second line continued to pile into Rodes's first, especially during the pause when the Yankees under Buschbeck made their last stand. Also the battle lines were becoming compressed, as by a funnel, narrowing from a mile and a half wide at the start of the charge to a half mile or so as they drove past Dowdall's Tavern. South of the Plank Road the abatis that fronted the Federal defenses further entangled and delayed the advance. As the formations entered the darkening woods beyond Dowdall's it became harder than ever to maintain control.

Finally, at about 7:15 P.M., General Rodes ordered a halt to reorganize. "Such was the confusion and darkness that it was not deemed advisable to make a farther advance," he would explain in his report. He sent word to Jackson recommending that A. P. Hill's troops in the third line come forward to take over the advance while he re-formed his brigades.

As a measure of the confusion, Rodes's order to halt did not reach some number of his men in the three leading brigades — Iverson's North Carolinians, O'Neal's Alabamians, Doles's Georgians. They continued on in pursuit through the woods and along the Plank Road, every man "his own commander, going as pleased him. . . ." Where they met resistance in the fading light they struck sparks.[8]

✻ ✻

ONE OF Hooker's headquarters dispatches had called for cavalry to help corral the fugitives from Howard's command; mounted men were thought to be best for halting panicked infantry. Just then all the cavalry was at Hazel Grove, waiting to join in the pursuit of the Rebel army. Major Pennock Huey's 8th Pennsylvania had been there some hours and was taking its ease, its officers enjoying a game of poker, when orders came to return to headquarters. The orders mentioned nothing of the attack on the Eleventh Corps, and no sound of battle had yet penetrated to Hazel Grove, and the troopers anticipated nothing out of the ordinary. The sun was just setting when the long column, two riders abreast, set off along the narrow woods road that ran northward three quarters of a mile to the Orange Plank Road.

After half a mile a byway came in from the left, from the direction of Dowdall's Tavern, and Major Huey saw some shadowy figures there but could not identify them. A little later, as they neared the Plank Road, he saw more figures crossing ahead of him and in the woods off to the left, and their uniforms were definitely butternut. Somehow, he thought, he had stumbled into an enemy force behind his own lines.

The road here was too narrow to reverse the column, and there was nothing for it but to charge ahead and gain the Plank Road and make a dash for Chancellorsville. Huey shouted the order, "Draw sabers and charge!" Behind him in the column was Captain Charles Wickersham, who the day before had narrowly escaped from the butternuts out on the Turnpike to the east. Wickersham wondered if today might not see the last of the 8th Pennsylvania cavalry.

Major Huey led the charge to the Plank Road and discovered it crowded with enemy troops to the right, toward Chancellorsville. Sawing his horse around, he led the troopers off to the left, hoping to find some way out of the ambush. They thundered down the road, sabers flashing at every Rebel soldier they encountered. They had gone about a hundred yards when the head of the column was abruptly riddled by a volley fired from the woods at point-blank range. Men and horses crashed to the ground or spilled into the trees. Three of the officers riding with Huey were killed instantly.

Those in the lead companies who survived this fire plunged into the forest to the north and tried to work their way back to Union lines. The trailing companies never reached the Plank Road but turned off instead into the woods to their right. Eventually the survivors reached safety at Fairview. Major Huey counted his casualties as 33 men and 80 horses, but in its ill-fated charge the regiment also lost all or most of the 76 men reported captured during the campaign. The Pennsylvania troopers did little harm to the Rebel infantry — this was Rodes's advancing guard — but still the warning went out to watch for surprise strikes by Yankee cavalry.[9]

Some 60 yards east of the entrance to the road Major Huey had followed from Hazel Grove, at right angles to the Plank Road, was a sturdy barricade of logs that Alpheus Williams's division had erected the day before. When Williams marched off that afternoon to reinforce Sickles at the Furnace, he left four companies of the 28th New York at the barricade to guard the division's baggage. Thus far their only action had been trying to halt the Eleventh Corps fugitives, but then Colonel Elliott

Cook and his men took heart when a goodly number of Howard's more stalwart troops joined them. "Then a strange thing happened," Sergeant Lucius Swift wrote. The newcomers were ordered away to continue their retreat, leaving the New Yorkers alone again in this strong defensive position. Retreat now struck Colonel Cook as his wisest course, and he had started his men toward the rear when a breathless courier arrived from General Williams. Hold on, he was told; the division was on the way back to its old position.

Dutifully Colonel Cook countermarched his little column. Then another column was seen in the dim light coming from the right, from the Plank Road, also heading for the barricade. A cheer rang out, and was answered. But as the two columns converged Sergeant Swift thought the other's flag looked wrong. "Those men are rebels!" he said to the colonel, who paid him no attention. Then it was too late: "They had the drop on us at close range." A crestfallen Colonel Cook was soon handing over his sword. Some in the rear rank managed to slip away, but sixty-seven men of the 28th New York were disarmed and marched away. In a final insult, soon afterward they were themselves stampeded by Federal artillery firing blindly in their direction.[10]

At the same time, a second band of Rodes's men was probing off to the southeast toward Hazel Grove. Hazel Grove had served as the staging area for Sickles's move to Catharine Furnace, and it was crowded with his batteries and divisional trains and cavalry and a mule train with the corps' reserve ammunition. Rebels of Doles's brigade — mostly from the 4th Georgia — swarmed out of the dark woods and set off another stampede. Terrified teamsters and muleteers set their charges on the run straight through batteries trying to unlimber to meet the threat. A great tangle of Third Corps wagons, ambulances, caissons, and runaway horses and mules rivaled the scene on the Plank Road. An artillery lieutenant described this throng "rushing through and through my battery, overturning guns and limbers, smashing my caissons, and trampling my horse-holders under them."

These latest fugitives, surging northeastward from Hazel Grove toward Chancellorsville, crossed the path of General Williams's Twelfth Corps division returning to its old position at the log barricade. Under threat of being swept away in the torrent, wrote the historian of the 27th Indiana, "Colonel Colgrove was equal to the emergency. He stood in his saddle-stirrups and shouted, in a voice as loud as a steam whistle, 'Steady John! Whoa, boys. Steady boys! Whoa, John.' The Colonel's horse was named John, but he and the 'boys' understood the commands all right, and acted accordingly."

Between them, the volleys of Sickles's men and Williams's, and the canister fired by the Hazel Grove batteries under Captain James Hunt-ington, drove the Rebels back into the woods. Orin Dority, a gunner in Huntington's Battery H, 1st Ohio Light, wrote in his diary, "I had hardly time to hitch up before the Rebs were singing out to us to surrender, 'You Yankee sons of bitches,' which of course we had no thought of doing until we had given them some of our medicine."

Much would be made of this repulse by all parties involved, each of whom claimed to have stopped Stonewall Jackson's attack single-hand-edly that night. General Pleasonton, ever ready to claim credit where none was due, sent off a dispatch to Hooker: "I had to stop a *stampede* & check Jackson — which we did handsomely. I think we got them." In truth, the stampede had been generated by hardly more than 200 of Doles's Georgians, scouting on their own, and the check of the Rebels' attack was by order of the Rebels themselves.[11]

It was 8 o'clock now and the twilight was dimming. On this night the moon was one day short of full and the sky was clear, and in the clearings around Chancellorsville there would be visibility through the night. In the dense woods, however, the visibility was fleeting at best. It was noticed that the rising moon seen through the battle smoke had a reddish cast, as if Mars, god of war, was lighting the scene. As General Williams put it, there was "just enough of its light to make darkness visible."

Under Hooker's goad the Federals were patching together a new line. At Hazel Grove to the south it was anchored powerfully by artillery — five Third Corps batteries and one horse battery, 34 pieces in all. Behind these guns, or coming up, were Sickles's two divisions, Birney's and Whipple's, that had been at the Furnace. To the north and east of this salient at Hazel Grove was Williams's Twelfth Corps division. Wil-liams had not made it back to his old position; he held the lower section of the log barricade and the Confederates the upper, westernmost sec-tion. A mix of Howard's more steadfast troops was near the Plank Road. North of the road were Berry's two Third Corps brigades and in support a brigade from the Second Corps. The point where this patchwork line crossed the Plank Road was three quarters of a mile west of the Chancel-lor house. At Fairview there was a second powerful array of artillery, under the command of Captain Best — seven batteries from three differ-ent corps, 37 pieces in total.[12]

Stonewall Jackson was not deterred in the least by the disorganization of his command or by the fading light or by the Yankee defenses. An enemy on the run must be kept on the run. He sent off staff aides with injunctions to straighten out the disorder. From Dowdall's Tavern he went forward himself, calling out, "Men, get into line! Get into line! Whose command is this? Colonel, get your men instantly into line!"

His intent was unchanged — drive straight for Chancellorsville along the axis of the Plank Road to link up with General Lee, while at the same time sweeping into the enemy's rear by the left flank. Only now A. P. Hill's division must take the advance. When Brigadier James Lane applied to him for orders, Jackson told him sharply, "Push right ahead, Lane!"

Jackson's artillery chief Stapleton Crutchfield brought up Captain William Carter's Virginia battery to relieve the horse battery that had been pacing the advance. In the clearing around the old schoolhouse a thousand yards beyond Dowdall's there was room enough for Carter to deploy three of his guns. He opened fire straight down the Plank Road. Immediately a battery of U.S. regulars posted at Fairview took up the challenge. The Yankee guns caught Lane's North Carolina brigade in the act of deploying from column into line to carry on the advance. The men dove into the woods along the margins of the road, and Lane sent back word that if Carter's guns would cease firing he thought the enemy's would too; then he could continue the deployment. Soon enough, as he predicted, the guns fell silent and the movement resumed.

Lane arranged his brigade with two regiments north of the Plank Road and two to the south, with his fifth regiment as advance skirmishers. As he was posting the right-hand troops, he was presented with a Yankee officer sent back by the skirmish line. The man had been waving a white handkerchief on a stick and calling out in the darkness asking whose troops these might be. Lieutenant Colonel Levi H. Smith, 128th Pennsylvania, was indignant that his truce flag was not honored. A small party of the 7th North Carolina under Lieutenant James Emack was sent forward to investigate, and returned with an additional 198 men of the 128th Pennsylvania. According to General Lane, they "had thrown down their arms & surrendered on representation made to them by Emack." The "representation" was that Stonewall Jackson had them surrounded.

These Pennsylvanians were a star-crossed outfit. The 128th was one of the Potomac army's nine-month regiments with (as its men well knew) only two more weeks to serve. The previous fall, raw and untrained, in the army hardly a month, it had been thrown into the worst of the fighting at Antietam and terribly mauled. On this day, in its second and last battle, it was terribly humiliated.[13]

The ill fate of the 128th Pennsylvania grew out of new orders from General Hooker. Realizing that if he lost the dominating ground at Fairview he could lose the entire Chancellorsville position, Hooker sent to Alpheus Williams to reoccupy his original posting at the log barricade, Fairview's first line of defense. Williams doubted his chances — "No one could tell friend from foe nor see a hidden enemy a rod away," he wrote — but orders were orders.

Joseph Knipe's brigade went forward in line of battle through the dark woods south of the Plank Road, and as it reached the barricade, Williams wrote, "got fairly enveloped. . . . It was a conflict of great confusion and came near losing me all of Knipe's brigade." The confusion was recorded by a man in the 5th Connecticut: "The Regt. got very much scattered in going into the works & running out again, & being very dark could not get together. . . ."

Already the 28th New York had lost its commander captured, and now the colonels of the 128th Pennsylvania and 5th Connecticut were captured as well. Major Cyrus Strous, leading Knipe's other regiment, was mortally wounded. All but one of the brigade's field officers were casualties. General Knipe too was a near-casualty. He went forward to try and get his bearings, one of his men wrote, "and we beheld him come out faster than he had gone in. . . ." Williams had to fall back to where he had started.[14]

Although Jim Lane's men had the best of this particular encounter, primarily because they had only to let the Yankees come to them in the deeply shadowed woods, theirs was not a comfortable or secure situation. Lane's 37th and 7th North Carolina were posted in line south of the Plank Road. The line was extended north of the road by the 18th and 28th North Carolina. The 33rd North Carolina remained out in front in skirmish formation. Here and there among the trees there were continued bursts of fire.

"When I gave my orders," General Lane explained, "I cautioned all of my regimental commanders to keep a bright lookout, as we were in front of everything & would soon be ordered forward to make a night attack." The Yankees in front of them did not seem to be running any longer, and in fact appeared to be acting aggressively. And an hour or so earlier, Rodes's men reported, there was that sharp brush with the Yankee cavalry. Admittedly, as one officer recalled, the prospect of a cavalry attack "in that dense country seemed to be as unlikely as an attack from a gun-boat." Still, Lane's men would be alert for anything.[15]

* *

STONEWALL JACKSON rode ahead on the Orange Plank Road toward the front. At the old schoolhouse where Carter's battery was posted he encountered A. P. Hill and a group of his staff. How soon would he be ready to advance, he asked Hill. "In a few minutes," Hill replied, "as soon as I can finish relieving General Rodes." Jackson then asked him if he knew the road from Chancellorsville to U.S. Ford. It would help if he had a guide, Hill said. Jackson detailed his engineering officer, Captain Keith Boswell, to guide the advance. Then looking intently at Hill he said, "General Hill, as soon as you are ready push right forward. Allow nothing to stop you. Press on to the United States Ford."

Leaving Hill to follow, Jackson rode slowly on up the Plank Road and past Jim Lane's deployed brigade. All that was ahead of him now was Lane's skirmish line and then the enemy. It was always Old Jack's way to lead like this from up front, to see the battlefield for himself rather than rely on others, and it was a habit that worried and exasperated his staff. The little party was about halfway between Lane's line of battle and his line of skirmishers when Sandie Pendleton nerved himself to ask, "General, don't you think this is the wrong place for you?" Jackson said in his abrupt way, "The danger is over. The enemy is routed. Go back and tell A. P. Hill to press right on."[16]

By the account of Captain Robert E. Wilbourn, Jackson's signal officer, the party was about a dozen strong. He rode on Jackson's left, and behind was another staff man, Lieutenant Joseph G. Morrison, and two signal corps men, Lieutenant W. T. Wynn and Sergeant William E. Cunliffe. Captain W. F. Randolph of the escort headed what Wilbourn remembered as five or six couriers.

No one in Lane's brigade — at least no officer — realized that Jackson's party, and then A. P. Hill's, were riding out ahead of the lines. Jim Lane was off to the right positioning his forces and knew nothing of it. Perhaps Jackson's party assumed that someone in Hill's would take the usual precaution of warning the troops; after all, Lane's brigade was in Hill's division. Perhaps Hill's party assumed someone in Jackson's had done so when passing through Lane's line. In any event, when he investigated later General Lane found none of his lieutenants had known that Jackson and Hill had gone out to the front, and in the darkness — it was after 9 o'clock now — they were not easily seen.

There was no real reason for Jackson to be where he was just then except his own impatience. He believed, as he told Sandie Pendleton, that there was no longer any danger here, and apparently he expected Lane's brigade to be advancing at any moment. Pushing ahead, skirmishers out front, the battle line would catch up with his party, which would move right along behind the line as it swept on toward Chancellorsville. A routed enemy must always be pressed so it could not catch its breath and make a stand. That was Old Jack's credo.

Jackson's party, riding slowly, reached an unfinished chapel building some 150 yards beyond Lane's line. Hill's party was some 50 or 60 yards behind Jackson's. When he was asked about it later, Hill said that since his superior officer was riding to the front he considered it his duty to accompany him. The firing from the clash between Knipe's brigade and Lane's had died out. In the darkness the silence was almost eerie, and they sat their horses and listened.

Abruptly, off to the right, there was a single shot. Captain Wilbourn thought it came from the right rear, but admitted it might have come directly from the right or even the right front — possibly a Yankee skirmisher, but it was hard to tell. Lieutenant Morrison was also uncertain of the direction. (Jackson would later say that it seemed to come from the right front, but he could not be sure either.) Then, in support or in reply, there was a spatter of shots and then a fusillade, as if set off by spontaneous combustion. There was no doubt this fire came from the right rear, where the 37th and 7th North Carolina of Jim Lane's brigade were nerving themselves for action.

Their fire tore through Hill's party and then Jackson's, and the Plank Road became a scene of desperate confusion. Men and horses went down; maddened horses bolted, some with riders, many without. In Hill's group Jackson's engineer Keith Boswell was killed instantly. Four others were killed or wounded, and two carried into the enemy lines by their panicked horses. Three officers of Hill's staff had their horses killed under them.

It was the same in Jackson's party: signalman Cunliffe killed, several men wounded, horses down or tearing off in every direction. Jackson was not hit. He and other survivors spurred across the Plank Road away from the fire and into the trees on the northern margin for shelter, and instinctively turned back to their own lines. The reaction by survivors in Hill's party was the same. The noise of their galloping horses, wrote Captain Alfred Tolar of Company K, 18th North Carolina, "seemed to the average infantryman like a brigade of cavalry."

At that the murderous fire redoubled. To Wilbourn it seemed to be an extension of the first fire from the right, leaping across the Plank Road and igniting the line of battle on the other side. It was aimed more at sound than sight. In the light of the muzzle flashes, some 30 or 40 yards away, Wilbourn saw men kneeling in line and firing, the classic infantry stance for repelling a cavalry charge. The men he saw lit by their own fire were the 18th North Carolina infantry.

Lieutenant Morrison had thrown himself off his wounded and panicked horse and now ran toward the infantry line screaming to cease fire: "You are firing into your own men!" A. P. Hill, too, had leaped from his horse into the roadway to escape the bullets, and was shouting the same order. Major John Berry, commanding this section of the infantry line,

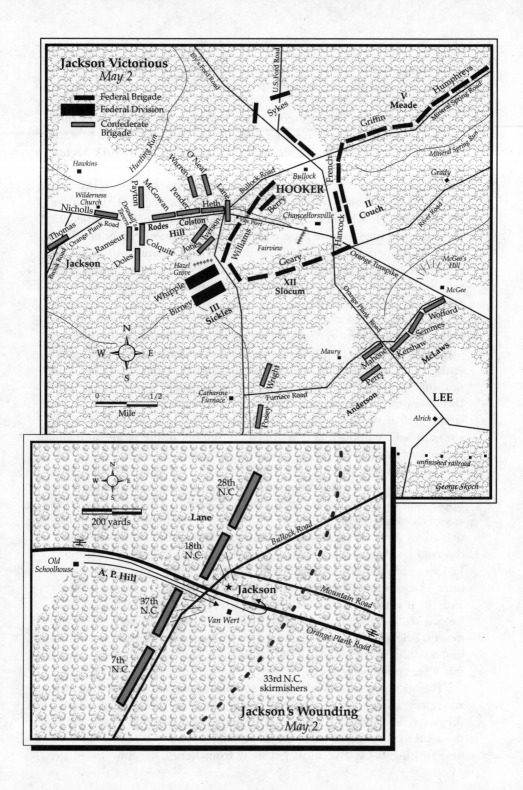

Jackson Victorious
May 2

▬ Federal Brigade
■ Federal Division
▬ Confederate Brigade

Ely's Ford Road
U.S. Ford Road
Hurling Run
Sykes
Humphreys
V
Meade
Griffin
Mineral Spring Road
Mineral Spring Run
Hawkins
O'Neal
Warren
Bullock
Grady
Wilderness Church
McGowan
Payton
Pender
Lane
Heth
Bullock Road
HOOKER
French
River Road
Nicholls
Donald's Tavern
Rodes
Hill
Colston
Iverson
Jones
Van Wert
Berry
Chancellorsville
Hancock
II
Couch
McGee's Hill
Thomas
Brock Road
Orange Plank Road
Ramseur
Colquitt
Williams
Fairview
Orange Turnpike
McGee
Jackson
Doles
Hazel Grove
Geary
XII
Slocum
Wofford
Semmes
Whipple
Birney
III
Sickles
Orange Plank Road
McLaws
Kershaw
Mahone
Maury
Perry
Wright
Anderson
LEE

N
W   E
S

0   1/2
Mile

Catharine Furnace
Furnace Road
Posey
Alrich

unfinished railroad
George Skoch

N
W   E
S

200 yards

28th
N.C.

Lane

18th
N.C.

Bullock Road

Old Schoolhouse

A. P. Hill

37th
N.C.

★ Jackson

Mountain Road

Van Wert

Orange Plank Road

7th
N.C.

33rd N.C.
skirmishers

Jackson's Wounding
May 2

suspecting a Yankee trick, called out, "Who gave that order? It's a lie! Pour it into them!" "I tried to stop them," cried an anguished aide of Hill's, "but they would fire. . . ."[17]

At last their firing was halted, but not before three bullets had struck Jackson. Once among the trees he had thrown up his right arm to ward off branches, and one bullet hit his right hand. A second struck his left forearm, and a third shattered the bone in his upper left arm near the shoulder. As his left arm fell uselessly at his side he lost the reins, and Little Sorrel, wounded and maddened by the fire, bolted back toward the Plank Road. A low branch nearly knocked Jackson out of the saddle. On the road the horse rushed away from the fire, toward the enemy, but Jackson grasped the reins with his injured right hand and regained control. Captain Wilbourn and signalman Wynn caught up and helped rein in the frantic animal. They were now at about the point in the road where they were first fired on.

Amazingly the Plank Road seemed empty but for the three of them, and there was no more firing. The general, Wilbourn wrote, seemed utterly stunned. "Gen. J. looked up the road towards our troops apparently much surprised at being fired at from that direction, but said nothing." Wilbourn told him, "Those certainly must be our troops," and Jackson nodded, still saying nothing. Asked if he was hurt badly, he finally spoke: "I fear my arm is broken." He was bleeding severely and losing strength, and Wilbourn and Wynn eased him out of the saddle and laid him under a small tree on the margin of the road.

Wynn was sent to find an ambulance and Dr. Hunter McGuire, the Second Corps' medical director, and Wilbourn bound the wound in the upper arm to try and stop the bleeding. "General, it is remarkable that any of us escaped," he said, to which Jackson agreed: "Yes, it is Providential." Now A. P. Hill and some of his staff and some of Jackson's staff, directed by Wynn, reached the scene. Forgetting his animosity toward Jackson, Hill said to him solicitously, "General, I hope you are not badly hurt." Jackson said his arm was broken, and to Hill's worried query added, "It is very painful." Hill took off Jackson's bloody gauntlets and helped Wilbourn bind the wound and fashion a sling, and sent off for the nearest brigade surgeon. When he arrived Jackson whispered to Hill, "Is that a skillful surgeon?" Assured that the man was well regarded, Jackson said, "Very good, very good."

The group was startled by the sudden appearance of two Yankee stragglers, apparently flushed out of the woods by the firing, and after they were taken away Lieutenant Morrison went forward to a low crest in the road to see if there were any more Yankees about. What he saw sent him rushing back. "We must get away from here," he announced urgently. "The Yankees are placing a battery in the road not a hundred yards from us." At that General Hill set off for his lines to take command of the leaderless army.

Jackson said he thought he could walk with their help, and they got him on his feet and started slowly back. Finally someone came with a litter, and with that they could carry the general at a better pace. Suddenly from the road behind them came a storm of fire. "Just then enemy opened battery," wrote Lieutenant James Power Smith of Jackson's staff, "raking road & shelling — road utterly swept." (This was a section of Lieutenant Justin Dimick's Battery H, 1st U.S. Artillery.)

They pressed on until one of the litter bearers was hit, and then they had to put Jackson down and shield him with their bodies until the fire slackened. Smith remembered the canister sparking and flashing as it struck rocks in the road. For better shelter they resumed their awkward march in the woods bordering the road. Here one of the bearers stumbled over a root or a vine and Jackson was spilled out of the litter. They were carrying it on their shoulders, and his fall, directly on his wounded arm, was a severe one. "For the first time he groaned, and groaned piteously," wrote one of the bearers. "He must have suffered excruciating agonies."

On they struggled, slowly drawing out of range, finally reaching their lines. They tried to keep the identity of their burden a secret, but one passing soldier insisted on satisfying his curiosity and drew close for a look. "Great God," he exclaimed, "that's old General Jackson!" A shocked Dorsey Pender, of Hill's division, also recognized Jackson. He was worried, Pender said, about the effect of the heavy enemy fire on his brigade. There were numerous Yankee guns in action now. Jackson roused himself enough to say, "General Pender, you *must* keep your men together, and hold your ground."

At last, after about half a mile, the litter party met Dr. McGuire with an ambulance. "I am badly injured, Doctor," Jackson said. "I fear I am dying." McGuire administered whiskey and morphine, and supervised placing the general in the ambulance. With him was his artillery chief, Stapleton Crutchfield, badly wounded by the Federal barrage. Torches were procured and the way cleared, and the ambulance proceeded carefully over the rough road westward to the newly established Second Corps field hospital at Wilderness Tavern.[18]

* *

JOE HOOKER had earlier ridden forward to Captain Clermont Best's artillery position at Fairview and (as Best phrased it) "kindly authorized me to open fire whenever I deemed it necessary." The fusillade from Lane's brigade that wounded Stonewall Jackson was taken by Captain Best as signaling an enemy attack, and he promptly deemed it necessary to open fire. Lieutenant Dimick's section had advanced along the Plank Road as an artillery picket, and after Dimick opened, the guns in the other six batteries at Fairview joined in. They did so, wrote General Williams, "with appalling vigor." They focused on the Plank Road, and for the Rebel troops massed in the roadway the effect was murderous.

"When the shells & grape shot come tearing through the ranks the scene is indescribeable," William Clegg of the 2nd Louisiana explained. "The men seemed almost panic stricken, the groans & shrieks of the wounded was heart rending, artillery horses riderless came thundering back with pieces & caissons, . . . all combined presented a most horrible spectacle." (For Yankee Justus Silliman, of the battered Eleventh Corps, the batteries' "thunderings and lightning was sweet music.")

General Francis Nicholls, commanding Corporal Clegg's brigade, had lost his left arm in the Valley campaign a year before and now he lost his left foot to a solid shot that tore right through his horse. An ambulance crew that found the unconscious Nicholls, seeing his empty sleeve and missing foot, left him for dead. He was later rescued by his men.

Another casualty of this barrage was A. P. Hill, struck across the back of the legs by a shell fragment. Unable to walk or ride, Hill felt obliged to turn over command of the Second Corps — a command he had held for a matter of minutes — to Robert Rodes. At the same time, Hill felt obliged to send for the only major general now left with the corps, Jeb Stuart, to take over for Rodes.

Jackson was not and could not be consulted about the command, and it would take too long to reach General Lee, so Powell Hill took the decision himself. To be sure, Stuart commanded cavalry rather than infantry, but he was a major general and he was known to the men. Brigadier General Rodes was commanding at the divisional level for the first time in this campaign and he was relatively unknown. Rodes himself noted, in his report, that General Stuart "was well and very favorably known to the army, and would tend, I hoped, to re-establish confidence." With the news of Jackson's wounding already racing through the ranks, just then confidence was a critical matter.

By his action of sending for Stuart, Hill was taking a second major decision. Stuart would be some time arriving — he was holding Ely's Ford on the Rapidan — and nothing could be undertaken in the mean-time. Very likely, had he not been wounded, Powell Hill would have felt obliged under Jackson's last orders to continue to press a night attack, despite the powerful Federal artillery. Now it was different. Now the army was in effect leaderless, and the word was quietly passed to stand down. The great flank attack was over.[19]

By way of securing the flanking column's flank, Jeb Stuart had taken his cavalry and an infantry regiment, the 16th North Carolina, back to Ely's Ford on the Rapidan. On the other side of the river they discovered the bivouac of William Averell's Yankee cavalry, recalled that morning by Hooker after Averell's hapless performance in Stoneman's raid. Apparently Averell believed there could be no enemy within miles, and his men were relaxing after the day's march. "Opposite we could see the camp fires, tents & long lines of horses tied up . . . ," Frank Robertson of Stuart's staff recalled. "From the hilarious sound, we judged the Averell horsemen were enjoying life."

Stuart was just positioning his troopers and the Tarheel infantry for attack when A. P. Hill's courier arrived with the summons to take over Jackson's command. Snapping out orders to fire three volleys and then follow him, Stuart wheeled and was gone. At the first volley, Lieutenant Robertson wrote, "we could see men rushing from the tents, horses falling & breaking away, running down tents & scattering fires. . . . It was an exhilarating & delightful show, *we* thought. . . ."

John Tidball of Averell's horse artillery recorded one dead and three wounded in the hit-and-run attack. John Follmer, 16th Pennsylvania cavalry, noted in his diary that their lieutenant colonel, at the first shot, "is said to have run behind a barn, and called to the men 'to rally on the barn.'" It was a rallying cry his troopers would never let him forget.[20]

Stuart reached the battlefront about midnight. Powell Hill was waiting for him, lying on a blanket under a tree by the Plank Road. Hill related what he knew of the situation and then he was carried off to a field hospital. Stuart set about acquainting himself with his new command. With Stapleton Crutchfield wounded, he called on Porter Alexander to direct the corps artillery. "As he had just taken command," Alexander wrote, "he could tell me nothing at all about the positions, or the roads, & I had to find out for myself about them, during the night." Stuart was doing the same.

Jackson's staff was scattered and demoralized by their chief's wounding, and in any event the secretive Jackson left little that told of his plans. Until daylight there could be little but generalities: Alexander was ordered "to be ready to attack the enemy at day break every where along the line." Francis Johnson of the 45th Georgia wrote his wife, "The night was clear and the moon shown bright but we could not sleep, the enemy could be heard very plainly in front throwing up breastworks and we knew we had to run them out in the morning."[21]

* *

DAN SICKLES, who liked to command with boldness and dash, had had a generally disappointing time of it so far on Day Six. His expedition to cut off the enemy's flight at Catharine Furnace had not come to much. He was checked by the Rebel artillery and had tangled painfully with Lee's infantry in the forest, and in the end he had only the capture of most of the 23rd Georgia to show for his efforts. Toward day's end he turned again to the bold move. He would make a night attack.

He felt he was in danger of being cut off after the collapse of the Eleventh Corps, and he wanted to recover his corps trains at Hazel Grove, not being aware that most of them had been stampeded. He got Hooker's approval for the night attack, and was promised (so he thought) the cooperation of the two divisions, under Williams and Berry, posted between him and Chancellorsville.

Sickles's plan was simple — an advance straight north along the axis of the woods road from Hazel Grove to the Orange Plank Road, the same road Major Huey and his 8th Pennsylvania cavalry had followed earlier. Except for the expectation that there were Confederates to the left and perhaps ahead and Federals to the right, Sickles had no knowledge of what he might find that night, and he sent out no scouts or skirmishers to find out. At midnight the word was passed quietly to go forward.

The men were decidedly nervous about the prospects. There was sufficient moonlight in the clearings but it was exceedingly dim in the woods. Obscuring mist rose from the marshy margins of nearby Lewis's Run. Earlier they had watched the awesome display of artillery light the sky above the dark forest to the north. "The sky seemed *full* of streams of molton fire as the lighted shells went flashing in every direction," Arthur Wilcox of the 7th Ohio told his family, "& their explosions scattered fire & death till it seemed as if nothing mortal could come out living from the midst of such an infernal volcano." George Marden of the sharpshooters believed "the 3rd Corps was surrounded with rebs. The only alternative was fight out or surrender."

David Birney's division mounted the attack, spearheaded by J. H. Hobart Ward's brigade. Bayonets were fixed and rifles uncapped; cold steel was thought decisive in a night battle. Rather than advancing in line the troops were deployed in parallel columns of companies. This was easy enough moving on the road or alongside it, but once in the woods on rough ground the men began to lose the line of march. When the firing began — and against orders was returned — direction was lost completely. Colonel Regis de Trobriand of the 38th New York remembered asking, "How can we find it again? We were fired on from all sides; from the front, from the right, from the left, and even from the rear. . . ." Columns surged ahead or fell back or off to the flanks, and excited men in the rear fired into the backs of those in front.[22]

The first reaction to the first fire in the darkness was panic, wrote John Haley of the 17th Maine. "The scare wasn't confined to the privates; officers dodged hither and thither, some of them so frightened that they couldn't have told their names." General Ward, he added, was in such haste to get to the rear that he rode down two of his men. The muzzle flashes of volleys in the dark were terrifying.

The first to fire were the surprised North Carolinians of Jim Lane's brigade, off to the Yankees' left. Sickles had warned Williams of his plan but not Williams's corps commander, General Slocum, who was at the Chancellor house when this gunfire exploded in the woods in front of Slocum's position. Quickly he called on Captain Best, commanding the artillery array at Fairview, to fight off another supposed Rebel assault. Best's gunners swung into action, firing into the massed troops of both sides wherever they saw the flash of musketry. The Rebel artillery soon added its share to the din.

As the firing spread on the left, many of Birney's men instinctively shifted to the right and collided with Alpheus Williams's line. Williams had warned his men there would be friendly troops on their front, but when they were fired upon they naturally fired back. Samuel Hayman, one of Birney's brigade commanders, noted dryly that the fire from friend as well as foe "no doubt checked the ardor" of his men. Captain Charles Bowers, watching and listening from a distance, told his daughter, "We could hear the huzzahs of our men and the horrid yells of the rebels as one or the other obtained some advantage." Another observer, Colonel Thomas Quincy, wrote his wife that after that night "I think I could write a fine description of Pandemonium. . . ."

The 3rd Michigan reached all the way to the Plank Road and charged a line of guns it believed was its tormentor and found it had captured a battery from Slocum's Twelfth Corps. Fortunately no one was hurt in the capture. At the height of the confusion the 3rd Wisconsin and the 13th New Jersey, both of General Ruger's Twelfth Corps brigade, unwittingly opened fire on each other. It was also recorded that General Knipe's brigade repelled two charges "by the enemy" and General Berry's command repelled one in this midnight battle. With Jim Lane's North Carolinians having all they could do to hold their own lines, in all likelihood Knipe and Berry were opposing friends and not foes.

Finally, abruptly, it was over. By General Williams's account, "almost on the instant, the tumult is hushed. . . . One would almost suppose that the combatants were holding their breath to listen for one another's movements. But the contest was not renewed." Sickles's men went back unhappily to where they had started. It was reported they rescued a gun and four caissons abandoned during the earlier stampede, but they would have been rescued in any event; Rodes's men had been unable to carry them off through the woods.

Casualties totaling 196 were reported for four of Birney's eleven regiments in the midnight battle. Whatever the actual total, a proportion was surely due to Union fire. "Whoever took part in the fizzle in the woods on the night of the 2nd of May," wrote a man in the 3rd Michigan, "will remember it as long as they live." Nothing at all had been gained by Dan Sickles's adventuring, although as a spectacle it was widely reported by an army of letter writers.[23]

*   *

DURING THESE nighttime hours Joe Hooker was working furiously to meet the mortal threat to his campaign. Already he had taken the best steps he could to gather defenses for the important high ground to the west and southwest of Chancellorsville, at Fairview and Hazel Grove. From the 23rd Georgia prisoners taken at the Furnace interrogators identified the force that had smashed the Eleventh Corps as Stonewall Jackson's. Knowing of Jackson raised Hooker's concern for the rear of his army. His only immediately available reserve was John Reynolds's First Corps. From where he was crossing at U.S. Ford Reynolds was directed to form a new line to block any attempt by Jackson to cut in behind the Potomac army and seize its river crossings.

The Rapidan enters the Rappahannock just over two miles above U.S. Ford, and a mile and a half up the Rapidan is Hunting Run, entering from the south. Hunting Run is a modest enough little stream but it offered the best natural defensive position in this woodland. Reynolds was ordered to post his three divisions behind the stream, facing west, from the Rapidan as far south as the crossing of the Ely's Ford Road. From there the Ely's Ford Road, where it ran southeasterly toward Chancellorsville, was to be the responsibility of George Meade's Fifth Corps. Meade's earlier position, off to the east behind the Mineral Spring Road, now appeared to be the most peaceful sector in the Federal line, and Otis Howard was told to man it with whatever troops he could reassemble from his broken command. "These lines," Hooker announced, "must be held at all hazard."

In the initial shock of Jackson's assault Hooker despaired that he could hold against the most pressing threat, especially at Hazel Grove. He put his engineers, Gouverneur Warren and Cyrus Comstock, to work laying out a new defensive line to the rear should the present line be breached. He would remember telling Warren and Comstock to do this immediately, that night, for he did not expect to be able to hold the present line "after the enemy should renew his attack the next morning."[24]

By 9 o'clock it was fully dark and the pressure of the attack had lessened and the defenses seemed to be holding, and Joe Hooker's confidence returned. He began to think how he might take advantage of the new situation.

As he explained it to General Warren, his plan for tomorrow, Sunday, was two-pronged. Jackson was massed on his right and, according to prisoners, was indeed intending to attack again at daybreak. "Genl. Hooker," Warren explained, "made his dispositions accordingly and intends to flank and destroy Jackson." The second half of the plan depended upon John Sedgwick and the Sixth Corps.

By all reports the assault on Howard had been a powerful one, apparently by Jackson's entire corps except Early's division, which Colonel Sharpe had placed at Fredericksburg. By Sharpe's accounting, that meant that on the front to the east Lee was facing the Federals with no more than the divisions of Anderson and McLaws. As the two armies were now positioned, after Jackson's attack, this one segment of Lee's army was squarely between the two segments of Hooker's.

General Hooker still did not have a firm grip on the location of Sedgwick's corps, and his order, sent at 9 o'clock, began by specifying that Sedgwick "cross the Rappahannock, at Fredericksburg, . . . and at once take up your line of march on the Chancellorsville road" until he connected with Hooker's forces. "You will probably fall upon the rear of the forces commanded by General Lee, and, between you and the major general commanding, he expects to use him up. Send word to General Gibbon to take possession of Fredericksburg. Be sure not to fail."

As a measure of its importance, Hooker had this order telegraphed directly to Sedgwick and another copy sent through Butterfield, and he sent two aides to the scene to be sure it was understood, but it seems that nothing could overcome this army's chronic communication lapses. Earlier the Signal Corps had started to extend the telegraph line from U.S. Ford to Chancellorsville, but in the chaos of the Eleventh Corps' collapse the line was knocked down and run over and cut and the Signal Corps party scattered, and there was nothing to do but rush dispatches by courier the five miles to the U.S. Ford station. And Sedgwick himself had crossed the river to carry out Hooker's earlier orders and it took time to find him. It was 11 o'clock before the order reached him.[25]

Whatever his confusion about where the Sixth Corps was just then, Hooker had seized on the earlier report that the Confederates had abandoned Fredericksburg and therefore all Sedgwick had to do was march his corps straight down the Orange Plank Road from Fredericksburg to Chancellorsville. Darkness would be no problem; the moonlight was so bright that night, he would later say, "that staff officers could see to write dispatches." Surely Sedgwick could be on the scene by daylight to fall on the enemy, and then together they would use up General Lee.

Had John Sedgwick shown the least bit of enterprise and initiative earlier that day, Hooker's expectations would likely have been met. Instead, even when he saw Early's forces leaving their lines during the afternoon, Sedgwick had refused to exercise his discretionary orders to attack. When finally he did act on Hooker's peremptory 4:10 P.M. order to "capture Fredericksburg with everything in it," it was sunset and Early's troops were on their way back to their lines and his chances for an easy victory were gone.

Sedgwick then contented himself with pushing Bully Brooks's division forward from its bridgehead below Fredericksburg. As Stonewall Jackson pursued the Eleventh Corps, Brooks's Yankees tangled with the 7th Louisiana holding the line of the River Road. An admiring Louisianian described "the gallant Seventh holding its ground manfully, until being flanked on both sides." With that the Confederates fell back a thousand yards to a new line behind the R.F. & P. Railroad. Sedgwick announced that General Brooks "will advance as long as he can see, and will then take position for the night."

That was the situation at Fredericksburg when Hooker's order for the Sixth Corps to march on Chancellorsville reached Sedgwick at 11 o'clock — Brooks below the town advanced across the River Road and bedding down for the night, and the divisions of Albion Howe and John Newton crossing the river to join the rest of the corps on the south bank. Thus Hooker's injunction for Sedgwick to cross "the Rappahannock at Fredericksburg on the receipt of this order" was puzzling.

There was not even a pontoon bridge at Fredericksburg — Reynolds's bridge taken up that morning was still piled on the bank downriver at Fitzhugh's Crossing — and for the whole corps to go back across the river, march up the north bank, lay a new bridge, and cross again was not something that could be done any time soon. Furthermore, a bridge thrown across at Fredericksburg would truly be overcrowded if it had to be used as well to carry out the rest of Hooker's plan — for

John Gibbon's division in Falmouth to cross and "take possession of Fredericksburg."

This conundrum would be much discussed by General Sedgwick in his later testimony before the Joint Committee on the Conduct of the War, but in fact he seems not to have taken it too seriously that night. Sedgwick had just met with Dan Butterfield on the matter of Hooker's confusing dispatches, and they apparently agreed simply to adapt them to the actual circumstances of the Sixth Corps. Since the entire corps was already on the south bank of the Rappahannock, it would march from there to Chancellorsville. (A chief of staff's duty is to keep his chief fully informed, but if Butterfield attempted that day to set Hooker straight on the postings of the Sixth Corps, it is not on record.)[26]

Sedgwick promptly issued marching orders for the advance. Newton's division would lead, followed by Burnham's Light Division and then Howe and Brooks. There would be no trains, only the pack mules carrying ammunition. The direction would be straight along the River Road on the south bank and into Fredericksburg, then west to Chancellorsville on the Orange Plank Road. It was two miles to Fredericksburg and ten from there to the Chancellor house.

The promptness of Sedgwick's orders suggests that he gave no thought to any other route. He might have thought to turn the enemy lines below the town and pass around behind it to reach the Plank Road, but if so the thought was a brief one. He knew nothing of the roads there, and it was dark. The Sixth Corps had been in the left wing in the December battle, and no one seemed to know anything of the terrain in and about Fredericksburg. General Sedgwick would require a guide even to get through the town and strike the Plank Road.

At 11:30 Captain Valarian Razderichin of Hooker's staff reached Falmouth with the first report of the surprise flank attack on the main army. Butterfield sent him across the river with his story as a way of inspiring Sedgwick's efforts. "Everything in the world depends upon the rapidity and promptness of your movement," Sedgwick was told. This ploy, Butterfield would admit ruefully, had just the opposite effect: "Razderichin's report of matters with Gen. Hooker made the movement of Gen. Sedgwick's column a little over cautious."

The advance of the Sixth Corps had not gone far before it was engaged by a swarm of Rebel skirmishers. Major Thomas Hyde of the 7th Maine wrote home that in the moonlight and the nightly Rappahannock fog "the skirmishing fire looked very pretty." General Sedgwick slowed and grew careful. It was 1:30 on the morning of May 3 when Sedgwick sent to Butterfield to outline the reality of the situation as he saw it.

"There is still a force in Fredericksburg," he explained. "We are marching as rapidly as possible but cannot reach Gen. Hooker by daylight."[27]

* *

SHORTLY AFTER 11 o'clock on the night of May 2, some two hours after he was wounded, Stonewall Jackson was gently placed on a cot at the Second Corps field hospital at Wilderness Tavern. He was in shock and weak from hemorrhaging; the fall from the litter had reopened the wounds. Dr. McGuire administered more whiskey as a stimulant and covered the general warmly and let him rest. Gradually his pulse strengthened until by 2:00 A.M. McGuire felt he was strong enough to undergo examination and treatment. He wakened Jackson and explained that his wound appeared serious enough that it might require amputation. "Yes, certainly, Dr. McGuire," the general said. "Do for me whatever you think right."

Chloroform was administered, and after confirming that the humerus in the left arm was shattered, McGuire and three surgeons consulting with him agreed that amputation was required. Swiftly, with the surgeons assisting and Lieutenant Smith of the staff holding a candle for light, Dr. McGuire performed a standard circular operation to amputate the arm two inches below the shoulder. It was done, McGuire wrote, "very rapidly and with slight loss of blood." (The Reverend Lacy would supervise the burial of the amputated arm in the family graveyard at Ellwood, the nearby home of Lacy's brother.)

Half an hour after the operation Jackson was awakened and given half a pint of coffee. "Very good; refreshing," he said to Lieutenant Smith. An hour later Sandie Pendleton of his staff arrived, sent by Jeb Stuart to ask the general "what his dispositions and plans were." Jackson greeted him, "Well, Major, I am glad to see you, very glad. I thought you were killed." Pendleton explained the position of the army and relayed Stuart's request. Jackson seemed to rouse himself to concentrate on the matter. "His eye flashed its old fire," Dr. McGuire wrote, but it was only for a moment. Then he fell back and said to Pendleton, "I don't know, I can't tell. Say to General Stuart that he must do what he thinks best."[28]

Meanwhile another Jackson aide, Robert Wilbourn, was reporting on events to General Lee. After helping deliver his wounded chief to the ambulance and Dr. McGuire, Wilbourn had been ordered to hurry to Lee to report the wounding of Jackson and Hill and the command devolving on Stuart. It was 3:00 A.M. when he reached Lee's bivouac close by the Plank Road east of Chancellorsville. Awakened by his inquiry among the staff, Lee called him to his side. As he had the night before,

Lee made his rude bed on the ground under a pine tree, and he bid the captain sit beside him and report.

"After telling of the fight & victory," Wilbourn wrote, "I told him Gen. J. was wounded, describing the wound &c when he said, 'Thank God it is not worse. God be praised that he is yet alive.' He then asked me some questions about the fight & said, 'Captain, any victory is dearly bought that deprives us of the services of Jackson even temporarily.'"

Wilbourn went on to say that A. P. Hill was also wounded and that Jeb Stuart had been sent for to take the command. After questioning the captain closely about the position of Jackson's command, Lee roused his staff for orders. Wilbourn heard him announce, "We must press these people right away."[29]

12

A Most Terribly Bloody Conflict

L ATE ON SATURDAY NIGHT, when the firing had died down, General Hooker called in Gouverneur Warren of his staff and briefed him on the situation and the plan for the next day, and then sent him off to counsel General Sedgwick. Sedgwick and his Sixth Corps had a crucial role to play on Day Seven. Since Hooker could not go himself and look over Sedgwick's shoulder, Warren must be his proxy. With his rank as a general officer, his knowledge of the terrain between Chancellorsville and Fredericksburg, and his friendship with Sedgwick, he must persuade that officer to act with extreme aggressiveness. On May 3 Sedgwick was to come up from Fredericksburg and fall on Lee's rear, and that order, Hooker said later, "was peremptory, and would have justified him in losing every man of his command in its execution." Warren's job was to be there with him in case "this latter important point might not be appreciated."

Despite Jackson's surprise attack and the destruction of the Eleventh Corps, Joe Hooker was sticking stubbornly to his tactic of fighting the battle defensively. Essentially, to his mind, the situation had not really changed. He was still on his chosen ground, or on most of it, he was well dug in, and by report Lee was determined to attack him there. Fighting from behind defenses would surely comfort all the short-term and new men in the ranks. And nothing would boost the spirits of the veterans more than to inflict a Fredericksburg-style defeat on their foes. He would not go over to the offensive except in concert with Sedgwick. Lee would be "held in check" to the east until Sedgwick was in position behind him. Then with the Sixth Corps as the upper stone and Couch's Second Corps as the nether, Lee would be ground to pieces. That should leave Jackson's command to the west isolated. And with Stoneman cutting their communications, the Rebels could not remain here much longer.

Sedgwick had 23,600 men under command, and John Gibbon cooperating with him added another 3,500. Wherever Jubal Early's division might be just now — whether in Fredericksburg or with Lee or somewhere in between — Colonel Sharpe's latest intelligence counted his force at 8,400 men. According to a Confederate officer captured on Sickles's front the evening before, there was only a single brigade of Early's actually in Fredericksburg. This intelligence was persuasive enough to be welcomed at the Chancellor house. (It was in fact correct, but outdated by events.) At 4:10 on Sunday morning Hooker's aide James Van Alen telegraphed Butterfield, "The General directs me to say that any force in front of Gen. Sedgwick must be a small one and must not check his advance."

But John Sedgwick would not be hurried. He would do as he was ordered, of course, but he was not going to act recklessly and sacrifice men of his command, men he cared deeply about, for the sake of acting out an unwanted independent role in this campaign. In any event, from the first the commanding general had never seemed to understand what the Sixth Corps was facing (or indeed sometimes even where it was). Certainly General Hooker did not appreciate what it was confronting in the Fredericksburg lines in the early morning hours of May 3. "The operations here are checked by a small but very active force" was how Warren diplomatically phrased it. Privately Warren would confide to Hooker afterward that had he not been there he did not believe Sedgwick would have moved at all; even then he seemed to lack confidence in himself and in what he was doing.[1]

One of Sedgwick's immediate concerns — which no doubt the commanding general did not appreciate — was how he was supposed to communicate with headquarters while he was on enemy ground. With the Sixth Corps ordered into active operations after four days of inaction, Dan Butterfield had suddenly remembered that the Rebels could read their signals. After all, it was on that premise that he had concocted his hoax message that paved the way for crossing the Rappahannock in the first place; it would never do now to reveal to the enemy the newest plans for the battle.

At night torches were substituted for flag telegraphy, and at 1:15 A.M. on May 3 Butterfield had his operator flash to Sedgwick across the river, "Don't let your signalman telegraph by signal as ordered when you pass Fredericksburg." In reply to Sedgwick's puzzled query, Butterfield explained, "The enemy read our signals."

With that Sedgwick's signalman Captain Edward Pierce dutifully shut down his operations. Butterfield neglected to tell his own signals chief, Samuel Cushing, of his edict, and when Cushing could not get any response from across the river he was ready to have Pierce arrested for neglect of duty. Finally an orderly crossed with Pierce's explanation and his plea, "What will we do?" Forehandedly Captain Cushing had developed a cipher system for flag and torch signaling, and he told Pierce to use the cipher for important messages. He added that Sedgwick could still use the old alphabetic flag code for messages about the Rebel positions, "which will not aid the enemy much, and may aid him." By the time all this was straightened out the morning was well advanced. The whole affair only increased John Sedgwick's distrust of headquarters and left him more cautious and careful than ever. For much of the day he was satisfied to communicate with Butterfield only by dispatches carried back and forth by Captain Razderichin of the staff. This was time-consuming, and Razderichin noted ruefully, "Time passed on without our advancing. . . ."[2]

It meanwhile appeared to John Gibbon that at last he was going to see some action. During the first days of the campaign his division had stayed quietly in its camps in Falmouth as a decoy while the rest of the army marched. Now came orders: cross the river right at Fredericksburg and occupy the town. After dark on May 2 the 50th New York engineers collected the First Corps pontoon bridge from Fitzhugh's Crossing and hauled it upriver to the Lacy house, one of the army's crossing places in the December battle. Silently two of Gibbon's brigades — his third brigade was still on guard at Banks's Ford — filed down to the river's edge for the crossing. "It was a lovely night," Lieutenant Frank Haskell of the staff wrote, "— not a cloud in the sky, and the moon, near the full, from the soft, hazy air shone down upon the ripples of the river, and the silent, lightless town, beautiful as a dream."

The plan was to assemble the bridge in darkness and at the first hint of daylight a storming party of volunteers — potentially a forlorn hope — would dash across to seize the opposite shore. Gibbon called for volunteers. To his surprise eighteen men of the 34th New York stepped forward. Two days earlier Gibbon had quelled the mutiny in the 34th; today, these men said, they were out to prove that their dispute with the War Department was protest, not mutiny. For John Gibbon that was a happy solution to the problem.

He was a good deal less happy with the officer in charge of the operation, Colonel Henry W. Hudson. After relieving Brigadier Alfred Sully for mishandling the 34th New York's mutiny — or protest — Gibbon had replaced him with Colonel Hudson, and now on the eve of battle the colonel showed up drunk. His speech was slurred and he reeled in the saddle and he smelled powerfully of liquor. "I was perfectly satisfied he was not in condition to attend to his duty," Gibbon testified, and put the man in arrest.

That at least proved to be the worst of General Gibbon's problems. "Boat after boat was pushed out & the timbers laid," wrote one of the bridge-builders, "with only an occasional shot from the other side, though we expected a volley every moment." Before that volley came an outburst of firing in the dark streets of the town, and then a vanguard of the Sixth Corps was there and yelling across that the Rebs were gone and the place was secure. "The day was just breaking, and we saw one of our signal flags waving in the lower end of the town. . . ." The bridge was soon completed and the storming party, now out of harm's way, trotted across and into the streets of Fredericksburg.[3]

In the Confederate lines back of Fredericksburg it was hardly a peaceful night, at least for the generals. It was late that Saturday before Early got all his troops back into the lines, and from their high ground they could see a good many Yankees who were too close for comfort. Colonel Benjamin Humphreys of the 21st Mississippi made his way up to Lee's Hill to search out his brigade commander, Brigadier General William Barksdale. He found Barksdale wrapped in a blanket at the base of a tree and whispered, "Are you asleep, General?" Barksdale's response was immediate and brusque: "No sir, who could sleep with a million of armed Yankees all around him!"

Before he bedded his men down for the night, Barksdale had put them to work bluffing the Yankees. They had been at this for several nights now and were practiced at it. A man in the 13th Mississippi explained how his brigade was posted "along the river about four miles, the companies stretched out raising tents and fires, to make them appear as regiments." Their effort was not without effect. General Sedgwick kept asking everyone from Hooker's staff he encountered where the commanding general was getting his idea that the Rebel force in front of him "must be a small one." It certainly did not look small to him.[4]

What Sedgwick, acting aggressively on his discretionary orders, might have accomplished at 6 o'clock Saturday evening he could not accomplish at 6 o'clock Sunday morning. Then the Rebels' Fredericksburg position was held by a single brigade. Now it was held by a division. Then it was supported by 15 guns. Now there were 40 in position.

Sedgwick's suspicions were soon enough confirmed by observers in the air and on the ground. Professor Lowe, aloft in the *Washington*, reported soon after sunrise, "The enemy have apparently increased their force during the night." Captain James Hall, using the powerful telescope at Station F at the Phillips house, reported infantry and artillery manning all their old sites on the heights opposite.

Butterfield sent this discouraging news on to Hooker. "Sedgwick, judging from the sound, is meeting with strong resistence," he added. "I have no reports from him yet." Then he did have a report from Sedgwick, sent shortly after sunrise, and it was not encouraging. "I am at Sumner's old battle ground, and am hotly engaged. Not sanguine of the result." Then there came still another report, relayed from the signal officer with Sedgwick: "Heavy firing heard in the direction of Chancellorsville."[5]

* *

JOHN SEDGWICK'S report that his column would not reach the Chancellorsville front by daylight Sunday morning, as ordered, was handed to General Hooker at the Chancellor house before daylight. The news set him back sharply. The night before, when the army recovered its balance after Jackson's assault, and when Hooker recovered his own equilibrium, he had taken a determined stance. He would hold the army right in its present position around the Chancellorsville crossroads, invite Lee to attack him there, then in concert with Sedgwick seize the initiative. Now, abruptly, he concluded he could not hold his present position after all if Sedgwick was going to be delayed for any appreciable time. He must contract his lines immediately.

Hooker's concern was for Dan Sickles in the salient at Hazel Grove. Porter Alexander, the Confederate artillerist, concisely captured the importance of the place. Hazel Grove, he wrote, "included a beautiful position for artillery, an open grassy ridge, some 400 yards long, extending N.E. and S.W. . . ." On May 2, Alexander admitted, he did not even know of Hazel Grove's existence; only on May 3 did he come to appreciate it. Joe Hooker, it seems, never came to appreciate it. Before first light that Sunday he called Sickles to the Chancellor house and ordered him to collect his two divisions and his batteries and march rapidly "by the most practicable route" back to Fairview.

This proved to be one of General Hooker's most fateful decisions of the campaign, yet oddly enough he never personally attempted to explain it. He would be forthcoming (in his own fashion) about his every other move but this one. "The position I abandoned was one that I had held at disadvantage" was all he would say about it.

One clue to his thinking in these pre-dawn hours is found in the description of the scene by historian Samuel P. Bates. After the war Hooker worked closely with Bates on his account of Chancellorsville, writing him two score letters on the subject, visiting him, visiting the battlefield with him, reading the manuscript as it progressed. Thus Bates was surely reflecting Hooker's views when he wrote that General Lee's force, "unbroken, and fresh for the conflict, was at hand and might at any moment move upon this part of the field." Sickles, he went on, "knew not at what moment the forces of Lee would strike him in rear, when he would have been between two fires and liable for capture. . . . General Hooker plainly saw the great danger. . . ."[6]

There was danger, to be sure, just as there was danger inherent in any position in the shape of a protruding salient. Losing here would leave Sickles with a particularly tortuous route for retreat. Yet there were seven brigades of veteran Yankee infantry here, and 38 guns. And whatever Dan Sickles might have lacked in military judgment he could make up for with military pugnaciousness. Furthermore, on Sickles's immediate left, facing Lee, were three more brigades under John Geary of the Twelfth Corps.

Joe Hooker was making a purely military judgment, and what he misread that morning was how critically important Hazel Grove would be, not only to him but to his enemy. Rebel batteries posted here in numbers — and Porter Alexander would see to that — would have a flanking fire on the Federal lines all the way to the Plank Road, and on the Federal artillery massed in the Fairview clearing. Rebel guns in numbers at Hazel Grove would put Fairview in jeopardy, which in turn would put the entire Chancellorsville position in jeopardy.

Perhaps Henry Hunt, the Potomac army's chief of artillery, might have made Hooker see this crucial reality about Hazel Grove, and might have talked him into making a fight for it. Perhaps Hunt's influence and gunnery expertise might have awakened Hooker to the grave risk to his own artillery. But in his dispute with Hunt before the campaign began Hooker had banished him — just now he was managing the reserve artillery at Banks's Ford — and artillery authority on this battlefield was scattered among the corps and divisional commanders. That morning of May 3, First Corps artillerist Charles Wainwright noted in his diary, "no one appeared to know anything, and there was a good deal of confusion."[7]

At first light on Day Seven the Federals in their altered position around Chancellorsville prepared for the battle they knew was coming. To the north, Reynolds's First Corps and Meade's Fifth manned a line running from the Rapidan south along Hunting Run and then southeasterly along the Ely's Ford Road. Opposite them, to the east, from the Rappahannock southward along the Mineral Spring Road, was Howard's Eleventh Corps. Between Reynolds and Meade on the west and Howard on the east ran the army's communications with U.S. Ford.

Couch's Second Corps continued the eastern face of the line, from

Howard on the north, past Chancellorsville, to Slocum's Twelfth Corps on the south. Geary's Twelfth Corps division faced south. At right angles to it and facing west, Williams's Twelfth Corps division ran from the corner of Hazel Grove up to the Plank Road. Beyond, north of the road, was Berry's Third Corps division, backed by a brigade from the Second Corps. Sickles's other two Third Corps divisions were in the Hazel Grove salient, forming a sort of extended southwestern corner of the position.

If the battle took up where it left off the previous night, as everyone expected it would, the Yankee troops immediately in the line of fire to the west were the Third and Twelfth corps — the divisions of Berry, Birney, and Whipple under command of Dan Sickles, and the divisions of Geary and Williams under Henry Slocum. William Hays's Second Corps brigade was posted just behind Berry. This force, all told, came to 33,400 men. Its two largest arrays of artillery were at Fairview and Hazel Grove.

In close support, if the attack indeed came from the west, would be the other elements of the Second Corps, about 15,000 men. It was said that nothing was expected of the Eleventh Corps but (this time) to hold its ground. Hooker's strategic reserve was the 32,000 troops in the First and Fifth corps. Joe Hooker would command on the field in person.

Facing this line on the west was Stonewall Jackson's command, led now by cavalryman Jeb Stuart. In front today were the six brigades of A. P. Hill's Light Division, now under Harry Heth. This line conformed to the Federals' line and was 500 to 700 yards from it. Colston's division formed the second line, and Rodes's the third. This time all the troops were at hand, giving Stuart some 31,900 of all arms, but no reserves to call upon. Initially the Federals had the best artillery positions, and the Confederates would have to improvise their artillery support. The 14,900 in the divisions of Anderson and McLaws, under Lee's direct command, would surely see action this day. Mr. Davis had never had to advise Robert E. Lee that in the next battle he should put in all his men.[8]

At midnight, after informing himself "of the state of affairs," Jed Hotchkiss had set off from Wilderness Tavern to report to General Lee. (He took as his guide on the dark roads Charles Wellford, who had earlier guided Jackson's column on the flank march. Thus closed one of the more eventful days of Wellford's life.) Hotchkiss reached Lee half an hour after Captain Wilbourn, and found that the general did not wish to hear further of Jackson's wounding. "He was much distressed and said he would rather a thousand times it had been himself," Hotchkiss recorded in his diary. His map and his account enabled Lee to evaluate the situation in detail for the first time.

From Lee's advanced line on the east, the brigades of Posey and Wright, it was about a mile and a quarter, in a straight line, to the most

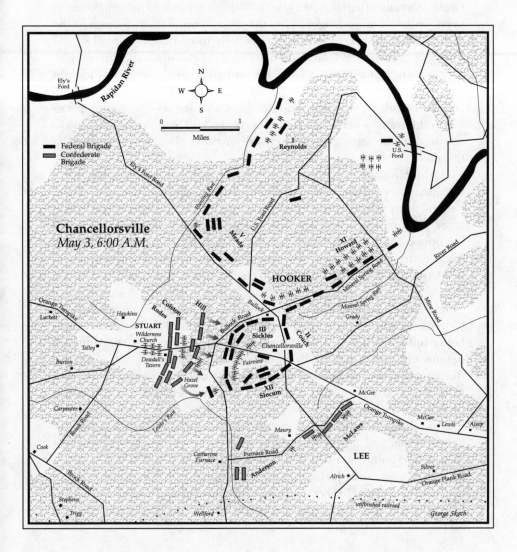

Chancellorsville
May 3, 6:00 A.M.

Federal Brigade
Confederate Brigade

N
W   E
S

0   1
Miles

Ely's Ford

Rapidan River

Ely's Ford Road

Hunting Run

U.S. Ford Road

U.S. Ford

I
Reynolds

V
Meade

XI
Howard

Mineral Spring Road

River Road

Mine Road

HOOKER

Bullock Road

Mineral Spring Run

Orange Turnpike

Luckett

Hawkins

Colston

Rodes

Hill

Bullock Road

Grady

STUART

Wilderness Church

Talley

Dowdall's Tavern

III
Sickles

Chancellorsville

II
Couch

McGee

Burton

Fairview

McGee

Lewis

Alsop

Hazel Grove

XII
Slocum

Carpenter

Brock Road

Lewis's Run

Maury

Orange Turnpike

McLaws

Cook

Catharine Furnace

Furnace Road

Anderson

LEE

Silver

Alrich

Orange Plank Road

Brock Road

Stephens

Trigg

Wellford

unfinished railroad

George Skoch

advanced of Stuart's troops. In between was the enemy massed at Hazel Grove. Already, after conferring with Wilbourn, Lee had written Stuart to press "with the utmost vigor . . . so that we can unite the two wings of the army. Endeavor, therefore, to disposess them of Chancellorsville. . . ." With the information from Hotchkiss he could be more specific, and he wrote again to Stuart, at 3:30 A.M. He wanted Stuart "to work by the right wing, turning the positions of the enemy, so as to drive him from Chancellorsville, which will again unite us." Lee stressed it — "continue pressing to the right" — and said that everything "will be done on this side to accomplish the same object." Beyond anything else, the army must be reunited.

From Hotchkiss's report and reports from Fredericksburg and from his own observations, it was apparent now to Lee that the bulk of the Federal army was in front of him. However he had decided to count that army, he knew he was substantially outnumbered. Withdrawal remained his option, and with nothing certain yet heard of the enemy's cavalry raiders, the way south was still open. Yet first, whatever the option, he must reunite the army, and to do that he must retain the initiative by attacking.

He must also retain the initiative so as to foreclose any attempt by General Hooker to seize it. The noise of axes and the sound of trees being felled during the night suggested that Hooker was still thinking defensively, and it was vitally important to Lee that Hooker continue thinking that way. Should the Federals strike out hard now at his divided army, Lee's gamble of Jackson's flank march might well end up losing him the entire game.

Assaulting an entrenched enemy with an inferior force was not the conventional way, but Lee had little choice that morning. His hope was that he and Stuart between them might find mismatches at the points of attack (as apparently Jackson had most emphatically found the evening before) and break Hooker's line and perhaps Hooker's spirit as well. As Lee recalled, that had been a most successful tactic against General McClellan.[9]

*　*

BEFORE HE could evacuate Hazel Grove, Dan Sickles had to clear a passage for his troops, especially for his artillery. The 105th Pennsylvania was detailed to corduroy a boggy section along a branch of Lewis's Run, and soon the troops were on the march back to Fairview. Whipple's division led, followed by Birney's. Staying to the last as rear guard at Hazel Grove were the six Pennsylvania regiments of Charles Graham's brigade. With Graham was James Huntington's Battery B, 1st Ohio

Light. It was daylight, wrote diarist Orin Dority of the Ohio battery, and "the Rebs are getting uneasy so they begin to sharpshoot a little. . . ." Huntington, out of canister after last night's fight, responded by ordering fuzes cut short on case shot for their 3-inch rifles so as to rain fragments like hail into the woods in front of them. "They didn't like it so they charged us," Dority wrote.

The men of A. P. Hill's division had been called to arms early on May 3, and at daylight they moved forward, skirmishers in advance. Porter Alexander would remember very few Confederate offensives in this war starting so promptly. In this instance there was little preliminary maneuvering, and the troops simply picked up their rifles and started ahead through the woods. They had breakfasted on whatever was left in their haversacks and whatever the fleeing Yankees had left behind the evening before. Although a commissary train made the roundabout journey to the Second Corps during the night, only Rodes's men in the third line had time to reprovision themselves before the fighting began. It was another nice morning, clear and pleasant, and men remembered birds singing as they moved among the trees.

James J. Archer's brigade — 1st, 7th, 14th Tennessee, 13th Alabama, 5th Alabama Battalion — was on the extreme right of the advance, and it was Archer's men gunner Dority was shooting at. H. T. Childs of the 1st Tennessee reported that his regiment went 50 yards and then halted to dress its lines. "Then General Archer's shrill, clear voice was heard along the line: 'Fix bayonets! Forward, guide center! Charge 'em boys!'" With the Rebel yell they charged. At the edge of the Hazel Grove clearing they clambered over an undefended breastwork and opened fire on Huntington's Ohio battery and its infantry supports.

In his midnight reconnaissance Porter Alexander had found an artillery position in what was little more than a wide spot in the woods road north of Hazel Grove and deployed two batteries there, and now they too opened on the Federals. The Rebel riflemen and artillerists made a short fight of it. Archer's line outflanked Graham's, and with that the Federals began to give way and join the withdrawal. His regiment fell back, wrote Captain James Ryan of the 63rd Pennsylvania, "which is, perhaps, excusable, considering the terrible flank fire it was under all the time."

Gunner Dority was not so charitable. "Our infantry support soon gave way," he complained, "and we were ordered to limber to the rear and get to the rear as best we could." All the while, he added, the Rebels were shooting down the artillery horses and calling out, "Surrender you Yankee so and so! . . ." By now the battery was in a fearful tangle, and three of Huntington's six guns were captured.

General Archer swung his brigade to the left to follow the retreating enemy and came up against what he took to be the second Yankee line. It was instead a section of the south-facing main line held by the 20th Connecticut and the 145th New York, of Alpheus Williams's division. These Yankees had never been in battle before, but they had the shelter of the log barricade built when the corps first manned this position. In the 145th nerves became frayed and it began to break, but General Williams was there to check it "before injury was done. It fought valiantly afterwards."

Archer's men pushed to within 70 yards of the barricade and then the fire became more than they could stand. They fell back, tried a second time and failed, and then Archer withdrew to Hazel Grove to await reinforcements. He would write home to complain that "the battle was half over before I received the least support, or even got a sight of any other of our troops." However that may be, it was 6:45 A.M. and the Confederates had Hazel Grove for their guns.[10]

General Archer had in fact made his gain against token resistance. The rest of A. P. Hill's division would not be that fortunate. With the dawn, fighting erupted all along the mile-wide battlefield that extended north from Hazel Grove and across the Plank Road nearly as far as the Bullock house. Berdan's Sharpshooters were just then falling back in rear of this line. "As we came along we had one of the fiercest battles of the war," wrote Lieutenant Marden of the sharpshooters. "Such cannonading and musketry I never heard. The roar was incessant. The slaughter was immense." General Williams was candid when he wrote, "I think the heaviest attack was against me, but as I was nearer and could see my own position best, and *hear* there the most, I may be mistaken." Every other Yankee general on the line might have said the same.

Samuel McGowan's South Carolina brigade was next to Archer, to the north, and in the advance the two brigades diverged and fought separately. McGowan's right first struck the hinge of the Federal line, near Hazel Grove, where it turned from facing south to facing west. The Rebel charge here caught one of Sickles's trailing regiments, the 37th New York, the Irish Rifles, in marching order instead of fighting order and sent it flying in confusion. The Irish Rifles would report a loss of 222 men, almost half of them prisoners, after scarcely firing a shot. Its lieutenant colonel would be all day trying to reassemble his command in the rear.

That was to be General McGowan's only easy victory. He now was facing Thomas Ruger's polyglot Twelfth Corps brigade — in the front row 27th Indiana, 2nd Massachusetts, and 3rd Wisconsin, backed by the 107th New York and 13th New Jersey — in a line of battle some 400 yards wide. The line was braced by a pair of Napoleons that Colonel Silas

Colgrove of the 27th Indiana had commandeered after the Third Corps stampede the evening before. The lieutenant of the battery was busy instructing the infantrymen Colgrove had detailed to serve the guns.

The Federals here were posted on a low open knoll. In front of them the ground sloped off to what was unusual in this Wilderness — fairly open woods, with little undergrowth, what out in Indiana (the 27th Indiana's historian explained) they called an "oak opening." By stooping a bit, he said, they could see through the trees for a good quarter of a mile. Ruger's gritty veterans watched calmly as the South Carolinians marched toward them through this woodland and into a depression at the base of the slope. Then they came into sight again. First their flags, then their hats, then their faces appeared. "They were the best dressed, tidiest and most soldierly-looking lot of rebels that we ever saw," the historian remembered.

Then he and his fellows opened fire and cut gaps in the Rebels' line but they closed up and came on. To the right the 2nd Massachusetts, which had been lying down, rose up as one man and added a ripping volley to the din. Then the two battle lines, perhaps 75 yards apart, on open ground, stood there and fired at each other, steadily and without pause for what both sides later agreed was 30 minutes.

"The advance was abandoned by us, the cheering was hushed," wrote J.F.J. Caldwell of the 1st South Carolina. "All on both sides addressed themselves to loading and firing as rapidly as possible." It was one of those dramas of war, wrote the 27th Indiana's historian, "which for cool, deliberate action and resolute, unflinching endurance, on both sides, has had few parallels. . . ." For Ruger's veterans there was the eerie recollection of another day, on another field, when they had stood exactly like this and slugged it out virtually toe-to-toe for possession of the bloody Cornfield at Antietam.

McGowan's men found they could not prevail in this savage firefight and finally, slowly, they fell back and took cover behind the log barricade behind them that Slocum's men had built earlier and then abandoned in the aftermath of Jackson's attack. General McGowan was wounded here, standing atop the works to rally his men, then his successor, Colonel Oliver Edwards, was mortally wounded doing the same thing. For both McGowan's command and Ruger's the respite would be brief. By now the entire first line of Hill's division was closely engaged, driving the thunderous musketry to a new pitch.[11]

The roar of the artillery doubled too, and then redoubled. The moment Archer's brigade had cleared Hazel Grove, Stuart was on the scene telling Porter Alexander to rush in his guns. "They were close at hand, & all ready, & it was done very quickly," Alexander wrote. Three

Virginia batteries he had posted close by the night before — Crenshaw's, McGraw's, and Davidson's — were first to roll into Hazel Grove, with 12 guns. Right behind came Page's 6-gun battery, and then three batteries from Alexander's own battalion, Parker's, Woolfolk's, and Moody's. Seven batteries, 28 guns, and all with an enfilading fire on all the targets they could want. From Hazel Grove they could even see the Chancellor house.

The Federals too were moving up guns, especially to the vital Fairview position. After rearrangements during the night, Captain Best had started the day here with four batteries. Before long he had eight, mounting 44 guns. Best was operating under large handicaps, however. To defend any part of the Federal lines he had to fire over the heads of his own infantry, and with the imperfect fuzes of the day that was dangerous and demoralizing. It was a practice normally avoided, but on this battlefield there was no alternative. It was a particular risk on the right of the gun line, near the Plank Road, where the ground was level and the trajectory of the cannon fire was highly uncomfortable for the infantrymen.

And being some 500 yards to the rear meant Best had to find other targets as soon as the opposing infantry lines began to close on each other. Finally, and most disconcerting to the Yankee gunners, Fairview was subject to a deadly converging fire from the enemy's guns. Alexander advanced 14 guns on the Plank Road to add to the fire from Hazel Grove to the south. It was just the sort of situation gunners dreamed of, and Willie Pegram, battalion commander at Hazel Grove, rejoiced. "A glorious day, Colonel, a glorious day!" he cried to Alexander.

What was missing this day at Fairview was the sure guiding hand of Henry Hunt. With tactical authority as chief of artillery, General Hunt would surely have directed the batteries there to ignore the infantry battle in front of them long enough to concentrate their full firepower on a single target — first the Rebel guns at Hazel Grove until they were silenced, then those on the Plank Road. The Federals had the guns, and the weight of metal, for the task. Hunt had done exactly that with his guns at Malvern Hill on the Peninsula the previous summer and all but destroyed Lee's artillery that day. But Clermont Best lacked Hunt's authority. Instead Best had to meet the demands of every divisional and corps commander, and their concerns were quite understandably their own. "It is not, therefore, to be wondered at," Hunt would observe, "that confusion and mismanagement ensued. . . ."[12]

A. P. Hill's other four brigades — Jim Lane's and Dorsey Pender's North Carolinians, E. L. Thomas's Georgians, and Harry Heth's Virginians commanded today by John Brockenbrough — drove hard against the Federal line where it straddled the Plank Road. The defenders here were mostly from Hiram Berry's division (the division Joe Hooker once commanded) of the Third Corps. North of the Plank Road were the brigades of Joseph Revere and Joseph Carr, and to the south was Gershom Mott's brigade. Mott was posted in support of two regiments from Samuel Ross's Twelfth Corps brigade in the front line. The Yankees in this sector had worked hard during the night throwing up breastworks. Their works tended to be low and crude, for often the only tools were bayonets and tin plates, but they offered some sense of security all the same.

Now, wrote a Yankee colonel, there was "no stopping, no breathing space, but a long, fierce, and desperate contest." Jim Lane's North Carolinians struck head-on Ross's two Twelfth Corps regiments, 123rd New York and 3rd Maryland, holding the line immediately south of the Plank Road. At the first spatterings of fire the New Yorkers' skirmishers came back at a run. "Get ready, boys," one of them yelled, "for they are coming and coming strong!" The attack was heralded by the Rebel yell, and there was also the cry "Remember Jackson!" When they sighted Lane's charge the batteries opened at Fairview, directly behind the Yankee line. "The noise was deafening as the shells went howling and singing over our heads," Rice Bull of the 123rd wrote, "and we nervously ducked as they went by."

The 3rd Maryland had seen some action before, but it had never faced anything like this rush of screaming men; also, its ranks were sprinkled with new replacements who had no combat experience at all. These men broke first, setting off what an officer in the second line described as a "premature and precipitate withdrawal." Lane's jubilant men broke over the abandoned breastworks and turned their fire on a suddenly exposed Federal battery on the Plank Road. This was Lieutenant Justin Dimick's section of Battery H, 1st United States, the same guns that had opened on the party carrying the wounded Stonewall Jackson the night before.

The infantry fire quickly silenced the battery and Dimick ordered it to retire. One gun was dragged off safely, but the horses of the other were shot down and the gun had to be left. The gun crews were shot down too, and Lieutenant Dimick was hit in the spine, a mortal wound. His successor, Lieutenant James Sanderson, saw the abandoned piece standing in the road between the hostile lines, galloped forward with a limber "amid a storm of musketry" to secure it, and hauled it to the rear. An infantry officer paid him tribute: "Not a braver act is recorded in the history of the war."[13]

North of the Plank Road the charge was taken up by Dorsey Pender's

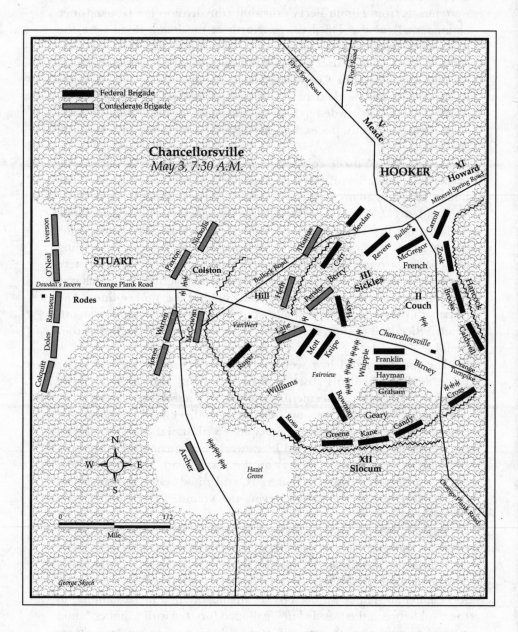

Federal Brigade
Confederate Brigade

Chancellorsville
May 3, 7:30 A.M.

HOOKER

V
Meade

XI
Howard

Fly's Ford Road

U.S. Ford Road

Mineral Spring Road

Iverson

O'Neal

STUART

Nicholls

Paxton

Colston

Berdan

Thomas

Carr

Bullock

Revere

McGregor

Carroll

Zook

French

Hancock

Brooke

Dowdall's Tavern

Orange Plank Road

Ramseur

Rodes

Bullock Road

Hill

Heth

Pender

Berry

III
Sickles

Hays

II
Couch

Doles

Jones

Warren

McGowan

VanWert

Lane

Mott

Knipe

Chancellorsville

Caldwell

Colquitt

Ruger

Williams

Fairview

Whipple

Franklin

Hayman

Birney

Orange
Turnpike

Graham

Bowman

Geary

Cross

Archer

Ross

Greene

Kane

Candy

Hazel
Grove

XII
Slocum

Orange Plank Road

N
W   E
S

0   1/2
Mile

George Skoch

North Carolinians and supported by the Virginians under John Brocken-brough. "My brigade behaved magnificently and got cut up terribly," General Pender told his wife. Six of his ten ranking field officers were casualties. In the 16th North Carolina both the colonel and lieutenant colonel were wounded. In the 22nd North Carolina Lieutenant Colonel Christopher Cole was killed and then Major Laban Odell was killed, and a captain took command. But in this grim competition of officer casualties, Pender's brigade could lay claim to killing one Yankee major general and capturing one Yankee brigadier general.

Down-Easter Hiram G. Berry, before the war a member of the Maine legislature and captain of a local militia company, was one of those amateur soldiers who had revealed a genuine talent for fighting. He had risen from colonel to major general of division after earning his spurs under such noted fighters as Phil Kearny and Joe Hooker. On the battlefield, much to the dismay of his staff, Berry insisted on delivering his orders in person. As Pender's assault now approached his lines he decided he had to check on one of his brigades. He crossed the Plank Road, gave his orders, and was returning to his headquarters north of the road when a bullet — said to be fired by a Rebel sharpshooter — found him. To his staff who rushed to his side he said calmly, "I am dying, carry me to the rear." He was borne back to the Chancellor house and presently he died.

Pender's regiments cut their way through this first line of defenders and came to the second line, manned by William Hays's brigade of the Second Corps. The 13th North Carolina, moving fast, turned the right flank of this brigade, much to the surprise of its commander. Lieutenant John R. Ireland and his Company E swept up the general and all but one of his staff before they could escape. Brigadier General Hays's name would head the list of Yankee officers captured at Chancellorsville that was featured on the front page of the *Richmond Examiner.*[14]

Farthest north in the attacking line were the Georgians of E. L. Thomas. Francis Johnson of the 45th Georgia described their attack in brief: "The Regiment then struck a trot yelled fiendishly never stopped until we had crossed their breastworks. . . ." Much of the ground here was heavily wooded, and the two sides groping for each other were guided as much by sound as by sight. Thomas's men knocked back the flank regiments of the first Yankee line and pushed ahead through the woods. The 132nd Pennsylvania was rushed up from the Second Corps to help fill the gap. When the Pennsylvanians entered the woods they revealed their presence by a crackling of leaves and branches, and the Georgians responded with a volley.

Major Frederick Hitchcock of the 132nd thought the enemy's volley "very hurriedly delivered," for it passed harmlessly over their heads. But in the still air the smoke of the volley, "not more than fifty yards away, hung like a chalk line and indicated their exact position." Major Hitchcock had the regiment aim just below this telltale line of smoke and fire a volley "by battalion," that is, in unison. He would remember it as the only time in his war experience that the regiment fired by battalion. It was effective enough, for when they went forward the enemy had fled, leaving only dead and wounded on its line.

It was 7:30 A.M. by now, and all up and down the mile-wide battlefield the Confederates' first line was fully engaged. Everywhere it had reached the Federal main line and in some places broken it and met the Federal supporting troops. The Light Division under Harry Heth engaged some 11,800 infantrymen that morning, about a third of the total force available to Jeb Stuart. The issue just now became which side could bring up fresh troops to feed the fighting, and how quickly.[15]

* *

JEB STUART was relishing his new command. Somewhere he had acquired a brand-new blue uniform coat — perhaps from some Federal headquarters overrun the evening before — and substituted a red artillery sash for his yellow cavalry one, and adorned his hat with red and black plumes. "His richly caparisoned steed, too, was worthy of the rider," wrote an admiring Harrison Griffith of the 14th South Carolina, "and the two together constituted the grandest figure of man and horse that I have ever seen." Surely, Griffith thought, the legendary Murat had never looked more dashing.

Stuart was everywhere that morning, seeing and being seen, leading troops forward and rallying them when they fell back. His battle tactics were not subtle. He had taken Jackson's corps where he found it at midnight, and under Lee's peremptory orders he felt obliged to attack at dawn, without waiting to rearrange his forces or to explore the enemy line for a weak spot. That Sunday, said Porter Alexander, Stuart "never seemed to hesitate or to doubt for one moment that he could just crash his way wherever he chose to strike."

Latter-day critics would find Stuart's tactics unimaginative, suggesting it would have been wiser to feint from the west and attack from the south, behind the batteries placed at Hazel Grove. Yet under General Lee's orders to attack immediately, Stuart had little real choice but to strike with his forces arranged as they were. And then to have left the Light Division engaged in a feint on the western battlefront, while he shifted Colston's and Rodes's divisions around to the southern flank, would have been to risk what in the event very nearly happened. For a time in this battle it would take every man Stuart could muster, in all three of his divisions, simply to hold on where he was against the aggressive defenders.

Under the particular conditions he inherited, then, it is hard to see how Jeb Stuart, in a new command, a cavalryman commanding infantry and artillery for the first time, could have done a better job. The astute Porter Alexander believed all credit was due: "Altogether, I do not think there was a more brilliant thing done in the war than Stuart's extricating that command from the extremely critical position in which he found it. . . ."[16]

Fighting Joe Hooker, too, was riding his lines that morning, and like Stuart he was seeing and being seen, encouraging his troops, ordering in fresh brigades to threatened positions. James T. Miller of the 111th Pennsylvania wrote home describing the commanding general: "I saw him on Sunday riding bareheaded rite into the thickest of the fight and cheering his men by his voice and steadying them by his example and at that point our men did fight more like devils incarnate than men. . . ."

Hooker's design was not being changed by the fierce heat of battle. The lines must continue to hold long enough for Sedgwick to reach the scene and attack Lee from the rear. He would make sure Sedgwick understood this. "You will hurry up your column," he telegraphed. "The enemy's right flank now rests near the Plank Road at Chancellorsville, all exposed. You will attack at once." (When General Sedgwick was handed this dispatch, he was some ten miles away and methodically preparing an attack on Marye's Heights back of Fredericksburg.)[17]

Just then the most immediate threat to Hooker's lines was being mounted by the northern wing of Stuart's offensive — E. L. Thomas's Georgians, along with the 13th North Carolina that had strayed from Pender's brigade. Curling around his opponents, rushing on "with the impetuosity of an avalanche" (as one of his men wrote), Thomas threatened to take the batteries at Fairview, just across the Plank Road, in the flank and even in the rear. His path was made immeasurably easier when Brigadier General Joseph J. Revere, to the bewilderment of his men and everyone nearby — "heedless of their murmers," was how Dan Sickles put it — marched his New York brigade right off the battlefield.

Revere's command was the celebrated Excelsior Brigade, New Yorkers originally recruited and led to glory by Dan Sickles. After his divisional commander Hiram Berry was killed, General Revere got it into his head that he was the senior brigadier — he was not — and therefore could act at his own discretion. His regiments were low on ammunition and out of rations, he explained, and "I moved them back down the road for the purpose of reorganizing and bringing them back to the field comparatively fresh. . . ." His six regiments — along with, for good measure, three regiments from a neighboring brigade — were then marched three miles away from the field and nearly to U.S. Ford. (Dan Sickles would relieve Revere on the spot, and in due course prefer charges, and he was court-martialed and cashiered. Mr. Lincoln lifted the sentence, allowing the unfortunate general to resign.) [18]

Joe Hooker took in the crisis — Thomas's advance was carrying him to within 800 yards of the Chancellor house — and cast about for troops to mend the break. He turned to the Second Corps and William H. French's division. General French, wrote a chronicler of the Army of the Potomac, looked "precisely like one of those plethoric French colonels, who are so stout, and who look so red in the face, that one would suppose some one had tied a cord tightly round their necks. . . ." French was fierce and hot-tempered, one of those generals best suited to obeying a direct order to do something directly in front of him. Hooker ordered him to "attack the enemy, and drive him through the woods," and General French set about doing that.

Calling seven regiments out of his entrenchments facing east, French sent them westward on a long slant toward the Plank Road. The three leading regiments under Brigadier Samuel Carroll were tough westerners — 14th Indiana, 4th Ohio, and 7th West Virginia, calling themselves the Granite Brigade. General Carroll, wrote Major William Houghton of the 14th Indiana, "in his soul stirring voice called 'Attention! Battalion. The battalion of direction — column forward!' The bugle sounded *March!* and the column moved. It was the finest sight I've witnessed." According to Houghton, no less than Major Generals Hooker, Meade, Howard, and French saw them off. In the woods they deployed and soon found the enemy "and gave the first volley and the first cheer. The rebels ran like a plague had fallen among them. . . ."

Thomas's Georgians by now had spent most of their ammunition and most of their impetus, and Carroll's attack outmanned them and sent them hurrying back through the trees. General French broadened the counterattack by sending in the other four regiments he had detailed. "I presume the thick woods protected us," the 45th Georgia's Francis Johnson commented to his wife, "as nearly every tree had a ball in it. . . ." General Thomas would express in his report the single most common complaint among officers on May 3, on both sides: "At this point, finding that there were no troops on my left and none in supporting distance on my right or rear, . . . I ordered the brigade to move back. . . ."

French's counterattack drove the entire Confederate position north of the Plank Road back across the line of breastworks captured earlier and on to the shelter of Slocum's log barricade where the Light

Division had started its advance at dawn. The Rebels held there and were braced by artillery and by troops from Colston's and Rodes's divisions. The Federals' charge soon spent itself. Now it was their turn to voice the familiar complaint. "We had no support on either side and were flanked," the 14th Indiana's Major Houghton wrote, "came near to being taken but formed . . . and came off in splendid order. . . ." The order was not everywhere splendid. The 14th's band had dutifully trailed along behind the advance to collect casualties, and when the enemy gunners opened they overshot somewhat and sent shells falling among the bandsmen. "It created considerable panic and very much demoralized the Band," musician George Lambert admitted in his diary, "so that we retreated back about a mile, where we knew they could not reach us."

To the north, diarist Henry Morrow of the 24th Michigan, First Corps, was listening to this unending din beyond the forest and watching the clouds of dirty battle smoke rise over the trees, and he felt the suspense of the moment. "It *seems* as if we are driving the enemy before us, but all is uncertain from where we are," he wrote. "The country is the worst possible for aggressive warfare. It is heavily wooded & is very broken. We cannot see a hundred yards in front of us."[19]

Just who held what in the dense smoky woodland was indeed far from settled. In their charge the Yankees had captured small groups of Rebels here and there and then passed on, and now these prisoners were being collected. Captain Samuel Fiske of French's division had rounded up several dozen and sent them to the rear, and had another squad of captives in hand when abruptly, in a little clearing, he came face to face with what struck him as "at least a whole regiment" of armed butternuts. At that one of his erstwhile prisoners turned to him with a grin and observed, "Cap'en, I reckon things is different from the way they was, and you'll hev to 'low you're our prisoner now." Ruefully Captain Fiske handed over his pistol and sword and agreed that things were different, "with a vengence."

During their attack, a man in the 4th Ohio wrote, "we could distinguish a number of Zouaves and 'blue coats' who had been taken prisoner. . . . The Zoo Zoos saw us coming, made a bold dash and most of them escaped." These Zoo Zoos — the 114th Pennsylvania — had had an eventful morning, and in their gaudy uniforms they were widely noticed.

During the fight on the Federal left, McGowan's South Carolinians remembered a bold charge on them by Zouaves. "It was a strange, sad sight," recalled Captain Griffith of the 14th South Carolina, "to see a few minutes afterwards, the ground covered with their prostrate bodies clad in their bright red trousers and writhing in agony or lying still in death."

Private Alfred Bellard of the 5th New Jersey recorded a less heroic sequel: "Before long a regt. of Red Legged Zouaves who were on the left of the first line broke, and running past our Regt. their officers called upon us to fire into them. We did not obey the order. . . ." At any event, a number of the Zouaves who had been taken prisoner were now liberated. They did not act properly grateful, grumbled the commander of the 7th West Virginia. In its charge, he reported, his regiment took a Rebel flag, but the freed Zouaves snatched it away and ran to the rear, "claiming it as theirs."[20]

On the other side of the Plank Road, to the south, the battle had also settled into a bitter struggle for the fought-over ground between the two lines of breastworks. Both lines were the handiwork of Henry Slocum's Twelfth Corps. The log barricade to the west, running in a long curve from Hazel Grove up to and across the Plank Road, had been started on April 30, when the Twelfth Corps first reached Chancellorsville. The breastworks to the east, distant 300 to 600 yards and put up only the night before, were less elaborate.

After their initial charge was checked, the brigades of Archer, McGowan, and Lane had fallen back and taken refuge behind the log barricade to fight off counterattacks, especially those of the Yankee brigade under the aggressive Tom Ruger. Lieutenant Colonel D.R.E. Winn of the 4th Georgia assured his wife that he had encountered that morning "the most stubborn resistance that has ever been made during the war."

In the 18th North Carolina at the barricade the feeling was growing that in this battle the regiment was star-crossed. The night before, they were told, it was their fire that had wounded Stonewall Jackson. Now this morning their colonel, Thomas J. Purdie, was killed by a bullet through his forehead and Lieutenant Colonel Forney George was wounded, and in the retreat the color bearer, Corporal Owen Eakins, was killed and the regimental flag was lost. The enemy was right on their heels and it could not be recovered, "at least, very unwise to attempt it."

Well before this, Colston's division in the second line was expected to be closed on the Light Division and pressing the assault, but all along Colston's line there were delays. Raleigh Colston, the least experienced of Lee's generals of division, proved painfully slow in directing his men into action.

Inexperience predominated in this division on this day. Only Frank Paxton of the Stonewall Brigade had ever led his command in combat before. Edward T. H. Warren, who had moved up to head Colston's brigade when Colston took over the division, had been wounded in Jackson's attack and Colonel Titus V. Williams now commanded. Brigadier Francis Nicholls, wounded at the head of the Louisiana brigade on May 2, was replaced by his senior colonel, Jesse M. Williams. Brigadier John R. Jones, already under a cloud for leaving two previous battlefields, now left this one with what he claimed was an ulcerated leg. He would never serve again in the Army of Northern Virginia. Colonel Thomas S. Garnett assumed command of Jones's Virginia brigade.

"As soon as it was fairly light we were at it and for two hours our brigade fought like devils," Colonel Samuel M. Quincy of Ruger's brigade told his wife. "Three times did the 27th Indiana the 2d Massachusetts & the 3rd Wisconsin break & drive the rebel lines, advancing over their dead & wounded." With their last cartridges they brought down the flag of the 1st South Carolina, he explained, and then held their position with the bayonet until relieved. "I had lost my horse but astonished to find myself alive. . . . All this time the battle thunder rose & fell & the column of yellow smoke rose above the trees & floated up in the clear sunshine. . . ."

Much of the struggle Colonel Quincy described took place at and around the thousand-yard-long log barricade between Hazel Grove and the Plank Road. In one of their charges Ruger's Yankees tangled savagely with Warren's brigade of Colston's division. Warren's replacement Colonel Titus Williams was soon down with a wound, and by battle's end 800 more men of the brigade were casualties.

Captain James Melhorn of the 10th Virginia recorded in his diary that the brigade came under severe shelling from the batteries at Fairview. The 10th's Lieutenant Colonel Samuel T. Walker was killed by a solid shot "passing through his body," and Major Joshua Stover was mortally wounded. "I was shot in the foot," Melhorn wrote, "and in 15 minutes after I was shot through the hip, which near disabled me. . . ." The Yankees called on him to surrender, and "I crawled over the breastworks & layed down." Suddenly the tide swung back and reinforcements arrived and as he was escaping he was hit a third time. "I made my exit from the field by the assistance of a friend. . . ." Among the 10th Virginia's 157 casualties were 17 of its officers.

On this blasted smoking field the charge and countercharge were so rapid that the contestants could not always carry off their wounded. Sergeant Franklin Marcha of the 122nd Pennsylvania looked out at the human wreckage left by one Rebel charge. "Here lies one . . . ," he wrote in his diary, "scratching the dirt in his last struggle for breath. Here is one praying and apparently happy. There is one praying but without any hope. Here is one moaning, there, one crying for help while there is no help. . . ."

Frank Paxton's Stonewall Brigade began the day posted in the second line north of the Plank Road, but in this new crisis it was hurried south across the road. Jeb Stuart rode out in front and "called out for the Old Stonewall to follow." As it was marched forward toward the log barricade, Garnett's brigade formed on its right. There were ten veteran Virginia regiments in the two brigades.

The barricade, built originally to protect Federals, was now protection for hundreds of Confederates crouched against its outer side. Many units were without organization, and others were without ammunition. Men were packed six and eight deep against the logs and their general feeling was that they had already done their share in this battle. Colonel John Funk of the 5th Virginia described "a large number of men of whom fear had taken the most absolute possession." He added that all attempts to persuade them to join the assault were fruitless. J.F.J. Caldwell of the 1st South Carolina took note of the Stonewall Brigade passing over them, "some of them saying, with not very pleasant levity, that they would show us how to clear away a Federal line."[21]

Frank Paxton, big, rough-hewn, called "Bull" since his youth, had long been what Randolph Barton of his staff described as "a rather profane and godless man." But then command of the Stonewall Brigade, Jackson's own, and also perhaps his association with Jackson, made him what Barton called "a new man." Bull Paxton's pocket Bible became his constant solace, and on the night before this battle he had admitted a premonition of his death and prepared himself for it. In the morning Barton saw the general complete his devotions, and placing his Bible "in a pocket just over his heart, with a face full of resolution, he awaited orders."

In this charge of the Stonewall Brigade, wrote Captain John Welsh of the 27th Virginia, "it seemed as if nothing but the hand of God could save a man. . . ." Paxton was squarely in the midst of a hail of musketry. They had to struggle through a thickly overgrown swale, all the time under a deadly plunging fire. Suddenly, Lieutenant Barton remembered, Paxton fell not two feet from him. "I placed my arm under him, when he muttered, 'Tie up my arm,' and died," Barton wrote. "He was not shot in the arm, but through the heart." Soon afterward, leading the other brigade in the assault, Colonel Thomas Garnett went down with a mortal wound.

Under their junior officers the Virginians tried to continue the charge. They closed to within 60 or 70 yards of the Yankee defenders at their breastworks — these were mostly Thomas Ruger's stubborn fighters — and then could go no farther and fell back to the log barricade where they had started. South Carolinian Caldwell, recalling the

Stonewall Brigade's boast to clear away the Federal line, remarked dryly, "But their reckoning was not accurate."

It was most likely this charge by Paxton's and Garnett's Virginians that Sergeant Ed Weller of the 107th New York, Ruger's brigade, was describing in a letter home a few days later. A fresh body of Rebels now came up, he wrote, "and had at their head a Genl. or Colonel, I could not tell which. He was on Horseback and as they came up in mass I showed the boys this officer and told them to let him have it. Immediately about twenty of us levelled our pieces at him and fired and Mr. Gen. or Col. fell, horse and all. Our whole Brigade then poured a terrible volley into them and they were obliged to fall back."

It was close to 8:30 now and in the battle there was a Federal tide running. French's counterattack north of the Plank Road had pushed back Stuart's offensive there. The strong fight put up by the Twelfth Corps, especially by Ruger's brigade, had blunted the enemy's advance south of the road. Hooker's design — to fight defensively from behind his works, with aggressive counterattacks of opportunity — seemed to be succeeding. Rufus Ingalls, the army's chief quartermaster, hurried to U.S. Ford to inform Butterfield. "A most terribly bloody conflict has raged since daylight," he telegraphed. "Enemy in great force in our front and on the right, but at this moment we are repulsing him on all sides. Carnage is fearful." To Joe Hooker's mind, however, everything still depended on John Sedgwick's Sixth Corps. "If possible communicate with Gen. Sedgwick," he telegraphed Butterfield. "We are driving the enemy & only need him to complete the job."[22]

* *

THE YANKEE infantrymen had been issued sixty rounds of ammunition (and some even eighty rounds) for this battle, but at the frantic pace of the fighting it was not long before they began to run short. The usual way in front-line units was to send back to higher authority for a replacement unit and as soon as it arrived to march to the rear to replenish cartridge boxes and then wait in reserve.

In some cases today, however — General Revere's being the most notorious — units marched to the rear without authority or without waiting for replacements to fill their places. This was often the action of flustered replacement officers. The 5th Connecticut, 46th Pennsylvania, and 128th Pennsylvania of Joseph Knipe's brigade, all of which had lost their commanders the night before, all now marched off the battlefield under the authority, "as we supposed," of a misguided junior officer.

"I had never seen such hot work," General Couch recalled, "some very brave officers were nearly demoralized, while others seemed to be inspired with superhuman courage. . . ." When his senior officer was wounded, Major Charles Mudge, 2nd Massachusetts, took his place. Mudge wrote his father afterward with relief that he felt he had met the test. "I was so astonished at my own coolness and courage that I could not help thanking and praising God for it in a loud voice while I sat there on my horse." In the 24th New Jersey, a nine-month regiment, it was reported that the regimental chaplain, William C. Stockton, "distinguished himself by his gallant bearing," setting out with the regiment on its charge and calling out encouragement "sometimes twenty or thirty feet in advance of the line." It was also officially reported that the chaplain of the 19th Mississippi, Reverend T. L. Duke, "remained in front of his regiment with his musket . . . and mainly directed the movements of the skirmishers. . . ."

But sometimes the primal urge for self-preservation took over. The lieutenant colonel of one of the two-year New York regiments, whose time was up in two weeks, was called to command after the colonel was wounded. The sequel was reported matter-of-factly by his next in command: "He said to me, 'Major, I am going to the rear to look after stragglers.' I said, 'I have sent after them, Sir!' After a few moments he remarked, 'I am going to the rear for ammunition.' I said, 'I have already sent for it.' He then remarked, 'I am worn out and going to the rear, you take command.' A few moments later I missed him and he did not again report for duty until the next day at noon."[23]

It was also common practice to bring ammunition up close to the front to replenish supplies directly. On this field, however, especially the open ground south of the Plank Road, it was nearly as dangerous in the rear as it was on the front line. Porter Alexander's guns at Hazel Grove blanketed the whole area. When he sent back for ammunition, General Williams wrote, the reply was "that I must furnish my own ammunition, which, of course, was not possible through that volcano of flame and roar with a mule pack-train." Men scavenged the cartridge boxes of the dead and wounded, friends and foes alike, and intrepid ordnance officers managed to push some supplies forward, but numerous Federal front-line troops grimly fixed bayonets and waited helplessly for the next attack.

Even more serious, and even more poorly resolved, was the ammunition problem for the Federal artillery. This was a problem with no ready solution, especially at Fairview, due to the lack of any centralized command over the guns. As soon as they ran out of shell and case and solid shot, batteries ceased firing, for they could not fire canister over the heads of their own troops. With central management of the guns — the sort of central management formerly exercised by artillery chief Henry Hunt — batteries lacking ammunition would simply be pulled back and replaced by fresh batteries held in reserve. Certainly in the Potomac army there was no shortage of batteries in reserve. However, there was no one on the scene in authority to make the exchange work.

For example, when Lieutenant Robert Sims's Battery B, New Jersey Light, exhausted its ammunition, Sims withdrew from Fairview on the authority of corps commander Dan Sickles. The other Third Corps batteries being already engaged, no one had the authority to replace Sims's with a battery from another corps. Thus the Fairview gun line was reduced by six pieces. This scene was soon repeated for other batteries. And among the guns in line at Fairview were a number with nothing but canister left in their chests. They could defend themselves against infantry attack, but now they were standing mute in the larger battle.

In striking contrast to the steadily collapsing artillery position at Fairview, the Confederate position at Hazel Grove grew steadily stronger. Colonel Alexander rolled in additional batteries from his reserve at Dowdall's Tavern until he had filled every available gun position. The moment batteries ran low on ammunition they were replaced by others with full chests. Alexander had some 50 guns employed here, with perhaps three dozen firing at any one time.

It would be said, upon reflection, that the volume of fire delivered from Hazel Grove that morning was never exceeded by the Confederate artillery. The best crews were getting off three rounds a minute, a firing pace the equal of the best-trained infantry. The gunners' single disappointment was (as always) the quality of their ammunition. What was described as an "extraordinarily large percentage" of shell and case shot either burst prematurely or failed to burst at all. Nevertheless, it was the weight of this gunnery — and the corresponding weakening of the Federal gunnery — that began gradually but steadily to shift the tide of battle back until it began to run in the South's favor.[24]

*   *

IN THIS third act of the drama the cast was changing. Alpheus Williams's Twelfth Corps brigades that had manned the front line south of the Plank Road so tenaciously were fought out now and out of ammunition, and Williams led them to the rear. The toll in his brigades that had borne the worst of the fighting, Samuel Ross's and Thomas Ruger's, came to over 1,100 men, about one in four. For Tom Ruger, the comparison with that earlier day at Antietam was chilling. The 614 men he had lost today was a higher percentage even than on that terrible field.

"The getting away was worse than the staying," General Williams

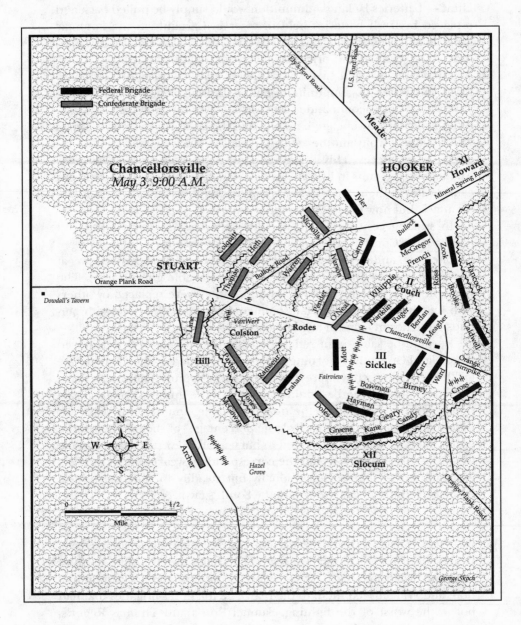

Chancellorsville
May 3, 9:00 A.M.

Federal Brigade
Confederate Brigade

STUART

Orange Plank Road

Dowdall's Tavern

Ely's Ford Road

U.S. Ford Road

V
Meade

HOOKER

XI
Howard

Mineral Spring Road

Tyler

Nicholls

Carroll

Bullock

McGregor

French

Zook

Ross

Hancock

Brooke

Iverson

Warren

Pender

O'Neal

Whipple

II
Couch

Franklin

Ruger

Berdan

Meagher

Caldwell

Colquitt

Heth

Bullock Road

Thomas

VanWert

Colston

Rodes

Chancellorsville

Orange
Turnpike

Lane

Ransseur

Mott

III
Sickles

Carr

Birney

Ward

Cross

Hill

Paxton

Graham

Fairview

Bowman

Jones

McGowan

Doles

Hayman

Geary

Candy

Greene

Kane

XII
Slocum

Archer

Hazel
Grove

N

W   E

S

0   1/2

Mile

Orange Plank Road

George Skoch

wrote. "Our line of retreat was over the ravine, up an exposed slope, and then for three-quarters of a mile over an open plain swept by artillery and infantry. . . . Many a poor fellow lost his life or limb in this fearful transit." Third Corps troops under Dan Sickles were ordered in to take their place. Where should he post his men, one of Sickles's colonels asked. "Fall in here with no reference to regiments, brigades, or divisions," Sickles told him grimly. "You are all my men! We must hold this line if every man of us should fall!"

On the Confederate side, Robert Rodes's division now came up from the third line to press the advance. They would have to do the job, for they were the last troops Stuart had. Alfred Iverson's North Carolinians and Edward O'Neal's Alabamians forced their way through the woods and back to the second line of Federal breastworks north of the Plank Road, where Colonel O'Neal was felled by a shell fragment. South of the road it was George Doles's Georgians and Dodson Ramseur's North Carolinians who took up the fight where Heth's and Colston's divisions had dropped it, at Slocum's log barricade. Jeb Stuart rode up to rally them, jauntily singing his new version of an old song: "Old Joe Hooker, won't you get out of the Wilderness!"[25]

"The aim was to dislodge the enemy from a very strong breastwork made of felled trees," Captain William Calder of the 2nd North Carolina, Ramseur's brigade, wrote his wife the next day. First Jones's brigade had tried it, he explained, "but were driven back. Then the Old Stonewall Brigade moved up with the like result. Now came our turn. . . ."

For Stephen Dodson Ramseur, a brigadier general at twenty-five, Chancellorsville was his first test in brigade command, and he was ambitious to succeed. When he came up behind Jones's Virginia brigade, which was under its third commander in twenty-four hours and freshly battered in the recent attack, he found the Virginians reluctant to renew the fight. Ramseur volunteered to Stuart to lead them if they would move and to march over them if they would not. He issued his orders and reported, "They did not move." To his brigade he called out, "Forward boys, walk right over them!" and the Tarheels pushed through the Virginians and over the log barricade and onto the shot-torn field in front. Pugnacious Bryan Grimes, commanding the 4th North Carolina, was disgusted with the scene. "I, myself, put my foot on the back and head of an officer of high rank, in mounting the work, and, through very spite, ground his face in the earth."

The replacement for Ruger's brigade at the breastworks here was Charles Graham's brigade of Pennsylvanians that had served earlier as rear guard during the evacuation of Hazel Grove. There was a savage and prolonged struggle at the breastworks. Ramseur drove his men at the double-quick, shortening the time they were exposed to the Federal artillery from Fairview; once they closed with the Yankee infantry the guns could no longer fire at them. "At the breastworks," Colonel Frank Parker of the 30th North Carolina told his wife, "the enemy would be lying on one side, and our men on the other; some dead, some dying, others badly wounded." Parker recorded two of his color bearers down wounded; the third survived narrowly, with "a hole put through the top of his hat."

At last the Federals' fire seemed to slacken somewhat and then, according to Captain Calder, "our men charged with a yell, driving them pell-mell from their breastworks." The Yankees' cartridge boxes were empty and there was no support in sight, and there was nothing for it but retreat. The Stonewall Brigade now came up on the right, securing that flank, and with that the Rebels had a firm lodgment that directly threatened the position at Fairview. Ramseur's brigade fell back to recuperate and resupply with ammunition. Jeb Stuart was there, waving his plumed hat and crying, "Three cheers for Ramseur's brigade!"

The cost of the victory here was very high. His thinned ranks left Dodson Ramseur distraught. "Is this all that is left of the Second?" he asked. "This is all, Sir," came the reply. The 2nd North Carolina had lost 259 dead, wounded, and missing, its Colonel William R. Cox had "five or six" wounds, and the regimental colors were lost when the entire color guard was struck down. In Company A, Lieutenant William Norman discovered, he and a private were the only survivors. The 4th North Carolina also had lost its flag, and 260 of the 327 men it took into battle, a casualty rate of just under 80 percent. Ramseur's brigade as a whole lost 788 of 1,509, over half its strength. (Their principal foe, Graham's Pennsylvanians, had only slightly fewer total casualties, 756.)[26]

Ramseur's fearfully bloody assault held the promise of being decisive. The iron ring Hooker had thrown around his army at Chancellorsville was broken now, and might be irreparable. The artillery at Fairview, threatened on the flanks by infantry, began pulling back to form a new gun line in the Chancellorsville clearing. Dan Sickles was in the midst of the tumult, walking about and smoking a cigar and smiling confidently. Colonel Trobriand, 38th New York, watched him: "'Everything is going well,' said he, in a loud voice, intending to be heard." But Sickles knew otherwise, and sent his aide Major Henry Tremain hurrying to the Chancellor house with an appeal for immediate support to mend the breach.

The Chancellor house, facing south, had a two-story porch supported by wooden pillars across much of its front. From prisoners Porter Alexander had learned it was Hooker's headquarters, and took it under fire with his rifled pieces. Already it had been hit several times.

General Hooker was on the porch near the front entrance, standing beside one of the pillars and observing the battle. Major Tremain rode up with Sickles's dispatch and was in the act of handing it to the general when a Confederate solid shot struck squarely against the pillar next to him.

He had his hand propped against the column at the time, Hooker would later write, "but as near as I can recollect was two or three paces from it." The shot split the heavy column lengthwise and hurled half of it "violently against me . . . which struck me in an erect position from my head to my feet." He crashed to the porch floor and lay inert. Major Tremain would write home saying he was somehow unhurt but had seen the commanding general "picked up for dead." Quickly word spread among the troops that Fighting Joe Hooker had been killed.[27]

13

Cavalcade of Triumph

A T THE MOMENT General Hooker was struck down, the battle of May 3 was beginning to tilt again in the Confederates' favor. Yet the outcome remained very much in the balance. Hooker had met earlier crises that morning by throwing in reinforcements at the threatened points; no doubt he would have responded to Sickles's call the same way. He had Second Corps brigades immediately at hand for that purpose. There were also the First and Fifth corps in reserve, although up to this time he had not issued orders for either one. Presumably he intended (as he had told Gouverneur Warren earlier) to strike the Confederates' exposed left flank at the appropriate moment with one or both of these corps. Despite his error in abandoning Hazel Grove and despite the mishandling of the artillery, in the blast and heat of this battlefield the commanding general was in every respect the Fighting Joe Hooker of earlier fields.

Sickles's call for help went unanswered. Hooker lay insensible from his injury for half an hour or more. For a time his medical director, Jonathan Letterman, doubted he would revive, but finally he regained consciousness. Hooker would later describe the entire right side of his body as "livid" from the blow of the shattered column, but it appears that the most serious consequence was a severe concussion. "The blow which the General received seems to have knocked all the sense out of him," Captain William Candler of his staff wrote home. "For the remainder of the day he was wandering, and was unable to get any ideas into his head. . . ."

As soon as he was conscious, Hooker attempted to mount his horse and show himself and reassure the troops, but soon he felt faint and had to be helped to dismount. He vomited and collapsed, and was laid on a blanket and given brandy as a stimulant by Dr. Letterman. After a time he recovered sufficiently to be carried to a safer place in the rear. Moments after he was helped away, a Rebel shell struck the blanket where he had lain. According to the First Corps' General Abner Doubleday, the commanding general "suffered great pain and was in a comatose condition for most of the time. His mind was not clear, and they had to wake him up to communicate with him."[1]

A commanding officer wounded or otherwise incapacitated on the battlefield was duty-bound to turn over command to the next-senior man. (Stonewall Jackson and A. P. Hill had both demonstrated that military convention the night before.) If not able to pass on the command — as Hooker was not able for at least half an hour after his injury — the head of staff was to call promptly for the second-in-command. Darius Couch, Second Corps commander and senior major general on the field, was indeed summoned, but only as an afterthought.

With Chief of Staff Butterfield in Falmouth, the staff at the Chancellor house was headed by Brigadier General James H. Van Alen. Political general Van Alen, a wealthy Republican businessman from New York, quite without military training or experience, had been inserted into Hooker's staff on General Halleck's order just ten days before. In this crisis he was neither as prepared nor as quick-witted as might be.

Hooker's injury occurred at 9 o'clock or a little after, and Couch was close by, but by the time he was called for, it was after 9:30 and he found the commanding general mounted and seemingly recovered. "Briefly congratulating him on his escape — it was no time to blubber or use soft expressions — I went about my own business," Couch recalled.

Hooker collapsed shortly after Couch left, but after a time recovered at least enough to be taken from the battlefield. The difficulty was calculating the extent of his head injury. Had he been wounded by a bullet or a shell fragment, a diagnosis could quickly follow and a decision taken about the command. But the nature and seriousness of his head injury was not so clear. General Van Alen, lacking the standing of chief of staff and not strong-willed to begin with, shied from making a judgment in the case. Dr. Letterman said only that the effects of the blow "lasted for some hours," and did not — or could not — judge the general as disabled for exercising command. Hooker apparently now seemed rational in speech; indeed it was he who finally roused himself enough to call Couch to his side again. But it was 10 o'clock by then, and for an hour — the most critical hour of the battle — the Army of the Potomac was without a head. Headquarters had been struck mute.[2]

*　*

THE ATTACK of Dodson Ramseur's North Carolina brigade, just before Hooker's injury, opened a breach in the Federal line that soon was widened. This exposed the flank of John Geary's Twelfth Corps division holding the south face of the line. George Doles's Georgians pushed into the breach and got in behind Geary and for a time directly threatened the Fairview batteries. "We had to go up to them in an open field . . . ," the 21st Georgia's Thomas Hightower wrote home, "and they threw grape, canister bombs, balls and nearly everything else. We had to fall back under the cover of a hill."

Although Doles's attack was blunted, he nonetheless kept pressure on Geary's position. Now Dick Anderson's troops were pushing forward as well, on General Lee's order, and Geary was under fire from both flank and front. They were shelled from Hazel Grove "like the very devil," wrote James Miller of the 111th Pennsylvania, "and then we had nothing to do but lay still and take it." That was always the hardest part in a battle, he added, "to lay still and be shelled."

Lacking any directions from the now silent headquarters, there was soon great confusion on Geary's front. To General Couch on his left Geary pleaded, "My division can't hold its place; what shall I do?" Couch could only reply, "I don't know, but do as we are doing; fight it out." The task was not made easier when General Geary lost his voice trying to shout over the din and had to turn over command to General George Sears Greene. What was so disconcerting to the Yankees here was that fire seemed to be aimed at them from all angles. There seemed nowhere safe.

Nathaniel Parmeter of the 29th Ohio, in Charles Candy's brigade, recorded in his diary the enemy trying to flank them out of their rifle pits: "Candies Brig. charged them back, they again rallied and charged us back, this was repeated several times but as they were gaining ground on the right, we had to fall back and form a new line, it was by quick time. . . ."

There became almost a pattern to it. G. H. Tarr of the 20th Connecticut explained that the Rebels would charge them, they would fight them off, and then when the two lines separated the Rebel artillery would pound them. "They poured the shells over into us in perfect showers." Then the sequence was repeated. That was when Tarr's comrade John Root was killed. "A shell burst just in the rear of him and threw him up in to the air tearing one side of him all away. He lived but a very few moments in great agony. May he meet a better fate in the world to come."

To William Aughinbaugh of the 5th Ohio, "it appeared as though we were completely surrounded, the enemy's missiles coming from every direction." First came orders to withdraw, then orders to retake their old position, then orders to withdraw. At that, "our men could have been seen running with all their might to the rear." In the woods Private Aughinbaugh so completely lost direction that he walked right into the enemy's lines. Summing up the whole experience in his journal, "I come to the conclusion that it was badly managed on our side."

One of Hooker's last orders before he was hurt had been to Geary to hold his position at all hazards, and now all hazards were here. The position was becoming as much of a salient as Hazel Grove had been, and the enveloping pressure was unbearable. Slocum finally ordered the division in. If the order was not quite executed "in a soldierly and masterly manner" (as General Geary claimed), there was staunch enough fighting before they decamped to cost the division some 1,100 casualties.

Geary's three brigades fell back north by east, passing around behind the Fairview batteries and toward Chancellorsville. The rear guard, 60th and 102nd New York, got into a terrific scrap with Doles's pursuing Georgians. The color guards of the 12th Georgia and the 102nd New York jousted personally, officers jabbing with swords, men swinging fists and rifle butts. The New Yorkers had the better of it and made off with the Rebels' battle flag, but in retreat that was their only comfort.[3]

The western face of the Federal line was meanwhile being tightly compressed as well. Sickles's Third Corps brigades took over for Williams's exhausted Twelfth Corps ones, but no actual reinforcement was directed there from the Chancellor house. Jeb Stuart's third (and last) line, Rodes's division, kept pressing forward, driving the Yankees away from their line of breastworks, forcing them to fight without this shelter. The prize for the winner would be Fairview.

There were hot little fights in every smoky clearing. Lieutenant James Mitchell of the 84th New York, Samuel Bowman's brigade, reported his regiment receiving a heavy fire from the woods on its left at the same time a force of Georgians charged them in front. Then "we received fire in the rear and discovered the rebels pouring over the knoll behind us, which we supposed was occupied by our men." Lines of battle evaporated; "here a squad of rebels could be seen, taking off some of our men, and not five rods off a few of our soldiers would be walking off with some captured rebels." In the shifting fortunes of this miniature war Lieutenant Mitchell and his small squad were captors, then captives, three times "before the rebels had undisputed possession of us." The struggle cost the 84th New York 55 percent of its men, two thirds of them as prisoners. Robert C. Lamberton of Company G would note in his diary, "A great many of our boys missing, only 5 present."

The 12th New Hampshire somehow became separated from the rest of Bowman's brigade in this fight and engaged in its own private war entirely alone. It blocked Doles's path to Fairview long enough and stubbornly enough to suffer 317 casualties, the greatest number in any regiment at Chancellorsville, North or South. Furthermore, fully 80 percent of this total were the New Hampshiremen's dead and wounded, giving credence to the oft-used claim that this or that regiment "retired from the field slowly and in good order." Having given as good as it got, the 12th New Hampshire was allowed to retire unmolested. "But the terrible experience of the last hour and a half," the regiment's chronicler wrote, "has taught them a lesson that each one is now practicing; for every man has his tree behind which he is fighting."[4]

Men would come away from this maelstrom of sound and smoke and rushing movement with vivid memories of narrow escapes. Colonel George Cobham of the 111th Pennsylvania could say he owed his life to the paymaster. A bullet caught him squarely in the chest and knocked him off his horse, but he was saved by a thick wad of greenbacks in his breast pocket, money he was carrying for his men to deliver home on a scheduled furlough. Colonel Henry Madill of the 141st Pennsylvania, his horse killed under him, picked himself up and counted seven harmless bullet holes in his coat. Georgian A. B. Barron assured his wife, "Nancy I did not get my skin toch with nary ball but one cut my hat brim and one struck my haver sack." Another Georgian, Micajah D. Martin, described a Yankee shell tearing off his haversack and carrying it "at least forty feet behind me, while my biscuits, bacon and sugar were scattered about promiscuously." Several comrades, he added, were hit by the flying biscuits and thought they had been wounded. The next day Corporal William Howell of the 124th New York wrote home, "I had a ball past through my canteen one through my pail three or four holes through my coattail one through the seat of my trousers but nary scratch."

Jeb Stuart had an escape that was unique. He was riding along close behind his advancing battle line when it was taken under fire from a wood on the left. That wood, Stuart thought, was held by his own men, and he spurred his horse straight at them and commanded "in a most peremptory manner" that they cease firing. That carried him close enough, however, to see that these troops were in blue, not butternut, but obediently they had lowered their rifles. What saved him was the blue officer's coat he was wearing that morning, and his ringing voice of authority. The charade ended when he wheeled abruptly and galloped hard for his own line. "Though hundreds of rifles were fired at him," a bystander reported, "he escaped unharmed."

Porter Alexander would remember May 3 for "the narrowest escape of my life from a shell taking my head clean off my shoulders." An artillery shell, he explained, "can only be seen if the eye is almost exactly in the line of its flight. I saw this plainly come out of the bushes within ten feet & it seemed to pass my ear within two inches."

Letter writers groping for the right image for the intense fighting wrote of hailstorms of bullets, of "bullets that fell like rain drops in a summer shower." Ohio Private Aughinbaugh reported, "men who had been at Antietam say that the roar of cannon there was not louder." Massachusetts Sergeant Charles Ward added, "such musketry was never heard by any of the old Peninsular men, they said."

The concentrated artillery fire was taking an unusually high toll in this battle. In his notes on the day's fighting, Colonel Regis de Trobriand of the 38th New York reported a caisson blown up by a Rebel shell; a gunner from the battery, terribly burned by the explosion, "runs shrieking towards the ambulances." Soon afterward he witnessed a lieutenant in the 3rd Maine cut in two by a bursting shell, "legs thrown to one side, the trunk to another." Brigadier Jim Lane of A. P. Hill's division came on a section of the battlefield pounded by the guns of first one side and then the other, "a ghastly & sickening sight. . . . Brave men were laying everywhere, . . . some with the backs of their heads blown off, others with their faces gone & still others with no heads at all." Federal surgeon John Shaw Billings, treating wounded at the Chancellor house, noted in his report, "At this place, the most extensive shell wounds that I have ever seen came under my notice. . . ."[5]

Stuart's pressure was unrelenting, especially after his attack was reinforced by Dick Anderson's brigades on the southern front. On the extreme left, north of the Plank Road, Stuart carried the battle forward with the Louisiana brigade of Colston's division, now under Colonel Jesse M. Williams. These Louisianians endured an especially brutal firefight in the woods. The 10th Louisiana would count six color bearers shot down that day, and the 1st Louisiana lost its flag. William Clegg of the 2nd Louisiana wrote home afterward that the battle had given him a new idea of destiny. He had made up his mind in advance that he would not survive, "and cared less about it than ever before," although he admitted, "I almost prayed to get a flesh wound at least. No such good luck for me." Good luck was simply surviving. Sergeant Clegg reported his regiment "numbering at the time about 175 guns." It lost in the fight 126 men, or almost three out of four. Just in time the reeling Louisiana brigade was reinforced by Alfred Colquitt's brigade from Rodes's third line. These Georgians were the last of Stuart's uncommitted reserves.

George Meade had been watching all this from his Fifth Corps line along the Ely's Ford Road to the north, and when General French sent back for help, Meade took it upon himself to send it. His nearest brigade was Erastus Tyler's, of Humphreys's division. Of Tyler's four Pennsylvania regiments, three were made up of nine-months' men due to be mustered out within the next two to three weeks. In spite of the generals' misgivings about them, the short-termers stood and fought well enough to create a standoff on this part of the field. Their 240 casualties included two regimental commanders wounded.[6]

In the center, in the area of the Orange Plank Road, there was a desperate scrambling fight for the clearing in front of the Fairview batteries. Officers on both sides patched together whatever forces they could lay their hands on. The attack was pressed by Ramseur's North Carolinians and O'Neal's Alabamians of the third line going in alongside fragments of Pender's North Carolinians and Brockenbrough's Virginians and Thomas's Georgians of the first line. The defenses were equally patchwork. There were troops here from Mott's and Carr's Third Corps brigades, supported at the last minute by a pair of regiments from Ross's Twelfth Corps brigade.

During the night the Fairview gunners, assisted by the army's pioneers, had dug in their guns behind earthen traverses along the gun line straddling the Plank Road. Not all the additional batteries run in at the start of the morning's fight had this protection, however. Those on the left or southern flank did not, and they were hardly a thousand yards from Porter Alexander's Rebel batteries at Hazel Grove.

That morning the six Napoleons of Lieutenant Francis Seeley of Battery K, 4th United States, were positioned on the far left by General Hooker himself, and Seeley would take one of the severest beatings of any Federal battery in any battle of the war. Forty-five of his 120 gunners were casualties, and 59 of his battery horses were killed or disabled that day. When finally he found the battery on his right gone, and his infantry supports gone, and the enemy "crowding in on both flanks," Seeley reported, "I limbered up my guns and moved off at a trot. . . ." If that were not enough, in due course he would learn that he was not done for the day.

Nearby were the six Parrott rifles of Battery F, Pennsylvania Light. Midway in the fight Alexander's barrage hit one of the Pennsylvanians' caissons and the explosion mortally wounded the battery commander, Captain Robert B. Hampton. Soon afterward Lieutenant Franklin B. Crosby, commanding Battery F, 4th United States, was killed by a sharpshooter's bullet through the heart. By day's end, of the eight battery commanders in this Fairview gun line, three would be dead and one a prisoner. One hundred fifty of their men would be casualties.

The fire of the Fairview batteries now began to drop off markedly. For lack of ammunition two batteries had already pulled out of line, reducing the count of guns there to thirty. There were no replacements. North of the Plank Road, Rodes's Alabamians and some of the 23rd North Caro-

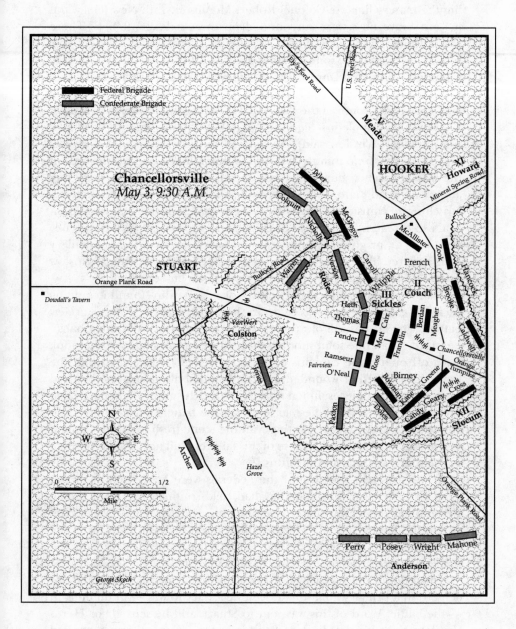

Chancellorsville
May 3, 9:30 A.M.

Federal Brigade
Confederate Brigade

Ely's Ford Road
U.S. Ford Road

V
Meade

HOOKER

XI
Howard

Mineral Spring Road

Tyler

Colquitt

McGregor

Nicholls

Bullock

McAllister

STUART

Bullock Road

Warren

Iverson

Rodes

Carroll

Whipple

French

Zook

Hancock

II
Couch

Brooke

Caldwell

Orange Plank Road

Dowdall's Tavern

Heth

Thomas

III
Sickles

Mott Carr

Berdan

Meagher

VanWert

Colston

Pender

Franklin

Chancellorsville

Ross

Jones

Ramseur

O'Neal

Fairview

Birney

Bowman

Kane

Greene

Cross

Orange Turnpike

N
W E
S

Paxton

Doles

Candy

Geary

XII
Slocum

Archer

Hazel
Grove

0   1/2
Mile

Orange Plank Road

Perry   Posey   Wright   Mahone

Anderson

George Skoch

lina they had picked up on the way drove off the Yankee infantry guarding the battery line. As Colonel Robert McAllister, 11th New Jersey, put it, "our brave boys were surrounded on three sides by Rebels. There was nothing left for us to do but to retreat, and we did. . . ." The 11th's retreat uncovered the four remaining guns in the battery of the mortally wounded Lieutenant Dimick. Quickly they were hauled to the rear.

This in turn uncovered Lieutenant George Winslow's Battery D, 1st New York Light, south of the Plank Road. The assault funneled in against Winslow's six Napoleons. Sighting the Rebels still in column ("in almost solid masses," Winslow said), he opened on them with solid shot. Deployed now, with no infantry to oppose them, they came trotting out of the woods barely a hundred yards ahead, defiantly planting their flag along the road "and commenced picking off my men and horses." Switching to canister, Winslow blew them back, but then they came on again to threaten both flanks as the batteries to his left withdrew. They were only 25 or 30 yards from his right-hand section when his artillery chief ordered him back. "I limbered from the left successively," Winslow wrote, "continuing to fire until my last piece was limbered."

Captain Charles F. Morse, Twelfth Corps staff, who "found I could be useful to Captain Best," was there in these last minutes of the Fairview battle. "The air was full of missiles, solid shot, shells, and musket balls," he wrote. "I saw one solid shot kill three horses and a man, another took a leg off one of the captains of the batteries. . . . More than half the horses were killed or wounded; one caisson had blown up, another had been knocked to pieces; in ten minutes more, the guns would have been isolated." But somehow, he marveled, all the batteries were gotten off, and without losing a gun. Writing with the scene fresh in mind, Captain Morse had no doubt of the cause of this failure: "Still not an infantry man was sent to the support of the guns."[7]

It was 10 o'clock now, and the Federals were being rapidly driven from virtually every position they had held south of the Plank Road. General Lee, watching these developments, rode over to Hazel Grove and found James Archer's brigade still in the position it had won in the first minutes of the fight. Seeing Fairview as the critical site on the battlefield, Lee ordered in Archer to help seize it.

In so doing the two wings of Lee's divided army were reunited. To achieve that primary goal it had been necessary to win — or all but win — the battle. Word of this was sent to Stuart, and he sent Major Heros Von Borcke of his staff back to Lee for orders. "General Lee expressed himself much satisfied with our operations," Von Borcke wrote, "and intrusted me with orders for Stuart, directing a general attack with his whole force, which was to be supported by a charge of Anderson's division on the left flank of the enemy."[8]

* *

AT FIRST light that morning the lead division of the Sixth Corps had marched through Fredericksburg's empty streets and pulled up in front of Marye's Heights. Glimpsed through the drifts and swirls of morning fog, the heights loomed up dark and silent and, for those Federals who remembered the December battle there, decidedly ominous. Beyond lay the road to Chancellorsville.

General Sedgwick ordered John Newton to probe ahead with his division and (in the military vernacular) "feel the enemy." From everything headquarters had been telling them, wrote Major Thomas Hyde of Sedgwick's staff, "it was not supposed that the works were occupied. . . ."

Newton called out four regiments from the head of the column — 62nd New York and 102nd Pennsylvania to be "thrown forward in open order," followed and supported by the 23rd and 93rd Pennsylvania. The two lead regiments, Major Hyde wrote, "moved off toward the hill in line, and they were soon swallowed up in the mist. . . ." They had closed to within twenty paces of a stone wall — *the* Stone Wall of terrible December memory — when without warning there came a Rebel yell and a blast of musketry and artillery virtually in their faces. "As they broke and ran, Gen. Sedgwick crys: 'Will some staff officer rally those men!'" Dutifully Major Hyde and Lieutenant Colonel Ford Kent "started at full gallop, fired at by the whole line, and succeeded in getting them into shape again by using our sabres freely."

General Sedgwick was "Uncle John" to everyone in the Potomac army, a large, slow-moving, comfortable sort of man who looked out for his troops and who shared the dangers of the battlefield with them. Today he was as usual right at the head of the column. He wore a red flannel shirt under his general's coat and an old slouch hat, and he tugged the brim of his hat low over his eyes and pondered the situation in front of him at length. The Confederate gunners were improving their aim with each shot, and finally Uncle John's staff persuaded him to turn back from his exposed position.[9]

The sun burned away the obscuring fog and it was soon apparent to Federal observers on both sides of the river that the heights behind Fredericksburg for their full length were manned by the enemy. In what force was not certain, but obviously it was greater than what the commanding general had been saying. The sharp response to the reconnaissance at Marye's Heights made it equally obvious that they would have a fight on their hands. As Sedgwick later testified, "The force displayed by the enemy was sufficient to show that the intrenchments could not be carried except at great cost." He set about mounting a full-dress attack.

General Warren and Captain Razderichin from Hooker's staff were there to advise Sedgwick on just what the commanding general expected of him. Not only was he to come up in the rear of Lee at Chancellorsville as quickly as possible, but he was to do so in a way that did not unite the Confederate forces at Fredericksburg with those at Chancellorsville. This severely limited Sedgwick's options. If he should attempt to turn the position on the left, below Fredericksburg, even if successful he would only drive Early's forces ahead of him to join with the rest of the army under Lee. That, Razderichin explained, "could not be what Gen. Hooker desired." The point of attack must therefore be on the right — against Marye's Heights or farther to the north — so as to break through between Early and Lee and prevent them from uniting.

His Antietam wounds had kept John Sedgwick from the fighting at Fredericksburg in December, but there were numerous witnesses to remind him of how much respect was due the Confederates' position on Marye's Heights. That respect added to the position's defensive strength. On December 13 Burnside had lost more than 6,000 men in front of the Stone Wall, and Uncle John Sedgwick swore he would avoid anything like that. His first thought was to turn the position on either or both flanks. Whatever weakness Marye's Heights had as a defensive posting was on its flanks, for it was by its topography a salient.

Marye's Heights is a ridgeline some 130 feet high and half a mile long north to south. Its southern end projects out some 800 yards ahead of the next high ground, Lee's Hill. Between these two heights is the valley of Hazel Run. At the northern end of the ridge the salient effect is less pronounced, but still it was susceptible to being flanked there. Running across the ridgeline to the north was Fredericksburg's Hanover Street and then the Orange Plank Road. To the south, the Telegraph Road from Richmond followed the valley of Hazel Run, then curved around and across the front of Marye's Heights; the road here, at the base of the heights, was fronted by the infamous Stone Wall. In the December battle Marye's Heights was well manned and its flanks well secured by artillery. On the morning of May 3 there were far fewer defenders and guns, although they were braced by the recollections of December.

One of those who defended Marye's Heights that day, Colonel Benjamin G. Humphreys, 21st Mississippi, reported an additional weakness of the position. At every other point in front of the Confederates' six-mile Fredericksburg line, he said, the Yankees could advance under cover no closer than 1,000 yards to form up for an assault. In front of the

Stone Wall, however, they could form up safely at 450 yards, and in front of the southern end of the salient, at 600 yards. Because of this, and because of the undermanned state of the defenses, Colonel Humphreys described matters that Sunday morning as "perilous."[10]

Not knowing Sedgwick's actual purpose in crossing his full corps to the Fredericksburg shore, Jubal Early assumed his division must be the Yankees' target. He was most vulnerable, he thought, to the south, toward Hamilton's Crossing, and he massed half his infantry there and a third of his guns. In the Lee's Hill sector at the center were a Louisiana regiment of Early's and two of William Barksdale's Mississippi regiments from McLaws's division. Defending Marye's Heights were the other two of Barksdale's Mississippi regiments. Moving to cover the northern flank were Early's remaining four Louisiana regiments, with support from Cadmus Wilcox's brigade from Dick Anderson's division. That morning Wilcox had determined to march from his posting at Banks's Ford to reinforce General Lee when he learned the Federals were in Fredericksburg. He promptly marched to the sound of the nearest guns.

To defend his six-mile front, then, Jubal Early had (with Wilcox) some 12,700 infantry and 46 guns. To defend the Marye's Heights sector there were perhaps 1,200 infantry and just 8 guns. In the December battle there had been considerably more infantry massed here, along with a substantial reserve, and twice the number of guns. General William Pendleton, in charge of the artillery guarding Early's left, seemed oblivious of any real danger here, and after the aborted withdrawal the day before he did not restore an adequate artillery defense to this sector. For his part, Early did not take the Federals' dawn thrust at Marye's Heights as a serious effort to seize the Plank Road route to Chancellorsville. Instead he dismissed it as a feint and continued to focus on his right. Like Pendleton, Old Jube did not believe the Yankees were foolish enough to repeat their December blunder of assaulting the Stone Wall.

When the 21st Mississippi's Colonel Humphreys pointed out the weakness of the line he was supposed to defend, General Barksdale told him, "Well sir, we must make the fight whether we hold it or are whipped." The general, however, did not let it go at that. He appealed to Early for more infantry and to artillery chief Pendleton for more guns. Neither was forthcoming.

To confront these defenders John Sedgwick set up his Sixth Corps divisions in a somewhat foreshortened opposing line. To the south Bully Brooks remained in about the same position he had been holding in the bridgehead since April 29, between Hamilton's Crossing and Fredericksburg. In the center was Howe's division, and in Fredericksburg were Newton's division and Burnham's brigade-sized Light Division.

When John Gibbon led his two Second Corps brigades across the new pontoon bridge at Fredericksburg after daylight, he was assigned the right or northern flank of the line. The addition of Gibbon's men raised Sedgwick's total to 27,100, with eleven batteries of 66 guns. To dislodge an entrenched enemy it was far from an overwhelming force. In order to better protect his communications, Sedgwick had the engineers move his two bridges from Franklin's Crossing upriver to Fredericksburg, giving the Federals three crossings there.[11]

* *

JOHN GIBBON had been with the Union forces that bloodlessly occupied Fredericksburg during the summer of 1862, and he was appalled by what he saw of the place now. "Fredericksburg is almost a desert," he wrote his wife that night, "some few women & children and old negroes remaining and nearly every house is crumbling into ruins. It is a sad sight." A man in the 93rd New York noted that the streets were "cut up by rifle pits running in every direction," and that every house he saw was more or less damaged. "The destruction of a once beautiful town like this is one of the dark pictures which war often produces," he concluded.

At 7:40 A.M. General Sedgwick sent a dispatch to Dan Butterfield outlining his plan: "I am about making a combined assault on their works, Gibbon on the right Newton the centre Howe on the left. If I fail I shall try again." Demonstrations up and down the line, he hoped, would prevent Early from reinforcing the Marye's Heights sector. Indeed, just then a thrust forward by Bully Brooks would set off a brisk artillery exchange and fix Early's attention toward his right.

Before any actual frontal attack on the Stone Wall, Sedgwick would try to flank the salient. Returning from delivering orders for the movements, Major Hyde found the generals "all in consultation at a beautiful house, where four streets met and where we had one piece of artillery." Since daylight the guns had been fitfully dueling here, and now a Rebel shell from one of the Marye's Heights batteries came spiraling into the group. It killed one gunner and wounded five others, and two artillery horses, Hyde wrote; wounded one of Sedgwick's staff and killed the horse of another; and wounded several men and horses in the headquarters cavalry escort, "not honoring me with a scratch. . . . So much damage could a well-directed spherical case inflict."[12]

Sedgwick and Gibbon initially pinned their hopes on a turning movement against the northern flank of the salient. Gibbon marched his two brigades in column through Fredericksburg and then off to the right where the ground was open and the way seemingly clear. But between them and the enemy line ran a canal and millrace that carried water from the Rappahannock to drive Fredericksburg's mills. The canal was thirty feet wide and too deep for troops to cross, and then it was discovered that the bridge they needed for crossing it had been torn up by the 21st Mississippi's pickets when they evacuated the town. The bridge framing was still standing, but the planking was taken up. The 19th Massachusetts was detailed to replace the bridge floor with siding torn from a nearby house, but the moment the Yankees set to work Rebel artillery took them under fire, wounding nine and driving them off. "They had all the advantage they could wish over us," according to Private Cyril Tyler.

By now it was 9 o'clock and becoming painfully obvious that even if the bridge could be repaired, the troop column would be shot to pieces as it funneled onto the narrow span. While this was being pondered, brigade commander Norman Hall had his men shelter behind a stone wall as the firing continued. "Their artillery opposite of us went to shelling us like the devil & they had a fair rake at us . . . ," Private Tyler wrote. These guns — two posted by Cadmus Wilcox and three by the Washington Artillery — were firing canister "& they bursted just in front of us & the balls just went over us so close they fairly blowed our caps off."

The 20th Massachusetts lay nearby, and Captain Oliver Wendell Holmes, Jr., described the scene for his homefolks: "Pleasant to see a d'd gun brought up to an earthwork deliberately brought to bear on you — to notice that your Co. is exactly in range — 1st discharge puff — second puff (as the shell burst) and my knapsack supporter is knocked to pieces . . . 2nd discharge man in front of me hit — 3rd whang the iron enters through garter & shoe into my heel." The future Supreme Court justice was helped off the field with his third wound of the war.

This same canal had balked the Federals in the December battle, and certainly headquarters knew of its existence from Professor Lowe and other observers. Yet no one in the Sixth Corps, which had been at the other extreme of the line in December, seemed to know anything about it. In any case, this was the first time anyone here had given thought to attacking Marye's Heights; John Sedgwick knew little enough about his role in this campaign as it was. What was needed at that moment was a powerful rank of artillery to protect the canal bridge-builders, but ten of Sedgwick's eleven batteries were posted elsewhere. Only one was available for the immediate support of Gibbon's movement.

Battery G, 1st Rhode Island Light, came up and unlimbered behind Gibbon's infantry to try and suppress the enemy fire. But the Rhode Islanders were on open ground while the Confederate guns were well sheltered and on higher ground, and they had much the better of the duel. These Rebels, wrote Yankee gunner James Barber, were "shooting down at the rate of one man and a horse a minute for 25 minutes nearly disabling us entirely." By the time it pulled back, Battery G had 5 dead and 18 wounded and 22 horses dead or disabled. The only thing that could now be said for John Gibbon's flanking movement was that it was occupying the attention of some number of Rebels opposite.[13]

Any attempt to swing around the salient at its southern end had the distinct disadvantage of exposing the flanking column's flank to enfilading artillery fire from Lee's Hill to the south. Reluctantly General Sedgwick came back to a frontal movement against Marye's Heights, "to carry the works by direct assault." He would combine it with an attack on the left at a narrow enough angle to give some protection from the enfilading fire. Gibbon was to maintain his demonstration on the right as at least a distraction.

Albion Howe contributed a brigade and a half to the southernmost flanking column. The forces for the frontal attack itself would come from Newton's division and Hiram Burnham's five-regiment Light Division, with Burnham supplying most of the first-line troops. The 5th Wisconsin's Thomas S. Allen was told his regiment must man the advanced skirmish line for the assault on the Stone Wall. "I then told Colonel Burnham that I did not 'hanker after' the position assigned me, honorable as it was." But Allen added that so long as his line had the proper support left and right, "we might be successful."

It took some time to shift troops into position and to ensure that everything was coordinated. All the while there was the steady, pounding rumble of gunfire from Chancellorsville ten miles to the west, and men had time (as one of them said) "to imagine how sweet it is to die for one's country. . . ." The stern word came down from the high command: make the charge at the double-quick, bayonets fixed, rifles uncapped so there would be no temptation to stop and return fire and break the momentum. This regulation to uncap rifles was winked at by some of the more sensible field officers, who simply told the men "on their honor" not to fire until the Stone Wall was reached. Colonel Burnham rode to where his troops were waiting and called out cheerfully, "Boys, I have got a government contract." What is it, they wanted to know. "One thousand rebels, potted and salted, and got to have 'em in less than five minutes. Forward! Guide center!"[14]

* *

IT WAS just after 10 o'clock, as Stuart's men and Lee's were smashing their way into Fairview, when John Sedgwick sent off a dispatch announcing "three strong columns of attack" were then starting forward against Marye's Heights. "I have good prospects of success."

Sedgwick's optimism stemmed from a fresh look at the enemy he was facing. The early morning reconnaissance had left several dozen Federal wounded right in front of the Stone Wall. Troops were always thought to be reluctant to charge over their own dead and wounded, so a front-line officer — probably one of Burnham's — had sent forward a flag of truce with a request to retrieve the wounded men. Colonel Thomas Griffin, commanding the 18th Mississippi posted behind the Stone Wall, incautiously agreed. As the Yankees carried off their wounded they took a good look at the thin rank of defenders in front of them. General Barksdale would feel it necessary to point out, in his report, "that Colo-nel Griffin, who is a brave and gallant officer, granted this flag of truce without consulting me."

The right-hand storming column coming straight out of Fredericks-burg on the Orange Plank Road was the signal for the general advance. Leading was the Light Division's 61st Pennsylvania, followed closely by the 43rd New York. The men were in columns of fours in light marching order, without knapsacks and haversacks. Waiting in support were two of Newton's regiments, 67th New York and 82nd Pennsylvania. The head of the column crossed a little bridge over the millrace and went to the double-quick, and then the Rebel guns opened on them.

This barrage — one piece of the Washington Artillery firing straight down the Plank Road and two others firing from off to the right — was deadly. The 61st's Colonel George C. Spear was killed instantly. His loss threw the Pennsylvanians into confusion, and they and the New Yorkers coming up behind them were checked by the sweeping hail of shell and canister.

The center column, charging out of Fredericksburg along Hanover Street, contained two of Newton's regiments, 7th Massachusetts and 36th New York. They were sheltered here by a dip in the ground until they came within rifle range of the Stone Wall. The 21st Mississippi's Colonel Humphreys watched from the heights as the Yankees "seemed to rise out of the earth, and rushed forward with demoniac shouts and yells." As they charged, their supporting batteries had to raise their aim from the wall to the redoubts above.

Behind the wall the 18th Mississippi, along with three companies of the 21st, opened a blast of musketry. The front rank of the 7th Massachu-setts was knocked to pieces, "the men dropping like leaves in autumn," as one of Sedgwick's aides put it. Colonel Thomas D. Johns went down with a wound, and of the 400 men in his regiment who made the charge, 22 were killed and 124 wounded. The center column, like the right column, was stymied. Gibbon's men off to the north were watching all this, and one of them wrote that just then "we gave up hope, the rebels on the

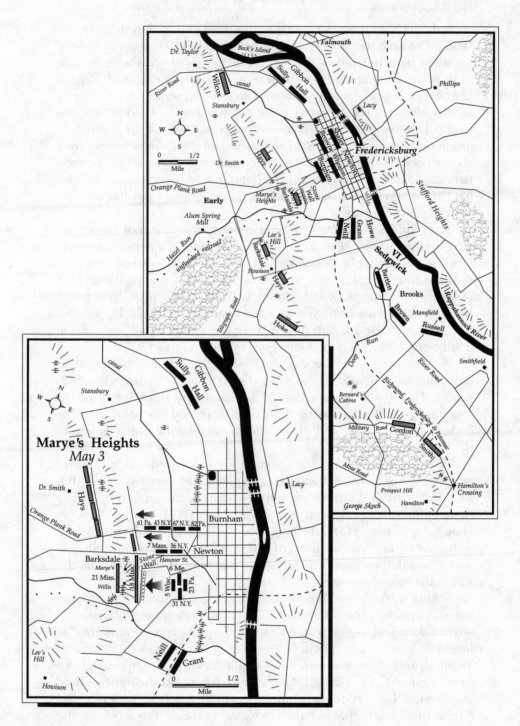

Dr. Taylor
Beck's Island
Falmouth
River Road
Wilcox
canal
Sully
Gibbon
Hall
Phillips
Stansbury
Lacy
N
W   E
S
0   1/2
Mile
Dr. Smith
Slater
Browne
Wheaton
Newton
Burnham
Fredericksburg
Hays
Stafford Heights
Orange Plank Road
Early
Marye's
Heights
Barksdale
Stone
Wall
Alum Spring
Mill
Neill
Grant
Howe
VI
Lee's
Hill
Barksdale
Sedgwick
Howison
Bartlett
Hazel Run
Hays
Brooks
unfinished railroad
Brown
Mansfield
Russell
Hoke
Telegraph Road
Deep Run
Smithfield
River Road
Richmond, Fredericksburg & Potomac
Rappahannock River
Bernard's
Cabins
Military   Road   Gordon
Smith
Mine Road
George Skoch
Prospect Hill
Hamilton
Hamilton's
Crossing

Marye's Heights
May 3

canal
Sully
Gibbon
Hall
Stansbury
N
W   E
S
Dr. Smith
Hays
Lacy
Orange Plank Road
61 Pa. 43 N.Y. 67 N.Y. 82 Pa.
Burnham
7 Mass. 36 N.Y.
Newton
Barksdale
Stone
Wall
Marye's
Hanover St.
21 Miss.
6 Me.
Willis
5 Wisc.
23 Pa.
18 Miss.
31 N.Y.
Lee's
Hill
Neill
Grant
Howison
0   1/2
Mile

other hand cheering all along the line & taunting us with numerous derisive questions. . . ."[15]

To the left of these two columns of attack and directly in front of the longest stretch of the Stone Wall, the rest of Burnham's Light Division was already deployed in line of battle. Shaken out in skirmish formation in front was the 5th Wisconsin, backed by the 31st New York and 6th Maine side by side. Coming up as a third line in support was the 23rd Pennsylvania, whose Colonel John Ely volunteered them for the duty. As the other storming parties came into view and engaged, it became their turn.

"Boys, you see those Heights," Colonel Allen told the 5th Wisconsin. "You have got to take them. You think you cannot do it, but you can and you will. When the signal 'Forward' is given, you will start at double-quick — you will not fire a gun — and you will not stop until you get the order to halt. You will never get that order." When the charge was sounded, Allen's men sprang forward with a yell. Thirty paces behind them, wrote Sergeant Benjamin Thaxter of the 6th Maine, "We all came to our feet with a tiger and soon caught up with the skirmishers."

For its entire length the Stone Wall was wreathed in smoke sparked with hundreds of muzzle flashes. In their redoubts on Marye's Heights above, the cannon boomed out with new fury. "The alternate charge and retreat of several lines of battle were plainly visible," wrote a watching Louisianian, "while the opposing shouts and cheers of the combatants . . . revealed the changing results of the battle. The whole scene lay like a panorama. . . ."

But the Confederates here were being relentlessly pressed from too many directions. The southernmost companies of the 18th Mississippi behind the wall had to contend with a brigade of Vermonters from Howe's division now beginning their advance. Above them, Lieutenant Thompson Brown's section of Parrott rifles from Parker's Richmond Battery also turned to defend the threatened southern flank of the salient. On the opposite flank, at the Plank Road and Hanover Street, the Mississippi riflemen at the wall and the guns behind them were occupied fighting off the other two Yankee storming columns. Left to face this new charge were eight companies of the 18th Mississippi behind the wall, and on the heights above infantry of the 21st Mississippi and three guns of the Washington Artillery. One of the gunners would write home that in those minutes he was "under a terrific fire which caused me often to think that my last days had come. . . ."

The Wisconsin men and the Maine men and the New Yorkers were rushing close to the Stone Wall now, those who were left on their feet. Albert Foster of the 5th Wisconsin would write his wife thanking Providence for his life. "The five next to me on the left fell in a space less than 10 ft. square, all killed but one," he told her, and added that the fifth man was wounded mortally. As they came up to the wall the enemy fire slackened abruptly, and men in butternut were seen scrambling up the slope back of the Telegraph Road to the works above. The Rebel artillerists could not depress their pieces enough to hit the attackers now.

Then Yankees in scores were vaulting the wall and stabbing at the remaining defenders with their bayoneted rifles. In these swirls of hand-to-hand combat Private George Brown of the 6th Maine was seen to bayonet two of the Mississippians and kill a third with his rifle butt. And in the turmoil it was said that men were killed in the act of surrendering. It was said, too, that numbers of the attackers had found their courage in a bottle, but a man who made the charge denied it. "Is there any intoxication like the joy of victory?" he asked. Of the 68 men of the 18th Mississippi killed or wounded in this struggle, most fell in these final moments. Colonel Thomas Griffin was among the 226 who surrendered.[16]

"Up went the stormers," wrote Frank Haskell of Gibbon's staff. "The rebel rifle pits flashed and puffed their smoke along the crests . . . but Sedgwick's men could not be stopped, they were for blood." Up the short and steep slope to Marye's Heights they raced. With the line at the Stone Wall broken, Federal parties to the left and right also stormed forward to finish the battle. Color Sergeant John Gray of the 6th Maine was first to plant the colors on the Heights, igniting great bursts of cheering from Sedgwick's men back in Fredericksburg.

The proud Washington Artillery of New Orleans, tracing its lineage back to 1838, had fought in the Mexican War and won renown on many battlefields of this war. Now it was about to be overwhelmed. There were Yankees from half a dozen regiments on the Heights now, with more coming, and they swarmed toward the guns in their redoubts. The gun crews worked to the end. One crew was shot down or taken trying to get off a last shot. "The rammer was left in the gun," wrote one of the captors. ". . . I must say that their artillery men was gritty." Captain Charles Squires, commanding the First Company in the same redoubt where it had fired with such effect in the December battle, saw Yankees break through on the left and come up on him from the rear, "cutting off all chance of escape. I waved my handkerchief and called out to them not to fire on us."

Six guns of the Washington Artillery were swept up, as well as the two guns of Lieutenant Brown's Richmond battery. Again, men were killed here in the act of surrendering. "It was, I think, done in the excitement and heat of battle," an aide to General Barksdale explained to a grieving father, "when men's passions set all restraint at defiance and was not the result of a deliberate determination to give no quarter."

The toll in the two Mississippi regiments and among the artillerists on Marye's Heights came to some 475, well over a third of the defenders there. The attackers — from Newton's and Howe's and Gibbon's divisions and Burnham's Light Division — lost nearly 1,100 men. Two thirds of these casualties fell on the regiments that led the charges. Burnham was especially hard hit, losing 30 percent of his men in these few minutes. "We remember the 13th of December with sorrow," Lieutenant Haskell wrote, "but we shall recall the 3d of May, with feelings that will partly efface it, at least." One of Barksdale's men wrote home, "The Mississippi Brigade had never been whipped before, and felt mighty bad; the Washington Artillery the same. . . ."

At 10:30 A.M., from his observation post at Station F north of the river, Captain James Hall signaled headquarters, "Our troops have just carried Maryes Hts and I think captured the guns." Twenty minutes later the news was on its way to General Hooker.[17]

*　*

AS THE BATTLE for Chancellorsville intensified that morning, General Meade had grown more and more frustrated. His Fifth Corps troops were drawn up to the north along the Ely's Ford Road, and it was apparent that the enemy columns, in driving eastward against Chancellorsville's defenders, were moving straight across his front. He was in the classic position for a devastating flank attack. He had Alexander Webb of his staff go forward to inspect the ground over which they might advance. Although on his own account he had sent Tyler's brigade to support the threatened line, still no orders came to him from headquarters. At about 9:45 A.M., as the Fairview position was collapsing, Meade took Webb with him to see the general commanding.

They found Hooker in his new field headquarters, a tent in a clearing near the Bullock house crossroads three quarters of a mile northwest of Chancellorsville. The general had just been brought from the front after his injury, and he was in the tent lying down. Although he was conscious and appeared to be aware of events, another visitor about this time thought he "seemed rather dull."

Meade explained his situation and proposed an attack on the enemy's left. Lieutenant Colonel Webb, he said, had already marked out the ground over which they would attack, and there need be no delay. "Meade begged to go in with our Corps and Reynolds' (5th & 1st) fresh, confident & anxious to fight," Webb wrote home, "but no, it could *not* be, just at the moment when any cool soldier felt that it must be done. . . . This was a grievous error, I think." By Meade's terse account, "I was *overruled*." If Hooker offered any reason for his overrule, neither Meade nor Webb recorded it. The course of events soon became clear, however, when at 10 o'clock General Couch arrived and entered the headquarters tent.

Hooker had called for Darius Couch, his second-in-command by seniority, to (as he put it) "exercise his office." But Couch was not to exercise it independently. As he remembered the conversation, Hooker told him, "I turn the command of the army over to you. You will withdraw it and place it in the position designated on this map." He handed him a field sketch marked with the defensive line that engineers Gouverneur Warren and Cyrus Comstock had laid out the night before.

As Couch emerged from the tent, Meade, standing with a group of officers nearby, looked at him inquiringly. Colonel N. H. Davis of Hooker's staff was heard to remark, "We shall have some fighting now!" Couch instead initiated a flurry of orders and actions to extract the reeling army from the battlefield.[18]

In the wake of Jackson's flank attack, Hooker had posted Meade's Fifth Corps and Reynolds's First on the Hunting Run–Ely's Ford Road line to guard against any Rebel attempt to cut the army off from its Rappahannock crossings. Jackson was indeed contemplating such a thrust when he was wounded. But according to Gouverneur Warren, when he left the Chancellor house late Saturday night to go to Sedgwick, Hooker's last words to him were of his intention "to flank and destroy Jackson." He was surely thinking of doing so with Meade's and Reynolds's corps, the only troops who were in a position to flank Jackson.

Yet now, with Meade's flank-attack plan the sole hope for salvaging the Fairview and Chancellorsville positions, and with it the battle, Hooker rejected Meade's scheme out of hand and without discussion. Possibly his was a rational decision — believing it was too late now to reverse the course of the battle and he would only endanger the army's sole reserves. More probably, in his stunned mental condition, he was unable (as his aide Captain Candler put it) "to get any ideas into his head." Perhaps, since periods of amnesia are symptomatic of severe concussion, he may not even have recalled his original plan for employing Meade and Reynolds. Seemingly the one simple thought he could grasp among this confusion was to save the army.

The fact of the matter is that due to the nature of his injury General Hooker was unable to understand his true condition and therefore unable to see it as his duty to relinquish command totally. He would later testify, "I may have been disqualified for command by the accident an hour or an hour and a half," during which time Couch carried on but acting on the commanding general's specific orders. Proud Joe Hooker would not — or could not — bring himself to surrender, even temporarily, the command he had pursued so long. And so the bloody struggle of May 3 played out its course, a course that now became inevitable.[19]

* *

AS THE FEDERAL front south of Fairview crumbled and fell away, Dick Anderson's fresh brigades — Carnot Posey's Mississippians and Rans Wright's Georgians and E. A. Perry's Floridians — rushed right on the heels of the retreating Yankees. They stormed onto the Fairview plateau and planted their flags over the entrenchments. Close behind came Porter Alexander's guns. From Hazel Grove the batteries careened down the rough track and across the ravine of Lewis's Run and up the long scarred slope to unlimber on the plateau, taking aim at the Chancellorsville clearing ahead. The Chancellor house was hardly 750 yards distant.

Alexander unlimbered seven batteries, 26 pieces, in this new Fairview position. From the Plank Road to the west a dozen more converged their fire on Chancellorsville. Alexander would remember the moment as an artilleryman's dream: ". . . We deployed on the plateau, & opened on the fugitives, infantry, artillery, wagons — everything — swarming about the Chancellorsville house, & down the broad road leading thence to the river." Veteran artillerists, Alexander said, called this "pie" — firing into fugitives who could not answer back. "One has usually had to pay for this pie before he gets it, so he has no compunctions of conscience or chivalry. . . ."[20]

Ever since the first clash of the armies on May 1, the Chancellor house had served as a field hospital, and now it overflowed with wounded. "They had taken our sitting room as an operating room," fourteen-year-old Sue Chancellor would remember, "and our piano served as an amputating table." She and her family and their neighbors, sixteen in all, were sheltering in the basement. "Upstairs they were bringing in the wounded, and we could hear their screams of pain." That Sunday they heard the roar of battle coming ever closer, and then Joe Dickinson of Hooker's staff came and said they would have to leave; the house had taken fire. As they left, Sue Chancellor saw piles of amputated arms and legs outside the sitting room windows, and in the yard row upon row of canvas-covered bodies.

In the Chancellorsville clearing the batteries were pounding away at the woods to the south and west and east, and men rushed about and riderless horses galloped in every direction while shells burst overhead or plowed up the ground about them. The din beat on their ears. With

Dickinson leading, the Chancellor party picked its way through the chaos to the road to U.S. Ford. "At our last look, our old home was completely enveloped in flames." Reaching the ford, Dickinson turned the party over to the chaplain of a New Jersey regiment, who promised to see them safely to the north bank. The colonel bid them godspeed and went back to the battle. "A nobler, braver, kindlier gentleman never lived," Sue Chancellor decided.[21]

It was the usual practice on both sides to spare any building flying a hospital flag, but not only was it known that the Chancellor house was Hooker's headquarters and thus a legitimate target, but the Yankee batteries were posted so close by that the Rebel gunners could not help but hit the house. Their shells soon set it ablaze in several places, but according to surgeon Cyrus Bacon, all the wounded were removed safely. "When we got there," wrote North Carolinian B. B. Carr, "there was one poor fellow out in the yard whose leg had been amputated below the knee; was in the second story when the building caught on fire and escaped without help. He was taken care of by our Hospital Corps. . . ." With the building fully alight it was like something out of Dante's *Inferno;* "the conflagration made a striking scene with our shells still bursting all around it," Porter Alexander wrote.[22]

Winfield Scott Hancock's Second Corps division had the task of holding open a corridor of retreat to the new battle line at the Bullock house clearing. Hancock already held the eastward-facing defenses that confronted McLaws's division. Now he formed a second line facing west a half mile from the first. The last of Geary's and Sickles's troops were funneling through this corridor toward the Bullock house line.

Hancock's division numbered just under 5,900 men, and he depended on the batteries in the Chancellorsville clearing for the primary firepower against the Rebels swarming in from the west and south and east. Colonel Edward Cross, commanding a demi-brigade under Hancock, wrote after the battle, "For about 40 minutes my command was under the heaviest fire it ever experienced." The corps historian gave a blunt summary: Hancock's position was "subjected to fire at once direct, enfilading, and reverse, receiving shot and shell from every direction except the north."

Darius Couch, slight and unimposing, quietly competent, rode straight into the heat of the battle to direct this fighting withdrawal. Twice he was nicked by bullets and his horse was killed under him. Soon afterward Colonel Trobriand saw him back in command and as cool as ever: "Couch passes by at a light trot, a little switch in his hand, as usual." Couch's lieutenant, Win Hancock, was by contrast big and expansive, with a great booming voice, who led by example. Hancock was always turned out in a clean white shirt; how he came by them on campaign no one could guess. His horse, too, was killed, and the remount found for him was so diminutive that his boots nearly touched the ground. The general rode on, one of his officers observed admiringly, "amidst this rain of shells utterly indifferent, not even ducking his head when one came close to him. . . ."[23]

The artillery array defending the Chancellorsville clearing was mostly a last-minute patchwork. There were sections and partial complements and full complements of eight different batteries here, from four different corps. They came up and went back as their ammunition was exhausted; there were never more than 16 guns in action at any one time. The Confederates firing from Fairview and from the Plank Road to the west outgunned them at all times. There was no overall management of the Chancellorsville guns. Each battery commander made his own fight, and the fight each made was as gallant as it was doomed. To Couch's chief of artillery, Lieutenant Colonel Charles Morgan, it was all a forlorn hope. The place could not be held, Morgan said, "by any number of guns I could have placed on the contracted ground near the Chancellor house."

Following its ordeal at Fairview, Lieutenant Seeley's Battery K, 4th U.S., was limping to the rear when it was intercepted by the Third Corps' chief of artillery and thrown into the defense of Chancellorsville. Seeley had only men enough left to work four of his six Napoleons. He took position to the west of the burning mansion. Under fire from two directions, he loaded canister and waited grimly for the Rebel infantry to advance into killing range. At 350 yards Seeley opened "with terrible effect, causing their troops to break and take to the cover of the woods. . . ."

These were Dick Anderson's men, and along with Alexander's guns they kept up a steady drumbeat of fire from longer range. Seeley retaliated by sending solid shot crashing through the trees. But he soon ran out of ammunition and hauled off his pieces with the few battery horses he had left. Lieutenant Seeley would not leave the field, however, until he had collected the harness from his fallen horses. He reported proudly, "the *debris* of my battery was drawn from the field, my men cheering. . . ."

When Lieutenant John Bucklyn was rushed into the line with his section of the 1st Rhode Island Light, he muttered, "Whoever goes up there will not live to return." He would man his guns only with volunteers. They fought until charging enemy infantry were 25 yards away. Every battery horse was down and there were enough crewmen to drag only one of the guns to safety. The other was lost. Lieutenant William

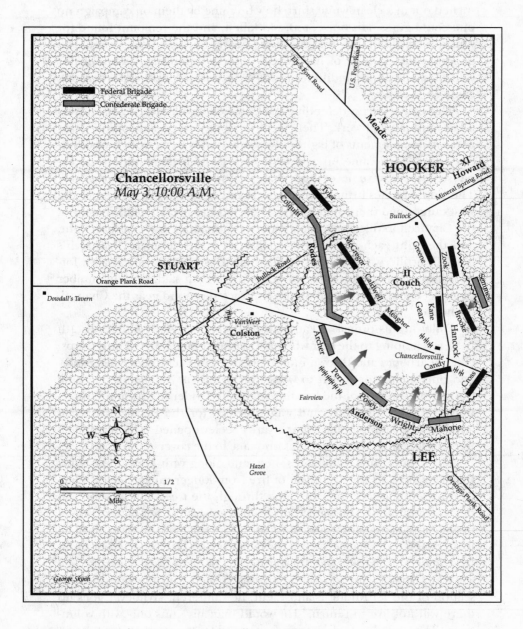

Chancellorsville
May 3, 10:00 A.M.

Federal Brigade
Confederate Brigade

Ely's Ford Road
U.S. Ford Road

V
Meade

HOOKER

XI
Howard

Mineral Spring Road

Bullock

Tyler

Colquitt

Rodes

McGregor

Greene

Zook

Caldwell

II
Couch

Kane

Sommers

STUART

Bullock Road

Meagher

Geary

Brooke

Orange Plank Road

Hancock

Dowdall's Tavern

VanWert

Colston

Archer

Chancellorsville

Candy

Cross

Perry

Fairview

Posey

Wright

Anderson

Mahone

LEE

N
W   E
S

Hazel
Grove

Orange Plank Road

0   1/2

Mile

George Skoch

O'Donohue, commanding three guns of Battery C, 4th United States, fell mortally wounded, one of fifteen Battery C casualties, but his guns were saved.

The crumbling gun line was braced for a time by two fresh batteries from the rear, one rounded up earlier on Hooker's order and the other called up by Couch. Captain Rufus Pettit's 10-pounder rifles of Battery B, 1st New York Light, were "within a very few moments" under fire from what Pettit counted as three batteries, firing at him from three directions. He had one caisson blown up and twelve men wounded and eight battery horses killed; still, he managed to fire nearly 600 rounds of shell and case shot that morning before withdrawing. Infantry helped haul his guns to the rear.

The First Corps' 5th Maine Light was marching to a position in John Reynolds's line when one of Hooker's staff came on it and diverted it to Chancellorsville. Its five Napoleons under Captain George Leppien took a position in front of a peach orchard in the rear of the Chancellor house. Leppien's battery was the last to reach the field and the last with any concerted firepower, and it became the target of "a most galling fire" from every Confederate gun within range.

Men and animals were hit and then Captain Leppien's leg was mangled by a shell, a wound that would prove mortal. General Couch was on the scene and directed Lieutenant Edmund Kirby of the regulars to take Leppien's place. Ammunition ran low and a limber chest was exploded and then Lieutenant Kirby was down with a wound that too proved mortal. The guns fell silent one by one and the gunners slipped back to the shelter of the orchard. Finally only Corporal James Lebroke and Private John Chase were left, methodically loading and firing their last rounds. Then a Confederate shell wrecked their piece.

Seeing the five guns standing silent on the smoking field, Win Hancock reached out for the nearest Second Corps infantry — 53rd, 116th, and 140th Pennsylvania — to haul off the guns. When they tried to carry Lieutenant Kirby to safety he refused to leave the field until the last gun was away. Twenty-eight men of the 5th Maine Light, better than a quarter of the battery's complement, had been killed or wounded. Many of these wounds from shellfire were grievous, and one of the Pennsylvania infantrymen was appalled to have mangled gunners plead with him "to shoot them, when you can't."[24]

The beleaguered troops of the Third and Twelfth corps had all escaped through the defensive corridor now, and all the batteries were being evacuated from the Chancellorsville clearing, and the word was passed for Hancock's division to join the retreat. Its job was done. Although the Rebel guns continued their fire against Hancock's columns, they were not immediately pressed by infantry. The road from the Chancellor house northward to the new Bullock house line ran through thick forest and the enemy shells arced down into the trees and the roadway and the marching men. "Our speed was rather faster than a walk after we got into the woods," admitted Captain Thomas Livermore of the 5th New Hampshire; "the time was quite trying." His company lost two men to the bursting shells on this march. At Bullock's, he wrote, "To the right and left of us as far as we could see, our troops occupied a line of battle. . . ." The time, he noted, was noon.

Amidst this tumult of musketry and bursting shells not every unit in Hancock's line had gotten the word to withdraw. The 27th Connecticut and part of the 145th Pennsylvania, holding the furthermost section of the line facing east, were left behind. Paul Semmes's Georgia brigade of McLaws's division was pressuring the Yankees here, and the 10th Georgia pushed through the vacated line and cut across their path of retreat. Before he ordered an attack, Lieutenant Colonel Willis Holt explained, "I thought that they might surrender, knowing them to be entirely cut off. . . ." Holt sent in a man under a flag of truce to call on them to give up. "The Rebel — a tall, rough specimen, and yet with the manner of a gentleman — announced himself as Lieutenant Bailey, of a Georgia regiment," wrote the 27th Connecticut's historian. Apparently no one disputed Lieutenant Bailey as to their predicament. But at least no one could say, a Connecticut soldier insisted, "that the 27th run; they stood their ground untill they were surrounded. . . ." The count of prisoners from the 27th Connecticut and 145th Pennsylvania came to 350.[25]

*　*

JEB STUART galloped into the Chancellorsville clearing at full tilt, shouting, "Go forward, boys! We have them running, and we'll keep them at it!" His infantry pushed in from the west, and Anderson's from the south and McLaws's from the east. Tossing battle flags crowded to the front. The smoldering battlefield was theirs.

"After the battle had ceased it was an awful sight to look at . . . ," wrote North Carolinian F. M. Nixon. "The ground was covered with guns & cartridge boxes, the men was laying thick in some places. You cant find a bush but what has been hit by a shell or a bullet. . . ." Hungry Rebels tore into abandoned Yankee knapsacks and haversacks in numbers beyond counting. There was booty beyond counting. "Our army," artilleryman Frank Coker would explain, "is entirely rigged out with overcoats, new clothes, India rubber blankets, oil cloths &c." John Garibaldi of the 27th Virginia marveled at the military captures: "I cant tell you how many small arms but we have got any number of them. . . ."

The grimmest scene of all was in the woods north of the Plank Road where the shelling had set fire to the dry leaves and underbrush and flames went scurrying through acres of woodland. The dead of both armies there were blackened and charred. Men wounded too badly to escape or those lying in thickets hidden from rescuers were burned to death. "We could plainly hear the poor fellows scream and yell," Yankee James Houghton noted in his diary that night. Corpses were found within little cleared spaces where wounded in their last moments had desperately pushed away the leaves and twigs as the flames approached. "I cant give you any idea what a sight it was to walk over the Battle Field and see men lying with their cloths burnt off their hair burnt close to their head their arms and legs all drawed up with the fire," Leonidas Torrence of the 23rd North Carolina wrote home. "I never saw such a distressing sight before and hope I may never see such another."[26]

When word of the capture of Chancellorsville reached him, General Lee rode from Hazel Grove up the track to the Orange Plank Road and turned eastward toward the day's final battlefield. His was a mile-long cavalcade of triumph. One of his staff thought it must have been like this in ancient times when the victorious warrior general took the salutes of his triumphant legions at battle's end. "With several other brigades we then formed in the road," wrote Lieutenant Francis Hillyer of the 3rd Georgia. "General Lee and staff coming down the road at this time, the troops opened to the right and left, and as the old Hero passed through, the line greeted him with tremendous cheers. He pulled off his hat in acknowledgment. . . ."

It was indeed a moment of high triumph. Beyond any doubt it was the greatest moment Robert E. Lee had experienced in his military life. Some forty hours earlier he had determined on his daring plan for Jackson's flank attack. Now Jackson's victory was sealed, and on this morning of May 3 the army was reunited and the enemy host driven from its strongly entrenched positions. The cheering Confederates could not know how important the injury they inflicted on Joe Hooker was to their victory — or how much, too, the Federals had contributed to their own downfall by their bungling response to that injury. Be that as it may, Lee and Jeb Stuart and their legions had amply earned their victory.[27]

The cost of victory was exceedingly high. Never had the Army of Northern Virginia lost so many men in battle in so short a time. The fighting that morning of May 3 cost the Confederates 8,962 dead, wounded, and missing. That was almost a thousand more than were lost at bloody Gaines's Mill on the Peninsula the spring before; only at Sharpsburg in September did more men fall — 10,318 — but the struggle at Sharpsburg lasted twelve hours. Chancellorsville on May 3 lasted five. This army had never experienced — and would never experience — a more intense, more furiously fought engagement.

Four out of five of the morning's casualties were from Stuart's command. Both A. P. Hill's and Rodes's divisions lost 24 percent of their numbers; Colston's loss was 29 percent. The toll of officers was staggering. Seven of Stuart's brigade commanders were hit, with three of them (Oliver Edwards, Frank Paxton, and Thomas Garnett) killed or mortally wounded. In Stuart's command and Lee's no fewer than forty regimental commanders or their battlefield replacements were casualties; eleven of the forty were killed or mortally wounded. At battle's end captains and lieutenants were leading regiments. The 55th Virginia was on its fifth commander, the 5th North Carolina, 5th Alabama, and 7th North Carolina on their fourth.

Considering the fact that the Federals fought from behind entrenchments for much of the time, their casualties at Chancellorsville on May 3 were surprisingly high — 8,623, only 339 fewer than their foes. The markedly superior tactics of the Rebel artillery contributed to this result, but in some instances so did a certain reluctance to continue fighting; a third of that total were taken prisoner.

One major general of division, Hiram Berry, was killed; two brigade commanders, Gershom Mott and Samuel Ross, were wounded; and one brigadier, William Hays, was captured. In all, thirty-two Federal regimental commanders or their replacements were casualties that morning — eight killed, eighteen wounded, and six who surrendered along with much of their commands. It is also estimated that as many as 5,000 Yankees were marched out of harm's way during the fighting by their misguided officers. With several notable exceptions, most particularly Brigadier Thomas Ruger of the Twelfth Corps, May 3, 1863, was not an outstanding day for the battlefield-level command of the Army of the Potomac.

Yet for the large majority of men in blue and butternut in the ranks, May 3 was a day of the staunchest kind of fighting. The combined casualties in the two armies of 17,585 in these five hours of combat had been exceeded before on only two days of this war — at Sharpsburg and at Fredericksburg — and both were all-day conflicts.[28]

14

Calling Upon General Sedgwick

EARLY THAT SUNDAY MORNING, some fifty miles to the south, General Stoneman set out to destroy General Lee's communications. Day Seven was the fifth day of Stoneman's march, and he announced that his cavalry raiders had "dropped in that region of country like a shell," and the shell was about to burst "in every direction . . . and thus magnify our small force into overwhelming numbers. . . ."

Stoneman's imagery was apt for Richmond at least. Sightings and rumor put hordes of Yankee cavalry at the city's gates. "When this was known the utmost consternation prevailed in the city," Josiah Gorgas, chief of the Ordnance Bureau, entered in his diary. "All our troops had been sent off to Lee. . . ." Church bells rang out the alarm. The militia was called to mobilize at City Hall. Citizens packed their trunks for evacuation, and Mary Chesnut burned her current outspoken journal lest it be captured and printed in the newspapers. A crowd gathering at the Richmond, Fredericksburg & Potomac depot on Broad Street to meet a train from Fredericksburg carrying sick and wounded from the army was stunned to learn that it had been captured by the Vandal cavalry.[1]

In point of fact, however, General Stoneman's actions that day and the next came to very little. Already he had fallen at least two days behind in approaching his primary target, the Richmond, Fredericksburg & Potomac. Now, when finally he attacked it, he did so weakly and entirely in the wrong place.

The R.F. & P. and the Virginia Central ran north from Richmond on parallel courses to Hanover Junction, where the Central turned west and crossed the R.F. & P. and went on to Gordonsville; the R.F. & P. continued northward to Fredericksburg. Army supplies and munitions were dispatched out of Richmond, but much additional food and forage from the western counties of the state were delivered by the Virginia Central to

Hanover Junction and stockpiled there for delivery to the army over the R.F. & P.

Thus to sever Lee's communications completely it was necessary to break the R.F. & P. at or north of Hanover Junction. To make it a lasting break it was necessary to destroy at least one of the railroad's major bridge crossings, three of which were just north of the Junction. Colonel Sharpe's B.M.I. had carefully charted both railroads, listing and locating all stations and crossings and describing the bridges in especial detail. Stoneman's instructions pointed him to Hanover Junction and assigned it first priority. When Hooker handed Stoneman his April 28 instructions at Morrisville, he surely reviewed them with him. Joe Hooker's indictment of George Stoneman was therefore fully justified: "no officer ever made a greater mistake in construing his orders, and no one ever accomplished less in so doing."[2]

From his headquarters in the field at Thompson's Crossroads on the South Anna River Stoneman sent one party of troopers under Colonel Percy Wyndham to do what damage they could to the James River Canal, west of Richmond. The raiders burned several bridges over the canal and several canal boats and did some other damage, but could make no impression on the masonry aquaduct that carried the canal over the Rivanna River. In any case blocking the James River Canal would benefit the Federals only in the long view. Wyndham's 400 men would have been of far more use against the much higher-priority R.F. & P.

Another 450 troopers under Colonel Judson Kilpatrick spent the entire day of May 3 in hiding, waiting for darkness to approach the R.F. & P.'s Hungary Station, less than ten miles from Richmond. Reaching there the next morning, they burned the depot and took up some two miles of track. Their technique was simply to pull the spikes and throw the rails aside; a track crew could put the line in order in about the same time it took the raiders to dismantle it. Kilpatrick went on to gaudy adventures, damaging the Virginia Central, running a Central train into the Chickahominy River, feeding the uproar in Richmond. His damage to the R.F. & P. was minimal.

Farther up the line, the 12th Illinois cavalry under Lieutenant Colonel Hasbrouck Davis reached Ashland, seventeen miles from Richmond and seven miles short of Hanover Junction, on the afternoon of May 3. The Illinois troopers cut the telegraph line and "tore up half a dozen rails" and burned a trestle so small that it was not on the B.M.I.'s list of the R.F. & P.'s bridges. It was Davis's troopers who captured the train carrying sick and wounded from Fredericksburg. They paroled their prisoners and disabled the engine. (One of the passengers, who managed to escape and make his way to Richmond, was Captain Joseph

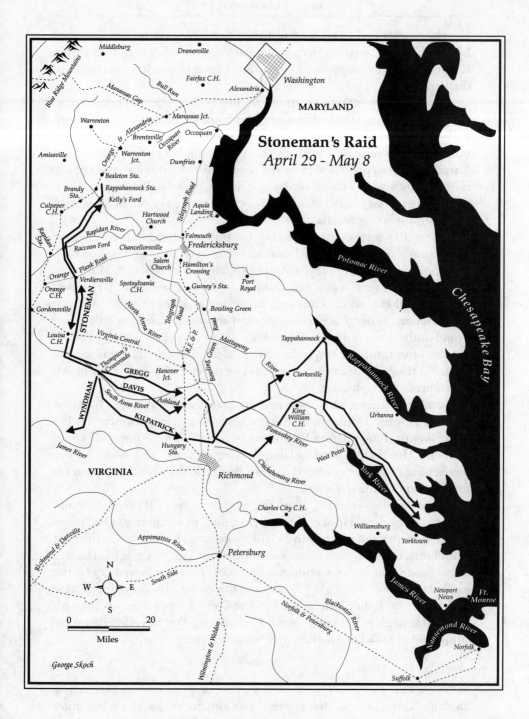

MARYLAND

Stoneman's Raid
April 29 - May 8

Middleburg

Dranesville

Fairfax C.H.

Alexandria

Washington

Blue Ridge Mountains

Manassas Gap

Bull Run

Manassas Jct.

Warrenton

Brentsville

Occoquan

Orange & Alexandria

Warrenton Jct.

Dumfries

Amissville

Bealeton Sta.

Telegraph Road

Aquia Landing

Brandy Sta.

Rappahannock Sta.

Culpeper C.H.

Kelly's Ford

Hartwood Church

Rapidan Sta.

Rapidan River

Hamilton's Crossing

Falmouth

Fredericksburg

Potomac River

Raccoon Ford

Chancellorsville

Salem Church

Plank Road

Orange

Verdiersville

Spotsylvania C.H.

Guiney's Sta.

Port Royal

Orange C.H.

North Anna River

Bowling Green

Gordonsville

STONEMAN

Telegraph Road

Tappahannock

Chesapeake Bay

Louisa C.H.

Virginia Central

Bowling Green Road

Mattapony

Clarksville

Rappahannock River

Thompson's Crossroads

Hanover Jct.

R.F. & P.

River

GREGG

DAVIS

Ashland

King William C.H.

Urbanna

WYNDHAM

South Anna River

KILPATRICK

Pamunkey River

James River

Hungary Sta.

West Point

York River

VIRGINIA

Richmond

Chickahominy River

Charles City C.H.

Williamsburg

Yorktown

Richmond & Danville

Appomattox River

Petersburg

South Side

Newport News

Ft. Monroe

N
W   E
S

0   20
Miles

Norfolk & Petersburg

Blackwater River

James River

Wilmington & Weldon

Nansemond River

Norfolk

George Skoch

Suffolk

Morrison, who had been sent to bring Anna Jackson to her wounded husband.) Davis went on to damage the Virginia Central and then, like Kilpatrick, led his command to the safety of the Union lines at the tip of the Peninsula.

A third party of Yankee troopers, under Brigadier General David Gregg, also reached the railroad near Ashland, after Davis's men had left, and "damaged things generally." Gregg detailed just 200 men to ride two miles north to seize and burn the 600-foot-long bridge over the South Anna River. That promised to be the most lasting accomplishment of the raid, but they were chased off by the bridge guard and Gregg did not pursue the matter further. After his Sunday's work he rejoined Stoneman at Thompson's Crossroads.

In less than forty-eight hours after the raiders left, track crews had the Richmond, Fredericksburg & Potomac running again. The Virginia Central would be open from Richmond to Gordonsville by May 8. Moreover, all during this time trains ran without interruption between Hanover Junction and Hamilton's Crossing, delivering supplies from the stocks at the Junction. Federal observers detailed to watch Hamilton's Crossing would dutifully record the arrival of the daily two trains on May 3 and no less than five trains on May 4. In all the calculations he made during the battle on the Rappahannock, General Lee never had to concern himself with a broken supply line.

Sunday morning, while investigating matters on Sedgwick's front for General Hooker, Gouverneur Warren learned from a prisoner that the man had just come up from Richmond by train. "This information would do Genl. Hooker no good today unless he succeeds and might be disheartening," Warren confided to Dan Butterfield. "I would not send it until he reports the day's results."

Later that day — and again on the next two days — Butterfield would have to tell General Hooker the disheartening news: there was still nothing heard from the cavalry, and Confederate trains were still arriving at Hamilton's Crossing with no apparent interruption. So far as Joe Hooker knew, Stoneman and his raiders might have been swallowed up by the earth, taking with them a key element in the grand plan for victory. In his frustration he lashed out at the only officer of Stoneman's within his reach, the hapless William Averell. He ordered Averell relieved and his command at Ely's Ford turned over to Alfred Pleasonton.[3]

* *

STONEWALL JACKSON awakened in the hospital tent at Wilderness Tavern about 9:00 A.M. that Sunday. The rumble of the battle five miles distant "could be very distinctly heard," Dr. McGuire wrote. The general drank some coffee with pleasure "and said he was sanguine of his recovery." He reported he was resting comfortably except for pain in his left side, caused he thought by the fall from the litter after his wounding. Dr. McGuire could find no evidence of injury there, "and the lung performed as far as I could tell, its proper function." Lieutenant James Power Smith remained with the general throughout the day, with Dr. McGuire looking in every hour or so between his rounds caring for the other wounded.

The Reverend Lacy arrived to commiserate with Jackson, but he would have none of it and insisted his wounding was the will of God. "You never saw me more perfectly contented than I am today," Jackson said. By late morning Smith was giving him reports of the successful course of the battle. General Stuart, he was told, had sent the Stonewall Brigade into action with the admonition "Charge and remember Jackson!" and the charge had gained a success. "Just like them to do so; just like them," the general said. "They are a noble set of men."

Speaking of his flank movement of the day before, Jackson observed that he would probably receive more credit for it than he deserved. Contrary to what "most men will think," he said, he had not planned it all out from the first. "I simply took advantage of circumstances, as they were presented to me in the providence of God. I feel that his hand led me."

Jackson dictated a dispatch to General Lee officially announcing his wounding and the transfer of command, and congratulating Lee on the victory. Pausing on the smoking battlefield of Chancellorsville, Lee dictated a reply: "I have just received your note informing me that you were wounded. I cannot express my regret at the occurrence. Could I have directed events, I should have chosen for the good of the country to have been disabled in your stead. I congratulate you upon the victory which is due to your skill and energy." When this was read to him, Jackson was silent for a time, and then said, "General Lee is very kind; he should give the glory to God."

Lee also sent orders that Jackson must be moved to a safer place for his recuperation. There was concern about Yankee cavalry raiding in the rear areas behind the army. It was decided to move the general the next day to Guiney's Station, on the railroad south of Fredericksburg. Lee specifically ordered Dr. McGuire to turn over his Second Corps duties and accompany his patient. That evening, as preparations were made for the journey, Jackson said the pain in his side had subsided. "He asked animatedly about the battle," McGuire wrote, "and the actions of the different troops engaged. . . ."[4]

It was approaching noon and General Lee was collecting and reorganizing his forces to continue the pursuit of Hooker's army — the victory would not be complete, he thought, until these people were driven into the Rappahannock — when a rider on a lathered horse came pelting down the Orange Plank Road from the direction of Fredericksburg. Lieutenant A. L. Pitzer of Jubal Early's staff brought ill tidings from Early's front.

Lieutenant Pitzer had been observing the battle there and witnessed Sedgwick's Yankees storm and capture Marye's Heights. With fine initiative he did not wait to notify Early first — Early would find out soon enough — but instead rode straight for General Lee to report that the enemy now had a clear path to the rear of the army.

The troops best positioned to face about to meet this new crisis were Lafayette McLaws's three brigades. (His fourth, William Barksdale's, had been at Marye's Heights.) Lee hurried to the Georgian's position and sent him off eastward. Mahone's brigade of Dick Anderson's division was ordered to follow. As McLaws was starting on his way, a second messenger from Early's command galloped up to report the collapse of the Fredericksburg line. He was the chaplain of the 17th Mississippi, the Reverend William Owen. In high excitement Reverend Owen started to pour out a tale of wrack and ruin when Lee calmed him and explained gently that Major Sedgwick was a nice gentleman and "I don't think he would hurt us very badly." (Major John Sedgwick had served under Colonel Robert E. Lee in the 1st Cavalry in the old army.) "I have just sent General McLaws to make a special call upon him."[5]

McLaws's brigades and Mahone's had been only lightly engaged (comparatively) in the morning's fighting, and Lee intended them to lead the pursuit of Hooker. Thus the news of Early's defeat necessarily forced the cancellation of any immediate operations on the Chancellorsville front. For the Confederates this was fortuitous. Lee believed the enemy was in flight for the river and was quite unaware of what awaited him beyond the forest in the direction of U.S. Ford. Had he thrown his wearied, bloodied army against the new Yankee line there, he would surely have met a disaster.

The defensive line that engineers Warren and Comstock had laid out the night before was in the form of a large salient some three and a half miles deep and three miles across at its base. The western arm was anchored on the Rapidan and the eastern arm on the Rappahannock, securely enclosing the pontoon bridges at U.S. Ford. Reynolds's First Corps held the westernmost section, posted behind Hunting Run from the Rapidan to where it crossed the Ely's Ford Road. The Fifth Corps under Meade took over from there to the intersection of the Ely's Ford and U.S. Ford roads. At the apex of the salient, at the Bullock house, was Sickles's Third Corps. The eastern arm, running along the

Everett B. D. Julio's monumental and symbolic *The Last Meeting of Lee and Jackson,* which he originally titled *The Heroes of Chancellorsville,* became a lasting icon of the Lost Cause.

Above, a photograph of the tangled Wilderness. Waud wrote on his drawing below that it showed the scene on the Union right in the early evening of May 2 "previous to the Germans running away." At center rear is Dowdall's Tavern, Howard's Eleventh Corps headquarters. General Howard's men are forming up to try and halt Jackson's assault approaching from the left.

Forbes caught the massive sweep of Jackson's flank attack in this drawing. On the Plank Road in the foreground, facing the onslaught, is Captain Hubert Dilger's 1st Ohio Light battery, the only one of General Howard's batteries that put up any serious resistance to Jackson.

Oliver Otis Howard

Above, Harry Fenn pictured veterans of Chancellorsville visiting the scene of Jackson's attack two decades later. Looking north, Wilderness Church is seen from the Plank Road; the Hawkins farm is at right rear. Below, Southern artist Allen Redwood depicted the same scene as it looked on May 2, 1863, with stampeded Eleventh Corps fugitives in full flight.

Artist Waud described his chaotic sketch above as Couch's Second Corps forming line of battle behind a line of guns "in the fields of Chancellorsville" to cover the Eleventh Corps "disgracefully running away," and listed those regiments he could identify in the rout.

Southern historical artist William Washington planned a painting of the mortally wounded Jackson being borne from the field, but completed only this 1864 study.

A. J. Russell took the two photographs on this page on the eve of Chancellorsville. Above, in a scene foreshortened by the camera lens, pickets of Barksdale's Mississippi brigade pose for Russell on the Fredericksburg end of the wrecked Rappahannock railroad bridge. Below are the 4.5-inch rifled cannon of the 1st Connecticut Heavy Artillery posted on Stafford Heights.

After Sedgwick's Sixth Corps established its bridgehead below Fredericksburg, Russell crossed to the Confederate shore to take these rarest of Civil War photographs — showing troops actually facing Rebel guns while on campaign. The men pictured here are from the division of William Brooks, dug in against Jubal Early's troops holding the River Road below Fredericksburg.

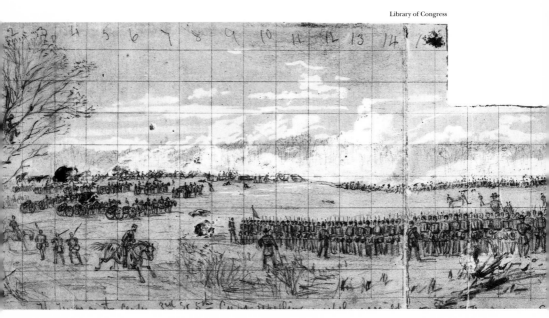

These two drawings by Alfred Waud picture elements of the savage, intense fighting around Chancellorsville on May 3. The scene above, marked for engravers at *Harper's Weekly*, depicts troops of Dan Sickles's Third Corps formed up in support of the artillery line at Fairview in the left background. General Sickles is with the corps flag at right. Below, artillery at left fires in support of an advanced infantry line. At center rear is the Bullock house.

Robert E. Rodes

James Ewell Brown Stuart

On May 3 Hooker ordered his army to fall back to a second line of defenses to the north of Chancellorsville, in the vicinity of the Bullock house. Forbes sketched the troops digging in on the new line as battle smoke from the continuing fighting rises over the trees.

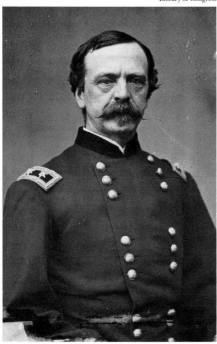

Daniel E. Sickles

Darius N. Couch

The 29th Pennsylvania of the Twelfth Corps, posted at the southernmost extremity of the Federal line, endures heavy shelling by Confederate guns at Hazel Grove. An officer of the Pennsylvania regiment commissioned this picture by Southern artist William Sheppard.

Cooke, *A Life of Gen. Robert E. Lee*

Newspaper artist Alfred Waud did the illustrations for an 1871 biography of General Lee by John Esten Cooke. Here, Waud shows Lee riding in triumph into the Chancellorsville clearing, to the cheers of his troops. The Chancellor house burns in the background.

The relentless artillery fire during the May 3 battle set portions of the Wilderness to the west and north of Chancellorsville on fire. Above, Forbes depicts rescuers' efforts to save wounded from the flames. The sketch below, also by Forbes, pictures a Federal field hospital and its patients, established along the U.S. Ford Road north of Chancellorsville.

Another Federal field hospital was set up at the Kalmbach sawmill, which also served as a depot for medical supplies; Waud sketched it above. Below, Forbes pictures a column of Confederate prisoners being taken to the rear on May 3; several appear by their clothes to be civilians. The cavalrymen heading the column display captured Rebel battle flags.

Within hours of the fight for Marye's Heights on May 3 Russell was there to photograph the battle-field. The Mississippians above died defending the Stone Wall. Below, wrecked caissons on the reverse slope of Marye's Heights. Railroad expert Herman Haupt stands at left.

Twenty years after the fighting there, Salem Church still bore the scars of battle. Men of the 9th Alabama holding the church were captured and then rescued in the shifting fortunes of the contest. Walton Taber made this drawing from a postwar photograph.

Jubal A. Early   John Sedgwick

Above is the Chandler estate office at Guiney's Station, where Stonewall Jackson was taken for care after his wounding, and where on May 10 he died. The general was taken to Lexington, Virginia, for burial. Below, mourners at Jackson's grave, photographed about 1866.

Mineral Spring Road, was held successively by Couch's Second, Howard's Eleventh, and Slocum's Twelfth corps.

After subtracting casualties, stragglers, and those demoralized or exhausted in the intense struggle of the morning, there were in these six corps perhaps 50,000 fighting men ready for action. Sixteen of Reynolds's and Meade's brigades had not yet fired a shot. Nor (that day) had Howard's six brigades. But the line's greatest strength was its guns. Placed in every eligible position were twenty-one batteries, 106 pieces. In the center, at the Bullock house, the most likely spot for the Confederates to press the pursuit, 48 pieces were massed. In reserve behind the lines were 140 more.

Colonel Wainwright, Reynolds's chief of artillery, managed to gain an audience with Hooker in one of his lucid moments after his injury. When the general asked him how the artillery was getting on, Wainwright replied boldly, "As badly as it well can . . . ; no one seems to know where to go." He started to elaborate, but Hooker cut him off: "Well, we have no time to talk now. You take hold and make it right." He dictated an order giving Wainwright "command of all the artillery and ammunition in this army," regardless of assignments to corps and divisions. This meant at last centralized control of the guns.

Later in the day Joe Hooker would silently acknowledge he had mishandled his artillery by calling Henry Hunt from across the river to take over the supervisory role. Had there been a serious renewal of the battle that afternoon, however, Charles Wainwright would have been in charge of the guns. How matters might have gone is suggested by an incident at about 3:00 P.M. Lee sent Raleigh Colston forward on the U.S. Ford Road to probe the Federals' positions. "Don't engage seriously," he told him, "but keep the enemy in check and prevent him from advancing." Colston promptly encountered a terrific fire from Wainwright's massed guns and was sent reeling back; he counted fifty men down in less than two minutes in one barrage. Yankee gunner Captain Stephen Weed, Wainwright noted in his diary, "was moving about among his guns with actual delight beaming on every feature of his face."[6]

* *

THROUGHOUT SUNDAY morning Jubal Early had posted himself toward the right of his Fredericksburg lines, where he expected Sedgwick to attack him, and so he was taken aback when it was reported that the Yankees had captured Marye's Heights on the left. Since he could not know Sedgwick's objective, Early continued to assume it was his division. With that thought in mind, he collected his main force and the troops scattered by the enemy's breakthrough and acting on Lee's earlier orders, fell back southward along the Telegraph Road so as to shield the army's railroad lifeline.

General Barksdale managed to evacuate the survivors of his brigade from the broken front ("Our center has been pierced, that's all," Barksdale announced cheerfully; "we will be all right in a little while.") and rallied them alongside Early. Two Georgia batteries, under Captains Henry Carleton and John Fraser, held off the foe while Barksdale's Mississippians made their escape. Harry Hays's Louisiana brigade, posted on the extreme left, could well have been cut off and taken entire by an aggressive Yankee pursuit. But the capture of Marye's Heights seemed to exhaust the Yankees' aggressiveness. Hays's four regiments made their way across to Early on the Telegraph Road without event. The Federals had to be content with picking up twenty-seven Louisiana stragglers.

Early fell back some two miles along the Telegraph Road to a road crossing at the Cox house, where the troops of his right and left wings could join him. There he drew a new defensive line, strongly bracing it with artillery. Except for the losses in Barksdale's brigade in the defense of Marye's Heights, Early's command was essentially intact. The eight guns lost in the assault could be made good from General Pendleton's reserve artillery. Once his position was re-established, Old Jube struck off northward to find the enemy. He discovered that the Orange Plank Road to the west was crowded with Yankees. "I rode out to a position across Hazel Run," he wrote, "from which I could see the moving column and discovered that it was moving very slowly, and that it finally halted."[7]

For Brigadier General Cadmus M. Wilcox, commanding the Alabama brigade of Dick Anderson's division, the campaign so far had been frustrating. From his position guarding Banks's Ford (where in fact he had been all winter), he watched the shifting fortunes of the battle for three days without once being engaged. A West Pointer, class of 1846 along with Stonewall Jackson, Wilcox had made a good fighting record in the 1862 campaigns. But his ambitions for promotion were thwarted, so much so that he had tried to leave the Army of Northern Virginia for greener pastures. Wilcox was therefore on the alert for any opportunity to shine, and now suddenly he saw that opportunity. The Yankees' seizure of Marye's Heights, he realized, "left the plank road open to the enemy to advance upon Gen'l Lee's rear and only 8 or 10 miles off." His was the only force that could do anything about that.

He first used his artillery to discourage the Federals for a time from pushing out beyond Marye's Heights. Wilcox then marched his command around by way of the River Road and a byway from that to reach the Plank Road at a toll gate three miles west of Fredericksburg. The enemy, he noted, seemed in no great hurry to advance, and he had ample time to deploy across the road ahead of them. As an advanced skirmish line he set out some fifty dismounted troopers of the 15th Virginia cavalry and two rifled guns under Lieutenant James S. Cobbs. Just then came the welcome news that General Lee was sending McLaws's brigades as a reinforcement.[8]

Paradoxically, his conquest of Marye's Heights had only made Uncle John Sedgwick more uncomfortable than ever in his independent-command role. Normal practice after breaking through an enemy's line, as he had, was to pursue the beaten fragments to complete the victory. But there was no change in Sedgwick's orders. Indeed, the first word he received from headquarters after taking the Heights only reiterated these orders.

All during May 3 the Potomac army's chief quartermaster, Rufus Ingalls, acted as a sort of unofficial backstairs link between Dan Butterfield and the battlefield. Ingalls would gallop from Hooker's headquarters to the station at U.S. Ford and exchange telegrams with Butterfield, then gallop back to deliver the reply. Ingalls tended to paint rosy pictures. "General Hooker is doing well," he told Butterfield in late morning as the Chancellorsville position was collapsing. They had gained no ground so far, he admitted, "yet our lines are strong." The enemy would surely make another desperate effort, and so "Sedgwick must press them fast. Answer here. I will take it to General Hooker. He wants Sedgwick to press them." Butterfield sent this dispatch on to Sedgwick and asked, "What answer can I send to General Hooker?"

Sedgwick was pondering his answer when Butterfield forwarded a second Ingalls dispatch. It did nothing to lift John Sedgwick's confidence. "Do not expect dispatches much from General Hooker at present," Ingalls announced. "He wishes to hear constantly from you but he is too engaged. He has been slightly hurt, but not at all severely. No firing for an hour. . . . The slaughter has been fearful on both sides."

The rosy picture was turning darker, but still there was no change in orders — nor from this did it appear there would be. Nor was there any hint in these Ingalls dispatches that Hooker was now making no pretense whatever of keeping Lee's attention fully focused on him, nothing to warn Sedgwick of possible danger from that direction. John Sedgwick was still obliged to march on Chancellorsville as rapidly as possible.

To do so, however, meant turning his back on the enemy he had just fought, and that made General Sedgwick nervous. The original idea had been to crush Lee's command between the two wings of the Federal army. Now, he could not help noticing, it was his Sixth Corps that was squarely between the two wings of the Confederate army. That inspired cautious John Sedgwick to further caution.

There was also concern that new counters might enter the game against him. Earlier a pair of deserters from Early's command spoke confidently to Yankee interrogators of Hood's and Pickett's divisions, from Longstreet's corps, "coming by way of Gordonsville." Then Captain Charles Squires of the Washington Artillery, captured that morning at Marye's Heights, assured his captors that the reinforcements were expected by nightfall. (By nightfall, in fact, Longstreet's corps would only be breaking off the siege of Suffolk to start north.) "The general impression of the prisoners," said the interrogators, "seems to be that we shall hear from Hood before long." And it was observed that the railroad was still operating to Hamilton's Crossing, raising the possibility that these reinforcements might arrive squarely in Sedgwick's rear. General Sedgwick was beginning to feel more like the hunted than the hunter.

At army headquarters at Falmouth there was little sense of such concern. Dan Butterfield expressed his regret at the news of Hooker's injury, but otherwise he was optimistic about Sedgwick's situation. He expected the enemy facing Sedgwick to make a desperate effort "as his custom is, toward dusk, if he lasts that long." He added, "Our troops are still advancing, cheering lustily." Indeed it was judged so peaceful that photographer Andrew Russell crossed the river in the afternoon and set up his camera to record the battlefield at Marye's Heights. Posing in one of Russell's pictures was the railroad man Herman Haupt, who was on the scene "ready to spring" with a replacement R.F. & P. bridge to span the Rappahannock. "Affairs seem to justify it now here," Butterfield announced.[9]

* *

ONCE THEY had finally sorted themselves out after their triumphant rush up Marye's Heights, Newton's division and Burnham's Light Division pushed ahead along the Plank Road a mile and a half to the country seat of George Guest. It was noon when General Sedgwick came up to the head of the column and determined that here was as far as this one third of his corps might safely go unsupported. (It was this column that Jubal Early saw advancing slowly and then halting.) Sedgwick took Mr. Guest's house for his field headquarters and set about rearranging his command before advancing any farther along the road to Chancellorsville.

Except for some skirmishing and artillery exchanges, Bully Brooks's division had not been engaged in the morning's fighting. That meant his was the freshest division in the corps, and it was decided that he should lead. To take the lead required Brooks to march up from below

Fredericksburg, through the town, and then westward on the Plank Road — a good five miles in all.

As they passed through the town the marchers saw the wounded in their hundreds being collected in dooryard field hospitals. Crossing Marye's Heights, New Yorker Clinton Beckwith wrote that "hundreds of human forms dotted the ground. . . . The dead were in every position, just as they had fallen." It was 2 o'clock before Brooks reached the Guest house. Behind him came Howe's division. Three and a half hours had passed since the Yankees swept over the crest of Marye's Heights, and Sedgwick's corps had advanced only a mile and a half beyond that point. To Chancellorsville was eight miles more.

Sedgwick did not understand if John Gibbon's two Second Corps brigades were his to command for this march, and Gibbon had no authority to join the march on his own, and so his 3,500 men remained behind to guard Fredericksburg and the bridges there. That left Sedgwick with some 22,500 troops. Acting as spearhead of the advance were two of Brooks's brigades. They moved out, wrote a man on Sedgwick's staff, "listening anxiously for the sound of firing from the main army. None was heard, however. . . ."[10]

Cadmus Wilcox's movement west to block the Plank Road in front of Sedgwick had not escaped the notice of Yankee observers. At 12:30, using a powerful telescope, Captain James Hall at Station F north of the river sighted Rebel infantry and artillery well out on the Plank Road, "in numbers about 1 Brigade." An hour later a Signal Corps observer at Banks's Ford reported infantry, a section of artillery, and two squadrons of cavalry "marching at double quick," a good description of Wilcox's command although overcounting it as 5,000 to 6,000 men. Both sightings were relayed to Sedgwick. McLaws's reinforcements marching from the Chancellorsville front were not sighted until later, however, and report of them did not reach Sedgwick until well after he committed to battle. Consequently, expecting to encounter no more than a single brigade of infantry, he marched straight into an ambush.

Wilcox had determined to take his stand on the crest of a low wooded ridge running at right angles to the Plank Road four miles from Fredericksburg. In a roadside clearing on the ridge was Salem Church, a sturdy Baptist edifice of brick, and a small log schoolhouse. McLaws's reinforcing brigades, coming up behind the ridge, would be able to deploy out of sight of the Yankees.

Wilcox had his advanced skirmish line posted on the Plank Road a mile to the east, at the toll gate, and to slow the enemy's advance and give McLaws time to deploy, he moved out ahead to open the fight there. By skirmishing at the toll gate and then falling back to Salem Church, he thought he could draw the Yankees into the ambush. Brigade commanders seldom had the chance to exercise much initiative and enterprise, and Cadmus Wilcox was seizing his moment.

Bully Brooks, like Wilcox, was a career army man, and like Wilcox it appeared to him that the impending fight on the Plank Road would be his best opportunity so far in this war to shine. Brooks had been wounded on the Peninsula and again at Antietam, but both times while playing inconsequential roles, and he was still under a cloud for his part in the generals' revolt in January. On this day, leading the Federal advance toward the toll gate, he was looking for a fight, yet he went into it considerably short of his full divisional strength.

General Brooks pushed ahead in a formation that was primed for battle. The ground here was open and level, and he advanced in columns of brigades — a column advancing along each side of the Plank Road in brigade strength, the regiments marching in double ranks, one behind the other. In the center, on the road, were two batteries. This was a slow-moving but compact formation, one that could be shaken out right and left into a line of battle without much delay. On the left, south of the road, was Joseph Bartlett with four of his five regiments. On the right was Henry Brown, also with four of five regiments. Their two absent regiments plus David Russell's entire brigade had covered the division while it disengaged from the Rebels below Fredericksburg, and now Brooks was going into action with nearly half his command off to the rear. One of his staff later admitted, "our people underestimated the number of the enemy in our front and on our flanks. . . ."[11]

At precisely 3:25 P.M. signalman Hall recorded the opening shot of the battle for Salem Church. Virginian James Cobbs, commanding two guns of the Pittsylvania Artillery posted at the toll gate, opened fire at 800 yards against Brooks's advance. Cobbs's second shot inflicted the first casualties of the contest. Exploding directly in front of Battery A of the Maryland Light Artillery, it seriously wounded Sergeant John Wormsley of the battery and Captain Theodore Read of the divisional staff. With that the Yankees deployed for battle.

Colonel Brown's New Jersey brigade swung smartly into line north of the Plank Road. Six companies of the 2nd New Jersey pushed out ahead in skirmish formation. Bartlett's New York, Maine, and Pennsylvania men formed a line on the left of the road. Battery A, Maryland Light, and Battery A, New Jersey Light, unlimbered straddling the road and returned Lieutenant Cobbs's fire.

The Rebel gunners and the dismounted troopers supporting them could not maintain this uneven contest. They began slowly to withdraw. Wilcox's Alabamians behind them loosed a few volleys and then they went back too, fading into a thick belt of woods 750 yards beyond the toll gate. The Federals pushed after them confidently. At 4:15 Lieutenant Charles Woolsey, traveling with Sedgwick, reported on events to Chief of Staff Butterfield. Their line of battle, he said, was half a mile wide "and meets with a *little* opposition." It was thought that the enemy would attempt a stand perhaps half a mile ahead. General Sedgwick "says we are 'getting along very well.'"

The belt of woods was 250 yards deep here and stretched right and left well beyond the battle lines. Wilcox's men slipped back through the trees and took position in the next clearing on the ridge. His battle line south of the road took cover in a farm lane behind a bordering brush and dirt fence. To the north, the troops formed up along the embankment of a little ravine. They had no time to entrench, but there was concealment and fair protection in these positions. Except for the passage of the Plank Road and the clearing containing Salem Church and the schoolhouse, the belt of woods completely hid the Confederates from the approaching Federals. The ridge sloping gradually away in front further concealed them from view.

In the line to the south Wilcox posted the 8th and 10th Alabama, with the 9th Alabama in reserve behind them. One company of the 9th was out ahead in the schoolhouse, and one company in Salem Church, with orders (as Wilcox put it) "to fire from the windows of the lower floor and from the windows of the gallery. . . ." Farther to the south, and completely concealed in the woods, were Kershaw's and Wofford's brigades of McLaws's division.

The line just north of the road was formed by Wilcox's 11th and 14th Alabama, and then the four Georgia regiments of Paul Semmes's brigade from McLaws. Mahone's brigade, from Anderson, formed the farthest-north extension of the line. Semmes and Mahone were late arrivals, hurrying into the line just as the action started. The Pittsylvania battery fell back from the toll gate to the new line, but its ammunition was soon exhausted and it was replaced by Captain Basil Manly's North Carolina battery. Manly took up the gun duel against the Maryland and New Jersey batteries. There had been no time for him to replenish ammunition after the morning's gunnery at Chancellorsville, however, and he too soon went to the rear, saving his last twelve rounds of canister for an emergency. For the Rebels it would now be purely an infantry fight.[12]

When the Yankees entered the belt of woods their artillery ceased firing. This woodland, an extension of the larger Wilderness to the west, was dense with tangled undergrowth that made it hard to keep any kind of formation. "I can remember now a strange sort of quiet in the ranks," Clinton Beckwith of the 121st New York recalled. "I had no idea, nor do

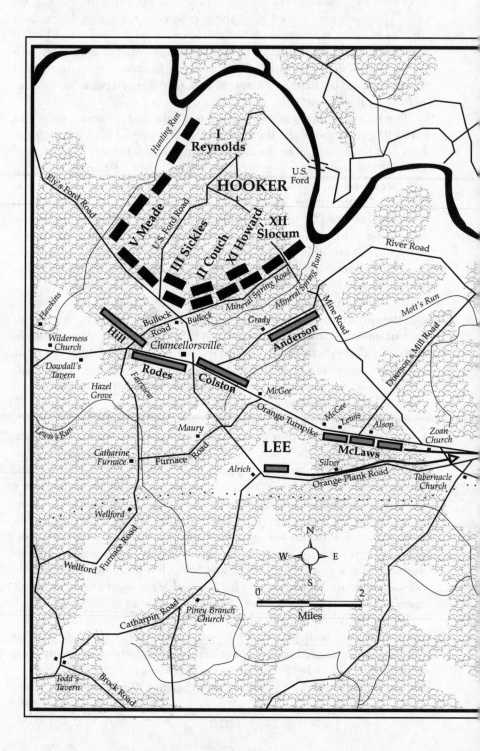

I
Reynolds

HOOKER

U.S.
Ford

V Meade

U.S. Ford Road

III Sickles

II Couch

XI Howard

XII
Slocum

Hunting Run

Ely's Ford Road

Mineral Spring Road

Mineral Spring Run

River Road

Hawkins

Hill

Bullock
Road

Bullock

Grady

Anderson

Mine Road

Mott's Run

Dierson's Mill Road

Wilderness
Church

Chancellorsville

Dowdall's
Tavern

Rodes

Colston

McGee

McGee

Lewis

Alsop

Zoan
Church

Hazel
Grove

Fairview

Orange Turnpike

Maury

LEE

McLaws

Silver

Lewis's Run

Catharine
Furnace

Furnace   Road

Alrich

Orange Plank Road

Tabernacle
Church

Wellford

Wellford

Furnace Road

Piney Branch
Church

Catharpin Road

N

W   E

S

0   2

Miles

Todd's
Tavern

Brock Road

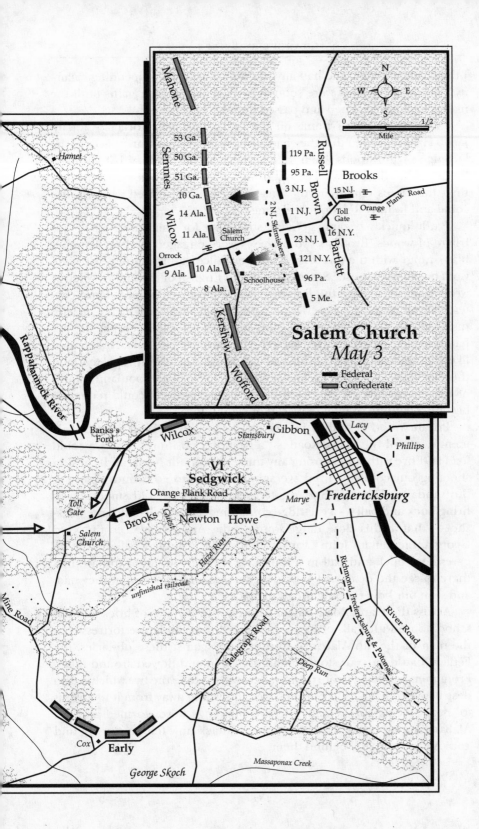

Salem Church
May 3

■ Federal
■ Confederate

N
W E
S

0 _____ 1/2
Mile

Mahone

53 Ga.
50 Ga.
51 Ga.
10 Ga.
14 Ala.
11 Ala.

Semmes

Wilcox

Salem
Church

Orrock

9 Ala.   10 Ala.

8 Ala.

Schoolhouse

Kershaw

Wofford

119 Pa.
95 Pa.
3 N.J.
1 N.J.

2 N.J. Skirmishers

23 N.J.
121 N.Y.
96 Pa.
5 Me.

Russell
Brown

Brooks

15 N.J.

Toll
Gate

16 N.Y.

Bartlett

Orange Plank Road

Hamet

Rappahannock River

Banks's
Ford

Wilcox

Stansbury

Gibbon

Lacy

Phillips

VI
Sedgwick

Orange Plank Road

Toll
Gate

Salem
Church

Brooks

Guest

Newton   Howe

Marye

Fredericksburg

Hazel Run

unfinished railroad

Mine Road

Telegraph Road

Deep Run

Richmond, Fredericksburg & Potomac

River Road

Cox   **Early**

Massaponax Creek

George Skoch

I think any one near me had any premonition of any impending calamity." Their skirmishers were soon at work, holding their gains until the main battle line reached and passed them.

In the 96th Pennsylvania on the left of the New Yorkers, Captain Jacob Haas recorded that they had advanced to within thirty paces of the far edge of the woods when "suddenly I saw two lines of battle of the 'Rebs' rise to their feet." The opposing lines fired simultaneously. "And then the circus commenced," Haas remarked. "We fired as fast as we could and Johnny Reb done the same."

Battle quickly became general, stretching for half a mile along this fringe of woods. Brooks's two brigades were engaged at virtually point-blank range with the two brigades under Wilcox and Semmes. "Now the work began in earnest," Sergeant Edmund English of the 2nd New Jersey wrote home, ". . . and the fighting came almost to a hand-to-hand contest. Never in all my experience have I seen or heard such a fearful fusillade." In the experience of John Wood of the 53rd Georgia, the din had been exceeded only at Malvern Hill on the Peninsula: "It sounded like a large cane brake on fire and a thunder storm with repeated loud thunder claps. . . ." With no breeze stirring in the thick woodland, clouds of battle smoke began to obscure everything. No one could see much beyond a handful of men to his left or right.

Private Wood described his regiment's posting behind the embankment north of the Plank Road as "a beautiful position . . . so we could load and fire without exposing any thing except our heads and arms. In shooting our company fired averaging from 15 to 20 rounds apiece at the vandals." These Georgians were equipped with old smoothbores firing buck and ball — a cartridge containing a lead ball and three buckshot — that at this close range were deadly. Another man in the 53rd Georgia, Lieutenant John Evans, told his wife, "you may believe that we gave them buck and ball in a hurry. . . . Molie you aught to have ben there to see the dead and wounded yankees and to see what they had, and seen our boys robbing their knapsacks."[13]

Across the Plank Road, Salem Church with its walls of brick and the schoolhouse with walls of logs were turned into miniature fortresses by the men of the 9th Alabama. Running up against these obstacles, the Federal battle line was stopped and then split and flowed around them. From their windows, wrote Clinton Beckwith, "came the fire which was so destructive to us . . . and our men were crowding away from it toward us to escape being hit." Finally the two buildings were stormed and the Alabamians captured. The thrust of the attack now fell on the 8th and 10th Alabama in line behind them.

Twenty-three-year-old Emory Upton, West Point class of 1861, recognized as one of the most promising young officers in the service (he would be a major general at twenty-five), was leading the 121st New York into its first battle. New men seemed to do best when there was no maneuvering to do under their first fire, and Upton led them straight ahead. His horse was shot but he leaped off and led on foot. "Fix bayonets and forward, double quick, charge!" came the order.

Beckwith loaded and fired as rapidly as he could, aiming in the direction the enemy fire seemed to be coming from, but it was so smoky now that he could see very little. Men began falling all around him. "Benny West who was next to me gave a terrible bound and pitched against me, shot dead." A man on the other side of him cried out that he was hit. "He mistook the water running from his canteen, which a bullet had pierced, for blood. I remember I laughed at the expression on his face at the time."

The main weight of this Yankee charge bowled into the 10th Alabama, which wavered and then broke. General Wilcox was watching alongside the 9th Alabama, his reserve force and his first command in this war. "Wilcox twice sang out, look at that damned 10th, steady 9th Alabama . . . ," Lieutenant William McClellan wrote in a letter home. "One solid sheet of flame awrose from this noble Reg., the enemy waver and return the fire. . . ." Then Major Jeremiah Williams shouted, "Forward, 9th Alabama!" and as the men rose to obey another volley hit them from a distance of forty paces. "This fire did most of the damage of the day," Lieutenant Edmund Patterson remembered. "Nine men of Co. K fell dead in their tracks without firing a gun, and almost twice as many suffered severely." Yet even this was not enough to stem the 9th's charge.

In falling back the 10th Alabama had exposed the flank of the 8th Alabama next to it. The 8th's commander, Young L. Royston, at six feet seven and a half inches one of the tallest men in Alabama, had gone down with a serious wound at the first fire, but Lieutenant Colonel Hilary Herbert saw the danger and had the two companies on the left of the line wheel back to face left, and they volleyed straight into the flank of the charging 121st New York. This fire from flank and front took a murderous toll. Colonel Upton claimed that in just seven minutes he lost 200 of the 453 men he led into battle that day. The bewildered survivors milled about in the woods. "Damn you, don't you know enough to fall back?" a staff man yelled at the rookies. With that they turned and went to the rear, losing men at every step.[14]

The 9th Alabama's determined countercharge into Colonel Upton's shattered regiment was the turning point. Yipping the Rebel yell, the rest of Wilcox's brigade joined in the charge against the surprised Yankee line. Catching the fever, the 10th and 51st Georgia joined in. (Semmes's other two regiments did not get the word and did not charge.)

Many of the Federals had already lost their bearings in the smoky woods and suddenly it seemed as if Rebels were coming at them from all sides. Corporal John S. Judd of the 3rd New Jersey entered in his diary, "After being in awhile found some one was firing into us from the rear. Went back to see who it was, found the enemy had flanked us and got in our rear. Ordered to surrender, as there was no help for it done so. . . ." Salem Church and the schoolhouse were overrun by the counterattack and their defenders freed. At first, wrote a man in the 14th Alabama, the Yankees "retreated slowly and sullenly, but our boys pressed them closely and they soon struck a trot to keep out of reach of our bayonets."

Brooks's formations spilled out of the belt of woods and went back across the open ground toward the toll gate and their supports. The Confederates swarmed after them. Watching with one of his aides, a stunned Bully Brooks said, "Twenty-five years in the army, Mr. Wheeler, and ruined at last!"

While there were substantial numbers of infantry back at the toll gate — the rest of Brooks's division and most of John Newton's — they were too far away to be anything more than a rallying point for the retreating Federals. Apparently Uncle John Sedgwick had anticipated nothing much more than an extended skirmish at Salem Church. Quickly the Maryland and New Jersey batteries, joined now by Battery D, 2nd United States, went into action. The Rebels, wrote one of Newton's men, "were advancing with a rush waving their old red rag of a battle flag and yelling like demons, but there was one stump for them to run against which they had not counted on. . . ." On Sedgwick's order firing shell and case shot over the heads of the returning men until their sights were clear, then switching to canister, the gunners broke the impetus of the counterattack. The massed infantry stopped it. Wilcox surveyed the solid ranks of infantry and the array of guns and noted the fast-fading light, and ordered the men back to their lines.[15]

They had won a striking victory. While nominally in command, McLaws deferred to the general on the scene and left tactical command largely to Wilcox. The brigades of Mahone, Kershaw, and Wofford, posted on the flanks in anticipation of a broader Federal assault, fired scarcely a shot.

Wilcox was exuberant over his carefully planned battle. McLaws asked him the identity of the regiment that initiated the counterattack. His old command, 9th Alabama, Wilcox told him proudly. "That is the best regiment I ever saw," McLaws was heard to say. "General," Wilcox said, "that is the best regiment on the American continent."

For Cadmus Wilcox the reasons behind the victory were clear. "My brigade acted nobly in this fight of the 3rd . . . ," he wrote his sister. "You can see how our men fight and how much better they fight than the Yankees." As for his ambitions, he told her, "If I am not promoted now I shall really be discouraged. . . ." Cadmus Wilcox's promotion to major general would come three months to the day after Salem Church.

John Sedgwick's almost constitutional inability to act or move swiftly had fated his men to fight a full-blooded battle at Salem Church rather than forcefully shouldering aside a single enemy brigade at midday (if indeed in that event Wilcox had managed to outmarch the Yankees after Marye's Heights). Federal accounts of the fighting here would speak of being outnumbered, or being overwhelmed by enemy reinforcements. In fact, of the opposing forces that did the actual fighting that day, the numbers were very nearly equal. Bully Brooks made his assault with two brigades, some 4,100 men. Wilcox's and Semmes's brigades met the assault with just over 4,000 men.

There was nothing second rate about these Union troops. Henry Brown's New Jersey brigade had originally been trained by Phil Kearny. The men of Joseph Bartlett's brigade were also veterans. Bartlett said this was the first time an attack of theirs had been repulsed, the first time they could not hold a position when ordered, the first time they had retired in the face of the enemy.

The Confederates' major advantage at Salem Church was receiving the Federals' attack from behind cover. To be sure, it was natural cover rather than man-made entrenchments, but it was superior to any cover the Yankees had. Federals complained that in the second-growth woodland they had to traverse there was not a single tree big enough to shelter behind. Brooks's men exhausted themselves attacking these lines, and were too weakened to resist a counterattack. And their closest support, as it happened, was a thousand yards distant.

Evidence of this Confederate advantage is the casualty lists. The Sixth Corps suffered 1,523 casualties in the Salem Church battle on May 3, the Confederates but 674, less than half as many. Colonel Mark W. Collet of the 1st New Jersey was killed and brigade commander Henry Brown wounded. Colonel Upton's 121st New York had 276 dead, wounded, and missing, second in the Federal army only to the 12th New Hampshire that lost 317 that morning at Chancellorsville. Upton's loss was nearly two thirds of the men he took into battle. (In an all too common scene in this war, the hamlet of Garrattsville in central New York State, where the

121st was recruited, mourned the loss of fifteen of its young men killed in these few hours at Salem Church.)[16]

* *

UNCLE JOHN SEDGWICK, recalled his chief of staff, Lieutenant Colonel Martin McMahon, "scarcely slept that night. . . . He would walk a few paces apart and listen; then returning would lie down again in the damp grass, with his saddle for a pillow, and try to sleep. The night was inexpressibly gloomy."

Sedgwick was painfully aware that he was in a no man's land. He was some three miles from the safety of his bridge crossings in Fredericksburg. He was somewhat closer to a new crossing at Banks's Ford, where late that afternoon a pontoon bridge had been laid by the engineers. Eight miles ahead was General Hooker with the main army, about which General Sedgwick knew very little. On two sides of him at least, to the west and to the south, lay the enemy in unknown force. What John Sedgwick wanted desperately just then was a firm set of orders telling him what to do in this predicament.

Sedgwick had reason to be concerned. At 7 o'clock that evening General Lee began laying plans to assail the Sixth Corps at the first opportunity the next day. He wrote to Early and McLaws urging them to coordinate forces. The two of them together, he told Early, "ought to be more than a match for the enemy." If McLaws attacked the enemy positions on the Plank Road, "and you could come upon their left flank, and communicate with General McLaws, I think you would demolish them." He had the same bold message for McLaws, adding, "It is necessary that you beat the enemy, and I hope you will do it." That this offensive some miles away on the Plank Road would leave him with barely half the army to confront Hooker's host in front of him appeared to concern General Lee not at all. He seemed to think the victorious effort at Chancellorsville that morning had immobilized his foe.[17]

The third actor in this evolving drama, Joe Hooker, was seldom taking any role at all in events that afternoon and evening. The effects of his concussion drove him to alternating periods of deep sleep and fitful wakefulness. For the most part Rufus Ingalls, his quartermaster, spoke for him.

At 1:30 P.M. Hooker roused himself enough to dictate a dispatch to the president, his first since the first day of the campaign. There had been two days of desperate fighting, he reported, "which has resulted in no success to us, having lost a position of two lines, which had been selected for our defense." The battle might resume at any moment. "I do not despair of success. If Sedgwick could have gotten up, there could

386

have been but one result." He could not forecast an outcome, but he praised his troops. "No general ever commanded a more devoted army."

This was not the report of a general who appeared to have any plan for reversing this grim picture. There was no trace of the outspoken optimism that had marked the Joe Hooker of weeks past. Rather it was the report of a general simply waiting for the next event to happen.

Before this dispatch reached him, President Lincoln had learned from Butterfield of the "fierce and terrible" morning's battle on the Rappahannock, and that General Hooker had been "slightly, but not severely, wounded." The concerned commander-in-chief wanted concrete answers. "Where is General Hooker?" he telegraphed brusquely. "Where is Sedgwick? Where is Stoneman?" Butterfield replied lamely, for he had only Ingalls's largely unfactual reports to go on, that Hooker was at Chancellorsville and that Sedgwick was three or four miles beyond Fredericksburg. "Lee is between. Stoneman has not been heard from."

As he usually did when a battle was in progress, Mr. Lincoln spent these evening hours of May 3 at the telegraph office in the War Department, where he could see the latest news from the field the moment it arrived. The slim diet of unhappy news from the Rappahannock resembled too many telegrams sent to Washington from too many battlefields of this war. In exasperation he began drafting a telegram demanding to know the specifics of the fight. "I assume that Howard, Meade, and Slocum were in the main fight with Hooker," he began. "Was Sickles in it? Was Couch in it? Was Reynolds in it? Where is Reynolds? Is Sedgwick fighting Lee's rear? . . ." Then no doubt with a sigh he gave it up and pigeonholed the telegram unsent. That night his secretary John Nicolay wrote his fiancée, "We know very little about what has been accomplished."[18]

Early that Sunday evening Captain William Folwell of the 50th New York engineers rode up to the front from his post at U.S. Ford. It was a slow passage, for the road was crowded with wounded and stragglers making for the rear. At the Bullock farm clearing he found the army's battle line stretching left and right as far as the eye could see. "The infantry were sitting and lying down, and the cannoniers resting on their guns," he explained to his wife. He met a staff man he knew and asked where General Hooker's headquarters might be. "'Right there' said he, pointing to a spot in the dirty and beaten road where two Major Generals were standing. I did not at first recognize Gen. Hooker. He and Gen. Meade stood there in the road, chatting coolly and pleasantly. They were both covered with dust and looked quite differently from the splendid gentlemen who figured at the reviews." To Captain Folwell, who did not know of Hooker's injury, nothing seemed unusual about the general commanding except his dusty appearance.

To those who did know of the injury, however, there was a definite change in the general's manner. A telegrapher who saw him that evening entered in his diary that Hooker seemed "extremely nervous." From the "terrible shock" of his injury, he wrote, "his mental faculties may almost be said to be temporarily impaired."

At about the same time, quartermaster Ingalls was making his final report to Dan Butterfield of the day's events at Hooker's headquarters. It was still quiet along the front, Ingalls said; "enemy remains in force, movements matter of conjecture." As for the army's future course, that too was conjecture, "if we are all right tomorrow which God grant may be our fortune."

Later in the evening Gouverneur Warren returned to headquarters after twenty-four eventful and exhausting hours on assignment with General Sedgwick and the Sixth Corps. He found Hooker asleep again and had difficulty waking him to report. The general, he said, appeared "very much exhausted." For the most part Hooker was unresponsive. Warren related events on Sedgwick's battlefields, and passed on Sedgwick's assertion that he had done all he could and could advance no farther.

By Warren's later testimony, Hooker offered nothing in return "and declined to give any special instructions to General Sedgwick. He said he had none to give, and gave me to infer that he would have to depend upon himself. . . ." As for the main army, Hooker said only that he hoped Lee would attack him the next day. Pressed for an opinion on General Hooker's condition, Warren could only say, "I should think the word 'tired' would express it."

Feeling obliged to give his friend John Sedgwick at least some guidance, Warren composed a midnight dispatch on his own responsibility. General Hooker, he explained, hoped the enemy would attack him on Monday. "If they will, he does not desire you to attack them again in force unless he attacks him at the same time." (This confusing instruction, which Warren blamed on his own exhaustion, was construed by Sedgwick to mean that he was to take the offensive only if General Hooker took the offensive first.) "He says you are too far away for him to direct."

Warren then added the one thing that John Sedgwick wanted to know above all else: he was to hold his communications with the bridges at both Fredericksburg and Banks's Ford. "Go to either place if you think it best to cross," Warren told him, and suggested that Banks's Ford would put him within supporting distance of the main army. This dispatch reached Sedgwick at 6:30 the next morning, and if it was not the firm set of orders he had wanted, it at least gave him the option to act as he thought best. Beyond that, it offered a cheerless prospect indeed.

So ended Day Seven of the Chancellorsville campaign. Except at Marye's Heights it had been a day of hard-won victory for the Confederates. The human cost of the three battles on May 3, 1863, was staggering. The toll of 21,357 for the two armies together would make it second only to Antietam as the bloodiest single day of the Civil War.[19]

15

Time the Yankees
Were Leaving

EVEN WHILE FOCUSING his attention on Sedgwick's Sixth Corps in his rear, Lee maintained a war of nerves against Hooker in his front. The more his opponent was distracted, the less likely he would be to take the offensive. On Monday, May 4, Day Eight of the campaign, one thing General Lee could not afford was an active and aggressive Fighting Joe Hooker.

Late Sunday afternoon, while Sedgwick was being challenged at Salem Church, Lee had ordered Dick Anderson and three brigades northward along the River Road. Anderson was to keep an eye on Hooker in his new lines back of Chancellorsville and discourage him from pushing eastward toward Banks's Ford and a link-up with Sedgwick. Lee told one of Anderson's artillerists, Major Robert A. Hardaway, to assemble a "rifle battalion" and go along and see what mischief he could do.

Hardaway was chosen because of his particular skill with rifled pieces, and he selected thirteen, from four different artillery battalions — a nice example of the flexibility of the Confederates' new artillery-command system. The Federals were seen to be resting quietly in their lines, and that evening Hardaway found some high open ground a third of a mile from the Rappahannock that overlooked the enemy positions north of the river at U.S. Ford. He concealed ten of his guns there and at 3 o'clock on the morning of May 4 unleashed a sudden barrage on the sleeping Yankee camps.

There were numerous supply trains crowded in here, and wounded men and a number of Confederate prisoners from the May 3 fighting and, in common with the backwash of any battlefield, a larger number of stragglers. The shells ignited a panic. Men and animals and wagons rushed in every direction. The prisoners were delighted. "They set up a loud yell for Jeff Davis," Alpheus Williams remarked, "and, I fear, laughed

somewhat at the general skedaddles on the part of our officers and men."
A disgusted Provost Marshal Patrick would comb about a thousand stragglers out of the bushes. With much satisfaction Major Hardaway limbered up and departed after 150 rounds.[1]

Hardaway's surprise bombardment was more spectacular than damaging — General Williams counted just three or four men killed by the
shelling — but it kindled a growing impression at Hooker's headquarters that day that no part of the army was secure. Hour by hour the
Rebels seemed to threaten from one direction and then another. A
signalman at U.S. Ford claimed he sighted enemy cavalry on the north
bank of the river, endangering the army's supply line. General Howard,
on the eastern flank of the line, reported probing movements against his
front. General Reynolds, on the western flank, signaled Hooker, "There
is no doubt but the enemy are massing their troops on our right for an
attack from the direction of Elys ford." Cavalryman Pleasonton raised
the alarm that a Rebel flanking force was moving downriver in the direction of Port Royal. "They may have a pontoon train down that way,"
he warned. But the most persistent alarms, and by far the most distract-
ing, had to do with the arrival of James Longstreet's two divisions from
the south.[2]

Deserters and prisoners were eager to tell their Yankee interrogators
that George Pickett's troops and John B. Hood's were close by the battlefield or even already there. Early Monday morning a deserter came
into John Gibbon's lines in Fredericksburg and announced that "Longstreet's forces are in the direction of Bowling Green," eighteen miles to
the south, "advancing in line of battle from that direction. . . ." Provost
Marshal Patrick had a deserter from the 16th Mississippi who insisted
that already Longstreet had "turned our right, would cross the river and
attack our rear. . . ." Dan Butterfield was told by a Fredericksburg citizen
that Hood's men were coming by rail by way of Gordonsville, while
Pickett's were coming north aboard the R.F. & P. Their scheduled arrival
had been May 3. "Railroads in good order yesterday," Butterfield added.
"Circumstances concurring with his statement convince me that it has
good foundation." Cavalryman Averell's earlier fear that 25,000 men
under Stonewall Jackson were lying in wait for him at Gordonsville was
somehow transmuted into a report that "25,000 men of Hood and Pickett's got off from the cars at Gordonsville. . . ."

George Sharpe and John Babcock of the Bureau of Military Information sorted through this welter of speculation and rumor to find the
facts of it. By May 3 no fewer than 824 prisoners and deserters had been
questioned but they had yet to find a single man who belonged to either
Pickett's or Hood's divisions. They concluded that there was "nothing

definite or certain as to any reinforcements of the enemy." Early on the afternoon of May 4 Babcock at Fredericksburg said he had no doubts that reinforcements "have arrived this morning on our front," but whether they were from the south or from Lee's army at Chancellorsville was uncertain; he still had no one from the divisions of Pickett or Hood.

The problem for Federal intelligence was that by the best reckoning reinforcements from Longstreet's corps could very well have reached the Rappahannock by Day Eight of the campaign. Indeed, if the Confederate high command had acted as promptly as it had to be given credit for acting, Hood and Pickett ought to have arrived from Suffolk by now. According to Hooker's original grand plan of campaign, by Day Eight the battle would already have been won over Lee and Hooker would be ready to meet Longstreet whenever he arrived. (To be sure, according to these same calculations Stoneman's raiders would have broken the railroads, delaying any reinforcements sent by Richmond. However, with each train seen arriving at Hamilton's Crossing hopes for that were dimming.)[3]

From the first, the various reports of Longstreet's supposed arrival were continually tested against what General Peck at Suffolk had to say about the matter. From the first, Peck insisted that Longstreet's entire command occupied the lines confronting Peck's besieged garrison. He documented his case with deserters from both Pickett's and Hood's divisions, with observations by his scouts, with captured enemy dispatches. Still, Dan Butterfield was not entirely convinced. He feared that somehow Pickett or Hood or both of them had slipped away without Peck seeing them. At 7:00 A.M. on May 4 he telegraphed Peck the latest Longstreet tales. While Butterfield admitted there was "nothing of positive nature" regarding Pickett and Hood, he asserted that nevertheless the Confederates on the Rappahannock "are being re-enforced in some measure from below. . . ."

At midday General Peck replied. In careful detail he pinpointed Longstreet's latest movements. At 9:30 on the evening of Sunday, May 3, he reported, "all his forces moved by different interior routes for the Blackwater. He had several hours the start." (General Peck had Longstreet's lifting of the siege of Suffolk almost to the minute.)

At Hooker's headquarters, however, the notion of Longstreet's thousands appearing any moment somewhere on the battlefield continued to be a matter of great concern. That night, for example, General Averell was sought out for the time those 25,000 troops of Pickett's and Hood's had gotten off the cars at Gordonsville, "and such other information as he may have." Clearly, the general commanding had Longstreet on his mind throughout the day on May 4. That was all the distraction General Lee could have hoped for.[4]

* *

AT 7 O'CLOCK that morning the Federal signalmen at Station F opposite Fredericksburg warned, "The enemy is advancing in line of battle towards our right. Are now on 2 ridges in rear of city. . . . About 1 brigade in sight." Ten minutes later their warning became more urgent: "Enemy will have works in about five or ten minutes if they are not resisted. I have informed Gen. Gibbon." Gibbon's aide, Lieutenant Frank Haskell, focused his binoculars and watched events unfold with growing astonishment: "The 'Telegraph Road' is full of the gray-backed devils, — on they come rapidly, regiment after regiment, pouring in like a torrent towards Fredericksburg . . . they rush along to the right into the vacant strongholds — one after another, — the whole heights swarm with them. . . ." The rumors must be true, Lieutenant Haskell concluded: Longstreet had arrived, and there was hell to pay.

This dramatic scene was in fact orchestrated by Jubal Early, who on May 4 was set on evening a score. Early sensed that he had been outgeneraled the day before, failing to anticipate where the Yankees would strike his Fredericksburg defenses. He sensed, too, a tone of rebuke from General Lee. "I very much regret the possession of Fredericksburg by the enemy," Lee had written him tersely Sunday night in urging Early to regain the initiative. Old Jube's response — a scheme to retake Marye's Heights and perhaps even Fredericksburg, and then to take Sedgwick in the rear — won Lee's prompt approval. That morning Early's opening move caught the Federals completely by surprise.[5]

John B. Gordon, new to the rank of brigadier general, new to the command of a brigade, new to service under Jubal Early, was impatient to start fighting that morning. Severely wounded at Sharpsburg, Gordon had only recently returned to the army and had barely acquainted himself with his brigade of Georgians. When he was selected to lead Early's column of attack on Monday, he assembled his troops and addressed them. He called on every man willing to follow him up Marye's Heights to raise his hat. According to Henry Walker of the 13th Georgia, the response was unanimous. "I don't want you to holler," Gordon told them. "Wait until you get up close to the heights. Let every man raise a yell and take those heights. . . . Will you do it? I ask you to go no farther than I am willing to lead!" On that ringing note he gave the order to march. "We all stepped off at quick time," Walker wrote.

Acting "under a mistake of my directions" (as Early phrased it), Gordon rushed off down the Telegraph Road toward Fredericksburg before the rest of the division could get into position. Early hurried up the other three brigades as best he could. For Gordon's troops primed for the charge what happened next was a decided anticlimax, but a welcome one. Lee's Hill was not occupied by the Yankees, nor was Marye's Heights. Reaching Sunday morning's battlefield, all they found were several Fredericksburg women on a mission of mercy, searching for any wounded still on the field, and several Mississippi scouts of Barksdale's brigade. In due course General Gordon would find a battle to join, but his first conquest on May 4 was a bloodless one.[6]

For the Federals this unhappy circumstance was the result of divided counsels. During the night and again after sunrise Sedgwick had pleaded for instructions. The enemy, he said, was in strong force in front of him and strongly posted. He predicted he would be attacked that morning. A courier he sent to Banks's Ford for directions had not returned. A second courier, according to Major Thomas Hyde, "came back to us some months after by way of Richmond and exchange." (Hyde, by heading there cross-lots, managed to reach Banks's Ford and return with a welcome report of the Federal bridgehead there.)

But not until 6:30 A.M. did Gouverneur Warren's midnight dispatch reach Sedgwick from Hooker's headquarters. Mainly it told him he was on his own, but at least he did not have to continue his advance and had the option of falling back on Fredericksburg or on Banks's Ford. Before Sedgwick could act on these instructions, Gordon's brigade had taken Marye's Heights and blocked his path to Fredericksburg.

Apparently no one in the Federal high command had given any further thought to Marye's Heights after its capture. John Gibbon's assignment was to hold Fredericksburg and the bridges there with his two brigades, and he deployed them on both sides of the river for that purpose. Gibbon assumed Sedgwick would be responsible for his own communications with his own Sixth Corps troops. But even after he was blocked at Salem Church and in obvious jeopardy, Sedgwick seemed to forget about his communications. Perhaps he thought Gibbon was guarding them, but he made no effort to find out if that was the case. And so Marye's Heights, won at such cost in blood on May 3, was lost without a fight on May 4.[7]

Early ordered Barksdale's Mississippians to take up their old line behind the Stone Wall at Marye's Heights and to test the Federals' hold on Fredericksburg. Barksdale pushed forward a strong line of skirmishers. The surprise of it set off a commotion. "The pickets rushed in, and for a few moments we had a wild time of it," wrote Lieutenant Henry

Ropes of the 20th Massachusetts, "but our regiment moved out and held the town and repulsed the enemy." Barksdale reported back to Early that the Yankees' infantry and their numerous guns were more than he could handle. He was given the task of preventing "any advance from town on the part of the enemy."

In his ardor John Gordon charged on ahead toward the west to find an enemy to fight. A Yankee supply and artillery train from Fredericksburg had just crossed Marye's Heights on the Plank Road when Gordon's Georgians spotted it. With a whoop Colonel Clement Evans's 31st Georgia dashed down a long slope to a little creek, splashed across, and charged up a hill on the other side toward the Plank Road. The train guard put up a brief fight and then scattered. His men, Colonel Evans wrote his wife proudly, "captured about 30 prisoners, several wagons full of stores, about 30 or 40 horses & mules, & drove everything before them." To the victors went the spoils: "My boys have helped themselves to Yankee fixins."

Gordon's brigade had gotten out ahead of the rest of Early's command, and now the 31st Georgia got out ahead of the rest of Gordon's brigade. Evans's men looked back and saw the other regiments far behind, saw their comrades waving their hats and yelling something they could not hear. Taking this for encouragement, they went on in pursuit of what they took to be the fleeing train guard and ran suddenly into a hail of fire from a fully manned Federal battle line. This was Thomas H. Neill's brigade of Albion Howe's division. The 31st went to ground and endured this for some time, I. G. Bradwell wrote, when "someone saw fit to send the 13th Virginia Regiment to assist us."

Early had ordered Extra Billy Smith's Virginia brigade after Gordon, and now Smith came up on the Georgians' left and sent the 13th forward in support. When it reached the beleaguered Georgians, Private Bradwell remembered, "they called out . . . to get up and help them drive the enemy out. To this our men replied in language more forcible than polite and informed them that what our regiment had failed to do they would be very far from doing." So it happened. The two regiments had to fall back out of range, leaving dead and wounded scattered across the hillside.

Still the uncoordinated assault continued. The 58th Virginia came up farther yet to the left and collided with the 7th Maine and 49th New York. Presently, to his dismay, the 58th's Colonel Francis Board discovered that everyone else had retired except his regiment. In the absence of an order from General Smith, "or its failure to reach me," Colonel Board passed the word to fall back.

At that moment the Federals counterattacked. The Rebels had come so close to their line, wrote Lieutenant Colonel Selden Connor of the 7th Maine, that now his men simply overran them, "routing them completely, and capturing the colors of the 58th Va. and some eighty prisoners." This little victory, Connor added, was the work of a single company of the 7th Maine and two companies of the 49th New York. To General Early, "It was now apparent that the hills were held in strong force," and he had everyone fall back and regroup for a second look at the situation. It was late morning now, and the poorly managed affair had cost Gordon and Smith 204 casualties, 101 of them in the 58th Virginia.[8]

* *

ONE ODD consequence of the Confederates' rush for Marye's Heights was to straighten out a signaling tangle that had plagued Sedgwick's command for the past twenty-four hours. When on Sunday morning Dan Butterfield put a ban on signaling across the river because the Rebels could read their signal code, it limited Sedgwick's communications with Falmouth headquarters to the speed of couriers. Butterfield's lame explanation that he was referring only to nighttime signaling by torch failed to persuade Sedgwick. If the Rebels could read nighttime torch signals, they could read daytime flag signals as well, for both used the same code. Sedgwick ordered his signalmen to remain mute.

It was sheer happenstance that finally resolved the matter. In their push across Marye's Heights the Confederates broke up and scattered a Union signal party, and signalmen Joseph Gloskoski and Paul Babcock, who escaped westward into Sedgwick's lines, knew nothing of the general's signal ban. Finding high ground near Sedgwick's headquarters at the Guest house, they uncased their flags and by 8:30 A.M. were in communication with Station F across the river. Their signals were going right over the heads of the enemy, but when Gloskoski and Babcock explained to General Sedgwick that they were using the Signal Corps' new cipher in place of the old flag code, he was appeased. Indeed he was grateful. For the first time he was receiving orders and intelligence within a matter of minutes. Uncle John Sedgwick might now say he was the best-informed general on the field.

A second flag station was soon established on Sedgwick's right, along the River Road, to communicate with the station across the river at Banks's Ford. The telegraph, now being worked with reliable Morse instruments, completed the circuit: by courier from Hooker's headquarters to the U.S. Ford station, from there by wire to Banks's Ford and to army headquarters at Falmouth. Captain Samuel Cushing, the army's chief signal officer, considered the new link-up on May 4 "of eminent importance," keeping General Sedgwick "thoroughly informed of the movements of the enemy. . . ."[9]

So far as enemy movements were concerned, Captain Cushing's appraisal was accurate. The Confederates on this battlefield had hardly any shelter from Yankee observers. Much of the forest here had been cleared, and with his telescope Captain Hall at Station F at the Phillips house could see far along the Orange Plank Road and the Telegraph Road and the valley of Hazel Run in between. Aeronauts Lowe in balloon *Washington* opposite Fredericksburg and E. S. Allen in the *Eagle* at Banks's Ford had good fields of vision. The two flag stations on Sedgwick's line also served as observation posts, reporting directly to the general. By 10 o'clock that morning Sedgwick knew that Rebels, "at least a full division," were forming up from the direction of the Telegraph Road to confront his line of battle. Professor Lowe estimated this force at 15,000. Albion Howe had beaten off the first assault without too much trouble, but surely there was more and worse to come.

Sedgwick thought himself to be in an awkward, uncomfortable position. After Sunday's fight at Salem Church he had remained there, poised to continue the advance toward Chancellorsville while he waited for further orders from the commanding general. These orders, embodied in Gouverneur Warren's dispatch that reached him at 6:30 Monday morning, were discretionary. As he had demonstrated repeatedly over the last three days, acting on discretionary orders was not John Sedgwick's long suit.

He faced three choices. He could stay where he was so as to act on Hooker's directive to attack toward Chancellorsville when — and if — Hooker took the offensive. He could fall back to the high ground behind Fredericksburg, securing the bridgehead there to hold his communications with the north bank. Or he could contract his lines to form a salient on Taylor's Hill and the high ground overlooking Banks's Ford and the bridges there (a second pontoon bridge was laid down at Banks's on May 4). This was the high ground that General Hooker, back on May 1, had hoped to seize to complete his grand turning movement. Hooker said he was too far away to direct; Sedgwick must decide these matters for himself.

The second alternative was almost immediately rendered unpalatable by Early's recapture of Marye's Heights. If Sedgwick wanted the Fredericksburg bridgehead now he would have to fight for it, retaking the high ground from the back side. If he acted quickly, however, before the Rebels formed up, he might swing back his center and right, the divisions of Brooks and Newton, to form a tight, compact, strong salient on the high ground overlooking the bridges at Banks's Ford. Instead he waited, cautiously pondering the situation, and then it was too late to move. The Confederates closed in on him tightly, making any pullback in daylight highly perilous. "My position is bad . . . ," he signaled Hooker at 11:15. "It was assumed for attack and not for defense. . . . Can you help me strongly if I am attacked?"[10]

What paralyzed Sedgwick was his conviction that he was facing (as he put it in his report) "immediate attack from vastly superior forces." After Sunday's fighting the Sixth Corps was left with just under 21,000 men. (Sedgwick, however, greatly overstating his losses, counted his numbers on May 4 as 17,000.) He described the enemy column that stormed up the Telegraph Road and retook Marye's Heights and struck at his left as "coming from the direction of Richmond." That had to be Longstreet. When with his inexpert eye Professor Lowe counted this column as 15,000 men — a considerable overcount of Early's 8,400 — it reinforced the illusion.

The prisoners taken in Gordon's and Smith's ragged morning assault might have cleared up the confusion, but no one thought to interrogate them; the B.M.I.'s John Babcock at army headquarters was now cut off from Sedgwick's command. Lieutenant Colonel Connor, 7th Maine, noted that the prisoners were talkative enough, warning the Yankees to skedaddle or they would "drive us into the river," but that they were Early's men and not Longstreet's escaped notice. By report, announced General Sedgwick at 1:40 that afternoon, the force that had cut him off from Fredericksburg was now two divisions strong. He said deserters put the total forces confronting him at 40,000.[11]

While Sedgwick gloomily contemplated his fate, the general commanding was contemplating a plan to recapture the initiative. Hooker went out to inspect his lines that morning, showing no outward signs of his Sunday injury and concussion. Captain Charles Bowers, 32nd Massachusetts, wrote his wife that the general "is looking finely and was out with us walking about. . . . The men are encouraged by his presence, confident that he is *the* man to direct." Apparently Hooker agreed.

It was now his thought to stay only one more day with his determination to fight the battle defensively. The evening before, Colonel Wainwright recorded in his diary, the general told him "he should give Lee tomorrow to attack him, and 'then if he does not,' said Hooker, 'let him look out.'"

Hooker did not at first articulate this new plan for the benefit of General Sedgwick — or perhaps the plan was still evolving. However that may be, Warren's dispatch under which Sedgwick was first acting on May 4 suggested that Hooker might take the offensive that day, in which event the Sixth Corps was cautioned to be ready to advance as well. That caution added to John Sedgwick's burden of cautions, and helped keep him right where he was for most of the day.

Should Lee not attack him in his prepared lines on Monday, Hooker intended to take the offensive himself on Tuesday. He would not attack Lee's lines at Chancellorsville head-on, which (as he later wrote) "I felt could be carried only at a frightful loss." Instead he would utilize the salient Sedgwick was holding on the Rappahannock — the high ground of Taylor's Hill and the area overlooking Banks's Ford and its bridges — for a turning movement. Once again Joe Hooker was choosing maneuver over needless dashes at the enemy.

Leaving a holding force in the lines facing Chancellorsville, he would slip away across U.S. Ford with the main force, march seven miles downriver to Banks's Ford, recross the river there, and drive into the unsuspecting flank of Lee's army. Hooker planned his maneuver to be completed during the morning of May 5. Thus Sedgwick would be required to hold the salient until afternoon of the fifth.

In several dispatches, delivered by several hands on May 4, Hooker tried to make the importance of all this clear to his lieutenant, yet at the same time he refused to spell out the whole plan for fear word of it would fall into the enemy's hands. (Butterfield told him he thought earlier dispatches intended for Sedgwick had been captured.) It was the commanding general's intention, Sedgwick was told, "to advance to-morrow. In this event the position of your corps on the south bank of the Rappahannock will be as favorable as the general could desire. It is for this reason that he desires that your troops may not cross the Rappahannock."

In reply to Sedgwick asking if he could expect substantial help if he was attacked in the meantime, Hooker offered cold comfort: "You must not count on much assistance without I hear heavy firing." Thus Uncle John Sedgwick was left to puzzle out just how important his salient really was to a commanding general who did not appear eager to help him defend it. Nevertheless he responded dutifully, "I shall do my utmost to hold a position on the right bank of the Rappahannock until tomorrow."[12]

To better manage this new operation, and simply to improve the workings of his field staff, Hooker made a personnel change on May 4. Dan Butterfield was told that the general commanding "cannot get along without you," and at 10:00 A.M. was called from Falmouth to run the headquarters staff. Hooker wasted no time sending the stand-in chief of staff, James Van Alen, back to Falmouth and lesser duties, and until Butterfield arrived cavalryman Alfred Pleasonton was pressed into duty as temporary chief of staff. Hooker complained that he had been "necessarily subjected to much trouble" running the army in the field and seemed confident that the efficient Butterfield would straighten matters out.

After the sharp morning's fight on Sedgwick's front — and after the thunderous din of the fighting the day before — the Chancellorsville battlefield at midday on Monday was eerily quiet. Too quiet, many in the Federal army thought. According to Provost Marshal Patrick, "the silence in front was ominous & I could not account for it." Colonel Wainwright, touring the army's artillery positions that morning, talked to numerous officers and found it the general opinion that, facing a divided army like this one, "it was Lee's business to attack the weaker division." And if Joe Hooker knew his business, they said, he would "move to the relief of the one attacked." Wainwright confided to his diary, "I can only hope that Hooker has something very wise and deep on hand for tomorrow, to fulfill his speech to me last night."[13]

* *

ROBERT E. LEE rarely displayed his temper, but when he did the anger registered ice cold and his lieutenants stayed out of his way. On this May 4 morning General Lee was in a temper. Porter Alexander had thought to volunteer some thoughts about moving against the enemy, "but the old man seemed to be feeling so real wicked, I concluded to retain my ideas exclusively in my own possession." Alexander was surprised at the display, and did not envy whoever might be the target of Lee's wrath.

If General Sedgwick was the best-informed general on the field this morning, General Lee was one of the worst informed. Today he particularly felt the absence of James Longstreet. Longstreet could be stubbornly opinionated at times, but he was never unprepared. He always managed his First Corps command efficiently, and was a careful reader of battlefields. Old Pete would never have permitted the situation Lee found when he reached Lafayette McLaws's headquarters on the Orange Plank Road near Salem Church at 11:00 A.M.

As Colonel Wainwright and his fellow officers surmised, Lee was making it his business this day to strike at the weaker portion of the divided Federal army. Before he could deal with Hooker's larger portion he must clear his rear of Sedgwick, and he wanted to do it quickly before Hooker took it in his head to intervene.

During the night Lee had given approval to Early's plan to cut Sedgwick off from Fredericksburg. In the morning he learned from McLaws of Early's next proposal, a joint assault on the enemy's flank and front by his and McLaws's divisions. McLaws had said he did not feel himself strong enough for his part in the plan and asked Lee for reinforcements.

Lee turned to Dick Anderson. Already two of Anderson's brigades, Cadmus Wilcox's and Little Billy Mahone's, were with McLaws at Salem Church. Now Lee told Anderson to go to McLaws with the rest of his command, the brigades of Rans Wright, Carnot Posey, and E. A. Perry. This would bring the total to three full divisions to deal with Sedgwick.

Anderson was reconnoitering the Yankee line in front of him along the Mineral Spring Road that morning, and it took him time to get organized for the march east to Salem Church. His troops first had to be relieved on their line by troops from A. P. Hill's division, and that took more time. It was not until 11:00 A.M. that Anderson reached McLaws's position with the first of his brigades, and the two others trailed in over the next few hours.

McLaws and Early had meanwhile each been waiting for the other to do something. Communicating at a distance raised more questions than were answered. Early had thought McLaws would be supporting his early morning movement of Gordon's and Smith's brigades, but heard "no sound of an engagement in that direction." For his part, McLaws expected Early to lead off their joint attack, and "General Early not attacking, as I could hear," had his men stand down. He waited patiently for Anderson's reinforcements.

Georgian Lafayette McLaws, the senior major general of the three on the field, was closest in military character to the man he was fighting, John Sedgwick. Like Sedgwick, McLaws was solid, dependable, and cautious; like Sedgwick, he was more comfortable obeying a direct order than acting on a discretionary one. Under Longstreet's watchful eye he had performed capably enough in previous fights. On this morning, called on for initiative to solve the puzzle of how to move against the enemy on his front, he was as paralyzed by indecision as Sedgwick.

Watching and listening to General Lee dig into this tangle, Porter Alexander thought he could identify the roots of the commanding general's anger. For one thing, a great deal of time had already been wasted and lost "by somebody, some how, no particulars being given." Furthermore, no one at Salem Church seemed to know just where the enemy was and where his lines ran, "& it was somebody's duty to know." Finally, it was devolving on Lee personally to use up more time finding out about the enemy "before we could move a peg." Old Pete would have seen to all this some time since, but Old Pete was not here and it was going on midday and General Lee's icy manner set everyone around him to becoming very busy.[14]

By skirmish probes and observation, it was found that the Yankee line was formed in the shape of a great horseshoe. Both flanks rested on the Rappahannock and enclosed Banks's Ford. Sedgwick's left flank ran from the river along the high ground of Taylor's and Stansbury's hills and across the Plank Road, then turned and ran south of and parallel to the Plank Road for some two miles, then turned northward again to cross the Plank Road at the toll gate and reach the Rappahannock upstream from Banks's.

Yankee strength was also analyzed. The march upriver of the Federal column from the bridgehead on May 2 — this was Reynolds's First Corps — had been reported by Confederate observers. That, combined with Early's sightings of the forces he contended with on Sunday and early Monday, made it clear that the enemy holding these lines could only be Sedgwick's Sixth Corps. Lee's view of Sedgwick that day was a good deal more realistic than Sedgwick's view of him.

During this scouting Lee was personally directing the troops into position. He rode over to Early's posting to discuss the plan with him. Early's four brigades, under Extra Billy Smith, John Gordon, Harry Hays, and Robert Hoke, formed the right of the Confederate line, extending westward from Marye's Heights and paralleling the Plank Road. The left remained as it had been after the Salem Church fighting on Sunday — a line a mile and three-quarters long, perpendicular to the Plank Road, consisting of McLaws's three brigades (Semmes, Kershaw, and Wofford), braced by the brigades of Mahone and Wilcox from Anderson. Barksdale's brigade, from McLaws, held Marye's Heights facing the Federals occupying Fredericksburg.

In the mile-and-a-half gap between Early and McLaws General Lee posted Wright, Posey, and Perry. This was time-consuming, for these brigades of Anderson's were slow coming up from Chancellorsville and then they had to march cross-lots over rough ground to reach their assigned positions. It all took longer than expected, which did nothing to improve Lee's temper.

Snowden Andrews's artillery battalion took up positions along the Telegraph Road to support Early on the right. Porter Alexander found high ground in the center, looking across Hazel Run, for his guns. On the extreme left, on Smith's Hill overlooking Banks's Ford, Major Hardaway's rifle battalion joined other batteries there to form an artillery array of twenty-one guns. The infantry strength of the three Confederate divisions came to just over 23,000 men. That, Lee thought, should be sufficient for an assault. It was, in fact, but 2,200 more men than Sedgwick commanded.

The plan was to break through the Federal left, using Early's division, and drive it back toward Anderson's advance. McLaws would join in against a Federal retreat and meanwhile stand between Hooker and any attempt he might make to relieve Sedgwick. The starting signal for the attack was to be three cannon shots fired in rapid succession. By the time everyone was finally in place the afternoon was fading into evening. Like Jackson's flank attack two days earlier, the attack of May 4 would be a race against darkness.[15]

* *

WHEN GENERAL LEE rode off to Salem Church that morning to deal with Sedgwick, he left Jeb Stuart at Chancellorsville with half the army to watch Hooker. After their fearful losses of the past two days — nearly 30 percent — Rodes, Colston, and A. P. Hill could muster but 21,000 infantrymen. Stuart spread them thinly, making the most of his defenses and the concealing Wilderness. "Our regt built breastworks until late Monday evening," Georgian John Wood explained. "They used their bayonets instead of picks and mattucks and their hands instead of shovels and spades, as shovels and spades could not be had." By massing his men in the clearings and blocking all the roads and byways, and leaving the intervening Wilderness undefended, Stuart presented a strong front wherever the Yankees looked, or so it seemed.

Morning patrols by Slocum's Twelfth Corps to the east met such aggressive picket fire that Slocum sent back a warning that he would need help to meet an attack on his lines. An hour later Fitz Lee's dismounted troopers put up so strong a fight from the west that John Reynolds raised the alarm of a possible breakthrough there. In the center Rebel sharpshooters perched in trees rained a deadly fire into the Yankee positions, "making it as much as life is worth to walk along our line," a Fifth Corps man wrote.

General Slocum, inspecting this front, had just turned away when a sergeant standing where he had been moments before was killed instantly by a sharpshooter. Brigadier General Amiel W. Whipple, commanding a division in the Third Corps, was in the act of ordering a detail of Berdan's Sharpshooters forward to deal with this harassing fire when a Confederate marksman put a bullet through his body. General Whipple was transported to Washington, where three days later he died. With Hiram Berry's death on Sunday, the Third Corps had now lost two divisional commanders to enemy sharpshooters in two days.[16]

In due course Berdan's Sharpshooters managed to halt this deadly harassment — and, so they claimed, kill the marksman who had hit General Whipple — but at an unexpected cost. Berdan's men maintained their picket line in a strip of woods between the lines, with the 11th New Jersey in immediate support. Through what the Jerseys' Colonel Robert McAllister claimed was a mixup in orders, the 11th started to withdraw just as Rebel gunners opened on the sharpshooters in the woods. Sunday had been the 11th New Jersey's first battle, when it was driven to the rear by the Rebels' attack on Fairview, and it was still somewhat unnerved. Now, under this sudden outburst, it "came back across the field in a decidedly short time," as an observer remarked. Seeing the Jerseys rushing toward them, the defenders in the main line opened fire on the woods and what they supposed were pursuing Confederates. In reaction the Confederates redoubled their fire.

Caught in the middle of this scything fire of musketry and canister was the detail of Berdan's Sharpshooters. "We found ourselves in a terrible position," Sergeant Wyman White remembered, forced to get out "the best way we could or be cut to pieces by missiles of both friend and foe." Dodging from tree to tree, then racing for their lines during a lull, the sharpshooters escaped with only five men wounded. But Sergeant White was unforgiving. The 11th New Jersey "retreated like cowards at nothing but noise. The whole regiment ought to have been punished."[17]

During the night and into the morning, Federal officers had worked industriously to round up stragglers and the thousands of men blown loose from their commands in Sunday's battle and to get them into their places in the new battle line. The more incorrigible stragglers had escaped across the river, but by noon the situation was in hand and there were perhaps 70,000 men with their units. Nevertheless, there was a good deal of gun-shyness running up and down the Union lines that day, especially among the new and short-term troops, as the hours passed and tensions rose.

This was most apparent in brigades like Gabriel Paul's of the First Corps, five regiments of nine-months' men. They had some six weeks to serve and had yet to experience battle. Paul's lines here were zigzag in shape, and it is recorded that a private "in his modesty" went well out to the front to answer a call of nature. As he returned through the trees he was taken for a butternut and fired on from one side of the angled line, which triggered a response from the facing side. The wild musketry went on for five minutes, and when it was over one man was dead and a half dozen wounded. The modest soldier escaped unscathed.

There were other such outbursts in the course of the day, and it troubled General Hooker. He was heard to remark on "the want of steadiness of some of our troops as exhibited by uncalled-for firing. . . ." From the start of the campaign Hooker had worried about the steadiness of the numerous new and short-term regiments, and had discounted as many as 40,000 men on that score. He could not have been pleased at the sight that afternoon of the 5th New York, Duryée's Zouaves, shouldering their rifles and marching out of the lines and across the bridges at

U.S. Ford to head for home. Their two years were up on May 9. May 4 was a day of "intense anxiety and suspense as to whether they were to be killed, perhaps an hour before the order for their relief should come," the regimental historian would write. (For Duryée's 237 three-year men detailed to serve out their remaining year in the 146th New York, May 4 was a day of bitterness.)

Not all the short-term regiments shared the 5th New York's relief to be leaving the battlefield, however. The 4th New York had been eligible to leave even as the campaign began, and the 123rd Pennsylvania could have left along with the Zouaves. Instead both elected to stay on and see the battle through.[18]

Monday, Day Eight of the campaign, was the last day of the rations the Yankee soldiers had carried all those miles from winter camp. By plan the battle should have been over by now, but that it was not did not create any supply worries. Numerous commissary and forage trains were parked north of the Rappahannock at U.S. Ford, and despite the Rebel major Hardaway's adventurous shelling before dawn, there would be no shortage of rations for man or beast in Hooker's main army. General Sedgwick had been resupplied with ammunition on Sunday, and had adequate rations for Monday.

The Army of the Potomac's quartermaster Rufus Ingalls told his lieutenants at the depots to stand fast: "We are in great trouble, but we shall fight out." Ingalls's concern was a raid on the army's supply base at Aquia Landing by Rebels who by report and rumor had the capability of crossing the Rappahannock with uncounted thousands at any point they chose. (In truth, General Lee's only bridge train was then far distant, at Orange Court House.)

The Federals' supply situation was made easier on May 4 by the completion of a third bridge at U.S. Ford. Engineer Henry Benham, sobered up after his unfortunate conduct at the laying of the bridges below Fredericksburg on April 29, had been carefully attending to business since then. The bridges laid at U.S. Ford and Banks's Ford on May 4 marked the nineteenth and twentieth times pontoon bridges were put down or taken up by Yankee engineers in the last seven days.[19]

Joe Hooker, granting Lee this final day, this Monday, to attack him in his defensive position, expected that if the attack came it would be from the west, against his right flank. In his best judgment, Jackson in attacking the Eleventh Corps on Saturday had been attempting to turn the Potomac army's right and cut it off from its bridge crossings. Not knowing of Jackson's wounding, Hooker assumed this still to be Jackson's intent. His first step therefore was to strengthen his defenses. Orders went out to chop and dig. Captain Jonathan Hager of the Fifth Corps put his men to enlarging their breastworks and slashing timber to form an abatis 400 feet wide along the entire length of his line. "We felt that we were impregnable & really half hoped we would be attacked," Hager confided to his diary. Hooker then ordered Reynolds and Meade to dispatch strong probes to the west and south to search out the enemy positions.

Reynolds first sent a scouting column made up of the 12th and 13th Massachusetts and a Maine battery westward along a forest track leading to the Ely's Ford Road. At the road intersection the column ran into sharp skirmish fire. General John Robinson satisfied himself that "the enemy was in force" there and returned the way he had come. His report seemed to mark the Rebels' left flank as extending as far west as the Ely's Ford Road. In fact Robinson encountered nothing more than an outpost manned by Fitz Lee's cavalry and a horse battery, running a bluff with the aid of the concealing Wilderness.

Next came a reconnaissance in force by James McQuade's Fifth Corps brigade. McQuade's lines were only a half mile from where the Rebels were thought to be, and so he went forward through the woods in line-of-battle formation, with the 4th Michigan out front deployed as skirmishers. "Our orders was to shoot the first live thing that we saw in front of us," Private James Houghton wrote in his journal. With "a wolverine yell" the Michigan men drove in the Rebel pickets and then struck the main force, arrayed behind stout breastworks and abatis. These were A. P. Hill's men, commanded today by Harry Heth, posted a mile west of Chancellorsville and well supported by artillery.

"When we got in about 20 or 30 rods of their breastworks they opened on us with grape & canister followed with volleys of musketry that extended both ways as far as we could see," Private Houghton wrote. A man in the 62nd Pennsylvania, Zerah C. Monks, took in this grim prospect and put the best face on it: "We got shelled most effectually, but made our point, drove the Rebels into their rifle pits, found out where their batteries were placed, and returned." Fortunately, he added, the Rebels were firing "a little too high, just over our heads." Still, the loss in McQuade's brigade in this episode was fifty-five killed and wounded.

Meanwhile Reynolds had sent Colonel Roy Stone's brigade of Pennsylvanians farther west along a forest track that led toward the Plank Road and Dowdall's Tavern. Except for a brief tangle with pickets and the capture of two Rebels from the 7th Tennessee of A. P. Hill's division, Stone's men heard more of the enemy than they saw. Colonel Stone, Reynolds reported to Hooker, "could hear the enemy on his right flank & front and wagons moving on to the Plank Road, & the enemy working on defences. . . ." Later Reynolds admitted privately that he had hoped

Stone would stir up enough of a fight to justify his going into action with the entire First Corps.

These reconnaissances only strengthened Hooker's resolve to attempt his turning movement by way of Banks's Ford the next day. He was adamantly against throwing his men into a frontal assault against fortifications like McQuade had encountered on the Chancellorsville line, and nowhere had the scouts found a flank to turn. Not realizing that Lee had shifted Anderson and McLaws to Sedgwick's front, Hooker assumed he was facing the same Confederates who had battled so ferociously on Sunday. Going on offense against that force was a daunting prospect indeed.

It was much the same dilemma Hooker believed he had faced on his march eastward from Chancellorsville on May 1 — how to mount an attack with "slender columns" advancing along the forest roads against a deployed or fortified enemy. In that event, he would testify, he felt certain the Confederates would destroy his columns "as fast as they were thrown on to his works." In any battle like that, Joe Hooker believed, the Wilderness was as much his enemy as Robert E. Lee's army.[20]

⋆ ⋆

MONDAY WAS another warm, pleasant May day, although it would cloud up and rain after nightfall. With no report of any threatening movement by the Federals, it was decided that morning to carry Stonewall Jackson to safer quarters. Jackson suggested he could recuperate at the home of an acquaintance, Thomas Coleman Chandler, near Guiney's Station on the R.F. & P. twelve miles south of Fredericksburg. Jed Hotchkiss plotted the route for the ambulance carrying Jackson: from Wilderness Tavern southeast on the Brock Road through Todd's Tavern and Spotsylvania Court House, south and then east from there to the Devenport Bridge Road and Guiney's Station on the railroad. It was a twenty-four-mile journey and would require the entire day.

Jackson was placed on a mattress in the ambulance along with his chief of artillery, Stapleton Crutchfield, whose shattered leg had been amputated. With them went Dr. McGuire, Chaplain Lacy, and Lieutenant Smith. Hotchkiss rode ahead with a party of pioneers to clear and patch and smooth the road. They passed crowds of walking wounded, Hotchkiss wrote, "each one wishing himself the badly wounded one instead of General Jackson." Supply trains they encountered hastily cleared the way when the ambulance's cargo was announced, the rough teamsters standing weeping by the roadside as it passed. "I wish it was me, Sir!" one of them called out. At Spotsylvania Court House the local residents offered food, and their prayers.

Hotchkiss entered in his diary that he thought the general "stood the ride very well." As they rolled slowly through the forest Jackson talked of Saturday's flank attack. His goal had been to seize a position between the Federals and their bridges at U.S. Ford, he said, obliging them to attack him there. In a situation like that, he observed with a smile, "My men sometimes fail to drive the Yankees from a position; they always fail to drive us away." He described Robert Rodes's leadership Saturday as "magnificent" and hoped it would promptly earn him rank. Battlefield promotions, Jackson thought, were "the greatest incentives to gallantry in others." Toward the end of the journey he tired and complained of nausea, but wet compresses on his stomach brought him relief.

At Fairfield, the Chandler home, Jackson was placed away from the main house in an estate office much like his winter quarters at Moss Neck. He ate a supper of bread and tea "with evident relish." Dr. McGuire would remain at his side, and report that the general seemed comfortable and slept well "throughout the entire night."[21]

Guiney's Station was also where captured Yankees were being collected. After Sunday's fighting their number had reached 4,400, and by day's end on Monday most of these had been marched to the station, to be held until they could be sent off to Richmond. In due course officer captives would reach Richmond's prisons by train; enlisted men would walk. "We were huddled up in separate squads and placed under guard," wrote prisoner Thomas Evans of the Eleventh Corps, and he complained that he had nothing to eat and only swamp water to drink. Those who had not saved their knapsacks or haversacks and canteens did go hungry and thirsty. Many others, before they reached Guiney's Station, had been relieved of food, possessions, and blankets by needy Rebels.

Almost half these 4,400 were nine-month or two-year men or men seeing battle for the first time. During the fighting these soldiers had surrendered in disproportionate numbers. Short-term and new regiments made up 26 percent of the total in the corps that had done the bulk of the fighting, but they accounted for 45 percent of the prisoners.

Here was evidence for Joe Hooker's mistrust of this portion of his army, and while he could not then know of these statistics he had at least anecdotal evidence of them. There was the case, for example, of the 283 nine-months' men of the 27th Connecticut who gave up on Sunday because a Confederate lieutenant told them, under a flag of truce, that they were cut off. Or the 199 short-termers of the 128th Pennsylvania who surrendered on Saturday on the word of another Confederate lieutenant that Stonewall Jackson had them surrounded.

Captain Samuel Fiske, captured by chance while he was himself collecting Rebel prisoners on Sunday's battlefield, noticed that almost without exception his fellow prisoners at Guiney's Station had the same story to tell. "The particular brigade or regiment or company of each man was captured because the enemy appeared in vast numbers on their flank or in their rear. They didn't fight much, because they were so unfortunately situated or surrounded, that there wasn't any use in resisting." Reflecting on this phenomenon, Captain Fiske decided he had never before heard of "so much cross-firing, and enfilading fire, and fire in the rear" on any battlefield he knew anything about.

However that may be, apparently it had been too much to expect regiments of new men, or men who had only days or weeks left to serve, to stand and fight to the last man or to press an attack to the bitter end. Awareness of this reality was one of the things preying on Joe Hooker's mind that Monday as he pondered his course for the rest of the battle.[22]

In the comparative calm there was time to care for the wounded. The Confederates, who at day's end on Sunday held considerably more of the battlefield than they held at dawn, had been able to evacuate their wounded to field hospitals with some promptness. Lee's men did not die that day for lack of care. Captain John Melhorn of the 10th Virginia, hit three times in the attack on Ruger's brigade, was carried back to what he described as "excellent quarters" near Wilderness Tavern. A Mr. Buckner of Raccoon Ford, he noted in his diary, "gave me some Stimulents and some very excellent bread & meat & eggs. His generosity furnished the hospital with two loads of prepared rations."

Not all the Federal wounded on this field were so fortunate. Those who fell on the battlefront south of the Plank Road on Sunday, many of them, could not be evacuated through the no man's land behind the lines while it was raked by Porter Alexander's guns. Twelfth Corps men there were carried no farther by the stretcher bearers than fifty yards or so behind the lines, to the shelter of a ravine carrying a branch of Lewis's Run.

"When I reached the stream its banks were already well lined with many dead and wounded," recalled New Yorker Rice Bull, who had two painful wounds. "Many were needlessly bleeding to death." When the Union front collapsed they were left behind, and then the Rebels stormed past them in pursuit. Next came Rebel stragglers, rifling the pockets of the dead and wounded until their provost guard came up and drove them away. The Federals had left no surgeons with this conclave of wounded, and the Confederates could spare none until their own wounded were cared for. Night came, Bull wrote, and "around us were suffering men and the air was filled with their cries and moans. . . . Before morning many died; we heard their cries no more."

On Monday the Confederates collected these Federal wounded in a makeshift field hospital near the Chancellorsville crossroads, where Bull estimated their number at 500. There was one surgeon here, from the Third Corps, but no medical supplies. Men did for themselves, and their comrades, as best they could. Finally, on May 5, surgeons and medical supplies arrived under a flag of truce. Forty-eight hours or more after they were hit these men received their first medical treatment. In time those fortunate enough to survive were returned to Union lines.

Wounded Yankees who did manage to make it safely to the rear during Sunday's battle were cared for in brigade field hospitals set up in clearings along the U.S. Ford Road. By Monday these busy places had quieted down. Every man who could be moved had been treated and sent across the river for further care. Surgeon Cyrus Bacon, who had worked ceaselessly at his operating table all day Sunday, noted in his diary on Monday, "Very warm, no work." In contrast, an attendant at a divisional hospital on the Warrenton Post Road north of the river recorded in his diary that Monday was a very busy day. In the hospital tents pitched in the yard at Oakland, the "residence of a rebel," Samuel Webster calculated that he "served coffee to several hundred men — about 700 I should think."

Stoneman's damage to the railroad delayed the sending of any Confederate wounded to Richmond until May 6. The first Union wounded from the fighting on Friday and Saturday reached Washington at nightfall on May 4. Walt Whitman watched from the wharf at the foot of Sixth Street. In the rain, by the light of flaring torches, in steady procession they were carried off the steamer. "All around — on the wharf, on the ground, out on side places — the men are lying on blankets, old quilts, etc. with bloody rags bound 'round heads, arms, and legs," Whitman wrote. Soon ambulances came to bear them off to Washington's military hospitals. "The men in charge told me the bad cases were yet to come. If that is so, I pity them — for these are bad enough."[23]

* *

FOR THE FIGHTING men in the two armies waiting tensely in their lines, the midday and afternoon hours of May 4 passed with agonizing slowness. On the twelve-mile-wide battlefield that stretched from Fredericksburg to Wilderness Church there were scattered outbursts of firing in one place and then another, but by late afternoon there had been no sustained fighting anywhere. With 140,000 armed men crowded onto this battlefield the sudden silences were uncanny.

General Hooker, hoping he would be attacked, waited in his fortified salient north of Chancellorsville. General Sedgwick, hoping with equal fervor he would not be attacked, waited in his salient guarding Banks's

Ford. General Lee, holding determinedly to the initiative, waited with growing impatience as his planned attack on Sedgwick slowly took shape and force. The somber faces of the officers, "always a barometer of success or defeat," filled the men with foreboding, wrote the Sixth Corps' Clinton Beckwith. "The day wore silently and listlessly away."

The afternoon was nearly gone and Lieutenant Colonel Selden Connor, commanding the 7th Maine, glanced at his watch and remarked to Major Thomas Hyde, "If the rebs want anything tonight it's time for them to commence." Recording this remark in a letter home, Connor added, "Hardly were the words out of my mouth when they *did* commence, charging our whole line in overwhelming force."

It was 5:30 when Porter Alexander signaled the attack with the agreed-upon three cannon shots. Six Confederate brigades, three of Early's and three of Anderson's, some 11,000 men, prepared to step off. There were considerably fewer men here than in Jackson's charge on Saturday evening, and somewhat fewer than in Harry Heth's on Sunday morning, yet as a spectacle of war it was the most visible of the three. For most of its length the Rebel line was entirely in the open as it started forward under its battle flags. "The whole hillside was alive with men," Major Hyde remembered. "A magnificent sight."[24]

Albion Howe's Sixth Corps division had not yet seen any real action in the campaign, except in beating off Gordon's thrust that morning, but with the dawn on Monday Howe had begun to suspect his turn was coming. Without waiting for Sedgwick's approval, he had swung his line back to face to the rear, at right angles to the Plank Road and mostly north of it and extending as far as the Rappahannock. "I carefully examined the ground," Howe testified, "and placed my troops so that they could best resist an attack from the left."

Howe had 6,200 men in two brigades, under Thomas H. Neill and Lewis A. Grant, and he arranged them in a defense in depth. Out ahead some 300 yards was Neill's skirmish line, backed by the rest of Neill's brigade holding higher ground. Some 500 yards back of this, behind the crests of a second ridgeline, was Grant's Vermont brigade, five veteran regiments of Green Mountain Boys onto which had been grafted the nine-months' men of the 26th New Jersey. In the intervals were twelve guns — a two-gun section of Lieutenant Leonard Martin's Battery F, 5th U.S., by the Plank Road, Captain James Rigby's six-gun Battery A, Maryland Light, in the center, and on the left the other two sections of Martin's battery. It was a skillfully arranged defense, making good use of the terrain and concealing its depth and strength.

Early aimed two brigades, under Harry Hays and Robert Hoke, against these lines of Howe's. A third brigade, John Gordon's, was di-

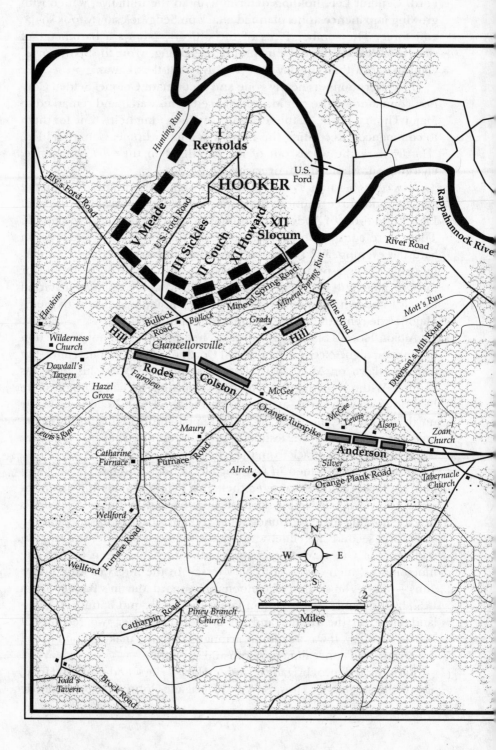

Reynolds

I

HOOKER

U.S. Ford

V Meade

III Sickles

II Couch

XI Howard

XII Slocum

Hunting Run

Ely's Ford Road

U.S. Ford Road

Rappahannock River

River Road

Mineral Spring Run

Mineral Spring Road

Hawkins

Wilderness Church

Hill

Bullock Road

Bullock

Grady

Hill

Mott's Run

Mine Road

Duerson's Mill Road

Chancellorsville

Dowdall's Tavern

Rodes

Fairview

Colston

McGee

McGee

Lewis

Alsop

Zoan Church

Hazel Grove

Orange Turnpike

Lewis's Run

Maury

Anderson

Silver

Catharine Furnace

Furnace Road

Alrich

Orange Plank Road

Tabernacle Church

Wellford

Furnace Road

N

W   E

S

Wellford

Catharpin Road

Piney Branch Church

0   2

Miles

Todd's Tavern

Brock Road

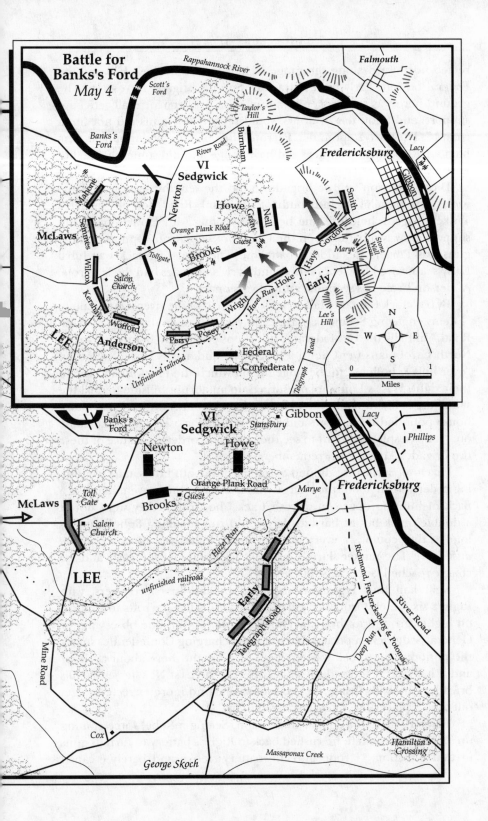

Battle for Banks's Ford
May 4

Rappahannock River

Falmouth

Scott's Ford

Banks's Ford

Taylor's Hill

Lacy

Burnham

River Road

Fredericksburg

Mahone

VI SEDGWICK

Howe

Smith

Gibbon

Newton

Grant

Neill

Semmes

Stone Wall

McLaws

Orange Plank Road

Gordon

Wilcox

Tollgate

Guest

Hays

Marye

Brooks

Salem Church

Kershaw

Wright

Hoke

Early

Wofford

Hazel Run

Anderson

Perry

Posey

Lee's Hill

LEE

N
W · E
S

Unfinished railroad

Telegraph Road

Federal
Confederate

0   1
Miles

Banks's Ford

VI SEDGWICK

Stansbury

Gibbon

Lacy

Phillips

Newton

Howe

Orange Plank Road

Marye

Fredericksburg

Toll Gate

Guest

Brooks

McLaws

Salem Church

Hazel Run

LEE

unfinished railroad

Early

Richmond, Fredericksburg & Potomac

River Road

Telegraph Road

Deep Run

Mine Road

Cox

Hamilton's Crossing

Massaponax Creek

George Skoch

rected northward along the range of hills toward Taylor's Hill and the Federal far left. Early held Extra Billy Smith's brigade in reserve. The ground here was too broken to advance his artillery for really effective support, and Snowden Andrews would report, "My guns did not fire a round." The two 20-pounder Parrott rifles of Captain Archibald Graham's 1st Rockbridge battery did have range and did some service, but Early's assault would essentially be an infantry affair.

Dick Anderson's three brigades faced the lengthy section of Sedgwick's line parallel to and south of the Plank Road. Joseph Bartlett's Yankee brigade held the line here, connecting with Howe's right and supported by two batteries on the Guest house plateau. Opposing these guns was Porter Alexander's battalion. The plan of attack was Jubal Early's, approved by General Lee, and Early's brigades had the lead role. Anderson's role was secondary and diversionary.

By 6 o'clock Captain Hall at Station F north of the river was signaling, "Enemy engaging Sedgwick hotly. Fight very severe on the Orange Plank Road." Initially the Confederate rush swept everything before it. Hoke's North Carolinians went down a long slope and across Hazel Run, then "over hills & hollows" to the ridgeline on which the Plank Road ran. To their right, Hays's Louisianians surged up an abrupt hillside toward the same target like a rising tide. Howe's batteries and those at the Guest house pounded them front and flank, but they closed ranks and came on. "It was a splendid sight to see the rapid and orderly advance of these two brigades," Jubal Early remembered.

Up close, Sergeant Edmund Stephens of the 9th Louisiana saw nothing orderly at all about the charge. Instead his regiment went at it like a pack of hunting dogs "on a fresh track," he wrote; "they went not at a double quick but as hard as they could run squalling & hollaring as loud as they could . . . every man for him self and *Old Yanks got up and dusted.* . . ." The Yankee skirmishers fell back fast under this rush, and the charge reached General Neill's line.[25]

Neill had four regiments deployed behind his skirmishers, with Rigby's six 3-inch Ordnance rifles and Martin's two Parrotts in support on higher ground to the rear. Thomas Hyde, on this line observing for General Sedgwick, reported that when the charging Confederates struck the position "the shock was terrible." "We fought there about an hour and a half," so it seemed to John Toffey of the 21st New Jersey, Neill's brigade, "the balls flying thick as hailstones. I no more expected to get out of that place alive than I expected to fly."

Major Hyde had a similar impression. Seeing a Rebel force coming up a ravine on the left, he rushed back to Rigby's battery to turn its guns in that direction. "I rode into the battery smoke and barely escaped being blown to pieces by one of our own shells." Coming up to rally his troops, General Neill had his horse killed under him. The 21st New Jersey's Colonel Gilliam Van Houten was mortally wounded.

Then Colonel Ernst von Vegesack of the 20th New York went down with a wound, and it seemed to break the fragile bonds holding his regiment together. Earlier in the campaign the 20th, a two-year regiment recruited from New York City's German population, had mutinied on the claim that its time was up, and 201 of its men were court-martialed and in custody. Whatever discipline remained evaporated with Colonel Vegesack's wounding, and (as Major Hyde put it) "The 20th New York disgracefully ran."

These fleeing Germans — soon to be known, along with Howard's Eleventh Corps, as the Flying Dutchmen — rushed through the neighboring 7th Maine and then through Rigby's battery. "They frightened my horses, and created so much confusion that I could do nothing," Captain Rigby complained. With his right flank turned by the New Yorkers' collapse, Neill had to order his brigade to fall back to the second line. "We retreated in the best order possible, turning and firing on the enemy at every opportunity," the 7th Maine's Selden Connor insisted. Rigby and Martin gave the order to limber their batteries to the rear. Hays's men and Hoke's rushed after them in pursuit, and it appeared that Jubal Early was about to break the Union line wide open.[26]

Old Jube's triumph was short-lived. Soon enough his offensive collapsed from a combination of its own misdirection and stubborn Yankee resistance. A key casualty began the collapse. General Hoke, crossing the Plank Road, was knocked off his horse with a severe wound in the left shoulder. Hoke had been told to pivot to his left once across the road so as to maintain a continuous front with Hays on his right, but Hoke's replacement, Colonel Isaac Avery, had been told nothing of the plan and the brigade lost its direction. The North Carolinians entered a patch of woodland on a collision course with the Louisianians, and the two brigades became entangled and fell into disorder. What was worse, the impetus of Hays's dashing charge had thrown his lead regiments well out ahead, and in the smoky confusion, Sergeant Stephens wrote, "they suffered for it, for our own men fired several volleys into the Brigade."

Lieutenant Henry Handerson, 9th Louisiana, summed up what happened to Hays's brigade at this critical moment in its attack. In a letter home, Handerson explained that "owing to the rapidity of our charge, the brigade became inextricably confused. One half the men were so broken down by previous hard marching as to be unable to keep up with the rest. Officers lost their companies, and companies their officers. Regiments had no commanders. No support was near us, and fresh bodies of the enemy flanking us on the right." In addition to these difficulties, Hays's men — and Hoke's too — had run up against the Green Mountain Boys.[27]

Colonel Grant's Vermont brigade was the Federals' last line of defense on this field, but it was also the strongest. Its most effective weapon proved to be surprise. Grant had his men lying concealed behind the crests of the ridgeline on which they were posted, and Hays's charging Louisianians came on them unexpectedly. Private Erastus Scott of the 3rd Vermont watched as "on they came like an avalanche to all appearance as though all would be swept before them." When they were within musket range, he went on, "all jumped to their feet & poured it into them as fast as we could load & fire." In the 2nd Vermont's line, according to Lieutenant Chester Leach, the Rebels "got almost in our faces when we opened on them & they were compelled to put back about as lively as they came up." The 6th Vermont followed its surprise volley with a surprise counterattack, and at that, a Vermonter wrote, the Rebels "turned en masse and fled, and then started a race. . . . It was the Green Mountain Boys versus the chivalry of Louisiana. . . ."

Harry Hays's men were already stretched to the end of their tethers getting this far, and the Vermonters' sudden fire stunned them. It was dusk now, and in the smoky twilight this blazing crash of gunfire was more than they could stand. Those Louisianians who did not or could not run or run far fell exhausted and surrendered. Of Hays's 445 casualties that day, 129 were taken prisoner — including, amazingly, three of Hays's five colonels, along with two lieutenant colonels and a major. Between them Hays and Hoke lost 852 men in their joint assault, and they fell back to the first position they had taken from the Yankees.[28]

At the same time, John Gordon's Georgians were pushing forward parallel to the river toward Taylor's Hill and the Federals guarding Banks's Ford. By the account of Henry Walker of the 13th Georgia, "About this time the boys raised a yell enough to frighten any living thing on earth" and drove the Yankees back at the double-quick "or sure thing a little faster, and it was all the skirmishers could do to keep in shooting distance." The movement (and perhaps the Rebel yell) caught the attention of the heavy batteries on the heights across the river at Falmouth. A watcher there marveled at the gunners' accuracy: "Several of our 20 pounders directed their shells directly in the midst of the masses, which scattered them in every direction. . . ." Captain W. R. Redding, 13th Georgia, labeled it "a tremendous shelling," costing two dead in his company killed by a single solid shot.

Major Hyde, in the line with the Vermonters in the center, saw Gordon's threatening rush toward the bridges and spurred back to Sixth

Corps headquarters for help. He was later told, he said, "that I presented a striking figure as I came down the road — sabre drawn, horse dripping and all blood and powder." Sedgwick sent him back at the double-quick with a battery and Frank Wheaton's Pennsylvania brigade, and with this reinforcement the Federal left blocked and then beat back Gordon's advance. Once again, Sedgwick's resilient Sixth Corps line had bent but not broken. The Confederates had to content themselves with Taylor's Hill, the most commanding ground in the area.[29]

To the west, Dick Anderson's advance also suffered from misdirection and never quite came to grips with the main Federal line defending the Plank Road. Rans Wright hurled his Georgia brigade forward vigorously enough but at an oblique angle, which only succeeded in masking the advance of Posey's and Perry's brigades to his left. Like many another Confederate on this May 4, General Wright spoke of "driving the enemy before me like chaff." In fact, like others, he was simply driving in the enemy's skirmish line. His assault was soon checked by the Yankee batteries. Their fire, Wright admitted, was "murderous." General Joseph Bartlett, commanding opposite Wright, summed it up tersely: "I was able to repel all attacks of the enemy on my front with artillery and skirmishers until after dark. . . ."

Harry G. Hore, an English volunteer serving on Sedgwick's staff, watched a battery of six Napoleons ordered up by Sedgwick open on the Rebels with canister. At the command "Depress pieces," Hore wrote home, "I felt quite sick. . . . Good God, dear girl, it was awful, the dead seemed piled heaps upon heaps, the shot went right through them, completely smashed the front of the columns." Sedgwick was watching too. "One more such repulse as that, my boys," Hore heard him say, and the day would be theirs.[30]

*　*

GENERAL SEDGWICK might indeed claim the day in this battle for Banks's Ford on May 4. His line had nowhere been broken and he inflicted about one quarter more casualties than he suffered — Early's grapple with Howe cost Early 1,200 casualties against Howe's 900. Even though he lost the high ground of Taylor's Hill, at the end of the evening's fight Sedgwick was in no greater danger than when he began it. Most of his troops had fought well, especially those under the skilled command of Albion Howe, and the Sixth Corps' small deficit in numbers that day was offset by its being able to fight defensively.

By pulling back after dark to form a more compact salient around his bridges, and digging in there, Sedgwick would present an even more formidable defensive front on Tuesday. In addition, he had thirty-four guns of the reserve artillery for support, firing from the north bank of the river. The position, General Howe would testify, "was less liable to a serious attack than it had been at any time before since the 6th corps crossed the Rappahannock; and I saw no occasion or necessity for re-crossing the river."

General Lee fully expected Sedgwick to hold his place. To McLaws he explained, "if we let them alone until morning we will find them again intrenched, so I wish to push them over the river tonight." Lee wanted to organize a night attack, something he had not attempted on any previous battlefield.

John Sedgwick, however, saw nothing optimistic, or at all promising, about his situation. He saw only danger and great risk. Like his mentor General McClellan, he credited his opponent with a phantom army. Repeatedly in this campaign Sedgwick measured what headquarters told him about the size of the enemy force confronting him and then rejected these estimates. Writing home soon afterward, Major Hyde said on that Monday it was the opinion of General Sedgwick and his headquarters that they were "very nearly surrounded" by Stonewall Jackson "and part of Longstreet's Corps. . . ." That night, after the fighting died out, Sedg-wick judged the day's result at best as a case of survival. In a dispatch marked 9:45 he announced to Hooker, "The enemy are pressing me. I am taking position to cross the river whenever necessary."[31]

One factor influencing Sedgwick just then was the commanding gen-eral's noncommittal response to the day's battle for Banks's Ford. Earlier Hooker had promised Sedgwick no assistance "without I hear heavy firing." Surely the firing that evening was heavy enough. Yet the only word from headquarters, sent when the firing was at its peak, was a request for a "full report" on Sedgwick's position and dispositions and the numbers of the enemy he was facing, so the general "may act advis-edly." There was no promise of reinforcements or assistance of any sort.

Ironically, the nearly daylong delay in mounting the attack on Sedg-wick that had so irritated General Lee ensured that when the attack finally was opened, there would be no interference from Hooker's main army. Unwittingly, and unintentionally, the Confederates guaranteed themselves a free hand to deal with Sedgwick.

At his headquarters near the Bullock house, Joe Hooker had pon-dered the choices facing him should he need to send assistance to Sedg-wick. To attack the enemy in the rear at Salem Church, he might attempt to smash through the Rebels at the Chancellor house and march east on the Turnpike or the Plank Road. This would be refighting Sunday's battle, however, assuming much risk and consuming much time. Alternatively, he might bypass the Chancellorsville crossroads by way of the Mine Road to reach the Turnpike at Zoan Church, some two miles from Salem Church. This too would mean fighting, against whatever force was blocking the Mine Road. A third way, following the River Road to Banks's Ford, also would involve a battle, with consequent delay. The only way to reach Sedgwick and reinforce him without fighting was to cross the Rappahannock at U.S. Ford and march to Banks's Ford along the north bank of the river. But that would require four or five hours.

None of these choices was inviting. Still, had the Confederates launched their attack on Sedgwick by midday, as Lee wanted, and had Sedgwick appealed to him in distress, Hooker would probably have felt obliged to act. If he chose one of the fighting alternatives, he might or might not have reached Sedgwick in time to do any good, but certainly he would have discovered the thinness of Stuart's lines in front of him. If he chose the river-crossing route it would at least have secured the Banks's Ford salient, assuming Sedgwick held out long enough for the reinforcements to reach him.

In the event, the Confederates' delay in launching the assault saved Joe Hooker from having to choose. He saw that darkness would close the fighting there before he could intervene to any effect. That truth did not lessen the suspense, or the distress, among his lieutenants. Colonel Wainwright noted in his diary that the fighting on Sedgwick's front "was plainly heard along our whole line for several hours after dark. Why we did not move I cannot say. . . ." Captain Hall at Station F signaled at 6:15: "Enemy are driving our forces at present"; and at 6:45: "It has become so smoky and dark that we cannot see the movements of either force." There was great relief, then, when two hours later engineer Benham at Banks's Ford reported Sedgwick's line still intact "where it has been for the last 24 hours."[32]

Thus when the first report on the fighting arrived from Sedgwick himself at about 11 o'clock — that he was being pressed by the enemy and was taking position to cross the river "whenever necessary" — it struck Hooker with the force of a blow. The new scheme he had nurtured all day, to cross the river on Tuesday with the bulk of the army and then recross at Banks's Ford to renew the battle, would fall to pieces if Sedgwick evacuated his salient.

Subsequent telegrams from engineer Benham at Banks's Ford seemed to make that a virtual certainty. Sedgwick's stragglers, Benham complained, "in regiments are pouring over my upper bridge." Soon the enemy artillery opened on the bridges, which he said he presumed Sedgwick could not prevent; then "a strong infantry fire has just burst out to the right and front. . . ." With real alarm now, Benham reported, "The enemy are shelling the whole place. . . . I fear the bridges will be destroyed."

(Before it had grown dark that evening, Porter Alexander made a point of getting the range and direction of Banks's Ford and, he wrote, "I sat up there all night long firing shell at that ford." The riverbank was too high for him to see the bridges and actually sight on them, and accurate indirect fire was unattainable with Civil War artillery. "Of course random fire like that could do no very serious harm," Alexander remarked. He would have been surprised, and elated, to learn the effect of his random fire on General Benham, and on General Sedgwick.)[33]

The prospect that Sedgwick would retreat across the river and abandon the Banks's Ford salient drove General Hooker to an agonizing decision. In later years a tale would be told that gained wide circulation: Fighting Joe Hooker confessing that the Battle of Chancellorsville took the course it did because he lost confidence in himself. In fact he never made such a confession. Instead, at that moment in the final hours of May 4, 1863, Fighting Joe Hooker simply lost confidence in his grand plan.

For eight days he had faithfully followed his plan — to secure an unopposed crossing of the Rappahannock and turn Lee's position; to force Lee out of his fortified lines to either flee or fight; to forgo bloody and costly head-on attacks; to fight only defensively and by maneuver on ground of his own choosing. But now, by all accounts, Stoneman had failed him and Sedgwick was failing him, and there were no options left in the plan. The plan was bankrupt, and he had nothing to put in its place.

For the first and only time in the campaign Hooker elected to involve his corps commanders in his decision-making. He called them together in his headquarters tent at the Bullock house. He would later insist this was not intended as a council of war, with any formal voting process. He only wanted to know, he said, "how they felt in regard to making what I considered a desperate move against the enemy in our front."

The conference opened at midnight, with corps commanders Meade, Reynolds, Howard, Sickles, and Couch present. Slocum could not immediately be found by the messenger sent for him and only arrived as they were adjourning. Hooker also called in Dan Butterfield and Gouverneur Warren. General Warren, by his account, had already that evening urged on Hooker "an attack in force" the next morning, and he hoped the conference would produce a plan of battle.

Hooker began by addressing the situation "as clearly as I could" on both their front facing Chancellorsville and on Sedgwick's front at

Banks's Ford. The "mode of attack" for an offensive from their salient, he told them, would have to be by slender, road-bound columns through the confining Wilderness, hurled against the fortified positions seen earlier that day. As for Sedgwick's front, he read them that general's dispatch announcing retreat.

Hooker was not entirely forthcoming, however. None of his listeners would remember him saying a word about his scheme to renew the battle on Tuesday by way of U.S. Ford and a recrossing at Banks's Ford. He also kept to himself the issues and intelligence in regard to Longstreet's divisions.

He did tell them of the instructions under which he was operating, and of the army's responsibility to protect Washington. He expressed concern at the "want of steadiness" of some of the troops. Finally he presented two propositions for action: a forward movement the next day on their front, presumably bringing on a battle; or a withdrawal of the army across U.S. Ford to the north bank of the Rappahannock — and an end to the campaign.[34]

Hooker then withdrew, along with Butterfield, leaving everyone free to express opinions "unembarrassed by his presence." Warren remained, thinking his knowledge of both battlefronts might be useful in the deliberations. George Meade, the most outspoken member of the gathering, would give it as his impression that the commanding general had already decided to withdraw the army before polling his corps commanders. Indeed, he later said as much to Hooker, and "he did not make any reply." No doubt Hooker hoped his lieutenants would reach the same conclusion he had, thereby reinforcing any explanations he had to make to Washington. Certainly his presentation had stressed the negatives of the situation at the expense of any positives. In the event, however, Joe Hooker misread the temper of the majority of his corps commanders.

Meade was very assertive (as Reynolds put it) "in favor of an advance in the direction of Fredericksburg at daylight the next morning. . . ." Meade thought the issue of Washington's safety had become a cliché for this army, and "threw that out of the question altogether." For his part, Reynolds said that although his corps had not yet been seriously engaged and therefore he would not urge his opinion, he voted for attack. Granting Meade his proxy, he then went to sleep.

Howard, too, was positive in his preference for an attack. It was the misconduct of his corps, he said, that in good measure had brought the army to the present crisis. His men were mortified, and now were "ready for the work." Howard insisted that the rout of the Eleventh Corps did not color his decision; he voted to fight because it was the right thing for the army to do.

Darius Couch, who was described by his divisional commander Win Hancock as "a person naturally very cautious about making a decision," said he did not feel competent to give an opinion because he did not have all the facts. In the end he would be counted as favoring retreat. Writing twenty years later, Couch assigned himself a bold stance at this midnight conference: he would favor the offensive only if he could select the point of attack rather than have General Hooker in command. At the time no one heard him take such a position, however.

Dan Sickles said he was not a professional soldier like the rest, and that might give any view in opposition to theirs less weight. But he would counsel retreat. It was a political question more than a military one, said political general Sickles. A reverse now for the Army of the Potomac would have grave consequences in the North. A victory over the enemy was "doubtful," Warren heard him say, "and a defeat would endanger Washington. The uncertainties are against us." Here was Dan Sickles echoing George McClellan. Sickles said he did not think the effect on the country of a withdrawal "would be fatal."

Hooker now rejoined the conference and polled each general for his opinion. Sickles brought up his concern about the army's supplies and its communications with the north bank. A hard shower earlier in the evening was a reminder of how swiftly the Rappahannock could rise and endanger the army's bridges. Meade, in advocating an offensive, made the additional argument that he doubted they could safely withdraw in the face of an aggressive enemy. The artillery especially would be at risk. Thus the risk in withdrawing was greater than the risk in attacking.

Hooker responded with one of his cocksure declarations: they could cross the river without the loss of a single man or gun. As Butterfield quoted him, "General Lee would throw up his hat to have us withdraw, and would not fire a gun or molest us at all; only be too glad to have us go back." (Hooker later claimed that by thus meeting Meade's objection he could count Meade as favoring withdrawal. Meade coldly rejected this sophistry.) After these arguments the vote of the corps commanders remained three to two in favor of making an attack.

However surprised he may have been at this vote, Joe Hooker had made up his mind and nothing his lieutenants said changed it. He took the responsibility for the decision, he said. The army would go back across the river at U.S. Ford; the necessary orders of march would follow. The meeting was dismissed. When he was awakened and told of the decision, Reynolds grumbled, "What was the use of calling us together at this time of night when he intended to retreat anyhow?"[35]

It was shortly before 1 o'clock in the morning — May 5 — when

Hooker was handed the dispatch from Sedgwick that he had been expecting. The Sixth Corps, Sedgwick announced, was "hemmed in upon the slope" in front of Banks's Ford, covered by General Hunt's guns north of the river. If his corps were his only responsibility, he said, he would withdraw it immediately. If Hooker's operations required him to jeopardize his command, he needed to know promptly "or I may be obliged to withdraw." Resignedly Hooker directed Butterfield to reply: "Dispatch this moment received. Withdraw. Cover the river, and prevent any force crossing."

Hooker hardly had time to absorb this blow when, minutes later, his hopes soared. A second telegram arrived from Sedgwick, with a complete change of heart: "I shall hold my position, as ordered, on south of Rappahannock." Hooker jumped at the reprieve: "Order to withdraw countermanded. Acknowledge. . . ."

John Sedgwick's change of heart came suddenly. Between 11:45 when he sent the first telegram, and about midnight when he sent the second, he was visited by engineer Benham, who came up from his posting at Banks's Ford to counsel his old friend. Benham warned Sedgwick most emphatically not to recross the river without Hooker's express sanction. Let the general commanding be responsible for the decision, he urged. Until then Sedgwick should simply obey his standing orders.

Sedgwick took the point. He hurried a second courier to the telegraph station at Banks's Ford with the dispatch saying he would hold position on the south bank. He assumed the second courier would overtake the first, and the second message be sent in place of the first one. The second courier did not have a fast enough horse, however; Sedgwick's two telegrams reached Hooker perhaps ten minutes apart.

By all rights this little mishap ought to have been of little consequence. Hooker's order for the Sixth Corps to recross the river was sent off at 1:00 A.M. and his countermanding order just twenty minutes later. Surely nothing irreversible could happen on Sedgwick's front in twenty minutes; surely the Banks's Ford salient would therefore still be in place for Joe Hooker to use on May 5. His scheme to open a new offensive from Banks's might salvage the campaign after all.

The previous Friday, the first day of fighting, Signal Corps' fumbling had blacked out Hooker's attempts to communicate with Sedgwick. On Saturday a bumbling courier so delayed Hooker's orders to Reynolds's First Corps that Howard's Eleventh was left to face Stonewall Jackson alone. Now, on Tuesday, yet another communications failure snuffed out Hooker's last hope for saving his campaign. General Hooker must have wondered if the Fates were conspiring against him.

The order to recross the river, sent at 1:00 A.M., reached Sedgwick at 2:00 A.M. Its one-hour delivery was typical of dispatches going between Hooker's headquarters and Sedgwick's that night. Sedgwick obeyed promptly and started his troops across the bridges. The order countermanding the retreat, sent at 1:20 A.M., only reached Sedgwick two hours later, at 3:20 A.M. The cause of this delay was never reported. At 3:20 it was far too late to turn back, Sedgwick said: "Almost my entire command has crossed over." By 5 o'clock it was dawn and he reported the bridges being swung and dismantled. At 7 o'clock his "much exhausted" command was in camp a mile back from the river.

"I was thwarted," was all Fighting Joe Hooker said about it. By General Meade's account, he was more affected than that. "Poor Hooker . . . ," Meade confided to his wife, "said to me, in the most desponding manner, that he was ready to turn over to me the Army of the Potomac; that he had enough of it, and almost wished he had never been born."[36]

∗　∗

THE MOMENT it was dark that Monday evening and when the firing died out, John Sedgwick had begun pulling his extended lines back toward Banks's Ford. The sky was clouded and in the early morning hours a thick ground fog formed. It was "dark as Egypt" in the pine thickets along the Rappahannock, a man remembered. Lieutenant Charles Brewster, 10th Massachusetts, had the "mighty dubious" honor of directing the rear guard in Newton's division. One regiment after another was drawn off the line and sent back to the river. They filed silently past, Brewster wrote, "and then we waited for the pickets quietly sitting on our horses with nothing between us and the Rebs." In due course the Rebel pickets discovered the pullback "and set up such a yelling as you never heard nor ever will." But the darkness was their shield and soon they were safely formed up in line of battle above the ford.

Irregular outbursts of firing would spark along the picket lines, and Porter Alexander lobbed his shells toward the bridges. The infantry waited quietly in the darkness, chewing their hardtack and trusting their generals to know what they were doing. Sedgwick and his staff had already worked out the agenda for the retreat, and the moment Hooker's withdrawal order arrived at 2:00 A.M. the word was passed to start the men across the bridges. Straw and earth were spread on the planking to deaden the noise of the wagons and guns. The men needed little urging to keep moving, and to keep quiet, and the retreat went swiftly.

Out on the picket lines the waiting was not easy. In the 6th Maine, acting as rear guard for Burnham's Light Division on the left, there was great bitterness at the actions of the 31st and 43rd New York pickets on their front. "The skirmishers in front of us, a parsel of N.Y. men," Sergeant Benjamin Thaxter wrote scornfully, "gave themselves up without firing a gun and told them that we were in the woods." The Maine men were able to extract themselves from this tangle, but only at considerable cost. The two New York regiments gave up 210 prisoners. Over on the right, when the pickets were finally called in, Chester Leach of the 2nd Vermont wrote his wife, "we could not find the bridge for some time & when we did find it, it was not there. . . . You can guess something how we felt." Finally pontoon boats were sent to bring them across.

Meanwhile all along the lines Confederates were prowling forward along the dark tracks and gathering prisoners in numbers. Some were stragglers, many were simply lost. Cadmus Wilcox estimated that two of his Alabama regiments "caught 350 of the enemy (woundless). . . ." Sergeant W. R. Montgomery said the Phillips Legion "fired a volley & you ought to have heard the Yanks beg for quarter — took a Lt Col & about half a Regt." The Sixth Corps would report 1,454 of its men captured in this campaign, with perhaps two thirds of them taken this night at Banks's Ford.

By 4:00 A.M. the infantry and artillery were across the two Banks's Ford bridges, and the engineers cut the cables on the south bank and let the current drift the bridge spans over to the north bank. "The night was dark and foggy," wrote engineer Stephen Weld, "and favorable for taking up the bridges." The river fog remained after daylight, allowing the engineers to dismantle the spans and shelter the pontoons in nearby creeks. The Sixth Corps went into camp, leaving a strong picket line on the shore to warn of any Rebel incursions.[37]

While Sedgwick's corps was being pulled back across the river in these early hours of Tuesday, it was suddenly remembered that John Gibbon still had a brigade on the south bank, occupying Fredericksburg. Gibbon was telegraphed to evacuate the town. Earlier, on Monday afternoon, he had taken up the lower of his three bridges, and now on Hooker's order he brought his troops back across at the Lacy house and the engineers swung the bridges there. "It was an anxious night," General Gibbon wrote his wife, but under cover of the dense fog the evacuation went well: "left without any trouble, the enemy firing only a few shots from his picket line."

One of Gibbon's men, Cyril H. Tyler, was stationed on picket duty opposite the town that Tuesday morning. Barksdale's Mississippians had reoccupied Fredericksburg almost as soon as the Yankees left, and they set out a picket line as well. Neither side was inclined to be aggressive, however, and an informal truce was soon established. "One of the rebs came down to the river," Tyler wrote his homefolks, "& I asked him what time it was, and he said it was time us Yankees was leaving."[38]

* *

GENERAL LEE was feeling just as aggressive on Tuesday as he had on Monday. The retreat of Sedgwick at Banks's Ford and of Gibbon at Fredericksburg during the night cleared the threat to his rear, something accomplished without further casualties. The Federals, it seemed, were obliging him. Captain W. R. Redding of Early's command counted the Yankees his regiment had captured that night, "which was not a great no. for they ran so fast that we could not catch them. . . ."

"We have reoccupied Fredericksburg," Lee signaled Richmond that morning, "and no enemy remains south the Rappahannock in its vicinity." To ensure that the enemy would not recross the river and renew the threat to his rear, Lee had Early take up his old line at Fredericksburg with his division and Barksdale's brigade. Lee discounted any threat of the enemy recrossing at Banks's Ford and began instead to mass his forces to again challenge Hooker's main army.

General Hooker, Lee told President Davis, "occupied a strong position in front of the U.S. Ford." This was confirmed by Jeb Stuart, whose reconnaissance that morning "discovered the enemy in force in earthworks, artillery and infantry." Stuart counted thirteen guns bearing on one point at the center of his line. Leaving Early on watch at Fredericksburg, Lee set about shifting his other five divisions for an attack on Hooker. He called on Jed Hotchkiss for a map of the roads to U.S. Ford. He intended to attack that day, May 5.[39]

Hooker was meanwhile carefully planning his retreat. He had determined to withdraw the army under cover of darkness. Engineers Warren and Comstock were told to prepare a new defensive line for the rear guard to occupy while the rest of the troops were crossing. This new line ran some three miles, from the Rappahannock on the east to the Rapidan on the west, enclosing a salient a mile and a half deep around the U.S. Ford bridges. The line was to be fortified and manned by two of Meade's Fifth Corps divisions, with his third division in reserve. General Hunt positioned forty-four guns on the north bank of the Rappahannock to cover the bridges. The engineers had laid three bridges at the crossing site, and were cutting new roads through the forest for the troops to reach them quickly. That morning Captain William Folwell, 50th New York engineers, wrote his wife, "I shudder at the idea, but can no longer suppress the suspicion that we are not able to hold our position over there and that the whole army will retire to this side. . . ."

John Babcock of the Bureau of Military Information, who had spent the night interrogating Confederate deserters and prisoners from the fighting on the Fredericksburg front, hurried his findings to Colonel Sharpe. As late as last evening, he explained, he had not found a single man of Longstreet's arrived from the south. "If they are up," he concluded, "they have gone over in your direction or toward Culpeper." Babcock was concise about the troops who had faced Sedgwick on May 4: "Early's, Anderson's, and McLaws'." (However expert such battlefield intelligence might be, it was by its very nature some hours after the fact — and in this instance, some hours after it might have persuaded General Sedgwick.)

This intelligence merely focused Hooker's concern about Longstreet toward the west. He had Butterfield inform the president of the impending withdrawal, giving as one reason the "possibility of enemy crossing river on our right flank and imperiling this army. . . ." Alfred Pleasonton, commanding his own cavalry and that of the deposed William Averell, was sent off to picket the river crossings and watch for Longstreet. Pleasonton conjured up alarms wherever he looked. "Perhaps they have a pontoon train we know nothing of," he said at one point. In the meantime, the signalman watching Hamilton's Crossing reported the arrival of three trains from the south during the night, and Butterfield noted, "This dispatch indicates no obstruction to the R.R. . . ." From a distraction Longstreet had grown into an obsession. (By late night on May 5 the first of Longstreet's troops from Suffolk reached Petersburg, twenty miles south of Richmond.)[40]

Hooker ordered the wounded to be taken back across the bridges first, starting immediately. Those too severely injured to be moved would have to be left to the enemy, along with surgeons and medical supplies. The artillery held in reserve was sent next. The infantry was not scheduled to move until dark, its batteries leading. Thus should Lee oblige Hooker by attacking any time in the daylight hours, he would confront not only the full infantry strength of six corps of infantry but 106 guns of the divisional and corps batteries.

The Fifth Corps would march first, falling back to the new defensive line covering the bridges. Then in sequence, from the left of the line and then from the right, the other corps would pass through the Fifth's line to the bridges. It was expected that the whole army would easily be across the river before daylight on May 6. But at 4 o'clock that afternoon it began to rain. Indeed, as Charles F. Morse of the Twelfth Corps put it, "it began to rain in torrents."

"This afternoon," Captain Jonathan Hager, 14th U.S. Infantry, recorded in his diary, "one of the heaviest & longest continued rainfalls I have ever seen. The whole country was flooded. Every shelter tent was swimming and officers & men were drenched to the skin." At nightfall General Williams termed it "darker than Erebus. We gathered around a big camp fire and piled on the wood, but the cold rain poured, and done up in our rubber coats and hats we looked most forlorn and felt quite so." Like the April storm that had delayed Hooker's first offensive, this storm originated to the west, where it set the headwaters of the Rappahannock and the Rapidan in flood. By 8 o'clock engineer Folwell had marked a six-foot rise in the Rappahannock at the bridges.

General Lee had been pressing his lieutenants to get the troops into position for an attack before dark. He planned a simultaneous assault on both enemy flanks, Anderson and McLaws striking from the east and Jeb Stuart's command from the west. This involved a good deal of shifting of forces and hard marching, and it went slowly. The men were tired, and when the storm hit, the roads turned to mud and they slowed to a crawl. John Wood of McLaws's division recorded a march that day of "3 or 4 miles up the road in the hardest rain that I have seen in Virginia. . . . We halted about sundown and pitched tents." Their consolation was that nearly every man had a shelter tent "captured from the Yanks." Lee surrendered to the storm and rescheduled his attack for morning on May 6.[41]

One of the first to cross to the north bank that evening was General Hooker, an action that surprised his aide William Candler. "It was so different from his former acts," Candler remarked. He decided General Hooker was not his former self. By 9 o'clock the Rappahannock was out of its banks and running over the bridges and they were impassable and the anchoring cables were barely holding. Hooker signaled by torch to Meade and Slocum, the generals nearest on the south bank, "Suspend movements for an hour or two. Trouble at the bridges."

To save the bridges, the engineers hit on the idea of taking up one of the spans and using its pontoons and planking to piece out the other two, extending and re-anchoring them so they would float on the flood. It was rough, dangerous work. Folwell said he "walked off into the river" and was saved from drowning only by catching a rope as he fell.

The engineers were still at work at midnight, and it was uncertain how soon their efforts might succeed. Meade spoke of an act of Providence and talked it over with Couch, the senior corps commander. On the specious argument that when Hooker crossed the river he left the troops "without a command in the presence of the enemy" — Hooker was clearly still in command, issuing orders through his signalmen — Couch suspended the movement to the bridges for the night. "The army should remain & fight it out," he said. Meade reported this to Hooker by signal at midnight: "The bridges being reported impassable — roads getting so — all the artillery not down & no definite intelligence of when the bridges would be ready Genl Couch, in your absence abandoned the movement for tonight. . . ."

What was happening here was another revolt of the generals, this time at the tactical level. Lieutenant Colonel Alexander S. Webb of Meade's staff caught the essence of it in a letter home a few days later. "Strong in our position we ought to have invited attack," he wrote. Then came the order to recross the river during the night. "We all prayed that the bridges might be washed away rather than have that order carried out."

The general commanding, Couch admitted, "showed plainly that my orders displeased him." General Hunt argued that the guns could not be gotten across before daylight, but Hooker would not listen. The engineers announced the bridges were secure, and at 1:20 A.M. a curt order was signaled to Couch: "The Genl directs that movements be continued as ordered."[42]

In steady procession the troop columns resumed their march through the dripping woods. Corporal Richard May of the 20th Connecticut remembered that it was 7 o'clock on that dark, cold, wet morning of May 6 when they reached the river. There was a large meadow there, half round in shape. "We found this field covered with troops as thick as they could stand. One could stand and see nearly all the battle flags of the Army of the Potomac there." There was only room to stand; the mud was six to twelve inches deep. Over each of the bridges "a column of troops was passing as rapidly as they could march. Even at this rate it did not thin out the mass but very slowly. We were obliged to stand there in that mud from seven until twelve, momentarily expecting an attack from the enemy."

But there was no attack. The Federal pickets stayed to the last, then came back at the double-quick. It was some time before Rebel skirmishers discovered their absence, and then they pushed forward cautiously. Except for a few exchanges between pickets there was no firing at all during the crossing. The Confederate batteries were silent.

Back on April 30, Day Four of the campaign, James Barnes's brigade from the Fifth Corps had advanced well out on the Turnpike beyond Chancellorsville before it was recalled on Hooker's order. Thus Barnes's men might say they had advanced the farthest of any Federals during the Chancellorsville campaign. Now, on Day Ten, they formed the army's rear guard and were the last Federals to leave the enemy shore. The engineers then dismantled the bridges, Captain Folwell recalled, "in quite a leisurely manner. I do not remember any excitement among the engineer detachment." With help from Barnes's infantry they dragged the bridge trains up the steep slope north of the river. With that, the Army of the Potomac marked the campaign as finished.

General Lee was coldly furious. He was preparing to issue the attack orders at his headquarters when General Dorsey Pender rode up to report that his skirmishers had gone forward and found the Yankee army gone. "This is the way that you young men are always doing," Lee snapped at him. "You have again let these people get away. I can only tell you what to do, and if you do not do it it will not be done. . . ."[43]

EPILOGUE

The Wages of Victory and Defeat

T HE ARMY OF THE POTOMAC marched back to its old camps around Falmouth in the mud and pounding rain. No straggling was reported, and there appeared to be little serious demoralization. "I heard neither officers nor men express even impatience of the movement . . . ," wrote engineer Folwell. "The ranks were dressed and closed and marched steadily and silently." Indeed, many of the troops thought this was just another of General Hooker's maneuvers — they were going to recross the river at some other point to renew the fight.

As was the case after every battle, men hurried off letters to their homefolks to let them know they were alive and uninjured. If there was a common thread in these letters, it was puzzlement. "The men were absolutely astonished at our move for every one felt that we had the best of the Rebs and could hold our position as the saying is till Hell froze over . . . ," Captain Henry Young, 7th Wisconsin, told his wife. "You cant make any person in this army believe we were whipped. . . ." Private Henry Howell, 124th New York, was of a like mind. "We had entrenchments put up there on all sides and I dont see how the Rebs could ever have driven us away from that place if we had not evacuated. But I suppose old Hooker knows what he is up to."

"We were in a dense wilderness and backed out in an immense storm," Colonel Edward Bragg wrote home. "I am alive — can eat — ride horseback — swear and smoke — that's about all the humanity that is left in me." Lieutenant George Marden of the sharpshooters asked himself, "Were we whipped? I dont know. What to make of it, I dont know." But of one thing he was certain. "I do know that Chancellorsville is the greatest battle of the war."[1]

Rations were issued and new equipment distributed — a careful quartermaster calculated that exactly 49.96 percent of the men in the

Twelfth Corps had lost their knapsacks — and the bands played and there were reviews, and there was time to reflect on what had happened in those ten days past. Newspapers were sought out for what they might tell about the battle, but they were not a great deal of help. The correspondents, it seemed, were as confused as everyone else and offered little enlightenment.

"It would seem that Hooker has beaten Lee, and that Lee has beaten Hooker . . . ," Major Charles T. Dix entered in his diary. "Everything seems to be everywhere, and everybody all over, and there is no getting at any truth." General Alpheus Williams, who had been at the center of the worst fighting, concluded that the newspapers' stories "so far as I have seen are mainly fictions." The *New York Herald* was at least certain that Chancellorsville was a Union defeat, and called for General Hooker's dismissal. The *Herald*'s startling choice for his replacement was the notorious Dan Sickles. After reading that, Dan Butterfield announced that in future any copies of the *Herald* delivered to the Army of the Potomac would be burned.

General Hooker issued a puzzling address to the army congratulating it for its achievements. "If it has not accomplished all that was expected, the reasons are well known to the army," he explained. He for one surely did not know those reasons, Captain Folwell grumbled, "and have met no one who does."[2]

However, there was one factor in the defeat — or in the lack of accomplishment, as General Hooker put it — that received far more mention that any other. James T. Miller of the 111th Pennsylvania, Slocum's Twelfth Corps, spoke for many of his fellow Yankees when he set out to explain the outcome of Chancellorsville in a letter home. Howard's Eleventh Corps, Miller wrote, "ran like a parcel of scart sheep.. . . I can tell you that for the present we think but very little of the dutch sons of bitches that used to brag that they fights mit Sigel and I dont know but they might have fought well with Sigel but they did not fight worth shit under Howard. . . ."

That the Dutchmen had run, or at least a good number of them, seemed to the rest of the army the one certain thing about this confusing battle. That also seemed the easiest explanation for the defeat. Indeed, for those who had no use for foreigners to begin with, particularly German foreigners, it was the logical explanation.

To the dismay of the Eleventh Corps, the issue became a public one. Accounts in the *Herald* and the *New York Times* in particular made much of the Eleventh's collapse on May 2. Alexander Schimmelfennig, one of Howard's generals of brigade, condemned the stories as "infamous falsehoods . . . poisonous slanders upon this heretofore honored corps." Howard told his troops, "Some obloquy has been cast upon us" and called for a renewal of their patriotic spirit. (Pious Howard believed the real author of their troubles was the general commanding. "Gen. Hooker is said to be impure. He swears . . . ," he wrote his clergyman brother. "Would that you would plead with our Father to convert the soul of Gen. Hooker. It is just what we need.") A mass meeting held in New York City sought to renew morale among German Americans in the army and at home, but to little avail. "The spirit of this corps is broken," Carl Schurz insisted. In German communities across the North support for the war was never the same after Chancellorsville.[3]

All this was most unfortunate for the misused troops of the Eleventh Corps, yet for the rest of the Army of the Potomac it was probably useful to have the Dutchmen for a target. The army had marched out of Falmouth on April 27 with high hopes for victory, and now it was back at Falmouth with those hopes dashed, and if there was something or someone to blame it eased the disappointment. That there might be other causes for the defeat was not nearly as clear or as easily understood.

Consequently there was virtually none of the widespread demoralization after Chancellorsville that had followed Fredericksburg in December. There were no wholesale desertions. The reforms Hooker had instituted remained in place, and there was none of the military mismanagement of the Burnside era that had left the men feeling so ill used. One disgusted man did write home that as to General Hooker, "the troops has not got half the confidence that they had in him," but even so that was half again as much confidence as they showed in General Burnside after Fredericksburg.

The Chancellorsville defeat was by no means being forgotten, but the men in the ranks of the Army of the Potomac were not dwelling on it. Most important, there was no one to say they were not ready for a fight if it should come to that. A Massachusetts soldier summed it up by insisting, "The morale of the Army of the Potomac was better in June than it had been in January," and he remembered "nothing of that spirit of insubordination and despondency. . . ."[4]

The news that Hooker had led the army back across the Rappahannock and ended the campaign came as a severe shock to President Lincoln. Newspaperman Noah Brooks was at the White House on the afternoon of May 6 when the president came in with Butterfield's dispatch. His face was ashen and he was obviously distraught. He handed the telegram to Brooks. "Read it — news from the Army." Then he began to pace the room, hands clasped behind his back, muttering, "What will the country say? Oh, what will the country say?"

Mr. Lincoln might worry initially about what the country would say, but in fact the country seemed to say very little. "Our people, though shocked and very much disappointed, are in better tone and temper than I feared they would be," Navy Secretary Welles noted in his diary. The news of the defeat came out slowly in the newspapers, seeping into the public's consciousness rather than smiting it in one blow. Thanks to Hooker's tight security and censorship of reporters, the battle was over, and the army safely back across the river, before many people even knew the campaign had started. And by report, the Rebels had suffered equally in the fighting — "likewise undergone a fearful clawing," was how New York diarist George Templeton Strong put it — and there was consolation in that. Strong thought the worst consequence of the defeat was a loss of faith in Fighting Joe Hooker, "when he seemed likely to be the man we have been so long trying to find. . . ."[5]

* *

A LOSS OF faith certainly marked the Army of the Potomac's officer corps. Here too the prevailing view was puzzlement, but blame was calculated and laid squarely on the general commanding. "Hooker who is so well known to possess personal bravery seems . . . to have shown a complete want of *backbone* at the wrong moment, to the surprise of every one," John Gibbon decided. The problem was a lack of "steady purpose," Gouverneur Warren thought. "We halted, we hesitated, wavered, retired. . . ." General Hancock told his wife he "had the blues ever since I returned from campaign. . . . Hooker's day is over." Fair-minded George Meade, who earlier had expressed respect for Hooker's generalship, was especially saddened. "General Hooker has disappointed all his friends by failing to show his fighting qualities at the pinch," he told Mrs. Meade. ". . . I think these last operations have shaken the confidence of the army in Hooker's judgment, particularly among the superior officers."

Coursing through the lower officer ranks at the same time was an undercurrent of malicious gossip. He had been told, said the cavalry's Captain George Armstrong Custer, that the commanding general was wounded during the fighting; if so, "it was a wound he received from a projectile which requires a cork to be drawn before it is servicable." That, tongues wagged, was the real cause of the defeat. As early as May 8, Washington insider Elizabeth Blair Lee had it from an acquaintance in the army that General Hooker "was drunk all the time & that after the first day's battle was unfit for duty"; it was Sunday, May 3, her acquaintance told her and "Hooker is stretched on the grass — the Staff standing around & the Army perfectly quiet in the rear. . . ."

What any such witnesses to Hooker's supposed intemperance had actually seen, of course, was the general after he was concussed by the Rebel cannon shot during Sunday's battle, when he was indeed "stretched on the grass" with his staff in attendance. Those who had been with Hooker during the fighting treated the tales of his drunkenness with the contempt they deserved. "When I saw him he shewed no signs of having drunk at all that I could see," Colonel Wainwright wrote in his diary, "and I saw a good deal of him on Sunday; the idea certainly never entered my head that day." When the charge persisted, so did Wainwright. "I cannot believe it, and do not hesitate to say he was perfectly sober every time I saw him on Sunday." Colonel Sharpe, who was at Hooker's side throughout the campaign, was blunt about it: anyone who said the commanding general was drunk at Chancellorsville "lies in his throat."[6]

Mr. Lincoln hastened down from Washington to investigate these and other matters, bringing General Halleck with him. They spent all day Thursday, May 7, at Falmouth with Hooker and his lieutenants. There was no attempt to dissect the failed campaign or to apportion blame. By Meade's account, Lincoln said that "the result was in his judgment most unfortunate; that he did not blame any one . . . the disaster was one that could not be helped." Still, the president thought its effect, at home and abroad, "would be more serious and injurious than any previous act of the war." At least he found the troops "none the worse for the campaign."

The Army of the Potomac's corps commanders seized on the president's visit to attempt yet another generals' revolt. This time the ringleaders were Henry Slocum and Darius Couch. Slocum sought to organize a cabal aimed at Hooker's overthrow, apparently anticipating support from at least a majority of his fellow corps commanders. Already the dissidents were coalescing around George Meade as their choice to replace Hooker. (Slocum, Couch, and Sedgwick, all senior to Meade, sent him word they would be willing to serve under him as commanding general.) Clearly Meade was the crucial figure in Slocum's scheme, but Meade would have none of it. "I refused to join Slocum, who desired to take action to have Hooker removed," he told his wife. While unwilling to join any movement against Hooker, Meade said that if asked his opinion by Mr. Lincoln officially, in a council of war, he would give it. He implied that if it came to that, he would not vote to retain Hooker in command.

Without Meade's name or tacit approval for his petition, Slocum backed away from approaching the president. Couch's role in the generals' revolt was less direct. As Meade explained it, "I declined to join Couch in a representation to the President . . . ," and there is nothing on record to suggest that Couch actually went ahead with any "representation" to Lincoln that day. He must have realized, as General Newton had realized back in December, that being singled out trying to have his superior relieved could be considered "manifestly improper" conduct, leading to his cashiering.

Couch instead took an indirect tack, and two days later made application to the president, through channels, to be relieved of his command in the Army of the Potomac. He let it be known he was unwilling to serve any longer under General Hooker. Darius Couch had a peculiar notion of duty. Hooker, "expressing great surprise," returned his application. (In due course, Couch would renew the application and see it accepted. Selflessly rejecting the high command for himself — he was the most senior of the corps commanders — he urged that it go to Meade. This erstwhile corps commander would direct Pennsylvania home guards in the Gettysburg campaign, and ended the war commanding a division in the western theater.)[7]

Although this latest revolt of the generals merely flickered and then burned out, it left a poisonous residue in the army's high command. The dissatisfaction in the officer corps leaked into the press, just as it had in Burnside's time. Reports of it reached the White House. "I must tell you," the president wrote Hooker, "that I have some painful intimations that some of your corps and division commanders are not giving you their entire confidence. This would be ruinous, if true. . . ." Undermining a superior was a familiar practice to Joe Hooker, and now it had come full circle. He did not want to accuse anyone, he said, and told the president to invite the ranking generals to call at the White House to "learn their views for his own information."

Treasury Secretary Chase, Hooker's staunchest ally in the Cabinet, thought there should be no room in the army for disaffected generals; far better to "make new generals of the best captains or lieutenants." He believed it a mistake for Hooker to let his generals go to Washington to tell their tales. Every man wants to be a hero, Chase observed, and claim how much better the results would have been "if his counsel or his ideas had been followed."

Secretary Chase's observation was prophetic. These generals painted a picture of Chancellorsville for Mr. Lincoln as a defeat engineered 100 percent by Fighting Joe Hooker. Gideon Welles noted in his diary, "The President says if Hooker had been killed by the shot which knocked over the pillar that stunned him, we should have been successful." However that might be, it was assigning blame for the defeat as unfairly as loading it entirely on the shoulders of the Eleventh Corps. Too many observers of the time — and of later times as well — shaped their verdict on Chancellorsville from faulty evidence.[8]

To be sure, Hooker as general commanding bore final responsibility for the defeat. To be sure, Hooker made serious mistakes during the campaign — poorly apportioning his cavalry between raiding and guarding the army; giving up Hazel Grove at the outset of the struggle for the Chancellorsville crossroads on May 3; muddling battlefield command of the artillery; staying a day too long with his determination to fight the battle defensively. Yet these mistakes, individually or added together, were not enough to lose the Battle of Chancellorsville. In the view of Gouverneur Warren, who witnessed a broader range of the fighting than any other Union general, "Our great weakness, in my opinion, is in the incompetency of many of our Corps Commanders. They don't know how to manage and fight troops." It must be said in defense of Joe Hooker that no Union general in any battle in this war was so badly served by his lieutenants.

Of the army's eight generals of corps, four failed Hooker's — and Warren's — test for competency. One was George Stoneman. The timely cutting of Lee's communications was pivotal to Hooker's plan, especially his determination to fight defensively, and Stoneman's blundering with the cavalry had larger consequences than simply failing to halt the flow of the enemy's supplies. Hooker found it incomprehensible that day after day Confederate trains should still be running, and he kept waiting — waiting too long — for this part of his plan to fall into place.

Hooker considered it equally incomprehensible that Otis Howard would ignore a direct order to prepare the Eleventh Corps for a flank attack on May 2, leaving Stonewall Jackson a virtually clear path nearly to the Chancellor house. That Saturday, too, Dan Sickles failed to organize a determined assault on Jackson's flanking column, and in the bargain misread what he saw and made the fateful announcement that Lee was giving up the field and retreating.

Fourth on the list of failures was John Sedgwick. Sedgwick's high character and warm reputation as "Uncle John" concealed a most ordinary level of generalship. His failure to act on his discretionary orders to break through Early's Fredericksburg lines on May 2, and his unnecessary retreat across the Rappahannock on the night of May 4, were the result of crippling caution and an unjustified belief in the enemy's capability and superior force. A general with any initiative — Hooker would say he wished he could have put John Reynolds in command of his left wing — would have delivered an attack on Lee's rear at Chancellorsville or at the very least have held the Banks's Ford bridgehead for future maneuvers.

Of all the actions in this campaign fought beyond his reach, Joe Hooker would write, "the trust I had reposed in commanders was not executed in a manner satisfactory to myself, and in a way that it would have been done could I have given the operations of these commanders my personal supervision." However much self-interest may have inspired that remark, it is nevertheless a damning indictment of the Army of the Potomac's high command.

After his brilliant opening moves, Hooker was repeatedly undone, too, by chance and mischance. Communications failures fatally delayed his promising advance from Chancellorsville on May 1. A negligent courier kept Reynolds's First Corps from being in position to confront Jackson's flank attack on May 2. The Rebel cannon shot that injured Hooker left the Potomac army leaderless when his leadership was most needed in the great battle of May 3. Yet another communications failure on May 6 lost the Banks's Ford bridgehead when it might have been saved.

With his campaign plan thus reduced to a shambles, in large measure by events not of his own making, Joe Hooker was left without resources. He had thrown all his energies and all his thought into his grand plan, followed it rigidly until it collapsed, and had nothing left with which to try and rescue victory from defeat. Consumed by his belief that his way was best, no other way would do. "The objection I have to Hooker," General Meade wrote, "is that *he did not and would not listen* to those around him; that he acted deliberately on his own judgment, and in doing so, committed, as I think, fatal errors."[9]

* *

THERE WAS still George Stoneman and his cavalry raiders to be accounted for. In Washington all that was known of the cavalry was what had been picked up from the Richmond newspapers. On Wednesday morning, May 6, not yet knowing of Hooker's decision to retreat and hoping to encourage his general, Mr. Lincoln passed on these papers' reports of Stoneman's depredations near Richmond, "which looks well." Hooker's response was sour. "Am glad to hear that a portion of the cavalry have at length turned up," he telegraphed from his old headquarters at Falmouth. "One portion did nothing." General Heintzelman, his ear always to the ground, speculated that when he did appear Stoneman would be in for a rough time. In his diary that night he observed, "Stoneman has also given dissatisfaction & will be relieved, when he returns, it is said."

Stoneman had decided on May 5 to start back with his command. Two of his raiding parties had already elected to head for Union lines on the Peninsula — they would reach there on May 6 — which left him with just 2,600 troopers at his field headquarters at Thompson's Crossroads on the South Anna River. He was a sixty-five-mile march from his starting point at Kelly's Ford. He had sent no word to Hooker and had received none, but rumors of the fighting on the Rappahannock were not encouraging. His rations were exhausted and man and beast were living off the country. This in itself was no particular hardship. Nathan Webb, 1st Maine cavalry, noted in his diary that day, "Chickens & ducks, ham & eggs, butter & milk and other delicacies we confiscated without judge or jury." Still, Stoneman was satisfied that he had now carried out his orders (or his interpretation of his orders), and without the expected reinforcement of Averell's division he was growing nervous. "I determined to make the best of our way back to the Army of the Potomac," he said.[10]

The way back he chose was the way he had come, and that decision saved him from ambush and attack. Rooney Lee's Confederate cavalry shadowing the raiders expected that Stoneman's entire force would make for Union lines on the Peninsula. While Lee planned a pursuit, Stoneman slipped away to the north. Rooney Lee's communications with General Lee were roundabout, and his warning arrived too late. Jeb Stuart organized an ambushing force of cavalry and infantry at Verdiersville on the Orange Plank Road for the morning of May 7, but found the quarry gone. Stoneman's column had plodded through the village the previous midnight.

It was a brutal march for the Yankee troopers. The violent storm that struck on the afternoon of May 5 turned the roads to rivers of mud and the streams to raging torrents. "The poor tired horses would splash, splash, through the mud, staggering along, hungry and almost gone," Nathan Webb wrote. "We were so sleepy that we cared for nothing and knew nothing." Raccoon Ford on the Rapidan was so deep, another trooper wrote, that it "took the horses up to the ears. We got awfully wet."

At nightfall on May 7 they reached Kelly's Ford on the Rappahannock, and the next day Stoneman reported that he "succeeded in getting everybody over except 1 man and 5 or 6 horses lost — drowned." They made camp and resupplied at Bealton Station on the Orange & Alexandria, and Stoneman telegraphed Hooker. His expedition, he explained, "has been an unusually severe one owing to the rains over head & mud under foot. . . . Its merits and results must be judged of by those competent to pass a judgment."

Joe Hooker did not hesitate to pass a judgment. He looked at Stoneman's casualty list — a total of 200 men, of which about 25 percent were lost in battle and the rest from straggling — and observed that for a general given the injunction to "fight, fight, fight," Stoneman seemed to have gone to great lengths to avoid fighting. The press was highly complimentary of Stoneman's exploits, however — the *Washington Daily Star*, for example, spoke of the "late brilliant cavalry raid" — and for the Yankee troopers it was at the least a memorable experience. According to the historian of the 1st Maine cavalry, "It was ever after a matter of pride with the boys that they were on 'Stoneman's Raid.'" When one of the boys was told that General Hooker was not pleased with the outcome, he had a ready answer: "Whether he was dissatisfied or not with our raid . . . I think we accomplished as much as he did."

For Joe Hooker there was only one fact about Stoneman's raid that mattered. He had sent off the bulk of his cavalry, 7,400 men, with an unmistakable first priority to sever Lee's supply line, yet on every day of the ten-day campaign Confederate trains were seen to arrive on schedule at Hamilton's Crossing. That was the true measure of Stoneman's failure. As late as Day Ten, Hooker said, had those trains stopped running, or had he learned they were soon to stop, it would have changed everything. "If Lee had been severed from his base of supplies, I certainly should not have retired across the River before giving him an old fashioned struggle for the ascendency." As a final expression of his displeasure, on May 22 General Hooker would relieve Stoneman of command of the cavalry.[11]

* *

IN HIS ADDRESS to the troops painting the best possible face on his defeat, Joe Hooker claimed the recent operations against the enemy had "placed *hors de combat* 18,000 of his chosen troops. . . ." Like much else in Hooker's address this represented a considerable leap of faith — Colonel Sharpe's B.M.I. would present the general with a more realistic estimate of Confederate losses — but at least it gave some perspective to the great battle on the Rappahannock. Chancellorsville would be accounted one of the costliest struggles these armies had fought in their two years of struggle.

Indeed, for the Army of the Potomac it was *the* costliest battle it had fought. That cost, when finally totted up, came to 1,694 dead, 9,672 wounded, and 5,938 missing, 17,304 in all. This eclipsed the losses in another stinging defeat, at Second Manassas the previous year. In terms of men killed and wounded, only at bloody Antietam had more Yankees — 282 more — fallen to enemy bullets and shells.

The toll fell very unevenly across the army. This reflected Hooker's failure to heed Mr. Lincoln's blunt caution that in the next battle "put in all of your men." The sole action for the men of Reynolds's First Corps was their forced river crossing below Fredericksburg on April 29; for the campaign as a whole the First's loss was but 300 men. The largest fight for Meade's Fifth Corps was the attempt by Sykes's regulars to advance eastward beyond Chancellorsville on May 1. That, and the engagement of a single brigade on May 3, added up to 700 casualties in the Fifth.

By contrast, the fierce struggle for Chancellorsville on May 3 fell most heavily on just two of the Potomac army's seven infantry corps — Sickles's Third and Slocum's Twelfth. Sickles lost 22 percent of his men on this day, Slocum 21 percent. Sickles's three divisions took a fearful pounding in Jeb Stuart's assaults on Sunday. Hiram Berry's division had 1,189 men killed and wounded, the largest number in that category in any Federal division in the campaign, and it cost the life of General Berry himself. The killed and wounded in Charles Graham's brigade of Birney's division came to 562, highest in any Federal brigade. In Amiel Whipple's little division, one man in five was killed or wounded, the highest percentage loss. The Third Corps' 4,124 total casualties — killed, wounded, and missing — were second only to the much larger Sixth Corps'.

Fighting shoulder to shoulder with Sickles's men on May 3, Slocum's Twelfth Corps took the same pounding. Alpheus Williams's division of the Twelfth totaled more men killed, wounded, and missing — 1,613 — than any other Federal division on the field. At the very center of the maelstrom on Sunday, Thomas Ruger's brigade lost 614 men in charge and countercharge, second only to Graham's Third Corps brigade that then took Ruger's place in the lines. As a measure of the fighting in this one sector of the May 3 battlefield, Ruger and Graham between them had 1,108 men killed and wounded, 10 percent of the entire killed-wounded loss suffered by the Potomac army in the campaign. Fighting nearby that day, two divisions of Couch's Second Corps, Hancock's and French's, added another 1,834 men to the Federal casualty rolls.

In all its complex maneuvering and fighting from Day Three to Day Nine, Sedgwick's Sixth Corps, largest in the army, suffered the largest casualty list — 4,611 killed, wounded, and missing. Bully Brooks lost 19 percent of his men and Albion Howe 21 percent of his, but the worst blow fell on Hiram Burnham's Light Division. More properly a light brigade, Burnham lost 808 men, 30 percent of his strength. The Light Division was wrecked in the assault on Marye's Heights on May 3 and never recovered; it was disbanded at the campaign's end.

For Howard's Eleventh Corps, the statistics had a largely negative connotation, bringing more abuse down on the heads of the poor Dutchmen. Charles Devens's division, bearing the brunt of Jackson's flank attack on May 2, recorded 45 percent of its loss in prisoners. Adolph Von Steinwehr's men behind them were overrun, and 50 percent of their casualties were prisoners. All told, the captured in Howard's corps came to 41 percent of its casualty list, the most in any corps at Chancellorsville.

The blame for such discouraging statistics, thought Herbert Mason of the 20th Massachusetts, had to be laid at the doorstep of the high command. "I feel assured that we can beat them, if we have the generals," he wrote, "but it is downright murder to keep sacrificing such a splendid army."[12]

Winning this battle cost Robert E. Lee dearly. His count of casualties came to 1,724 dead, 9,233 wounded, and 2,503 missing, a total of 13,460. While this was 3,844 fewer than Hooker's loss, the largest share of that difference was Federals missing in action, the most of them prisoners. Counting only the dead and wounded, a truer measure of the severity (and the closeness) of the fighting, there were actually more Confederates killed at Chancellorsville — 30 more — than Federals, and only 439 fewer wounded.

Although virtually every infantryman in the Army of Northern Virginia was thrown into the ten-day battle, the heaviest losses fell on the divisions of A. P. Hill and Robert Rodes. Their losses were virtually the same — Hill's 3,030, Rodes's 3,009. Hill's Light Division, fighting from start to finish in Sunday's battle for the Chancellorsville crossroads, suffered for it. Jim Lane's brigade lost 910 men, 43 percent of his numbers and the highest brigade count in the army. Another of Hill's brigades, Dorsey Pender's, lost 35 percent.

Rodes, who spearheaded Jackson's flank attack on May 2 and supplied the finishing blows on May 3, had equally severe casualties. O'Neal's brigade, with 818 killed, wounded, and missing, lost 35 percent of its force. Ramseur's brigade loss was 789, a staggering 52 percent. Overall, Hill lost 25 percent of his infantry and Rodes 29 percent.

Raleigh Colston's division, the smallest in the army, had the highest ratio of divisional casualties to men present, 31 percent. Dick Anderson and Lafayette McLaws, fighting with their divisions on both battlefronts, lost 1,498 and 1,889 men respectively. Jubal Early, whose duty it was to keep watch on Sedgwick's corps at Fredericksburg, lost 1,548. A nearly flawless performance cost the army's artillery arm 199 men among the forty-five batteries engaged.

With the much smaller army, General Lee had to face the sobering statistic that victory at Chancellorsville was achieved at a cost of better than 23 percent of his infantry. That was second only to the slaughter at Sharpsburg in September.

The ten days of Chancellorsville, including the fighting on both the eastern and western battlefronts and Stoneman's raid, involved just under 200,000 men. The combined cost to the two armies was 30,764 men

— 3,418 dead, 18,905 wounded, 8,441 missing. Only the Seven Days at Richmond ten months before had cost more. Veterans of the two campaigns ranked them equally as hell on earth.[13]

* *

EVEN WHEN he learned the enemy was back across the Rappahannock, General Lee had not been certain the campaign was over. He hurried divisions to their old postings all along the river in case Hooker should attempt another crossing somewhere else.

This was an army that was bone tired. The men, most of them, had been marching or fighting without pause day after day with little rest, many living only on what they could find in Yankee knapsacks. This latest march in the drenching rain was particularly wearing. "We were all verry near broke down when we got here," Leonidas Torrence wrote from his old camp on May 7. "We rested but once on the way and that was not more than 5 minutes," and he grumbled, "I dont think there was any use in marching us so hard. . . ." Georgian John Wood was equally unhappy after he discovered his regiment's old camp "had been plundered by citizens and stragglers. We all lost everything. . . ."

The true measure of the victory was some time sinking in. One day the enemy was there, strong and menacing, the next day he was gone, and there was uncertainty about exactly what had been accomplished. A Virginian in Dick Anderson's division boasted to his wife, "The enemy has been badly, ignominiously whipped . . . and driven back over the river in disgrace." This man had been in the rear with the commissary, however, and experienced none of the fighting. The view of those Confederates in the battle lines was more sobering.

Except perhaps for the victims of Jackson's flank attack on May 2, not many Yankees could be said to have been ignominiously whipped. "What has either side gained," G. W. Poindexter of Early's division wanted to know. "How much more does it look like peace than before — both sides back in their old camps, and their pickett posts in the same place. Just say we have not gained anything nor the Yankees. . . ." Captain S. G. Pryor of Rodes's division admitted to his wife, "I feel more sad since the last battle than I ever have after one. Everything ahead looks like war and nothing else." Doubtless there was victory here to claim, and to celebrate, but with the Federal army safely back across the river it was clear that there was still some way to go for the final victory.[14]

The Southern press, by contrast, was quick to rank the Chancellorsville victory very highly. The *Charleston Mercury* thought it significant that in his dispatch to the president General Lee had spoken of "a great victory." The paper pointed out that in no previous dispatch announcing a victory had the general used the word "great." The *Richmond Sentinel* was of a like mind. "It is now certain that the late victories near Fredericksburg were the most decisive of the war. Gen. Lee himself has so declared." According to the *Richmond Daily Dispatch,* the battles of Saturday and Sunday ranked "amongst the most brilliant in the annals of the Southern Confederacy, already illuminated with triumphs which, for number and magnitude, are not surpassed in history."

When he reflected on it, General Lee was of a very different mind. He thought such public sentiment, as expressed by newspapers, of little significance. So it had been after Fredericksburg, he pointed out to a Richmond official. "At Chancellorsville we gained another victory; our people were wild with delight — I, on the contrary, was more depressed than after Fredericksburg; our loss was severe, and again we had gained not an inch of ground and the enemy could not be pursued." For Robert E. Lee, claiming the battlefield was not enough.[15]

"You Carrie, nor any one else who has not witnessed it, can't form any idea of a battle field," Allie Clack of the 23rd North Carolina wrote his wife. "On the one side, you will see a large body of woods, completely torn to pieces by artillery, trees two & three feet in diameter shot through & through or broken off. On the other side where the growth is smaller, trees are worn to a complete *frazzle* by the incessant pounding of the minie balls. For miles the ground is strewn with blankets, knapsacks, haversacks, canteens, guns, cartridge boxes & every thing else pertaining to a soldier. . . . You could have gotten anything you might want. . . ."

Indeed, the Army of Northern Virginia resupplied itself after Chancellorsville. Thirteen pieces of artillery and 19,500 Federal rifles and a "large quantity" of ammunition were gleaned from the battlefield. There was almost nothing a man could want that he could not find. Georgian William Stillwell told his wife he did not draw any rations "but I had plenty, captured my rations from the Yankees." He catalogued his booty: "I got me needles, thread, pins, hair brush, comb, portfolio to keep my paper in, good canteen, two of the best blankets worth $10 apiece. Also I captured books, hymn and testament by the wholesale, so I made the trip very profitable, if I did suffer."

Not every booty hunter had such an easy time of it. Artillerist Frederick Colston, searching the battlefield for one of the highly prized India-rubber blankets issued to Yankee soldiers, discovered one tied to several muskets to form a last shelter for a dead Yankee. "So I dismounted and was untying it," Colston wrote, "when the supposed corpse opened his eyes and said reproachfully, 'I ain't dead yet.' I was dreadfully startled but managed to say, 'Excuse me, Sir, I thought you were dead,' mounted my horse and rode away."

Holding the field, the Confederates had the task of burying the dead. They buried their own with decent care but were less scrupulous with the enemy's. After a time, Virginian Thomas Smiley admitted, the burial details simply grew tired. "There were so many that our men could not dig graves for them but just threw a few shovelfulls of dirt over them . . . remarking as they did so that if they had staid home as they should have done they might probably have gotten a decent burial."

When Lieutenant Colonel John C. Mounger, commander of the 9th Georgia of Hood's division, reached the Rappahannock from Suffolk several days after the battle, he was told that his son, Captain Terrell T. Mounger, 14th Georgia, had been mortally wounded in Sunday's fighting. Colonel Mounger wrote his wife on May 23 that he had finally found their son's grave. "I put a small fence around his grave and wrote his name plainly on the head board drew the dirt up on the grave solomnly invoked the blessing of God on his departed soul. . . ." Less than two months after learning of her son's death at Chancellorsville, Mrs. Mounger would learn of her husband's death at Gettysburg.[16]

In the course of time Chancellorsville would come to be considered Robert E. Lee's greatest victory, and properly so. Certainly the odds against him in a major battle were never longer than when he determined he would challenge Hooker's army on May 1. Yet it must be said too that throughout the course of this battle Lee was repeatedly blessed with astonishingly good fortune.

Lee's decision to send Jackson on his flank march was an act as desperate as it was bold, and Joe Hooker insisted that under any kind of normal circumstances "ninety nine chances out of a hundred Genl Jackson's Corps would have been destroyed" on May 2. However far off he was statistically, Hooker's point was well taken. It required an improbable combination of pure chance and Union blundering for Jackson's secret march to go virtually unchallenged and for his assault to be so weakly met. "I trust that an ever kind Providence will bless us," said Jackson as he prepared to attack, and so it seemed.

Chance doubly favored Lee on May 2. His misunderstood order for Early to abandon Fredericksburg was rendered harmless by Sedgwick's negligent caution; indeed, Early's starting to withdraw fed the illusion the Confederates were retreating. And it was surely good fortune for Lee on May 3 when he was distracted that afternoon from his intended assault on Hooker's newly fortified and powerful lines behind the Chancellor house.

On May 4 the delay forced on an impatient Lee in attacking Sedgwick was fortuitous, leaving Hooker no time to intervene. The next day chance smiled again on Lee: the storm forced him to postpone his assault on Hooker's fortified lines, an assault Hooker was waiting for with anticipation. Then, on May 6, Hooker elected to wait no longer to be attacked and retreated — leaving Lee no target for his impending attack.

Thus it would appear that chance favored General Lee at least as often as it turned against General Hooker. However, in the end chance — or Dame Fortune or Fate or Providence or whatever name might be applied to it — came into singular balance between the two sides with the blast of gunfire that brought down Stonewall Jackson.[17]

* *

IN THOMAS CHANDLER'S small whitewashed estate office at Guiney's Station, Hunter McGuire watched in growing anguish as Stonewall Jackson sickened and failed. At first Dr. McGuire had been satisfied and even encouraged by his patient's progress. For two days after he was brought to Chandler's, May 5 and 6, the general's recovery seemed to proceed routinely. The amputation was healing, and he was alert and cheerful, pressing the doctor on how long a recuperation he would require.

On these days he passed much of the time in discussion of religious matters. It was a favorite subject of his, and he had willing listeners in Chaplain Lacy and Lieutenant Smith of his staff, a former theological student. "Every act of a man's life should be a religious one," Jackson said to Lacy at one point. "Religion makes every man better in every lawful calling: a better general, a better shoemaker." In the case of the general, it calmed perplexity, putting "mind and heart in tune."

On Thursday, May 7, however, Jackson took an abrupt turn for the worse. At about 1:00 A.M. he awakened with nausea and renewed pain in his side that had been injured in the fall from the litter the night of his wounding. Dr. McGuire, exhausted from his constant ministrations, lay asleep on a cot close by, but Jackson would not disturb him. Instead he quietly called on his servant Jim Lewis for wet compresses to relieve the discomfort. This had brought him relief during the journey to Chandler's, but today it did not. Still, Jackson insisted that Dr. McGuire's sleep not be disturbed until morning.

When he examined his patient at daylight that Thursday, McGuire was deeply disturbed. "I found him suffering with great pain in his side, and difficulty of breathing," he wrote. His diagnosis was prompt — pneumonia, "doubtless caused by the fall from the litter." There must be a contusion of the lung, he thought, and "effusion of blood in the chest was then produced, which lay dormant until full reaction had been established, & then inflammation resulted."

This remains the probable, if not the positively known, cause of the pneumonia. However that may be, it was linked directly to Jackson's wounding; at the very least the pneumonia took hold as it did because of his body's traumatized, seriously weakened condition. And there can be no doubt that pneumonia was the general's deadly affliction. Dr. McGuire had called in Dr. Samuel B. Morrison, chief surgeon of Early's division and the Jacksons' prewar physician, to assist him, and Morrison concurred in the diagnosis. So did a specialist in pneumonia, Dr. David Tucker, hurriedly called from Richmond by McGuire as a consultant.

In that day there was no known effectual treatment for pneumonia. The best Dr. McGuire could attempt was cupping — drawing blood to the affected area by means of glass cups held to the chest and partially evacuated by heating — and administering opiates — mercury, antimony, opium. The general appeared to rally the next morning, raising everyone's hopes. He believed he would get well, he announced. "I believe God has yet a work for me to perform. . . ." But the rally was short-lived. Under the opiates Jackson's mind began to drift and wander, and his breathing grew increasingly labored. The sole recourse now seemed to be prayer.[18]

There was no lack of that. General Lee, when he was told by Chaplain Lacy that Jackson's condition had become "threatening," replied that he was confident that God would not take General Jackson "at such a time when his country so much needed him." He asked Lacy to give the general "my affectionate regards and say to him, He has lost his left arm, but I my right arm."

Word of Stonewall Jackson's wounding had raced across the South, and prayer services were held in city, town, and hamlet. "Every heart is agonized lest his injuries may prove fatal," the *Savannah Republican* editorialized, "and one universal prayer will ascend that his precious life may be spared to the country."

Anna Jackson was brought from Richmond, and as much as she had prepared herself, still she was shocked to find her husband "terribly changed, face sunken, complexion bad, respiration terribly difficult, & under the influence of a strong anodyne." He roused himself at her presence and told her, "Now Anna, don't wear a long face." In another of his lucid periods he said to McGuire, "I see, Doctor, from the number of physicians that you think my condition dangerous, but I thank God, if it is his will, that I am ready to go. I am not afraid to die. . . ." In periods of delirium he was back on the battlefield. "Tell Major Hawks to send forward provisions for the men . . . ," he called out, and at another time, "Major Pendleton, send in and see if there is higher ground back of Chancellorsville. . . ."

By Sunday, May 10, it was evident that Stonewall Jackson would not survive the day. Chaplain Lacy preached at well-attended morning services at army headquarters. Afterward General Lee sought him out to say he was sure the prayers offered that day would be answered. "When you return I trust you will find him better. When a suitable occasion offers, tell him that I prayed for him last night, as I never prayed, I believe, for myself." Overcome by emotion, he turned away.

At about 10 o'clock that warm, pleasant morning, Dr. McGuire told Anna Jackson that her husband would live but a few hours. She determined she must inform him of his fate. He had told her several times, she said, that while he was willing enough to die any time that God willed it, he desired a few hours to prepare. He hoped, too, that when that time came, it would be on a Sunday.

She went to his bedside and said, "Do you know that the doctors say you must very soon be in heaven? . . . Before this day closes, you will be with the blessed Saviour in his glory." Then she asked if the Saviour's presence was with him and he answered distinctly, "Yes." He called for Dr. McGuire. "Doctor, Anna says you have told her that I am to die today. Is it true?" It was too true, McGuire said. After a time Jackson said, as of old, "Very good, very good. It is all right."

The child Julia was brought in for a last farewell, and then the warm midday hours passed slowly. The general lay quiet, and the room was shaded and hushed. Once, at about 2:30, he suddenly roused to call out, "Order A. P. Hill to prepare for action! Pass the infantry to the front! Tell Major Hawks. . . ." Then he fell silent again. Just before 3:15 he spoke out again. Clearly and firmly he said, "Let us cross over the river, and rest under the shade of the trees." Presently, peacefully and without struggle, he died.[19]

* *

THE SOUTH mourned, and the two armies settled into their old lines along the Rappahannock. Except for the some 30,000 fewer men in the ranks, little seemed to have changed since the quiet days of late April. The days grew longer and hotter. On the opposing picket lines on the riverbanks the informal truce was re-established, and with it the bantering exchanges. "I say, Yank," a Rebel called across one day. "Where is Fighting Joe Hooker now?" The Yank called back, "Oh, he's gone to Stonewall Jackson's funeral!"

"What next?" President Lincoln asked his general, but Joe Hooker was without ideas. He spoke vaguely of another Rappahannock crossing, this time to fight where he "had elbow room," keeping the entire army "within my personal supervision." But he came up with no new grand plan. He did not want to undertake anything, he said, until all the short-term men were gone from the camps and the Army of the Potomac could operate without that distraction.

Mr. Lincoln listened to this, and to the dissident generals, and whatever the justice of it, he recognized that as commanding general Joe Hooker was compromised. He watched and waited, and when the opportunity came — it was just four days before the two armies met on the hot fields and ridges of Gettysburg — he replaced Fighting Joe Hooker with George Gordon Meade.

General Lee had not been content to wait again for his opponent. He understood that in war the initiative was precious, especially for the smaller army; he had won it and would keep it. The previous September he had found General McClellan back in command of the Army of the Potomac, and having taken McClellan's measure once, was eager to do so again. He marched north, intending to force McClellan to battle on ground of his choosing in Maryland or Pennsylvania. But Sharpsburg had not been the decisive victory he sought. Now the circumstances were repeated, and he would repeat the experiment.

He would build on the victory won at Chancellorsville, demoralizing the enemy. This time Longstreet would be with him. (At Chancellorsville, Lee told General Hood, "had I had the whole army with me, General Hooker would have been demolished.") He considered the men of the Army of Northern Virginia to be all but invincible. ("There never were such men in an army before," he told Hood.) He had taken the measure of Mr. F. J. Hooker once; he would do so again. A month after Chancellorsville, Robert E. Lee set his army on the roads to Pennsylvania.

"Our course led us by the field of Chancellors where our memory of the great contest was forcibly refreshed by sight of new made graves, blackened ruins & rotting horses . . . ," Virginia artillerist Ham Chamberlayne wrote home. "We may reasonably hope, I think, to thrash Hooker and to possess the country — Gen Lee's designs are too deep & far reaching however for guessers to follow. . . ."[20]

APPENDIX I

The Armies at Chancellorsville

This tabulation of forces in the two armies in the Chancellorsville campaign is compiled from tables in the *Official Records,* supplemented by data from documents and correspondence in those volumes and from other primary and manuscript sources. Commanders and their ranks, and unit designations, are as of the commencement of the campaign. In the notation of officer casualties, (k) stands for killed, (mw) for mortally wounded, (w) for wounded, and (c) for captured.

ARMY OF THE POTOMAC
Maj. Gen. Joseph Hooker

Chief of Artillery: Brig. Gen. Henry J. Hunt
Signal Corps: Capt. Samuel T. Cushing
Engineer Brigade: Brig. Gen. Henry W. Benham
    15th New York Engineers: Col. Clinton G. Colgate
    50th New York Engineers: Col. Charles B. Stuart
    U.S. Engineer Battalion: Capt. Chauncey B. Reese

FIRST CORPS: Maj. Gen. John F. Reynolds
Chief of Artillery: Col. Charles S. Wainwright
Escort: 1st Maine Cavalry, 1 Co.: Capt. Constantine Taylor

First Division: Brig. Gen. James S. Wadsworth
  First Brigade: Col. Walter Phelps, Jr.
    22nd New York: Maj. Thomas J. Strong
    24th New York: Col. Samuel R. Beardsley
    30th New York: Col. William M. Searing
    84th New York: Col. Edward B. Fowler
  Second Brigade: Brig. Gen. Lysander Cutler
    7th Indiana: Lt. Col. Ira G. Grover
    76th New York: Col. William P. Wainwright

95th New York: Col. George H. Biddle
147th New York: Col. John G. Butler
56th Pennsylvania: Col. J. William Hofmann
Third Brigade: Brig. Gen. Gabriel R. Paul
22nd New Jersey: Col. Abraham G. Demarest
29th New Jersey: Col. William R. Taylor
30th New Jersey: Col. John J. Cladek
31st New Jersey: Lt. Col. Robert R. Honeyman
137th Pennsylvania: Col. Joseph B. Kiddoo
Fourth Brigade: Brig. Gen. Solomon Meredith
19th Indiana: Col. Samuel J. Williams
24th Michigan: Col. Henry A. Morrow
2nd Wisconsin: Col. Lucius Fairchild
6th Wisconsin: Col. Edward S. Bragg
7th Wisconsin: Col. William W. Robinson
Artillery: Capt. John A. Reynolds
1st New Hampshire Light: Capt. Frederick M. Edgell
1st New York Light, Battery L: Capt. John A. Reynolds
4th United States, Battery B: Lt. James Stewart
Second Division: Brig. Gen. John C. Robinson
First Brigade: Col. Adrian R. Root
16th Maine: Col. Charles W. Tilden
94th New York: Capt. Samuel A. Moffett
104th New York: Col. Gilbert G. Prey
107th Pennsylvania: Col. Thomas F. McCoy
Second Brigade: Brig. Gen. Henry Baxter
12th Massachusetts: Col. James L. Bates
26th New York: Lt. Col. Gilbert S. Jennings
90th Pennsylvania: Col. Peter Lyle
136th Pennsylvania: Col. Thomas M. Bayne
Third Brigade: Col. Samuel H. Leonard
13th Massachusetts: Lt. Col. N. Walter Batchelder
83rd New York: Lt. Col. Joseph A. Moesch
97th New York: Col. Charles Wheelock
11th Pennsylvania: Col. Richard Coulter
88th Pennsylvania: Lt. Col. Louis Wagner
Artillery: Capt. Dunbar R. Ransom
2nd Maine Light: Capt. James A. Hall
5th Maine Light: Capt. George F. Leppien (w)
                     Lt. Edmund Kirby (mw)
                     Lt. Greenleaf T. Stevens
Pennsylvania Ind. Light, Battery C: Capt. James Thompson
5th United States, Battery C: Capt. Dunbar R. Ransom
Third Division: Maj. Gen. Abner Doubleday
First Brigade: Brig. Gen. Thomas A. Rowley
121st Pennsylvania: Col. Chapman Biddle
135th Pennsylvania: Col. James R. Porter
142nd Pennsylvania: Col. Robert P. Cummins
151st Pennsylvania: Col. Harrison Allen

Second Brigade: Col. Roy Stone
    143rd Pennsylvania: Col. Edmund L. Dana
    149th Pennsylvania: Lt. Col. Walton Dwight
    150th Pennsylvania: Col. Langhorne Wister
Artillery: Maj. Ezra W. Matthews
    1st Pennsylvania Light, Battery B: Capt. James H. Cooper
    1st Pennsylvania Light, Battery F: Lt. R. Bruce Ricketts
    1st Pennsylvania Light, Battery G: Capt. Frank P. Amsden

SECOND CORPS: Maj. Gen. Darius N. Couch
Chief of Artillery: Lt. Col. Charles H. Morgan
Escort: 6th New York Cavalry, 2 Co's: Capt. Riley Johnson

First Division: Maj. Gen. Winfield S. Hancock
  First Brigade: Brig. Gen. John C. Caldwell
    61st New York: Col. Nelson A. Miles (w)
               Lt. Col. K. Oscar Broady
    66th New York (attached): Col. Orlando H. Morris
    148th Pennsylvania: Col. James A. Beaver (w)
               Maj. George A. Fairlamb
  Second Brigade: Brig. Gen. Thomas F. Meagher
    28th Massachusetts: Col. Richard Byrnes
    63rd New York: Lt. Col. Richard C. Bentley
    69th New York: Capt. James E. McGee
    116th Pennsylvania: 4 Co's: Maj. St. Clair A. Mulholland
  Third Brigade: Brig. Gen. Samuel K. Zook
    52nd New York: Col. Paul Frank
               Lt. Col. Charles G. Freundenberg
    57th New York: Lt. Col. Alford B. Chapman
    140th Pennsylvania: Col. Richard P. Roberts
  Fourth Brigade: Col. John R. Brooke
    27th Connecticut: Col. Richard S. Bostwick (c)
    2nd Delaware: Lt. Col. David L. Stricker
    64th New York: Col. Daniel G. Bingham
    53rd Pennsylvania: Lt. Col. Richards McMichael
    145th Pennsylvania: Col. Hiram L. Brown
  Fifth Brigade (attached): Col. Edward E. Cross
    5th New Hampshire: Lt. Col. Charles E. Hapgood
    81st Pennsylvania: Col. H. Boyd McKeen (w)
    88th New York: Col. Patrick Kelly
  Artillery: Capt. Rufus D. Pettit
    1st New York Light, Battery B: Capt. Rufus D. Pettit
    4th United States, Battery C: Lt. Evan Thomas
Second Division: Brig. Gen. John Gibbon
  First Brigade: Brig. Gen. Alfred Sully
               Col. Henry W. Hudson
               Col. Byron Laflin
    19th Maine: Col. Francis E. Heath

15th Massachusetts: Maj. George C. Joslin
1st Minnesota: Lt. Col. William Colville, Jr.
34th New York: Col. Byron Laflin
     Lt. Col. John Beverly
82nd New York: Col. Henry W. Hudson
     Lt. Col. James Huston
Second Brigade: Brig. Gen. Joshua T. Owen
 69th Pennsylvania: Col. Dennis O'Kane
 71st Pennsylvania: Col. Richard P. Smith
 72nd Pennsylvania: Col. De Witt C. Baxter
 106th Pennsylvania: Col. Turner G. Morehead
Third Brigade: Col. Norman J. Hall
 19th Massachusetts: Lt. Col. Arthur F. Devereux
 20th Massachusetts: Lt. Col. George N. Macy
 7th Michigan: Capt. Amos E. Steele, Jr.
 42nd New York: Col. James E. Mallon
 59th New York: Lt. Col. Max A. Thoman
 127th Pennsylvania: Col. William W. Jennings
Artillery
 1st Rhode Island Light, Battery A: Capt. William A. Arnold
 1st Rhode Island Light, Battery B: Lt. T. Frederick Brown
Sharpshooters
 1st Company Massachusetts: Capt. William Plumer
Third Division: Maj. Gen. William H. French
 Provost Guard: 10th New York, 4 Co's: Maj. G. F. Hopper
First Brigade: Col. Samuel S. Carroll
 14th Indiana: Col. John Coons
 24th New Jersey: Col. William B. Robertson
 28th New Jersey: Lt. Col. John A. Wildrick (c)
     Maj. Samuel K. Wilson
 4th Ohio: Lt. Col. Leonard W. Carpenter
 8th Ohio: Lt. Col. Franklin Sawyer
 7th West Virginia: Col. Joseph Snider
     Lt. Col. Jonathan H. Lockwood
Second Brigade: Brig. Gen. William Hays (c)
     Col. Charles J. Powers
 14th Connecticut: Maj. Theodore G. Ellis
 12th New Jersey: Col. J. Howard Willets (w)
     Maj. John T. Hill
 108th New York: Col. Charles J. Powers
     Lt. Col. Francis E. Pierce
 130th Pennsylvania: Col. Levi Maish (w)
     Maj. Joseph S. Jenkins
Third Brigade: Col. John D. MacGregor
     Col. Charles Albright
 1st Delaware: Col. Thomas A. Smyth
 4th New York: Lt. Col. William Jameson
 132nd Pennsylvania: Col. Charles Albright
     Lt. Col. Joseph E. Shreve

Artillery
    1st New York Light, Battery G: Lt. Nelson Ames
    1st Rhode Island Light, Battery G: Capt. George W. Adams
Corps Reserve Artillery
    1st United States, Battery I: Lt. Edmund Kirby (mw)
    4th United States, Battery A: Lt. Alonzo H. Cushing

THIRD CORPS: Maj. Gen. Daniel E. Sickles
Chief of Artillery: Capt. George E. Randolph

First Division: Brig. Gen. David B. Birney
    First Brigade: Brig. Gen. Charles K. Graham
                Col. Thomas W. Egan
        57th Pennsylvania: Col. Peter Sides
        63rd Pennsylvania: Lt. Col. William S. Kirkwood (mw)
                        Capt. James F. Ryan
        68th Pennsylvania: Col. Andrew H. Tippin
        105th Pennsylvania: Col. Amor A. McKnight (k)
                        Lt. Col. Calvin A. Craig
        114th Pennsylvania: Col. Charles H. T. Collis
                        Lt. Col. Frederick F. Cavada
        141st Pennsylvania: Col. Henry J. Madill
    Second Brigade: Brig. Gen. J. H. Hobart Ward
        20th Indiana: Col. John Wheeler
        3rd Maine: Col. Moses B. Lakeman
        4th Maine: Col. Elijah Walker
        38th New York: Col. Regis de Trobriand
        40th New York: Col. Thomas W. Egan
        99th Pennsylvania: Col. Asher S. Leidy
    Third Brigade: Col. Samuel B. Hayman
        17th Maine: Lt. Col. Charles B. Merrill
                Col. Thomas A. Roberts
        3rd Michigan: Col. Byron R. Pierce (w)
                Lt. Col. Edwin S. Pierce
        5th Michigan: Lt. Col. Edward T. Sherlock (k)
                Maj. John Pulford
        1st New York: Lt. Col. Francis L. Leland
        37th New York: Lt. Col. Gilbert Riordan
    Artillery: Capt. A. Judson Clark
        New Jersey Light, Battery B: Lt. Robert Sims
        1st Rhode Island Light, Battery E: Lt. Pardon S. Jastram
        3rd United States, Battery F–K: Lt. John G. Turnbull
Second Division: Maj. Gen. Hiram G. Berry (k)
            Brig. Gen. Joseph B. Carr
    First Brigade: Brig. Gen. Joseph B. Carr
            Col. William Blaisdell
        1st Massachusetts: Col. Napoleon B. McLaughlen
        11th Massachusetts: Col. William Blaisdell
                        Lt. Col. Porter D. Tripp
        16th Massachusetts: Lt. Col. Waldo Merriam

11th New Jersey: Col. Robert McAllister
26th Pennsylvania: Col. Benjamin C. Tilghman (w)
                  Maj. Robert L. Bodine
Second Brigade: Brig. Gen. Joseph W. Revere
              Col. J. Egbert Farnum
70th New York: Col. J. Egbert Farnum
              Lt. Col. Thomas Holt
71st New York: Col. Henry L. Potter
72nd New York: Col. William O. Stevens (k)
              Maj. John Leonard
73rd New York: Maj. Michael W. Burns
74th New York: Lt. Col. William H. Lounsbury (w)
              Capt. Henry M. Alles (w)
              Capt. Francis E. Tyler
120th New York: Lt. Col. Cornelius D. Westbrook
Third Brigade: Brig. Gen. Gershom Mott (w)
              Col. William J. Sewell
5th New Jersey: Col. William J. Sewell
              Maj. Ashbel W. Angel (w)
              Capt. Virgil M. Healy
6th New Jersey: Col. George C. Burling (w)
              Lt. Col. Stephen R. Gilkyson
7th New Jersey: Col. Louis R. Francine
              Lt. Col. Francis Price
8th New Jersey: Col. John Ramsey (w)
              Capt. John G. Langston
2nd New York: Col. Sidney W. Park (w)
              Lt. Col. William A. Olmsted
115th Pennsylvania: Col. Francis A. Lancaster (k)
              Maj. John P. Dunne
Artillery: Capt. Thomas W. Osborn
    1st New York Light, Battery D: Lt. George B. Winslow
    4th New York Independent Light: Lt. George F. Barstow
              Lt. William T. McLean
    1st United States, Battery H: Lt. Justin E. Dimick (mw)
              Lt. James A. Sanderson
    4th United States, Battery K: Lt. Francis W. Seeley
Third Division: Brig. Gen. Amiel W. Whipple (mw)
              Brig. Gen. Charles K. Graham
First Brigade: Col. Emlen Franklin
86th New York: Lt. Col. Barna J. Chapin (k)
              Capt. Jacob H. Lansing
124th New York: Col. A. Van Horne Ellis
122nd Pennsylvania: Lt. Col. Edward McGovern
Second Brigade: Col. Samuel M. Bowman
12th New Hampshire: Col. Joseph H. Potter (w)
              Lt. Col. John F. Marsh (w)
              Maj. Moses H. Savage (w)
84th Pennsylvania: Lt. Col. Milton Opp

110th Pennsylvania: Col. James Crowther (k)
                                    Maj. David M. Jones (w-c)
Third Brigade: Col. Hiram Berdan
   1st U.S. Sharpshooters: Lt. Col. Casper Trepp
   2nd U.S. Sharpshooters: Maj. Homer R. Stoughton
Artillery: Capt. Albert A. Von Puttkammer
      Capt. James F. Huntington
   10th New York Independent Light: Lt. Samuel Lewis
   11th New York Independent Light: Lt. John E. Burton
   1st Ohio Light, Battery H: Capt. James F. Huntington

     FIFTH CORPS: Maj. Gen. George G. Meade
     Chief of Artillery: Capt. Stephen H. Weed
     Escort: 17th Penn. Cavalry, 2 Co's: Capt. William Thompson

First Division: Brig. Gen. Charles Griffin
  First Brigade: Brig. Gen. James Barnes
     2nd Maine: Col. George Varney
     18th Massachusetts: Col. Joseph Hayes
     22nd Massachusetts: Col. William S. Tilton
        2nd Co. Massachusetts Sharpshooters (attached)
     1st Michigan: Col. Ira C. Abbott
     13th New York, 2 Co's: Capt. William Downey
     25th New York: Col. Charles H. Johnson
     118th Pennsylvania: Col. Charles M. Prevost
  Second Brigade: Col. James McQuade
          Col. Jacob B. Sweitzer
     9th Massachusetts: Col. Patrick R. Guiney
     32nd Massachusetts: Lt. Col. Luther Stephenson
     4th Michigan: Col. Harrison H. Jeffords
     14th New York: Lt. Col. Thomas M. Davies
     62nd Pennsylvania: Col. Jacob B. Sweitzer
          Lt. Col. James C. Hull
  Third Brigade: Col. Thomas B. W. Stockton
     20th Maine: Lt. Col. Joshua L. Chamberlain
     16th Michigan: Lt. Col. Norval E. Welch
        Brady's Co. Michigan Sharpshooters (attached)
     12th New York: Capt. William Huson
     17th New York: Lt. Col. Nelson B. Bartram
     44th New York: Col. James C. Rice
     83rd Pennsylvania: Col. Strong Vincent
  Artillery: Capt. Augustus P. Martin
     Massachusetts Light, Battery C: Capt. Augustus P. Martin
     Massachusetts Light, Battery E: Capt. Charles A. Phillips
     1st Rhode Island Light, Battery C: Capt. Richard Waterman
     5th United States, Battery D: Lt. Charles E. Hazlett
Second Division: Maj. Gen. George Sykes
  First Brigade: Brig. Gen. Romeyn B. Ayres
     3rd United States, 6 Co's: Capt. John D. Wilkins
     4th United States, 4 Co's: Capt. Hiram Dryer

12th United States, 8 Co's: Maj. Richard S. Smith
14th United States, 8 Co's: Capt. Jonathan B. Hager
                              Maj. Grotius R. Giddings
Second Brigade: Col. Sidney Burbank
2nd United States, 5 Co's: Capt. Salem S. Marsh (k)
                           Capt. Samuel A. McKee
6th United States, 5 Co's: Capt. Levi C. Bootes
7th United States, 4 Co's: Capt. David P. Hancock
10th United States, 4 Co's: Lt. Edward G. Bush
11th United States, 8 Co's: Maj. DeLancey Floyd-Jones
17th United States, 7 Co's: Maj. George L. Andrews (w)
Third Brigade: Col. Patrick H. O'Rorke
5th New York: Col. Cleveland Winslow
140th New York: Lt. Col. Louis Ernst
146th New York: Col. Kenner Gerrard
Artillery: Capt. Stephen H. Weed
1st Ohio Light, Battery L: Capt. Frank C. Gibbs
5th United States, Battery I: Lt. Malbone F. Watson
Third Division: Brig. Gen. Andrew A. Humphreys
First Brigade: Brig. Gen. Erastus B. Tyler
91st Pennsylvania: Col. Edgar M. Gregory (w)
                     Lt. Col. Joseph H. Sinex
126th Pennsylvania: Lt. Col. David W. Rowe (w)
129th Pennsylvania: Col. Jacob G. Frick
134th Pennsylvania: Col. Edward O'Brien
Second Brigade: Col. Peter H. Allabach
123rd Pennsylvania: Col. John B. Clark
131st Pennsylvania: Maj. Robert W. Patton
133rd Pennsylvania: Col. Franklin B. Speakman
155th Pennsylvania: Lt. Col. John H. Cain
Artillery: Capt. Alanson M. Randol
1st New York Light, Battery C: Capt. Almont Barnes
1st United States, Battery E–G: Capt. Alanson M. Randol

SIXTH CORPS: Maj. Gen. John Sedgwick
Chief of Artillery: Col. Charles H. Tomkins
Escort: Maj. Hugh H. Janeway
1st New Jersey Cavalry, 1 Co.
1st Pennsylvania Cavalry, 1 Co.

First Division: Brig. Gen. William T. H. Brooks
Provost Guard: 4th New Jersey, 3 Co's: Capt. Charles Ewing
First Brigade: Col. Henry W. Brown (w)
               Col. Samuel L. Buck (w)
               Col. William H. Penrose
1st New Jersey: Col. Mark W. Collet (k)
               Lt. Col. William Henry, Jr.
2nd New Jersey: Col. Samuel L. Buck
               Lt. Col. Charles Wiebecke
3rd New Jersey: Maj. J.W.H. Stickney

15th New Jersey: Col. William H. Penrose
    Lt. Col. Edward L. Campbell
23rd New Jersey: Col. E. Burd Grubb
Second Brigade: Brig. Gen. Joseph J. Bartlett
  5th Maine: Col. Clark S. Edwards
  16th New York: Col. Joel J. Seaver
  27th New York: Col. Alexander D. Adams
  121st New York: Col. Emory Upton
  96th Pennsylvania: Maj. William H. Lessig
Third Brigade: Brig. Gen. David A. Russell
  18th New York: Col. George R. Myers
  32nd New York: Col. Francis E. Pinto
  49th Pennsylvania: Lt. Col. Thomas M. Hulings
  95th Pennsylvania: Col. Gustavus W. Town (k)
    Lt. Col. Elisha Hall (k)
    Capt. Theodore H. McCalla
  119th Pennsylvania: Col. Peter C. Ellmaker
Artillery: Maj. John A. Tomkins
  Massachusetts Light, Battery A: Capt. William H. McCartney
  New Jersey Light, Battery A: Lt. Augustin N. Parsons
  Maryland Light, Battery A: Capt. James H. Rigby
  2nd United States, Battery D: Lt. Edward B. Williston
Second Division: Brig. Gen. Albion P. Howe
  Second Brigade: Col. Lewis A. Grant
  2nd Vermont: Col. James H. Walbridge
  3rd Vermont: Col. Thomas O. Seaver
    Lt. Col. Samuel E. Pingree
  4th Vermont: Col. Charles B. Stoughton
  5th Vermont: Lt. Col. John R. Lewis
  6th Vermont: Col. Elisha L. Barney
  26th New Jersey: Col. Andrew J. Morrison
    Lt. Col. Edward Martindale
Third Brigade: Brig. Gen. Thomas H. Neill
  7th Maine: Lt. Col. Selden Connor
  21st New Jersey: Col. Gilliam Van Houten (mw)
    Lt. Col. Isaac S. Mettler
  20th New York: Col. Ernst von Vegesack (w)
  33rd New York: Col. Robert F. Tayler
  49th New York: Col. Daniel B. Bidwell
  77th New York: Lt. Col. Winsor B. French
Artillery: Maj. J. Watts de Peyster
  1st New York Independent Light: Capt. Andrew Cowan
  5th United States, Battery F: Lt. Leonard Martin
Third Division: Maj. Gen. John Newton
  First Brigade: Col. Alexander Shaler
  65th New York: Lt. Col. Joseph E. Hamblin
  67th New York: Col. Nelson Cross
  122nd New York: Col. Silas Titus
  23rd Pennsylvania: Col. John Ely
  82nd Pennsylvania: Maj. Isaac C. Bassett

Second Brigade: Col. William H. Browne (w)
 Col. Henry L. Eustis
 7th Massachusetts: Col. Thomas D. Johns (w)
  Lt. Col. Franklin P. Harlow
 10th Massachusetts: Col. Henry L. Eustis
  Lt. Col. Joseph B. Parsons
 37th Massachusetts: Col. Oliver Edwards
 36th New York: Lt. Col. James J. Walsh
 2nd Rhode Island: Col. Horatio Rogers, Jr.
Third Brigade: Brig. Gen. Frank Wheaton
 62nd New York: Lt. Col. Theodore B. Hamilton (w)
 93rd Pennsylvania: Capt. John S. Long
 98th Pennsylvania: Capt. John F. Ballier (w)
  Lt. Col. George Wynkoop
 102nd Pennsylvania: Col. Joseph M. Kinkead
 139th Pennsylvania: Col. Frederick H. Collier
Artillery: Capt. Jeremiah McCarthy
 1st Pennsylvania Light, Battery C–D: Capt. Jeremiah McCarthy
 2nd United States, Battery G: Lt. John H. Butler
Light Division: Brig. Gen. Calvin E. Pratt
 Col. Hiram Burnham
 6th Maine: Lt. Col. Benjamin F. Harris
 31st New York: Col. Frank Jones
 43rd New York: Col. Benjamin F. Baker
 61st Pennsylvania: Col. George C. Spear (k)
  Maj. George W. Dawson
 5th Wisconsin: Col. Thomas S. Allen
 3rd New York Independent Light: Lt. William A. Harn

ELEVENTH CORPS: Maj. Gen. Oliver O. Howard
 Chief of Artillery: Lt. Col. Louis Schirmer
 Escort: 1st Indiana Cavalry, 2 Co's: Capt. Abram Sharra

First Division: Brig. Gen. Charles Devens, Jr. (w)
 Brig. Gen. Nathaniel C. McLean
 Provost Guard: 8th New York, 1 Co.: Lt. Herman Rosenkranz
First Brigade: Col. Leopold Von Gilsa
 41st New York: Maj. Detleo von Einsiedel
 45th New York: Col. George von Amsberg
 54th New York: Lt. Col. Charles Ashby (c)
  Maj. Stephen Kovacs
 153rd Pennsylvania: Col. Charles Glanz (c)
  Lt. Col. Jacob Dachrodt
Second Brigade: Brig. Gen. Nathaniel C. McLean
 Col. John C. Lee
 17th Connecticut: Col. William H. Noble (w)
  Maj. Allen G. Brady
 25th Ohio: Col. William P. Richardson (w)
  Maj. Jeremiah Williams

55th Ohio: Col. John C. Lee
Lt. Col. Charles B. Gambee
75th Ohio: Col. Robert Reily (k)
Capt. Benjamin Morgan
107th Ohio: Col. Seraphim Meyer (w-c)
Lt. Col. Charles Mueller
Artillery
13th New York Independent Light: Capt. Julius Dieckmann
Second Division: Brig. Gen. Adolph Von Steinwehr
First Brigade: Col. Adolphus Buschbeck
29th New York: Lt. Col. Louis Hartmann (w)
Maj. Alex von Schluembach
154th New York: Col. Patrick H. Jones (w)
Lt. Col. Henry C. Loomis
27th Pennsylvania: Lt. Col. Lorenz Cantador
73rd Pennsylvania: Lt. Col. William Moore (w)
Second Brigade: Brig. Gen. Francis C. Barlow
33rd Massachusetts: Col. Adin B. Underwood
134th New York: Col. Charles R. Coster
136th New York: Col. James Wood, Jr.
73rd Ohio: Col. Orland Smith
Artillery
1st New York Light, Battery I: Capt. Michael Wiedrich
Third Division: Maj. Gen. Carl Schurz
Unattached: 82nd Ohio: Col. James S. Robinson
First Brigade: Brig. Gen. Alexander Schimmelfennig
82nd Illinois: Col. Frederick Hecker (w)
Maj. Ferdinand H. Rolshausen (w)
Capt. Jacob Lasalle
68th New York: Col. Gotthilf Bourry
157th New York: Col. Philip B. Brown, Jr.
61st Ohio: Col. Stephen J. McGroarty
74th Pennsylvania: Lt. Col. Adolph von Hartung
Second Brigade: Col. Wladimir Krzyzanowski
58th New York: Capt. Frederick Braun (mw)
Capt. Emil Koenig
119th New York: Col. Elias Peissner (k)
Lt. Col. John T. Lockman
75th Pennsylvania: Col. Francis Mahler
26th Wisconsin: Col. William H. Jacobs
Artillery
1st Ohio Light, Battery I: Capt. Hubert Dilger
Corps Reserve Artillery: Lt. Col. Louis Schirmer
2nd New York Independent Light: Capt. Hermann Jahn
1st Ohio Light, Battery K: Capt. William L. DeBeck
1st West Virginia Light, Battery C: Capt. Wallace Hill

TWELFTH CORPS: Maj. Gen. Henry W. Slocum
Chief of Artillery: Capt. Clermont L. Best
Provost Guard: 10th Maine, 3 Co's: Capt. John D. Beardsley

First Division: Brig. Gen. Alpheus S. Williams
First Brigade: Brig. Gen. Joseph F. Knipe
5th Connecticut: Col. Warren W. Packer (c)
Lt. Col. James A. Betts
Maj. David F. Lane
28th New York: Lt. Col. Elliott W. Cook (c)
Maj. Theophilus Fitzgerald
46th Pennsylvania: Maj. Cyrus Strous (mw)
Capt. Edward L. Witman
128th Pennsylvania: Col. Joseph A. Mathews (c)
Maj. Cephas W. Dyer
Second Brigade: Col. Samuel Ross (w)
Brig. Gen. Joseph F. Knipe
20th Connecticut: Lt. Col. William B. Wooster (c)
Maj. Philo B. Buckingham
3rd Maryland: Lt. Col. Gilbert P. Robinson
123rd New York: Col. Archibald L. McDougall
145th New York: Col. E. Livingston Price (w)
Capt. George W. Reid
Third Brigade: Brig. Gen. Thomas H. Ruger
27th Indiana: Col. Silas Colgrove
2nd Massachusetts: Col. Samuel M. Quincy
13th New Jersey: Col. Ezra A. Carman
Maj. John Grimes (w)
Capt. George A. Beardsley
107th New York: Col. Alexander S. Diven
3rd Wisconsin: Col. William Hawley
Artillery: Capt. Robert H. Fitzhugh
1st New York Light, Battery K: Lt. Edward L. Bailey
1st New York Light, Battery M: Lt. Charles E. Winegar (c)
Lt. John D. Woodbury
4th United States, Battery F: Lt. Franklin B. Crosby (k)
Lt. Edward H. Muhlenberg
Second Division: Brig. Gen. John W. Geary
First Brigade: Col. Charles Candy
5th Ohio: Lt. Col. Robert L. Kilpatrick (w)
Maj. Henry E. Symmes
7th Ohio: Col. William R. Creighton
29th Ohio: Lt. Col. Thomas Clark
66th Ohio: Lt. Col. Eugene Powell
28th Pennsylvania: Maj. Lansford F. Chapman (k)
Capt. Conrad U. Meyer
147th Pennsylvania: Lt. Col. Ario Pardee
Second Brigade: Brig. Gen. Thomas L. Kane
29th Pennsylvania: Lt. Col. William Richards, Jr.

109th Pennsylvania: Col. Henry J. Stainrook (k)
Capt. John Young, Jr.
111th Pennsylvania: Col. George A. Cobham, Jr.
124th Pennsylvania: Lt. Col. Simon Litzenberg
125th Pennsylvania: Col. Jacob Higgins
Third Brigade: Brig. Gen. George S. Greene
60th New York: Col. John C. O. Redington
78th New York: Maj. Henry R. Stagg
Capt. William H. Randall
102nd New York: Col. James C. Lane
137th New York: Col. David Ireland
149th New York: Maj. Abel G. Cook (w)
Capt. Oliver T. May
Lt. Col. Koert S. Van Voorhis
Artillery: Capt. Joseph M. Knap
Pennsylvania Light, Battery E: Lt. Charles A. Atwell (w)
Lt. James D. McGill
Pennsylvania Light, Battery F: Capt. Robert B. Hampton (mw)
Lt. James P. Fleming

CAVALRY CORPS: Brig. Gen. George Stoneman

First Division: Brig. Gen. Alfred Pleasonton
First Brigade: Col. Benjamin F. Davis
8th Illinois: Lt. Col. David R. Clendenin
3rd Indiana: Col. George H. Chapman
8th New York: Lt. Col. William L. Markell
9th New York: Col. William Sackett
Second Brigade: Col. Thomas C. Devin
1st Michigan, 1 Co.: Lt. John K. Truax
6th New York: Lt. Col. Duncan McVicar (k)
Capt. William E. Beardsley
8th Pennsylvania: Maj. Pennock Huey
17th Pennsylvania: Col. Josiah H. Kellogg
Artillery
6th New York Independent Light: Lt. Joseph W. Martin
Second Division: Brig. Gen. William W. Averell
First Brigade: Col. Horace B. Sargent
1st Massachusetts: Lt. Col. Greely S. Curtis
4th New York: Col. Louis P. Di Cesnola
6th Ohio: Maj. Benjamin C. Stanhope
1st Rhode Island: Lt. Col. John L. Thompson
Second Brigade: Col. John B. McIntosh
3rd Pennsylvania: Lt. Col. Edward S. Jones
4th Pennsylvania: Lt. Col. William E. Doster
16th Pennsylvania: Lt. Col. Lorenzo D. Rogers
Artillery
2nd United States, Battery A: Capt. John C. Tidball

Third Division: Brig. Gen. David McM. Gregg
    First Brigade: Col. Judson Kilpatrick
        1st Maine: Col. Calvin S. Donty
        2nd New York: Lt. Col. Henry E. Davies, Jr.
        10th New York: Lt. Col. William Irvine
    Second Brigade: Col. Percy Wyndham
        12th Illinois: Lt. Col. Hasbrouck Davis
        1st Maryland: Lt. Col. James M. Deems
        1st New Jersey: Lt. Col. Virgil Brodrick
        1st Pennsylvania: Col. John P. Taylor
    Reserve Cavalry: Brig. Gen. John Buford
        6th Pennsylvania: Maj. Robert Morris, Jr.
        1st United States: Capt. R.S.C. Lord
        2nd United States: Maj. Charles J. Whiting
        5th United States: Capt. James E. Harrison
        6th United States: Capt. George C. Cram
    Horse Artillery: Capt. James M. Robertson
        2nd United States, Battery B–L: Lt. Albert O. Vincent
        2nd United States, Battery M: Lt. Robert Clarke
        4th United States, Battery E: Lt. Samuel S. Elder
General Headquarters
    Provost Guard: Brig. Gen. Marsena R. Patrick
        93rd New York: Col. John S. Crocker
        8th United States, 6 Co's: Capt E.W.H. Read
        6th Pennsylvania Cavalry, 2 Co's: Capt. James Starr
        Regular Cavalry Detachment: Lt. Tattnall Paulding
    Guards and Orderlies
        Oneida (New York) Cavalry: Capt. Daniel P. Mann
    Patrick's Brigade: Col. William F. Rogers
        21st New York: Lt. Col. Chester W. Sternberg
        23rd New York: Col. Henry C. Hoffman
        35th New York: Col. John G. Todd
        80th New York: Col. Theodore B. Gates
        Maryland Light, Battery B: Capt. Alonzo Snow
        12th Ohio Independent Light: Capt. Aaron C. Jonnson
    Reserve Artillery: Capt. William M. Graham
                Brig. Gen. Robert O. Tyler
        1st Connecticut Heavy, Battery B: Lt. Albert F. Brooker
        1st Connecticut Heavy, Battery M: Capt. Franklin A. Pratt
        5th New York Independent Light: Capt. Elijah D. Taft
        15th New York Independent Light: Capt. Patrick Hart
        29th New York Independent Light: Lt. Gustav von Blucher
        30th New York Independent Light: Capt. Adolph Voegelee
        32nd New York Independent Light: Lt. George Gaston
        1st United States, Battery K: Lt. Lorenzo Thomas, Jr.
        3rd United States, Battery C: Lt. Henry Meinell
        4th United States, Battery G: Lt. Marcus P. Miller
        5th United States, Battery K: Lt. David H. Kinzie
        32nd Massachusetts Infantry, 1 Co.: Capt. Josiah C. Fuller

Ordnance Detachment: Lt. John R. Edie
Train Guard
    4th New Jersey, 7 Co's: Col. William Birney
                Capt. Robert S. Johnston

ARMY OF NORTHERN VIRGINIA
Gen. Robert E. Lee

FIRST CORPS: Gen. Robert E. Lee
Chief of Artillery: Col. John B. Walton

Anderson's Division: Maj. Gen. Richard H. Anderson
  Mahone's Brigade: Brig. Gen. William Mahone
    6th Virginia: Col. George T. Rogers
    12th Virginia: Lt. Col. Everard M. Feild
    16th Virginia: Lt. Col. Richard O. Whitehead
    41st Virginia: Col. William A. Parham
    61st Virginia: Col. Virginius D. Groner
  Posey's Brigade: Brig. Gen. Carnot Posey
    12th Mississippi: Lt. Col. Merry B. Harris (w)
                Maj. Samuel B. Thomas
    16th Mississippi: Col. Samuel E. Baker
    19th Mississippi: Col. Nathaniel H. Harris
    48th Mississippi: Col. Joseph M. Jayne (w)
  Perry's Brigade: Brig. Gen. E. A. Perry
    2nd Florida: Maj. Walton R. Moore (w)
    5th Florida: Maj. Benjamin F. Davis (w)
    8th Florida: Col. David Lang
  Wilcox's Brigade: Brig. Gen. Cadmus M. Wilcox
    8th Alabama: Col. Young L. Royston (w)
                Lt. Col. Hilary A. Herbert
    9th Alabama: Maj. Jeremiah H. J. Williams
    10th Alabama: Col. William H. Forney
    11th Alabama: Col. John C. C. Sanders
    14th Alabama: Lt. Col. Lucius Pinckard (w)
  Wright's Brigade: Brig. Gen. Ambrose R. Wright
    3rd Georgia: Maj. John F. Jones (w)
                Capt. Charles H. Andrews
    22nd Georgia: Col. Joseph Wasden
    48th Georgia: Lt. Col. Reuben W. Carswell
    2nd Georgia Battalion: Maj. George W. Ross
  Garnett's Artillery Battalion: Lt. Col. John J. Garnett
                Maj. Robert A. Hardaway
    Grandy's Norfolk (Virginia) Blues Battery: Capt. C. R. Grandy
    Lewis's Pittsylvania (Virginia) Battery: Lt. Nathan Penick
    Maurin's Donaldsonville (Louisiana) Battery: Capt. Victor Maurin
    Moore's Norfolk (Virginia) Battery: Capt. Joseph D. Moore

McLaws's Division: Maj. Gen. Lafayette McLaws
 Kershaw's Brigade: Brig. Gen. Joseph B. Kershaw
  2nd South Carolina: Col. John D. Kennedy
  3rd South Carolina: Maj. Robert C. Maffett
  7th South Carolina: Lt. Col. Elbert Bland
  8th South Carolina: Col. John W. Henagan
  15th South Carolina: Lt. Col. Joseph F. Gist
  3rd South Carolina Battalion: Lt. Col. William G. Rice
 Semmes's Brigade: Brig. Gen. Paul J. Semmes
  10th Georgia: Lt. Col. Willis C. Holt
  50th Georgia: Lt. Col. Francis Kearse
  51st Georgia: Col. W. M. Slaughter (mw)
   Lt. Col. Edward Ball (w)
   Maj. Oliver P. Anthony
  53rd Georgia: Col. James P. Simms
 Wofford's Brigade: Brig. Gen. William T. Wofford
  16th Georgia: Col. Goode Bryan
  18th Georgia: Col. S. Z. Ruff
  24th Georgia: Col. Robert McMillan
  Cobb's Georgia Legion: Lt. Col. Luther J. Glenn
  Phillips's Georgia Legion: Lt. Col. E. S. Barclay, Jr.
 Barksdale's Brigade: Brig. Gen. William Barksdale
  13th Mississippi: Col. James W. Carter
  17th Mississippi: Col. William D. Holder
  18th Mississippi: Col. Thomas M. Griffin (c)
  21st Mississippi: Col. Benjamin G. Humphreys
 Cabell's Artillery Battalion: Col. Henry C. Cabell
   Maj. S. P. Hamilton
  Carleton's Troup (Georgia) Battery: Capt. Henry H. Carlton
  Fraser's Pulaski (Georgia) Battery: Capt. John C. Fraser
  McCarthy's Richmond Howitzers, 1st Co.: Captain Edward S. McCarthy
  Manly's North Carolina Battery: Capt. Basil C. Manly
First Corps Reserve Artillery
 Alexander's Battalion: Col. E. Porter Alexander
   Maj. Frank Huger
  Eubank's Bath (Virginia) Battery: Lt. Osmond B. Taylor
  Jordan's Bedford (Virginia) Battery: Capt. Tyler C. Jordan
  Moody's Madison (Louisiana) Battery: Capt. George V. Moody
  Parker's Richmond Battery: Capt. William W. Parker
  Rhett's Brooks (South Carolina) Battery: Capt. A. B. Rhett
  Woolfolk's Ashland (Virginia) Battery: Capt. Pichegru Woolfolk, Jr.
 Washington (Louisiana) Battalion: Col. James B. Walton
  Squires's First Company: Captain Charles W. Squires (c)
   Lt. C.H.C. Brown
  Richardson's Second Company: Capt. John B. Richardson
  Miller's Third Company: Capt. Merritt B. Miller
  Eshleman's Fourth Company: Capt. Benjamin F. Eshleman

SECOND CORPS: Lt. Gen. Thomas J. Jackson (mw)
Maj. Gen. A. P. Hill (w)
Brig. Gen. Robert E. Rodes
Maj. Gen. J.E.B. Stuart
Chief of Artillery: Col. Stapleton Crutchfield (w)
Col. E. Porter Alexander
Col. J. Thompson Brown

Hill's Light Division: Maj. Gen. A. P. Hill
Brig. Gen. Henry Heth (w)
Brig. Gen. William D. Pender (w)
Brig. Gen. James J. Archer
Heth's Brigade: Brig. Gen. Henry Heth
Col. John M. Brockenbrough
40th Virginia: Col. John M. Brockenbrough
Lt. Col. Fleet W. Cox (w)
Capt. T. E. Betts
47th Virginia: Col. Robert M. Mayo
55th Virginia: Col. Francis Mallory (k)
Lt. Col. William S. Christian (w)
Maj. Andrew D. Saunders (k)
Lt. R. L. Williams
Maj. Evan Rice
22nd Virginia Battalion: Lt. Col. Edward P. Tayloe
Pender's Brigade: Brig. Gen. William D. Pender
13th North Carolina: Col. Alfred M. Scales (w)
Lt. Col. Joseph H. Hyman
16th North Carolina: Col. John S. McElroy (w)
Lt. Col. Wiliam A. Stowe (w)
22nd North Carolina: Lt. Col. Christopher C. Cole (k)
Maj. Laben Odell (k)
Capt. George A. Graves
34th North Carolina: Col. William L. J. Lowrance
38th North Carolina: Col. William J. Hoke
McGowan's Brigade: Brig. Gen. Samuel McGowan (w)
Col. Oliver E. Edwards (mw)
Col. Abner Perrin
Col. Daniel H. Hamilton
1st South Carolina: Col. Daniel H. Hamilton
Capt. Washington P. Shooter
1st South Carolina Rifles: Col. James M. Perrin (mw)
Lt. Col. F. E. Harrison
12th South Carolina: Col. John L. Miller
13th South Carolina: Col. Oliver E. Edwards
Lt. Col. Benjamin T. Brockman
14th South Carolina: Col. Abner Perrin
Lt. Col. Joseph N. Brown

Lane's Brigade: Brig. Gen. James H. Lane
   7th North Carolina: Col. Edward G. Haywood (w)
                     Lt. Col. Junius L. Hill (k)
                     Maj. William L. Davidson (w)
                     Capt. N. A. Pool
   18th North Carolina: Col. Thomas J. Purdie (k)
                     Lt. Col. Forney George (w)
                     Maj. John D. Berry
   28th North Carolina: Col. Samuel D. Lowe
   33rd North Carolina: Col. Clark M. Avery (w)
                     Capt. Joseph H. Saunders
   37th North Carolina: Col. William M. Barbour (w)
Archer's Brigade: Brig. Gen. James J. Archer
                 Col. Birkett D. Fry
   1st Tennessee: Lt. Col. Newton J. George
   7th Tennessee: Col. John A. Fite (w)
   14th Tennessee: Col. William McComb (w)
                     Capt. R. C. Wilson
   13th Alabama: Col. Birkett D. Fry
   5th Alabama Battalion: Capt. S. D. Stewart (k)
                     Capt. A. N. Porter
Thomas's Brigade: Brig. Gen. E. L. Thomas
   14th Georgia: Col. Robert W. Folsom
   35th Georgia: Capt. John Duke
   45th Georgia: Lt. Col. Washington L. Grice
   49th Georgia: Maj. Samuel T. Player
Walker's Artillery Battalion: Col. Rueben L. Walker
                 Maj. William J. Pegram
   Brunson's Pee Dee (South Carolina) Battery: Capt. Ervin B. Brunson
   Crenshaw's Virginia Battery: Lt. John H. Chamberlayne
   Davidson's Letcher (Virginia) Battery: Capt. Greenlee Davidson (mw)
                     Lt. Thomas A. Brander
   McGraw's Purcell (Virginia) Battery: Lt. Joseph McGraw
   Marye's Fredericksburg (Virginia) Battery: Capt. Edward A. Marye
Rodes's Division: Brig. Gen. Robert E. Rodes
                 Brig. Gen. Stephen D. Ramseur
   O'Neal's Brigade: Col. Edward A. O'Neal (w)
                 Col. Josephus M. Hall
   3rd Alabama: Capt. M. F. Bonham
   5th Alabama: Col. Josephus M. Hall
                  Lt. Col. E. Lafayette Hobson (w)
                  Capt. W. T. Renfro (mw)
                  Capt T. M. Riley
   6th Alabama: Lt. Col. James N. Lightfoot
   12th Alabama: Col. Samuel B. Pickens
   26th Alabama: Lt. Col. John S. Garvin (w)
                  Lt. Miles J. Taylor
Doles's Brigade: Brig. Gen. George Doles
   4th Georgia: Col. Philip Cook (w)
                 Lt. Col. D.R.E. Winn

12th Georgia: Col. Edward S. Willis
21st Georgia: Col. John T. Mercer
44th Georgia: Col. John B. Estes
Iverson's Brigade: Brig. Gen. Alfred Iverson
    5th North Carolina: Col. Thomas M. Garrett (w)
                 Lt. Col. John W. Lea (w)
                 Maj. William J. Hill (w)
                 Capt. S. B. West
    12th North Carolina: Maj. David P. Rowe (mw)
                 Lt. Col. Robert D. Johnston
    20th North Carolina: Col. Thomas F. Toon (w)
                 Lt. Col. Nelson Slough
    23rd North Carolina: Col. Daniel H. Christie
Colquitt's Brigade: Brig. Gen. Alfred H. Colquitt
    6th Georgia: Col. John T. Lofton
    19th Georgia: Col. Andrew J. Hutchins
    23rd Georgia: Col. Emory F. Best
    27th Georgia: Col. Charles T. Zachry
    28th Georgia: Col. Tully Graybill
Ramseur's Brigade: Brig. Gen. Stephen D. Ramseur (w)
              Col. Francis M. Parker
    2nd North Carolina: Col. William R. Cox (w)
    4th North Carolina: Col. Bryan Grimes
    14th North Carolina: Col. R. Tyler Bennett
    30th North Carolina: Col. Francis M. Parker
Carter's Artillery Battalion: Lt. Col. Thomas H. Carter
    Reese's Jeff Davis Alabama Battery: Capt. William J. Reese
    Carter's King William (Virginia) Battery: Capt. William P. Carter
    Fry's Orange (Virginia) Battery: Capt. Charles W. Fry
    Page's Morris Louisa (Virginia) Battery: Capt. R.C.M. Page
Early's Division: Maj. Gen. Jubal A. Early
    Gordon's Brigade: Brig. Gen. John B. Gordon
        13th Georgia: Col. James M. Smith
        26th Georgia: Col. Edmund N. Atkinson
        31st Georgia: Col. Clement A. Evans
        38th Georgia: Col. James D. Mathews
        60th Georgia: Col. William H. Stiles
        61st Georgia: Col. John H. Lamar
    Hoke's Brigade: Brig. Gen. Robert F. Hoke (w)
              Col. Isaac E. Avery
        6th North Carolina: Col. Isaac E. Avery
                    Maj. Samuel M. Tate
        21st North Carolina: Lt. Col. William S. Rankin
                    Col. William W. Kirkland
        54th North Carolina: Col. James C. S. McDowell (mw)
                    Lt. Col. Kenneth M. Murchison
        57th North Carolina: Col. Archibald C. Godwin (w)
        1st Battalion North Carolina Sharpshooters: Maj. R. W. Wharton
    Smith's Brigade: Brig. Gen. William Smith
        13th Virginia: Lt. Col. James B. Terrill

49th Virginia: Lt. Col. Jonathan C. Gibson
52nd Virginia: Col. Michael G. Harman
58th Virginia: Col. Francis H. Board
Hays's Brigade: Brig. Gen. Harry T. Hays
5th Louisiana: Col. Henry Forno
6th Louisiana: Col. William Monaghan
7th Louisiana: Col. Davidson B. Penn (c)
8th Louisiana: Col. Trevanion D. Lewis (c)
9th Louisiana: Col. Leroy A. Stafford (c)
Andrews's Artillery Battalion: Lt. Col. R. Snowden Andrews
Brown's Fourth Maryland Chesapeake Battery: Capt. W. D. Brown
Carpenter's Alleghany (Virginia) Battery: Capt. Joseph Carpenter
Dement's First Maryland Battery: Capt. William F. Dement
Raine's Lee (Virginia) Battery: Capt. Charles J. Raine
Colston's Division: Brig. Gen. Raleigh E. Colston
Paxton's Brigade: Brig. Gen. E. F. Paxton (k)
Col. John H. S. Funk
2nd Virginia: Col. J.Q.A. Nadenbousch (w)
Lt. Col. Raleigh T. Colston
4th Virginia: Maj. William Terry
5th Virginia: Col. John H. S. Funk
Lt. Col. Hazael J. Williams
27th Virginia: Col. James K. Edmondson (w)
Lt. Col. Daniel M. Shriver
33rd Virginia: Lt. Col. Abraham Spengler
Jones's Brigade: Brig. Gen. John R. Jones
Col. Thomas S. Garnett (mw)
Col. A. S. Vandeventer
21st Virginia: Maj. John B. Moseley
42nd Virginia: Lt. Col. R. W. Withers
44th Virginia: Maj. Norvell Cobb (w)
Capt. Thomas R. Bucker
48th Virginia: Col. Thomas S. Garnett
Maj. Oscar White
50th Virginia: Col. A. S. Vandeventer
Maj. Lynville J. Perkins
Capt. Frank W. Kelly
Warren's Brigade: Col. Edward T. H. Warren (w)
Col. Titus V. Williams (w)
Lt. Col. Hamilton A. Brown
1st North Carolina: Col. John A. McDowell (w)
Capt. Jarrette N. Harrell (w)
Capt. Louis C. Latham
3rd North Carolina: Lt. Col. Stephen D. Thruston (w)
Maj. William M. Parsley
10th Virginia: Lt. Col. Samuel T. Walker (k)
Maj. Joshua Stover (mw)
Capt. A. H. Smals
23rd Virginia: Lt. Col. Simeon T. Walton
37th Virginia: Col. Titus V. Williams

Nicholls's Brigade: Brig. Gen. Francis T. Nicholls (w)
        Col. Jesse M. Williams
    1st Louisiana: Capt. Edward D. Willett
    2nd Louisiana: Col. Jesse M. Williams
        Lt. Col. Ross E. Burke
    10th Louisiana: Lt. Col. John M. Legett (k)
        Capt. A. Perrodin
    14th Louisiana: Lt. Col. David Zable
    15th Louisiana: Capt. William C. Michie
Jones's Artillery Battalion: Lt. Col. Hilary P. Jones
    Carrington's Charlottesville Battery: Capt. James McD. Carrington
    Garber's Staunton (Virginia) Battery: Lt. Alexander H. Fultz
    Latimer's Courtney (Virginia) Battery: Capt. W. A. Tanner
    Thompson's Louisiana Guard Battery: Capt. Charles Thompson
Second Corps Reserve Artillery
    Brown's Battalion: Col. J. Thompson Brown
        Capt. David Watson
        Capt. Willis J. Dance
    Brooke's Warrenton (Virginia) Battery: Capt. James V. Brooke
    Dance's Powhatan (Virginia) Battery: Capt. Willis J. Dance
    Graham's 1st Rockbridge (Virginia) Battery: Capt. Archibald Graham
    Hupp's Salem (Virginia) Battery: Capt. Abraham Hupp
    Watson's Richmond Howitzers, 2nd Co.: Capt. David Watson
    Smith's Richmond Howitzers, 3rd Co.: Capt. Benjamin H. Smith, Jr.
    McIntosh's Battalion: Maj. D. G. McIntosh
    Hurt's Alabama Battery: Capt. William P. Hurt
    Johnson's Richmond Battery: Capt. Marmaduke Johnson
    Lusk's 2nd Rockbridge (Virginia) Battery: Capt. John A. M. Lusk
    Wooding's Danville (Virginia) Battery: Capt. George W. Wooding
Army Reserve Artillery: Brig. Gen. William N. Pendleton
    Cutts's Battalion: Lt. Col. A. S. Cutts
    Ross's Sumter (Georgia), Battery A: Capt. Hugh M. Ross
    Patterson's Sumter (Georgia), Battery B: Capt. George M. Patterson
    Nelson's Battalion: Lt. Col. William Nelson
    Kirkpatrick's Amherst (Virginia) Battery, Capt. T. J. Kirkpatrick
    Massie's Fluvanna (Virginia) Battery: Capt. John L. Massie
    Milledge's Georgia Battery: Capt. John Milledge, Jr.

CAVALRY CORPS: Maj. Gen. J.E.B. Stuart

Second Brigade: Brig. Gen. Fitzhugh Lee
    1st Virginia: Col. James H. Drake
    2nd Virginia: Col. Thomas T. Munford
    3rd Virginia: Col. Thomas H. Owen
    4th Virginia: Col. Williams C. Wickham
Third Brigade: Brig. Gen. W.H.F. Lee
    2nd North Carolina: Maj. C. M. Andrews
    5th Virginia: Col. Thomas L. Rosser
    9th Virginia: Col. Richard L. T. Beale
    10th Virginia: Col. J. Lucius Davis

13th Virginia: Col. John R. Chambliss, Jr.
15th Virginia: Lt. Col. John Critcher
Horse Artillery: Maj. Robert F. Beckham
   Lynchburg (Virginia) Beauregard's Battery: Capt. M. N. Moorman
   1st Stuart Horse Artillery: Capt. James Breathed
   2nd Stuart Horse Artillery: Capt. William N. McGregor
   Washington (South Carolina) Battery: Capt. James F. Hart

Casualties at Chancellorsville

The following listing of Federal casualties from all operations in the Chancellorsville campaign (April 27–May 8) is derived from the casualty returns in the *Official Records* (25:1, pp. 172–92), with certain adjustments and corrections from other primary sources. The comparable casualty return for the Army of Northern Virginia, compiled by that army's medical director, Dr. Lafayette Guild (*OR*, 25:1, pp. 806–9), is incomplete, undercounting Lee's casualties by nearly 25 percent. A more definitive count is derived here from the individual Confederate regimental (and in some cases, brigade) casualty returns. These are taken from three sources: included with commanders' reports in the *Official Records*, preserved in manuscript in the National Archives (RG 109, M-863), or printed in Richmond newspapers following the battle (Hooker Papers, Huntington Library).

ARMY OF THE POTOMAC

	dead	wounded	missing	total
Headquarters Staff		1		1
Signal Corps		2		2
Engineer Brigade		6	1	7
Total		9	1	10

FIRST CORPS: Reynolds
  First Division: Wadsworth
    First Brigade: Phelps

	dead	wounded	missing	total
22nd New York		10		10
24th New York		2		2
30th New York		2		2
84th New York	1	22		23
Total First Brigade	1	36		37

	dead	wounded	missing	total
Second Brigade: Cutler				
7th Indiana	1	4		5
76th New York		3		3
95th New York		4	5	9
147th New York		6		6
56th Pennsylvania	2	8		10
Total Second Brigade	3	25	5	33
Third Brigade: Paul				
22nd New Jersey		6		6
29th New Jersey	2	7		9
30th New Jersey		5		5
Total Third Brigade	2	18		20
Fourth Brigade: Meredith				
19th Indiana	1	4		6
24th Michigan	4	20		24
2nd Wisconsin		5	1	6
6th Wisconsin	3	13		16
7th Wisconsin	3	5	1	9
Total Fourth Brigade	11	47	3	61
Artillery				
1st New York Light, Battery L		8		8
4th United States, Battery B	1		2	3
Total Artillery		9	2	11
Total First Division	17	135	10	162
Second Division: Robinson				
First Brigade: Root				
94th New York		1		1
104th New York		3		3
107th Pennsylvania		1		1
Total First Brigade		5		5
Second Brigade: Baxter				
12th Massachusetts		3	5	8
90th Pennsylvania	1	7		8
136th Pennsylvania	1	5		6
Total Second Brigade	2	15	5	22

	dead	wounded	missing	total
Third Brigade: Leonard				
13th Massachusetts	2	7		9
83rd New York		4	1	5
88th Pennsylvania		2		2
Total Third Brigade	2	13	1	16
Artillery				
5th Maine Light	6	22		28
Pennsylvania Ind. Light, Battery C	1	3		4
Total Artillery	7	25		32
Total Second Division	11	58	6	75
Third Division: Doubleday				
First Brigade: Rowley				
121st Pennsylvania		2	1	3
135th Pennsylvania		4	26	30
151st Pennsylvania	1	6	9	16
Total First Brigade	1	12	36	49
Second Brigade: Stone				
143rd Pennsylvania		1		1
149th Pennsylvania		1		1
150th Pennsylvania		1		1
Total Second Brigade		3		3
Artillery				
1st Pennsylvania Light, Battery G		9	2	11
Total Third Division	1	24	38	63
Total First Corps	29	217	54	300
SECOND CORPS: Couch				
Corps Staff		1		1
Escort		2		2
Total		3		3
First Division: Hancock				
First Brigade: Caldwell				
Brigade Staff		1		1
61st New York	1	16	10	27
66th New York	1	10	59	70
148th Pennsylvania	31	119	14	164
Total First Brigade	33	146	83	262

	dead	wounded	missing	total
Second Brigade: Meagher				
28th Massachusetts		11	5	16
63rd New York	1	3	2	6
69th New York	3	7		10
116th Pennsylvania	1	19	4	24
Total Second Brigade	5	40	11	56
Third Brigade: Zook				
52nd New York	4	30	9	43
57th New York	2	28	1	31
140th Pennsylvania	7	28	9	44
Total Third Brigade	13	86	19	118
Fourth Brigade: Brooke				
27th Connecticut	1	7	283	291
2nd Delaware	2	19	40	61
64th New York	15	21	8	44
53rd Pennsylvania		8	3	11
145th Pennsylvania	2	8	112	122
Total Fourth Brigade	20	63	446	529
Fifth Brigade (attached): Cross				
5th New Hampshire		22	3	25
81st Pennsylvania	4	38	19	61
88th New York	3	23	20	46
Total Fifth Brigade	7	83	42	132
Artillery				
1st New York Light, Battery B		12		12
4th United States, Battery C	3	12		15
Total Artillery	3	24		27
Total First Division	81	442	601	1,124
Second Division: Gibbon				
First Brigade: Sully				
15th Massachusetts		2		2
1st Minnesota		9		9
34th New York		2	1	3
82nd New York		3	3	6
Total First Brigade		16	4	20

	dead	wounded	missing	total
Third Brigade: Hall				
19th Massachusetts		9		9
20th Massachusetts	2	14	1	17
7th Michigan		7		7
42nd New York		9		9
59th New York	1	7	7	15
127th Pennsylvania	1	9		10
Total Third Brigade	4	55	8	67
Total Second Division	4	71	12	87
Third Division: French				
First Brigade: Carroll				
14th Indiana	8	49	7	64
24th New Jersey	3	21	12	36
28th New Jersey	1	29	29	59
4th Ohio	14	55	4	73
8th Ohio	1	10	1	12
7th West Virginia	3	17	4	24
Total First Brigade	30	181	57	268
Second Brigade: Hays				
Brigade Staff		4	1	5
14th Connecticut	1	36	19	56
12th New Jersey	24	132	22	178
108th New York	3	39	10	52
130th Pennsylvania		29		29
Total Second Brigade	28	240	52	320
Third Brigade: MacGregor				
1st Delaware	6	39	10	55
132nd Pennsylvania	2	41	1	44
Total Third Brigade	8	80	11	99
Artillery				
1st Rhode Island Light, Battery G	5	18		23
Total Third Division	71	519	120	710
Corps Reserve Artillery				
1st United States, Battery I	1	1		2
Total Second Corps	157	1,033	733	1,923

	dead	wounded	missing	total
THIRD CORPS: Sickles				
Corps Staff		1		1
First Division: Birney				
Division Staff		2		2
First Brigade: Graham				
57th Pennsylvania	10	43	18	71
63rd Pennsylvania	10	70	38	118
68th Pennsylvania	4	34	37	75
105th Pennsylvania	9	64	3	76
114th Pennsylvania	20	123	38	181
141st Pennsylvania	23	152	60	235
Total First Brigade	76	486	194	756
Second Brigade: Ward				
20th Indiana	1	19	4	24
3rd Maine	4	17	42	63
4th Maine	2	16	10	28
38th New York	2	17	18	37
40th New York	1	40	29	70
99th Pennsylvania	1	16	9	26
Total Second Brigade	11	125	112	248
Third Brigade: Hayman				
17th Maine	10	65	38	113
3rd Michigan	7	46	20	73
5th Michigan	7	43	28	78
1st New York	3	18	59	80
37th New York	3	111	108	222
Total Third Brigade	30	283	253	566
Artillery				
New Jersey Light, Battery B	3	7		10
1st Rhode Island Light, Battery E	2	13	2	17
3rd United States, Battery F–K	1	6	1	8
Total Artillery	6	26	3	35
Total First Division	123	922	562	1,607

	dead	wounded	missing	total
Second Division: Berry				
Division Staff	2	2		4
First Brigade: Carr				
1st Massachusetts	9	46	40	95
11th Massachusetts	8	65	3	76
16th Massachusetts	8	57	8	73
11th New Jersey	18	146	5	169
26th Pennsylvania	11	71	9	91
Total First Brigade	54	385	65	504
Second Brigade: Revere				
Brigade Staff		1		1
70th New York	4	11	17	32
71st New York	1	15	23	39
72nd New York	12	30	59	101
73rd New York	3	31	4	38
74th New York	3	22	15	40
120th New York	4	49	13	66
Total Second Brigade	27	159	131	317
Third Brigade: Mott				
Brigade Staff		3		3
5th New Jersey	13	102	6	121
6th New Jersey	7	52	8	67
7th New Jersey	7	40		47
8th New Jersey	18	101	6	125
2nd New York	4	44	6	54
115th Pennsylvania	11	78	22	111
Total Third Brigade	60	420	48	528
Artillery				
1st New York Light, Battery D	2	12		14
1st United States, Battery H	3	18		21
4th United States, Battery K	7	38		45
Total Artillery	12	68		80
Total Second Division	155	1,034	244	1,433

	dead	wounded	missing	total
Third Division: Whipple				
Division Staff	2			2
First Brigade: Franklin				
86th New York	8	68	1	77
124th New York	29	160	15	204
122nd Pennsylvania	11	75	16	102
Total First Brigade	48	303	32	383
Second Brigade: Bowman				
12th New Hampshire	41	213	63	317
84th Pennsylvania	5	59	151	215
110th Pennsylvania	5	18	22	45
Total Second Brigade	51	290	236	577
Third Brigade: Berdan				
1st U.S. Sharpshooters	11	51	6	68
2nd U.S. Sharpshooters	1	9	6	16
Total Third Brigade	12	60	12	84
Artillery				
10th New York Independent Light		13	5	18
11th New York Independent Light	2	8	1	11
1st Ohio Light, Battery H		5	3	8
Total Artillery	2	26	9	37
Total Third Division	115	679	289	1,083
Total Third Corps	393	2,636	1,095	4,124
FIFTH CORPS: Meade				
First Division: Griffin				
First Brigade: Barnes				
2nd Maine		3		3
18th Massachusetts	1	10	2	13
22nd Massachusetts	1			1
1st Michigan	2	12	1	15
13th New York		4	1	5
25th New York		3		3
118th Pennsylvania		8		8
Total First Brigade	4	40	4	48

	dead	wounded	missing	total
Second Brigade: McQuade				
9th Massachusetts		13		13
32nd Massachusetts	1	5	5	11
4th Michigan	6	12	2	20
14th New York		3		3
62nd Pennsylvania	2	13		15
Total Second Brigade	9	46	7	62
Third Brigade: Stockton				
16th Michigan	1	6		7
17th New York	1	4		5
44th New York		4		4
83rd Pennsylvania		4		4
Total Third Brigade	2	18		20
Artillery				
1st Rhode Island Light, Battery C	2	4	2	8
Total First Division	17	108	13	138
Second Division: Sykes				
First Brigade: Ayres				
3rd United States, 6 Co's.		4	5	9
4th United States, 4 Co's.	1	2	1	4
12th United States, 8 Co's.		5	18	23
14th United States, 8 Co's.	3	6	6	15
Total First Brigade	4	17	30	51
Second Brigade: Burbank				
2nd United States, 5 Co's.	1	27		28
6th United States, 5 Co's.	1	21	6	28
7th United States, 4 Co's.	2	9	5	16
10th United States, 4 Co's.		12		12
11th United States, 8 Co's.	7	16	5	28
17th United States, 7 Co's.	7	22	6	35
Total Second Brigade	18	107	22	147
Third Brigade: O'Rorke				
140th New York	2	12	7	21
146th New York	2	17	31	50
Total Third Brigade	4	29	38	71

	dead	wounded	missing	total
Artillery				
1st Ohio Light, Battery L	2	8	1	11
5th United States, Battery I		5		5
Total Artillery	2	13	1	16
Total Second Division	28	166	91	285
Third Division: Humphreys				
First Brigade: Tyler				
91st Pennsylvania	10	41	25	76
126th Pennsylvania	5	57	15	77
129th Pennsylvania	4	32	6	42
134th Pennsylvania	4	34	7	45
Total First Brigade	23	164	53	240
Second Brigade: Allabach				
123rd Pennsylvania		7	1	8
131st Pennsylvania		4		4
133rd Pennsylvania	1	10		11
155th Pennsylvania	3	10	1	14
Total Second Brigade	4	31	2	37
Total Third Division	27	195	55	277
Total Fifth Corps	72	469	159	700
SIXTH CORPS: Sedgwick				
Corps Staff		1	1	2
First Division: Brooks				
Division Staff		1		1
Provost Guard		1		1
Total		2		2
First Brigade: Brown				
Brigade Staff		2		2
1st New Jersey	7	71	27	105
2nd New Jersey	4	36	9	49
3rd New Jersey	11	69	15	95
15th New Jersey	24	126	4	154
23rd New Jersey	20	57	31	108
Total First Brigade	66	361	86	513

	dead	wounded	missing	total
Second Brigade: Bartlett				
5th Maine	12	57	27	96
16th New York	23	70	49	142
27th New York	3	13	3	19
121st New York	49	172	55	276
96th Pennsylvania	16	54	9	79
Total Second Brigade	103	366	143	612
Third Brigade: Russell				
18th New York		1	33	34
32nd New York	1	2	40	43
49th Pennsylvania	1	3	5	9
95th Pennsylvania	23	113	20	156
119th Pennsylvania	11	77	38	126
Total Third Brigade	36	196	136	368
Artillery				
Massachusetts Light, Battery A	1	1		2
New Jersey Light, Battery A		1		1
Maryland Light, Battery A		3		3
2nd United States, Battery D	1			1
Total Artillery	2	5	.	7
Total First Division	207	928	365	1,500
Second Division: Howe				
Second Brigade: Grant				
2nd Vermont	18	114		132
3rd Vermont	3	22		25
4th Vermont	4	27	22	53
5th Vermont	3	11	9	23
6th Vermont	5	54	15	74
26th New Jersey	7	66	51	124
Total Second Brigade	40	294	97	431
Third Brigade: Neill				
7th Maine	12	49	31	92
21st New Jersey	10	60	141	211
20th New York	6	92	110	208
33rd New York	18	129	74	221
49th New York	1	16	18	35
77th New York	7	46	30	83
Total Third Brigade	54	392	404	850

	dead	wounded	missing	total
Artillery				
5th United States, Battery F		8	1	9
Total Second Division	94	694	502	1,290
Third Division: Newton				
First Brigade: Shaler				
65th New York	1	13	3	17
67th New York	2	16	11	29
122nd New York		7		7
23rd Pennsylvania	4	17	40	61
82nd Pennsylvania	1	32	13	46
Total First Brigade	8	85	67	160
Second Brigade: Browne				
Brigade Staff		1		1
7th Massachusetts	22	125	3	150
10th Massachusetts	10	57	2	69
37th Massachusetts	1	10	5	16
36th New York	2	18	6	26
2nd Rhode Island	8	67	6	81
Total Second Brigade	43	278	22	343
Third Brigade: Wheaton				
62nd New York	10	55	55	120
93rd Pennsylvania	8	53	18	79
98th Pennsylvania	8	20	13	41
102nd Pennsylvania	12	54	103	169
139th Pennsylvania	12	53	11	76
Total Third Brigade	50	235	200	485
Artillery				
1st Pennsylvania Light, Battery C–D	1	4	4	9
2nd United States, Battery G			14	14
Total Artillery	1	4	18	23
Total Third Division	102	602	307	1,011

	dead	wounded	missing	total
Light Division: Burnham				
6th Maine	24	110	35	169
31st New York	13	53	87	153
43rd New York	15	53	136	204
61st Pennsylvania	9	63	16	88
5th Wisconsin	36	121	36	193
3rd New York Independent Light		1		1
Total Light Division	97	401	310	808
Total Sixth Corps	500	2,626	1,485	4,611
ELEVENTH CORPS: Howard				
First Division: Devens				
Division Staff		2		2
First Brigade: Von Gilsa				
41st New York	2	28	31	61
45th New York	7	25	44	76
54th New York	1	24	18	43
153rd Pennsylvania	6	40	39	85
Total First Brigade	16	117	132	265
Second Brigade: McLean				
Brigade Staff		1	2	3
17th Connecticut	4	38	69	111
25th Ohio	15	106	31	152
55th Ohio	10	86	57	153
75th Ohio	13	61	66	140
107th Ohio	6	53	74	133
Total Second Brigade	48	345	299	692
Artillery				
13th New York Independent Light		11	2	13
Total First Division	64	475	433	972
Second Division: Von Steinwehr				
First Brigade: Buschbeck				
29th New York	4	53	39	96
154th New York	38	42	160	240
27th Pennsylvania	6	31	19	56
73rd Pennsylvania	10	64	29	103
Total First Brigade	58	190	247	495

	dead	wounded	missing	total
Second Brigade: Barlow				
33rd Massachusetts		4	3	7
134th New York		3	5	8
136th New York		1	5	6
73rd Ohio		1	1	2
Total Second Brigade		9	14	23
Artillery				
1st New York Light, Battery I	1	10	2	13
Total Second Division	59	209	263	531
Third Division: Schurz				
Division Staff		1		1
82nd Ohio (unattached)	9	47	25	81
Total	9	48	25	82
First Brigade: Schimmelfennig				
82nd Illinois	30	87	38	155
68th New York	3	18	33	54
157th New York	13	66	19	98
61st Ohio	33	27		60
74th Pennsylvania	8	14	30	52
Total First Brigade	87	212	120	419
Second Brigade: Krzyzanowski				
58th New York	1	10	20	31
119th New York	12	66	42	120
75th Pennsylvania	1	7	51	59
26th Wisconsin	25	133	40	198
Total Second Brigade	39	216	153	408
Artillery				
1st Ohio Light, Battery I	1	10		11
Total Third Division	136	486	298	920
Corps Reserve Artillery				
1st Ohio Light, Battery K		3		3
Total Eleventh Corps	259	1,173	994	2,426

	dead	wounded	missing	total
TWELFTH CORPS: Slocum				
Corps Staff		1		1
Provost Guard		2	1	3
Total		3	1	4
First Division: Williams				
Division Staff			1	1
First Brigade: Knipe				
5th Connecticut	1	19	43	63
28th New York	1	6	71	78
46th Pennsylvania	3	15	81	99
128th Pennsylvania		13	199	212
Total First Brigade	5	53	394	452
Second Brigade: Ross				
Brigade Staff		2	1	3
20th Connecticut	11	60	98	169
3rd Maryland	12	44	29	85
123rd New York	17	113	18	148
145th New York	4	33	58	95
Total Second Brigade	44	252	204	500
Third Brigade: Ruger				
Brigade Staff		1		1
27th Indiana	21	125	4	150
2nd Massachusetts	21	110	7	138
13th New Jersey	18	99	24	141
107th New York	5	54	24	83
3rd Wisconsin	18	74	9	101
Total Third Brigade	83	463	68	614
Artillery				
1st New York Light, Battery K		8		8
1st New York Light, Battery M	5	13	4	22
4th United States, Battery F	2	9	5	16
Total Artillery	7	30	9	46
Total First Division	139	798	676	1,613

	dead	wounded	missing	total
Second Division: Geary				
First Brigade: Candy				
5th Ohio	6	52	24	82
7th Ohio	16	62	21	99
29th Ohio	2	42	28	72
66th Ohio	3	40	30	73
28th Pennsylvania	18	61	24	103
147th Pennsylvania	13	57	24	94
Total First Brigade	58	314	151	523
Second Brigade: Kane				
Brigade Staff		1		1
29th Pennsylvania	6	13	2	21
109th Pennsylvania	4	16	2	22
111th Pennsylvania	5	14	7	26
124th Pennsylvania	1	16	3	20
125th Pennsylvania	1	29	19	49
Total Second Brigade	17	89	33	139
Third Brigade: Greene				
Brigade Staff		1		1
60th New York	9	44	13	66
78th New York	12	51	68	131
102nd New York	10	41	39	90
137th New York	3	15	36	54
149th New York	15	68	103	186
Total Third Brigade	49	219	260	528
Artillery				
Pennsylvania Light, Battery E	1	8		9
Pennsylvania Light, Battery F	2	7		9
Total Artillery	3	15		18
Total Second Division	127	637	444	1,208
Total Twelfth Corps	266	1,435	1,120	2,821
CAVALRY CORPS: Stoneman				
First Division: Pleasonton				
First Brigade: Davis				
8th Illinois			2	2
3rd Indiana	1	3	20	24
8th New York		5		5
Total First Brigade	1	8	22	31

	dead	wounded	missing	total
Second Brigade: Devin				
6th New York	5	17	53	75
8th Pennsylvania	5	24	76	105
17th Pennsylvania		9	5	14
Total Second Brigade	10	50	134	194
Artillery				
6th New York Independent Light	2	4		6
Total First Division	13	62	156	231
Second Division: Averell				
First Brigade: Sargent				
1st Massachusetts	1		2	3
1st Rhode Island		5		5
Total Second Division	1	5	2	8
Third Division: Gregg				
First Brigade: Kilpatrick				
1st Maine	1	1	24	26
Total First Brigade				36
Second Brigade: Wyndham				
12th Illinois	2	3	30	35
1st Maryland			10	10
Total Second Brigade	2	3	40	45
Total Third Division	3	4	64	71
Reserve Cavalry: Buford				
6th Pennsylvania			2	2
1st United States			18	18
2nd United States			11	11
5th United States	1	3	33	37
6th United States			11	11
Total Reserve Cavalry	1	3	75	79
Total Cavalry Corps	18	74	297	389

	dead	wounded	missing	total
ARMY OF THE POTOMAC				
Headquarters		9	1	10
First Corps	29	217	54	300
Second Corps	157	1,033	733	1,923
Third Corps	393	2,636	1,095	4,124
Fifth Corps	72	469	159	700
Sixth Corps	500	2,626	1,485	4,611
Eleventh Corps	259	1,173	994	2,426
Twelfth Corps	266	1,435	1,120	2,821
Cavalry Corps	18	74	297	389
Total	1,694	9,672	5,938	17,304

ARMY OF NORTHERN VIRGINIA

	dead	wounded	missing	total
FIRST CORPS: Lee				
Anderson's Division				
Mahone's Brigade				
6th Virginia	8	33	6	47
12th Virginia	5	31	50	86
16th Virginia	1	17	19	37
41st Virginia	6	23	19	48
61st Virginia	4	30	3	37
Total Mahone's Brigade	24	134	97	255
Posey's Brigade				
Brigade Staff		1		1
12th Mississippi	3	38	23	64
16th Mississippi	22	57	25	104
19th Mississippi	6	39	6	51
48th Mississippi	10	50	11	71
Total Posey's Brigade	41	185	65	291
Perry's Brigade				
Brigade Staff		1		1
2nd Florida	5	30		35
5th Florida	8	20		28
8th Florida	10	36		46
Total Perry's Brigade	23	87		110

	dead	wounded	missing	total
Wilcox's Brigade				
8th Alabama	9	43	4	56
9th Alabama	23	89	1	113
10th Alabama	18	54	28	100
11th Alabama	16	75	24	115
14th Alabama	13	104	34	151
Total Wilcox's Brigade	79	365	91	535
Wright's Brigade				
3rd Georgia	10	129		139
22nd Georgia	5	54		59
48th Georgia	7	65		72
2nd Georgia Battalion	3	23		26
Total Wright's Brigade	25	271		296
Garnett's Artillery Battalion				
Grandy's Norfolk Blues Battery	1	3		4
Lewis's Pittsylvania Battery		6		6
Maurin's Donaldsonville Battery		1		1
Total Garnett's Artillery	1	10		11
Total Anderson's Division	193	1,052	253	1,498
McLaws's Division				
Kershaw's Brigade				
2nd South Carolina				
3rd South Carolina	1			
7th South Carolina	1			
8th South Carolina				
15th South Carolina	9			
3rd South Carolina Battalion	1			
Total Kershaw's Brigade	12	90	2	104
Semmes's Brigade				
10th Georgia	23			
50th Georgia	17			
51st Georgia	30			
53rd Georgia	15			
Total Semmes's Brigade	85	492	26	603

	dead	wounded	missing	total
Wofford's Brigade				
16th Georgia	18			
18th Georgia	14			
24th Georgia	14			
Cobb's Georgia Legion	24			
Phillips's Georgia Legion	4			
Total Wofford's Brigade	74	479	9	562
Barksdale's Brigade				
13th Mississippi	5			
17th Mississippi	10			
18th Mississippi	25	43	226	294
21st Mississippi	3			
Total Barksdale's Brigade	43	208	341	592
Cabell's Artillery Battalion				
Carleton's Troup Battery	1	10		11
Fraser's Pulaski Battery	1	2	2	5
McCarthy's Richmond Howitzers, 1st Co.	2	2		4
Manly's North Carolina Battery	1	7		8
Total Cabell's Artillery	5	21	2	28
Total McLaws's Division	219	1,290	380	1,889
First Corps Reserve Artillery				
Alexander's Artillery Battalion				
Eubank's Bath Battery				
Jordan's Bedford Battery				
Moody's Madison Battery				
Parker's Richmond Battery	1		24	
Rhett's Brooks Battery				
Woolfolk's Ashland Battery				
Total Alexander's Artillery	6	35	24	62
Washington Artillery Battalion				
Squires's First Company	3		27	30
Richardson's Second Company				
Miller's Third Company				
Eshleman's Fourth Company				
Total Washington Artillery	4	8	27	45
Total Corps Reserve Artillery	10	43	54	107
Total First Corps	422	2,385	687	3,494

	dead	wounded	missing	total
SECOND CORPS: Jackson				
Corps Staff	3	2		5
Hill's Light Division				
Division Staff	2	2		4
Heth's Brigade				
Brigade Staff		1		1
40th Virginia	14	71	9	94
47th Virginia	3	47	3	53
55th Virginia	20	90	10	120
22nd Virginia Battalion	6	23	16	45
Total Heth's Brigade	43	232	38	313
Pender's Brigade				
13th North Carolina	31	178	7	216
16th North Carolina	17	73	15	105
22nd North Carolina	30	129	15	174
34th North Carolina	18	110	20	148
38th North Carolina	18	84	11	113
Total Pender's Brigade	114	574	68	756
McGowan's Brigade				
Brigade Staff	1	1		2
1st South Carolina	12	88	4	104
1st South Carolina Rifles	20	91	2	113
12th South Carolina		2		2
13th South Carolina	6	84	1	91
14th South Carolina	8	137		145
Total McGowan's Brigade	47	403	7	457
Lane's Brigade				
7th North Carolina	49	148	13	210
18th North Carolina	34	99	21	154
28th North Carolina	14	91	2	107
33rd North Carolina	32	101	68	201
37th North Carolina	36	194	8	238
Total Lane's Brigade	165	633	112	910

	dead	wounded	missing	total
Archer's Brigade				
1st Tennessee	9	51	1	61
7th Tennessee	10	49	3	62
14th Tennessee	7	56	3	66
13th Alabama	15	117	8	140
5th Alabama Battalion	3	32	1	36
Total Archer's Brigade	44	305	16	365
Thomas's Brigade				
14th Georgia	8	67		75
35th Georgia	6	28	4	38
45th Georgia	4	36	1	41
49th Georgia	4	30	4	38
Total Thomas's Brigade	22	161	9	192
Walker's Artillery Battalion				
Brunson's Pee Dee Battery				
Crenshaw's Virginia Battery	1	5		6
Davidson's Letcher Battery	2	5		7
McGraw's Purcell Battery				
Marye's Fredericksburg Battery	2	6		8
Total Walker's Artillery	5	28		33
Total Hill's Light Division	442	2,338	250	3,030
Rodes's Division				
O'Neal's Brigade				
Brigade Staff		1		1
3rd Alabama	16	127	16	159
5th Alabama	24	133	121	278
6th Alabama	26	122	14	162
12th Alabama	13	79	10	102
26th Alabama	12	77	27	116
Total O'Neal's Brigade	91	539	188	818
Doles's Brigade				
4th Georgia	29	115	11	155
12th Georgia	12	58	2	72
21st Georgia	15	64	10	89
44th Georgia	20	96	5	121
Total Doles's Brigade	76	333	28	437

	dead	wounded	missing	total
Iverson's Brigade				
5th North Carolina	8	61	9	78
12th North Carolina	12	96	11	119
20th North Carolina	15	67	18	100
23rd North Carolina	32	106	35	173
Total Iverson's Brigade	67	330	73	470
Colquitt's Brigade				
6th Georgia	2	29	2	33
19th Georgia	3	33	11	47
23rd Georgia		3	296	299
27th Georgia	2	39	1	42
28th Georgia	2	24	2	28
Total Colquitt's Brigade	9	128	312	449
Ramseur's Brigade				
Brigade Staff		1		1
2nd North Carolina	55	155	49	259
4th North Carolina	47	155	58	260
14th North Carolina	23	120		143
30th North Carolina	26	99	1	126
Total Ramseur's Brigade	151	530	108	789
Carter's Artillery Battalion				
Reese's Jeff Davis Battery				
Carter's King William Battery	4	12		16
Fry's Orange Battery				
Page's Morris Louisa Battery				
Total Carter's Artillery	9	37		46
Total Rodes's Division	406	1,894	709	3,009
Early's Division				
Gordon's Brigade				
Brigade Staff		1		1
13th Georgia	4	54	28	86
26th Georgia	3	21		24
31st Georgia	3	22	1	26
38th Georgia	2	18		20
60th Georgia	5	30	4	39
61st Georgia		32	3	35
Total Gordon's Brigade	17	178	36	231

	dead	wounded	missing	total
Hoke's Brigade				
Brigade Staff		1		1
6th North Carolina	8	42	17	67
21st North Carolina	16	72	43	131
54th North Carolina	7	37	49	93
57th North Carolina	12	64	57	133
1st Batt. North Carolina Sharpshooters		20		20
Total Hoke's Brigade	43	236	166	445
Smith's Brigade				
13th Virginia	6	35	17	58
49th Virginia	1	16		17
52nd Virginia	4	9		13
58th Virginia	2	28	71	101
Total Smith's Brigade	13	88	88	189
Hays's Brigade				
5th Louisiana	11	37	28	76
6th Louisiana	14	68	99	181
7th Louisiana	7	75	36	118
8th Louisiana	17	64	89	170
9th Louisiana	21	53	42	116
Total Hays's Brigade	70	297	294	661
Andrews's Artillery Battalion				
Brown's Fourth Maryland Battery	1	4		5
Carpenter's Alleghany Battery	1	3		4
Dement's First Maryland Battery	3	6		9
Raine's Lee Battery	1	3		4
Total Andrews's Artillery	6	16		22
Total Early's Division	149	815	584	1,548
Colston's Division				
Division Staff	1	5		6
Paxton's Brigade				
Brigade Staff	1			1
2nd Virginia	8	58		66
4th Virginia	18	148	3	169
5th Virginia	9	111	5	125
27th Virginia	9	63	1	73
33rd Virginia	10	50		60
Total Paxton's Brigade	55	430	9	494

	dead	wounded	missing	total
Jones's Brigade				
Brigade Staff	1			1
21st Virginia	4	40		44
42nd Virginia	15	120		135
44th Virginia	15	62		77
48th Virginia	19	84	9	112
50th Virginia	8	110		118
Total Jones's Brigade	62	416	9	487
Warren's Brigade				
Brigade Staff		2		2
1st North Carolina	32	140	27	199
3rd North Carolina	39	176	17	232
10th Virginia	25	107	25	157
23rd Virginia	10	70	2	82
37th Virginia	22	101	9	132
Total Warren's Brigade	128	596	80	804
Nicholls's Brigade				
Brigade Staff		1		1
1st Louisiana	7	29	10	46
2nd Louisiana	15	90	21	126
10th Louisiana	15	51	20	86
14th Louisiana	4	60	17	81
15th Louisiana	5	37	62	104
Total Nicholls's Brigade	46	268	130	444
Jones's Artillery Battalion				
Carrington's Charlottesville Battery				
Garber's Staunton Battery				
Latimer's Courtney Battery				
Thompson's Louisiana Guard Battery				
Total Jones's Artillery		21		21
Total Colston's Division	292	1,736	228	2,256

	dead	wounded	missing	total
Second Corps Reserve Artillery				
Brown's Artillery Battalion				
Brooke's Warrenton Battery				
Dance's Powhatan Battery	1	5		6
Graham's 1st Rockbridge Battery	1	5	2	8
Hupp's Salem Battery				
Watson's Richmond Howitzers, 2nd Co.				
Smith's Richmond Howitzers, 3rd Co.				
Total Brown's Artillery	2	16	2	20
McIntosh's Artillery Battalion				
Hurt's Alabama Battery				
Johnson's Richmond Battery				
Lusk's 2nd Rockbridge Battery				
Wooding's Danville Battery				
Total McIntosh's Artillery		18		18
Total Corps Reserve Artillery	2	34	2	38
Total Second Corps	1,294	6,819	1,773	9,886
Army Reserve Artillery				
Cutts's Artillery Battalion				
Patterson's Sumter, Battery B		3		3
Total Army Reserve Artillery		3		3
CAVALRY CORPS: Stuart				
Fitzhugh Lee's Brigade				
1st Virginia				
2nd Virginia				
3rd Virginia		15		15
4th Virginia	1	1	4	6
Total Fitzhugh Lee's Brigade	4	16	4	24
W.H.F. Lee's Brigade				
2nd North Carolina				
5th Virginia				
9th Virginia		4		4
10th Virginia				
13th Virginia				
15th Virginia				
Total W.H.F. Lee's Brigade		4	31	35

	dead	wounded	missing	total
Horse Artillery				
1st Stuart Horse Artillery	1			1
2nd Stuart Horse Artillery	3	6	8	17
Total Horse Artillery	4	6	8	18
Total Cavalry Corps	8	26	43	77

ARMY OF NORTHERN VIRGINIA

	dead	wounded	missing	total
First Corps				
Anderson's Division	193	1,052	253	1,498
McLaws's Division	219	1,290	380	1,889
First Corps Reserve Artillery	10	43	54	107
Second Corps				
Corps Staff	3	2		5
Hill's Light Division	442	2,338	250	3,030
Rodes's Division	406	1,894	709	3,009
Early's Division	149	815	584	1,548
Colston's Division	292	1,736	228	2,256
Second Corps Reserve Artillery	2	34	2	38
Army Reserve Artillery		3		3
Cavalry Corps	8	26	43	77
Total	1,724	9,233	2,503	13,460

APPENDIX III

The Romances of Chancellorsville

IT WAS Theodore A. Dodge, in an 1886 paper delivered to the Military Historical Society of Massachusetts, who coined the phrase "the romances of Chancellorsville." It was his euphemism for "constantly reiterated misstatements and misconceptions" respecting the battle. Dodge had served in the Army of the Potomac and fought at Chancellorsville in the much-maligned Eleventh Corps and had written a history of the battle, and he told his audience he would "oppose bald misstatements by vigorous denial."

A number of such aspects of the campaign that have generated controversy are discussed in their context within the narrative — Hooker's decision to recall his advance on the afternoon of May 1, for one example; or the matter of warnings of Jackson's flank attack on May 2, for another. Both were on Dodge's list. Others are better suited to discussion here, outside the narrative, under the heading of Dodge's coinage.

There are more romances of Chancellorsville than Theodore Dodge imagined in 1886, but it is well to begin with General Alfred Pleasonton, whom Dodge described as "the chief romancer of this campaign." Yankee cavalryman Pleasonton was well known to his own men as — not to put too fine a point on it — a habitual liar. Colonel Charles Russell Lowell's contemporaneous judgment is apt: ". . . it is the universal opinion that P's own reputation and P's late promotions are bolstered by systematic lying." Pleasonton's motive during the war seems to have been self-promotion; after the war it was self-acclamation.[1]

During Hooker's turning movement, for example, Pleasonton claimed, in an article in *Battles and Leaders,* that at Germanna Ford on April 29 he captured a Confederate diary that furnished him such telling insights into Lee's thinking that he pressed on Hooker the "correct" strategy for the campaign — strategy that of course was not followed. No trace of such a diary has been found, and Pleasonton failed to mention his important find in either his report or his journal of operations.[2]

He also claimed, in his article and in congressional testimony, to have captured a dispatch written by General Lee at noon on April 30 addressed to Anderson (addressed to McLaws in *Battles and Leaders*) reading, "I have just received reliable information that the enemy have crossed the river in force. Why have you not kept me informed? . . ." Pleasonton said this helped him deduce the proper strategy for winning the battle, but again Hooker ignored his advice. Since Lee had already been in communication with both Anderson and McLaws on this subject the day before, he would not have sent such a dispatch on April 30. And of course Pleasonton did not produce the dispatch.[3]

Pleasonton's boast, in his congressional testimony and in his *Battles and Leaders* article, that he had contributed mightily to stopping Jackson's flank attack on May 2 attracted the most derision by his contemporaries. He claimed he ordered Major Huey's cavalry charge to buy time enough for him (Pleasonton) to put the Hazel Grove artillery into action. As the narrative points out, however, Huey's charge was a spontaneous and desperate act; the artillery at Hazel Grove was commanded by Captain Huntington (Pleasonton at best had authority over Martin's horse battery); and neither was instrumental in stopping Jackson.

The *Battles and Leaders* editors ran refutations of Pleasonton, he was refuted in the "Annals of the War" series in the *Philadelphia Weekly Times,* and Theodore Dodge added the final touches in his 1886 paper. Dodge was particularly offended because originally, in his Chancellorsville history (1881), he had accepted Pleasonton's claims.[4]

* *

HISTORIANS HAVE taken a wary approach to how General Hooker reacted to Lincoln's famous letter to him of January 26, 1863. The editors of Lincoln's papers felt that Hooker's reception of the president's views had "not been adequately recorded. All accounts known to the editors reveal an abundance of conjecture and rationalized recollections after the fact." Hooker's biographer Walter H. Hebert suggested that Noah Brooks's well-known recollection of Hooker's reaction ("That is just such a letter as a father might write to his son.") was "strictly out of character" for the general to have said. It was more likely, Hebert thought, that Hooker accepted the letter as a rebuke.

In fact, however, the earliest record of Hooker's reaction seems to mirror Brooks's recollection. At the army review at Falmouth early in

April, Hooker showed Lincoln's letter to Dr. Anson G. Henry, a close friend of the president's, with the remark that it "ought to be printed in letters of gold."

Following the war, Hooker was at pains to preserve the letter and to ensure its publication. In 1878 he sent it to Samuel P. Bates for publication in Bates's forthcoming *The Battle of Chancellorsville,* and to Robert N. Scott for publication in the *Official Records.* Its actual first publication, with Hooker's blessing, was in the *Providence Journal* for May 6, 1879, some six months before Hooker's death.[5]

* *

NOTHING HAS BEEN more damaging to General Joseph Hooker's military reputation than this, from John Bigelow's *The Campaign of Chancellorsville* (1910):

"A couple of months later, when Hooker crossed the Rappahannock [actually, the Potomac] with the Army of the Potomac in the campaign of Gettysburg, he was asked by General Doubleday: 'Hooker, what was the matter with you at Chancellorsville? Some say you were injured by a shell, and others that you were drunk; now tell us what it was.' Hooker answered frankly and good-naturedly: 'Doubleday, I was not hurt by a shell, and I was not drunk. For once I lost confidence in Hooker, and that is all there is to it.'"

This admission, given credence by appearing in Bigelow's authoritative volume, became a keystone of virtually every latter-day account of Chancellorsville and every analysis of Hooker's generalship — boastful Hooker publicly confessing he lost the battle because he lost his nerve. This in Herman Hattaway and Archer Jones's *How the North Won: A Military History of the Civil War* is typical: "Hooker's nerve failed. As he said of himself: 'For once I lost confidence in Hooker.'"[6]

In fact, Joe Hooker's confession fully qualifies as one of the romances of Chancellorsville.

Bigelow was quoting a letter of one E. P. Halstead, written April 19, 1903, and acquired by Bigelow as research for his book. Halstead was very specific about Hooker's admission. The occasion was just after the army had crossed the Potomac in pursuit of Lee, and just before Hooker resigned his command. That puts it on one of three days, June 25–27. Halstead, on the staff of Abner Doubleday's First Corps division, records that Hooker joined Doubleday on the march, and as they rode along together he overheard the exchange between the two generals. After chatting a few minutes more, Hooker rode on ahead and they "saw no more of Gen. Hooker during the campaign."

It must be observed that such a demeaning admission to a subordinate would be totally out of character for Joe Hooker. Nor, certainly, would he have said that he was not hurt by the shell at the Chancellor house on May 3; he made certain his injury was known widely. Be that as it may, the exchange quoted by Halstead did not take place as he described it because it could not have taken place.

Tracking the routes of both Hooker's headquarters and Doubleday's on these three days reveals them dozens of miles apart, with never an opportunity for an encounter. Indeed there was never an opportunity for the two to meet like this at *any* time during the march toward Gettysburg.

Halstead waited until both Hooker and Doubleday were dead before he retailed his tale. Doubleday, whose history of the Chancellorsville campaign was published in 1882, left not even a hint in his volume that Hooker's loss of nerve, confessed or otherwise, caused his defeat.

It can only be concluded that forty years after the event, elderly ex–staff officer Halstead was at best retailing some vaguely remembered campfire tale, and at worst manufacturing a role for himself in histories of the campaign. (The rest of his letter is a garbled account of the First Corps' role at Chancellorsville.) Whatever Joe Hooker's failings at Chancellorsville, he did not publicly confess them.[7]

* *

TESTIFYING BEFORE the Joint Committee on the Conduct of the War in 1864, Dan Butterfield was asked if he had ever seen General Hooker under the influence of liquor, "or known of his being so." Like all the other Potomac-army generals asked this question by the committee, Butterfield replied, "Never." When he was asked about the source of the rumors of the general being drunk, Butterfield elaborated on his answer:

"I do not know, unless it is malice; upon the general principle that when a man attains a high position people are always found to carp at him and endeavor to pull him down." He noted this had happened to McDowell, McClellan, Pope, and Burnside before Hooker — "some have been called drunkards, some cowards, some fools. It is the nature of our people. . . ."

The tales that Joe Hooker was drunk at Chancellorsville quickly drew investigators. Members of the joint committee visited Falmouth a week after the battle and could find no basis for the tales. Nor could Thaddeus Stevens, the eagle-eyed congressman from Pennsylvania, who made his own investigation and then branded the stories "atrociously false." The *New York Tribune*'s George Smalley visited Falmouth on the story and probed all his sources in the Army of the Potomac, including Joe Hooker. "If I am to be investigated, it might as well be by you as anybody," Hooker said grimly. "I asked everybody likely to know," Smalley reported, "and not one witness could testify to having seen General Hooker the worse for whiskey."

When private testimony of such reliable and unbiased witnesses as George Meade and Charles Wainwright and George Sharpe is added to these public investigations, it becomes clear enough that Fighting Joe Hooker was sober throughout the Chancellorsville campaign. It seems that the only liquor that touched his lips was the brandy administered as a stimulant by Dr. Letterman after his injury on May 3. It was Hooker's near-comatose condition after this injury, of course, that inspired the "eyewitness" stories of his lying insensible with drink that day.

Darius Couch, in an article on the battle that appeared in *Battles and Leaders,* agreed that the commanding general was sober on the Chancellorsville battlefield, but he then argued a case repugnant in its own right. General Hooker habitually took his courage from a bottle, Couch suggested, and at Chancellorsville all might have turned out well had he "continued in his usual habit in that respect." Couch, whose military career went rapidly downhill after the battle, apparently had no compunction, after Hooker's death, in using his pen to avenge himself on his old commander.[8]

Until recent times the tale of Hooker's drunkenness was relegated to a footnote in studies of the campaign. Then Robert G. Carter and Washington A. Roebling were called up as late witnesses to Hooker's intemperance. Carter, a Massachusetts private at the time of the battle, was a self-righteous sort who, decades later, without a shred of evidence, charged that Hooker "had been *drunk* all *winter*"; seeing the fallen general comatose after his injury and concussion on May 3, he labeled the scene a "drunken debauch." He boasted, "No one had dared to tell the truth about this until I myself published it." In fact, the truth about this is that Robert Carter was a mendacious gossip.

Roebling was little better. His account of Chancellorsville, dating from about the turn of the century, is bitter, careless of fact, and twisted with self-importance. For example, he said he learned (by hearsay) that at 9:00 A.M. on May 1 Hooker was still sleeping off the previous night's drunk and missed a chance for victory that day. In fact, the evidence is incontrovertible that Hooker had been up for hours that morning, riding his lines.

Carter and Roebling, then, only contributed to making the story of Hooker's drunkenness the longest running of the romances of Chancellorsville.[9]

* *

EXACTLY WHAT was discussed by Generals Lee and Jackson at their Wilderness conference on the evening of May 1, and which of them originated the idea of the bold flanking march, became another subject of later misstatements and misconceptions. After Lee's death in 1870, the question became entangled in the efforts of Lee partisans to make the general the dominant figure of the Lost Cause and Confederate historiography.

As there was no single witness to the entirety of the generals' lengthy conversation that evening, misunderstandings were perhaps inevitable. For example, Hunter McGuire, Jackson's medical director, said as late as 1896 that he still believed the flank march originated with Jackson, "but I have no positive proof of it; it was the common belief of our staff that he did it. I remember, Pendleton, Crutchfield, and myself often discussed it, and we all simply accepted it as a move proposed by Jackson."

In his memoir Confederate general John B. Gordon said he had it by the authority of the Reverend Lacy that Lee actually opposed the flank-march idea that night, and Jackson persuaded him otherwise. Indeed, Jackson was blunt about it, saying "this is not the best way to move on Hooker" and that Lee was "mistaken" to rely on his engineers' advice. "Move on the flank — move on the flank," Jackson insisted — apparently Lee had proposed and then rejected that — and finally the commanding general gave in: "Then you will at once make the movement, Sir."

Such improbability was not restricted to the Jackson camp, however. Charles Marshall, Lee staff officer and a leader of the postwar "Lee cult," remembered Jackson insisting, at the May 1 conference, that Hooker would be gone from Chancellorsville by morning. Marshall has Jackson "expressing the opinion very decidedly, and repeating it more than once, that the enemy would recross the Rappahannock before morning." The more perceptive Lee doubted this would happen, and said they must plan a strategy.

Having just finished inspecting (with Captain Haskell) the massed and well-entrenched Yankees in their Chancellorsville lines, it is highly unlikely Jackson would have drawn that conclusion or expressed that opinion. In this case, as in other of the romances of Chancellorsville, self-interest was dictating latter-day recollections.[10]

* *

NOT SURPRISINGLY, the wounding of Stonewall Jackson on the evening of May 2 generated suspect accounts. The most durable is that of David J. Kyle, who claimed to have been Jackson's guide on that fateful evening. According to cavalryman Kyle, a local man, the site of Jackson's wounding was the Mountain Road rather than the Orange Plank Road as narrated in Chapter 11. Written thirty-three years after the event, Kyle's account is unsupported and unsupportable.

None of the dozen witnesses to the event, or some aspect of it, mentions Kyle; surely a role as extensive as he paints his could not have been entirely overlooked. Every eyewitness account, regardless of variations in detail, places the incident on the Plank Road; surely they cannot all have been in error. Indeed, because of its planking the Orange Plank Road was one of the few readily identifiable features in the Wilderness. When eyewitnesses said that Jackson was wounded while on the Plank Road, they could hardly have been mistaken in their identification of the location.

There could have been no logic in Jackson's asking to be guided down the Mountain Road. It was a poor, narrow woods track, paralleling the Plank Road and probably unusable for artillery and certainly going nowhere of interest to the Confederates. Jackson's objective was Chancellorsville and a link-up with Lee; only then might he consider trying to turn the Federals' right. Finally, after Kyle's account was published in *Confederate Veteran* in 1896, it was explicitly rejected by two credible witnesses, James Power Smith and Jed Hotchkiss.

What has given Kyle's account longevity is its acceptance by Douglas Southall Freeman in his *Lee's Lieutenants*. Apparently Freeman was influenced by the vouched-for credibility of Kyle by a respected friend who had known the old soldier in his later years. But to accept Kyle is to bend out of shape all of the contemporaneous accounts, most especially the one written within a matter of days by Richard Wilbourn, who was at Jackson's side every minute that evening — an account unknown to Freeman.

The best that may be said of David Kyle's story is that it is all true — except for Jackson's presence in it. The young 9th Virginia cavalryman may have been (as he said) acting as a courier that day, may have delivered a dispatch to Jackson from Stuart, and, having grown up nearby, may have been sent to scout north of the Plank Road. His was the most minor of roles that eventful evening, however, and to persuade *Confederate Veteran*'s editors to print his "recollections," Kyle (in effect) took Stonewall Jackson with him down the Mountain Road.[11]

Also in connection with Jackson's wounding, there is the story of the "solitary rider" seen just moments after the general was hit. He appears first, quite prosaically, in Wilbourn's initial account, written soon after the event to John Esten Cooke. Just after they helped the wounded Jackson rein in his horse, Wilbourn wrote, "Wynn saw a man on horseback near by and told him to 'ride back & see what troops those are,' pointing in the direction of our troops, and he rode off at once."

Cooke's account of this, in a Richmond newspaper, dramatized the figure's presence at the scene as a "singular circumstance," and he concluded, "Who this silent personage was is left to conjecture." Conjecture there was. (Douglas Freeman thought he might have been David Kyle, thus legitimizing Kyle's presence at the scene.) Wilbourn complained that Cooke had taken his account and made "it appear more like a romance than reality." Most likely the man was one of the couriers who scattered after the attack.

The role of the solitary rider was even claimed by a Federal general, Joseph W. Revere, at the time in command of a brigade in the Third Corps. Revere, a grandson of the Revolution's Paul Revere, said he was scouting out in front of his lines that evening and therefore was the "silent personage" of Cooke's account. Jubal Early took the measure of Revere's claim in the pages of the *Southern Historical Society Papers* and demolished it. (It required gall on Revere's part to raise this matter. He had been court-martialed for incompetence at Chancellorsville and forced to resign from the service.)[12]

After reading of Jackson's death, men in Berry's Federal brigades that were posted near the Plank Road claimed to remember firing at a group of horsemen on their front that night. These marksmen seemed mostly to come from the 1st Massachusetts. Their colonel related that the party rode right into their lines and his men without orders "opened a terrific fire. . . ." There was never a doubt in the colonel's mind that it was this fire that killed Stonewall Jackson, "and he so reported it to the Adjutant General of Massachusetts." Another regiment making the claim was the 73rd New York. These theories, like Revere's (and Kyle's), have nothing whatever to support them.[13]

* *

STEPHEN CRANE'S *The Red Badge of Courage* is most certainly not one of the romances of Chancellorsville — quite the opposite — yet there has been much speculation and questioning about the setting and sources for the novel. Recent research into these matters offers more answers than ever to these intriguing questions.

Stephen Crane was born six years after the end of the war he described so memorably. He was only twenty-one, with his first novel, *Maggie: A Girl of the Streets*, just published (at his own expense), when he set out to write what he described as a "historical romance, a pot-boiler" about the Civil War. By about the time he turned twenty-two, on November 1, 1893, he had finished the manuscript. Just under two years later, on October 5, 1895, *The Red Badge of Courage: An Episode of the American Civil War* was published. Crane's potboiler became both a bestseller and a classic of American literature.

Crane was deliberately unspecific about the battle his young antihero, Henry Fleming, experienced. It was essential to his purpose, he wrote, "that I should make my battle a type and name no names. . . ." Yet the setting and scenes have such a ring of authenticity about them that it was hard to believe they could be made up, and veterans who read the novel quickly recognized Chancellorsville as the battle. In his typically indirect way Crane confirmed it. In a story called "The Veteran," published within a year of *The Red Badge of Courage,* Crane wrote of Henry Fleming in old age, remembering that first battle of his youth, when fear had sent him running. "That was at Chancellorsville," Henry says.

Where did Stephen Crane learn about the Civil War in general and Chancellorsville in particular? During the winter of 1892–93 Crane lived a bohemian life with three artist friends in a cramped studio on New York's East Twenty-third Street. Among their possessions was a stack of decade-old *Century* magazines containing the "Battles and Leaders of the Civil War" series. Crane pored over these old issues, absorbing much about the battles, fixing them visually from the multitude of illustrations that *Century* had commissioned for its war papers. Yet these participants' accounts, most of them by former officers, left him unsatisfied: "I wonder that *some* of these fellows don't tell how they *felt* in those scraps! They spout eternally of what they *did* but they are emotionless as rocks!"

Crane began work on his novel in March or April of 1893 in the New York studio, but soon moved to his brother William's lodge called Hartwood, in Sullivan County near Port Jervis, New York. For Crane this was almost a homecoming, and it was a critical step in the creation of *The Red Badge of Courage.* For Henry Fleming's introduction to war Crane enlisted him in the fictional 304th New York, and it was in Port Jervis that he found the model for the 304th.[14]

Crane's father, a Methodist pastor, had moved his family to Port Jervis when Stephen was seven years old. In 1862, when it was formed, the 124th New York had recruited men from Port Jervis, and in the postwar years the old soldiers would gather at the 124th's monument in the town park to reminisce about the war. A favorite reminiscence was their first battle, at Chancellorsville. The youthful Stephen Crane was an avid listener to these war stories.

At Hartwood and in Port Jervis Crane found what he needed for Henry Fleming's story. His brother William was expert in the histories of Chancellorsville and Gettysburg, and his library would have been invaluable to Stephen. The 124th New York's regimental history had been published in 1877. Another book believed useful to Crane was Wilbur F. Hinman's irreverent *Corporal Si Klegg and his "Pard"* (1889), rich with army slang and soldier dialect.

The closest student of this subject, Charles J. LaRocca, has discovered still another probable stock of source material for *The Red Badge of Courage* in the files of a local wartime newspaper called the *Whig Press* that had published soldiers' letters from the battlefronts. LaRocca found passages in these letters that parallel settings in the novel, and Crane seems to have recognized his debt to the *Whig Press* and its editor, John Hasbrouck, by naming an officer in Henry Fleming's company Lieutenant Hasbrouck.

There can be little doubt that Crane modeled Henry Fleming's regiment on the 124th New York. LaRocca demonstrates that the Chancellorsville record of the 124th of Franklin's brigade, Whipple's division, Third Army Corps, forms a framework for Henry Fleming's experiences in his first battle — the first battle, too, for the 124th. Henry's comrade Jim Conklin, whose death is so strikingly depicted by Crane, has as his namesake Private James H. Conklin on the roster of the 124th New York in this campaign.

As apparent as these sources and influences are, it is equally apparent that Stephen Crane crafted and shaped this material to his own use. And he stepped out of context when it suited him. There is a vivid scene during Henry's flight from the battle line when he stumbles into a hidden glade deep in the woods and finds there the moldering corpse of a Federal soldier. This was not characteristic of Chancellorsville — the two armies had not fought there before — but rather of the 1864 campaign in the same area, and the image may have been suggested to Crane by a Herman Melville war poem titled "The Armies of the Wilderness."

Stephen Crane was concerned that men from the war would reject his story of the war because (as he put it) "This damned young fool was not there." But he was at pains to absorb all he could from those who had been there, and then transcend what they told him with his own vision. Stephen Crane may not have been at Chancellorsville, but Henry Fleming certainly was.[15]

ACKNOWLEDGMENTS

The Joseph Hooker Papers, at the Huntington Library, are essential to an understanding of Chancellorsville, and I was privileged to have Edwin C. Fishel's expert guidance to their contents. I was privileged, too, to have prepublication access to his ground-breaking study of Civil War military intelligence, *The Secret War for the Union,* which is also essential to understanding Chancellorsville. On these and many other counts, my debt to Edwin Fishel is great.

Many other people were exceedingly generous with their time and expertise. Chief Historian Robert K. Krick at the Fredericksburg & Spotsylvania National Military Park shared his encyclopedic knowledge of the campaign and granted me a prepublication look at his study of Jackson at Chancellorsville, and he and Donald C. Pfanz guided me through the battlefield park's manuscript holdings. John J. Hennessy generously shared his important work on the Army of the Potomac in advance of publication, and led me to important research sources. William Marvel did the same, especially with the change of command from Burnside to Hooker. A. Wilson Greene allowed me an early look at his study of morale in the Army of the Potomac and his definitive paper on Stoneman's raid.

Peter Cozzens let me see the James S. Mitchell memoir, used here by courtesy of William Fleming and Frances Gaines Bales. Arthur Candenquist solved the mystery of "Union time" and "Confederate time." Russell B. Bailey shared source material on Cadmus M. Wilcox, Arthur Ruitberg on Berdan's Sharpshooters, Donald Wickman on the Vermont brigade, Earl McElfresh on the Clinton Beckwith memoir, Mark H. Dunkelman on the 154th New York. Others who kindly guided me to research sources and material were Margaretta Barton Colt, Daniel R. Weinberg, Bryce A. Suderow, Herbert M. Schiller, and Lauren Cook Burgess.

Once again, Betty L. Krimminger furnished invaluable research assistance. Others who helped with the research were Andrew Darien, Vesta Lee Gordon, and Jane G. Nardy.

George Skoch skillfully resolved the complexities of mapping this most complex of campaigns.

I am greatly indebted to the curatorial staffs of the manuscript collections used in this study. Particular thanks are due Michael P. Musick, the National Archives; Thomas Knoles, American Antiquarian Society; Margaret R. Goostray, Boston University Library; Susan Ravdin, Bowdoin College Library; M. N. Brown, John Hay Library, Brown University; Philip N. Cronenwett, Dartmouth College Library; James J. Holmberg, the Filson Club; Charlotte Ray, Georgia Department of Archives and History; Melissa Bush, Hargrett Library, University of Georgia; Karen E. Kearns, the Huntington Library; Eric L. Mundell, Indiana Historical Society; Retha W. Stephens, Kennesaw Mountain National Battlefield; Mary M. Ison and Harry Katz, Prints and Photographs Division, Library of Congress; Mary Linn Bandaries, Northwestern State University of Louisiana; Virginia H. Smith, Massachusetts Historical Society; Robert S. Cox, William L. Clements Library, University of Michigan; Nancy Bartlett, Bentley Historical Library, University of Michigan; Hampton Smith, Minnesota Historical Society; Michael Hennen, Mississippi Department of Archives and History; James Corsaro, New York State Library.

Also, John White, Southern Historical Collection, University of North Carolina; Gary J. Arnold, Ohio Historical Society; William F. Hannah, Old Colony Historical Society; Edward Skipworth, Rutgers University Libraries; Henry G. Fulmer, South Caroliniana Library; Richard J. Sommers and Michael J. Winey, U.S. Army Military History Institute; Jeffrey D. Marshall, University of Vermont Library; Diane B. Jacob, Virginia Military Institute; Laura Katz Smith, Virginia Polytechnic Institute and State University Libraries; Ervin L. Jordan, Jr., Alderman Library, University of Virginia; Wayne C. Mann, Western Michigan University; Ann K. Sindelar, Western Reserve Historical Society; Harold L. Miller, State Historical Society of Wisconsin; Judith Ann Schiff, Yale University Library; Teresa Roane, Valentine Museum; Corrine P. Hudgins, Museum of the Confederacy.

NOTES

Works cited by author and short title in the Notes will be found in full citation in the Bibliography. The abbreviation *OR* stands for: U.S. War Department, *The War of the Rebellion: A Compilation of the Official Records of the Union and Confederate Armies,* Series One, unless otherwise noted.

1: The Revolt of the Generals

1. Stephen W. Sears, *George B. McClellan: The Young Napoleon,* p. 329; Franklin and Smith to Lincoln, Dec. 20, 1862, *OR,* 21, p. 868; Lincoln to Franklin and Smith, Dec. 22, Lincoln, *The Collected Works of Abraham Lincoln,* ed. Roy P. Basler, 6, p. 15; James Longstreet in *Battles and Leaders of the Civil War,* eds. Robert U. Johnson and Clarence C. Buel, 3, p. 81; *OR,* 21, pp. 142, 899; Franklin testimony, *Report of the Joint Committee on the Conduct of the War,* 1 (1863), p. 712; Smith letter in *Magazine of American History,* 15 (1886), p. 197.

2. Newton, Cochrane testimony, *Report of Joint Committee,* 1 (1863), pp. 730–40, 740–46; John Cochrane, *The War for the Union: Memoir of Gen. John Cochrane* (New York, 1875), pp. 48–51; Lincoln to Burnside, Dec. 30, 1862, Lincoln, *Collected Works,* 6, p. 22.

3. Sears, *George B. McClellan,* pp. 235, 264–65; Burnside to Halleck, Dec. 17, 1862, *OR,* 21, pp. 66–67; *New York Times,* Dec. 23; Warren to fiancée, Apr. 15, 1863, Warren Papers, New York

State Library; Meade to wife, Jan. 26, George G. Meade, *The Life and Letters of George Gordon Meade,* 1, p. 351.

4. Burnside to Lincoln, Dec. 30, 1862, *OR,* 21, p. 900; Dec. 31, Gideon Welles, *Diary of Gideon Welles,* ed. Howard K. Beale (New York: Norton, 1960), 1, p. 211; Burnside testimony, *Report of Joint Committee,* 1 (1863), pp. 716–18.

5. Burnside to Lincoln, Jan. 1, 1863, W. F. Smith to Franklin, May 29, *OR,* 21, pp. 941–42, 1011; Burnside testimony, *Report of Joint Committee,* 1 (1863), p. 718; Burnside memorandum, May 25, RG 94, U.S. Generals' Reports, National Archives; William Marvel, *Burnside,* pp. 209–11; Franklin to Halleck, May 27, Halleck to Franklin, May 29, Burnside to Lincoln, Jan. 5, *OR,* 21, pp. 1008, 1009, 944–45. Burnside's chronology varied in his recountings of this episode, but the sequence narrated here — Burnside meeting alone with Lincoln on Dec. 31, writing his resignation letter dated Jan. 1 that night, then meeting Lincoln, Stanton, and Halleck on the morning of Jan. 1 — is confirmed by other sources.

6. Lincoln to Halleck, Jan. 1, 1863, Lin-

coln, *Collected Works*, 6, p. 31; Halleck to Burnside, Jan. 7, Halleck to Stanton, Jan. 1, *OR*, 21, pp. 953–54, 940–41.

7. Franklin to Halleck, June 6, 1863, *OR*, 21, p. 1011; Meade to wife, Jan. 2, Meade, *Life and Letters*, 1, pp. 394–95; Warren to brother, Dec. 18, 1862, Warren Papers, New York State Library; McClellan to Army of the Potomac, Mar. 14, 1862, McClellan, *The Civil War Papers of George B. McClellan*, ed. Stephen W. Sears, p. 211; William H. Withington to sister, Dec. 23, Michigan Historical Collections, Bentley Historical Library, University of Michigan; George W. Lambert diary, Dec. 16, Indiana Historical Society.

8. Samuel P. Heintzelman diary, Jan. 5, 1863, Heintzelman Papers, Library of Congress; Samuel Ward to S.L.M. Barlow, Jan. 5, Barlow Papers, Huntington Library; Henry Villard, *Memoirs of Henry Villard* (Boston: Houghton Mifflin, 1904), 1, p. 348; Salmon P. Chase, *Inside Lincoln's Cabinet: The Civil War Diaries of Salmon P. Chase*, ed. David Donald (New York: Longmans, Green, 1954), pp. 153–66; Hooker to Stanton, Dec. 4, 1862, Stanton Papers, Library of Congress; Hooker testimony, *Report of Joint Committee*, 1 (1863), pp. 670–71; Marsena R. Patrick diary, Jan. 17, 1863, Patrick Papers, Library of Congress.

9. *New York Times*, Jan. 13, 1863; Herman Haupt to Lincoln, Dec. 22, 1862, Stanton Papers, Library of Congress; Bruce Catton, *The Centennial History of the Civil War: Never Call Retreat*, pp. 60–63.

10. Lucius Fairchild to wife, Dec. 30, 1862, State Historical Society of Wisconsin; Edwin O. Wentworth to wife, Feb. 13, 1863, Library of Congress; Isaac Mann to wife, Jan. 23, Huntington Library; Hugh P. Roden to parents, Feb. 16, Schoff Collection, Clements Library, University of Michigan; Feb. 3, George Templeton Strong, *The Diary of George Templeton Strong: The Civil War, 1860–1865*, eds. Allan Nevins and Milton H. Thomas, p. 294; Joseph Medill to Elihu Washburne, Jan. 14, Washburne Pa-

pers, Library of Congress; Oliver Morton to Stanton, Feb. 9, Stanton Papers, Library of Congress; *Congressional Globe*, 37th Congress, 3rd Session, 1, p. 284–90.

11. William O. Stoddard in Gabor S. Boritt, *Lincoln and the Economics of the American Dream* (Memphis: Memphis State University Press, 1978), p. 271; Henry L. Abbott to George Perry, Dec. 21, 1862, Abbott, *Fallen Leaves: The Civil War Letters of Major Henry Livermore Abbott*, ed. Robert Garth Scott, p. 154.

12. Edward H. Wade to sister, Jan. 2, 1863, Schoff Collection, Clements Library, University of Michigan; Darius Couch memoir, p. 127, Old Colony Historical Society; Hubert Dilger to Lincoln, Mar. 25, Lincoln Papers, Library of Congress; M. Bain Folwell to mother, Jan. 24, Minnesota Historical Society; Henry Ropes to father, Jan. 5, Boston Public Library.

13. James A. Huston, "Logistical Support of Federal Armies in the Field," *Civil War History*, 7:1 (Mar. 1961), p. 40; Daniel G. McNamara, *The History of the Ninth Regiment Massachusetts Volunteer Infantry* (Boston: E. B. Stillings, 1899), p. 276; Perley report, *OR*, 21, p. 958; *Congressional Globe*, 37th Congress, 3rd Session, 1, p. 215; John T. Boyle to Peter Filbert, Jan. 13, 1863, U.S. Army Military History Institute; Carl Schurz to Lincoln, Jan. 24, Lincoln Papers, Library of Congress; Robert Goodyear to "Sarah," Feb. 14, U.S. Army Military History Institute.

14. McClellan to Lincoln, July 14, 1862, McClellan, *Civil War Papers*, p. 357; John E. Ryder to sister, Jan. 4, 1863, Michigan Historical Collections, Bentley Historical Library, University of Michigan; Sanford N. Truesdell to sister, Jan. 26, University of Chicago Library; Charles H. Brewster to sister, Feb. 12, Brewster, *When This Cruel War Is Over: The Civil War Letters of Charles Harvey Brewster*, ed. David W. Blight, p. 212.

15. Patrick diary, Dec. 26, 1862, Jan. 2, 11, 17, 1863, Library of Congress; Abner

R. Small, *The Sixteenth Maine Regiment in the War of the Rebellion, 1861–1865,* p. 93; Henry L. Abbott to George Perry, Feb. 1, Abbott, *Fallen Leaves,* p. 168; Regis de Trobriand, *Four Years with the Army of the Potomac,* p. 418; George H. Sharpe to Daniel Butterfield, Mar. 22, RG 393, Part 1, Entry 3980, National Archives; William C. Wiley to sister, Feb. 1, Pattee Library, Pennsylvania State University.

16. Hooker general orders, Jan. 30, 1863, Hooker to War Dept., Feb. 15, *OR,* 25:2, pp. 11–12, 77–78; Nov. 10, 1862 return, *OR,* 19:2, p. 569; Jan. 31, 1863 return, RG 94, Entry 65, National Archives; Halleck to Stanton, Feb. 18, Stanton Papers, Library of Congress; John Bigelow, Jr., *The Campaign of Chancellorsville,* p. 36; Hooker testimony, *Report of Joint Committee,* 1 (1865), p. 112; S. M. Carpenter to Frederic Hudson, Feb. 2, James Gordon Bennett Papers, Library of Congress. The one-in-ten desertion ratio (extrapolated by Bigelow from a now missing War Dept. document) and the Jan. 31 total of absentees (based on the original return in the National Archives rather than the return abstract in *OR,* 25:2, p. 15) apply only to the rolls of the eight Army of the Potomac corps then in the field, and excludes the Washington garrison.

17. George W. Barr to wife, Jan. 25, 1863, Schoff Collection, Clements Library, University of Michigan; Burnside general order, Jan. 20, *OR,* 21, p. 127; Henry W. Raymond, ed., "Excerpts from the Journal of Henry J. Raymond," *Scribner's Monthly,* 19:3 (Jan. 1880), p. 421; Jan. 19, 20, Charles S. Wainwright, *A Diary of Battle: The Personal Journals of Colonel Charles S. Wainwright, 1861–1865,* ed. Allan Nevins, pp. 157–58.

18. Samuel S. Partridge to brother, Jan. 25, 1863, Fredericksburg & Spotsylvania National Military Park; William Swinton in Frank Moore, ed., *The Rebellion Record: A Diary of American Events,* 6, Documents, p. 399; George H. Nichols to father, Jan. 25, Schoff Collec-

tion, Clements Library, University of Michigan; Alpheus S. Williams to daughter, Jan. 24, Williams, *From the Cannon's Mouth: The Civil War Letters of General Alpheus S. Williams,* ed. Milo M. Quaife, p. 159; Cornelius Van Santvoord, *The One Hundred and Twentieth Regiment, New York State Volunteers* (Roundout, N.Y.: Kingston Freeman, 1894), pp. 33–34.

19. Henry Ropes to father, Jan. 23, 1863, Boston Public Library; Raymond, "Excerpts from the Journal of Henry J. Raymond," *Scribner's Monthly,* 19:3 (Jan. 1880), pp. 420–22, 19:5 (Mar. 1880), pp. 703–4; Burnside general order (unissued), Jan. 23, *OR,* 21, pp. 998–99; Patrick diary, Jan. 4, Library of Congress; Burnside memorandum, May 24, RG 94, U.S. Generals' Reports, National Archives; Burnside testimony, *Report of Joint Committee,* 1 (1863), p. 720; Burnside to Lincoln, Jan. 23, *OR,* 21, p. 998. Hooker meant "dictator" not in its modern sense of tyrant, but in its more benign Roman sense as a general accepting supreme command, then selflessly relinquishing it after the crisis was past.

20. Stephen W. Sears, "The Court-Martial of Fitz John Porter," *MHQ,* 5:3 (Spring 1993), pp. 70–79; Porter to Manton Marble, Dec. 27, 1862, Marble Papers, Library of Congress; Porter to McClellan, Jan. 13, 1863, McClellan Papers, Library of Congress; Charles Russell Lowell to H. L. Higginson, Jan. 21, Edward W. Emerson, *Life and Letters of Charles Russell Lowell,* p. 232.

21. William F. Smith, *Autobiography of Major General William F. Smith, 1861–1864,* ed. Herbert M. Schiller, pp. 65–66; Smith letter in *Magazine of American History,* 15 (1886), p. 198; Burnside testimony, *Report of Joint Committee,* 1 (1863), p. 720; *New York Herald,* Jan. 25, 1863; Raymond, "Excerpts from the Journal of Henry J. Raymond," *Scribner's Monthly,* 19:5 (Mar. 1880), p. 705.

22. Halleck to Franklin, May 29, 1863, *OR,* 21, pp. 1008–9; Burnside testimony,

Report of Joint Committee, 1 (1863), pp. 721–22; Raymond, "Excerpts from the Journal of Henry J. Raymond," Scribner's Monthly, 19:5 (Mar. 1880), pp. 706–7; Smith, Autobiography, p. 66. Charles F. Benjamin's account (Battles and Leaders, 3, pp. 239–40) of an elaborately orchestrated change of command is undocumented and written long after the event, and is flatly contradicted by (among others) Halleck's contemporaneous account.

2: General Lee Knows His Business

1. Dunbar Rowland, ed., Jefferson Davis, Constitutionalist: His Letters, Papers and Speeches (Jackson: Mississippi Department of Archives and History, 1923), 5, pp. 390–95; Charleston Mercury, Dec. 15, 1862.
2. John Esten Cooke, A Life of Robert E. Lee (New York: D. Appleton, 1871), p. 184; Lee to daughter, July 28, 1862, Robert E. Lee, The Wartime Papers of R. E. Lee, ed. Clifford Dowdey, p. 240; John G. Walker in Battles and Leaders, 2, pp. 605–6; James Longstreet in Battles and Leaders, 3, p. 70; Lee to wife, Feb. 23, 1863, Lee, Wartime Papers, p. 408.
3. Francis E. Pierce, "Civil War Letters of Francis Edwin Pierce of the 108th New York Volunteer Infantry," ed. Blake McKelvey, Rochester Historical Society Publications, 22 (1944), pp. 160–61; Feb. 16, 1863, John S. Tucker, "The Diary of John S. Tucker: Confederate Soldier from Alabama," ed. Gary Wilson, Alabama Historical Quarterly, 43:1 (Spring 1981), p. 22; Jedediah Hotchkiss to wife, Dec. 21, 1862, Jan. 21, 1863, Hotchkiss Papers, Library of Congress; Jan. 7, Jedediah Hotchkiss, Make Me a Map of the Valley: The Civil War Journal of Stonewall Jackson's Topographer, ed. Archie P. McDonald, p. 107; J. B. Walton to Longstreet, Dec. 23, 1862, OR, 51:2, pp. 665–66.
4. U.S. Coast Survey, Rappahannock River, RG 77, Z-423, National Archives. Although Fredericksburg's frontage on the Rappahannock actually faces northeast, for purposes of clarity this narrative refers throughout to the left (Federal) bank of the Rappahannock as the north bank, and the right (Confederate) bank as the south bank.
5. Angus James Johnston II, Virginia Railroads in the Civil War, pp. 4, 115–16; Report on Railroads, 1863, Joseph Hooker Papers, Huntington Library; Douglas Southall Freeman, R. E. Lee: A Biography, 2, p. 441; Lee to Davis, Jan. 13, 1863, OR, 21, p. 1092; Alexander S. Pendleton to mother, Jan. 20, Apr. 26, in Susan Pendleton Lee, Memoirs of William Nelson Pendleton, pp. 252, 256–57; Jedediah Hotchkiss to wife, Jan. 21, Hotchkiss Papers, Library of Congress.
6. Dec. 31, 1862 return, OR, 21, p. 1082 (the figure 91,093 is "aggregate present," or all those requiring rations); Johnston, Virginia Railroads, pp. 128, 132, 158; June 8, 20, 1863, J. B. Jones, A Rebel War Clerk's Diary, ed. Howard Swiggett, 1, pp. 343, 354; Lee to Jackson, Feb. 7, OR, 51:2, p. 678. By the fall of 1864 superintendent Ruth's disloyalty was certain, but there is as well evidence of at least inefficiency in the railroad's operations during the winter of 1862–63 (Meriwether Stuart, "Samuel Ruth and General R. E. Lee: Disloyalty and the Line of Supply to Fredericksburg, 1862–63," Virginia Magazine of History and Biography, 71:1 [Jan. 1963], pp. 35–109). Gen. McLaws reported the speed limit on the R.F. & P. reduced to ten miles an hour (McLaws to wife, Apr. 11, Southern Historical Collection, University of North Carolina).
7. Lee to Agnes Lee, Feb. 6, 1863, Lee to wife, Feb. 23, Lee, Wartime Papers, pp. 400, 407–8.
8. Lee general order, Dec. 24, 1862, OR, 21, p. 1077; Pendleton to Lee, Feb. 11, 1863, Lee to Pendleton, Apr. 6, OR, 25:2, pp. 618, 709; Frank M. Coker to wife, Mar. 18, Heidler Collection, Hargrett Library, University of Georgia; John Hampden Chamberlayne to

mother, Jan. 1, Feb. 11, Chamberlayne, *Ham Chamberlayne—Virginian: Letters and Papers of an Artillery Officer,* ed. C. G. Chamberlayne, pp. 151, 156; Dec. 27, 1862, Jan. 5–14, Feb. 8, 13, 1863, Henry Robinson Berkeley, *Four Years in the Confederate Artillery: The Diary of Private Henry Robinson Berkeley,* ed. William H. Runge, pp. 40–41, 43, 44.

9. Lee to G.W.C. Lee, [Feb.] 5, 1863, Lee Papers, Perkins Library, Duke University; Lee to Seddon, Jan. 26, *OR,* 25:2, p. 598; Seddon to Lee, Feb. 15, Lee to Longstreet, Mar. 16, *OR,* 18, pp. 878, 922; Dec. 31, 1862 return, *OR,* 21, p. 1082; Mar. 9–10, 1863 returns, *OR,* 18, pp. 915–16. The total of 20,076 ordered south was "aggregate present," those requiring rations.

10. Richard D. Goff, *Confederate Supply,* pp. 17–18, 79; Lee to Seddon, Mar. 27, 1863, *OR,* 25:2, p. 687; W. R. Montgomery to aunt, Apr. 19, South Caroliniana Library; William Calder to mother, Apr. 13, Southern Historical Collection, University of North Carolina; Edgar Allan Jackson to sister, Mar. 10, Virginia State Library; Bell Irvin Wiley, *The Life of Johnny Reb,* pp. 104–5; S. G. Pryor to wife, Mar. 8, Pryor, *A Post of Honor: The Pryor Letters, 1861–63,* ed. Charles R. Adams, Jr., p. 323; Thomas M. Hightower to fiancée, Jan. 29, Georgia Department of Archives and History.

11. S. G. Pryor to wife, Feb. 20, 1863, Pryor, *Post of Honor,* pp. 316–17; Frank M. Coker to wife, Mar. 21, Heidler Collection, Hargrett Library, University of Georgia; Jubal A. Early, *Autobiographical Sketch and Narrative of the War Between the States,* pp. 188–89; Apr. 17, John P. Oden, "The End of Oden's War: A Confederate Captain's Diary," ed. Michael Barton, *Alabama Historical Quarterly,* 43:2 (Summer 1981), p. 77; Lee to Seddon, Mar. 27, *OR,* 25:2, p. 687; Sidney J. Richardson to parents, Mar. 31, Georgia Department of Archives and History; Robert K. Krick, *Parker's Virginia Battery C.S.A.,* p. 110; George P. Wallace to sister, Mar. 31, West Virginia Collection, West Virginia University Library; Leonidas Torrence to brother, Feb. 9, Torrence, "The Road to Gettysburg: The Diary and Letters of Leonidas Torrence of the Gaston Guards," ed. Haskell Monroe, *North Carolina Historical Review,* 36 (Oct. 1959), p. 502; Alfred Zachry memoir, *Civil War Times Illustrated,* 33:4 (Sept.–Oct. 1994), pp. 72–73; Elias Davis to wife, Apr. 10, Southern Historical Collection, University of North Carolina.

12. Leonidas Torrence to sister, Apr. 12, 1863, Torrence, "The Road to Gettysburg," p. 505; Harrison P. Griffith, *Variosa: A Collection of Sketches, Essays and Verses,* p. 53; William H. Hill diary, Jan.–Mar. 1863, Mississippi Department of Archives and History; Jim Mobley to brother, Feb. 1, Mills Lane, ed., *"Dear Mother: Don't grieve about me . . .": Letters from Georgia Soldiers in the Civil War,* pp. 220–21; D. Augustus Dickert, *History of Kershaw's Brigade,* pp. 206–7; John W. Melhorn diary, Feb. 24, Stanford University Libraries; Charles M. Blackford to daughter, Feb. 2, in Susan Leigh Blackford, ed., *Letters from Lee's Army,* pp. 165–66; Barry G. Benson memoir, Southern Historical Collection, University of North Carolina; Edgar Allan Jackson to sister, Mar. 10, Virginia State Library.

13. John W. Melhorn diary, Jan. 21, 1863, Stanford University Libraries; Hotchkiss to wife, Jan. 11, Hotchkiss Papers, Library of Congress; New report, *OR,* 21, p. 1098; diary, Jan. 6, Hotchkiss, *Make Me a Map,* p. 106; Charles M. Blackford to wife, Jan. 10, in Susan Blackford, *Letters from Lee's Army,* pp. 157–58; William H. Hill diary, Feb. 21, 23, Mississippi Department of Archives and History; William M. Owen, *In Camp and Battle with the Washington Artillery of New Orleans,* pp. 205–6; G. Moxley Sorrel, *Recollections of a Confederate Staff Officer,* ed. Bell Irvin Wiley (New York: Neale, 1905), pp. 134–35; Barry G. Benson memoir, Southern Historical Collection, University of North Carolina. The Washington Artillery re-

peated its program that fall, on October 22, in Petersburg.

14. William G. Morris to wife, Dec. 28, 1862, Southern Historical Collection, University of North Carolina; Charles B. Fairchild, *History of the 27th Regiment N.Y. Vols.* (Binghamton, N.Y.: Carl & Matthews, 1888), p. 137; Dec. 23, Charles B. Haydon, *For Country, Cause & Leader: The Civil War Journal of Charles B. Haydon*, ed. Stephen W. Sears (New York: Ticknor & Fields, 1993), p. 300; Edmund S. Stephens to parents, Mar. 17, 1863, Northwestern State University of Louisiana; Rufus R. Dawes, *Service with the Sixth Wisconsin Volunteers*, p. 142; J. S. Graham to sister, Jan. 6, Janice Bartlett Reeder McFadden, ed., *Aunt and the Soldier Boys from Cross Creek Village, Pennsylvania*, pp. 62–63; Frederick L. Hitchcock, *War from the Inside*, p. 185.

15. William H. Hill diary, Jan. 5, Apr. 8, 18, 1863, Mississippi Department of Archives and History; John S. Apperson diary, Mar. 7, Virginia Polytechnic Institute and State University Libraries; Robert A. Moore, *A Life for the Confederacy, as Recorded in the Pocket Diaries of Pvt. Robert A. Moore*, ed. James W. Silver, pp. 138–42. Hospital steward Apperson listed 12 smallpox deaths in the Second Corps in March (Apperson diary, Apr. 1).

16. R. B. Hudgens to uncle, Apr. 12, 1863, Boatright Papers, Southern Historical Collection, University of North Carolina; Wiley, *Life of Johnny Reb*, pp. 182–83; B. T. Lacy narrative, R. L. Dabney Papers, Southern Historical Collection; William H. Hill diary, Feb. 19, Mar. 15, Mississippi Department of Archives and History.

17. Frank M. Parker to wife, Apr. 11, 1863, North Carolina State Archives; William P. Lloyd diary, Apr. 30, Southern Historical Collection, University of North Carolina; Lee to Seddon, Feb. 11, *OR*, 51:2, p. 680; Mar. 31 return, Bigelow, *Chancellorsville*, p. 49.

18. Mar. 21, 1863, Edmund D. Patterson, *Yankee Rebel: The Civil War Journal of Edmund DeWitt Patterson*, ed. John G. Barrett, pp. 96–97; W. D. Pender to W. H. Taylor, Apr. 23, *OR*, 25:2, pp. 746–47; Z. B. Vance to Jefferson Davis, May 13, *OR*, 51:2, p. 709; Charles E. DeNoon to parents, Jan. 16, DeNoon, *Charlie's Letters: The Correspondence of Charles E. DeNoon*, ed. Richard T. Couture, p. 118; Feb. 28, Mar. 16, Bartlett Y. Malone, *Whipt 'em Everytime: The Diary of Bartlett Yancey Malone*, ed. William Whatley Pierson, Jr. (Jackson, Tenn.: McCowat-Mercer Press, 1960), pp. 73–74; Leonidas Torrence to mother, Mar. 28, Torrence, "Road to Gettysburg," p. 504; John F. Coghill to father, Mar. 29, Southern Historical Collection, University of North Carolina; Spencer G. Welch to wife, Mar. 5, Welch, *A Confederate Surgeon's Letters to His Wife*, pp. 44–45; Frank Paxton to wife, Feb. 20, Paxton, *The Civil War Letters of General Frank "Bull" Paxton, CSA*, ed. John Gallatin Paxton, p. 74.

19. *Richmond Dispatch*, May 29, 1862; *Charleston Mercury*, July 25, 1861; *Richmond Daily Whig*, June 16, 1862; C. Vann Woodward, ed., *Mary Chesnut's Civil War*, p. 375; Peter W. Alexander, "Confederate Chieftains," *Southern Literary Messenger*, 35 (Jan. 1863), pp. 36–37; *New Orleans Crescent*, Feb. 15, 1862.

20. James Power Smith, "Stonewall Jackson in Winter Quarters at Moss Neck," Hotchkiss Papers, Library of Congress; James Power Smith, "With Stonewall Jackson in the Army of Northern Virginia," *Southern Historical Society Papers*, 43 (1920), pp. 37–39, 41. Some accounts have Jackson hosting Christmas dinner in the outbuilding on the Moss Neck property he used as his military office, but that space was far too small for the number of guests described by Smith. The dinner was surely held in the main house.

21. *Charleston Mercury*, June 20, 1862; Hampton report, *OR*, 21, p. 696.

22. Stuart report, *OR*, 21, pp. 731–35; diary, Jan. 2, 1863, Moore, *A Life for the Confederacy*, p. 128; Channing Price to sister, Jan. 2, Southern Historical Col-

lection, University of North Carolina; *Richmond Examiner,* Jan. 2; Williams to daughter, Dec. 31, 1862, Williams, *From the Cannon's Mouth,* p. 156. According to Channing Price, the Federals "were in great alarm, and orders were telegraphed to destroy everything in case of our attacking them." Apparently these messages were sent uncoded.

23. Lee to Seddon, Feb. 14, 1863, Lee to Davis, Feb. 18, *OR,* 25:2, pp. 623, 631; Fitzhugh Lee, Averell reports, *OR,* 25:1, pp. 24–25; Lee to Seddon, Feb. 28, *OR,* 25:2, p. 646.

24. Douglas Southall Freeman, *Lee's Lieutenants: A Study in Command,* 2, pp. 414–19, 504–9; Lenoir Chambers, *Stonewall Jackson,* 2, pp. 316–17; James I. Robertson, Jr., *The Stonewall Brigade,* p. 18.

25. A. P. Hill to R. H. Chilton, Jan. 29, 1863, *OR,* 19:2, p. 733; Jackson to Lee, Apr. 24, in Freeman, *Lee's Lieutenants,* 2, p. 514. The Jackson–A. P. Hill feud is detailed in James I. Robertson, Jr., *General A. P. Hill: The Story of a Confederate Warrior.*

26. Stephen W. Sears, *To the Gates of Richmond: The Peninsula Campaign,* p. 321; Pendleton to Lee, Feb. 11, 1863, *OR,* 25:2, pp. 614–18; Lee to Seddon, Dec. 5, 1862, *OR,* 21, p. 1047. The composition of the Confederate artillery battalions is in Appendix I.

27. Lee to Trimble, Mar. 8, 1863, *OR,* 25:2, p. 658; McLaws to wife, Apr. 13, Southern Historical Collection, University of North Carolina.

3: Joe Hooker Takes Command

1. Walter H. Hebert, *Fighting Joe Hooker,* pp. 25–33, 39–40; *McClellan's Own Story* draft, McClellan Papers, Library of Congress; Sept. 9, 1863, John Hay, *Lincoln and the Civil War in the Diaries and Letters of John Hay,* ed. Tyler Dennett (New York: Dodd, Mead, 1939), p. 86. For investigations into Hooker's alleged drinking, see Appendix III.

2. Halleck to William T. Sherman, Sept. 16, 1864, in Sherman, *Memoirs* (1885; Library of America edition, 1990), p. 590; Hooker to Samuel P. Bates, June 28, 1878, Bates Collection, Pennsylvania Historical and Museum Commission, Pennsylvania State Archives; Hooker testimony, *Report of Joint Committee,* 1 (1865), p. 112.

3. Hebert, *Fighting Joe Hooker,* pp. 47–50, 91, 123; Lincoln to J.F.K. Mansfield, June 19, 1861, Lincoln, *Collected Works,* 4, p. 413; *San Francisco Chronicle,* Nov. 1, 1879; John Pope in *Battles and Leaders,* 2, p. 465; Bigelow, *Chancellorsville,* p. 6; Henry F. Young to wife, Apr. 11, 1863, State Historical Society of Wisconsin; *Harper's Weekly,* Feb. 7; Daniel Larned memorandum, Larned Papers, Library of Congress; Hooker testimony, *Report of Joint Committee,* 1 (1863), p. 668.

4. Jan. 26, 1863, Orville H. Browning, *The Diary of Orville Hickman Browning,* eds. Theodore C. Pease and James G. Randall (Springfield: Illinois State Historical Library, 1925, 1933), 1, p. 619; Lincoln to Hooker, Jan. 26, Lincoln, *Collected Works,* 6, pp. 78–79.

5. Burnside, Hooker general orders, Jan. 26, 1863, *OR,* 25:2, pp. 4–5; Daniel Larned to Mary B. Burnside, Jan. 28, Larned Papers, Library of Congress; Zenas R. Bliss memoir, 4, pp. 48–49, U.S. Army Military History Institute; Patrick diary, Jan. 26, Library of Congress.

6. Noah Brooks, *Washington in Lincoln's Time,* p. 56; Horace Emerson to brother, Dec. 31, 1862, Schoff Collection, Clements Library, University of Michigan; David Leigh to Henry Drumgold, Mar. 3, 1863, Special Collections, Dartmouth College Library; William H. Folwell to fiancée, Feb. 3, Minnesota Historical Society; John E. Ryder to sister, Mar. 5, Michigan Historical Collections, Bentley Historical Library, University of Michigan; John L. Smith, *History of the Corn Exchange Regiment, 118th Pennsylvania Volunteers,* pp. 166–67.

7. Henry L. Abbott to father, Jan. 27,

1863, Abbott, *Fallen Leaves,* p. 165; Henry Ropes to father, Jan. 26, Boston Public Library; Charles Francis Adams, Jr. to father, Jan. 30, Worthington Ford, ed., *A Cycle of Adams Letters* (Boston: Houghton Mifflin, 1920), 1, pp. 249–50; John Gibbon, *Personal Recollections of the Civil War,* p. 107; Meade to wife, Jan. 26, Apr. 12, Meade, *Life and Letters,* 1, pp. 351, 365; Jan. 31, Wainwright, *Diary of Battle,* pp. 161–62; Margaret Leech, *Reveille in Washington, 1860–1865* (New York: Harper & Brothers, 1941), p. 264. The term "hooker" for a prostitute long pre-dated the Civil War (*The American Heritage Dictionary,* 3rd edition, p. 869). By one account, Washington's Second Ward brothels were still referred to as Hooker's Division a half century later (E. N. Gilpin to James H. Wilson, Apr. 7, 1911, Bigelow Papers, Library of Congress).

8. Jan. 26, 1863, Strong, *Diary,* p. 290; Elizabeth Blair Lee to Samuel P. Lee, Jan. 27, Lee, *Wartime Washington: The Civil War Letters of Elizabeth Blair Lee,* ed. Virginia Jeans Laas, p. 237; *New York Times,* Feb. 12.

9. Heintzelman diary, Jan. 26, 1863, Library of Congress; Heintzelman to Halleck, Jan. 26, War Dept. general order, Feb. 2, *OR,* 25:2, pp. 3–4, 42; Hooker testimony, *Report of Joint Committee,* 1 (1865), p. 111; Jan. 31 return, *OR,* 25:2, p. 29. In addition to a separate Department of Washington, the Middle Department headquartered in Baltimore was reorganized at this time, removing an additional 7,596 garrison troops on the upper Potomac from the rolls of the Army of the Potomac (Jan. 20 return, *OR,* 21, p. 987).

10. War Dept. general order, Jan. 25, 1863, *OR,* 25:2, p. 3; Sumner testimony, *Report of Joint Committee,* 1 (1863), p. 660; Hooker special order, Feb. 4, *OR,* 25:2, p. 53; Hooker to Stanton, Feb. 25, 1864, *OR,* 32:2, p. 468; Hooker testimony, *Report of Joint Committee,* 1 (1865), pp. 111–12; Halleck to Francis Lieber, Aug. 4, 1863, Lieber Papers, Huntington Library.

11. Hooker to Bates, May 29, June 29, 1878, Bates Collection, Pennsylvania Historical and Museum Commission; Patrick diary, Feb. 9, 1863, Library of Congress; Hooker to Stanton, Apr. 23, *OR,* 25:2, pp. 855–56. For Hooker's response to Lincoln's letter, see Appendix III.

12. Hooker to Lorenzo Thomas, Jan. 26, 1863, RG 107, M-473:52, National Archives; Stephen W. Sears, "The Ordeal of General Stone," *MHQ,* 7:2 (Winter 1994), pp. 46–56; Hooker general order, Jan. 29, *OR,* 25:2, p. 6; Julia L. Butterfield, *A Biographical Memorial of General Daniel Butterfield,* pp. 10, 120; Joseph L. Whitney and Stephen W. Sears, "The True Story of Taps," *Blue & Gray,* 10:6 (Aug. 1993), pp. 30–33; Hebert, *Fighting Joe Hooker,* p. 172.

13. Hooker general order, Feb. 5, 1863, *OR,* 25:2, p. 51; John J. Hennessy, "The Forgotten Legion: The Subordinate Command of the Army of the Potomac."

14. Sigel to Hooker, with Lincoln endorsement, Feb. 12, 1863, *OR,* 25:2, pp. 70–71; Hooker to Stanton, Mar. 20, RG 107, M-473:52, National Archives; Schurz to Lincoln, Apr. 6, Lincoln Papers, Library of Congress; Oliver Otis Howard, *Autobiography of Oliver Otis Howard,* pp. 348–49; Elijah H. C. Cavins to wife, Apr. 1, Cavins, *The Civil War Letters of Col. Elijah H. C. Cavins, 14th Indiana,* ed. Barbara A. Smith, p. 150.

15. Thomas J. Fleming, "A Husband's Revenge," *American Heritage,* 18:3 (Apr. 1967), pp. 65–75. Army of the Potomac order of battle: Dec. 11, 1862, *OR,* 21, pp. 48–61 — Dec. 31, 1862, *OR,* 21, pp. 925–38 — Jan. 31, 1863, *OR,* 25:2, pp. 16–28 — May 1, 1863, *OR,* 25:2, pp. 156–70.

16. Hooker general order, Feb. 5, 1863, *OR,* 25:2, p. 51; Stoneman general order, Feb. 12, *OR,* 25:2, pp. 71–72; Army of the Potomac order of battle, May 1, *OR,* 25:2, pp. 169–70; Stephen Z. Starr, *The Union Cavalry in the Civil War,* 1, pp. 339–40.

17. Hunt testimony, *Report of Joint Commit-*

tee, 1 (1865), pp. 89–94; Hunt report, *OR*, 25:1, p. 252; Hooker to Bates, Aug. 28, 1876, Bates Collection, Pennsylvania Historical and Museum Commission.

18. Hooker general order, Mar. 30, 1863, *OR*, 25:2, p. 167; Butterfield testimony, *Report of Joint Committee*, 1 (1865), p. 74; Edwin C. Fishel, "Pinkerton and McClellan: Who Deceived Whom?" *Civil War History*, 34:2 (June 1988), pp. 115–42; Hooker to Patrick, Feb. 4, RG 393, Part 1, Entry 3980, National Archives; Patrick diary, Feb. 10, 11, Library of Congress. The development of the Bureau of Military Information is described in the definitive work by Edwin C. Fishel, *The Secret War for the Union: The Untold Story of Military Intelligence in the Civil War*, Ch. 12.

19. Hooker general order, Jan. 30, 1863, Hooker to War Dept., Feb. 15, S. Williams to Adams Express Co., Feb. 13, Butterfield to Samuel Magaw, Feb. 1, *OR*, 25:2, pp. 11–12, 79–80, 73, 36–37; Hooker to Patrick, Jan. 28, Patrick to John A. Kennedy, Feb. 5, RG 393, Part 1, Entry 3980, National Archives; S. Williams to A. S. Williams, Feb. 18, Hooker to War Dept., Feb. 6, *OR*, 25:2, pp. 86, 52; president's proclamation, Mar. 10, Lincoln, *Collected Works*, 6, pp. 132–33; Hooker to War Dept., Mar. 20, *OR*, 25:2, p. 149; Joshua R. Giddings to Stanton, Mar. 9, RG 107, M-221:228, National Archives; Mar. 31 return, Bigelow, *Chancellorsville*, p. 49.

20. James W. Geary, *We Need Men: The Union Draft in the Civil War* (De Kalb: Northern Illinois University Press, 1991), pp. 65–67; Edwin Weller to father, Mar. 29, 1863, Weller, *A Civil War Courtship: The Letters of Edwin Weller from Antietam to Atlanta*, ed. William Walton, p. 30; John E. Ryder to mother, Mar. 25, Michigan Historical Collections, Bentley Historical Library, University of Michigan.

21. Hooker general order, Jan. 30, 1863, *OR*, 25:2, pp. 11–12; Chester K. Leach to wife, Mar. 19, Special Collections, University of Vermont Library; Hooker to Bates, Dec. 8, 1876, Bates Collection, Pennsylvania Historical and Museum Commission; Sanford N. Truesdell to sister, Mar. 10, 1863, University of Chicago Library.

22. Julia Butterfield, *Memorial of General Butterfield*, pp. 116–17; Hooker to Bates, Dec. 8, 1876, Bates Collection, Pennsylvania Historical and Museum Commission; Hooker circular, Mar. 21, 1863, Hooker to War Dept., Feb. 2, *OR*, 25:2, pp. 152, 38.

23. Hooker general orders, Feb. 7, Mar. 3, 1863, *OR*, 25:2, pp. 57, 119–22; Huston, "Logistical Support of Federal Armies," pp. 40–41; Williams to daughter, Mar. 20, Williams, *From the Cannon's Mouth*, p. 169; Jesse B. Young, *What a Boy Saw in the Army* (Boston: Hunt and Eaton, 1894), p. 212; William W. Folwell to fiancée, Feb. 18, Minnesota Historical Society.

24. Lee to Isaac Trimble, Mar. 8, 1863, *OR*, 25:2, p. 658; Herman Haupt, *Reminiscences of General Herman Haupt*, pp. 165–66; McCallum to Stanton, Apr. 7, *OR*, Series Three, 3, pp. 119–20.

25. Hooker to Stanton, Dec. 4, 1862, Stanton Papers, Library of Congress; Hooker to Bates, June 7, 1877, Bates Collection, Pennsylvania Historical and Museum Commission; Butterfield memorandum, Feb. 27, 1863, *OR*, 25:2, p. 110; J. Cutler Andrews, *The North Reports the Civil War*, p. 343; Patrick diary, Mar. 16, 18, Library of Congress; Hooker general order, Apr. 30, *OR*, 25:2, p. 316; Hooker to Associated Press, June 18, *OR*, 27:2, p. 192.

26. Matthew Marvin to brother, Dec. 24, 1862, Minnesota Historical Society; William Aughinbaugh diary, Jan. 2, 1863, Schoff Collection, Clements Library, University of Michigan; Lucius L. Shattuck to "Gill," Feb. 6, Michigan Historical Collections, Bentley Historical Library, University of Michigan; Nathaniel Parmeter diary, Apr. 15, Ohio Historical Society; Samuel Fiske, *Mr. Dunn Browne's Experiences in the Army*, pp. 134–35; Feb. 8, 19, Wainwright, *Diary of Battle*, pp. 164, 167;

Apr. 2, Robert S. Robertson, "Diary of the War," eds. Charles N. and Rosemary Walker, *Old Fort News*, 28:2 (Apr.–June 1965), pp. 88–89.

27. John D. Billings, *Hardtack and Coffee, or The Unwritten Story of Army Life*, pp. 113–17; Horace Emerson to brother, Feb. 23, 1863, Schoff Collection, Clements Library, University of Michigan; Jan. 1, Isaac L. Taylor, "Campaigning with the First Minnesota: A Civil War Diary," ed. Hazel C. Wolf, *Minnesota History*, 25 (Sept. 1944), p. 240; Edward H. Wade to sister, Jan. 25, Schoff Collection; Edwin O. Wentworth to wife, Mar. 31, Library of Congress; Samuel S. Partridge to brother, Feb. 10, Fredericksburg & Spotsylvania National Military Park; Henry Ropes to father, Mar. 14, Boston Public Library; John V. Hadley to Mary Jane Hill, Feb. 7, Hadley, "An Indiana Soldier in Love and War: The Civil War Letters of John V. Hadley," ed. James I. Robertson, Jr., *Indiana Magazine of History*, 59:3 (Sept. 1963), pp. 228–29.

28. Henry M. Howell to mother, Mar. 8, 1863, Charles J. LaRocca, ed., *This Regiment of Heroes: A Compilation of Primary Materials Pertaining to the 124th New York State Volunteers*, p. 105; Chester Ballard to parents, Apr. 3, Schoff Collection, Clements Library, University of Michigan; Chester K. Leach to wife, Mar. 19, Special Collections, University of Vermont Library; Matthew Marvin diary, Feb. 16, Minnesota Historical Society.

29. Charles Ward to family, Mar. 5, 1863, American Antiquarian Society; James M. Madden and Ronald P. McGovern, "A Wedding in Camp," *Blue & Gray*, 9:3 (Feb. 1992), pp. 22–24.

30. Thomas F. Galwey, *The Valiant Hours* (Harrisburg, Pa.: Stackpole, 1961), pp. 77–79; D. P. Conyngham, *The Irish Brigade and Its Campaigns* (New York: P. Donahoe, 1867), pp. 373–74; Peter Welsh to wife, Mar. 19, 1863, Welsh, *Irish Green and Union Blue: The Civil War Letters of Peter Welsh*, ed. Lawrence Frederick Kohl (New York: Fordham University Press, 1986), p. 79; Edward

K. Gould, *Major-General Hiram G. Berry*, pp. 241–43; James S. Mitchell memoir, William Fleming Collection; Charles E. Goddard to mother, Mar. 26, Minnesota Historical Society; Trobriand, *Four Years with the Army of the Potomac*, pp. 427–28; Samuel S. Partridge to brother, Mar. 29, Fredericksburg & Spotsylvania National Military Park; Mar. 28, Wainwright, *Diary of Battle*, pp. 174–75.

31. H. N. Hunt to wife, Apr. 17, 1863, Samuel S. Partridge to brother, Apr. 10, Fredericksburg & Spotsylvania National Military Park; Samuel E. Pingree letter, Apr. 9, Kelly A. Nolin, ed., "The Civil War Letters of S. E. and S. M. Pingree, 1862–1864," *Vermont History*, 63:2 (Spring 1995), pp. 92–93; Elijah H. C. Cavins to wife, Jan. 19, Cavins, *Civil War Letters*, p. 132; Adrian R. Root to mother, Apr. 5, Buffalo and Erie County Historical Society; Solomon Newton to mother, Apr. 12, Newton, "Letters to Mother from a Union Volunteer," *Yankee Magazine* (June 1961), p. 29.

32. George T. Stevens, *Three Years in the Sixth Corps* (New York: D. Van Nostrand, 1870), p. 183; Alfred Bellard, *Gone for a Soldier: The Civil War Memoirs of Private Alfred Bellard*, ed. David Herbert Donald, p. 210; Cyrus R. Stone to parents, Mar. 11, Minnesota Historical Society.

33. James T. Miller to brother, Mar. 28, 1863, Schoff Collection, Clements Library, University of Michigan; John E. Ryder to sister, Mar. 29, Michigan Historical Collections, Bentley Historical Library, University of Michigan; George Fairfield diary, Mar. 26, State Historical Society of Wisconsin; Sanford McCall to niece, Mar. 10, Archives and Regional History Collections, Western Michigan University.

34. Edmund English memoir, Huntington Library; Couch memoir, p. 128, Old Colony Historical Society; Henry L. Abbott to George Perry, Mar. 10, 1863, Abbott, *Fallen Leaves*, p. 170; William W. Folwell to fiancée, Mar. 6, Minne-

sota Historical Society; Charles Ward to mother, Apr. 14, American Antiquarian Society; *New York Times,* Mar. 1.

35. Schurz to Lincoln, Jan. 24, 1863, Lincoln Papers, Library of Congress; Alexander K. McClure, *Recollections of Half a Century* (Salem, Mass.: Salem Press, 1902), p. 347; Selden Connor to father, Mar. 25, John Hay Library, Brown University.

4: The Highest Expectations

1. D. M. Gilmore, "Cavalry: . . . The Engagements at Kelly's Ford and Gettysburg," Minnesota MOLLUS, *Glimpses of the Nation's Struggle,* 2nd Ser. (St. Paul, 1890), pp. 38–44; Frank Moore, ed., *Anecdotes, Poetry and Incidents of the War, North and South, 1860–1865* (New York, 1867), p. 305; Averell report, *OR,* 25:1, pp. 47–48; A. B. Isham, "The Cavalry of the Army of the Potomac," Ohio MOLLUS, *Sketches of War History, 1861–1865,* 5 (Cincinnati, 1903), p. 313; Isaac Silver report, Mar. 13, 1863, "Organization and strength of force comprising the present Army of Northern Virg.," Apr. 28, RG 393, Part 1, Entry 3980, Bureau of Military Information, National Archives.

2. Fitzhugh Lee report, *OR,* 25:1, pp. 60–61; John Bigelow, Jr., "The Battle of Kelly's Ford," *Cavalry Journal,* 21 (1910), pp. 5–11; Frederic Denison, *Sabres and Spurs: The First Regiment Rhode Island Cavalry in the Civil War, 1861–1865* (Central Falls, R.I., 1876), p. 202; Averell report, *OR,* 25:1, p. 48; Jacob B. Cooke, "The Battle of Kelly's Ford, March 17, 1863," *Personal Narratives of Events in the War of the Rebellion,* Rhode Island Soldiers and Sailors Historical Society, 3rd Ser. (Providence, 1887), No. 19.

3. Fitzhugh Lee, "Chancellorsville," *Southern Historical Society Papers,* 7 (1887), p. 555; Stuart, Fitzhugh Lee reports, *OR,* 25:1, pp. 59, 61–62; R. E. Lee report, *OR,* 21, p. 547; H. H. Matthewe, "Major John Pelham, Confederate Hero," *Southern Historical Society Papers,* 38 (1910), p. 382, Averell report, *OR,* 25:1, pp. 49–52; Harry Gilmor, *Four Years in the Saddle* (New York: Harper & Brothers, 1866), pp. 58–69.

4. Frank W. Hess, "The First Cavalry Battle at Kelly's Ford, Va.," *First Maine Bugle* (1893), 3:3, pp. 3–16, 3:4, pp. 8–22; Bigelow, "Battle of Kelly's Ford," pp. 12–28; H. B. McClellan, *The Life and Campaigns of Major-General J.E.B. Stuart,* pp. 202–17; *New York Times,* Mar. 22, 1863.

5. Hooker to War Dept., May 13, 1863, *OR,* 25:1, p. 1073; Moore report, *OR,* 25:2, p. 147. Casualties: *OR,* 25:1, pp. 53, 63.

6. *New York Tribune,* Mar. 21, 1863; *New York Herald,* Mar. 20; *New York Times,* Mar. 16; Chester K. Leach to wife, Mar. 12, Special Collections, University of Vermont Library; Jeffry D. Wert, *Mosby's Rangers* (New York: Simon & Schuster, 1990), pp. 17–22; John S. Mosby, *The Memoirs of Colonel John S. Mosby* (Boston: Little, Brown, 1917), p. 173; *New York Times,* Mar. 11. Although his brigadier general's commission expired four days before his capture, Stoughton was still exercising command on Mar. 9.

7. Lee to Stuart, Mar. 12, 1863, *OR,* 25:2, p. 664; Lee to wife, Apr. 3, Lee, *Wartime Papers,* p. 427; Longstreet to Lee, Mar. 18, Longstreet to D. H. Hill, Mar. 18, *OR,* 18, pp. 924, 925; Stuart to Lee, Mar. 17, *OR,* 51:2, p. 685; Lee to Cooper, Mar. 18, *OR,* 25:2, p. 672; Jeffry D. Wert, *General James Longstreet,* p. 232.

8. Longstreet to D. H. Hill, Mar. 18, 1863, Lee to Longstreet, Mar. 30, *OR,* 18, pp. 926, 907.

9. Lee to wife, Mar. 6, 1863, R. E. Lee Papers, Library of Congress; Lee to wife, Mar. 9, 27, Apr. 3, 5, 12, Lee, *Wartime Papers,* pp. 413, 419, 427, 428, 432. Freeman, *R. E. Lee,* 4, pp. 524–25, offers an analysis of Lee's heart ailments by Dr. Lewellys F. Baker.

10. Steven A. Cormier, *The Siege of Suffolk: The Forgotten Campaign, April 11–*

May 4, 1863, pp. 265, 308–11; Longstreet to Lee, Mar. 19, 1863, *OR*, 18, pp. 926–27.

11. Lee to Seddon, Mar. 27, Apr. 17, 1863, *OR*, 25:2, pp. 687, 730; Lee to Longstreet, Mar. 19, *OR*, 18, p. 927; Cormier, *The Siege of Suffolk*, pp. 39, 175–76; Longstreet to Lee, Mar. 19, *OR*, 18, p. 926.

12. Lee to Longstreet, Mar. 21, 27, 1863, Longstreet to Lee, Mar. 30, Apr. 4, *OR*, 18, pp. 933–34, 943–44, 950, 960; Lee to Seddon, Apr. 9, *OR*, 25:2, pp. 713–14; Longstreet to Seddon, Apr. 17, 27, *OR*, 18, pp. 997, 1025. It was Longstreet who proposed sending his First Corps troops to Tennessee (Seddon to Longstreet, Apr. 16, 1875, Longstreet Papers, Perkins Library, Duke University).

13. "Distances on Roads from Fredericksburg," Hooker Papers, Huntington Library; Caroline County map, 1863, Gilmer Collection, Virginia Historical Society; Ralph Happel, "The Chancellors of Chancellorsville," *Virginia Magazine of History and Biography*, 71:3 (July 1963), pp. 259–77; Noel G. Harrison, *Chancellorsville Battlefield Sites*, pp. 16–17. Any macadamized surfacing on the Orange Turnpike had disappeared by 1863. Regis de Trobriand, referring to the Turnpike, wrote of "the principal road, called the Macadamized road (although it is not) . . ." (*Four Years with the Army of the Potomac*, p. 435). Here and elsewhere in this narrative, distances are measured over the roads (and railroads) as of 1863, often using the tables compiled by Hooker's topographical engineers and preserved in the Hooker Papers. Distances on rivers are measured by tracing their courses.

14. These various planning studies are in the Hooker Papers, Huntington Library.

15. Lowe to Butterfield, Mar. 22, 1863, Comstock to Sharpe, Feb. 27, RG 94, Entry 168, National Archives; Hooker special order, Apr. 7, *OR*, Series Three, 3, p. 302.

16. Milton Cline report, Mar. 1863, Isaac Silver report, Mar. 13, Sharpe report, Mar. 15, RG 393, Part 1, Entry 3980, B.M.I., National Archives; J. E. Hammond to S.L.M. Barlow, Apr. 22, Barlow Papers, Huntington Library; J. Willard Brown, *The Signal Corps, U.S.A. in the War of the Rebellion*, 1, p. 214. For the breaking of the Confederate signal-flag code, see James S. Hall to Samuel T. Cushing, Nov. 28, 1862, RG 111, Entry 27, National Archives. These various Federal espionage operations were first uncovered by Edwin C. Fishel, who details them in *The Secret War for the Union*, Chs. 13, 14.

17. Lee to wife, Mar. 21, 1863, Lee, *Wartime Papers*, p. 416; Mar. 31 return, *OR*, 25:2, p. 180 (corrected to include headquarters staff and signal corps); Hooker to L. Thomas, Apr. 22, 25:2, p. 243; Sedgwick to sister, Apr. 30, John Sedgwick, *Correspondence of John Sedgwick, Major General*, 2, p. 91. The count of the two-year and the nine-month regiments, and the number of men in them, is compiled from data in: *OR*, 25:2, p. 532; *OR*, Series Three, 3, pp. 760, 775; *Report of Joint Committee*, 1 (1865), p. 219; Frederick H. Dyer, *A Compendium of the War of the Rebellion* (Des Moines, Iowa, 1908).

18. Patrick diary, Mar. 23, 27, 1863, Library of Congress; Lee to Trimble, Mar. 8, S. Williams memorandum, Mar. 30, *OR*, 25:2, pp. 658, 167–68.

19. Samuel P. Bates, *History of Pennsylvania Volunteers, 1861–65* (Harrisburg, 1869–71), 2, p. 410; Butterfield to Salmon P. Chase, Nov. 26, 1862, Julia Butterfield, *Memorial of General Butterfield*, p. 112; Hooker special order, Mar. 7, 1863, Meigs memorandum, Jan. 2, 1862, *OR*, 25:2, pp. 487–88, 489–91.

20. Flying-column board memorandum, Mar. 1863, post-campaign memoranda by Butterfield, Ingalls, corps quartermasters, *OR*, 25:2, pp. 488–89, 486–87, 544–62; George Fairfield diary, Apr. 14, State Historical Society of Wisconsin; Hooker circular, Apr. 13, *OR*, 25:2, pp. 202–3; Daniel D. Jones to Jonathan Jordan, Apr. 7, Historical Society of

Pennsylvania; Mar. 25, Wainwright, *Diary of Battle*, p. 174.

21. Samuel C. Hodgman to mother, Mar. 7, 1863, Archives and Regional History Collections, Western Michigan University; Samuel D. Webster diary, Apr. 2, Huntington Library; Henry Aplin to sister, Apr. 8, Schoff Collection, Clements Library, University of Michigan; John E. Ryder to sister, Apr. 19, Michigan Historical Collections, Bentley Historical Library, University of Michigan; Hooker testimony, *Report of Joint Committee*, 1 (1865), p. 113.

5: *My Plans Are Perfect*

1. Hall Tutwiler to sister, Apr. 3, 1863, Southern Historical Collection, University of North Carolina; Emory M. Thomas, *The Confederate State of Richmond: A Biography of the Capital*, pp. 118–22; Mar. 27, Jones, *Rebel War Clerk's Diary*, 1, p. 280; William C. Davis, *Jefferson Davis: The Man and His Hour*, p. 497; Varina H. Davis, *Jefferson Davis, Ex-President of the Confederate States of America: A Memoir by His Wife* (New York: Belford, 1890), 2, pp. 374–76; Jonathan Withers to W. S. Morris, Apr. 2, *OR*, 18, p. 958.

2. Davis proclamation, Apr. 10, 1863, *OR*, Series Four, 2, pp. 475–77; Cormier, *The Siege of Suffolk*, pp. 290–91; Johnston, *Virginia Railroads*, pp. 126, 284–85.

3. Lee to Longstreet, Apr. 27, 1863, *OR*, 18, pp. 1024–25; Lee to wife, Apr. 19, Lee, *Wartime Papers*, pp. 437–38; Lee general order, Mar. 21, Lee to Davis, Apr. 2, *OR*, 25:2, pp. 681–82, 700–701.

4. Lee to Halleck, Jan. 10, 1863, *OR*, Series Three, 3, pp. 10–11; Lee to Seddon, Apr. 9, Imboden to Lee, Mar. 2, *OR*, 25:2, pp. 713–14, 652–53; Lee to W. E. Jones, Feb. 13, Mar. 26, Lee to Gilmer, Apr. 11, *OR*, 25:2, pp. 622, 685, 715; William H. Mills, "Chancellorsville," *Magazine of American History*, 15 (1886), p. 378.

5. Lee to Davis, Apr. 16, 1863, *OR*, 25:2,

pp. 724–25; Stephen W. Sears, "The Last Word on the Lost Order," *MHQ*, 4:3 (Spring 1992), pp. 66–72. Lee first learned of the Lost Order from Northern newspapers, possibly in January 1863 but more probably in April when McClellan's testimony to the Joint Committee on the Conduct of the War was published.

6. Lee to Longstreet, Apr. 27, 1863, *OR*, 18, pp. 1024–25; Lee to Cooper, Apr. 16, *OR*, 25:2, p. 726. The March 31 count of 61,520 "present for duty" in the Army of Northern Virginia is drawn from data in: March [31] return, *OR*, 25:2, p. 696; March 31 return abstract (misdated Apr. 30), *OR*, Series Four, 2, p. 530. Artillery manpower is detailed in Bigelow, *Chancellorsville*, pp. 132–33. The count of conscripts for April (3,500) is from E. P. Alexander, *Military Memoirs of a Confederate*, p. 322. There is no April return for the Army of Northern Virginia.

7. Sears, *To the Gates of Richmond*, pp. 156–57; Sears, *George B. McClellan*, p. 181; Lafayette McLaws to wife, Apr. 26, 1863, Southern Historical Collection, University of North Carolina; William D. Pender to wife, Apr. 23, Pender, *The General to His Lady: The Civil War Letters of William Dorsey Pender to Fanny Pender*, ed. William W. Hassler, p. 229; Lee to Davis, Apr. 16, *OR*, 25:2, p. 725.

8. Lincoln to Hooker, Apr. 3, 1863, Lincoln, *Collected Works*, 6, p. 161; Hooker to Lincoln, Apr. 3, Lincoln Papers, Library of Congress; Brooks, *Washington in Lincoln's Time*, pp. 51–55; Apr. 6, Edward Bates, *The Diary of Edward Bates, 1859–1866*, ed. Howard K. Beale (Washington: Government Printing Office, 1933), p. 288; Robert McAllister to family, Apr. 7, McAllister, *The Civil War Letters of General Robert McAllister*, ed. James I. Robertson, Jr., p. 282; Patrick diary, Apr. 6, Library of Congress.

9. Henry Howell diary, Apr. 8, 1863, LaRocca, *This Regiment of Heroes*, p. 42; John D. Wilkins to wife, Apr. 8, Schoff Collection, Clements Library, University of Michigan; Brooks, *Washington in*

Lincoln's Time, pp. 54–56; Dawes, *Service with the Sixth Wisconsin,* pp. 131–32n; Stephen M. Weld, *War Diary and Letters of Stephen Minot Weld,* p. 170n.

10. Meade to wife, Apr. 9, 1863, Meade, *Life and Letters,* 1, p. 364; Lincoln to Hooker, c. Apr. 7, Lincoln, *Collected Works,* 6, pp. 164–65; Anson G. Henry to wife, Apr. 12, Illinois State Historical Library; Noah Brooks, "Personal Reminiscences of Lincoln," *Scribner's Monthly,* 15 (March 1878), p. 673; Couch in *Battles and Leaders,* 3, p. 155; Couch memoir, p. 128, Old Colony Historical Society; Bates to James B. Eads, Apr. 1863, Eads Papers, Missouri Historical Society.

11. Comstock to Hooker, Feb. 3, 8, Apr. 12, 1863, *OR,* 51:1, pp. 980–81, 984, 1003–4; Hooker testimony, *Report of Joint Committee,* 1 (1865), p. 115; Lincoln to Halleck, Nov. 27, 1862, Lincoln, *Collected Works,* 5, pp. 514–15; Heintzelman diary, Apr. 11, 1863, Library of Congress; Heintzelman special order, Apr. 11, *OR,* 51:1, pp. 1002–3.

12. Hooker testimony, *Report of Joint Committee,* 1 (1865), pp. 115, 144; Sharpe to Butterfield, Mar. 21, 1863, Silver report, Apr. 1, RG 393, Part 1, Entry 3980, B.M.I., National Archives; *Harper's Weekly,* Feb. 7.

13. Julia Butterfield, *Memorial of General Butterfield,* p. 155; Hooker to Lincoln, Apr. 11, 1863, Lincoln Papers, Library of Congress; Lincoln to Hooker, Apr. 12, *OR,* 25:2, p. 200.

14. Charles Sumner to Francis Lieber, May 3, 1863, Lieber Papers, Huntington Library; Apr. 22, Strong, *Diary,* p. 312; Hooker testimony, *Report of Joint Committee,* 1 (1865), p. 145; Hooker to Samuel Ross, Feb. 28, 1864, in *Battles and Leaders,* 3, p. 223; Haupt, *Reminiscences,* p. 193; H. Seymour Hall, "Fredericksburg and Chancellorsville," Kansas MOLLUS, *War Talks in Kansas* (Kansas City, Mo., 1906), p. 194.

15. Hooker to Stoneman, Apr. 12, 1863, *OR,* 25:1, pp. 1066–67; Hooker notes, Apr. 12, Hooker Papers, Huntington Library; Hooker to Bates, Mar. 24,

1879, Bates Collection, Pennsylvania Historical and Museum Commission; Sawtelle report, *OR,* 25:1, p. 1067; Sickles to John Bigelow, Apr. 10, 1911, Bigelow Papers, Library of Congress; Stoneman circular, Apr. 11, 1863, *OR,* 25:2, p. 198.

16. S. Williams to Stoneman, Apr. 12, 1863, *OR,* 25:1, p. 1066; Butterfield ruse message, [Apr. 13], RG 111, Entry 27, National Archives; Cushing to Butterfield, Apr. 14, RG 393, Part 1, Entry 3980, B.M.I., National Archives; Lee to W. E. Jones, Apr. 14, *OR,* 25:2, p. 721. Butterfield's ruse is detailed by its discoverer, Edwin C. Fishel, in *The Secret War for the Union,* Ch. 15.

17. Hooker directives, Apr. 12, 1863, Hooker circulars, Apr. 13, 14, *OR,* 25:2, pp. 202, 203–4, 211; James T. Miller to father, Apr. 16, Schoff Collection, Clements Library, University of Michigan; Henry F. Young to wife, Apr. 11, State Historical Society of Wisconsin; Rufus Ingalls to postmaster, Apr. 14, S. Williams to Samuel Magaw, Apr. 13, Halleck to Hooker, Apr. 14, *OR,* 25:2, pp. 209, 203, 210; Hooker to Lincoln, [Apr. 13], Lincoln Papers, Library of Congress; Alexander S. Webb to wife, Apr. 14, Webb Papers, Yale University Library.

18. S. Williams to Stoneman, Apr. 12, 1863, *OR,* 25:1, p. 1066; Stoneman circular, Apr. 13, *OR,* 25:2, pp. 204–5; Apr. 14, 15, Samuel Cormany and Rachel Cormany, *The Cormany Diaries: A Northern Family in the Civil War,* ed. James C. Mohr (Pittsburgh: University of Pittsburgh Press, 1982), p. 306; Patrick diary, Apr. 15, Library of Congress; Apr. 19, Wainwright, *Diary of Battle,* p. 182; W.H.F. Lee, Buford reports, *OR,* 25:1, pp. 86, 1088.

19. Hooker to Lincoln, Apr. 15, 1863 (two), Lincoln to Hooker, Apr. 15, Hooker to Lincoln, Apr. 17, *OR,* 25:2, pp. 213–14, 220.

20. William N. Pendleton to wife, Apr. 15, 1863, Susan Lee, *Memoirs of Pendleton,* p. 255; Lee to Longstreet, Apr. 17, *OR,* 18, p. 996; Lee to W. E. Jones, Apr. 14,

OR, 25:2, p. 721; McClellan, *Life and Campaigns of Stuart*, p. 220. The Jones-Imboden raid set off on Apr. 20. It is detailed in Bigelow, *Chancellorsville*, pp. 460–72.

21. Lee to Davis, Apr. 16, 1863, Lee to Stuart, Apr. 17, 19, 25, Stuart to Mosby, Apr. 25, 26, *OR*, 25:2, pp. 724–25, 730, 736–37, 749–50, 860.

22. William Calder to mother, Apr. 20, 1863, Southern Historical Collection, University of North Carolina; Samuel C. Hodgman to brother, Apr. 21, Archives and Regional History Collections, Western Michigan University; Lee to Stuart, Apr. 20, *OR*, 25:2, p. 738.

23. *Philadelphia Inquirer,* Apr. 25, 1863; Hooker to Stanton, Apr. 27, Jonathan Letterman to Hooker, Apr. 4, Joseph R. Smith to W. A. Hammond, Apr. 23, Hooker to Stanton, Apr. 21, Hooker general order, Apr. 30, *OR*, 25:2, pp. 269–70, 239–40, 239, 316; Lee to Davis, Apr. 27, Lee to Seddon, May 10, *OR*, 25:2, pp. 752, 790.

24. McLaws to wife, Apr. 12, 26, 1863, Southern Historical Collection, University of North Carolina; James T. McElvany to sister, Apr. 20, Georgia Department of Archives and History; John Hampden Chamberlayne to mother, Apr. 16, Chamberlayne, *Ham Chamberlayne*, p. 168; J. J. Wilson to brother, Apr. 27, Mississippi Department of Archives and History.

25. Alfred M. Scales to wife, Apr. 19, 1863, North Carolina State Archives; Mary Anna Jackson, *Memoirs of Stonewall Jackson*, pp. 408–9; Hotchkiss to wife, Apr. 24, Hotchkiss Papers, Library of Congress.

26. Washington A. Roebling to father, Apr. 15, 1863, Roebling Papers, Rutgers University Libraries; S. Williams to Stoneman, Apr. 18, *OR*, 25:2, p. 228; Stoneman to S. Williams, Apr. 19, Lincoln Papers, Library of Congress; William L. Candler letter, Apr. 24, in Bigelow, *Chancellorsville*, p. 164.

27. Stanton to Hooker, Apr. 18, 1863, Halleck to Stanton, May 18, *OR*, 25:2, pp. 227, 506; Patrick diary, Apr. 20, Library of Congress; Henry W. Bellows to John Bigelow, Sr., Apr. 20, Bigelow Papers, Library of Congress.

28. Warren report, *OR*, 25:1, pp. 195–96; William W. Folwell to wife, Apr. 17, 20, 1863, Minnesota Historical Society; Apr. 14, Weld, *War Diary and Letters*, p. 176; Hooker to Lincoln, Apr. 21, *OR*, 25:2, p. 238.

29. "Organization . . . Army of Northern Virg.," Apr. 28, 1863, RG 393, Part 1, Entry 3980, B.M.I., National Archives; B.M.I., "Organization of the Rebel Army of N. Va.," May 10, Civil War Papers, Southern Historical Collection, University of North Carolina. From internal evidence, both these documents were in use at Hooker's headquarters before their "corrected to" dates. The two uncounted brigades were Perry of Anderson's division and Kershaw of McLaws's. Of Babcock's list of 116 Confederate infantry regiments, 103 were correctly identified and located, 7 were misidentified, and 6 were identified but mislocated. For sources of the actual April figures for Lee's army, see Note 6 above.

30. Isaac Silver report, Apr. 15, 1863, Milton Cline report, Mar., RG 393, Part 1, Entry 3980, B.M.I., National Archives.

31. Hooker to Lincoln, Apr. 27, 1863, Lincoln Papers, Library of Congress; Hooker testimony, *Report of Joint Committee*, 1 (1865), pp. 116, 137.

32. Diary, Apr. 26, 1863, Taylor, "Campaigning with the First Minnesota," *Minnesota History*, 25 (Dec. 1944), p. 344; Edward H. Wade to sister, Apr. 25, Schoff Collection, Clements Library, University of Michigan; Apr. 23, George W. Bailey, *The Civil War Diary and Biography of George W. Bailey*, ed. Gerald R. Post, p. 33; John J. Pullen, *The Twentieth Maine: A Volunteer Regiment in the Civil War* (Philadelphia: Lippincott, 1957), p. 74; Hooker to Bates, Aug. 29, 1876, Bates Collection, Pennsylvania Historical and Museum Commission. The count of 134,858 for the Army of the Potomac is derived from the Apr. 30 return "present for duty

equipped" (*OR*, 25:2, p. 320), with the addition of the Fifth Corps escort, the engineer brigade, and the signal corps unit.

33. Hooker to Peck, Apr. 21, 1863, *OR*, 25:2, p. 241; Doubleday report, Hooker Papers, Huntington Library; Port Royal report, *OR*, 25:1, p. 137; Lucius L. Shattuck to family, Apr. 26, Michigan Historical Collections, Bentley Historical Library, University of Michigan; Lee to wife, Apr. 24, Lee, *Wartime Papers*, pp. 439–40; Lee to Jackson, Apr. 23, *OR*, 25:2, p. 959.

34. William W. Folwell to wife, Apr. 25, 1863, Minnesota Historical Society; Meade to wife, Apr. 26, Meade, *Life and Letters*, 1, p. 369; Hooker to Bates, Apr. 2, 1877, Bates Collection, Pennsylvania Historical and Museum Commission.

6: Army on the March

1. Diary, Apr. 26, 1863, Hotchkiss, *Make Me a Map*, p. 134; Mary Anna Jackson, *Memoirs of Stonewall Jackson*, p. 411; John W. Daniels to grandfather, Apr. 27, Alderman Library, University of Virginia; John S. Cooper diary, Apr. 26, Perkins Library, Duke University.

2. Twelfth Corps circular, Apr. 25, 1863, S. Williams to Howard and Slocum, Apr. 26, S. Williams to Meade, Apr. [26], *OR*, 25:2, pp. 250, 255–56, 262; Warren testimony, *Report of Joint Committee*, 1 (1865), p. 43.

3. Hooker testimony, *Report of Joint Committee*, 1 (1865), pp. 116, 164; Hooker to Peck, Apr. 26, 1863, *OR*, 25:2, pp. 256–57; Hooker to Lincoln, Apr. 27, Lincoln Papers, Library of Congress.

4. Hooker to Bates, Aug. 8, 29, 1876, Bates Collection, Pennsylvania Historical and Museum Commission; Apr. 30 return, *OR*, 25:2, p. 320; Bigelow, *Chancellorsville*, p. 36. The Army of the Potomac winter encampments are in Bigelow, Map 2. The record of the units making up the Eleventh and Twelfth corps can be traced in Frank J. Welcher,

The Union Army, 1861–1865: Organization and Operations, 1 (Bloomington: Indiana University Press, 1989).

5. Hooker to Bates, Aug. 29, 1876, Bates Collection, Pennsylvania Historical and Museum Commission; S. Williams to Howard and Slocum, Apr. 26, 1863, S. Williams to Meade, Apr. [26], S. Williams to Comstock, Apr. 27, *OR*, 25:2, pp. 255–56, 262, 264; Apr. 30 return, *OR*, 25:2, p. 320; John D. Wilkins to wife, Apr. 27, Schoff Collection, Clements Library, University of Michigan. For data on the new and short-term troops, see Chapter 4 Note 17. In his congressional testimony (*Report of Joint Committee*, 1 [1865], p. 120) Hooker gave the number in the flanking column as 36,000, but failed to include Pleasonton's cavalry brigade and apparently assumed that more short-term men were left behind than was the case.

6. Hooker to Lincoln, Apr. 27, 1863, Lincoln Papers, Library of Congress; Hooker to Bates, Apr. 2, 1877, Bates Collection, Pennsylvania Historical and Museum Commission; Apr. 30, 1863, return, *OR*, 25:2, p. 320; S. Williams to Sedgwick, Apr. 27, S. Williams to Couch, Apr. 27, *OR*, 25:2, pp. 268, 266–67.

7. Justus M. Silliman to mother, May 8, 1863, Silliman, *A New Canaan Private in the Civil War: Letters of Justus M. Silliman, 17th Connecticut Volunteers,* ed. Edward Marcus, p. 25; Charles E. Bowers to wife, Apr. 27, Massachusetts Historical Society; Rice C. Bull, *Soldiering: The Civil War Diary of Rice C. Bull, 123rd New York Volunteer Infantry,* ed. K. Jack Bauer, p. 37; John J. Cate to wife, May 1, Fredericksburg & Spotsylvania National Military Park; Fifth Corps circular, Apr. 27, *OR*, 25:2, p. 269; Eleventh Corps journal of operations, Schoff Collection, Clements Library, University of Michigan; Fifth and Twelfth corps journals of operations, Hooker Papers, Huntington Library.

8. Williams to daughter, May 18, 1863, Williams, *From the Cannon's Mouth,*

p. 179; flying-column memorandum, Mar. 1863, *OR,* 25:2, pp. 488–89; Justus M. Silliman to mother, May 8, Silliman, *New Canaan Private,* p. 25; James Houghton diary, Apr. 27, Michigan Historical Collections, Bentley Historical Library, University of Michigan; Fifth Corps circular, Apr. 27, *OR,* 25:2, p. 269; Darwin D. Cody to parents, May 9, Fredericksburg & Spotsylvania National Military Park; diary, Apr. 28, Cyrus Bacon, Jr., "A Michigan Surgeon at Chancellorsville One Hundred Years Ago," eds. Frank Whitehouse, Jr., and Walter M. Whitehouse, *The University of Michigan Medical Bulletin,* 29:6 (Nov.–Dec. 1963), p. 317.

9. John S. Cooper diary, Apr. 24, 1863, Perkins Library, Duke University; J. B. Brooks to B. F. Fisher, Mar. 14, Hooker Papers, Huntington Library; Patrick diary, Apr. 27, Library of Congress; Thomas L. Livermore, *Days and Events, 1860–1866,* p. 189; William Child, *A History of the Fifth Regiment New Hampshire Volunteers,* p. 181; Bigelow, *Chancellorsville,* p. 179; Devin report, *OR,* 25:1, p. 777; Stuart to Mosby, Apr. 25, 26, *OR,* 25:2, p. 860.

10. Thomas K. Stephens diary, Apr. 29, 1863, U.S. Army Military History Institute; Bigelow, *Chancellorsville,* p. 179; Hooker to Lincoln, Apr. 27, Lincoln Papers, Library of Congress; Lincoln to Hooker, Apr. 27, Hooker to Lincoln, Apr. 27, *OR,* 25:2, p. 263; Couch memoir, p. 129, Old Colony Historical Society; Butterfield to Hooker, Apr. 28, *OR,* 25:2, pp. 276–77.

11. William H. Hill diary, Apr. 27, 1863, Mississippi Department of Archives and History; Charles W. McArthur to James W. Vaughan, May 23, Kennesaw Mountain National Battlefield; Lee to Davis, Apr. 27, *OR,* 25:2, pp. 752–53; diary, Apr. 27, Hotchkiss, *Make Me a Map,* p. 135.

12. Rufus R. Dawes to family, Apr. 28, 1863, Rufus D. Beach Collection; Eleventh Corps journal of operations, Schoff Collection, Clements Library, University of Michigan; Justus M. Silliman to mother, May 8, Silliman, *New Canaan Private,* p. 25; Alfred Davenport, *Camp and Field Life of the Fifth New York Volunteer Infantry,* pp. 378–79; Williams to daughter, May 18, Williams, *From the Cannon's Mouth,* p. 180.

13. James B. Heazlitt diary, Apr. 28, 1863, Huntington Library; William Aughinbaugh diary, Apr. 28, Schoff Collection, Clements Library, University of Michigan; Humphreys report, *OR,* 25:1, p. 550; W. R. Hopkins to Rufus Ingalls, May 23, *OR,* 25:2, p. 558; Williams to daughter, May 18, Williams, *From the Cannon's Mouth,* pp. 179–80; Eleventh Corps journal of operations, Schoff Collection; Howard, *Autobiography,* p. 353. Fifty-eight wagons was the "official" count of the Eleventh Corps quartermaster (Le Duc to Ingalls, May 24, *OR,* 25:2, p. 555).

14. Cushing report, *OR,* 25:1, pp. 317–18; Brown, *Signal Corps,* 1, pp. 348–49. Reports of Federal signal officers are in *OR,* 25:1, pp. 217–46; a considerably more complete file is in the Hooker Papers, Huntington Library. The Phillips house itself was in ruins, destroyed that winter in a fire. Battlefield telegraphy was first used in this war by McClellan at Gaines's Mill in June 1862. No one before Hooker, however, had attempted to use the telegraph to coordinate the movements of widely separated columns during a battle.

15. First, Second, Third, Sixth corps journals of operations, Hooker Papers, Huntington Library; Charles H. Brewster to mother, Apr. 30, 1863, Brewster, *When This Cruel War Is Over,* pp. 220–21; diary, Apr. 28, Dawes, *Sixth Wisconsin Volunteers,* p. 135; Patrick diary, Apr. 28, 29, Library of Congress; Judith Yandoh, "Mutiny at the Front," *Civil War Times Illustrated,* 34:2 (June 1995), pp. 35–36, 69; James R. Strong to brother, May 1, State Historical Society of Wisconsin.

16. William W. Folwell diary, Apr. 28, 1863, Minnesota Historical Society; Taylor to Cushing, Apr. 28, Hooker Papers, Huntington Library; Sharpe to But-

terfield, Apr. 28, RG 393, Part 1, Entry 3980, B.M.I., National Archives.

17. B.M.I., "Organization of Rebel Army," May 10, 1863, Civil War Papers, Southern Historical Collection, University of North Carolina (see Chapter 5 Note 29); Hooker to Stoneman, Apr. 26, Candler to Slocum, Apr. 28, *OR*, 25:2, pp. 254, 273–74. For sources of the actual April figures for Lee's army, see Chapter 5 Note 6.

18. Mark H. Dunkelman and Michael J. Winey, *The Hardtack Regiment: An Illustrated History of the 154th Regiment, New York State Infantry Volunteers*, pp. 51–52; Charles H. Howard to brother, May 1, 1863, C. H. Howard Papers, Bowdoin College Library; O. O. Howard report, *OR*, 25:1, p. 627; Comstock report, Hooker Papers, Huntington Library.

19. Carl Schurz, *The Reminiscences of Carl Schurz*, 1, pp. 408–9; Stuart report, *OR*, 25:1, pp. 1045–46; McClellan, *Life and Campaigns of Stuart*, pp. 225–26; Candler to Slocum, Apr. 28, 1863, *OR*, 25:2, pp. 273–74. Stuart's report has Schenofsky giving Howard's strength as 20,000 men. On the morning of Apr. 29, however, Lee gave Howard's strength (obviously reported to him by Stuart) as 14,000 men and six batteries (Lee to Cooper, Apr. 29, Lee, *Wartime Papers*, pp. 441–42).

20. James Power Smith in *Battles and Leaders*, 3, p. 203; *Richmond Dispatch*, May 1, 1863; diary, Apr. 29, Moore, *A Life for the Confederacy*, pp. 142–43.

21. S. Williams to Sedgwick, Apr. 27, 1863, *OR*, 25:2, p. 268; Benham report, *OR*, 25:1, pp. 205–6; McMahon to Brooks, Apr. 28, *OR*, 51:1, p. 1015; Stephen M. Weld to father, Apr. 29, Weld, *War Diary and Letters*, pp. 187–90.

22. John S. Cooper diary, Apr. 29, 1863, Perkins Library, Duke University; Russell report, *OR*, 25:1, p. 591; William Byrnes diary, Apr. 29, Perkins Library; R. F. Halsted to Emily Sedgwick, May 13, in Sedgwick, *Correspondence*, 2, pp. 112–13; Early, *Autobiographical Sketch*, p. 193; Rollin P. Converse to niece, May 13, Fredericksburg & Spot-

sylvania National Military Park; Benham report, *OR*, 25:1, p. 215.

23. Stephen M. Weld diary, Apr. 29, 1863, Weld, *War Diary and Letters*, pp. 186, 200; Benham, Meredith reports, *OR*, 25:1, pp. 212, 266–67; James W. Latta diary, Apr. 29, Library of Congress; Rufus R. Dawes to sister, May 1, Rufus D. Beach Collection; William Speed to wife, May 10, Schoff Collection, Clements Library, University of Michigan.

24. Apr. 29, 1863, Wainwright, *Diary of Battle*, pp. 185–86; Stephen M. Weld to father, Apr. 29, Weld, *War Diary and Letters*, p. 190; diary, Apr. 29, Hotchkiss, *Make Me a Map*, p. 136; Henry C. Walker to John W. Johnston, May 9, Lane, *Letters from Georgia Soldiers*, p. 233.

25. Apr. 29, 1863, Wainwright, *Diary of Battle*, p. 186; Rufus R. Dawes to sister, May 1, Rufus D. Beach Collection; William Speed to wife, May 10, Schoff Collection, Clements Library, University of Michigan; Edward S. Bragg to wife, May 8, State Historical Society of Wisconsin.

26. Alan T. Nolan, *The Iron Brigade: A Military History*, p. 214; "Confederate States Army Casualties," RG 109, M-836:6, National Archives.

27. Charles W. McArthur to James W. Vaughan, May 23, 1863, Kennesaw Mountain National Battlefield; William J. Seymour, *The Civil War Memoirs of Captain William J. Seymour: Reminiscences of a Louisiana Tiger*, ed. Terry L. Jones, p. 49; Mary Anna Jackson, *Memoirs of Stonewall Jackson*, pp. 415–17; Early, *Autobiographical Sketch*, pp. 194–95; diary, Apr. 29, Hotchkiss, *Make Me a Map*, p. 135; Mar. 31 return, *OR*, 25:2, p. 696. This March return gives Jackson 35,895 infantry, but his share of the 3,500 April conscripts would have raised his total to more than 38,000. The downriver extension of the River Road, as it was called locally, ran eastward from Fredericksburg paralleling the Rappahannock for six miles. At the six-mile pole the Bowling Green Road branched off to the south; the eastward extension was called the Port Royal

Road. In some accounts the full length of this road east from Fredericksburg and then south is labeled the Bowling Green Road (or the Old Stage Road).

28. Lee report, *OR*, 25:1, p. 796; Lee to Stuart, Apr. 17, 1863, *OR*, 25:2, pp. 736–37; Lee to Cooper, Apr. 29, Lee, *Wartime Papers*, pp. 442–43; Edward Porter Alexander, *Fighting for the Confederacy: The Personal Recollections of General Edward Porter Alexander*, ed. Gary W. Gallagher, p. 194; B. T. Lacy narrative, Dabney Papers, Southern Historical Collection, University of North Carolina; Pendleton to Eshleman, Apr. 29, *OR*, 51:2, p. 698. Lee's report misdated the Federals' downstream crossing as Apr. 28, which led him to misdate some information from Stuart.

29. Lee to Cooper, Apr. 29, 1863, Lee to Davis, Apr. 29, Lee, *Wartime Papers*, pp. 441–42, 443; McLaws to wife, Apr. 29, Southern Historical Collection, University of North Carolina. Stuart's Apr. 29 dispatches are not on record, and their content must be inferred from Lee's reports to Richmond. Lee's telegram to Cooper did not specifically name Gordonsville as Howard's target, but in repeating the telegram to Longstreet, Cooper included the phrase "making toward Gordonsville" after Howard's name (Cooper to Longstreet, Apr. 29, *OR*, 25:2, p. 758). Richmond had relayed Stuart's original telegram to Lee, from which no doubt the Gordonsville phrase was taken.

30. Candler to Slocum, Apr. 28, 1863, *OR*, 25:2, pp. 273–74; Williams to daughter, May 18, Williams, *From the Cannon's Mouth*, p. 181.

31. Candler to Stoneman, Apr. 28, 1863, *OR*, 25:1, p. 1065; Candler to Comstock, Apr. 28, *OR*, 25:2, p. 275.

32. Slocum to Hooker, Apr. 28, 1863, Hooker Papers, Huntington Library; Justus M. Silliman to mother, May 9, Silliman, *New Canaan Private*, pp. 27–28; Stuart report, *OR*, 25:1, p. 1046; R. T. Hubard, "Operations of General J.E.B. Stuart Before Chancellorsville,"

Southern Historical Society Papers, 8 (1880), pp. 251–52.

33. Frank Robertson memoir, Virginia Historical Society; Ruger, Quincy, Hawley reports, *OR*, 25:1, pp. 707, 714, 719; Williams to daughter, May 18, 1863, Williams, *From the Cannon's Mouth*, pp. 182–83; "Confederate States Army Casualties," RG 109, M-836:5, National Archives; *OR*, 25:1, p. 864; Slocum to Hooker, Apr. 29, Hooker Papers, Huntington Library.

34. E. R. Brown, *The Twenty-seventh Indiana Volunteer Infantry in the War of the Rebellion*, p. 310; Darwin D. Cody to parents, May 9, 1863, Fredericksburg & Spotsylvania National Military Park; Williams to daughter, May 18, Williams, *From the Cannon's Mouth*, p. 183; Slocum to Hooker, Apr. 29, Hooker Papers, Huntington Library; H. B. Scott to John Bigelow, May 20, June 24, 1911, Bigelow Papers, Library of Congress; W. A. Croffut and John M. Morris, *The Military and Civil History of Connecticut During the War of 1861–65*, p. 360; Eleventh Corps journal of operations, Schoff Collection, Clements Library, University of Michigan.

35. Meade, Humphreys reports, *OR*, 25:1, pp. 505–6, 545; Meade to Hooker, Apr. 29, 1863, Hooker Papers, Huntington Library; Charles Ward to mother, May 7, American Antiquarian Society; James Houghton diary, Apr. 29, Michigan Historical Collections, Bentley Historical Library, University of Michigan; Timothy J. Reese, *Sykes' Regular Infantry Division, 1861–1864: A History of Regular United States Infantry Operations in the Civil War's Eastern Theater*, p. 209; Howard Thomas, *Boys in Blue from the Adirondack Foothills* (Prospect, N.Y.: Prospect Books, 1960), pp. 132–33; Jonathan B. Hager memoir, Alderman Library, University of Virginia; Charles E. Bowers to wife, May 1, Massachusetts Historical Society.

36. Stoneman report, *OR*, 25:1, pp. 1058–59; A. Wilson Greene, "Stoneman's Raid," in Gary W. Gallagher, ed., *Chancellorsville: The Battle and Its Aftermath;*

Hooker to Bates, Apr. 2, 1877, Bates Collection, Pennsylvania Historical and Museum Commission; Candler to Stoneman, Apr. 28, 1863, *OR*, 25:1, p. 1065; Edward P. Tobie, *History of the First Maine Cavalry, 1861–1865* (Boston: Emery & Hughes, 1887), p. 134; John Follmer diary, Apr. 29, Michigan Historical Collections, Bentley Historical Library, University of Michigan; Stuart report, *OR*, 25:1, p. 1046; Hubard, "Operations of Stuart," pp. 251–52. That Stuart's intelligence did not reach Lee until after daylight on Apr. 30 is evident from Lee's telegram to Davis, received in Richmond at 8:30 A.M. Apr. 30, relaying that intelligence (Robert E. Lee, *Lee's Dispatches*, eds. Douglas Southall Freeman and Grady McWhiney, pp. 85–86).

37. John F. Sale to aunt, May 10, 1863, Alderman Library, University of Virginia; Posey report, *OR*, 25:1, pp. 870–71; Lee to Davis, Apr. 29, Lee to McLaws, Apr. 29, Lee to Anderson, Apr. 29, *OR*, 25:2, pp. 756–57, 759, 759–60.

38. Patrick diary, Apr. 29, 1863, Library of Congress; Butterfield to Sedgwick, Apr. 29, Alexander Moore to Hooker, Apr. 29, Hooker Papers, Huntington Library; Second, Third Corps journals of operations, Hooker Papers; S. Williams to Couch, Apr. 29, *OR*, 25:2, p. 291; J. Franklin Marcha diary, Apr. 29, Fredericksburg & Spotsylvania National Military Park. The Army of the Potomac's Apr. 30 return (*OR*, 25:2, p. 320) gives "present for duty equipped" figures by corps only. Figures by division may be extrapolated from the more detailed return of Apr. 17 (copied by Henry Hunt, McClellan Papers, Library of Congress). Expressing the divisional figures on the Apr. 17 return as percentages of corps' totals, then applying those percentages to the corps' totals on the Apr. 30 return, gives a realistic estimate of Federal divisional strength at Chancellorsville.

39. Hunt report, *OR*, 25:1, pp. 246–47; George Breck in *Rochester Union & Advertiser*, May 4, 1863, courtesy John J.

Hennessy; Sedgwick to Hooker, Apr. 29, Hooker Papers, Huntington Library; Butterfield to Sedgwick, Apr. 29, *OR*, 25:2, p. 292.

40. Hooker to Peck, Apr. 29, 1863, Peck to Hooker, Apr. 29, *OR*, 25:2, p. 293; Taylor to Cushing, Apr. 29, Hooker Papers, Huntington Library; Sharpe to Butterfield, Apr. 29, RG 393, Part 1, Entry 3980, B.M.I., National Archives; Lowe to Allen, Apr. 29, Butterfield to Lowe, Apr. 29, *OR*, Series Three, 3, pp. 310–11.

41. Hooker testimony, *Report of Joint Committee*, 1 (1865), p. 120; Samuel P. Bates, *The Battle of Chancellorsville*, p. 55; Alexander, *Fighting for the Confederacy*, p. 195.

7: Day of Decisions

1. G. Moxley Sorrel, *Recollections of a Confederate Staff Officer*, ed. Bell Irvin Wiley (Jackson, Tenn.: McCowat Mercer, 1958), p. 128; Anderson, Mahone, Posey reports, *OR*, 25:1, pp. 849–50, 862, 870–71; Lee to Anderson, Apr. 29, 1863, *OR*, 25:2, pp. 759–60; Thomas E. Dardin to Mary Collins, May 24, Rowley-Gifford-Clegg Papers, Filson Club.

2. Stuart, Beckham reports, *OR*, 25:1, pp. 1046, 1051; Justus Scheibert, *Seven Months in the Rebel States During the North American War, 1863*, ed. Wm. Stanley Hoole, p. 56; Hubard, "Operations of Stuart," p. 252. Lee's directive to Stuart is not on record; its contents are inferred from Stuart's report. Since on Apr. 29 Lee lacked intelligence on the weight of the Federal flanking column, the decision on how to divide the cavalry force was surely Stuart's.

3. Lee to Anderson, Apr. 29, 1863, *OR*, 25:2, pp. 759–60; Anderson report, *OR*, 25:1, p. 850.

4. Freeman, *R. E. Lee*, 2, p. 512; Lee to Davis, Apr. 30, 1863, *OR*, 25:2, p. 761; Cormier, *Siege of Suffolk*, pp. 251–53; Wert, *James Longstreet*, pp. 238–39; Anderson, Alexander reports, *OR*, 25:1,

pp. 850, 820; William Allan, "Fredericksburg," *Papers of the Military Historical Society of Massachusetts* (Boston, 1903), 3, p. 145; William Allan, interview with General Lee, 1868, Lee Papers, Leyburn Library, Washington and Lee University. Cormier and Wert effectively refute charges that Longstreet unduly delayed his return to the Rappahannock.

5. Jonathan B. Hager memoir, Alderman Library, University of Virginia; J. E. Carpenter in *Philadelphia Weekly Times,* June 29, 1878; Charles E. Bowers to wife, May 1, 1863, Massachusetts Historical Society; John F. Sale to aunt, May 10, Alderman Library; George S. Bernard, *War Talks with Confederate Veterans,* p. 50; Devin, Huey, Mahone reports, *OR,* 25:1, pp. 779–80, 783, 862.

6. Meade report, *OR,* 25:1, p. 506; Charles E. Bowers to wife, May 1, 1863, Massachusetts Historical Society; Jonathan B. Hager memoir, Alderman Library, University of Virginia; Cyrus Bacon diary, Apr. 30, Bacon, "A Michigan Surgeon," p. 318; William W. Folwell to wife, May 1, Minnesota Historical Society; Alexander Moore to Butterfield, Apr. 30, Theme Prints catalog (May 1988); Hooker to Haupt, Apr. 30, *OR,* 25:2, p. 301.

7. Williams to daughter, May 18, 1863, Williams, *From the Cannon's Mouth,* p. 184; Stuart, Chapman reports, *OR,* 25:1, pp. 1046, 743–44; Hubard, "Operations of Stuart," pp. 252–53; McClellan, *Life and Campaigns of Stuart,* pp. 228–29. Casualties: *OR,* 25:1, p. 172.

8. Justus M. Silliman to mother, May 9, 1863, Silliman, *New Canaan Private,* p. 29; Darwin D. Cody to parents, May 9, Fredericksburg & Spotsylvania National Military Park; Williams to daughter, May 18, Williams, *From the Cannon's Mouth,* p. 184.

9. Williams to daughter, May 18, Williams, *From the Cannon's Mouth,* p. 184; Happle, "The Chancellors of Chancellorsville," pp. 259–60; Sue M. Chancellor, "Personal Recollections of the Battle of Chancellorsville," *Register of the Kentucky Historical Society,* 66:2 (Apr. 1968), pp. 137–41; Smith, *History of Corn Exchange Regiment,* p. 171.

10. Richard M. Bache, *Life of General George Gordon Meade, Commander of the Army of the Potomac* (Philadelphia: H. T. Coates, 1897), p. 260; Alexander S. Webb to father, May 12, 1863, James C. Biddle to Webb, Dec. 10, 1885, Webb Papers, Yale University Library; Butterfield to Slocum, Apr. 30, 1863, Ulric Dahlgren to Hooker, Apr. 30, Hooker Papers, Huntington Library; Butterfield to Warren, Apr. 30, *OR,* 25:2, p. 305; Barnes report, *OR,* 25:1, pp. 514–15; Meade to wife, Apr. 30, Meade, *Life and Letters,* 1, p. 370. Where the Orange Turnpike and the Orange Plank Road ran as one between Chancellorsville and Wilderness Church, most of the local people elected to call it by its newer name, the Plank Road, and it will be so called here. The other section where the newer Plank Road overlay the older Turnpike, between Fredericksburg and Tabernacle Church, was also usually known in 1863 as the Plank Road; that usage, too, will be followed here.

11. Hooker to Bates, Apr. 2, 1877, Bates Collection, Pennsylvania Historical and Museum Commission; Reynolds to Butterfield, Apr. 30, 1863 (two), Reynolds to Hooker, Apr. 30, Hooker Papers, Huntington Library.

12. Stoneman, Averell reports, *OR,* 25:1, pp. 1059–60, 1077–78; Nathan Webb diary, Apr. 30, 1863, Schoff Collection, Clements Library, University of Michigan; John C. Tidball journal, Apr. 30, Hooker Papers, Huntington Library; G. W. Beale in *Southern Historical Society Papers,* 34 (1906), p. 208; Averell to headquarters, May 1 (misdated Apr. 30 by Averell in his report), Hooker Papers. Stoneman sent back 500 men.

13. Warren report, *OR,* 25:1, p. 197; William W. Folwell to wife, Apr. 29, May 1, 1863, Minnesota Historical Society; George W. Lambert diary, Apr. 30, Indiana Historical Society; Weld, *War Di-*

ary and Letters, pp. 176–77; Folwell to John Bigelow, Oct. 10, 1911, Bigelow Papers, Library of Congress.

14. Butterfield to Sickles, Apr. 30, 1863, *OR,* 25:2, p. 314; Henry N. Blake, *Three Years in the Army of the Potomac* (Boston: Lee and Shepard, 1865), p. 170.

15. Hall to Cushing, Apr. 30, 1863, Pierce to Cushing, Apr. 30, *OR,* 25:2, pp. 301, 304; Lowe to Butterfield, Apr. 30 (two), *OR,* Series Three, 3, p. 312; S. Williams to Sedgwick, Apr. 30, *OR,* 25:2, p. 206; Sedgwick to Hooker, Apr. 30, Hooker Papers, Huntington Library; John Babcock, "Jackson's Corps," RG 393, Part 1, Entry 3980, B.M.I., National Archives.

16. Charles H. Brewster to mother, Apr. 30, 1863, Brewster, *When This Cruel War Is Over,* p. 221; William D. Pender to wife, Apr. 30, Pender, *The General to His Lady,* p. 233; Marion H. Fitzpatrick to wife, Apr. 30, Fitzpatrick, *Letters to Amanda from Sergeant Major Marion Hill Fitzpatrick, 1862–1865,* ed. Henry Mansel Hammock, p. 54.

17. Thomas W. Hyde to mother, May 7, 1863, Hyde, *Civil War Letters by General Thomas W. Hyde,* p. 70; Sedgwick to Butterfield, Apr. 30, *OR,* 25:2, p. 311; Samuel D. Webster diary, Apr. 30, Huntington Library; Orel Brown diary, Apr. 30, U.S. Army Military History Institute; Small, *The Sixteenth Maine,* pp. 101–2.

18. Butterfield to Hooker, May 1, 1863, *OR,* 25:2, p. 326; Heintzelman diary, Apr. 30, Library of Congress; *New York Herald,* Apr. 30. In the code used by the *New York Times* correspondent, for example, "Will send you twelve pages tonight" stood for "Hooker will fight today" (Andrews, *The North Reports the Civil War,* p. 711 n86).

19. Reynolds to Sedgwick, Apr. 30, 1863, S. Williams to Benham, Apr. 30, Butterfield to Gibbon, Apr. 30, Butterfield to Sedgwick, Apr. 30, *OR,* 25:2, pp. 309, 308, 312, 306–7; Cushing report, *OR,* 25:1, pp. 218–19.

20. Lee to Anderson, Apr. 30, 1863, *OR,* 25:2, p. 761; Freeman, *R. E. Lee,* 2,

p. 514; Charles E. DeNoon to brother, May 7, DeNoon, *Charlie's Letters,* p. 140.

21. Charles Marshall, "Events Leading up to the Battle of Gettysburg," *Southern Historical Society Papers,* 23 (1895), p. 210; Fitzhugh Lee, "Chancellorsville," *Southern Historical Society Papers,* 7 (1879), p. 562; Randolph Barton memoir, Margaretta Barton Colt, *Defend the Valley: A Shenandoah Family in the Civil War,* pp. 235–36; Lee to War Dept., [May 1], 1863, Lee, *Wartime Papers,* p. 449; Lee special orders, Apr. 30, *OR,* 25:2, p. 762; Lee to McLaws, Apr. 30, Lee, *Wartime Papers,* pp. 447–48.

22. John Esten Cooke, *Stonewall Jackson: A Military Biography* (New York: D. Appleton, 1866), p. 394; William Allan memoir, Allan Papers, Southern Historical Collection, University of North Carolina; diary, Apr. 30, May 1, 1863, Hotchkiss, *Make Me a Map,* pp. 136–37. In entering in his diary Jackson's call for a map, Hotchkiss described it as "embracing the region between the Rapidanne and the Rappahannock and reaching back to the Virginia Central Railroad. . . ." He surely meant the Orange & Alexandria rather than the Virginia Central, which was some 25 miles south of the focus of the map.

23. Hillman A. Hall, *History of the Sixth New York Cavalry* (Worcester, Mass.: Blanchard Press, 1908), pp. 102–3; Stuart report, *OR,* 25:1, p. 1047; McClellan, *Life and Campaigns of Stuart,* pp. 230–31; Scheibert, *Seven Months in the Rebel States,* pp. 57–58; Bigelow, *Chancellorsville,* p. 226; E. C. Adams to Thomas T. Munford, 1909, Adams to William F. Graves, Jan. 18, 1909, M. T. Rucker to Graves, Jan. 18, 1909, Bigelow Papers, Library of Congress; James W. Watts to Munford, Sept. 1, 1897, *OR Supplement,* 4, pp. 678–79; Jedediah Hotchkiss and William Allan, *The Battle-Fields of Virginia: Chancellorsville,* p. 32.

24. Casualties: *OR,* 25:1, p. 172, Robert T. Hubard memoir, Alderman Library, University of Virginia.

25. Williams to daughter, May 18, 1863,

Williams, *From the Cannon's Mouth,*
p. 185; Winfield Scott Hancock to wife,
May 7, Almira R. Hancock, *Reminiscences of Winfield Scott Hancock, By His Wife* (New York: Charles L. Webster, 1887), pp. 94–95; Cyrus Bacon diary, Apr. 30, Bacon, "A Michigan Surgeon," pp. 318–19.

26. Hooker general order, Apr. 30, 1863, *OR,* 25:1, p. 171; Williams to daughter, May 18, Williams, *From the Cannon's Mouth,* p. 185; Justus M. Silliman to mother, May 9, Silliman, *New Canaan Private,* p. 30; Charles E. Bowers to wife, May 1, Massachusetts Historical Society; William Houghton to father, May 1, Nancy Niblack Baxter, *Gallant Fourteenth: The Story of an Indiana Civil War Regiment,* p. 138; Charles H. Eoger to wife, May 1, U.S. Army Military History Institute.

8: To Repulse the Enemy

1. Hotchkiss and Allan, *Chancellorsville,* p. 40; Hotchkiss to G.F.R. Henderson, 1897, Hotchkiss Papers, Library of Congress; Robert K. Krick, "Lee's Greatest Victory," *American Heritage,* 41:2 (Mar. 1990), pp. 69–70; Harrison, *Chancellorsville Battlefield Sites,* p. 57.

2. Paul J. Scheips, "Union Signal Communications: Innovation and Conflict," *Civil War History,* 9:4 (Dec. 1963), pp. 402–3, 407–9; Cushing report, *OR,* 25:1, p. 223.

3. Cushing, Beardslee reports, *OR,* 25:1, pp. 217–19, 223, 228–29.

4. Jerome report, Hooker Papers, Huntington Library; William R. Plum, *The Military Telegraph During the Civil War in the United States,* 2, p. 97; Butterfield to Hooker, May 1, 1863 (two), *OR,* 25:2, pp. 326, 338.

5. Alexander, *Fighting for the Confederacy,* pp. 195–96, 581n; Alexander, McLaws reports, *OR,* 25:1, pp. 820, 824–25; Robert Stiles, *Four Years Under Marse Robert,* p. 168; William M. Dame to mother, May 2, 1863, Fredericksburg & Spotsylvania National Military Park.

Lee and Jackson may only have been together somewhat later in the day than Alexander remembered; still his reaction is credible.

6. Diary, May 1, 1863, Hotchkiss, *Make Me a Map,* p. 137; Lee special order, Apr. 30, *OR,* 25:2, p. 762; Lee to War Dept., [May 1], Lee, *Wartime Papers,* p. 449; Alexander, *Fighting for the Confederacy,* p. 196. For data on the numbers in Lee's army, see Chapter 5 Note 6.

7. Hooker to Bates, Apr. 2, 1877, Bates Collection, Pennsylvania Historical and Museum Commission; Fiske, *Dunn Browne in the Army,* p. 142; diary, May 1, 1863, Bacon, "A Michigan Surgeon," p. 319.

8. Hooker circular, May 1, 1863, *OR,* 25:2, p. 324; Butterfield to Sedgwick, Apr. 30 (two), Butterfield to Gibbon, Apr. 30 (two), Butterfield to Sickles, Apr. 30, *OR,* 25:2, pp. 306–7, 312, 343–44, 314; Hooker to Butterfield, May 1, *OR,* 25:2, p. 338.

9. Hooker to Bates, Apr. 2, 1877, Bates Collection, Pennsylvania Historical and Museum Commission; Hooker memorandum, Mar. 21, 1877, courtesy Abraham Lincoln Book Shop; Butterfield to Hooker, May 1, 1863, *OR,* 25:2, p. 322; Warren, Meade, Humphreys reports, *OR,* 25:1, pp. 198, 507, 546; Lowe to Sedgwick, May 1, Hooker circular, May 1, *OR,* 25:2, pp. 336, 324; John W. De Peyster, "The Plan of Chancellorsville," in Frank Allaben, *John Watts De Peyster,* 2, p. 113. Hooker's circular was certainly prepared before its 11:00 A.M. time marked in the *Official Records,* and was supplemented and modified by verbal orders to Meade and Slocum (De Peyster, pp. 113–14).

10. Robert T. Hubard memoir, Alderman Library, University of Virginia; Couch, RG 94, U.S. Generals' Reports, National Archives; Williams to daughter, May 18, 1863, Williams, *From the Cannon's Mouth,* p. 186.

11. Meade report, *OR,* 25:1, p. 507; Charles E. Bowers to wife, May 2, 1863, Massachusetts Historical Society; Walter Carter letter, May 2, in Robert G. Carter,

Four Brothers in Blue, pp. 246–47; Oliver W. Norton to sister, May 8, Norton, *Army Letters, 1861–1865,* p. 149; James C. Biddle letter, May 7, in Alexander S. Webb, "Meade at Chancellorsville," *Papers of the Military Historical Society of Massachusetts,* 3, p. 233. The side-road advance Bowers mentions was on the Duerson's Mill Road. Another Meade contingent made a short advance down the Mine Road.

12. Bernard, *War Talks,* p. 69; Harrison, *Chancellorsville Battlefield Sites,* pp. 26–27, 35–36, 39; Charles I. Wickersham, "Personal Recollections of the Cavalry at Chancellorsville," Wisconsin MOLLUS, *War Papers,* 3 (Milwaukee, 1903), pp. 456–57; Westwood A. Todd memoir, Southern Historical Collection, University of North Carolina.

13. Diary, May 1, 1863, Bacon, "A Michigan Surgeon," p. 319; Burbank, Bush, Andrews reports, *OR,* 25:1, pp. 533, 537, 540; Reese, *Sykes' Regular Infantry,* pp. 210–12; Harrison, *Chancellorsville Battlefield Sites,* p. 32; George Merryweather to parents, May 9, Chicago Historical Society.

14. Westwood A. Todd memoir, Southern Historical Collection, University of North Carolina; Jonathan B. Hager memoir, Alderman Library, University of Virginia.

15. Semmes, McLaws, Warren, Sykes reports, *OR,* 25:1, pp. 833–34, 825, 198, 525; John Wood to aunt, May 10, 1863, Georgia Department of Archives and History; Reese, *Sykes' Regular Infantry,* p. 213; Stuart to Jackson, May 1, Jackson to Stuart, May 1, *Southern Historical Society Papers,* 11 (1883), pp. 137–38.

16. Warren, Slocum, Williams reports, *OR,* 25:1, pp. 198–99, 670, 677; Bull, *Soldiering,* pp. 44–45; William Aughinbaugh diary, May 7, 1863, Schoff Collection, Clements Library, University of Michigan.

17. Joseph Dickinson memoir, in Henry E. Tremain, *Two Days of War,* pp. 432–33; Hooker to Butterfield, May 1, 1863, *OR,* 25:2, p. 328; Warren report, *OR,* 25:1, p. 199; Butterfield to Hooker, May 1 (10:25 A.M.), Hooker Papers, Huntington Library; Butterfield to Hooker, May 1 (11:32 A.M.), *Report of Joint Committee,* 1 (1865), p. 129; Butterfield to Hooker, May 1 (12:30 P.M., 1:45 P.M.), *OR,* 25:2, pp. 325, 326; Hooker to Butterfield, May 1 (11:30 A.M.), *Report of Joint Committee,* 1 (1865), p. 128. Possibly other such dispatches also reached Hooker. In the *Official Records* and the Hooker Papers are half a dozen additional sightings made before noon of Jackson's columns by signal officers or by Lowe.

18. Hooker to Bates, Apr. 2, 1877, Bates Collection, Pennsylvania Historical and Museum Commission; Hancock report, *OR,* 25:1, p. 311; Hooker testimony, *Report of Joint Committee,* 1 (1865), p. 125; Hooker to Butterfield, May 1, 1863, *OR,* 25:2, p. 326; Hooker to Sykes, May 1, in Francis A. Walker, *History of the Second Army Corps,* p. 221; De Peyster, "Plan of Chancellorsville," p. 114; Dickinson memoir, Tremain, *Two Days of War,* p. 434; Charles F. Morse to John Bigelow, Jan. 13, 1912, Bigelow Papers, Library of Congress; Couch, RG 94, U.S. Generals' Reports, National Archives; Couch memoir, p. 129, Old Colony Historical Society. Couch later claimed Warren went back to Hooker a second time to protest the withdrawal (*Battles and Leaders,* 3, p. 159). This is unlikely, for the order to Sykes to withdraw is in Warren's handwriting; his protest, if any, would surely have been made at the time of the order's writing. In neither his report nor in his congressional testimony did Warren comment on the withdrawal order. It was also claimed in retrospect that Slocum went back to protest directly to Hooker (Washington A. Roebling memoir, Bigelow Papers, Library of Congress). No contemporaneous evidence supports this.

19. Hooker to Bates, Apr. 2, 1877, Bates Collection, Pennsylvania Historical and Museum Commission; Bigelow, *Chancellorsville,* pp. 254–55; Washington A. Roebling memoir, Bigelow Papers, Li-

20. George Merryweather to parents, May 9, 1863, Chicago Historical Society; Harrison, *Chancellorsville Battlefield Sites,* pp. 28–29; Billings report, *OR Supplement,* 4, pp. 616–17; Williams to daughter, May 18, Williams, *From the Cannon's Mouth,* p. 187; Walker, *Second Army Corps,* p. 222; Couch in *Battles and Leaders,* 3, p. 159.

21. George Breck in *Rochester Union & Advertiser,* May 4, 1863, courtesy John J. Hennessy; Cyrus R. Stone to parents, May 1, Minnesota Historical Society; Selden Connor to father, May 1, John Hay Library, Brown University.

22. Walter Clark, ed., *Histories of the Several Regiments and Battalions from North Carolina in the Great War, 1861–'65,* 4, p. 172; Samuel W. Eaton diary, May 1, 1863, Southern Historical Collection, University of North Carolina; Early, *Autobiographical Sketch,* pp. 197–99; Pendleton report, *OR,* 25:1, pp. 810–11; R. Snowden Andrews report, RG 109, M-836:6, National Archives; May 1, Henry W. Wingfield, "Diary of Capt. H. W. Wingfield," ed. W. W. Scott, *Bulletin of the Virginia State Library,* 16 (July 1927), p. 25; Urbanus Dart, Jr., in *Brunswick* (Ga.) *News,* May 4, Georgia Department of Archives and History; Butterfield to Hooker, May 1, *OR,* 25:2, p. 327; Edmund D. Halsey diary, May 1, U.S. Army Military History Institute.

23. Sedgwick to Butterfield, May 1, 1863, Hooker Papers, Huntington Library; Sedgwick to Butterfield, May 1, *OR,* 25:2, p. 338; Burnham report, *OR,* 51:1, p. 180; Reynolds to Sedgwick, May 1, Hooker to Butterfield, May 1, Butterfield to Hooker, May 1, *OR,* 25:2, pp. 337, 326; Hooker to Butterfield, May 1, *Report of Joint Committee,* 1 (1865), p. 128; Sedgwick to Reynolds, May 1, *OR,* 25:2, p. 341; Butterfield to Sedgwick, May 1, Hooker Papers.

24. Matthew Marvin diary, May 1, 1863, Minnesota Historical Society; Gibbon, *Recollections of the Civil War,* pp. 112–14; Isaac L. Taylor diary, May 1, Taylor, "Campaigning with the First Minnesota," p. 345; Gibbon special order, May 1, Sully court of inquiry, May 16, *OR,* 25:1, pp. 351, 352.

25. Hooker to Butterfield, May 1, 1863, *OR,* 25:2, p. 330; Hooker to Bates, Aug. 28, 1876, Mar. 24, 1879, Apr. 2, 1877, Bates Collection, Pennsylvania Historical and Museum Commission; S. Williams to Stoneman, Apr. 12, 1863, Candler to Stoneman, Apr. 28, *OR,* 25:1, pp. 1066–67, 1065; Report on Railroads, 1863, Hooker Papers, Huntington Library.

26. Stoneman, Gregg, Averell, W.H.F. Lee reports, *OR,* 25:1, pp. 1060, 1082, 1078–79, 1098; Nathan Webb diary, May 2, 1863, Schoff Collection, Clements Library, University of Michigan; John C. Tidball journal, May 1, Hooker Papers, Huntington Library; Candler to Averell, May 1, *OR,* 25:1, p. 1080. The fire did not in fact destroy the Rapidan Station railroad bridge.

27. Morrison to McLaws, May 1, 1863, *OR,* 25:2, p. 764; Bryan Grimes memoir, Grimes, *Extracts of Letters of Major-General Bryan Grimes to His Wife,* p. 28; Geary, Slocum reports, *OR,* 25:1, pp. 729, 670; Thomas M. Hightower to wife, May 8, Georgia Department of Archives and History; Alexander, *Fighting for the Confederacy,* p. 198.

28. Grandy report, *OR,* 25:1, p. 883; John Wood to aunt, May 10, 1863, Georgia Department of Archives and History; Joseph A. Graves, *The History of the Bedford Light Artillery* (Bedford, Va., 1903), p. 29; William M. Dame to mother, May 2, Fredericksburg & Spotsylvania National Military Park; Watson, Arnold, Morgan, Hancock reports, *OR,* 25:1, pp. 545, 360, 309, 311; Thomas E. Dardin to Mary Collins, May 24, Rowley-Gifford-Clegg Papers, Filson Club; J. S. Graham to aunt, May 8,

McFadden, *Aunt and the Soldier Boys,* p. 83; Reese, *Sykes' Regular Infantry,* p. 215.

29. Wright, McDougall reports, *OR,* 25:1, pp. 866, 704–5; Joseph L. Akerman diary, May 1, 1863, Perkins Library, Duke University; Williams to daughter, May 18, Williams, *From the Cannon's Mouth,* p. 187; Bull, *Soldiering,* pp. 45–47; S. Atwood in *Salem* (N.Y.) *Press,* May 26, courtesy John J. Hennessy. Lewis's Run was also known as Lewis's Creek and Scott's Run.

30. Beckham, Fitzhugh, Woodbury reports, *OR,* 25:1, pp. 1049, 723, 725; Brown, *Twenty-seventh Indiana,* p. 316; Frank Robertson memoir, Virginia Historical Society; Marcellus N. Moorman in *Southern Historical Society Papers,* 30 (1902), p. 110; Scheibert, *Seven Months in the Rebel States,* p. 60; Thomas E. Dardin to Mary Collins, May 24, 1863, Rowley-Gifford-Clegg Papers, Filson Club; Heros Von Borcke, *Memoirs of the Confederate War for Independence,* 2, pp. 220–21.

31. Williams to daughter, May 18, 1863, Williams, *From the Cannon's Mouth,* p. 187. Sykes's losses are compiled from his officers' reports in the *Official Records.*

32. Couch in *Battles and Leaders,* 3, p. 161; T.M.R. Talcott, "General Lee's Strategy at the Battle of Chancellorsville," *Southern Historical Society Papers,* 34 (1906), p. 12.

9: My Troops Will Move at Once

1. Williams to daughter, May 18, 1863, Williams, *From the Cannon's Mouth,* p. 187.

2. Butterfield to Hooker, May 1, 1863, Hunt to Butterfield, May 1, Butterfield to Hooker, May 1, *OR,* 25:2, pp. 332, 327–28, 331; Butterfield to Gibbon, May 1, Hunt to Hooker, May 1, Hooker Papers, Huntington Library.

3. Hooker circular, May 1, 1863, *OR,* 25:2, p. 328; Warren, Graham reports, *OR,* 25:1, pp. 199, 413; Candler to Slo-

cum and Howard, May 1, *OR,* 25:2, p. 334; Couch memoir, p. 130, Old Colony Historical Society.

4. Fortescue to Cushing, May 1, 1863, Hooker Papers, Huntington Library; Butterfield to Hooker, May 1, Butterfield to Peck, May 1, *OR,* 25:2, pp. 327, 345; Peck to Butterfield, May 1, Hooker Papers; Peck to Butterfield, May 2, *OR,* 25:2, p. 370.

5. Sharpe to Babcock, May 2, 1863, Hooker Papers, Huntington Library; Butterfield to Sedgwick, May 2, *OR,* 25:2, p. 362; J. L. McPhail to Sharpe, May 2 (two), RG 393, Part 1, Entry 3980, B.M.I., National Archives (the dispatch in *OR,* 25:2, p. 329 is misdated May 1). The spy Maddox is identified in Edwin C. Fishel, *The Secret War for the Union.*

6. Butterfield to Hooker, May 1, 1863, Hooker to Butterfield, May 2, Butterfield to Hooker, May 2, Butterfield to Reynolds, May 2, *OR,* 25:2, pp. 342, 351, 368–69; Sedgwick to Butterfield, May 2, Hooker Papers, Huntington Library; Sedgwick, Hooker testimony, *Report of Joint Committee,* 1 (1865), pp. 95, 129. Col. Hiram Burnham replaced the resigned Brig. Gen. Calvin E. Pratt in command of the Light Division on Apr. 30. In his testimony concerning his order to Sedgwick on May 2 to cross the river, Hooker explained that it was written "under the impression that his corps was on the north bank of the Rappahannock. . . ." The head of Reynolds's column did not start upriver until 9:00 A.M., four to five hours later than Hooker intended, and was across U.S. Ford at 5:30 P.M. (Root report, *OR,* 25:1, p. 279).

7. William Allen, interview with General Lee, 1868, Lee Papers, Leyburn Library, Washington and Lee University; Lee to Stuart, May 1, 1863, *OR,* 25:2, p. 764; W.H.F. Lee report, *OR,* 25:1, p. 1098; Louise Haskell Daly, *Alexander Cheves Haskell: The Portrait of a Man,* pp. 100–101; Talcott, "Lee's Strategy," p. 17; Krick, *Parker's Virginia Battery,* pp. 123–24.

8. T.M.R. Talcott in A. L. Long, *Memoirs of Robert E. Lee: His Military and Personal History*, p. 254; Lee to Davis, May 2, 1863, *OR*, 25:2, p. 765; Lee to Mary Anna Jackson, Jan. 25, 1866, Lee Papers, Leyburn Library, Washington and Lee University (the manuscript was R. L. Dabney's). The accounts of this May 1 conference are summarized in Talcott's "Lee's Strategy," *Southern Historical Society Papers*, 34 (1906), pp. 1–27, and Douglas Southall Freeman's "Who Devised the Left Flank Movement at Chancellorsville?" in his *R. E. Lee*, 2, pp. 584–89. See Appendix III.

9. Talcott, "Lee's Strategy," pp. 16–17; James Power Smith to Hotchkiss, 1897, Hotchkiss Papers, Library of Congress; Fitzhugh Lee, "Chancellorsville," p. 567; Beckham, Schurz reports, *OR*, 25:1, pp. 1049, 650; John Gill to John Bigelow, Jan. 4, 1909, Bigelow Papers, Library of Congress; Long, *Memoirs of Lee*, p. 252; Lee to Davis, May 2, 1863, *OR*, 25:2, p. 765.

10. Hotchkiss to G.F.R. Henderson, 1897, J. P. Smith to Hotchkiss, Apr. 16, 1897, Hotchkiss Papers, Library of Congress; B. T. Lacy narrative, Southern Historical Collection, University of North Carolina. This early morning conference on May 2 was in a different clearing than the conference the evening before, and by all accounts only at the morning conference were the famous Yankee hardtack (or cracker) boxes utilized.

11. Candler letter, May 2, 1863, in Bigelow, *Chancellorsville*, p. 271; Hooker circular, May 1, *OR*, 25:2, p. 328.

12. Harrison, *Chancellorsville Battlefield Sites*, pp. 11, 74; Candler to Averell, May 1, 1863, *OR*, 25:1, p. 1080. At the time of the battle the James Hatch family was living at Talley's, which in some accounts is called the Hatch house.

13. Howard in *Battles and Leaders*, 3, p. 195; Justus M. Silliman to mother, May 9, 1863, Silliman, *New Canaan Private*, p. 30; Sickles, Von Gilsa, Schurz reports, *OR*, 25:1, pp. 385, 636, 651; Bruce Catton, *Glory Road: The Bloody*

Route *from Fredericksburg to Gettysburg*, p. 195; Hooker testimony, *Report of Joint Committee*, 1 (1865), p. 125; Bigelow, *Chancellorsville*, p. 258.

14. Joseph L. Akerman diary, May 2, 1863, Perkins Library, Duke University; Richard T. Auchmuty to mother, May 2, Auchmuty, *Letters of Richard Tylden Auchmuty, Fifth Corps, Army of the Potomac*, p. 86.

15. Griffith, *Variosa*, p. 62; diary, May 2, 1863, Hotchkiss, *Make Me a Map*, p. 139; J.F.J. Caldwell, *The History of [Gregg's] Brigade of South Carolinians*, p. 74; Oliver C. Hamilton to father, May 17, Eli Spinks Hamilton Papers, Southern Historical Collection, University of North Carolina; John S. Brooks to father, May 8, Southern Historical Collection; Pegram, Knap reports, *OR*, 25:1, pp. 937–38, 771; James B. Heazlitt diary, May 2, Huntington Library.

16. John B. Imboden in *Battles and Leaders*, 2, p. 297. For the calculation of numbers in the Army of Northern Virginia, see Chapter 5 Note 6. The difference from Bigelow's May 2 figures (*Chancellorsville*, p. 273) is in accepting Alexander's count of April reinforcements (*Military Memoirs*, p. 322), and the correction of placing Graham's 1st Rockbridge Battery with Early at Fredericksburg (Early, *Autobiographical Sketch*, p. 197). One of McLaws's regiments, the 8th South Carolina, was detailed to Jackson, but as it guarded a portion of the upper Furnace Road on May 2 it is credited here to Lee's force (Lacy narrative, Southern Historical Collection, University of North Carolina). Lee's force lacked one brigade from Anderson's division, Wilcox's, that was guarding Banks's Ford on May 2.

17. Rodes report, *OR*, 25:1, p. 940; Alexander, *Military Memoirs*, p. 329; James Power Smith in *Battles and Leaders*, 3, p. 205; G.F.R. Henderson, *Stonewall Jackson and the American Civil War*, p. 666. The Federals first sighted the flanking column at Catharine Furnace

about 8:00 A.M., some two miles (an hour's march) from Colquitt's camp on the Plank Road. Confederate reports on the starting time are vague, Rodes saying the march was "resumed" at 8 o'clock.

18. Alexander, *Military Memoirs,* p. 330; Jackson general order, Apr. 13, 1863, *OR,* 25:2, p. 719; Griffith, *Variosa,* p. 67. Neither Hotchkiss nor Lacy left a specific description of the flank-march route as originally planned. But since the only purpose in following Wellford's recommended route was to detour unseen past the Carpenter farm, it seems certain Jackson believed the Federals' right flank to be located there. His subsequent reconnaissance eastward on the Orange Plank Road suggests that, too, was part of the intended route.

19. Hunter McGuire, "Career and Character of General T. J. Jackson," *Southern Historical Society Papers,* 25 (1897), p. 110; B. B. Carr memoir, North Carolina State Archives; Alexander, *Fighting for the Confederacy,* pp. 201–2; Thomas T. Munford to John Bigelow, Dec. 24, 1908, Bigelow Papers, Library of Congress; Thomas T. Munford memoir, Perkins Library, Duke University; Caldwell, *Gregg's Brigade,* p. 76; Griffith, *Variosa,* p. 67; Archer report, *OR,* 25:1, p. 924.

20. Butterfield to Hooker, May 2, 1863 (two), Hooker Papers, Huntington Library (the 8:55 A.M. telegram is miscopied in the *Official Records*); Peck to Hooker, May 2, *OR,* 25:2, p. 370; May 2, Wainwright, *Diary of Battle,* pp. 190–91; Andrews report, RG 109, M-836:6, National Archives; Paul report, *OR,* 25:1, pp. 265–66; First Corps journal of operations, Hooker Papers; Reynolds to Sedgwick, May 2, *OR,* 51:1, p. 1034.

21. Butterfield to Lowe, May 2, 1863, Lowe to Butterfield, May 2, *OR,* Series Three, 3, p. 314; E. S. Allen to Paul Oliver, May 2, Hooker Papers, Huntington Library; Randolph Barton to John Bigelow, Jan. 8, 1909, Bigelow Papers, Library of Congress; Barry G. Benson memoir, Southern Historical Collection, University of North Carolina.

22. Birney, Clark, Randolph, Sickles, Best reports, *OR,* 25:1, pp. 408, 443, 404, 386, 979; William W. Chamberlain memorandum, 1908, Bigelow Papers, Library of Congress; William Allan memoir, Southern Historical Collection, University of North Carolina; John S. Apperson diary, May 2, 1863, Virginia Polytechnic Institute and State University Libraries.

23. The 9:30 A.M. Van Alen dispatch to Howard is from the "Letters Received" file of the Eleventh Corps, copied by Howard's clerk on June 30, 1863 (with H. M. Kellogg to Hooker, July 7, 1872, Bates Collection, Pennsylvania Historical and Museum Commission). The 9:30 circular is in the *Report of the Joint Committee,* 1 (1865), p. 126. The Catharine Furnace clearing was not visible to Hooker from the Chancellor house. Thus the scene with Hooker watching the movement and soliloquizing, "If not retreat, what is it? Lee is trying to flank me" (Bigelow, *Chancellorsville,* p. 276), is apocryphal.

24. Schurz to Hooker, Apr. 22, 1876, in *Battles and Leaders,* 3, pp. 219–20; Schurz, *Reminiscences,* 1, pp. 416–18; O. O. Howard in *Battles and Leaders,* 3, p. 196; Howard to Hooker, May 2, 1863, in Bates, *Chancellorsville,* p. 90; Castle report, Hooker Papers, Huntington Library. For Hooker's warning to Howard, see Note 23 above. Schurz remembered the warning arriving about noon, but the time of Howard's reply (10:50 A.M.) places it earlier. And the 10:50 was surely a reply: the sighting from Talley's was too distant to tell friend from foe, giving Howard no reason to speak of meeting an attack from the west before receiving Hooker's warning. Hooker wrote that the warning was delivered "certainly within an half an hour. . . ." (Hooker to Bates, June 26, 1876, Bates Collection, Pennsylvania Historical and Museum Commission.) It was usual practice to

post corps artillery near headquarters, rather than in this case a response by Howard to Hooker's warning.

25. Sickles, Bodine, Tripp, Hamilton, Miles reports, *OR*, 25:1, pp. 385, 459, 454, 844, 323; Charles E. Bowers to wife, May 2, 1863, Massachusetts Historical Society.

26. Butterfield to Hooker, May 2, 1863, Van Alen to Butterfield, May 2 (two), *OR*, 25:2, pp. 353, 362; Hooker to Bates, Apr. 2, 1877, Bates Collection, Pennsylvania Historical and Museum Commission.

27. Early, *Autobiographical Sketch*, pp. 200–202; Stiles, *Four Years Under Marse Robert*, p. 189; Pendleton report, *OR*, 25:1, pp. 811–12. Early thought Chilton arrived with Lee's order about 11:00 A.M., and Pendleton remembered it as between 11:00 and 12:00. From Federal sightings of Early's movements it was probably closer to 10 o'clock.

28. Lowe to Butterfield, May 2, 1863, *OR*, Series Three, 3, p. 314; Fortesque to Butterfield, May 2, Hall to Butterfield, May 2, Sedgwick to Butterfield, May 2, Butterfield to Hooker, May 2, Hooker Papers, Huntington Library.

29. McLaws report, *OR*, 25:1, p. 825; Lee to [Wilcox], May 2, 1863, Palmer Collection, Western Reserve Historical Society; Lee to Davis, May 2, *OR*, 25:2, p. 765.

30. Butterfield to Hooker, May 1, 1863, Stanton to Hooker, May 2, *OR*, 25:2, pp. 326, 351; May 2, Heintzelman diary, Library of Congress; Elizabeth Blair Lee to Samuel P. Lee, Apr. 30, Laas, *Wartime Washington*, p. 265; May 2, Patrick diary, Library of Congress; Robert McAllister to wife, May 2, McAllister, *Civil War Letters*, p. 296; diary, May 2, Bacon, "A Michigan Surgeon," p. 320; Williams to daughter, May 18, Williams, *From the Cannon's Mouth*, p. 188. Heintzelman referred to a *New York Tribune* extra published May 1.

31. Butterfield to Keyes, May 2, 1863, *OR*, 25:2, p. 370; Butterfield to Hooker, May 2, Butterfield to Van Alen, May 2,

Hooker Papers, Huntington Library; Greene, "Stoneman's Raid," in Gallagher, *Chancellorsville;* Nathan Webb diary, May 2, Schoff Collection, Clements Library, University of Michigan; Stoneman report, *OR*, 25:1, p. 1060.

32. Sickles report, *OR*, 25:1, p. 385; William Allan memoir, Southern Historical Collection, University of North Carolina; John S. Apperson diary, May 2, 1863, Virginia Polytechnic Institute and State University Libraries. At Todd's Tavern, according to Apperson, the corps ambulance train went north on the Brock Road and followed the Wellford "detour" the rest of the column was using. By Allan's account, the corps ordnance train, apparently due to crowding along this route, continued on the Catharpin Road four miles or so beyond Todd's Tavern before turning north to reach the Orange Plank Road at Parker's Store, then turned east.

33. Best report, *OR*, 25:1, p. 980; H. S. Fuller in *Confederate Veteran*, 26:11 (Nov. 1918), p. 473; James S. Mitchell memoir, William Fleming Collection; Bigelow, *Chancellorsville*, 280–81; George Marden letter, May 8, 1863, Special Collections, Dartmouth College Library; Sickles to Dickinson, May 2, Hooker Papers, Huntington Library.

34. R. E. Lee, Moore, Archer, Sickles, Best reports, *OR*, 25:1, pp. 798, 934, 924, 386–87, 980; H. S. Fuller in *Confederate Veteran*, 26:11 (Nov. 1918), p. 473; George Marden letter, May 8, 1863, Special Collections, Dartmouth College Library; Bull, *Soldiering*, pp. 49–50; John L. Collins in *Battles and Leaders*, 3, p. 183; Asa W. Bartlett, *History of the Twelfth Regiment New Hampshire Volunteers in the War of the Rebellion*, p. 448.

35. Thomas T. Munford to John Bigelow, Dec. 24, 1908, James Breckinridge to Bigelow, Feb. 12, 1909, M. T. Rucker to Bigelow, Jan. 18, 1909, Bigelow Papers, Library of Congress; Fitzhugh Lee, "Chancellorsville," pp. 572–73; Sandie Pendleton statement, July 18, 1863, John Esten Cooke Papers, Alderman

Library, University of Virginia; Augustus C. Hamlin, *The Battle of Chancellorsville*, pp. 14–15.

36. Alexander, *Fighting for the Confederacy*, p. 202; Jackson to Lee, May 2, 1863, in *Battles and Leaders*, 3, p. 206.

10: They Were Flying in Great Disorder

1. Griffith, *Variosa*, p. 68; W. H. May memoir, Georgia Department of Archives and History; Rodes, Colston reports, *OR*, 25:1, pp. 940–41, 1004. Rodes's entire division participated in the attack except the 23rd Georgia, left at Catharine Furnace.

2. Frank Robertson memoir, Virginia Historical Society; Marcellus N. Moorman in *Southern Historical Society Papers*, 30 (1902), p. 111.

3. Couch memoir, p. 130, Old Colony Historical Society; Alexander S. Webb to wife, May 2, 1863, Webb Papers, Yale University Library; Howard to J. E. Rankin, Aug. 5, 1869, O. O. Howard Papers, Bowdoin College Library; Howard to John A. Owens, Aug. 15, 1881, Chicago Historical Society; Howard report, *OR*, 25:1, p. 630; Schurz, *Reminiscences*, 1, pp. 405–6; Hamlin, *Chancellorsville*, pp. 35, 64; Alfred E. Lee, John C. Lee in *Philadelphia Weekly Times*, Nov. 23, 1887, Feb. 1, 1888.

4. Butterfield to Hooker, May 2, 1863, Hooker circular, May 2, Hooker Papers, Huntington Library. A dozen dispatches, in the Hooker Papers and the *Official Records*, detail Early's movements previous to Butterfield's 4:45 announcement.

5. Howard to Hooker, May 2, 1863, in Bates, *Chancellorsville*, p. 90; Croffut and Morris, *Military and Civil History of Connecticut*, p. 361; Norvell Cobb memorandum, Dabney Papers, Southern Historical Collection, University of North Carolina; John C. Lee in Hamlin, *Chancellorsville*, p. 58; Hartwell Osborn, "On the Right at Chancellorsville," Illinois MOLLUS, *Military Essays*

and Recollections, 4 (Chicago, 1907), pp. 185–86; Hamlin, *Chancellorsville*, pp. 58–60, 145; Elias R. Monfort, "The First Division, Eleventh Corps, at Chancellorsville," *G.A.R. War Papers* (Cincinnati, 1891), p. 62. John C. Lee's articles appeared in *National Tribune*, May 19, 1885, and *Philadelphia Weekly Times*, Feb. 1, 1888.

6. Williams to daughter, May 18, 1863, Williams, *From the Cannon's Mouth*, p. 188; A. B. Searles in *Boston Journal*, n.d., Fredericksburg & Spotsylvania National Military Park; Owen Rice, "Afield with the Eleventh Corps at Chancellorsville," Ohio MOLLUS, *Sketches of War History*, 1 (Cincinnati, 1885), p. 23; Hamlin, *Chancellorsville*, p. 61; Schurz, Castle reports, *OR*, 25:1, pp. 654, 231; J. H. Stine, *History of the Army of the Potomac*, p. 350; Hamlin, *Chancellorsville*, pp. 56–57; Catton, *Glory Road*, pp. 200–201.

7. Hamlin, *Chancellorsville*, p. 144; Alfred E. Lee in *Philadelphia Weekly Times*, Nov. 23, 1887; John C. Lee in Hamlin, *Chancellorsville*, p. 58; Devens report, *OR*, 25:1, pp. 633–34; Howard, *Autobiography*, p. 366; Hooker to Bates, June 26, 1876, Bates Collection, Pennsylvania Historical and Museum Commission.

8. Slocum report, *OR*, 25:1, p. 670; Van Alen to Butterfield, May 2, 1863, *OR*, 25:2, p. 363.

9. Schurz, *Reminiscences*, 1, p. 419; Monfort, "First Division, Eleventh Corps," pp. 62–63; Schurz report, *OR*, 25:1, pp. 652, 654; May 4, 1863, Daniel G. Brinton, "From Chancellorsville to Gettysburg: A Doctor's Diary," ed. D. G. Brinton Thompson, *Pennsylvania Magazine of History and Biography*, 89 (1965), p. 300; Howard to S. Williams, May 10, Hooker Papers, Huntington Library; Frank Robertson memoir, Virginia Historical Society.

10. Eleventh Corps return, May 21, 1863, *OR*, 25:1, p. 660; Charles Parker to Edgar Van Hoesen, May 15, Schoff Collection, Clements Library, University of Michigan; Humphreys report, *OR*,

25:1, p. 550; Warren testimony, *Report of Joint Committee*, 1 (1865), p. 45; Francis Stofflet in *Easton* (Pa.) *Daily Free Press*, May 3, 1913, Ropes Collection, Boston University Library; Thomas Evans memoir, Civil War Collection, Ohio State Museum.

11. Hamlin, *Chancellorsville*, p. 144; Howard to Hooker, May 2, 1863, in Bates, *Chancellorsville*, p. 90; Hooker testimony, *Report of Joint Committee*, 1 (1865), pp. 127, 137; Howard in *Battles and Leaders*, 3, p. 197; Schurz, *Reminiscences*, 1, p. 421; Francis Stofflet in *Easton* (Pa.) *Daily Free Press*, May 3, 1913, Ropes Collection, Boston University Library; diary, May 4, 1863, Brinton, "From Chancellorsville to Gettysburg," p. 300; Thomas Evans memoir, Civil War Collection, Ohio State Museum.

12. James Power Smith in *Battles and Leaders*, 3, p. 208. Although Hotchkiss's diary (Hotchkiss, *Make Me a Map*, p. 138) sets the start of Jackson's attack "at precisely 6 o'clock," it appears that "Confederate time" as set at Fredericksburg from Richmond was half an hour faster than "Union time" set at Washington. Newspaperman Whitelaw Reid noted this in his May 2 dispatch from Falmouth (James G. Smart, ed., *A Radical View: The "Agate" Dispatches of Whitelaw Reid, 1861–1865* [Memphis: Memphis State University Press, 1976], 1, p. 264). Just arrived from Washington, Reid remarked that the church clocks in Fredericksburg struck the hours "just half an hour faster with their Richmond-regulated time. . . ." Arthur Candenquist's researches suggest that the R.F. & P. Railroad set its own "railroad time" in Richmond to regulate traffic on the road, and as a matter of convenience time-setters in Fredericksburg followed the railroad's lead. For benchmarks the R.F. & P. probably used a less than accurate almanac, while Washington time was regulated by the more accurate Naval Observatory. Since in this narrative such benchmarks as sunrise and sunset are Naval Observatory calculations, the timing of other events is adjusted accordingly — thus a starting time of 5:30 for Jackson's attack.

13. John S. Brooks to father, May 8, 1863, Southern Historical Collection, University of North Carolina; Doles, Von Gilsa reports, *OR*, 25:1, pp. 967, 636; Hamlin, *Chancellorsville*, p. 65; Francis Stofflet in *Easton* (Pa.) *Daily Free Press*, May 3, 1913, Ropes Collection, Boston University; Thomas H. Hightower to fiancée, May 8, 1863, Georgia Department of Archives and History.

14. John C. Lee in Hamlin, *Chancellorsville*, p. 59; Alfred E. Lee in *Philadelphia Weekly Times*, Nov. 23, 1887; McLean, Devens, Brady reports, *OR*, 25:1, pp. 637, 635, 639–40; Hamlin, *Chancellorsville*, pp. 66–67; Thomas Evans memoir, Civil War Collection, Ohio State Museum; Luther B. Mesnard memoir, U.S. Army Military History Institute; Justus M. Silliman to mother, May 9, 1863, Silliman, *New Canaan Private*, p. 31. In his report (*OR*, 25:1, p. 642) Colonel Lee received these orders directly from Devens, but in his later account, used here, he more properly received them through his brigade commander.

15. Howard, *Autobiography*, pp. 370–71; Howard to wife, May 9, 1863, O. O. Howard Papers, Bowdoin College Library; Schurz, *Reminiscences*, 1, pp. 406–7; Schurz report, *OR*, 25:1, pp. 654–55; Adam Muenzenberger to wife, May 7, Fredericksburg & Spotsylvania National Military Park; Sandie Pendleton statement, July 18, John Esten Cooke Papers, Alderman Library, University of Virginia; Henry Camp letter in *Queens County* (N.Y.) *Sentinel*, May 14, courtesy John J. Hennessy.

16. Schurz report, *OR*, 25:1, pp. 656–57; Darwin D. Cody to parents, May 9, 1863, Fredericksburg & Spotsylvania National Military Park; Howard to wife, May 9, 12, O. O. Howard Papers, Bowdoin College Library; *New York Herald*, May 7.

17. Robert K. Garnett to brother, May 19, 1863, Perkins Library, Duke University;

William Clegg to Mary Collins, May 8, Rowley-Gifford-Clegg Papers, Filson Club; Clark, *North Carolina Regiments*, 1, p. 145; Robert E. Park in *Southern Historical Society Papers*, 2 (1876), p. 26; Alexander, *Fighting for the Confederacy*, p. 203; Rodes, Iverson reports, *OR*, 25:1, pp. 941, 984–85; B. B. Carr memoir, North Carolina State Archives; Osborn, "On the Right at Chancellorsville," p. 189.

18. Henry Heth memoir, *Civil War History*, 8:3 (Sept. 1962), p. 301; Oliver C. Hamilton to father, May 17, 1863, Eli Spinks Hamilton Papers, Southern Historical Collection, University of North Carolina; William Clegg to Mary Collins, May 8, Rowley-Gifford-Clegg Papers, Filson Club; Griffith, *Variosa*, pp. 69–70.

19. Rodes, Colquitt, Ramseur reports, *OR*, 25:1, pp. 941, 975, 995; James O. Coghill to sister, May 10, 1863, Perkins Library, Duke University; Hamlin, *Chancellorsville*, pp. 74–76; James D. Emmons to sister, May 12, in Dunkelman and Whiney, *The Hardtack Regiment*, p. 61.

20. R. E. Wilbourn to [John Esten Cooke], May 1863, Charles J. Faulkner Papers, Virginia Historical Society; Wilbourn to R. L. Dabney, Dec. 13, 1863, Dabney Papers, Southern Historical Collection, University of North Carolina; McClellan, *Life and Campaigns of Stuart*, p. 234; Schurz, *Reminiscences*, 1, p. 426; Alexander, *Fighting for the Confederacy*, p. 201.

11: The Fate of Stonewall Jackson

1. Lee to Jackson, May 2, 1863, J.E.B. Stuart Papers, Huntington Library; Bernard, *War Talks*, p. 72; Lewis E. Warren memoir, Woodruff Library, Emory University; *London Times*, June 16; McLaws, Mahone, Mueller reports, *OR*, 25:1, pp. 826, 863, 644.

2. Lee, Pendleton reports, *OR*, 25:1, pp. 800, 814; Early, *Autobiographical Sketch*, p. 203; Butterfield to Sedgwick,

May 2, 1863 (two), Van Alen to Butterfield, May 2, Butterfield to Hooker, May 2 (misdated May 1), *OR*, 25:2, pp. 355, 364, 363, 329; May 31, Wainwright, *Diary of Battle*, p. 213. Sedgwick's later testimony (*Report of Joint Committee*, 1 [1865], p. 95) and Early's later autobiography are unclear as to the timing of these events. Telegrams cited and in the Hooker Papers have it that Hooker's 4:10 P.M. order was relayed to Sedgwick at 5:50 and received by him at 6:15, and that his advance was under way by 6:45. Early's operations are not easily reconstructed due to a lack of reports. His report (*OR*, 25:1, pp. 1000–2) is sketchy, and there are no reports by any of his infantry commanders on record.

3. Hamlin, *Chancellorsville*, p. 148; Hooker testimony, *Report of Joint Committee*, 1 (1865), p. 126; Charles Parker to Edgar Van Hoesen, May 15, 1863, Schoff Collection, Clements Library, University of Michigan.

4. William C. Wiley letter, May 1863, Patee Library, Pennsylvania State University; Swinton, *Campaigns of the Army of the Potomac*, p. 288; Robert McAllister to wife, May 1863, McAllister, *Civil War Letters*, pp. 300–1; James F. Rusling, *Men and Things I Saw in the Civil War Days* (New York: Eaton & Mains, 1899), p. 303; Patrick A. Guiney to wife, May 7, Dinand Library, College of the Holy Cross.

5. Henry N. Blake, *Three Years in the Army of the Potomac* (Boston: Lee & Shepard, 1865), p. 180; Hamlin, *Chancellorsville*, p. 78; Walker, *Second Army Corps*, pp. 228–29; Charles F. Morse letter, May 7, 1863, Bigelow Papers, Library of Congress; Francis A. Walker, *General Hancock* (New York: Appleton, 1894), p. 83; Hitchcock, *War from the Inside*, p. 218.

6. William Aughinbaugh diary, May 7, 1863, Schoff Collection, Clements Library, University of Michigan; Darwin D. Cody to parents, May 9, Fredericksburg & Spotsylvania National Military Park; Williams to daughter, May 18,

Williams, *From the Cannon's Mouth,* p. 190; Lucius B. Swift memoir, Bigelow Papers, Library of Congress. At most perhaps one third of the Eleventh Corps' twenty-three regiments retired in tolerably good order; in his report (*OR,* 25:1, p. 657) Schurz listed only four: 26th Wisconsin, 82nd Illinois, 82nd Ohio, 157th New York.

7. Francis C. Barlow to family, May 8, 1863, Massachusetts Historical Society; *San Francisco Chronicle,* Mar. 18, 1873. Eleventh Corps casualties were 248 killed, 1,183 wounded, and 993 captured, a total of 2,424; Bigelow counts but one of these after May 2. The count of 814 casualties in Jackson's attack does not include the 23rd Georgia's loss at Catharine Furnace (Bigelow, *Chancellorsville,* p. 505).

8. Slocum, Sickles, Reynolds, Meade reports, *OR,* 25:1, pp. 670, 387, 255, 507; Hooker testimony, *Report of Joint Committee,* 1 (1865), p. 126; Rodes report, *OR,* 25:1, p. 941; Hamlin, *Chancellorsville,* p. 81; B. B. Carr memoir, North Carolina State Archives.

9. Pennock Huey, Andrew B. Wells in *Battles and Leaders,* 3, pp. 186–87; Hamlin, *Chancellorsville,* pp. 90–92; Wickersham, "Recollections of the Cavalry at Chancellorsville," pp. 460–61.

10. Hamlin, *Chancellorsville,* pp. 97–98; Lucius B. Swift memoir, Bigelow Papers, Library of Congress.

11. Hamlin, *Chancellorsville,* pp. 93–95; Winn, Martin reports, *OR,* 25:1, pp. 970, 787; Brown, *Twenty-seventh Indiana,* p. 322; May 2, 1863, Orin G. Dority, "The Civil War Diary of Orin G. Dority," *Northwest Ohio Quarterly,* 37:1 (Winter 1964–65), pp. 14–15; Pleasonton to Hooker, May 2, Hooker Papers, Huntington Library.

12. Daly, *Alexander Cheves Haskell,* p. 102; Williams to daughter, May 18, 1863, Williams, *From the Cannon's Mouth,* p. 194; Bigelow, *Chancellorsville,* pp. 312–13, 318. Sunset on May 2 was at 6:49, and the end of evening nautical twilight (400 yards' visibility) was at 7:52 (U.S. Naval Observatory calcula-

tions, in Mark M. Boatner III, *The Civil War Dictionary,* pp. 819–21).

13. Norvell Cobb memorandum, Dabney Papers, Southern Historical Collection, University of North Carolina; James H. Lane in *Southern Historical Society Papers,* 8 (1880), pp. 493–94; Carter report, *OR,* 25:1, p. 999; Lane to A. C. Hamlin, 1892, Lane Papers, Auburn University Library; Marcellus N. Moorman in *Southern Historical Society Papers,* 30 (1902), p. 113.

14. Williams to daughter, May 18, 1863, Williams, *From the Cannon's Mouth,* pp. 191–92; Knipe report, *OR,* 25:1, pp. 686–87; John H. Brewster to John Bigelow, Nov. 21, 1910, Bigelow Papers, Library of Congress; Alexander W. Selfridge in *Philadelphia Weekly Times,* Apr. 1, 1882.

15. Lane report, *OR,* 25:1, p. 916; Lane to A. C. Hamlin, 1892, Lane Papers, Auburn University Library; Randolph Barton to Bigelow, Dec. 28, 1908, Bigelow Papers, Library of Congress.

16. Murray F. Taylor in *Confederate Veteran,* 12:10 (Oct. 1904), p. 493; Joseph G. Morrison in *Confederate Veteran,* 13:5 (May 1905), p. 231; Sandie Pendleton statement, July 18, 1863, John Esten Cooke Papers, Alderman Library, University of Virginia.

17. Robert E. Wilbourn to [John Esten Cooke], May 1863, Charles J. Faulkner Papers, Virginia Historical Society; Wilbourn to Cooke, Dec. 12, John Esten Cooke Papers, Alderman Library, University of Virginia; Wilbourn to R. L. Dabney, Dec. 12, Dabney Papers, Southern Historical Collection, University of North Carolina; Joseph G. Morrison to Dabney, Oct. 29, Dabney Papers, Southern Historical Collection; James H. Lane in Clark, *North Carolina Regiments,* 5, p. 95; W. H. Palmer, Joseph G. Morrison in *Confederate Veteran,* 13:5 (May 1905), pp. 230–33; W. F. Randolph in *Southern Historical Society Papers,* 29 (1901), p. 334; Hunter McGuire to Jubal Early, Mar. 6, 1873, Early Papers, Library of Congress; Jubal Early in *Southern Historical Society*

Papers, 6 (1878), p. 278; Alfred H. H. Tolar in Clark, *North Carolina Regiments,* 5, p. 99; James Power Smith statement, Dabney Papers, Southern Historical Collection. The unfinished chapel (or house) was known as Van Wart's (Harrison, *Chancellorsville Battlefield Sites,* p. 89).

18. Wilbourn and Morrison manuscripts in Note 17 above; Morrison to Spier Whitaker, Jan. 27, 1900, Virginia Historical Society; James Power Smith statement, Dabney Papers, Southern Historical Collection, University of North Carolina; Smith statement, John Esten Cooke Papers, Alderman Library, University of Virginia; Benjamin W. Leigh to wife, May 12, 1863, Hotchkiss Papers, Library of Congress; Dabney, *Life and Campaigns of Jackson,* p. 690; Hunter McGuire statement, New-York Historical Society. See Appendix III.

19. Best, A. P. Hill, Rodes reports, *OR,* 25:1, pp. 675, 885–86, 942–43; Williams to daughter, May 18, 1863, Williams, *From the Cannon's Mouth,* p. 192; William Clegg to Mary Collins, May 8, Rowley-Gifford-Clegg Papers, Filson Club; Justus M. Silliman to mother, May 9, Silliman, *New Canaan Private,* p. 32; Terry L. Jones, *Lee's Tigers: The Louisiana Infantry in the Army of Northern Virginia,* pp. 146–47.

20. McClellan, *Life and Campaigns of Stuart,* p. 235; Frank Robertson memoir, Virginia Historical Society; John C. Tidball journal, May 2, 1863, Hooker Papers, Huntington Library; John Follmer diary, May 2, Michigan Historical Collections, Bentley Historical Library, University of Michigan.

21. William Allan memoir, Southern Historical Collection, University of North Carolina; Alexander, *Fighting for the Confederacy,* p. 206; Francis S. Johnson to wife, May 5, 1863, Hargrett Library, University of Georgia.

22. Sickles, Birney, Ward reports, *OR,* 25:1, pp. 389, 409, 429; Arthur T. Wilcox to family, May 16, 1863, U.S. Army Military History Institute; George Marden

letter, May 8, Special Collections, Dartmouth College Library; Trobriand, *Four Years with the Army of the Potomac,* p. 451.

23. John Haley, *The Rebel Yell & the Yankee Hurrah: The Civil War Journal of a Maine Volunteer,* ed. Ruth L. Silliker, p. 80; Slocum, Hayman, Pierce, Hawley, Knipe, Berry, Merrill reports, *OR,* 25:1, pp. 670, 433, 437, 720, 687, 449, 435; Williams to daughter, May 18, 1863, Williams, *From the Cannon's Mouth,* pp. 194–95; Charles E. Bowers to daughter, May 3, Samuel M. Quincy to wife, May 14, Massachusetts Historical Society; D. G. Crotty, *Four Years Campaigning in the Army of the Potomac* (Grand Rapids: Dygert, 1874), p. 84.

24. Hooker circular, May 2, 1863, Van Alen to Reynolds, May 2, *OR,* 25:2, pp. 359, 364; Hooker testimony, *Report of Joint Committee,* 1 (1865), p. 127.

25. Warren to Butterfield, May 3, 1863, Sharpe to Babcock, May 2, Hooker Papers, Huntington Library; Van Alen to Sedgwick, May 2, *Report of Joint Committee,* 1 (1865), p. 129; Van Alen to Butterfield, May 2, *OR,* 25:2, p. 365; Cushing report, *OR,* 25:1, p. 220; Jerome to Cushing, May 3, Hooker Papers; Sedgwick testimony, *Report of Joint Committee,* 1 (1865), p. 95.

26. Butterfield to Hooker, May 2, 1863, Hooker Papers, Huntington Library; Hooker, Sedgwick testimony, *Report of Joint Committee,* 1 (1865), pp. 129, 95–96; Van Alen to Butterfield, May 2, Sedgwick to Butterfield, May 2, *OR,* 25:2, pp. 363, 364; Seymour, *Civil War Memoirs,* p. 51.

27. Sixth Corps circular, May 2, 1863, *Report of Joint Committee,* 1 (1865), p. 109; Sedgwick to Butterfield, May 2, 3, Butterfield to Sedgwick, May 3, Hooker Papers, Huntington Library; Razderichin report, Butterfield memorandum, Hooker Papers; Thomas Hyde to mother, May 7, Hyde, *Civil War Letters,* p. 71.

28. Hunter McGuire statement, New-York Historical Society; McGuire in *Southern Historical Society Papers,* 14 (1886),

pp. 156–58; James Power Smith statement, B. T. Lacy statement, Dabney Papers, Southern Historical Collection, University of North Carolina; Sandie Pendleton statement, John Esten Cooke Papers, Alderman Library, University of Virginia. The three assisting doctors were R. T. Colman, John William Walls, and Harvy Black.

29. Robert E. Wilbourn to [John Esten Cooke], May 1863, Charles J. Faulkner Papers, Virginia Historical Society; Wilbourn to R. L. Dabney, Dec. 12, 1863, Dabney Papers, Southern Historical Collection, University of North Carolina.

12: A Most Terribly Bloody Conflict

1. Warren report, *OR*, 25:1, p. 201; Hooker, Sedgwick testimony, *Report of Joint Committee*, 1 (1865), pp. 129, 96; Warren to Butterfield, May 3, 1863, Van Alen to Butterfield, May 3, Razderichin report, Hooker Papers, Huntington Library; John Babcock, "Jackson's Corps," RG 393, Part 1, B.M.I., Entry 3980, National Archives; Hooker to Bates, Apr. 2, 1877, Bates Collection, Pennsylvania Historical and Museum Commission. The Confederate prisoner claimed to be from the 50th Mississippi (Razderichin report), a unit not in the Confederate army. He was perhaps a plant.

2. Butterfield to Sedgwick, May 3, 1863, Hooker Papers, Huntington Library; Sedgwick to Butterfield, May 3, *OR*, 25:2, p. 384; Pierce to Cushing, May 3, Cushing to Pierce, May 3, *OR*, 25:1, p. 220; Cushing report, *OR*, 25:1, p. 220; Razderichin report, Hooker Papers.

3. Frank A. Haskell to brother, May 3, 1863, Haskell, *Haskell of Gettysburg: His Life and Civil War Papers*, eds. Frank L. Byrne and Andrew T. Weaver, p. 70; Gibbon, *Recollections*, pp. 114–15; Laflin report, *OR*, 25:1, pp. 352–53; Henry W. Hudson court-martial, May 8, Lincoln Papers, Library of Con-

gress; May 3, Robertson, "Diary of the War," pp. 94–95.

4. Benjamin G. Humphreys, "Recollections of Fredericksburg, 1863," *The Land We Love*, 3:6 (Oct. 1867), p. 448; "J.S.K." in *Mobile Advertiser*, May 22, 1863, Fredericksburg & Spotsylvania National Military Park; Razderichin report, Hooker Papers, Huntington Library.

5. Lowe to Butterfield, May 3, 1863, *OR*, Series Three, 3, p. 315; Hall to Butterfield, May 3 (two), Sedgwick to Butterfield, May 3, Hooker Papers, Huntington Library; Butterfield to Hooker, May 3, *OR*, 25:2, p. 386.

6. Butterfield to Hooker, May 3, 1863, *OR*, 25:2, p. 385; Alexander, *Fighting for the Confederacy*, pp. 204, 206–7; Tremain report, *OR Supplement*, 4, p. 594; Sickles report, *OR*, 25:1, p. 390; Hooker testimony, *Report of Joint Committee*, 1 (1865), p. 127; Bates, *Chancellorsville*, p. 120. Hooker did not specifically deal with this issue in his forty-odd letters to Bates, but he did not criticize Bates's handling of it when reading the manuscript (Bates Collection, Pennsylvania Historical and Museum Commission). They most likely discussed it during one of their visits.

7. May 3, 1863, Wainwright, *Diary of Battle*, p. 193. In addition to Birney's three brigades and Whipple's three at Hazel Grove, there was Barlow's Eleventh Corps brigade.

8. Apr. 30 return, *OR*, 25:2, p. 320. For calculation of Federal numbers by division, see Chap. 6 Note 38. For Confederate numbers, see Chap. 5 Note 6, and Chap. 9 Note 16. Wilcox's brigade of Anderson's division remained at Banks's Ford, and would fight on May 3 at Salem Church.

9. Diary, May 2, 3, 1863, Hotchkiss, *Make Me a Map*, pp. 138–39; Hotchkiss to G.F.R. Henderson, July 1897, Hotchkiss Papers, Library of Congress; Lee to Stuart, May 3 (two), *OR*, 25:2, p. 769.

10. Sickles, Graham, Stuart, Archer, Ryan reports, *OR*, 25:1, pp. 390, 414, 887, 925, 419; May 3, 1863, Dority, "Civil

War Diary," p. 15; James F. Huntington, "The Battle of Chancellorsville," *Papers of the Military Historical Society of Massachusetts*, 3, pp. 177–79; Alexander, *Fighting for the Confederacy*, p. 208; Spencer G. Welch to wife, May 9, Welch, *A Confederate Surgeon's Letters*, pp. 50–51; H. T. Childs in *Confederate Veteran*, 28:6 (June 1920), p. 221; Williams to daughter, May 18, Williams, *From the Cannon's Mouth*, p. 196; James J. Archer to sister, June 14, Archer, "The James J. Archer Letters: A Marylander in the Civil War," ed. C. A. Porter Hopkins, *Maryland Historical Magazine*, 56 (June 1961), pp. 148–49. A fourth gun of Huntington's was abandoned but later recovered (Huntington report, *OR*, 25:1, p. 504).

11. George Marden letter, May 8, 1863, Special Collections, Dartmouth College Library; Williams to daughter, May 18, Williams, *From the Cannon's Mouth*, p. 195; Riordon, Colgrove reports, *OR*, 25:1, pp. 440–41, 711; Brown, *Twenty-seventh Indiana*, pp. 329–33; Caldwell, *History of Gregg's Brigade*, p. 79; Spencer G. Welch to wife, May 9, Welch, *Confederate Surgeon's Letters*, pp. 51–52.

12. Alexander, *Fighting for the Confederacy*, p. 209; Alexander, Pegram, Best, Hunt reports, *OR*, 25:1, pp. 823, 938, 675, 252; Bates, *Chancellorsville*, p. 124; Robert K. Krick, *The Fredericksburg Artillery* (Lynchburg, Va.: H. E. Howard, 1986), pp. 51–53; F. M. Colston in *Confederate Veteran*, 5:6 (June 1897), p. 288.

13. Robert McAllister to wife, May 1863, McAllister, *Civil War Letters*, p. 303; Bull, *Soldiering*, pp. 54–55; Trobriand, *Four Years with the Army of the Potomac*, p. 458; Robinson, Poland, Osborn reports, *OR*, 25:1, pp. 703, 450, 484–85.

14. William D. Pender to wife, May 7, 1863, Pender, *The General to His Lady*, p. 235; Pender, French reports, *OR*, 25:1, pp. 935, 363; Edward K. Gould, *Major-General Hiram G. Berry*, pp. 266–67; Edwin B. Houghton, *Campaigns of the Seventeenth Maine* (Portland: Short & Loring, 1866), p. 61; *Richmond Examiner*, May 9.

15. Francis S. Johnson to wife, May 9, 1863, Hargrett Library, University of Georgia; Thomas report, *OR*, 25:1, 913; Shreve report, *OR Supplement*, 4, p. 584; Hitchcock, *War from the Inside*, pp. 223–24.

16. Griffith, *Variosa*, pp. 81–82; Alexander to H. B. McClellan, May 16, 1885, in McClellan, *Life and Campaigns of Stuart*, p. 255; Bigelow, *Chancellorsville*, pp. 374–75.

17. James T. Miller to brother, May 12, 1863, Schoff Collection, Clements Library, University of Michigan; Hooker to Sedgwick, May 3, Sedgwick to Butterfield, May 3, Hooker Papers, Huntington Library.

18. Thomas, Sickles, Revere reports, *OR*, 25:1, pp. 913, 392, 460, 462; S. B. David to parents, May 9, 1863, Fredericksburg & Spotsylvania National Military Park; Revere court-martial, *OR*, 25:1, p. 460; Sickles to Dickinson, May 3, Hooker Papers, Huntington Library; Joseph J. Revere, *A Statement of the Case of Brigadier-General Joseph J. Revere* (New York: C. A. Alvord, 1863).

19. Theodore Lyman, *Meade's Headquarters, 1863–1865*, ed. George R. Agissiz, p. 10; French, Carroll, Thomas reports, *OR*, 25:1, pp. 363, 365, 913; William Houghton to father, May 8, 1863, Nancy Niblack Baxter, ed., *Gallant Fourteenth: The Story of an Indiana Civil War Regiment*, pp. 140–41; Francis S. Johnson to wife, May 9, Hargrett Library, University of Georgia; George W. Lambert diary, May 3, Indiana Historical Society; Henry A. Morrow diary, May 3, *Civil War Times Illustrated*, 14:9 (Jan. 1976), p. 19.

20. Fiske, *Mr. Dunn Browne's Experiences*, pp. 147–48; "Laird" letter, May 10, 1863, George S. Lester Papers, Hill Memorial Library, Louisiana State University; Griffith, *Variosa*, p. 80; Bellard, *Gone for a Soldier*, pp. 213–14; Lockwood report, *OR*, 25:1, p. 374. The 114th Pennsylvania's actions are not easily accounted for. According to General Graham, the report of its colonel

"is a complete romance from the beginning to the end" (Collis report, *OR*, 25:1, pp. 422–25).

21. D.R.E. Winn to wife, May 9, 1863, Woodruff Library, Emory University; George, Heth, Colston, Smals, Funk reports, *OR*, 25:1, pp. 920, 893, 1005, 1036, 1013; Samuel M. Quincy to wife, May 14, Massachusetts Historical Society; John W. Melhorn diary, May 3, Stanford University Libraries; J. Franklin Marcha diary, May 3, Fredericksburg & Spotsylvania National Military Park; Ted Barclay to family, May 8, Barclay, *Ted Barclay, Liberty Hall Volunteers: Letters from the Stonewall Brigade*, ed. Charles W. Turner, p. 78; Caldwell, *History of Gregg's Brigade*, p. 80.

22. Randolph Barton memoir, Colt, *Defend the Valley*, p. 242; John P. Welsh to family, May 8, 1863, W. G. Bean, ed., "A House Divided: The Civil War Letters of a Virginia Family," *Virginia Magazine of History and Biography*, 59:4 (Oct. 1951), p. 413; Colston report, *OR*, 25:1, p. 1006; Caldwell, *History of Gregg's Brigade*, p. 80; Edwin Weller to Netty Watkins, May 13, Weller, *A Civil War Courtship*, p. 42; Ingalls to Butterfield, May 3, *OR*, 25:2, p. 377; Van Alen to Butterfield, May 3, Hooker Papers, Huntington Library.

23. Bigelow, *Chancellorsville*, p. 351; Witman, Posey reports, *OR*, 25:1, pp. 695, 873; Darius Couch, William B. Tibbitts, RG 94, U.S. Generals' Reports, National Archives; Charles R. Mudge to father, May 5, 1863, Mudge, *In Memoriam: Charles Redington Mudge, Lieut.-Col. Second Mass. Infantry* (Cambridge, 1863), p. 24; William B. Robertson letter, June 2, Hooker Papers, Huntington Library.

24. Williams to daughter, May 18, 1863, Williams, *From the Cannon's Mouth*, p. 198; Charles F. Morse to John Bigelow, Jan. 13, 1912, Bigelow Papers, Library of Congress; Clark, Randolph reports, *OR*, 25:1, pp. 444, 405; Alexander, *Military Memoirs*, pp. 347–48; Jennings C. Wise, *The Long Arm of Lee*,

or the History of the Artillery of the Army of Northern Virginia, 2, pp. 509–10.

25. Williams to daughter, May 18, 1863, Williams, *From the Cannon's Mouth*, pp. 198–99; Robert McAllister to wife, May 7, McAllister, *Civil War Letters*, p. 398; McClellan, *Life and Campaigns of Stuart*, p. 251.

26. William Calder to wife, May 4, 1863, Southern Historical Collection, University of North Carolina; Ramseur to Funk, May 22, *OR Supplement*, 4, p. 692; Calder to mother, May 10, Southern Historical Collection; Bryan Grimes memoir, Grimes, *Letters of Grimes*, p. 32; Rodes, Ramseur, Gales reports, *OR*, 25:1, pp. 944, 947–49, 996, 998; Frank M. Parker to wife, May 9, North Carolina State Archives; William M. Norman, *A Portion of My Life* (Winston-Salem: John F. Blair, 1959), p. 173.

27. Trobriand, *Four Years with the Army of the Potomac*, p. 460; Frank M. Coker to wife, May 8, 1863, Heidler Collection, Hargrett Library, University of Georgia; Hooker to Bates, Dec. 24, 1878, Bates Collection, Pennsylvania Historical and Museum Commission; Hooker memorandum, Mar. 21, 1877, courtesy Abraham Lincoln Book Shop; Henry E. Tremain letter, May 7, 1863, Tremain, *Two Days of War*, p. 328. In Washington A. Roebling's imagined and self-serving account, he put himself at the Chancellor house, warned Hooker of the approaching shot, and saved his life: "Oh, would that I had kept silent and allowed him to be killed. The battle of Chancellorsville might still have been saved!" (Roebling memoir, Bigelow Papers, Library of Congress).

13: Cavalcade of Triumph

1. Warren to Butterfield, May 3, 1863, Hooker Papers, Huntington Library; Hooker testimony, *Report of Joint Committee*, 1 (1865), p. 128; Hooker memorandum, Mar. 21, 1877, courtesy Abraham Lincoln Book Shop; Hooker in *Battles and Leaders*, 3, p. 221; William

Candler letter, May 7, 1863, in Bigelow, *Chancellorsville*, p. 363n; Haley, *The Rebel Yell*, p. 82; Meade to wife, May 23, Meade, *Life and Letters*, 1, p. 380; Bates, *Chancellorsville*, pp. 126–27; Doubleday memorandum, Doubleday Papers, New-York Historical Society.

2. HQ of the Army special order, Apr. 24, 1863, *OR*, 25:2, p. 249; Couch in *Battles and Leaders*, 3, p. 167; Couch, RG 94, U.S. Generals' Reports, National Archives; Jonathan Letterman, *Medical Recollections of the Army of the Potomac*, p. 137.

3. Doles, Geary, Lane reports, *OR*, 25:1, pp. 968, 731, 765; Thomas M. Hightower to fiancée, May 8, 1863, Georgia Department of Archives and History; James T. Miller to brother, May 12, William Aughinbaugh diary, May 7, Schoff Collection, Clements Library, University of Michigan; Couch in *Battles and Leaders*, 3, p. 168; Nathaniel Parmeter diary, May 3, Ohio Historical Society; G. H. Tarr letter, May 4, Virginia Polytechnic Institute and State University Libraries; George S. Greene, RG 94, U.S. Generals' Reports, National Archives; Moore, *Rebellion Record*, 7, Incidents, pp. 7–8.

4. James S. Mitchell memoir, William Fleming Collection; Robert C. Lamberton diary, May 3, 1863, Western Reserve Historical Society; Bowman report, *OR*, 25:1, pp. 500–501; William F. Fox, *Regimental Losses in the American Civil War, 1861–1865* (Albany, 1889), p. 144; Asa W. Bartlett, *History of the Twelfth Regiment New Hampshire Volunteers in the War of the Rebellion*, pp. 82–83.

5. David Monat, "Three Years in the 29th Penna. Vols.," Fredericksburg & Spotsylvania National Military Park; David Craft, *History of the 141st Regiment Pennsylvania Volunteers, 1861–1865* (Towanda, 1885), pp. 79, 83; A. B. Barron to wife, May 14, 1863, Georgia Department of Archives and History; Micajah D. Martin to parents, May 8, Martin, "Chancellorsville: A Soldier's Letter," ed. Abbott C. Martin, *Virginia Magazine of History and Biography*, 37:3 (July

1929), p. 226; William H. Howell to mother, May 4, LaRocca, *This Regiment of Heroes*, p. 124; Griffith, *Variosa*, pp. 84–85; Alexander, *Fighting for the Confederacy*, p. 208; John B. Crawford to wife, May 7, Mississippi Department of Archives and History; William Aughinbaugh diary, May 7, Schoff Collection, Clements Library, University of Michigan; Charles Ward to mother, May 7, American Antiquarian Society; Trobriand, *Four Years with the Army of the Potomac*, pp. 460–61; James H. Lane memoir, Auburn University Library; Billings report, *OR Supplement*, 4, p. 617.

6. Jones, *Lee's Tigers*, pp. 147–48; William Clegg to cousin, May 24, 1863, Rowley-Gifford-Clegg Papers, Filson Club; Meade report, *OR*, 25:1, p. 508.

7. Osborn, Selley, Knap, Winslow reports, *OR*, 25:1, pp. 484, 490, 771, 488; Robert McAllister to wife, May 1863, McAllister, *Civil War Letters*, p. 304; Charles F. Morse letter, May 7, Bigelow Papers, Library of Congress. Bigelow (*Chancellorsville*, p. 306) gives Seeley four guns, but Seeley's count of his personnel indicates he had six.

8. Archer report, *OR*, 25:1, p. 925; Heros Von Borcke, *Memoirs of the Confederate War for Independence* (New York: Peter Smith, 1938), 2, p. 239.

9. Newton report, *OR Supplement*, 4, pp. 632–33; Thomas W. Hyde to mother, May 7, 1863, Hyde, *Civil War Letters*, p. 71; Thomas W. Hyde, *Following the Greek Cross, or Memories of the Sixth Army Corps*, pp. 123–24; Bigelow, *Chancellorsville*, p. 385.

10. Sedgwick testimony, *Report of Joint Committee*, 1 (1865), p. 96; Razderichin report, Hooker Papers, Huntington Library; Humphreys, "Recollections of Fredericksburg, 1863," p. 450. Properly speaking, Marye's Heights comprises Marye's Hill on the north and Willis's Hill on the south, but by wartime usage the entire ridge was known as Marye's Heights (Krick, *Parker's Battery*, pp. 135–36). For convenience, the narrative throughout refers to the

north (Federal) bank and the south (Confederate) bank of the Rappahannock, but it should be noted that on the battleground behind Fredericksburg the opposing forces faced each other along a north-south axis. Thus on May 3 the Federals here were attacking westward.

11. Early, *Autobiographical Sketch*, pp. 205–6; Humphreys, "Recollections of Fredericksburg, 1863," pp. 447–49; Cadmus M. Wilcox to sister, May 16, 1863, Wilcox Papers, Library of Congress; Alexander, *Military Memoirs*, p. 303; Sedgwick report, *OR*, 25:1, pp. 558–59. The number of Marye's Heights defenders can only be estimated. Clerk William H. Hill's diary (Mississippi Department of Archives and History) gives Barksdale's brigade strength as "barely 2700," from which two regiments might total 1,350 infantry. Humphreys's count of "400 muskets" in the 21st Mississippi (and assuming the same in the 18th Mississippi, plus officers and gunners) gives a total of approximately 1,000. The actual count was probably about 1,200.

12. John Gibbon to wife, May 3, 1863, Fredericksburg & Spotsylvania National Military Park; May 3, Robertson, "Diary of War," p. 96; Sedgwick to Butterfield, May 3, Hooker Papers, Huntington Library; Early, *Autobiographical Sketch*, pp. 205–6; Sedgwick testimony, *Report of Joint Committee*, 1 (1865), p. 96; Thomas W. Hyde to mother, May 7, Hyde, *Civil War Letters*, p. 71; Hyde, *Following the Greek Cross*, p. 125.

13. Warren, Hall reports, *OR*, 25:1, pp. 201–2, 358; Frank Haskell letter, May 3, 1863, Haskell, *Haskell of Gettysburg*, p. 71; Humphreys, "Recollections of Fredericksburg, 1863," p. 449; Cyril H. Tyler to father, May 7, Perkins Library, Duke University; Oliver Wendell Holmes, Jr., to mother, May 3, Holmes, *Touched with Fire: Letters and Diary of Oliver Wendell Holmes, Jr.*, ed. Mark DeWolfe Howe (Cambridge: Harvard University Press, 1946), p. 92; James A. Barber memoir, John Hay Library,

Brown University; Adams report, *OR Supplement*, 4, pp. 582–83.

14. Sedgwick report, *OR*, 25:1, p. 559; Newton report, *OR Supplement*, 4, pp. 633–34; Thomas S. Allen, "Storming of Marye's Heights," ed. George B. Engle, pp. 11–13, State Historical Society of Wisconsin; Hyde, *Following the Greek Cross*, p. 126.

15. Sedgwick to Butterfield, May 3, 1863, Hooker Papers, Huntington Library; Barksdale, Dawson reports, *OR*, 25:1, pp. 840, 626; Shaler, Newton reports, *OR Supplement*, 4, pp. 646, 633–34; Humphreys, "Recollections of Fredericksburg, 1863," p. 451; Huntington W. Jackson in *Battles and Leaders*, 3, p. 229; Henry L. Abbott to father, May 5, Abbott, *Fallen Leaves*, p. 174. Some accounts have the flag of truce incident occurring during a pause in the main assault. But since by Sedgwick's dispatch the assault began at 10:05 and by signalman Hall's dispatch (Note 17 below) it succeeded by 10:30 (signalmen were careful to time their dispatches), there would not have been time for a flag of truce during those 25 minutes.

16. Harris, Ely reports, *OR*, 51:1, pp. 186, 188; Allen, "Storming of Marye's Heights," p. 16; Benjamin R. J. Thaxter to Elinor Comer, May 21, 1863, Albert Foster to wife, May 7, Fredericksburg & Spotsylvania National Military Park; Henry E. Handerson, *Yankee in Gray: The Civil War Memoirs of Henry E. Handerson*, p. 56; Krick, *Parker's Battery*, pp. 141–42; Andrew Hero to father, May 14, Hill Memorial Library, Louisiana State University; Humphreys, "Recollections of Fredericksburg, 1863," pp. 451–52; Ira S. Dodd, *The Song of the Rappahannock: Sketches of the Civil War* (New York: Dodd, Mead, 1898), p. 17.

17. Frank Haskell letter, May 3, 1863, Haskell, *Haskell of Gettysburg*, pp. 72–73; Burnham report, *OR*, 51:1, p. 184; William Stowe to parents, May 15, "J.S.K." in *Mobile Advertiser and Register*, May 22, Fredericksburg & Spotsylvania National Military Park; Charles W. Squires

memoir, *Civil War Times Illustrated*, 14:2 (May 1975), p. 22; Krick, *Parker's Battery*, pp. 142–44; John A. Barksdale to Oscar J. E. Stuart, June 29, Mississippi Department of Archives and History; Hall to Butterfield, May 3, Hooker Papers, Huntington Library. Confederate casualties are from *OR*, 25:1, p. 806, and (for prisoners) the Hooker Papers. Federal casualties for the Fredericksburg front are broken out for May 3 from individual reports and accounts.

18. Alexander S. Webb, "Meade at Chancellorsville," *Papers of the Military Historical Society of Massachusetts*, 3, pp. 222, 231; Couch in *Battles and Leaders*, 3, pp. 169–70; Alexander S. Webb to father, May 12, 1863, Webb Papers, Yale University Library; Meade to wife, May 8, Meade, *Life and Letters*, 1, p. 372. A letter to the *New York Times*, June 3, 1867, from "Eye Witness" (Henry E. Tremain, formerly of Sickles's staff) charged that Meade "declined to fight" on May 3. Tremain's false accusation, a ploy in the ongoing Meade-Sickles controversy over Gettysburg, was exposed by Webb in his "Meade at Chancellorsville."

19. Warren to Butterfield, May 3, 1863, Hooker Papers, Huntington Library; Hooker testimony, *Report of Joint Committee*, 1 (1865), p. 128.

20. Alexander, Pegram, Hardaway reports, *OR*, 25:1, pp. 851, 938, 878; Alexander, *Fighting for the Confederacy*, p. 210.

21. Sue Chancellor, "Personal Recollections," pp. 141–43. The Chancellor party found refuge at a home in Stafford County, and afterward spent the war years in Charlottesville.

22. Bacon, "A Michigan Surgeon at Chancellorsville," p. 322; B. B. Carr memoir, North Carolina State Archives; Alexander, *Fighting for the Confederacy*, p. 210.

23. Hancock testimony, *Report of Joint Committee*, 1 (1865), pp. 67–68; Child, *Fifth New Hampshire*, p. 186; Walker, *Second Army Corps*, pp. 236, 246; Trobriand, *Four Years with the Army of the Potomac*, p. 460; Lyman, *Meade's Headquarters*, p. 107; Josiah M. Favill, *The Diary of a Young Officer Serving with the Armies of the United States During the War of the Rebellion*, p. 234.

24. Morgan, Seeley, Clark, Pettit, Stevens, Hancock reports, *OR*, 25:1, pp. 310, 490, 444, 349–50, 285, 314; L. Van Loan Naisawald, *Grape and Canister: The Story of the Field Artillery of the Army of the Potomac*, pp. 311–14; Field report, *OR Supplement*, 4, p. 670; Second Army Corps diary, May 3, Fredericksburg & Spotsylvania National Military Park.

25. Livermore, *Days and Events*, pp. 206–7; Morris, Holt reports, *OR*, 25:1, pp. 334–35, 838; Winthrop D. Sheldon, *The "Twenty-seventh": A Regimental History* (New Haven: Morris & Benham, 1866), p. 53; Charles J. Morris to family, May 16, 1863, Perkins Library, Duke University.

26. Caldwell, *History of Gregg's Brigade*, pp. 83–84; F. M. Nixon to uncle, May 20, 1863, Perkins Library, Duke University; Frank M. Coker to wife, May 8, Heidler Collection, Hargrett Library, University of Georgia; John Garibaldi to wife, May 7, Virginia Military Institute Archives; James Houghton diary, May 3, Michigan Historical Collections, Bentley Historical Library, University of Michigan; Leonidas Torrence to mother, May 8, Torrence, "Road to Gettysburg," p. 507.

27. Charles Marshall, *An Aide-de-Camp of Lee*, ed. Frederick Maurice, p. 173; Francis F. Hillyer to father, May 7, 1863, Fredericksburg & Spotsylvania National Military Park.

28. May 3 casualties for Chancellorsville are extrapolated from Appendix II and the sources therein. The 5,000 Federals marched from the field is Bigelow's estimate (*Chancellorsville*, p. 377).

14: Calling Upon General Sedgwick

1. Stoneman report, *OR*, 25:1, p. 1060; May 3, 1863, Josiah Gorgas, *The Civil War Diary of General Josiah Gorgas*, ed. Frank E. Vandiver (University: University of Alabama Press, 1947), p. 36; May

6, Robert G. H. Kean, *Inside the Confederate Government: The Diary of Robert Garlick Hill Kean,* ed. Edward Younger (New York: Oxford University Press, 1957), pp. 55–56; Woodward, *Mary Chesnut's Civil War,* p. 453; *Richmond Daily Examiner,* May 4.

2. Virginia railroads report, April 1863, Hooker Papers, Huntington Library; Hooker testimony, *Report of Joint Committee,* 1 (1865), p. 140. It was common knowledge in the cavalry command (Stoneman apparently excepted) that Hanover Junction was the raiders' primary target. See George A. Custer to George B. McClellan, May 6, 1863, McClellan Papers, Library of Congress.

3. Wyndham, Kilpatrick, Davis, Gregg reports, *OR,* 25:1, pp. 1085, 1084, 1086, 1082; Greene, "Stoneman's Raid," in Gallagher, *Chancellorsville;* Nathan Webb diary, May 4, 1863, Schoff Collection, Clements Library, University of Michigan; Virginia railroads report, April 1863, Hooker Papers, Huntington Library; Joseph Morrison in *Confederate Veteran,* 13:5 (May 1905), p. 232; Johnston, *Virginia Railroads,* pp. 149–50; Fortescue to Butterfield, May 3–5, Butterfield to Hooker, May 3–5, Warren to Butterfield, May 3, Van Alen to Pleasonton, May 3, Hooker Papers.

4. Hunter McGuire statement, New-York Historical Society; Beverly Tucker Lacy statement, James Power Smith statement, Dabney Papers, Southern Historical Collection, University of North Carolina; Lee to Jackson, May 3, 1863, Lee, *Wartime Papers,* pp. 452–53.

5. Early, *Autobiographical Sketch,* p. 211; McLaws report, *OR,* 25:1, p. 826; Stiles, *Four Years Under Marse Robert,* pp. 177–78.

6. Bigelow, *Chancellorsville,* pp. 509–10; May 3, 1863, Wainwright, *Diary of Battle,* pp. 193–94, 196; Hunt to Butterfield, May 3, Hooker Papers, Huntington Library; Colston in *Battles and Leaders,* 3, p. 233; Colston report, *OR,* 25:1, p. 1007.

7. Early, *Autobiographical Sketch,* pp. 209–11; Owen, *In Camp and Battle with the Washington Artillery,* pp. 218–19; Jones, *Lee's Tigers,* p. 152.

8. Freeman, *Lee's Lieutenants,* 2, pp. 619–20; Cadmus M. Wilcox to sister, May 16, 1863, Wilcox Papers, Library of Congress; Wilcox report, *OR,* 25:1, p. 857.

9. Ingalls to Butterfield, May 3, 1863, *OR,* 25:2, p. 391; Ingalls to Butterfield, May 3, Sharpe to Babcock, May 2, Hooker Papers, Huntington Library; Butterfield to Hooker, May 3 (two), *OR,* 25:2, p. 381, 377–78. Although Captain Cushing ran a telegraph wire across the pontoon bridge into Fredericksburg on May 3, Sedgwick made little or no use of it (Cushing report, *OR,* 25:1, pp. 220–21). Copies of these Ingalls dispatches went instead from Butterfield to Sedgwick by courier; that announcing Hooker's injury reached Sedgwick about 2:00 P.M. (Hooker Papers). By Bigelow's account (*Chancellorsville,* p. 397), Butterfield was so dissatisfied with Sedgwick's progress that he "started three times to relieve him from command." Bigelow gives no source for this allegation, and no documentation in the *Official Records* or the Hooker Papers supports it. Indeed, Butterfield lacked the authority to relieve Sedgwick, and nothing indicates that Hooker had granted him such authority.

10. Newton report, *OR Supplement,* 4, p. 635; Burnham report, *OR,* 51:1, p. 182; Clinton Beckwith memoir, in Isaac O. Best, *History of the 121st New York State Infantry,* p. 66; Hyde, *Following the Greek Cross,* p. 128.

11. Hall to Butterfield, May 3, 1863, Denicke to Cushing, May 3, Stone to Cushing, May 3, Hooker Papers, Huntington Library; Wilcox, Warren, Brooks reports, *OR,* 25:1, pp. 857, 203, 567–68; D. D. Wheeler in Camille Baquet, *History of the First Brigade, New Jersey Volunteers,* pp. 248–49. Aeronaut E. S. Allen in balloon *Eagle* at Banks's Ford failed to sight McLaws's force on May 3 — or much else either. There is but a single message from Allen on re-

cord that day (Hooker Papers), on a matter of little consequence.

12. Hall to Butterfield, May 3, 1863, Woolsey to Butterfield, May 3, Hooker Papers, Huntington Library; Rigby, Brooks, Wilcox reports, *OR*, 25:1, pp. 596, 567–68, 858; Tomkins, Manly reports, *OR Supplement*, 4, pp. 626, 674–75; Hotchkiss and Allen, *Chancellorsville*, p. 86; John L. G. Wood to aunt, May 10, Georgia Department of Archives and History.

13. Clinton Beckwith memoir, in Best, *121st New York Infantry*, pp. 68–69; Jacob W. Haas to brother, May 12, 1863, in David A. Ward, "Of Battlefields and Bitter Feuds: The 96th Pennsylvania Volunteers," *Civil War Regiments*, 3:3 (1993), p. 24; Edmund English to brother, May 6, Huntington Library; John L. G. Wood to aunt, May 10, Georgia Department of Archives and History; John B. Evans to wife, May 8, Perkins Library, Duke University.

14. Clinton Beckwith memoir, in Best, *121st New York Infantry*, pp. 69–70; Upton, Wilcox reports, *OR*, 25:1, pp. 589, 858; William C. McClellan to father, May 10, 1863, Buchanan-McClellan Papers, Southern Historical Collection, University of North Carolina; Edmund D. Patterson journal, May 3, Patterson, *Yankee Rebel*, p. 102; Hilary A. Herbert in Baquet, *First New Jersey Brigade*, p. 243; Eliza Wilkes to Charles Wilkes, May 20, Wilkes Family Papers, Perkins Library, Duke University.

15. Wilcox, Semmes, Rigby, McLaws reports, *OR*, 25:1, pp. 858–59, 835–36, 596, 827; John S. Judd diary, May 3, 1863, Kansas State Historical Society; [14th Alabama], Tomkins reports, *OR Supplement*, 4, pp. 677, 626; D. D. Wheeler in Baquet, *First New Jersey Brigade*, p. 250; Charles A. Brewster to daughter, May 10, Brewster, *When This Cruel War Is Over*, p. 226.

16. William C. McClellan to father, May 10, 1863, Buchanan-McClellan Papers, Southern Historical Collection, University of North Carolina; Cadmus M. Wilcox to sister, May 16, Wilcox Papers,

Library of Congress; Bartlett report, *OR*, 25:1, pp. 581–82; Mather Cleveland, *New Hampshire Fights the Civil War* (New London, 1969), p. 7. Union losses are for Brown's and Bartlett's brigades, plus the 95th and 119th Pennsylvania of Russell's brigade and the 2nd Rhode Island and 10th Massachusetts of Newton's division that helped halt the counterattack. Confederate losses are for Wilcox's and Semmes's brigades.

17. Martin T. McMahon, "The Sixth Army Corps," *United States Service Magazine*, 5 (1866), p. 211; Benham to Butterfield, May 3, 1863, Hooker Papers, Huntington Library; Lee to Early, May 3, Lee to McLaws, May 3, *OR*, 25:2, p. 770.

18. Hooker to Lincoln, May 3, 1863, Butterfield to Lincoln, May 3 (two), Lincoln to Butterfield, May 3, *OR*, 25:2, pp. 378–79; Lincoln to Butterfield, May 3 (unsent), Lincoln, *Collected Works Supplement*, pp. 186–87; John G. Nicolay to Therena Bates, May 3, Nicolay Papers, Library of Congress.

19. William W. Folwell to wife, May 3, 1863, Minnesota Historical Society; J. H. Emerick diary, May 3, in Plum, *Military Telegraph*, 1, p. 367; Ingalls to Butterfield, May 3, Hooker Papers, Huntington Library; Warren, Hooker, Sedgwick testimony, *Report of Joint Committee*, 1 (1865), pp. 48–49, 148, 97; Warren to Sedgwick, May 3, *OR*, 25:2, p. 396; Warren report, *OR*, 25:1, p. 203.

15: Time the Yankees Were Leaving

1. Anderson, Hardaway reports, *OR*, 25:1, pp. 851–52, 879–80; Williams to daughter, May 18, 1863, Williams, *From the Cannon's Mouth*, p. 200; Patrick diary, May 6, Library of Congress.

2. Tuckerman to Fisher, May 4, 1863, Hooker Papers, Huntington Library; Butterfield to Sedgwick, May 4, *OR*, 25:2, p. 404; Reynolds to Hooker, May 4, Pleasonton to S. Williams, May 4, Hooker Papers.

3. Gibbon to Butterfield, May 4, 1863,

Hooker Papers, Huntington Library; Patrick to Sharpe, May 4, RG 393, Part 1, B.M.I., Entry 3980, National Archives; Butterfield to Hooker, May 4, Averell to headquarters, May 1, Hooker Papers; Van Alen to Butterfield, May 4, Thomas Dolan Papers, New-York Historical Society; Butterfield to Hooker, May 4, Babcock to Sharpe, May 4, Hooker Papers.

4. Peck to Butterfield, May 2, 4, 1863, Butterfield to Peck, May 4, *OR*, 25:2, pp. 370, 371, 415, 414; Peck to Hooker, May 4, S. Williams to Averell, May 4, Hooker Papers, Huntington Library. Van Alen's query regarding the 25,000 men of Pickett and Hood reported at Gordonsville was written at 10:00 A.M. on May 4 but not forwarded to Averell until 10:45 P.M. Thus the report was still current at day's end.

5. Taylor to Butterfield, May 4, 1863, Hall to Butterfield, May 4 (two), Hooker Papers, Huntington Library; Frank Haskell to brother, May 4, Haskell, *Haskell of Gettysburg*, pp. 75–76; Lee to Early, May 3, *OR*, 25:2, p. 769; Early, *Autobiographical Sketch*, p. 220.

6. Henry C. Walker to John W. Johnston, May 9, 1863, Lane, *Letters from Georgia Soldiers*, p. 234; Early to Lee, Nov. 20, 1868, Lee Headquarters Papers, Virginia Historical Society; Humphreys, "Recollections of Fredericksburg, 1863," p. 458. Although Gordon's nomination as brigadier general was not confirmed until May 11, he served as such throughout the campaign.

7. Sedgwick to Hooker, May 4, 1863, Sedgwick to Butterfield, May 4, *OR*, 25:2, pp. 402–3; Hyde, *Following the Greek Cross*, p. 129; Warren to Sedgwick, May 3, *OR*, 25:2, p. 396; Gibbon, *Personal Recollections*, pp. 116–17.

8. Barksdale, Neill, Board reports, *OR*, 25:1, pp. 841, 609–10, 1002–3; Henry Ropes to father, May 5, 1863, Boston Public Library; Early, *Autobiographical Sketch*, pp. 224–26; I. G. Bradwell in *Confederate Veteran*, 20:10 (Oct. 1915), p. 447; Butler report, *OR Supplement*, 4,

p. 657; Clement A. Evans to wife, May 5, Evans, *Intrepid Warrior: Clement Anselm Evans, Confederate General from Georgia*, ed. Robert Grier Stephens, Jr., p. 151; Selden Connor to father, May 10, John Hay Library, Brown University; Sedgwick to Hooker, May 4, *OR*, 25:2, p. 405. Confederate casualties: RG 109, M-836:6, National Archives.

9. Butterfield to Sedgwick, May 3, 1863, Hooker Papers, Huntington Library; Butterfield to Sedgwick, May 4, *OR*, 25:2, p. 385; Brown, *Signal Corps*, 1, p. 97; Gloskoski report, Hooker Papers; Babcock, Denicke, Lyon, Cushing reports, *OR*, 25:1, pp. 240–41, 235, 237, 221.

10. Hall to Sedgwick, May 4, 1863, Lowe to Butterfield, May 4, Warren to Sedgwick, May 3, Sedgwick to Hooker, May 4, *OR*, 25:2, pp. 407, 409, 396, 408. Banks's Ford was actually two crossings, an upper one near a sharp bend in the Rappahannock, and a lower one (sometimes called Scott's Ford) a half mile downstream. The two Federal pontoon bridges, 300 yards apart, were near the lower crossing.

11. Sedgwick report, *OR*, 25:1, p. 560; Sedgwick to Hooker, May 4, 1863, Lowe to Butterfield, May 4, *OR*, 25:2, pp. 406, 409; Selden Connor to father, May 10, John Hay Library, Brown University; Sedgwick to Hooker, May 4, *Report of Joint Committee*, 1 (1865), p. 99. Despite the loss of Marye's Heights, Sedgwick retained a roundabout connection with Fredericksburg by way of the River Road.

12. Charles E. Bowers to wife, May 4, 1863, Massachusetts Historical Society; May 3, Wainwright, *Diary of Battle*, p. 197; Warren to Sedgwick, May 3, *OR*, 25:2, p. 396; Hooker to Bates, Apr. 2, 1877, Bates Collection, Pennsylvania Historical and Museum Commission; Hunt testimony, *Report of Joint Committee*, 1 (1865), p. 90; Van Alen to Butterfield, May 4, Hooker Papers, Huntington Library; Van Alen to Sedgwick, May 4, Hooker to Sedgwick, May 4, Sedgwick to Hooker, May 4, Butterfield to

Hooker, May 4, *OR*, 25:2, pp. 408, 409, 410, 403.

13. Van Alen to Butterfield, May 4, 1863 (two), Hooker Papers, Huntington Library; May 6, Patrick diary, Library of Congress; May 4, Wainwright, *Diary of Battle*, p. 199.

14. Alexander, *Fighting for the Confederacy*, p. 213; Anderson report, *OR*, 25:1, p. 852; Taylor to McLaws, May 3, 1863, *OR*, 25:2, p. 770; McLaws, Early reports, *OR*, 25:1, pp. 827, 1001.

15. Cadmus M. Wilcox to sister, May 16, 1863, Wilcox Papers, Library of Congress; Early, *Autobiographical Sketch*, pp. 227–28; Andrews report, RG 109, M-836:6, National Archives; Alexander, Hardaway reports, *OR*, 25:1, pp. 821, 881. Lee's listing of the Federals he faced on May 4 as "one army corps and part of another" in his report (*OR*, 25:1, p. 801) referred to Sedgwick's corps plus Gibbon's division; and when the battle was fought Gibbon was known to be in Fredericksburg.

16. John Wood to aunt, May 10, 1863, Georgia Department of Archives and History; Van Alen to Slocum, May 4, *OR*, 25:2, p. 402; Reynolds to Hooker, May 4, Hooker Papers, Huntington Library; Richard T. Auchmuty to mother, May 4, Auchmuty, *Letters*, pp. 89–90; Charles F. Morse letter, May 7, Bigelow Papers, Library of Congress; George Marden letter, May 8, Special Collections, Dartmouth College Library. The mortally wounded Whipple was promoted major general, to date from May 3.

17. H. T. Peck, "Historical Sketch of the 118th Regiment Pennsylvania Volunteers, 'Corn Exchange Regt.'" (1884), p. 202; McAllister, Berdan reports, *OR*, 25:1, pp. 458, 503; Haley, *Rebel Yell*, p. 84; Wyman S. White, *The Civil War Diary of First Sergeant Wyman S. White of the 2nd United States Sharpshooter Regiment*, ed. Russell C. White (Baltimore: Butternut & Blue, 1992), pp. 78–79.

18. May 4, 1863, Wainwright, *Diary of Battle*, p. 199; Warren memorandum, May

1863, *OR*, 25:1, p. 512; Hooker testimony, *Report of Joint Committee*, 1 (1865), p. 113; Davenport, *Fifth New York*, pp. 386–88; Humphreys report, *OR*, 25:1, p. 549.

19. Warner to Tomkins, May 4, 1863, Patrick to Van Alen, May 4, Hooker Papers, Huntington Library; Ingalls to Rankin, May 4, Ingalls to Thompson, May 4, Gilmer to Lee, Apr. 19, *OR*, 25:2, pp. 401, 400, 735; Benham report, *OR*, 25:1, p. 215.

20. May 31, 1863, Wainwright, *Diary of Battle*, p. 212; Jonathan B. Hager memoir, Alderman Library, University of Virginia; Robinson, McQuade, Stone reports, *OR*, 25:1, pp. 277, 518, 296; James Houghton diary, May 4, Michigan Historical Collections, Bentley Historical Library, University of Michigan; Zerah C. Monks to Hannah Rohrer, May 7, Woodruff Library, Emory University; Reynolds to Hooker, May 4, Hooker Papers, Huntington Library; Stuart to Lee, May 4, *OR*, 25:2, p. 702; Thomas Chamberlain, *History of the One Hundred and Fiftieth Regiment Pennsylvania Volunteers* (Philadelphia: Lippincott, 1895), p. 95; Hooker testimony, *Report of Joint Committee*, 1 (1865), p. 133.

21. Diary, May 4, 1863, Hotchkiss, *Make Me a Map*, p. 140; James Power Smith statement, Beverly Tucker Lacy statement, Dabney Papers, Southern Historical Collection, University of North Carolina; Hunter McGuire statement, New-York Historical Society; McGuire in *Southern Historical Society Papers*, 14 (1886), p. 160. The route of Jackson's ambulance can be traced on the 1863 Confederate Engineers' map of Caroline and surrounding counties (Gilmer Collection, Virginia Historical Society). Robert Rodes would be promoted major general on May 7, to date from May 2.

22. Thomas Evans diary, May 5, 1863, Library of Congress; Fiske, *Mr. Dunn Browne's Experiences*, p. 152.

23. John W. Melhorn diary, May 4, 1863, Stanford University Libraries; Bull, *Soldiering*, pp. 58–63, 73; diary, May 4, Ba-

con, "A Michigan Surgeon," p. 322; Samuel D. Webster diary, May 4, Huntington Library; Dix to Halleck, May 7, *OR*, 18, p. 706; Walter Lowenfels, ed., *Walt Whitman's Civil War* (New York: Knopf, 1960), pp. 65–66.

24. Clinton Beckwith memoir in Best, *121st New York*, p. 73; Selden Connor to father, May 10, 1863, John Hay Library, Brown University; Hyde, *Following the Greek Cross*, p. 130; Thomas W. Hyde to mother, May 9, Hyde, *Civil War Letters*, p. 74.

25. Howe testimony, *Report of Joint Committee*, 1 (1865), p. 20; Neill, Grant reports, *OR*, 25:1, pp. 609–10, 604; Early, *Autobiographical Sketch*, pp. 228–29; Andrews report, RG 109, M-836:6, National Archives; Hall to S. Williams, May 4, 1863, Hooker Papers, Huntington Library; S. W. Eaton diary, May 4, Southern Historical Collection, University of North Carolina; Edmund S. Stephens to father, May 1863, Northwestern State University of Louisiana.

26. John J. Toffey to parents, May 9, 1863, Fredericksburg & Spotsylvania National Military Park; Thomas W. Hyde to mother, May 9, Hyde, *Civil War Letters*, p. 75; Rigby report, *OR*, 25:1, p. 597; Selden Connor to father, May 10, John Hay Library, Brown University.

27. Early, *Autobiographical Sketch*, pp. 229–30; Edmund S. Stephens to father, May 1863, Northwestern State University of Louisiana; Henry E. Handerson to father, May 13, Handerson, *Yankee in Gray*, p. 102.

28. Grant report, *OR*, 25:1, pp. 604–5; Erastus H. Scott to father, May 18, 1863, Chester K. Leach to wife, May 9, Special Collections, University of Vermont Library; "A.A.C." in *Rutland* (Vt.) *Daily Herald*, May 16, courtesy Donald Wickman; William J. Seymour, *The Civil War Memoirs of Captain William J. Seymour*, ed. Terry L. Jones (Baton Rouge: Louisiana State University Press, 1991), p. 54. Confederate casualties: RG 109, M-836:6, National Archives.

29. Henry C. Walker to John W. Johnston, May 9, 1863, Lane, *Letters from Georgia*

Soldiers, p. 234; Robert S. Robertson diary, May 4, Robertson, "Diary of the War," p. 97; W. R. Redding to wife, May 8, Southern Historical Collection, University of North Carolina; Thomas W. Hyde to mother, May 9, Hyde, *Civil War Letters*, p. 75; Hotchkiss and Allan, *Chancellorsville*, p. 93.

30. Perry, Wright, Bartlett reports, *OR*, 25:1, pp. 876, 869, 582; Harry G. Hore to cousin, May 10, 1863, Fredericksburg & Spotsylvania National Military Park.

31. Howe testimony, *Report of Joint Committee*, 1 (1865), p. 21; Lee to McLaws, May 4, 1863, Lee, *Wartime Papers*, p. 455; Thomas W. Hyde to mother, May 9, Hyde, *Civil War Letters*, p. 74; Sedgwick to Hooker, May 4, 9:45 P.M. (printed erroneously 9:45 A.M. in the *Official Records*), Hooker Papers, Huntington Library. Confederate casualties: RG 109, M-836:6, National Archives. Federal casualties for Howe (*OR*, 25:1, p. 190) totaled 1,290, of which 399 were men taken prisoner in the subsequent retreat.

32. Hooker to Sedgwick, May 4, 1863, Butterfield to Sedgwick, May 4, *OR*, 25:2, pp. 409, 411; May 4, Wainwright, *Diary of Battle*, p. 199; Hall to S. Williams, May 4 (two), Benham to Hooker, May 4, Hooker Papers, Huntington Library.

33. Sedgwick to Hooker, May 4, 1863, Hooker Papers, Huntington Library (see Note 31 above); Benham to Butterfield, May 4 (two), *OR*, 25:2, p. 411; Benham to Hooker, May 4 (two), Hooker Papers; Alexander, *Fighting for the Confederacy*, p. 214.

34. Hooker testimony, *Report of Joint Committee*, 1 (1865), pp. 134–35, 144; Warren memorandum, May 1863, *OR*, 25:1, p. 512. For Hooker's "confession," see Appendix III.

35. Butterfield testimony, *Report of Joint Committee*, 1 (1865), p. 78; Warren memorandum, May 1863, *OR*, 25:1, p. 512; Meade to wife, May 19, Meade, *Life and Letters*, 1, pp. 377–78; Reynolds to Meade, May 24, *OR*, 25:1, p. 510; Howard to T. H. Davis, Sept. 14, 1875, Bates Collection, Pennsylvania Histori-

cal and Museum Commission; Hancock, Hooker testimony, *Report of Joint Committee*, 1 (1865), pp. 70, 135; Couch in *Battles and Leaders*, 3, p. 171; Sickles to Meade, May 26, 1863, *OR*, 25:1, p. 511.

36. Sedgwick to Hooker, May 4, 1863, 11:45 P.M., *Report of Joint Committee*, 1 (1865), p. 132; Butterfield to Sedgwick, May 5, 1:00 A.M., Sedgwick to Hooker, May 4, 12:00 P.M., Hooker to Sedgwick, May 5, 1:20 A.M., *OR*, 25:2, pp. 418–19; Abner Doubleday, *Chancellorsville and Gettysburg*, pp. 66–67; Hooker testimony, *Report of Joint Committee*, 1 (1865), p. 133; Sedgwick to Hooker, May 5, 3:20 A.M., Sedgwick to Butterfield, May 5, 5:00, 7:00 A.M., *OR*, 25:2, p. 419; Meade to wife, May 8, Meade, *Life and Letters*, 1, p. 373. Sedgwick's 11:45 P.M. telegram saying he would have to retreat is marked received at 1:00 A.M. in the *Official Records*, but it must have arrived a few minutes ahead of his second telegram, at about 12:50, or it would not have been replied to separately. The council of war had already adjourned, or else the exchange with Sedgwick would have been deliberated.

37. Charles H. Brewster to sister, May 10, 1863, Brewster, *When This Cruel War Is Over*, p. 227; Elisha H. Rhodes diary, May 5, Rhodes, *All for the Union: A History of the 2nd Rhode Island Volunteer Infantry*, p. 107; Benjamin R. J. Thaxter to Elinor Comer, May 21, Fredericksburg & Spotsylvania National Military Park; Harris report, *OR*, 51:1, p. 187; Chester K. Leach to wife, May 9, Special Collections, University of Vermont Library; Wilcox to Lee, 1867, Lee Headquarters Papers, Virginia Historical Society; W. R. Montgomery to family, May 7, South Caroliniana Library; May 5, Weld, *War Diary and Letters*, pp. 192–93.

38. John Gibbon to wife, May 1863, Gibbon, *Recollections of the Civil War*, p. 118; John S. Cooper diary, May 5, Cyril H. Tyler to father, May 7, Perkins Library, Duke University.

39. W. R. Redding to wife, May 8, 1863, Southern Historical Collection, University of North Carolina; Lee to Davis, May 5, Lee, *Wartime Papers*, p. 455; Lee report, *OR*, 25:1, p. 802; Stuart to Taylor, May 5, *OR*, 51:2, p. 702; diary, May 5, Hotchkiss, *Make Me a Map*, p. 141.

40. Warren, Benham reports, *OR*, 25:1, pp. 204, 214; Bigelow, *Chancellorsville*, p. 422; William W. Folwell to wife, May 5, 1863, Minnesota Historical Society; Babcock to Sharpe, May 5 (two), Butterfield to Lincoln, May 5, Pleasonton to Butterfield, May 5, *OR*, 25:2, pp. 421, 417, 421–22, 423; Fortesque to Butterfield, May 5, Hooker Papers, Huntington Library; Cormier, *Siege of Suffolk*, p. 310.

41. Butterfield to Letterman, May 5, 1863, retreat instructions, May 5, Hooker Papers, Huntington Library; Charles F. Morse letter, May 7, Bigelow Papers, Library of Congress; Jonathan B. Hager memoir, Alderman Library, University of Virginia; Williams to daughter, May 18, Williams, *From the Cannon's Mouth*, p. 201; William W. Folwell to wife, May 7, Minnesota Historical Society; Lee report, *OR*, 25:1, p. 802; John L. G. Wood to aunt, May 10, Georgia Department of Archives and History.

42. William L. Candler letter, May 7, 1863, in Bigelow, *Chancellorsville*, p. 428; Hooker to Meade and Slocum, May 5, Hooker Papers, Huntington Library; William W. Folwell to wife, May 7, Minnesota Historical Society; May 5, Wainwright, *Diary of Battle*, p. 200; Couch, U.S. Generals' Reports, RG 94, M-1098:5, National Archives; Meade to Hooker, May 5, Hooker Papers; Cushing report, *OR*, 25:1, p. 222; Alexander S. Webb to father, May 12, Webb Papers, Yale University Library; Theodore A. Dodge, *The Campaign of Chancellorsville*, p. 230; Butterfield to Couch, May 6, Hooker Papers.

43. Richard E. May memoir, Huntington Library; Barnes report, *OR*, 25:1, p. 516; William W. Folwell to John Bigelow, Oct. 10, 1911, Bigelow Papers, Library of Congress; Jed Hotchkiss to G.F.R. Henderson, 1896, Hotchkiss Papers, Library of Congress.

Epilogue: The Wages of Victory and Defeat

1. William W. Folwell to wife, May 7, 1863, Minnesota Historical Society; Henry F. Young to wife, May 13, Edward S. Bragg to wife, May 10, State Historical Society of Wisconsin; Henry F. Howell to mother, May 7, LaRocca, *This Regiment of Heroes*, p. 132; George Marden letter, May 8, Special Collections, Dartmouth College Library.

2. Charles T. Dix diary, in Morgan Dix, *Memoirs of John Adams Dix* (New York: Harper & Brothers, 1883), 2, p. 57; Twelfth Corps QM report, Hooker Papers, Huntington Library; Williams to daughter, May 18, Williams, *From the Cannon's Mouth*, p. 202; *New York Herald*, May 8; Patrick diary, May 10, Library of Congress; Army of the Potomac G.O. 49, May 6, *OR*, 25:1, p. 171; William W. Folwell to wife, May 12, Minnesota Historical Society.

3. James T. Miller to brother, May 12, 1863, Schoff Collection, Clements Library, University of Michigan; Schimmelfennig to Schurz, May 10, Howard G.O. 9, May 10, *OR*, 25:1, pp. 662, 631; Howard to Rowland Howard, May 16, O. O. Howard Papers, Bowdoin College Library; Schurz to Hooker, May 17, Schurz Papers, Library of Congress; William L. Burton, *Melting Pot Soldiers: The Union's Ethnic Regiments* (Ames: Iowa State University Press, 1988), p. 100.

4. Arthur A. Harmon to parents, May 10, 1863, Woodruff Library, Emory University; Andrew E. Ford, *The Story of the Fifteenth Regiment Massachusetts Volunteer Infantry* (Clinton, Mass.: W. J. Coulter, 1898), p. 253.

5. Brooks, *Washington in Lincoln's Time*, pp. 60–62; Noah Brooks, "Personal Reminiscences of Lincoln," *Scribner's Monthly*, 15 (March 1878), p. 678; May 7, 1863, Welles, *Diary*, 1, p. 294; May 7, Strong, *Diary*, p. 319.

6. Gibbon to George B. McClellan, May 18, 1863, Custer to McClellan, May 6, McClellan Papers, Library of Congress; Warren to fiancée, May 11, Warren Papers, New York State Library; Hancock to wife, May 1863, Almira R. Hancock, *Reminiscences of Hancock*, pp. 94–95; Meade to wife, May 8, 10, Meade, *Life and Letters*, 1, pp. 372, 373; Elizabeth Blair Lee to husband, May 8, Lee, *Wartime Washington*, p. 266; May 7, 31, Wainwright, *Diary of Battle*, pp. 202, 214; George Sharpe clipping, Hooker Papers, Huntington Library.

7. Meade to wife, May 8, 10, 20, 1863, Meade, *Life and Letters*, 1, pp. 372, 373, 379; Montgomery C. Meigs diary, May 7, Meigs Papers, Library of Congress; Alexander S. Webb to brother, May 1863, Yale University Library; Heintzelman diary, May 13, Library of Congress; Walker, *Second Army Corps*, pp. 254–55; Couch, U.S. Generals' Reports, RG 94, M-1098:5, National Archives. Charles F. Benjamin's assertion that Halleck returned from Falmouth with Hooker's offer to resign (*Battles and Leaders*, 3, p. 241) is undocumented. That Hooker gave such a proxy to his archenemy Halleck is highly unlikely; no doubt this is as untrustworthy as Benjamin's account of Hooker's appointment to command (Chapter 1 Note 22).

8. Lincoln to Hooker, May 14, 1863, *OR*, 25:2, p. 479; Hooker testimony, *Report of Joint Committee*, 1 (1865), p. 151; Chase to Hooker, May 23, in Hebert, *Fighting Joe Hooker*, p. 229; June 20, Welles, *Diary*, 1, p. 336. It is probable that the dissident generals vented their views of Hooker to a sympathetic General-in-Chief Halleck, who stayed on several days at Falmouth and who no doubt represented their views to Lincoln.

9. Warren to brother, May 8, 1863, Warren Papers, New York State Library; Hooker to Bates, Nov. 29, Dec. 24, 1878, Bates Collection, Pennsylvania Historical and Museum Commission; Meade to wife, May 23, 1863, Meade, *Life and Letters*, 1, p. 380.

10. Lincoln to Hooker, May 6, 1863, Lincoln, *Collected Works*, 6, p. 198; Hooker to Lincoln, May 6, *OR*, 25:2, p. 435;

Heintzelman diary, May 6, Library of Congress; Greene, "Stoneman's Raid," in Gallagher, *Chancellorsville*, pp. 93–96; Nathan Webb diary, May 5, Schoff Collection, Clements Library, University of Michigan; Stoneman report, *OR*, 25:1, p. 1062.

11. Sedden to W. H. F. Lee, May 5, 1863, *OR*, 25:2, p. 776; Stuart to Colston, May 7, Colston Papers, Southern Historical Collection, University of North Carolina; Nathan Webb diary, May 6, Schoff Collection, Clements Library, University of Michigan; James Brisbin to wife, May 9, Van Sickle Military Books catalog (1989); Stoneman report, *OR*, 25:1, p. 1063; Stoneman to S. Williams, May 9, Hooker Papers, Huntington Library; S. Williams to Stoneman, Apr. 22, *OR*, 25:1, p. 1066; *Washington Daily Star*, May 9; Edward P. Tobie, *History of the First Maine Cavalry* (Boston: Emery & Hughes, 1887), pp. 143–44; Hooker to Bates, Dec. 24, 1878, Aug. 28, 1876, Bates Collection, Pennsylvania Historical and Museum Commission.

12. Army of the Potomac G.O. 49, May 6, 1863, *OR*, 25:1, p. 171; Sharpe to Hooker, May 30, Hooker Papers, Huntington Library; Couch in *Battles and Leaders*, 3, p. 155; Herbert C. Mason to father, May 7, Fredericksburg & Spotsylvania National Military Park. Federal casualties are analyzed from Appendix II. The B.M.I.'s estimate of Confederate losses was 14,348.

13. Confederate casualties are based on figures in Appendix II and the sources listed there. The cavalry reports from both armies are inadequate and incomplete, and there were surely more losses than recorded therein. It is equally likely that there were a good many more Confederates marked "missing" in this campaign than the nominal reports used here indicate. A half-dozen brigades list no missing men at all or a suspiciously low number.

14. Leonidas Torrence to mother, May 7, 1863, Torrence, "The Road to Gettysburg," p. 507; John L. G. Wood to aunt, May 10, Georgia Department of Archives and History; Thomas C. Elder to wife, May 8, Virginia Historical Society; G. W. Poindexter to uncle, May 9, Perkins Library, Duke University; S. G. Pryor to wife, May 12, Pryor, *Post of Honor*, p. 354.

15. Lee to Davis, May 3, 1863, *OR*, 25:2, p. 768; *Charleston Mercury*, May 9; *Richmond Sentinel*, May 8; *Richmond Daily Dispatch*, May 7; Lee quoted by John Sedden, July 1863, in *Southern Historical Society Papers*, 4 (1877), pp. 153–54.

16. Allie Clack to wife, May 23, 1863, Frederick H. Colston memoir, Southern Historical Collection, University of North Carolina; Lee report, *OR*, 25:1, p. 804; William R. Stillwell to wife, May 10, Lane, *Letters from Georgia Soldiers*, pp. 234–35; Thomas M. Smiley to aunt, May 12, Alderman Library, University of Virginia; John C. Mounger to wife, May 23, Georgia Department of Archives and History.

17. Hooker to Bates, Dec. 24, 1878, Bates Collection, Pennsylvania Historical and Museum Commission; Jackson to Lee, May 2, 1863, in *Battles and Leaders*, 3, p. 206.

18. Hunter McGuire statement, New-York Historical Society; B. T. Lacy statement, James Power Smith statement, Dabney Papers, Southern Historical Collection, University of North Carolina; Samuel B. Morrison to William Brown, May 13, 1863, Special Collections, Florida State University Library; William E. Thompson letter, 1988, in *Blue & Gray*, 6:2 (Dec. 1988), pp. 4–6. Dr. McGuire's detailed medical records did not survive the war, and in his published account of Jackson's last days he wrote of "pleuro-pneumonia of the right side" (*Richmond Medical Journal*, May 1866, in *Southern Historical Society Papers*, 14 [1886], p. 160). Surely he meant Jackson's left side. In McGuire's manuscript statement used here, he mentions neither right nor left, and from eyewitness Smith's manuscript statement, it was certainly Jackson's left side that was injured in the fall from the litter on May 2.

19. B. T. Lacy statement, Anna Jackson statement, Dabney Papers, Southern Historical Collection, University of North Carolina; *Savannah Republican,* May 5, 1863; Hunter McGuire statement, New-York Historical Society. Dr. McGuire recorded Jackson's last words in his manuscript statement as told to him by "those who remained" — the doctor had left the sickroom to control his emotions. Anna Jackson, in her manuscript narrative, has her husband saying, "Let us pass over the river . . . ," but in her published narrative (*Memoirs of Stonewall Jackson,* p. 457) she adopted McGuire's phrasing.

20. John G. Nicolay to Therena Bates, May 17, 1863, Nicolay Papers, Library of Congress; Lincoln to Hooker, May 7, Hooker to Lincoln, May 7, 13, *OR,* 25:2, pp. 438, 473; Hooker testimony, *Report of Joint Committee,* 1 (1865), p. 134; Lee to Hood, May 21, Lee, *Wartime Papers,* p. 490; Ham Chamberlayne to mother, June 25, Chamberlayne, *Ham Chamberlayne — Virginian,* pp. 188–89.

Appendix III: The Romances of Chancellorsville

1. Theodore A. Dodge, "The Romances of Chancellorsville," *Papers of the Military Historical Society of Massachusetts,* 3, pp. 192, 193, 202; Dodge, *The Campaign of Chancellorsville,* 1881; Charles Russell Lowell in Emerson, *Life and Letters of Charles Russell Lowell,* p. 279.

2. Alfred Pleasonton, "The Successes and Failures of Chancellorsville," *Battles and Leaders,* 3, pp. 173–75; Bigelow, *Chancellorsville,* pp. 197–98n; Pleasonton report, *OR,* 25:1, pp. 774–75; Pleasonton journal of operation, Hooker Papers, Huntington Library. Lt. Thomas Price of Stuart's staff apparently lost a diary or letterbook to the Federals, but its contents fail to match Pleasonton's claim (Blackford, *War Years with Stuart,* pp. 205–6; Williams, *From the Cannon's Mouth,* p. 184).

3. Pleasonton, "Successes and Failures," p. 174; Pleasonton testimony, *Report of Joint Committee,* 1 (1865), pp. 26–27.

4. Pleasonton testimony, *Report of Joint Committee,* 1 (1865), p. 28; Pleasonton, "Successes and Failures," pp. 179–80; *Battles and Leaders,* 3, pp. 183–88; W. E. Parmelee in *Philadelphia Weekly Times,* Nov. 24, 1886; Dodge, *Chancellorsville,* pp. 202–17.

5. Lincoln, *Collected Works,* 6, p. 79; Hebert, *Fighting Joe Hooker,* p. 170; Brooks, *Washington in Lincoln's Time,* pp. 57–58; Anson G. Henry to wife, Apr. 12, 1863, Illinois State Historical Library; Hooker to Bates, May 29, July 2, 1878, Bates Collection, Pennsylvania Historical and Museum Commission; Hebert, *Hooker,* p. 329 n33.

6. Bigelow, *Chancellorsville,* pp. 477–78n; Herman Hattaway and Archer Jones, *How the North Won: A Military History of the Civil War* (Urbana: University of Illinois Press, 1983), p. 382. Bigelow (per Halstead's letter) surely meant to refer to Hooker's crossing of the Potomac rather than the Rappahannock.

7. E. P. Halstead to W.F.H. Godson, Apr. 19, 1903, Bigelow Papers, Library of Congress; Doubleday, *Chancellorsville and Gettysburg,* 1882. Halstead authorized Godson to pass the letter on to Bigelow. Halstead had earlier related a similar tale to J. H. Stine for his *The Army of the Potomac,* p. 368. The marches of the two headquarters may be traced in *OR,* 27:3.

8. Butterfield testimony, *Report of Joint Committee,* 1 (1865), p. 84; Patrick diary, May 15, 1863, Library of Congress; Thaddeus Stevens letter, May 18, Stevens Papers, Library of Congress; Andrews, *North Reports the Civil War,* pp. 372–73; George W. Smalley, *Anglo-American Memories* (New York: Putnam's, 1911), p. 158; Couch in *Battles and Leaders,* 3, p. 170 (first published in *Philadelphia Weekly Times,* Jan. 22, 1881).

9. Robert G. Carter marginal notations in Dodge, *Campaign of Chancellorsville,* Fredericksburg & Spotsylvania Na-

tional Military Park; Carter, *Four Brothers in Blue*, pp. 270–72; Washington A. Roebling memoir, Bigelow Papers, Library of Congress.

10. Stephen W. Sears, "Getting Right With Robert E. Lee," *American Heritage*, 42:3 (May–June 1991), pp. 58–72; Hunter McGuire to Jed Hotchkiss, May 19, 1896, Hotchkiss Papers, Library of Congress; John B. Gordon, *Reminiscences of the Civil War* (New York: Scribner's, 1903), pp. 96–97; Charles Marshall in Fitzhugh Lee, "Chancellorsville," *Southern Historical Society Papers*, 7 (1879), p. 567.

11. David J. Kyle in *Confederate Veteran*, 4:9 (Sept. 1896), pp. 308–9; James Power Smith to Jed Hotchkiss, July 21, 1897, Hotchkiss to G.F.R. Henderson, July 1897, Hotchkiss Papers, Library of Congress; Freeman, *Lee's Lieutenants*, 2, p. 563n; Richard E. Wilbourn to [John Esten Cooke], May 1863, Charles J. Faulkner Papers, Virginia Historical Society.

12. Richard E. Wilbourn to [John Esten Cooke], May 1863, Charles J. Faulkner Papers, Virginia Historical Society; Cooke, Wilbourn, Joseph W. Revere, Early in *Southern Historical Society Papers*, 6 (1878), pp. 269, 271, 262–63, 279–80; Freeman, *Lee's Lieutenants*, 2, p. 569; *OR*, 25:1, p. 460n. Revere made his claim in his *Keel and Saddle, a Retrospect of Forty Years of Military and Naval Service* (Boston: Osgood, 1872).

13. *Boston Evening Transcript*, May 22, 1863; Carter, *Four Brothers in Blue*, pp. 263–64; William F. Fox, *Regimental Losses in the American Civil War* (Albany, 1898), p. 155.

14. Robert Stone introduction, Stephen Crane, *The Red Badge of Courage: An Episode of the American Civil War* (New York: The Library of America edition, 1990), p. xi; Robert W. Stallman, *Stephen Crane: A Biography* (New York: George Braziller, 1968), p. 167; Harold R. Hungerford, "'That Was at Chancellorsville': The Factual Framework of *The Red Badge of Courage*," *American Literature*, 34:4 (Jan. 1963), p. 520; Christopher Benfey, *The Double Life of Stephen Crane* (New York: Knopf, 1992), p. 104.

15. Charles J. LaRocca, "Stephen Crane's Inspiration," *American Heritage*, 42:3 (May–June 1991), p. 108; Charles H. Weygant, *History of the 124th Regiment, N.Y.S.V.* (Newburgh, N.Y., 1877); Wilbur F. Hinman, *Corporal Si Klegg and his "Pard"* (Cleveland: N. G. Hamilton, 1889); H. T. Webster, "Wilbur F. Hinman's *Corporal Si Klegg* and Stephen Crane's *Red Badge of Courage*," *American Literature*, 11 (1939), pp. 285–93; Charles J. LaRocca, *The Red Badge of Courage: Stephen Crane's Novel of the Civil War. An Historically Annotated Edition* (Fleischmanns, N.Y.: Purple Mountain Press, 1995), pp. xiii–xiv; Herman Melville, *Battle-Pieces*, 1866; Stallman, *Stephen Crane*, p. 167.

Map Sources

The maps in this volume are derived from these sources: John Bigelow, *The Campaign of Chancellorsville;* Jedediah Hotchkiss and William Allan, *Chancellorsville;* Michael Jeck, Topography of Chancellorsville Battlefield, National Park Service; Troop Movement Maps, Chancellorsville, National Park Service; Confederate Engineers' Maps, Gilmer collection, Virginia Historical Society; *Official Records Atlas;* Civil War Map File, RG 77, National Archives. Unit commanders labeled on the maps are as of the start of the campaign.

BIBLIOGRAPHY

This selective Bibliography lists the primary sources, manuscript and printed, of general interest to the study of the Chancellorsville campaign and what led up to it. Numerous additional sources of narrower focus, both manuscript and printed, are cited in full in the Notes.

MANUSCRIPT SOURCES

American Antiquarian Society, Worcester, Mass.
  Charles Ward letters
Auburn University Library, Auburn, Ala.
  James H. Lane Papers
Boston Public Library
  Henry Ropes letters
Boston University Library
  John C. Ropes Collection: Papers of the Military Historical Society of
    Massachusetts
Special Collections, Bowdoin College Library, Brunswick, Me.
  C. H. Howard Papers
  O. O. Howard Papers
John Hay Library, Brown University, Providence, R.I.
  James A. Barber memoir
  Selden Connor letters
Chicago Historical Society
  George Merryweather letter
  O. O. Howard letter
University of Chicago Library·
  Sanford N. Truesdell letters

Special Collections, Dartmouth College Library, Hanover, N.H.
 David Leigh letters
 George Marden letter
William L. Perkins Library, Duke University, Durham, N.C.
 Joseph L. Akerman diary
 William Byrnes diary
 James O. Coghill letters
 John S. Cooper diary
 John B. Evans letter
 Robert K. Garnett letter
 Charles J. Morris letter
 Thomas T. Munford memoir
 F. M. Nixon letter
 G. W. Poindexter letter
 Cyril H. Tyler letter
 Wilkes Family Papers
Robert W. Woodruff Library, Emory University, Atlanta
 Arthur A. Harmon letter
 Zerah C. Monks letters
 Lewis E. Warren memoir
 D.R.E. Winn letters
Filson Club, Louisville, Ky.
 William Clegg letters, Thomas E. Dardin letters: Rowley-Gifford-Clegg Papers
Fredericksburg & Spotsylvania National Military Park, Fredericksburg, Va.
 John J. Cate letter
 Darwin D. Cody letter
 Rollin P. Converse letter
 William M. Dame letters
 S. B. David letter
 Albert Foster letters
 John Gibbon letter
 Francis F. Hillyer letter
 H. N. Hunt letter
 "J.S.K." letter
 J. Franklin Marcha diary
 Herbert C. Mason letter
 David Monat memoir
 Adam Muenzenberger letter
 Samuel S. Partridge letters
 William Stowe letter
 Benjamin R. J. Thaxter letter
 John J. Toffey letter
Georgia Department of Archives and History, Atlanta
 A. B. Barron letter
 Urbanus Dart, Jr., letters
 Thomas M. Hightower letters
 James T. McElvany letter
 W. H. May memoir
 John C. Mounger letter
 Sidney J. Richardson letters

John L. G. Wood letters
Hargrett Library, University of Georgia, Athens
    Frank M. Coker letters: Florence Hodgson Heidler Collection
    Francis S. Johnson letters
Dinand Library, College of the Holy Cross, Worcester, Mass.
    Patrick A. Guiney letters
Huntington Library, San Marino, Calif.
    Samuel L. M. Barlow Papers
    Edmund English Papers
    James B. Heazlitt diary
    Joseph Hooker Papers
    Richard E. May memoir
    J.E.B. Stuart Papers
    Samuel D. Webster diary
Indiana Historical Society, Indianapolis
    George W. Lambert diary
Kansas State Historical Society, Topeka
    John S. Judd diary
Kennesaw Mountain National Battlefield, Marietta, Ga.
    Charles W. McArthur letter
Manuscript Division, Library of Congress, Washington
    John Bigelow, Jr., Papers
    Bruce Catton research notes (E. B. Long), Doubleday & Co.
    Jubal Early Papers
    Samuel P. Heintzelman diary
    Jedediah Hotchkiss Papers
    James W. Latta diary
    Abraham Lincoln Papers
    T.S.C. Lowe Papers
    George B. McClellan Papers
    Marsena R. Patrick diary
    Edwin M. Stanton Papers
    Edwin O. Wentworth letters
    Cadmus M. Wilcox Papers
Northwestern State University of Louisiana, Natchitoches
    Edmund S. Stephens letters
Hill Memorial Library, Louisiana State University, Baton Rouge
    Andrew Hero letter
    "Laird" letter: George S. Lester Papers
Massachusetts Historical Society, Boston
    Francis C. Barlow letters
    Charles E. Bowers letters
    Samuel M. Quincy letters
James S. Schoff Civil War Collection, William L. Clements Library, University of
        Michigan, Ann Arbor
    Henry Aplin letters
    William Aughinbaugh letters
    Chester Ballard letters
    Horace Emerson letters
    James T. Miller letters

George H. Nichols letters
Charles Parker letters
William Speed letters
Edward H. Wade letters
Nathan Webb diary
John D. Wilkins letters

Michigan Historical Collections, Bentley Historical Library, University of Michigan, Ann Arbor
John Follmer diary
James Houghton diary
John E. Ryder letters
Lucius L. Shattuck letters
William H. Withington letters

Minnesota Historical Society, St. Paul
William W. Folwell Papers
Charles E. Goddard letters
Matthew Marvin diary
Cyrus R. Stone letters
Isaac L. Taylor diary

Mississippi Department of Archives and History, Jackson
John A. Barksdale letter
John B. Crawford letter
William H. Hill diary
J. J. Wilson letters

National Archives, Washington
Record Group 94: Records of the Office of the Adjutant General; U.S. Generals' Reports
Record Group 107: Records of the Office of the Secretary of War
Record Group 109: Confederate Records
Record Group 111: Records of the Office of the Chief Signal Officer
Record Group 393: Army of the Potomac; Bureau of Military Information

National Park Service, Washington
Topography of Chancellorsville battlefield, by Michael Jeck
Troop Movement Maps, Chancellorsville

New-York Historical Society, New York City
Thomas Dolan Papers
Abner Doubleday Papers
Hunter McGuire Papers

New York State Library, Albany
G. K. Warren Papers

Southern Historical Collection, University of North Carolina, Chapel Hill
William Allan Papers
Barry G. Benson memoir
John S. Brooks letters
William Calder letters
Civil War Papers
Allie Clack letter
John F. Coghill letter
Frederick H. Colston memoir
R. L. Dabney Papers

    Elias Davis letters
    Samuel W. Eaton diary
    Eli Spinks Hamilton Papers
    B. T. Lacy Papers
    William C. McClellan letter
    Lafayette McLaws Papers
    Channing Price letters
    W. R. Redding letter
    Westwood A. Todd memoir
    Hall Tutwiler letter
North Carolina State Archives, Raleigh
    B. B. Carr memoir
    Frank M. Parker letters
    Alfred M. Scales letters
Ohio Historical Society, Columbus
    Nathaniel Parmeter diary
Ohio State Museum, Columbus
    Thomas Evans memoir: Civil War Collection
Old Colony Historical Society, Taunton, Mass.
    Darius Couch Papers
Pennsylvania Historical and Museum Commission, Pennsylvania State Archives,
      Harrisburg
    Joseph Hooker letters: Samuel P. Bates Collection
Pattee Library, Pennsylvania State University, University Park
    William C. Wiley letters
Rutgers University Libraries, New Brunswick, N.J.
    Washington A. Roebling Papers
South Caroliniana Library, University of South Carolina, Columbia
    W. R. Montgomery letters
Stanford University Libraries, Stanford, Calif.
    John W. Melhorn diary
U.S. Army Military History Institute, Carlisle Barracks, Pa.
    Zenas R. Bliss memoir
    John T. Boyle letters
    Orel Brown diary
    Charles H. Eoger letter
    Robert Goodyear letters
    George E. Hagar diary
    Edmund D. Halsey diary
    Luther B. Mensard memoir
    Thomas K. Stephens diary
    Arthur T. Wilcox letter
Special Collections, University of Vermont Library, Burlington
    Chester K. Leach letters
    Erastus H. Scott letter
Virginia Historical Society, Richmond
    Thomas C. Elder letter
    Charles J. Faulkner Papers
    Confederate Engineers' Maps: Jeremy Francis Gilmer Collection
    Lee Headquarters Papers

  Joseph G. Morrison letters
  Frank Robertson memoir
Virginia Military Institute Archives, Lexington
  John Garibaldi letters
Virginia Polytechnic Institute and State University Libraries, Blacksburg
  John S. Apperson diary
  G. H. Tarr letter
Virginia State Library, Richmond
  Edgar Allan Jackson letters
Alderman Library, University of Virginia, Charlottesville
  John Esten Cooke Papers
  John W. Daniels letters
  Jonathan B. Hager memoir
  Robert T. Hubard memoir
  John F. Sale letters
  Thomas M. Smiley letter
Leyburn Library, Washington and Lee University, Lexington, Va.
  Robert E. Lee Papers
Archives and Regional History Collections, Western Michigan University, Kalamazoo
  Samuel C. Hodgman letters
  Sanford McCall letters
Western Reserve Historical Society, Cleveland
  Robert E. Lee letter, Robert C. Lamberton diary: William Palmer Collection
West Virginia University Library, Morgantown
  George P. Wallace letter: West Virginia Collection
State Historical Society of Wisconsin, Madison
  Thomas S. Allen memoir
  Edward S. Bragg letters
  Lucius Fairchild letters
  George Fairfield diary
  James R. Strong letters
  Henry F. Young letters
Yale University Library, New Haven, Conn.
  Alexander W. Webb Papers

BOOKS AND ARTICLES

Abbott, Henry L. *Fallen Leaves: The Civil War Letters of Major Henry Livermore Abbott.* Ed. Robert Garth Scott. Kent, Ohio: Kent State University Press, 1991.

Alexander, Edward Porter. *Fighting for the Confederacy: The Personal Recollections of General Edward Porter Alexander.* Ed. Gary W. Gallagher. Chapel Hill: University of North Carolina Press, 1989.

Alexander, Edward Porter. *Military Memoirs of a Confederate.* New York: Scribner's, 1907.

Andrews, J. Cutler. *The North Reports the Civil War.* Pittsburgh: University of Pittsburgh Press, 1955.

Andrews, J. Cutler. *The South Reports the Civil War.* Princeton: Princeton University Press, 1970.

Archer, James J. "The James J. Archer Letters: A Marylander in the Civil War." Ed. C. A. Porter Hopkins. *Maryland Historical Magazine*, 56 (June 1961), pp. 125–49.

Auchmuty, Richard T. *Letters of Richard Tylden Auchmuty, Fifth Corps, Army of the Potomac*. Ed. Ellen S. Auchmuty. New York, 1895.

Bacon, Cyrus, Jr. "A Michigan Surgeon at Chancellorsville One Hundred Years Ago." Eds. Frank Whitehouse, Jr., and Walter M. Whitehouse. *The University of Michigan Medical Bulletin*, 29:6 (Nov.–Dec. 1963), pp. 315–31.

Bailey, George W. *The Civil War Diary and Biography of George W. Bailey*. Ed. Gerald R. Post. Colleyville, Texas, 1990.

Baquet, Camille. *History of the First Brigade, New Jersey Volunteers, from 1861 to 1865*. Trenton: MacCrellish & Quigley, 1910.

Barclay, Ted. *Ted Barclay, Liberty Hall Volunteers: Letters from the Stonewall Brigade*. Ed. Charles W. Turner. Natural Bridge Station, Va.: Rockbridge Publishing, 1992.

Bartlett, Asa W. *History of the Twelfth Regiment New Hampshire Volunteers in the War of the Rebellion*. Concord: C. Evans, 1897.

Bates, Samuel P. *The Battle of Chancellorsville*. Meadville, Pa., 1882.

Battles and Leaders of the Civil War. Eds. Robert U. Johnson and Clarence C. Buel. 4 vols. New York: Century, 1887–88.

Baxter, Nancy Niblack. *Gallant Fourteenth: The Story of an Indiana Civil War Regiment*. 2nd ed. Indianapolis: Guild Press, 1986.

Beale, James. *Chancellorsville*. Philadelphia: United Service Club, 1892.

Bean, W. G., ed. "A House Divided: The Civil War Letters of a Virginia Family." *Virginia Magazine of History and Biography*, 59:4 (Oct. 1951), pp. 397–422.

Ballard, Alfred. *Gone for a Soldier: The Civil War Memoirs of Private Alfred Ballard*. Ed. David Herbert Donald. Boston: Little, Brown, 1975.

Berkeley, Henry Robinson. *Four Years in the Confederate Artillery: The Diary of Private Henry Robinson Berkeley*. Ed. William H. Runge. Chapel Hill: University of North Carolina Press, 1961.

Bernard, George S. *War Talks with Confederate Veterans*. Petersburg, Va.: Fenn & Owen, 1892.

Best, Isaac O. *History of the 121st New York State Infantry*. Chicago: W. S. Conkey, 1921.

Bigelow, John, Jr. "The Battle of Kelly's Ford." *Cavalry Journal*, 21 (1910), pp. 5–28.

Bigelow, John, Jr. *The Campaign of Chancellorsville*. New Haven: Yale University Press, 1910.

Billings, John D. *Hardtack and Coffee, or the Unwritten Story of Army Life*. Boston: G. M. Smith, 1887.

Blackford, Susan Leigh, ed. *Letters from Lee's Army*. New York: Scribner's, 1947.

Blackford, W. W. *War Years with Jeb Stuart*. New York: Scribner's, 1945.

Brewster, Charles H. *When This Cruel War Is Over: The Civil War Letters of Charles Harvey Brewster*. Ed. David W. Blight. Amherst: University of Massachusetts Press, 1992.

Brinton, Daniel G. "From Chancellorsville to Gettysburg: A Doctor's Diary." Ed. D. G. Brinton Thompson. *Pennsylvania Magazine of History and Biography*, 89 (July 1965), pp. 292–315.

Brooks, Noah. *Washington in Lincoln's Time*. Ed. Herbert Mitgang. New York: Rinehart, 1958.

Brown, E. R. *The 27th Indiana Volunteer Infantry in the War of the Rebellion*. Indianapolis, 1899.

Brown, J. Willard. *The Signal Corps, U.S.A. in the War of the Rebellion*. 2 vols. Boston: U.S. Veteran Signal Corps Association, 1896.

Bull, Rice C. *Soldiering: The Civil War Diary of Rice C. Bull, 123rd New York Volunteer Infantry.* Ed. K. Jack Bauer. San Rafael, Calif.: Presidio Press, 1977.

Butterfield, Julia L. *A Biographical Memorial of General Daniel Butterfield.* New York: Grafton Press, 1894.

Caldwell, J.F.J. *The History of [Gregg's] Brigade of South Carolinians.* Philadelphia: King & Baird, 1866.

Camerer, C. B. "The Last Days of 'Stonewall' Jackson." *The Military Surgeon,* 78 (Feb. 1936), pp. 135–40.

Carpenter, John A. *Sword and Olive Branch: Oliver Otis Howard.* Pittsburgh: University of Pittsburgh Press, 1964.

Carter, Robert G. *Four Brothers in Blue.* Washington: Gibson Press, 1913.

Catton, Bruce. *The Centennial History of the Civil War: Never Call Retreat.* New York: Doubleday, 1965.

Catton, Bruce. *Glory Road: The Bloody Route from Fredericksburg to Gettysburg.* New York: Doubleday, 1952.

Cavins, Elijah H. C. *The Civil War Letters of Col. Elijah H. C. Cavins, 14th Indiana.* Ed. Barbara A. Smith. Owensboro, Ky.: Cook-McDowell, 1981.

Chamberlayne, John Hampden. *Ham Chamberlayne — Virginian: Letters and Papers of an Artillery Officer.* Ed. C. G. Chamberlayne. Richmond, 1932.

Chambers, Lenoir. *Stonewall Jackson.* 2 vols. New York: Morrow, 1959.

Chancellor, Sue M. "Personal Recollections of the Battle of Chancellorsville." *Register of the Kentucky Historical Society,* 66:2 (April 1968), pp. 137–46.

Child, William. *A History of the Fifth Regiment New Hampshire Volunteers in the American Civil War, 1861–1865.* Bristol, N.H.: R. W. Musgrove, 1893.

Clark, Walter, ed. *Histories of the Several Regiments and Battalions from North Carolina in the Great War, 1861–'65.* 5 vols. Raleigh: State of North Carolina, 1901.

Colt, Margaretta Barton. *Defend the Valley: A Shenandoah Family in the Civil War.* New York: Orion Books, 1994.

Confederate Veteran. Nashville, Tenn.: 1–40 (1893–1932).

Cormier, Steven A. *The Siege of Suffolk: The Forgotten Campaign.* Lynchburg, Va.: H. E. Howard, 1989.

Croffut, W. A., and John M. Morris. *The Military and Civil History of Connecticut During the War of 1861–65.* New York: Ledyard Bill, 1868.

Dabney, Robert L. *Life and Campaigns of Lieut.-Gen. Thomas J. Jackson.* New York: Blelock & Co., 1866.

Daly, Louise Haskell. *Alexander Cheves Haskell: The Portrait of a Man.* 1934; Wilmington, N.C.: Broadfoot Publishing, 1989.

Davenport, Alfred. *Camp and Field Life of the Fifth New York Volunteer Infantry (Duryee Zouaves).* New York: Dick and Fitzgerald, 1879.

Davis, William C. *Jefferson Davis: The Man and His Hour.* New York: HarperCollins, 1991.

Dawes, Rufus R. *Service with the Sixth Wisconsin Volunteers.* Marietta, Ohio, 1890.

DeNoon, Charles E. *Charlie's Letters: The Correspondence of Charles E. DeNoon.* Ed. Richard T. Couture. Farmville, Va., 1982.

De Peyster, John W. "The Plan of Chancellorsville," in Frank Allaben, *John Watts De Peyster,* vol. 2. New York, 1908.

Dickert, D. Augustus. *History of Kershaw's Brigade.* Newberry, S.C.: E. A. Aull, 1899.

Dodge, Theodore A. *The Campaign of Chancellorsville.* 2nd ed. Boston: Ticknor & Fields, 1881.

Dority, Orin G. "The Civil War Diary of Orin G. Dority." *Northwestern Ohio Quarterly,* 37:1 (Winter 1964–65), pp. 7–26.

Doubleday, Abner. *Chancellorsville and Gettysburg.* Scribner's, 1882.

Dunkelman, Mark H., and Michael J. Winey. *The Hardtack Regiment: An Illustrated History of the 154th Regiment, New York State Volunteer Infantry.* Rutherford, N.J.: Fairleigh Dickinson Press, 1981.

Early, Jubal A. *Autobiographical Sketch and Narrative of the War Between the States.* Philadelphia: Lippincott, 1912.

Emerson, Edward W. *Life and Letters of Charles Russell Lowell.* Boston: Houghton Mifflin, 1907.

Evans, Clement A. *Intrepid Warrior: Clement Anselm Evans, Confederate General from Georgia: Life, Letters and Diaries of the War Years.* Dayton, Ohio: Morningside House, 1992.

Farwell, Byron. *Stonewall: A Biography of General Thomas J. Jackson.* New York: Norton, 1992.

Favill, Josiah M. *The Diary of a Young Officer Serving in the Armies of the United States During the War of the Rebellion.* Chicago: Donnelley, 1909.

Fishel, Edwin C. "Pinkerton and McClellan: Who Deceived Whom?" *Civil War History,* 34:2 (June 1988), pp. 115–42.

Fishel, Edwin C. *The Secret War for the Union: The Untold Story of Military Intelligence in the Civil War.* Boston: Houghton Mifflin, 1996.

[Fiske, Samuel]. *Mr. Dunn Browne's Experiences in the Army.* Boston: Nichols & Noyes, 1866.

Fitzpatrick, Marion H. *Letters to Amanda from Sergeant Major Marion Hill Fitzpatrick, 1862–1865.* Ed. Henry Mansel Hammock, Culloden, Ga., 1976.

Freeman, Douglas Southall. *Lee's Lieutenants: A Study in Command.* 3 vols. New York: Scribner's, 1942–44.

Freeman, Douglas Southall. *R. E. Lee, A Biography.* 4 vols. New York: Scribner's, 1934–35.

Furgurson, Ernest B. *Chancellorsville 1863: The Souls of the Brave.* New York: Knopf, 1992.

Gallagher, Gary W., ed. *Chancellorsville: The Battle and Its Aftermath.* Chapel Hill: University of North Carolina Press, 1996.

Gallagher, Gary W., ed. *Lee the Soldier.* Lincoln: University of Nebraska Press, 1996.

Gibbon, John. *Personal Recollections of the Civil War.* New York: Putnam's, 1928.

Goff, Richard D. *Confederate Supply.* Durham, N.C.: Duke University Press, 1969.

Gould, Edward K. *Major-General Hiram G. Berry.* Rockland, Me., 1899.

Griffith, Harrison P. *Variosa: A Collection of Sketches, Essays and Verses.* 1911.

Grimes, Bryan. *Extracts of Letters of Major-General Bryan Grimes to His Wife.* Raleigh, N.C.: Edwards, Broughton, 1883.

Haley, John. *The Rebel Yell & the Yankee Hurrah: The Civil War Journal of a Maine Volunteer.* Ed. Ruth L. Silliker. Camden, Me.: Down East Books, 1985.

Hamlin, Augustus C. *The Battle of Chancellorsville.* Bangor, Me., 1896.

Hancock, Almira R., ed. *Reminiscences of Winfield Scott Hancock.* New York: Webster, 1887.

Handerson, Henry E. *Yankee in Gray: The Civil War Memoirs of Henry E. Handerson.* Ed. Clyde Lottridge Cummer. Cleveland: Press of Western Reserve University, 1962.

Hannah, William F. "Major General Darius N. Couch: A Civil War Profile." *Lincoln Herald,* 86:1 (Spring 1984), pp. 25–31.

Happel, Ralph. "The Chancellors of Chancellorsville." *Virginia Magazine of History and Biography,* 71:3 (July 1963), pp. 259–77.

Harrison, Noel G. *Chancellorsville Battlefield Sites.* Lynchburg, Va.: H. E. Howard, 1990.

Haskell, Frank A. *Haskell of Gettysburg: His Life and Civil War Papers.* Eds. Frank L. Byrne and Andrew T. Weaver. Kent, Ohio: Kent State University Press, 1989.

Haupt, Herman. *Reminiscences of General Herman Haupt.* Milwaukee: Wright & Joys, 1901.

Hebert, Walter H. *Fighting Joe Hooker.* Indianapolis: Bobbs-Merrill, 1944.

Henderson, G.F.R. *Stonewall Jackson and the American Civil War.* New York: Longmans, Green, 1936.

Hermance, W. L. "The Cavalry at Chancellorsville, May, 1863." *Journal of the United States Cavalry Association,* 4:13 (June 1891), pp. 107–13.

Hitchcock, Frederick L. *War from the Inside.* Philadelphia: Lippincott, 1904.

Hotchkiss, Jedediah. *Make Me a Map of the Valley: The Civil War Journal of Stonewall Jackson's Topographer.* Ed. Archie P. McDonald. Dallas: Southern Methodist University Press, 1973.

Hotchkiss, Jedediah, and William Allan. *The Battle-Fields of Virginia: Chancellorsville.* New York: D. Van Nostrand, 1867.

Howard, Oliver Otis. *Autobiography of Oliver Otis Howard.* 2 vols. New York: Baker & Taylor, 1907.

Hubard, R. T. "Operations of General J.E.B. Stuart Before Chancellorsville." *Southern Historical Society Papers,* 8 (1880), pp. 249–54.

Humphreys, Benjamin G. "Recollections of Fredericksburg, 1863." *The Land We Love,* 3:4 (Oct. 1867), pp. 443–60.

Huston, James A. "Logistical Support of Federal Armies in the Field." *Civil War History,* 7:1 (March 1961), pp. 36–47.

Hyde, Thomas W. *Civil War Letters by General Thomas W. Hyde.* 1933.

Hyde, Thomas W. *Following the Greek Cross, or Memories of the Sixth Army Corps.* Boston: Houghton Mifflin, 1895.

Jackson, Mary Anna. *Memoirs of Stonewall Jackson.* Louisville, Ky.: Prentice Press, 1895.

Johnston, Angus James. *Virginia Railroads in the Civil War.* Chapel Hill: University of North Carolina Press, 1961.

Jones, John B. *A Rebel War Clerk's Diary at the Confederate States Capital.* Ed. Howard Swiggett. 2 vols. New York: Old Hickory Bookshop, 1935.

Jones, Terry L. *Lee's Tigers: The Louisiana Infantry in the Army of Northern Virginia.* Baton Rouge: Louisiana State University Press, 1987.

Krick, Robert K. "Lee's Greatest Victory." *American Heritage,* 41:2 (March 1990), pp. 66–79.

Krick, Robert K. *Parker's Virginia Battery C.S.A.* 2nd ed. Wilmington, N.C.: Broadfoot Publishing, 1989.

Lane, Mills, ed. *"Dear Mother: Don't grieve about me . . .": Letters from Georgia Soldiers in the Civil War.* Savannah: Beehive Press, 1977.

LaRocca, Charles J., ed. *This Regiment of Heroes: A Compilation of Primary Materials Pertaining to the 124th New York State Volunteers.* 1991.

Lee, Elizabeth Blair. *Wartime Washington: The Civil War Letters of Elizabeth Blair Lee.* Ed. Virginia Jeans Laas. Urbana: University of Illinois Press, 1991.

Lee, Fitzhugh. "Chancellorsville." *Southern Historical Society Papers,* 7 (1879), pp. 545–85.

Lee, Robert E. *The Wartime Papers of R. E. Lee.* Ed. Clifford Dowdey. New York: Bramhall House, 1961.

Lee, Susan Pendleton. *Memoirs of William Nelson Pendleton.* Philadelphia: Lippincott, 1893.

Letterman, Jonathan. *Medical Recollections of the Army of the Potomac.* New York: D. Appleton, 1866.

Lincoln, Abraham. *The Collected Works of Abraham Lincoln.* Ed. Roy P. Basler. 9 vols. New Brunswick, N.J.: Rutgers University Press, 1953–55.

Livermore, Thomas L. *Days and Events, 1860–1866.* Boston: Houghton Mifflin, 1920.

Long, A. L. *Memoirs of Robert E. Lee: His Military and Personal History.* New York: J. M. Stoddart, 1886.

Lyman, Theodore. *Meade's Headquarters, 1863–1865.* Ed. George G. Agassiz. Boston: Atlantic Monthly Press, 1922.

McAllister, Robert. *The Civil War Letters of General Robert McAllister.* Ed. James I. Robertson, Jr. New Brunswick, N.J.: Rutgers University Press, 1965.

McClellan, George B. *The Civil War Papers of George B. McClellan: Selected Correspondence, 1860–1865.* Ed. Stephen W. Sears. Boston: Ticknor & Fields, 1989.

McClellan, H. B. *The Life and Campaigns of Major-General J.E.B. Stuart.* Boston: Houghton Mifflin, 1885.

McFadden, Janice Bartlett Reeder, ed. *Aunt and the Soldier Boys from Cross Creek Village, Pennsylvania.* Santa Cruz, Calif., 1970.

McGuire, Hunter. "Death of Stonewall Jackson." *Southern Historical Society Papers,* 14 (1886), pp. 154–63.

McIntosh, David Gregg. *The Campaign of Chancellorsville.* Richmond: W. E. Jones, 1915.

Marshall, Charles. *An Aide-de-Camp of Lee.* Ed. Frederick Maurice. Boston: Little, Brown, 1927.

Martin, Micajah D. "Chancellorsville: A Soldier's Letter." Ed. Abbott C. Martin. *Virginia Magazine of History and Biography,* 37:3 (July 1929), pp. 221–28.

Marvel, William. *Burnside.* Chapel Hill: University of North Carolina Press, 1991.

Meade, George Gordon. *The Life and Letters of George Gordon Meade.* Ed. George Meade. 2 vols. New York: Scribner's, 1913.

Military Historical Society of Massachusetts. *Campaigns in Virginia, Maryland and Pennsylvania, 1862–1863.* Boston, 1903.

Military Historical Society of Massachusetts. *Petersburg, Chancellorsville, Gettysburg.* Boston, 1906.

Mills, William H. "Chancellorsville." *Magazine of American History,* 15 (1886), pp. 371–81.

Moe, Richard. *The Last Full Measure: The Life and Death of the First Minnesota Volunteers.* New York: Henry Holt, 1993.

Monfort, Elias R. "The First Division, Eleventh Corps, at Chancellorsville." *G.A.R. War Papers,* pp. 60–75. Cincinnati, 1891.

Moore, Frank, ed. *The Rebellion Record: A Diary of American Events,* vol. 6. New York: Putnam's, 1863.

Moore, Robert A. *A Life for the Confederacy, as Recorded in the Pocket Diaries of Pvt. Robert A. Moore.* Ed. James W. Silver. Jackson, Tenn.: McCowat-Mercer, 1959.

Naisawald, L. Van Loan. *Grape and Canister: The Story of the Field Artillery of the Army of the Potomac.* New York: Oxford University Press, 1960.

Neely, Mark E., Jr. "Wilderness and the Cult of Manliness: Hooker, Lincoln, and Defeat," in Gabor W. Boritt, ed., *Lincoln's Generals,* pp. 51–77. New York: Oxford University Press, 1994.

Nelson, A. H. *The Battles of Chancellorsville and Gettysburg.* Minneapolis, 1899.

Nolan, Alan T. *The Iron Brigade: A Military History.* New York: Macmillan, 1961.

Norton, Oliver W. *Army Letters, 1861–1865.* Chicago, 1903.

Oden, John P. "The End of Oden's War: A Confederate Captain's Diary." Ed. Michael Barton. *Alabama Historical Quarterly,* 43:2 (Summer 1981), pp. 73–98.

Osborn, Hartwell. "On the Right at Chancellorsville." Illinois MOLLUS, *Military Essays and Recollections,* vol. 4, pp. 171–92. Chicago, 1907.

Owen, William M. *In Camp and Battle with the Washington Artillery of New Orleans.* Boston: Ticknor & Co., 1885.

Patrick, Marsena R. *Inside Lincoln's Army: The Diary of Marsena Rudolph Patrick, Provost Marshal General, Army of the Potomac.* Ed. David S. Sparks. New York: Yoseloff, 1964.

Patterson, Edmund D. *Yankee Rebel: The Civil War Journal of Edmund DeWitt Patterson.* Ed. John G. Barrett. Chapel Hill: University of North Carolina Press, 1966.

Paxton, Frank. *The Civil War Letters of General Frank "Bull" Paxton, CSA.* Ed. John Gallatin Paxton. Hillsboro, Texas: Hill Junior College Press, 1978.

Peabody, James H. "Battle of Chancellorsville." *G.A.R. War Papers,* pp. 49–75. Cincinnati, 1891.

Pender, William D. *The General to His Lady: The Civil War Letters of William Dorsey Pender to Fanny Pender.* Ed. William W. Hassler. Chapel Hill: University of North Carolina Press, 1965.

Pfanz, Donald C. "Negligence on the Right: The Eleventh Corps at Chancellorsville." *Morningside Notes.* Dayton, Ohio, 1984.

Philadelphia Weekly Times: Annals of the War, 1878–1888.

Plum, William R. *The Military Telegraph During the Civil War in the United States.* 2 vols. Chicago: Janson, McClurg, 1882.

Pryor, S. G. *A Post of Honor: The Pryor Letters, 1861–63.* Ed. Charles R. Adams, Jr. Fort Valley, Ga.: Garret Publications, 1989.

Raymond, Henry W., ed. "Excerpts from the Journal of Henry J. Raymond." *Scribner's Monthly,* 19:3 (Jan. 1880), pp. 419–24, 19:3 (Mar. 1880), pp. 703–10.

Reese, Timothy J. *Sykes' Regular Infantry Division, 1861–1864: A History of Regular United States Infantry Operations in the Civil War's Eastern Theater.* Jefferson, N.C.: McFarland, 1990.

Report of the Joint Committee on the Conduct of the War. Washington: Government Printing Office, vol. 1 (1863), vol. 1 (1865).

Rhodes, Elisha Hunt. *All for the Union: A History of the 2nd Rhode Island . . . as Told by the Diary and Letters of Elisha Hunt Rhodes.* Ed. Robert Hunt Rhodes. Lincoln, R.I.: Andrew Mowbray, 1985.

Rice, Owen. "Afield with the Eleventh Corps at Chancellorsville." Ohio MOLLUS, *Sketches of War History,* vol. 1, pp. 358–91. Cincinnati, 1885.

Richardson, Charles. *The Chancellorsville Campaign: Fredericksburg to Salem Church.* New York: Neale, 1907.

Robertson, James I., Jr. *General A. P. Hill: The Story of a Confederate Warrior.* New York: Random House, 1987.

Robertson, James I., Jr. *The Stonewall Brigade.* Baton Rouge: Louisiana State University Press, 1963.

Robertson, Robert S. "Diary of the War." Eds. Charles N. and Rosemary Walker. *Old Fort News,* 28:2 (April–June 1965), pp. 58–118.

Royster, Charles. *The Destructive War: William Tecumseh Sherman, Stonewall Jackson, and the Americans.* New York: Knopf, 1991.

Scheibert, Justus. *Seven Months in the Rebel States During the North American War, 1863.* Ed. Wm. Stanley Hoole. Tuscaloosa, Ala.: Confederate Publishing Co., 1958.

Scheips, Paul J. "Union Signal Communications: Innovation and Conflict." *Civil War History,* 9:4 (Dec. 1963), pp. 399–421.

Schurz, Carl. *The Reminiscences of Carl Schurz.* 3 vols. New York: Doubleday, Page, 1909.

Sears, Stephen W. *To the Gates of Richmond: The Peninsula Campaign.* New York: Ticknor & Fields, 1992.

Sears, Stephen W. *George B. McClellan: The Young Napoleon.* New York: Ticknor & Fields, 1988.

Sedgwick, John. *Correspondence of John Sedgwick, Major General.* 2 vols. New York, 1903.

Seymour, William J. *The Civil War Memoirs of Captain William J. Seymour: Reminiscences of a Louisiana Tiger.* Ed. Terry L. Jones. Baton Rouge: Louisiana State University Press, 1991.

Silliman, Justus. *A New Canaan Private in the Civil War: Letters of Justus M. Silliman, 17th Connecticut Volunteers.* Ed. Edward Marcus. New Canaan, Conn.: New Canaan Historical Society, 1984.

Skoch, George. "'Stonewall' Jackson's Last March." *Civil War Times Illustrated,* 28:3 (May 1989), pp. 22–27.

Small, Abner R. *The Sixteenth Maine Regiment in the War of the Rebellion, 1861–1865.* Portland, Me.: B. Thurston, 1886.

Smith, Beverly C. "The Last Illness and Death of Thomas Jonathan (Stonewall) Jackson." *VMI Alumni Review,* Summer 1975, pp. 8–13.

Smith, Gene. "The Destruction of Fighting Joe Hooker." *American Heritage,* 44:6 (Oct. 1993), pp. 95–103.

Smith, James Power. "With Stonewall Jackson in the Army of Northern Virginia." *Southern Historical Society Papers,* 43 (1920), pp. 1–99.

Smith, John L. *History of the Corn Exchange Regiment, 118th Pennsylvania Volunteers.* Philadelphia, 1888.

Smith, William F. *Autobiography of Major General William F. Smith, 1861–1864.* Ed. Herbert M. Schiller. Dayton, Ohio: Morningside House, 1990.

Southern Historical Society Papers. Richmond: 1–52 (1876–1959).

Stackpole, Edward J. *Chancellorsville: Lee's Greatest Battle.* Harrisburg: Stackpole, 1958.

Starr, Stephen Z. *The Union Cavalry in the Civil War,* vol. 1. Baton Rouge: Louisiana State University Press, 1979.

Stiles, Robert. *Four Years Under Marse Robert.* New York: Neale, 1903.

Stine, J. H. *History of the Army of the Potomac.* 2nd ed. Washington, 1893.

Strong, George Templeton. *The Diary of George Templeton Strong: The Civil War, 1860–1865.* Eds. Allan Nevins and Milton H. Thomas. New York: Macmillan, 1952.

Stuart, Meriwether. "Samuel Ruth and General R. E. Lee: Disloyalty and the Line of Supply to Fredericksburg, 1862–63." *Virginia Magazine of History and Biography,* 71:1 (Jan. 1963), pp. 35–109.

Swanberg, W. A. *Sickles the Incredible.* New York: Scribner's, 1956.

Talcott, T.M.R. "General Lee's Strategy at the Battle of Chancellorsville." *Southern Historical Society Papers,* 34 (1906), pp. 1–27.

Taylor, Isaac I. "Campaigning with the First Minnesota: A Civil War Diary." Ed. Hazel C. Wolf. *Minnesota History,* 15 (1944), pp. 224–57, 342–61.

Thomas, Emory M. *Bold Dragoon: The Life of J.E.B. Stuart.* New York: Harper & Row, 1986.

Thomas, Emory M. *The Confederate State of Richmond: A Biography of the Capital.* Austin: University of Texas Press, 1971.

Torrence, Leonidas. "The Road to Gettysburg: The Diary and Letters of Leonidas

Torrence of the Gaston Guards." Ed. Haskell Monroe. *North Carolina Historical Review,* 36 (Oct. 1959), pp. 476–517.

Tremain, Henry E. *Two Days of War.* New York: Bonnell, Silver & Bowers, 1905.

Trobriand, Regis de. *Four Years with the Army of the Potomac.* Boston: Ticknor & Co., 1889.

Tucker, John S. "The Diary of John S. Tucker: Confederate Soldier from Alabama." Ed. Gary Wilson. *Alabama Historical Quarterly,* 43:1 (Spring 1981), pp. 5–33.

U.S. War Department. *The War of the Rebellion: A Compilation of the Official Records of the Union and Confederate Armies.* 128 parts in 70 vols. and atlas. Washington: Government Printing Office, 1880–1901. *Supplement.* Wilmington, N.C.: Broadfoot Publishing, 1994–.

Vandiver, Frank E. *Mighty Stonewall.* New York: McGraw-Hill, 1957.

Von Borcke, Heros. *Memoirs of the Confederate War for Independence.* 2 vols. New York: Peter Smith, 1938.

Wainwright, Charles S. *A Diary of Battle: The Personal Journals of Colonel Charles S. Wainwright.* Ed. Allan Nevins. New York: Harcourt, Brace & World, 1962.

Walker, Francis A. *History of the Second Army Corps.* New York: Scribner's, 1887.

Welch, Spencer G. *A Confederate Surgeon's Letters to His Wife.* New York: Neale, 1911.

Weld, Stephen M. *War Diary and Letters of Stephen Minot Weld, 1861–1865.* 2nd ed. Boston: Massachusetts Historical Society, 1979.

Weller, Edwin. *A Civil War Courtship: The Letters of Edwin Weller from Antietam to Atlanta.* Ed. William Walton. New York: Doubleday, 1980.

Wells, Gideon. *Diary of Gideon Welles.* Ed. Howard K. Beale. 3 vols. New York: Norton, 1960.

Wert, Jeffry D. *General James Longstreet.* New York: Simon & Schuster, 1993.

Wickersham, Charles I. "Personal Recollections of the Cavalry at Chancellorsville." Wisconsin MOLLUS, *War Papers,* vol. 3, pp. 453–62. Milwaukee, 1903.

Wiley, Bell Irvin. *The Life of Billy Yank.* Indianapolis: Bobbs-Merrill, 1952.

Wiley, Bell Irvin. *The Life of Johnny Reb.* Indianapolis: Bobbs-Merrill, 1943.

Williams, Alpheus S. *From the Cannon's Mouth: The Civil War Letters of General Alpheus S. Williams.* Ed. Milo M. Quaife. Detroit: Wayne State University Press, 1959.

Wilson, James Harrison. *The Campaign of Chancellorsville, by Major John Bigelow: A Critical Review.* Wilmington, Del., 1911.

Wingfield, Henry W. "Diary of Capt. H. W. Wingfield." Ed. W. W. Scott. *Bulletin of the Virginia State Library,* 16 (July 1927), pp. 7–47.

Winslow, Richard E., III. *General John Sedgwick: The Story of a Union Corps Commander.* Novato, Calif.: Presidio Press, 1982.

Wise, Jennings C. *The Long Arm of Lee, or the History of the Artillery Arm of the Army of Northern Virginia.* 2 vols. Lynchburg, Va.: J. B. Bell, 1915.

Woodward, C. Vann, ed. *Mary Chesnut's Civil War.* New Haven: Yale University Press, 1981.

INDEX

abatis, 85, 180, 287, 406
Abbot, Capt. Henry L., 14, 59, 81
Adams, Sgt. C. E., 191
Adams, Capt. Charles Francis, Jr., 59
aerial reconnaissance, Federal, 69–70,
    100–101, 130, 134, 144, 170, 184, 244,
    251, 311, 397
Akerman, Pvt. Joseph, 221
Alabama troops: regiments, 3rd, 260; 5th,
    366; 8th, 379, 382, 383; 9th, 44, 379,
    382, 383; 10th, 38, 379, 382, 383; 13th,
    317; 14th, 379, 384; 5th Battalion, 317
Alabama Warrior Guards, 278
Alexander, Peter, 45–46
Alexander, Col. E. Porter, 52, 160, 171,
    175, 188, 196–97; May 1, 199, 219–20,
    230; May 3, 312–44 passim, 359, 360,
    361; May 4, 400–402, 411, 424
Alexandria, Va., 74
Allen, Col. William, 189, 190, 241
Allen, E. S., 170, 244, 397
Allen, Col. Thomas S., 352, 355
Alrich, John (farm), 208, 213, 220
Alsop, Hugh (farm), 190, 191
Alsop, Joseph (farm), 203–4
American Express Co., 63
Amherst Artillery, 34
Anderson, Maj. Gen. Richard H., 130, 172,
    178, 232, 303, 340, 343; April 29, 161,
    167; April 30, 172–75, 187–89; May 1,
    197, 198, 212; May 3, 314, 347, 349,
    359, 361, 372, 374, 390; May 4, 400–
    402, 414, 417; May 5, 428, 442
Andrews, Lt. Col. R. Snowden, 402, 414

Antietam, battle of, 27–28, 52, 57, 112,
    187, 249, 319, 333, 343, 348, 365, 366,
    378, 389
Aquia Landing, Va., 129, 138; Federal sup-
    ply base, 15, 18, 31, 47, 52–53, 74, 104,
    405
Archer, Brig. Gen. James J., 246, 317–18,
    328, 346
Army of Northern Virginia, 26–27, 232,
    365, 374; casualties, 27, 90, 158, 164,
    441–42, 561n27; supply problems, 31,
    32–38, 109–11; winter quarters, 38–43;
    religious revival, 42–43; deserters, 43–
    45; strength, 112–13, 130, 151, 159,
    531n27; defenses, 121–22, 124–26, 131,
    132, 140, 144–45, 155, 187. See also artil-
    lery, Confederate; cavalry, Confederate;
    communications, Confederate; entries for
    states
Army of the Ohio, 24
Army of the Potomac, 11–16, 562n19; un-
    der Burnside, 2–3, 6–7; loyalty to McClel-
    lan, 9–10; deserters, 16–19, 70–71, 138,
    146, 216–17, 516n16; Mud March, 19–
    22; supplies, 47, 73–74, 332–33, 405;
    Hooker's reforms, 63–75, 80–82; Ger-
    man soldiers, 64–65, 115, 139, 269–70,
    286, 415, 432–33; corps badges, 72; casu-
    alties, 90, 155, 158, 164, 185, 440–42;
    short-term troops, 103–4, 113, 291, 132–
    33, 139–40, 146, 150; flying column,
    104–6, 132, 139, 140; strength, 132,
    140, 169, 236–37, 529n5; winter quar-
    ters, 140